To the brave men and women of the Houston
Police Department who have given their lives
in the line of duty.

Houston Police Officers Killed In The Line Of Duty

#	Pg.	Name	Date Of Death	Date Of Birth	Age	Location Of Death	How Killed	*100 Club Marker Cemetery	Location Of Burial
1	12	Foley, C. Edward	03/10/1860			Market Area-Downtown	Shot		
2	14	Snow, Richard	03/17/1882			Fifth Ward	Shot		
3	16	Williams, Henry	08/08/1886			Preston Avenue	Shot	Glenwood	Houston
4	19	Fenn, James	03/15/1891			Bill Davis Dive-Downtown	Shot	Washington	Houston
5	24	Weiss, Willie	7/30/1901	03/07/1870	31	Congress @ San Jacinto	Shot	*Glenwood	Houston
6	26	Youngst, Herman	12/12/1901		58	Congress @ San Jacinto	Shot	*Washington	Houston
7	26	James, John C.	12/12/1901	08/00/1867	34	Congress @ San Jacinto	Shot	Washington	Houston
8	30	Murphy, William	4/1/1910	03/10/1862	48	904 Preston Avenue	Shot	Evergreen	Houston
9	33	Cain, John Morris	8/3/1911	03/04/1881	30	Northside Railroad Crossing	Shot	*Magnolia	Houston
10	36	Parson, Isaac	5/24/1914	09/29/1885	28	Barron St. (5th Ward)	Shot	Black Evergreen	Houston
11	38	Daniels, Rufus	8/23/1917		56	Camp Logan Riot	Shot/mutilated	*Glenwood	Houston
12	38	Meinecke, Edwin G.	8/23/1917	11/26/1893	23	Camp Logan Riot	Shot	*Pilgrims Rest	Bellville, Tx.
13	38	Moody, Horace	8/23/1917	09/02/1869	47	Camp Logan Riot	Shot	Hollywood	Houston
14	38	Raney, Ira D.	8/23/1917	04/19/1878	39	Camp Logan Riot	Shot/mutilated	*Evergreen	Houston
15	38	Patton, D. Ross	9/8/1917	03/21/1888	29	Camp Logan Riot	Shot	*Oates-Mcgee	Houston
16	48	Davidson, Johnnie	2/19/1921	02/26/1886	34	3405 Liberty Road	Shot	Evergreen	Houston
17	49	Young, Jeter	6/19/1921	03/14/1888	33	Preston @ Louisiana	Auto	*Hollywood	Houston
18	51	Murdock, David D.	6/27/1921	08/31/1884	36	1508 George Street	Shot	*Oak Lawn	Rockdale, Tx.
19	53	Etheridge, John Clark	8/23/1924	07/12/1898	26	Main @ Mcgowen	Motorcycle	For. Prk-Lawndale	Houston
20	54	Corrales, Pete	1/21/1925	04/08/1876	48	2003 Congress	Shot	Holy Cross	Houston
21	56	Chavez, E.C.	9/17/1925	10/13/1885	39	#13 Woods Alley	Shot	Washington	Houston
22	57	Jones, Perry Page	1/25/1927	07/03/1893	33	400 Milam	Shot	*Fields Store	Waller County
23	61	Wells, Rodney Q.	7/30/1927	10/29/1876	50	Labranch @ Elgin	Auto	*East Sandy	New Waverly, Tx.
24	62	Greene, Carl	3/14/1928	05/27/1893	34	E. Montgomery Road	Shot	For. Prk-Lawndale	Houston
25	63	Whitlock, Paul W.	4/17/1928	1/27/1901	27	400 Caroline	Shot	For, Prk-Lawndale	Houston
26	64	Davis, Albert Worth	6/17/1928	10/17/1897	30	Genessee @ Andrews	Shot	*Hollywood	Houston
27	66	Hope, Oscar E.	6/22/1929	08/17/1897	31	408 Bayou Street	Shot	For. Prk-Lawndale	Houston
28	68	Jones, Ed	9/13/1929	01/01/1880	49	3527 Mcgregor Avenue	Shot	Olivewood	Houston
29	69	Thomas, C.F. (Osburn)	12/17/1929	5/8/1906	23	Texas @ Caroline	Motorcycle	For. Prk-Lawndale	Houston
30	70	Fitzgerald, Edward D.	9/20/1930	2/1/2003	27	Milam @ Anita	Shot	*Barbers Hill	Barbers Hill, Tx.
31	70	Phares, William Bonner	9/30/1930	2/29/1904	26	Milam @ Anita	Shot	*Glendale	Lufkin, Tx.
32	74	Landry, J.D.	12/3/1930	11/23/1895	35	Tuam @ Genessee	Motorcycle	New Iberia	Louisiana
33	75	Mereness, Harry T.	10/18/1933	09/15/1894	39	Old Galv. Rd/Broadway	Motorcycle	Ypsalanti	Michigan
34	76	Sullivan, Rempsey H.	3/9/1935	7/8/1900	34	1917 Dowling	Shot	For. Prk-Lawndale	Houston
35	79	Gambill, James T.	12/1/1936	08/27/1887	49	2700 Calhoun	Heart	Resthaven	Houston
36	81	Martial, Adolph P.	11/8/1937	01/24/1883	54	Woodland Heights	Auto	Hollywood	Houston
37	82	Palmer, Marion E.	3/24/1938		47	1512 Heights Blvd.	Shot	For. Prk-Lawndale	Houston
38	83	Edwards, George D.	6/30/1939	04/25/1899	40	1200 Franklin	Shot	*Rock Springs	Dialville, Tx.
39	86	Hammond, Howard B.	8/18/1946	6/12/2013	33	3700 Dowling	Shot	*New Providence	Longview, Tx.
40	88	Kent, Smith A. (Buster)	1/12/1954	3/29/2006	47	6300 Navigation	Motorcycle	For. Prk-Lawndale	Houston
41	90	Maddox, Fred Jr.	2/24/1954	3/10/2024	29	5318 Laura Koppe	Shot	Brookside	Houston
42	92	Beets, Jack B.	4/30/1955	2/14/2025	30	3003 1/2 Nance	Shot	*Kaufman	Kaufman, Tx.
43	92	Gougenheim, Charles R. Jr.	4/30/1955	6/23/2001	53	3003 1/2 Nance	Shot	South Park	Pearland, Tx.
44	95	Kellogg, Frank L.	11/30/1955	1/1/2019	36	119 N. Bryan	Shot	For. Prk-Lawndale	Houston
45	97	Schultea, Robert J.	8/25/1956	12/3/2027	28	4315 Navigation	Shot	*Resthaven	Houston
46	99	Miller, Noel Ray	6/6/1958	3/30/1930	28	2813 Canfield	Shot	For. Prk-Lawndale	Houston
47	101	Branon, Claude E.	3/20/1959	11/18/2026	32	8700 Gulf Freeway	Motorcycle	For. Prk-Lawndale	Houston
48	103	Suttle, John W. (Jack)	8/23/1959	6/6/1935	24	4800 Gulf Freeway	Auto-pedestrian	Brookside	Houston
49	106	Gonzalez, Gonzalo Q.	2/23/1960	12/23/1931	28	Pease/Chenevert	Auto	For. Prk-Lawndale	Houston
50	108	Walker, James T.	3/8/1963	1/18/2022	41	6100 North Freeway	Heart	For. Prk-Lawndale	Houston
51	109	Mcdaniel, Charles R.	8/4/1963	8/31/1932	40	14300 Hempstead Hwy.	Auto	Woodlawn	Houston
52	111	Willis, James F.	7/1/1964	6/15/2025	39	9000 Market	Auto	*Galloway	Galloway, Tx.
53	112	Planer, Herbert N.	2/18/1965	3/3/1932	32	5000 Navarro	Shot	VA Cemetery	New Jersey
54	128	Deloach, Floyd T. Jr.	6/30/1965	10/20/1936	28	650 W. Crosstimbers	Shot	For. Prk-Lawndale	Houston
55	130	Sander, Louis Lyndon	1/21/1967	2/10/1942	24	900 Hardy	Shot	*Resthaven	Houston
56	134	Kuba, Louis R.	5/17/1967	3/12/1942	25	3200 Wheeler	Shot	For. Prk-Lawndale	Houston
57	137	Gerhart, Ben Eddie	6/26/1968	7/14/2022	45	1000 West Loop N.	Shot	Memorial Oaks	Houston
58	137	James, Bobby L.	6/26/1968	12/1/2029	38	16000 Beaumont Hwy.	Auto	Brookside	Houston
59	140	Moody, Kenneth Wayne	11/26/1969	12/19/1932	36	139 E. 20th	Shot	*Resthaven	Houston
60	142	Griggs, Leon	1/31/1970	2/19/2028	41	2616 Blodgett	Shot	*Cemetery Beautiful	Houston
61	145	Lee, Robert Wayne	1/31/1971	12/21/1935	35	5702 Gulf Freeway	Shot	*Resthaven	Houston

4

#	Pg.	Name	Date Of Death	Date Of Birth	Age	Location Of Death	How Killed	*100 Club Marker Cemetery	Location Of Burial
62	147	Beck, Claude Ronnie	12/10/1971	12/29/1947	23	S.W.Frwy/Montrose	Auto-pedestrian	*Oakland	Arkansas
63	150	Noel, David Franklin	6/17/1972	9/22/1943	28	316 N. Nagle	Stabbed	*Zavalla	Zavalla, Tx.
64	153	Spruill, Jerry Leon	10/26/1972	3/27/1943	29	616 Westheimer	Shot	VA Cemetery	Houston
65	157	Guzman, Antonio Jr.	1/9/1973	9/18/1942	30	6700 Telephone	Shot	VA Cemetery	Houston
66	159	Huerta, David	9/19/1973	4/11/1946	27	918 Heights	Shot	For. Prk-Lawndale	Houston
67	162	Riley, Jerry Lawrence	6/18/1974	3/30/1950	24	2800 Old Galveston Rd.	Auto	*South Park	Pearland, Tx.
68	164	Bamsch, Johnny Terrell	1/30/1975	9/10/1947	27	4600 Yale	Shot	Rosewood	Humble, Tx.
69	167	Wright, Francis Eddie	8/2/1975	10/26/1942	32	4500 S.W. Freeway	Auto-pedestrian	Brookside	Houston
70	170	Calhoun, Richard Howard	11/10/1975	8/4/1940	35	9410 Avenue J	Shot	For. Prk-Lawndale	Houston
71	172	Rojas, George Garza	1/28/1976	2/23/1946	29	7035 Harrisburg	Stabbed	Brookside	Houston
72	174	Kilty, James Frederick	4/8/1976	11/11/1940	35	2929 S.W. Freeway	Shot	Memorial Oaks	Houston
73	176	Hearn, Timothy Lowe	6/8/1978	11/8/1949	28	6800 Harrisburg	Shot	*Corinth	Buckholts, Tx.
74	178	Baker, Charles Henry	8/16/1979	12/27/2027	51	10200 Silvercrest	Shot	*Copeland Chapel	Conroe, Tx.
75	181	Wells, Victor Ray III	10/2/1980	12/18/1946	33	6800 Harrisburg	Shot	Brookside	Houston
76	183	Zamarron, Jose A.	4/18/1981	2/9/1953	28	12700 Market	Auto-pedestrian	For. Prk-Lawndale	Houston
77	185	Rawlins, Winston J.	3/29/1982	8/1/1958	23	8400 South Loop East	Motorcycle	*Paradise North	Houston
78	187	Deleon, William E.	3/29/1982	10/3/1946	35	1300 S.W. Freeway	Motorcycle	For. Prk-Lawndale	Houston
79	190	Shirley, Daryl W. (Wayne)	4/28/1982	9/1/1947	34	2802 Rolido	Shot	For. Prk-Lawndale	Houston
80	193	Harris, James Donald	7/16/1982	10/17/1952	29	4800 Walker	Shot	For. Prk-Lawndale	Houston
81	196	Schaefer, Kathleen (Kathy)	8/18/1982	2/24/1948	34	2505 W.Bay Area Blvd.	Shot	Brookside	Houston
82	200	Coates, Charles Robert	2/23/1983	4/8/1946	36	12600 Memorial Drive	Auto-pedestrian	Florissant	Missouri
83	201	Moss, William	9/12/1983	8/17/1941	42	17900 J.F.K. Blvd.	Auto		New York
84	202	Groves, Maria Michelle	4/10/1987	11/13/1964	22	10800 Katy Freeway	Auto-pedestrian	*Garden Of Memories	Lufkin, Tx.
85	204	Winzer, Andrew	2/18/1988	6/24/1957	30	Franklin/Louisiana	Auto-drowning	*Paradise North	Houston
86	207	Howard, Elston M.	7/19/1988	9/18/1963	24	4330 Richmond	Shot	*Calvary	Houston
87	211	Garcia, Florentino M. Jr.	11/10/1989	1/9/1962	27	3000 Canal	Motorcycle	VA Cemetery	Houston
88	214	Boswell, James Charles	12/9/1989	11/29/1960	29	9300 Main	Shot	Meridian Mem'l. Park	Mississippi
89	218	Irby, James B. (Jim)	6/27/1990	5/25/1953	37	4600 Airline	Shot	For. Prk-Lawndale	Houston
90	223	Salvaggio, John Anthony	11/25/1990	7/23/1951	39	8500 Katy Freeway	Auto-pedestrian	For. Prk-Westheimer	Houston
91	226	Soboleski, Bruno D.	4/12/1991	2/5/1958	33	6600 Calhoun	Shot	*Oak Hill	Pennsylvania
92	230	Roman, Michael Paul	1/6/1994	9/24/1966	27	North Main/East 28th	Auto	Brookside	Houston
93	232	Gaddis, Guy Patrick	1/31/1994	3/21/1969	24	8100 Chimney Rock	Shot	South Park	Pearland, Tx.
94	236	Healy, David M.	11/12/1994	7/25/1968	26	6600 South Freeway	Auto	Cremation	
95	237	Erickson, Dawn S.	12/24/1995	1/15/1973	22	2900 Unity Drive	Auto-pedestrian	For. Prk-Westheimer	Houston
96	238	Thrinh, Cuong H. (Tony)	4/6/1997	5/18/1971	25	2716 Westerland	Shot	For. Prk-Westheimer	Houston
97	240	Kincaid, Kent	5/23/1998	8/17/1957	40	7600 Plum Crk. Forest	Shot	Stockton	Kansas
98	243	Blando, Troy	5/19/1999	7/31/1959	39	6800 S.W. Freeway	Shot	Woodlawn	Houston
99	245	Stowe, Jerry Keith	9/20/2000	2/1/1953	47	1605 Robin	Beaten	Brookside	Houston
100	248	Holmes, Dennis	1/10/2001	5/1/1955	45	6400 Bourgeois	Heart	Calvary	Houston
101	250	Vasquez, Alberto	5/22/2001	4/16/1969	32	6200 Marinette	Shot	*Resthaven	Houston
102	253	Dees, Keith Alan	3/7/2002	10/19/1956	45	100 Gulf Freeway	Motorcycle	For. Prk-Westheimer	Houston
103	254	Clark, Charles R. (Charlie)	4/3/2003	10/24/1957	45	5700 South Loop East	Shot	Cremation	
104	259	Cantu, Francisco	3/26/2004	5/12/1961	42	Dunlavy @ W. Gray	Auto	Cremation	
105	260	Deleon, Rueben B.	10/26/2005	7/4/1974	31	9707 South Gessner	Shot	Greenlawn Memorial	Rosenberg, Tx.
106	262	Johnson, Rodney J.	9/21/2006	10/24/1965	40	9300 Randolph	Shot	Resthaven	Houston

Foreword

No society can long endure without the existence of rules designed to ensure the reasonable expectation of the safety and security of its members. Most members of society obey these rules, and enact them as laws governing the conduct of all who share the inalienable right to life, liberty and the pursuit of happiness. Some do not obey the rules. For this reason, society has found it necessary to create institutions to give meaning to the law. In the vanguard of society's reaction to law-breakers are law enforcement officers, waging a never-ending war against those who would threaten the freedoms we hold dear.

The war against law-breakers carries a price, often spelled out in the blood-stained bar-rooms, sidewalks and back alleys of our cities. There are men and women willing to risk their lives to give meaning to the law. They are the street cops, beat officers, men and women in marked patrol units, detectives in street clothes and undercover agents seeking to penetrate the heart of criminal cartels. This is the story of 106 of these officers in one city in one state of our Country, of 106 families who knelt before the graves of a loved one who paid the supreme sacrifice so that we might live as free men and women. It is also the story of their brothers and sisters in arms who doggedly pursued those who had caused a hero to be laid on the sacrificial altar of freedom.

Houston police officers pledge to never forget the ultimate sacrifices made by their fellow men and women in blue in the 166-year history of the mighty law enforcement organization known as the Houston Police Department. Since 1841, the city's best records show that 106 officers died in the line of duty. Some met their early demise by accident; others were murdered in cold blood by career criminals who received far more quarter from the Texas criminal justice system than they provided their victims.

Each of these senseless deaths became an HPD homicide case file. It seems only natural that an HPD Homicide lieutenant would devote endless off-duty hours to ferreting out the details of each and every case, telling the stories of each officer, literally from cradle to grave. In 2004, Lieutenant Nelson Zoch, who retired from HPD after 36 years, which were mostly in Homicide, doggedly researched these details, tracking down surviving family members in often obscure parts of Texas and the rest of the nation. Lieutenant Zoch also initiated a special partnership with the 100 Club of Houston and the Houston Police Officers Union to provide and install special grave markers that denote the fact that here lies a Houston police officer who died in the line of duty. By agreement, the 100 Club pays for the markers and the HPOU pays for the often complicated installation process.

Locating the gravesites of dozens of these men and women would not have been possible without Zoch's tireless effort. He often searched in his spare time when he was on out-of-town trips. In one such case, the off-duty lieutenant located the grave of one officer in an obscure, seldom-used cemetery on the far northeastern edge of the Bayou City, only to find the gate locked and no contact number posted anywhere. It was almost as if this sacred acreage was in a section of land totally forgotten and barely visible on a Key Map. Undeterred and with the strong determination of typical Houston Homicide personnel, Zoch later returned to the scene with a ladder he used to get over the fence. He had no map or any hint of where the gravesite was. But in typical Zoch fashion, he found the grave just before sundown and proceeded through the paper-intensive process to get the go-ahead to put a special marker down. Zoch had to work not only with the 100 Club and HPOU but also with the officer's family and cemetery operators.

LT. NELSON ZOCH AND CHIEF HARRY CALDWELL IN 1977

Even though a few of these unforgettable police officers are buried in other cities in other states, Zoch went the extra mile, always on his own long-distance nickel, to speak with family members or cemetery managers to verify existent grave markers or to ascertain whether the installation of the 100 Club/HPOU marker would be in compliance with cemetery policies. In ironing out such details, Zoch found that Houston funeral and cemetery operators were diligent in their actions to see that the officers buried in their plots are indeed not forgotten. Forest Park Lawndale, the largest cemetery in Texas, contains the remains of 21 Houston police officers killed in the line of duty. Cemetery officials there created and installed the special markers at no cost to the 100 Club or HPOU. The same policy held forth in Earthman's Resthaven on Interstate 45, where seven of Houston's finest were laid to rest.

The stories of each of these men and women have appeared in the monthly editions of the Badge & Gun, the Union's official publication, since 1998, when Lieutenant Zoch set a goal to nail down every possible detail in every line of duty death case. As late as 2006, Zoch uncovered the facts in the case of Officer Paul W. Whitlock, accidentally shot to death on the police shooting range on Tuesday, April 17, 1928. Without Zoch's persistent attention to every detail, HPD and the city of Houston might not have discovered that this officer belonged on this too-long but distinguished roll.

From Zoch's diligence we learn that a line of duty death could happen at any time on any given shift. The line of fire could find solo officers, sergeants and even a deputy chief in the crosshairs. Yet, generally, the officers on patrol – those first-line defenders of the people – are far more apt to take the slug in a vital organ or be struck and killed by a careless vehicle. We learn that most of the shooters or provocateurs are captured and receive the appropriate punishment. History shows us – thanks to Zoch's research – that one cop killer was lynched by a small civilian mob and another spent only 69 days on the Texas Death Row before being executed in the electric chair. The less-sophisticated era administered justice far more quickly than that of today, when the latest count in 2007 shows that the 10 men on Death Row for the murder of nine Houston police officers have spent an average of 12.5 years there since they committed these heinous crimes. The current appellate process will see to it that they spend even longer periods before they make the list of scheduled executions.

It is sad that law-abiding citizens in Houston, Texas and the rest of civilization also must note that a few of these dangerous killers got away unpunished but for the judgment of God.

While compiling these often frustrating facts, Zoch doesn't fail to put the emphasis where it properly belongs – with the families of fallen officers and the manner in which they have coped with their tragic losses. We learn that both of Officer Daryl Shirley's sons entered the law enforcement field, serving the people in two different parts of the country, while Shirley's killer has been on Death Row 24 years and counting. We also learn that widows raise their young children into adulthood with the aid of the 100 Club or help from other police officers.

Thanks to Zoch, this book provides everything the reader could possibly want to know about everyone from C. Edward Foley, killed in the line of duty on March 10, 1860, to Rodney Johnson, murdered on duty on September 21, 2006. And thanks to him, we will never forget names like Snow, Fenn, Weiss and Murphy, Meinke, Moody, Patton and Raney, Corrales, Davis, Sullivan, Gambill and Martial, Gonzalez, Planer, Kuba, Griggs, and Beck, Noel, Guzman, Huerta, Bamsch, Kilty and Hearn, Schaefer, Groves, Howard, Boswell, Irby, Salvaggio and Soboleski, Thrinh, Dees, Clark and Cantu. In sad cases of coincidence, two different Houston officers with the respective names of Jones, Moody, Wells, James and DeLeon are on this unforgettable list.

We all wish that the last page of this book would mark the end of the story of officers who make the ultimate sacrifice to preserve and protect the people of Houston. We can only hope and pray that it will be many decades before even the slightest revisions are necessary.

Good job, Lieutenant Zoch!

Harry Caldwell
Chief of Police (Retired)
Houston Police Department

Introduction

A number of people have asked me how and why I came to have a desire to write stories about Houston Police Officers who had been killed in the LINE OF DUTY.

Well, for a number of years, I thought about learning to write. I took several courses in Fiction Writing at a community college, and learned how to, if nothing else, impress the instructor in order to obtain a good grade.

Then, one day, the thought arose about writing a synopsis of a WHO DUN IT Police Officer Murder. One in particular had always intrigued me as it occurred in the patrol district I was working in January, 1970. That was the Murder of Officer Leon Griggs at the Sacco Brothers Food Market on Blodgett. While this offense occurred in the late afternoon, I was working the night shift. Shortly after this tragic day, many of us on all three patrol shifts in that area of town became exposed to a very interesting learning experience regarding the use of informants and how information from the public became useful in an investigation. Citizens and other folks, who needed help in their criminal justice problems, were coming forward with clues you could not even imagine, and Homicide Detectives were contacting patrol officers requesting assistance in solving this crime.

Due to the involvement of the street officers and the diligent efforts of a number of Homicide Detectives, this Capital Murder was eventually solved and brought to a successful conclusion. So, in 1998, I decided to write a synopsis of this case. I did so, and it was published in the **Badge and Gun**. Not being unlike many other people, a little praise and a few compliments usually help to motivate a person. And so, the story of Officer Johnny Bamsch followed, and then, the story of Officer Robert W. Lee. I knew both of these men and came to experience the satisfaction that came with meeting family and friends while researching these stories.

During this time, I received the utmost cooperation and support from the Houston Police Officer's Association, now the HPOU. My stories were printed in their publication, the **Badge and Gun**, and when the fledgling Houston Police Retired Officer's Association began their bimonthly newspaper, the **Retired Badge**, again their cooperation was extended to me as another outlet for these stories.

Somewhere along the way, the thought arose in my mind that it would be a worthwhile accomplishment late in my career to do something to repay HPD and my fellow Officers for the benefits I had received. This has been a career that I have so very much enjoyed and from which I have greatly benefited. When the first story was written in late 1998, the death of Sergeant Kent Kincaid earlier that year brought to ninety-six the number of HPD Officers classified as KILLED IN THE LINE OF DUTY. Unfortunately, here in late 2006, we are now at the tragic number of one hundred and six.

As the research continued, I began to make more and more friendships in the way of personally meeting family, friends, and fellow Officers of these slain comrades. To me, this was the most rewarding part of my efforts. When I think of the many, many people whom I would have never met had it not been for this project, all of the work, all of the high times and low times, suddenly, the effort all becomes worthwhile.

While I do not mean to refer to my efforts as a project, my wife and son, as well as several other well-meaning people, have openly referred to this as an obsession. And, that reference has likely been correct.

I will now attempt to bring to mind the people that have supported and assisted me throughout the past eight plus years:

To my wife, Mary Sue, and my son Andy, thank you for all that you have endured by way of my obsession. I spent much time away from both of you, but you always helped me with your moral support. Thank you for that support, especially at those times when I felt I was beating my head against a brick wall, wondering if this was ever going to work out. Mary Sue and Andy, you told me that I could do it, and with your help, WE DID IT. Both of you helped me at times in loading and unloading those grave markers and in setting them. Mary Sue, thanks for your help in Kaufman, and Andy, thanks for your strong back in helping me dig holes and setting them in Lufkin, New Waverly, Fields Store, Evergreen, and Oates. And, also thank you both for your ideas. The very important job of photoediting and much of the computer work was accomplished by Mary Sue and Andy as well as the design of a website for this publication. The bureaucratic problems in obtaining copyright and other necessary government registration was accomplished by Mary Sue. I love you both.

To my friend, Mr. Tom Kennedy, a former Houston Post reporter whose friendship was renewed when he came on board as the Editor of the **Badge and Gun**. I am very proud of this relationship that has developed throughout this effort. Tom, thank you for your assistance and the professional editing job you performed, even though we disagreed at times. My many thanks to you. You hung tough, even though I admit I was very disappointed in your pick and shovel skills in the rock-hard ground of Dialville, Texas.

To my friend and coworker, Retired Officer Henry (Butch) Chisholm, who early on in this project assisted me greatly in the public record research of convicted suspects.

To HPD Family Assistance Officers Matt Perales and Mike Newsome, who went the extra mile to assist me at times with information that they were allowed to provide.

To Roger Demny, an Academy classmate of mine from Class #37 in 1968. Roger retired as a Lieutenant from HPD and went on to another exemplary career with the Texas Department of Criminal Justice. There were times when his assistance became invaluable providing clues for me to continue tracking the histories of TDCJ inmates.

To Sherwood (Tom) Bradshaw, Bobby Brooks, and Matt Fowler at the Photo Lab. These men bent over backwards to assist me with information they were allowed to provide regarding the photos of slain Officers.

To Retired Officer Jerry Wright: Jerry observed me struggling with a four to five page spread of Big Chief tablet books one day in my office. I had them all laid out in perfect form when Jerry, in his own Golden Triangle drawl asked, "What are you doing?" I very thoroughly explained to him that I was in the process of tracking the investigation and research of over 100 HPD Officers that had been KILLED IN THE LINE OF DUTY. Jerry then politely told me that he could assist me in a more efficient manner of tracking this information. He proceeded to set up a database which I still rely heavily on to this day. Thanks, Jerry, for this Microsoft Access database, and more importantly, your lasting friendship.

To my newfound friends, Bernice and Gus Mistrot, Cathy Finch, and Martha Peterson of Washington and Glenwood Cemeteries. These fine people assisted me with the more complicated genealogy research and also with searching newspaper archives online. Without their able assistance, I would not have found some of the information on the very old Officer Deaths.

And now, without a doubt, the most difficult words I have written in this entire book. However, I wish to include the following:

To my two Police Officer brothers, both now retired and deceased-LEROY N. ZOCH, HPD CAPTAIN, 1954-1987, passed away in 2005, and HERMAN A. (JOHN) ZOCH, HPD DETECTIVE, 1955-1983, passed away in 1990: What I wouldn't give to go on one more fishing trip on the Colorado River or at Bastrop/Christmas Bay with both of you, to go on one more trip with you, John, to Centerville or Lake Livingston, or to listen to one more batch of stories about policing in your day, and to drink just one more cold beverage with each of you. THANKS TO BOTH OF YOU. You never told me anything but the truth when I asked for it about this job and career. I know GOD is with both of you.

GRAVEMARKER PROJECT INTRO

To Mr. Russell Allen, Manager of Forest Park Lawndale Cemetery:

To Mr. David Dettling, SCI Corporation:

To Mr. John B. Earthman, Area Manager of Earthman Funeral Homes and Cemeteries:

To Mr. Rick Hartley, Executive Director of the 100 Club of Houston and Harris County.

To Officer Mark Clark, Executive Director, and

To Officer Hans Martucic, President of the Houston Police Officer's Union (HPOU);

Early on in this endeavor, I became aware that there were some Houston Police Officers who were killed in the LINE OF DUTY and had not received a proper marker to commemorate their final resting place. While many were marked, very few markers portrayed any indication of how these men and women died, which was an honorable death-IN THE LINE OF DUTY. While some had badge numbers, I really felt that these men and women were deserving of more. I made these feelings known to Tom Kennedy and as a result, Tom and I requested meetings with the above named gentlemen.

The first meeting was with Mr. Rick Hartley, who was supportive of the idea of a special gravemarker from the beginning. With his approval, he had an artist work with us and we came up with a design-a 1' X 2' X 4" granite marker, which is depicted in this introduction. The 100 Club agreed to bear the expense of the marker.

The next meeting, I believe, was with Officers Mark Clark and Hans Marticuc of the HPOU. They were very supportive of this idea and readily offered to cover the installation expense of these markers. To date, the HPOU has covered the installation expenses of twenty-six of these markers.

Sample Gravemarker

At this point, it was realized that nearly one-fifth of all Houston Police Officers KILLED IN THE LINE OF DUTY were interred at the Forest Park Lawndale Cemetery. Tom and I were able to gain an audience with Mr. Russell Allen, the Manager of that vast facility, which is the final resting place for over 130,000 people. Forest Park has long been known as being not only easy to work with for law enforcement, but also very generous. This generosity was once again exhibited when Mr. Russell Allen made a most unbelievable offer-his organization would donate fifteen of these such markers along with the installation. Naturally, this offer was accepted and the parameters of their rules and regulations were carefully followed and today, nine markers have been placed.

At the time, Resthaven Cemetery on the North Freeway was the final resting place of five HPD LINE OF DUTY DEATHS. Rick Hartley suggested that contact be made with Mr. John B. Earthman, who was a regional Vice President of the Earthman Company, owners of Resthaven. Tom and I met with Mr. Earthman and again, the cooperation and generosity of this man and his organization was fantastic. Mr. Earthman, when advised that five of our Officers were buried there that met the LINE OF DUTY criteria, generously contributed those five markers and the installations. There are now seven of our slain officers buried at Earthman.

Glenwood Cemetery has donated the installation fees for three such markers at Glenwood and Washington Cemeteries.

Each and every cemetery, by law or by policy, has rules and regulations which they enforce very stringently, and rightfully so. Even with the above two named facilities, notarized approvals were required from surviving family members who had ownership of the plots. These details were worked out and as a result, forty-three 100 Club LINE OF DUTY gravemarkers have been placed in memory of our slain Officers to date. A number of these are out of the Houston area and their locations are listed in the main index of this publication.

Again, my utmost thanks is extended to these organizations for their generosity and cooperation in having these markers available to our fallen heroes.

About the Author

Nelson J. Zoch served the City of Houston Police Department for thirty-six years from 1968-2004. His service included stints on the night shift in Radio Patrol as a street officer in the Third Ward of Houston and later as a Park Place Radio Patrol Shift Lieutenant. He also served in the Homicide Division from 1972-1977 as a Detective investigating murders and other Homicide related investigations. His return to the Homicide Division in 1980 continued a distinguished career in the Homicide Division where he served as a Murder Squad Lieutenant for over twenty-four years until his retirement in 2004.

In 1998, Nelson began writing about the lives and deaths of Houston Police Officers who had given their lives in the line of duty. The overwhelmingly positive reception of his first article about the Capital Murder of Officer Leon Griggs provided Nelson with the confidence needed to continue regarding the deaths of other HPD Officers. Nelson soon came to realize the personal fulfillment in meeting and speaking with the families of these slain officers, some of which Nelson knew. Those families that he did not know, he eventually came to know.

As a result of his research and documentation about slain Houston Police Officers, Nelson has been recognized and received many awards, including The Houston Police Officers' Union Local No. 2 OFFICER OF THE MONTH, September, 2001; Houston Police Department CHIEF OF POLICE COMMENDATION, 2002; The National Law Enforcement Memorial Fund OFFICER OF THE MONTH, FEBRUARY, 2003; and most recently, the LAW ENFORCEMENT COMMENDATION MEDAL by the NATIONAL SOCIETY OF THE SONS OF THE AMERICAN REVOLUTION, March 2007.

Following his retirement from HPD in 2004, Nelson and his wife Mary Sue reside in the Kingwood area where he has continued his research with the able assistance of his wife, a special education schoolteacher, and their son, Andrew, who in 2007 is in his third year of study at Texas A&M University in College Station.

This publication is a culmination of nearly nine years of diligent research and the compilation of that research into published form.

1

Officer C. Edward Foley
Saturday, March 10, 1860

Officer Foley Murdered in Market Area by Local Citizen- Talk of a Lynching was Quelled

From the Houston Weekly Telegraph, Tuesday, March 13, 1860:

ATROCIOUS DEED-POLICEMAN KILLED
WHILE ON DUTY

"This morning while Policeman Foley was attending to his duties in the market, Michael Flock attempted to interfere, when the policeman struck him. Flock made off at once, got a double-barrelled gun, and shot Foley dead on the spot. A good deal of excitement was manifested and some talk of lynching him at once, but the police hurried the prisoner off to the calaboose, and it is hoped the law will be justly dealt to him. He had no business to interfere with a policeman on duty, in the first place, and we have yet to hear any excuse attempted for the deed. The coroner's jury have (sic) returned the following verdict":

"We, the jury, duly empanelled, tried and sworn, this the 10th of March, 1860, to sit upon the body of one deceased, Edward Foley, having heard the evidence of several witnesses, say that the deceased came to his death by wounds received by a double barrelled gun, discharged from the hands of Michael Flock".

The Houston Weekly Telegraph, Tuesday, March 20, 1860:

"Michael Flock, who killed Edward Foley last Saturday, was arrested and brought before an examining court on Monday, when, after an extended trial, was admitted to bail in the sum of $8,000. Some dissatisfaction, being expressed by the public at the bail, he was re-arrested and brought before Chief Justice Shearn, by whom the bail was raised to $15,000. Many think it was not a bailable case, but a deliberate murder. It does not become us editorially to pass any judgement upon it. We confess we were struck with horror when the details of the case were made known to us, and from all we could hear, were inclined to regard it as a crime technically known as murder-a crime, rarely if ever, committed in Texas. We presume some considerable paliatory circumstances must have appeared on the trial to justify bail being allowed. Not having heard the evidence, we are of course, ignorant of what they were. As Mr. Flock has submitted to the laws, the people should submit also, and let his trial be full and fair".

While the above were verbatim from newspaper accounts of the day, the story continues:

Michael Flock was indicted for the Murder of Officer C. Edward Foley in the 11th District Court of Harris County on May 7, 1860. This began a most unusual chain of events which saw legal proceedings occur over the next six years without any final disposition. Harris County Sheriff's Deputy Doug M. Hudson, HPD Retired, provided this author with extensive research he compiled into the court proceedings. I have reviewed these documents with Deputy Hudson and we are unable to determine not only a final disposition, but a plausible reason for this obvious miscarriage of justice.

Page 137 of proceedings: May 15, 1860

In this case on motion of the District Attorney, it is ordered that a special venue facias issue returnable on Tuesday next the 15th of May directed to the Sheriff of Harris County.

Page 159 of proceedings:

He appeared in court with five men who severely acknowledge themselves indebted to the State of Texas in the sum of $400.00 each to be made and levied on their respective property for the use of the State of Texas. Wording is such that it appears that these five men were made to appear in open court any time that Michael Flock was ordered to appear.

Next page-four more named men under same proceedings.

May 16, 1860, page 161-ten more men added to the bond.

Thursday, December 13, 1862-Continued, April 29, 1863-continued, and on 12/4/1863-continued.

Thursday, 12/21/1865-Reba and Martin Floeck appeared and severely acknowledged themselves indebted to the State of Texas in the amount of $15,000.00.

NOTE: There is a discrepancy in the original newspaper articles and the later court proceedings. This difference was in the name of FLOCK and FLOECK. However, this is believed to be the same person, merely a difference in the spelling of the name in that era. Also, please note the lost years, from 1862-1865, these being the primary years of the War Between the States.

There are more lost years, as the name of Michael Floeck does not resurface in newspaper accounts until 1885. A summary of his activities, as printed in the Galveston Daily News, are as follows:

March, 1885-in Michael Floeck's show window on Travis Street, there is exhibited a gold and silver medal to be awarded in an upcoming shooting competition.

July, 1885-an assault and battery charge was dismissed against Michael Floeck.

August, 1885-a burglar was captured by police and several weapons belonging to Michael Floeck and another local businessman were recovered. Indications were that these items were taken from Michael Floeck's place on business on Travis.

September, 1886-Michael Floeck was on a streetcar with another well known businessman when this man was assassinated. Floeck was also in the company of other well-connected businessman leaving a theatre performance.

August, 1887-Michael Floeck was making considerable improvements to property owned by him.

April, 1888-Mike Floeck was crowned the King in a shooting competition among the town's elite at a local shooting club.

October, 1888-Mike Floeck was chosen as a delegate from Houston's Second Ward to a local political convention.

August and September, 1890-Michael Floeck was again mentioned as a convention delegate.

May, 1891-he was listed as a witness in a local civil court proceeding.

Galveston Daily News, July 10, 1891-FUNERAL OF MIKE FLOECK-"This forenoon at 10 o'clock the funeral of the late Mike Floeck took place from the residence of Mr. William Riter, in the Second Ward. The remains were laid to rest in the Catholic section of Glenwood Cemetery. He had lived in Houston since his childhood, and served through the late war with much credit. He died at the age of 52 years. Nearly all his life, except during the war, was spent in this city".

Why and How did Michael Floeck escape justice? Or did he?

There seems to have been a complete turnaround in the plight of Michael Floeck. He was nearly lynched on the spot for his murdering Officer Foley. Note the above change of tune in the newspaper articles in just the passing of one week. The newspaper changed from "He had no business to interfere with a policeman doing his duty" to "It does not become us to pass judgement upon him". One can only wonder what must have happened in just a short week for the newspaper to lighten its stand against this Michael Floeck.

It is known that Floeck was a member of a prominent family in Houston at the time involved in the beer brewing business and very likely, a family of some wealth. It appears from the above newspaper stories that a number of businessmen came forward to guarantee his bail. The disposition of the case seemed to stall during the Civil War years. His funeral notice indicated that he served during the war "with much credit".

While this is speculation on the part of this writer, it seems to be a possible (but certainly not justifiable) explanation that Michael Floeck went off to the Civil War in some type of attempt to amend for his murderous actions in taking the life of an Officer of the Law. Could he have done this to redeem himself and then continued as a businessman and political newcomer in the years following the war? Just as well, he could have served some time for his murderous deed after the war and prior to his name resurfacing in 1885. It would seem rather unusual for a convicted criminal to begin a new business 20 years later and be successful in that endeavor without family connections.

At this time, more importantly, nothing is known about Officer Foley's family nor about his final resting place. May Houston Police Officer C.Edward Foley continue to REST IN PEACE.

2

Officer Richard Snow
March 17, 1883

Campbell Kills Officer Richard Snow at 5th Ward Church Festival, Later Gets a Stay of Execution

The tragic events surrounding the death of Officer Richard Snow have been pieced together from 1883 newspaper accounts, which contain the descriptive language common to the era. The chronology begins with March 18 and 20 reports from The Houston Daily Post.

On Saturday night, March 17, 1883, Officer Richard Snow was at the home of Austin Johnson, a colored man, in the 5th Ward, near the International Compress Company. He was at this location to keep the peace at a church festival. It is believed that this was a departmental assignment. Around 10:30 p.m., Officer Snow sensed trouble from the crowd and he sent for another officer to come help him preserve order.

Snow felt he recognized one of the troublemakers at this party and began questioning the man about his true identity. This man, a colored man named Henry Campbell, resisted Officer Snow's inquiries. He became exasperated when he realized that Officer Snow knew his name to be Henry and the officer was persistent in his questioning.

Campbell then assaulted Officer Snow, knocking him down and thrusting him out the door. Snow returned inside and at about 11 p.m., Campbell began flourishing a pistol in this house. Snow attempted to arrest Campbell, but couldn't control this individual. He drew his pistol and during the struggle, while being held by members of the crowd, accidentally fired a shot that struck a small girl in the hand.

Campbell fired his gun directly at Officer Snow, striking him just above an eye. The wounded officer fell, got up on his feet and out into the yard, where he fell again. It was there that other officers picked him up. Special Officer William Humble had arrived just before the tragic shooting. Pandemonium followed and the crowd was so large that Officer Humble was forced to retreat as he was pursued by a crowd shouting, "We'll kill the other son of a b____ too." Humble, while probably not needing to justify his actions, later did so by saying that "self preservation is the first law of nature."

More help arrived. Deputy Sheriffs Keegan and Glasscock and Deputy Marshall Glass, along with others, went over and arrested Henry Campbell. These lawmen recovered a pistol, described as a "three barrel little .38 calibre five-shooting Ranger Number 2," from Campbell's room where he was arrested. Campbell also had in his possession a "hoodoo" bag, which he regretted very much to give up.

Initially, there were witnesses who did not want to admit that they had seen Campbell shoot Officer Snow. Some of them said that a white man had shot Officer Snow. However, it was later learned that Snow and Special Officer Humble were the only white men present prior to all of the other officers arriving later to make the arrest.

One star witness, John Green (colored), said he saw the suspect take deliberate aim and snap the first barrel of the weapon, then revolve the cylinder with his finger, shove the pistol almost into the officer's face, shoot and kill him. After Green told officers what he had seen, they recalled the fact that one barrel of the recovered weapon had a cap bursted but the barrel still loaded, while the one next to it manifestly had been discharged. On the strength of this statement, Green was asked to come to the station to make sure that Henry Campbell was the right man. In an 1883 version of a lineup, all of the prisoners on the lower floor of the jail were turned into the corridor. Officers instructed Green to come see if the suspect was the right man.

Almost instantly, Green pointed to Campbell as being the proper one, even though Campbell attempted to stand behind several others in the back part of the corridor.

The Daily Post commented with the following editorial statement: "A shooting and killing under any circumstances is bad enough, but when an officer is shot down in the discharge of his duty, the affair becomes cloaked in a different garb, and the grossest indignity is perpetuated against the government in its endeavor the protect the public welfare."

A reporter interviewed Henry Campbell in jail. Campbell denied being the shooter, saying that he didn't know he had an enemy in the Fifth Ward and couldn't understand why the colored people there would falsely accuse him. He told the reporter that he wanted to have a trial as early as possible.

The March 21, 1883 edition of The Daily Post reported that in a directly related incident, another tragedy occurred on Monday night, March 19, 1883, at the same location in the Fifth Ward. At around 8 p.m., someone knocked on the door of Austin Johnson's residence, asking him to come outside.

Johnson refused to open the door as he recognized a voice among the four white men who showed up wanting to speak to him. The voice was that of Special Officer Will Humble. When Johnson did not comply, four shots were fired through the front door, one of which struck and killed Mrs. Matilda Johnson, Johnson's wife.

That same night, Justice Bringhurst went to this location and empanelled a jury to assist him in conducting this inquest. The result was that the death of Mrs. Matilda Johnson was declared a homicide and Justice Bringhurst ordered Sheriff Fant to arrest Will Humble and place him in jail. After a hearing, Will Humble was ordered to be arrested and held without bail.

The Daily Post reported in its edition of Sunday, March 25 that the case of Henry Campbell was not placed on preliminary trial due to the absence of the city attorney prosecuting the case. The following Tuesday's edition (March 27) said that the murder of Officer Snow was declared cold-blooded and it is believed that the police have Henry Campbell "dead to rights." He was reported to have bold, brazen countenance and does not seem to be aware of the enormity of the crime committed. He is likely, they say, to dance the "airline jig."

..... Further developments:

San Antonio Daily Express (March 29):

In Houston, preliminary trial of Henry Campbell for killing Policeman Snow was held today, and he was held to await the action of the grand jury without bail.

Galveston Daily News (October 17):

The case was continued on affidavit of the defendant owing to the absence of attached witnesses, who were required to give a $300 appearance bond to appear in the next term of the court.

Galveston Daily News (December 15):

Houston is destined soon to have another hanging. Henry Campbell was tried for killing Officer Richard Snow. The jury was out only a half hour when they returned a verdict of murder in the first degree and sentenced Campbell to death.

Galveston Daily News (December 17):

Counsel for Henry Campbell filed an appeal. The motion will probably be argued tomorrow, and in the event of its being overruled, an appeal will be taken.

Galveston Daily News (March 7, 1884):

The action of the Court of Appeals, in affirming the death sentence passed by the Criminal Court upon Henry Campbell for the killing of Policeman Richard Snow, gives Houston the prospect of having another hanging in the near future. Final sentences will be passed at the April term of the Criminal Court, when the time of the execution will be fixed.

Galveston Daily News (April 28):

Prisoners will be sentenced on Thursday, among them Henry Campbell, who will receive his death sentence for the murder of Officer Snow.

Galveston Daily News (May 2):

While this case has gone to the upper court and the sentence has been affirmed, yet it is more than probable that Campbell's sentence will be commuted, as the killing was not of that premeditated, malicious character necessary to make that crime murder in the first degree. The crime, though heinous enough, was perpetrated in the heat of passion at a negro dance, surrounded by more or less excitement. It is understood that the officers of the court, the district attorney, and the court itself, if their opinion be solicited, would favor a commutation of the sentence.

Galveston Daily News (May 3):

Henry Campbell's execution was set for Friday, July 11, 1884. When called to the bar and asked if he had anything to say why the sentence of the law should not be passed upon him, Campbell protested that he was innocent and was not there when Snow was killed; but said if he had to be hunged (sic), he wanted it to be done publicly. He was prepared to meet his God and he wanted everybody to see that he was going to die happy. The judge then pronounced the sentence, and the small audience that had gathered to see how the murderer would look when listening to his own death sentence, quietly disappeared and the court adjourned for the term.

Galveston Daily News (June 24):

Sheriff Fant received the death warrant for Henry Campbell, scheduled to be executed here next month.

What brought about the change of attitude toward this crime? Later reports indicated that the small child in the house was killed, not just shot in the hand as first reported. In retrospect, this may have been a major turning point in this case. However, at the same time, it did not change the fact that Officer Richard Snow was killed while enforcing the law and attempting to maintain the peace.

Galveston Daily News (July 4):

A LEASE ON LIFE – Henry Campbell, the negro who stands convicted of murder in the first degree and was to be hanged on the 11th, has been granted a respite of 30 days. Governor Ireland issued and sent to Sheriff Fant an order not to hang the murderer until Friday, the 11th of August. This is probably done in order that the executive may have sufficient time to consider the merits of the case, as it is definitely one calling for the interpretation of executive clemency, as the killing was done in the heat of excitement at a ball. The crime was not attended by that premeditation and malice necessary to make the crime murder in the first degree.

Galveston Daily News (July 31):

Sheriff Fant received today a proclamation from Governor Ireland, commuting the death sentence of the negro Henry Campbell, who was to have been hanged on August 11, to a life sentence in the penitentiary. Campbell was originally sentenced to be hanged July 11, but the governor gave a respite for 30 days. The commutation gives no surprise to intelligent people here, who are conversant with all the facts connected with the crime for which Campbell was condemned to lose his life, and at the time of the sentence a commutation was predicted in these columns, as the facts in the case did not justify the verdict of murder in the first degree. Judge Cook was of the opinion at the time, and many argue from this that he should have then set the verdict aside.

The crime for which Campbell was convicted was the killing of Police Officer Snow at a negro dance in the fifth ward something over a year ago. At the time of the killing everything was in a state of excitement. Officer Snow had fired the first shot and killed a young colored child and was in turn shot by Campbell, with whom he was in a difficulty. With such surrounding circumstances the killing could scarcely be construed into murder in the first degree and the facts when laid before Governor Ireland, resulted in a commutation of the sentence. A NEWS correspondent accompanied Sheriff Fant when he went to the jail this evening to convey the intelligence to Campbell to note the effect of the good news. Campbell was brought from his cell into the Sheriff's room and before being told of his commutation conversed quite freely and seemed in excellent good spirits, despite the fact of his being cognizant of his near approaching end. He has all along denied the killing but the proof against him is too strong to make his denials plausible, even on the part of his own witnesses, and no such plea as that of his being innocent of the killing was made by his friends in their intercession for executive clemency. The prisoner laughed and talked for quite a while in his ignorant way before being informed of his commutation, and when Sheriff Fant did break the good news to him it had scarcely any perceptible effect, he merely remarking, in almost an indifferent way, that he was much obliged. He will be sent to the penitentiary in a few days.

Special Officer Will Humble was charged with the murder of Mrs. Matilda Johnson, who along with her husband resided at the location of the murder of Officer Richard Snow. Research into this disposition is listed from the Galveston Daily News for the following dates:
- October 4, 1883 – Case set for trial on October 23.
- October 23, 1883 – Case reset.
- December 7, 1883 – Case docketed for Saturday, December 22.
- December 22, 1883 – Case docketed for trial tomorrow in the Court of Judge Gustave Cook.

Research may continue at a later date. However, the fact remains that Officer Richard Snow was killed in the performance of his duty and his killer's death sentence was commuted.

3

Officer Henry Williams
February 8, 1886

Officer Henry Williams Shot and Killed By Member of a Well-to-do Area Family

A headline from the New York Times of Tuesday, February 9, 1886 read:
A POLICEMAN MURDERED-THE CRIME OF A MAN DRIVEN CRAZY BY STRONG DRINK

From that same day, a headline from the Galveston Daily News read:
SLAIN WITH A SIX-SHOOTER-MORE BLOODSHED IN THE BAYOU CITY

Other newspapers in Dallas and Houston basically told the tragic story of how a drunken young man from a prominent family took the life of one of the Houston Police Department's finest, Officer Henry Williams.

Kyle Terry, a tall, well-built and handsome young man from a prominent family in Richmond, Fort Bend County, had been in Houston for several days. It was reported that he had been indulging in liquor rather freely and had become extremely intoxicated. Officer Henry Williams confronted him for a city ordinance violation. Officer Williams, aware of Kyle Terry's reputation, used caution in dealing with him. He summoned Officer Jack White to assist him, figuring that Terry would resist any attempt to being arrested but would likely go peacefully with the more personally familiar Officer White.

On this Monday night, February 8, 1886, officers arrested Kyle Terry and took him to the station house. There, they removed a pistol from his possession and filed an additional charge relating to the weapon. Probably partially due to his family connections, he was released on bond with orders to appear in court the following morning at 10 o'clock to answer the charges levied against him.

After leaving the court and before going home for the night, he returned to the scene of his arrest. There, in one of the local bars, he met up with some of his drinking buddies. They added fuel to the already hot fire between him and Officer Williams. These "friends" were apparently successful when they prodded Terry on, telling him that Officer Williams had made verbal threats against Terry and obviously was "out to get him."

Terry arrived early for his court session the following morning. Being impatient, he admitted later that he desired a drink and left the courthouse to go to the bar. En route, he encountered Officer Henry Williams on Preston Street at the south corner of Market Square. Williams, who had likely been on duty the entire night, was on his way to do his duty by testifying against Terry regarding the arrest of the previous night.

Witnesses abounded at this daytime confrontation. An independent witness, A. F. Lazier, was very close to the tragic event. The Galveston Daily News wrote of his account: Lazier observed a disturbance between Officer Williams and several men. He started across the street and saw Terry there and heard him making some threatening remarks to the officer. He then saw Terry draw a revolver from his pocket and point it toward the officer, saying something like, "I am determined to kill." Everyone nearby scattered and ran. Terry rushed toward the officer, and from a distance of only four or five feet, fired one shot and then several more. Kyle Terry was heard to say something to the effect, "I have killed you, you SOB."

Constable Perkins grabbed Kyle Terry and tried to hold him, pleading for someone in the crowd to come and help him. Eventually, another officer, Dan Scanlan, stepped in and assisted Constable Perkins in the arrest of Terry.

There were numerous other witnesses to this murder and they were all consistent with Mr. Lazier. These independent witnesses stated that as Terry saw Officer Williams, he shouted to him while pulling his pistol, "there is the sonofabitch who is wanting to kill me." Whether this was true, it was apparently what Kyle Terry believed, especially after having been fired up the night before by his "friends." The only area in which these witnesses differed was whether Officer Williams was felled by the first shot or had already fallen when he was shot the first time.

All were in agreement that Kyle Terry fired more shots after Williams was on the ground. Another point of consistency in the witness accounts was that Williams had not drawn nor fired his weapon. One witness was quoted as hearing Terry shout "Get back all of you. Give me equal break or I will dose you all."

Unfortunately, the damage was done. Officer Williams died almost instantly in the gutter. He was taken at once to Justice Railey's office, where a jury of inquest was impaneled. The inquest, conducted by Dr. T. J. Boyles, determined that Williams was struck by one ball of ammunition near the left nipple, passing through the aorta and lodging at the junction of the ninth rib and the spinal column, causing almost instant death. Second and third balls struck his body, rendering the victim completely helpless and immobile.

The verdict of the inquest jury: "We, the jury, believe from the evidence before us that the deceased, Henry Williams, came to his death from a gunshot wound inflicted by one Kyle Terry, and that said pistol was held and fired by Kyle Terry, on February 8, 1886, in the City of Houston, Harris County." The jurors were listed as John Lang, J. B. Perkins, J. J. Sullivan, A. O. Harnett, J. A. Railey and H. Yungst (It is unknown whether this was HPD Officer Herman Youngst, who was killed in the line of duty in 1901).

Authorities took Kyle Terry to the county jail. As would be expected, the suspect's accounts differed greatly from those of the witnesses: Terry stated that as he met Williams on the street, the officer pulled his pistol. Terry also freely stated that several of his "friends" told him that Williams was "dogging him" and had made threats against his life.

The Galveston Daily News of February 9, 1886 contained an interview with Terry, who told the reporter that he was in Usener's saloon playing pool between 7 and 8 p.m. with James Freeman, Judge Cox and A. C. Bonds, all family friends from Brazoria County. A slight disagreement took place with Freeman. "We left and went over to Charley Tharonat's saloon when Officer Williams came in after us and displayed his nippers (slang for handcuffs), caught hold of me, and said, 'I want you.' I told him, 'You can take me if you treat me like a gentleman, but you can not take me under any other circumstances."

The party then left the saloon and scattered to different points, with Kyle Terry going to Jones' saloon. "Officer Williams followed me," Terry said, "and I told him that if I was to be arrested, I would go with Officer Jack White."

The defendant later said that Williams pulled his pistol on him the next morning on the street, a point that all of the witnesses disputed with their accounts.

One of the night-before witnesses was listed as Mike Floeck, believed to be the same individual who shot and killed Officer C. Edward Foley on March 10, 1860. While there was a strong movement to lynch Floeck on the same day he killed Officer Foley, unfortunately cooler heads prevailed. The reasons why Floeck was never properly processed through the Houston legal system remain a mystery to this day

Kyle Terry (White Male, 31) conducted business in Fort Bend County and resided in the Fifth Ward with his family. He was the son of General Frank Terry of Confederate Army renown, the namesake of the famed Terry's Rangers from the Civil War days. The defendant Terry also came from a fighting family, being a nephew of Judge A. W. Terry of California. He was a first cousin of a member of the most prominent law firm in Texas, that of Balinger, Molt and Terry of Galveston. After his arrest, he called this lawyer cousin for consultation. This might explain the considerable news coverage given to this Houston incident by the Galveston newspapers of the day.

Several conditions became apparent after numerous sworn witness statements involved a number of reputable citizens. Henry Williams and Kyle Terry had irreconcilable differences and were destined to meet a tragic fate. Terry thought Williams was out to get him and Williams, a man of some stature himself, had told several other officers that Terry had embarrassed him in the eyes of officers and citizens. Something had to give, and it did.

The funeral took place on the afternoon of February, 10, 1886. The remains were escorted to the gravesite at Glenwood Cemetery by the police force in uniform as well as relatives and a large number of friends. The pallbearers from the police force were Captain Jack White, Dan Scanlan, A. C. Moreland, James Furlong, J. Fitzgerald and George Gorham.

The station house was draped inside and outside with white and black streamers, and on the brick front was a large green wreath with fourteen in the center in black figures. The whole force showed deep respect for the memory of its dead comrade. Wall and Noland Undertaking took charge of the proceedings and conducted the funeral procession from Officer Williams' house in the Fourth Ward.

Henry Williams lived in Houston from boyhood. He was considered a reliable officer and at the time of his death held one of the most responsible night beats in the city. His home was in the northern section of the ward, where he left a wife and two or three children. With obviously no pension or official support for the family, a newspaper article of February 17, 1886 said, "Theo Pereira and Henry Ross donated a large oil painting to be raffled off for the benefit of the widow of Henry Williams. It is now framed and on display in the Two Orphans Saloon. Alex Erichson started the list by taking ten chances at $1 each. Five hundred chances are to be taken. It is believed that all the chances will be secured within the next few days."

While the entire life of Kyle Terry has not been researched, it should be noted that this was certainly not his first brush with the law. The Houston Daily Post of April 6, 1883 listed one Kyle Terry on the Criminal Court docket of Harris County on an assault charge.

The criminal proceedings in the Williams case began as early as February 17, 1886. The prosecution was in the hands of Major Frank Spencer, who had but few equals in the South as a prosecutor. Kyle Terry, seated dressed in a black suit, looked cool and collected and did not seem to manifest any uneasiness during the proceedings. He was represented by Messrs. Hutcheson and Carrington, two of the finest lawyers in the State of Texas. A number of witnesses testified at the preliminary hearing in this case. It seemed like a case that could easily be proved as a murder. However, due to the defendant's family ties, strange things started to happen.

The Galveston Daily News edition of Friday, March 5, contained a headline that read, "KYLE TERRY GRANTED BAIL IN THE SUM OF $5,000 BY THE COURT OF APPEALS."

The story read verbatim:

"It is a well known fact that whenever the duties of an honest, upright and conservative judge call him to sit in judgment upon a friend or a friend's relative, who is charged with a crime, his endeavor to mete out justice impartially and faithfully to his trust extends beyond the middle line and goes to the opposite extreme. A better illustration of this fact cannot be found than in the instance in which Judge Gustav Cook refused bail in the Kyle Terry case.

When the application for a writ of habeas corpus was made on behalf of Terry to Judge Cook, his friends were confident that bail would be granted, both for the reason that they thought the evidence justified such, and that Judge Cook would be lenient on account of his friendship with Colonel Frank Terry, the father of Kyle Terry who was an old army friend and who was succeeded in command of the Eighth Texas Regiment by Judge Cook.

Not fully appreciating the effect of the above rule, they were much surprised when Judge Cook refused Kyle Terry bail. They thereupon appealed his decision to the Court of Appeals, to which court the case was submitted upon the record and argument of counsel Wednesday.

The case was immediately considered by the Court of Appeals and yesterday, Judge Willson delivering the opinion, the court reversed the judgment of Judge Cook and granted Terry bail in the sum of $5000, to be taken by the Sheriff of Harris County. Judge Willson did not discuss the evidence in detail, nor intimate any opinion about it, but after citing section 11 of the bill of rights remarks, that as presented by the record the court could not say that the "proof is evident" that the prisoner is guilty of murder in the first degree, and therefore he is entitled to bail.

Papers necessary to be issued before the sheriff could accept bail were immediately forwarded to Houston by the first train.

The citizens of Houston and especially the family and fellow officers of Officer Williams must have been devastated. It would not be a stretch of the imagination to believe that "the fix was in." Unfortunately, it would only get worse.

The Galveston Daily News edition of Saturday, March 6, 1886 contained the headline, "KYLE TERRY RELEASED." The story read:

Early this morning a number of gentlemen presented themselves in Sheriff John Fant's office and stated that they were ready to go on the bond of Kyle Terry, held for killing Henry Williams. After preliminaries that lasted until 11 o'clock the bond of $5,000 was finally arranged and placed before the bondsmen, who signed their names as follows: J. D. Freeman, F. Whitesides, G. K. Sessner and Judge Cox.

Three of these gentlemen arrived from the country this morning for the express purpose of going on Kyle Terry's bond. All the signers are men of high standing and ample means. After the signing of the bond, Sheriff Fant issued an order for the release of the prisoner. When the doors of the cell and corridor were thrown open, he walked out into the open air, and after receiving congratulations of his friends, took a carriage ride and was driven by his wife to the Fifth Ward. He will remain at home until Monday, when he will leave for the plantation that he has in charge.

The Judge Cox assisting in making bail for Kyle Terry is the same Judge Cox with whom Kyle was drinking with the night before this tragedy.

Kyle Terry's journey through the legal system proceeded at a slow pace. After a number of continuances, the case finally went to trial in the court of Judge Kittrell in December 1886. The evidence was completed on the late evening of December 30. Courthouse observers felt that Terry would be acquitted. However, the jury returned a verdict of guilty of murder in the second degree and assessed a penalty of two years. To no one's surprise, Terry appealed this verdict and sentence and was immediately released on bail.

He returned to his plantation in Fort Bend County where he became heavily involved in politics. Terry's later activities are found to be rather intriguing.

In Fort Bend County after the Civil War, a rather infamous political feud brewed between two groups commonly known as the Jaybirds and Woodpeckers. On June 21, 1889, Kyle Terry went to Wharton, where he gunned down one of his political rivals, L. E. Gibson, in an obvious case of murder with which he was charged and released on bail. Sounds rather familiar.

The Gibson family also was well connected and the rival factions of the Jays and the Peckers both participated in the Riot of Richmond several months later. A number of people were killed. As a result, a federal grand jury indicted a large number of individuals. The case was such a political mess that somehow Galveston County wound up with the Terry murder case from Wharton County on a change of venue as well as the federal charges.

On January 21, 1890, an armed Kyle Terry arrived at the Galveston County Courthouse. His attorneys advised the local authorities that his life was in danger. However, no special precautions were taken and that morning, L. E. Gibson's brother, Volney, showed up and shot and killed Kyle Terry inside the Galveston County Courthouse. Volney Gibson was charged with murder, but the eventual disposition of the case was unknown.

Kyle Terry was buried at Glenwood Cemetery in Houston, the same resting place of his famous father as well as that of Houston Police Officer Henry Williams. In death, just as in his life, Kyle Terry was accompanied by people of wealth who were friends of his father. Terry's path of destruction through life was finally over at the age of thirty-four.

There is no marker at Glenwood for Officer Henry Williams, whose remains have laid there at rest since 1886, 120 years ago. With the cooperation of the 100 Club, the Houston Police Officers Union and Glenwood Cemetery, the grave will finally get an appropriate marker – the 100 Club's LINE OF DUTY headstone that marks the final resting places for Houston officers who paid the ultimate price to keep the community safe from wrong doers, especially cold-blooded killers.

4

Officer James E. Fenn
March 15, 1891

Officer James E. Fenn Shot to Death In 5th Ward 'Dive,' His Killer Hanged

On Saturday night, March 14, 1891, Houston Police Officer James E. Fenn was on duty, assigned to a Negro dance hall commonly known as the "Bill Davis dive." While there, he observed an individual known to him and also known to usually carry a pistol. He approached this man and upon doing so, was shot. He was taken down the street to the offices of Dr. Duffau for medical treatment.

He gradually sank after reaching there, but remained in a semiconscious condition up to almost the last moment. He passed away as his wife and three children were being rushed to him in a hack. He was not able to see them, having passed away at 1:30 a.m. Sunday, March 15, 1891. Officer Fenn was only thirty-five years old.

Police Chief Charles Wichman immediately headed up an investigation at the Bill Davis "dive" and dance hall. A key witness, Joe Walker, related the following:

"I was standing behind one of the violinists when Officer Fenn came over to me and said, 'Hello, Joe, I thought you had gone home.' I told him, 'I thought I would stay a while longer.' Officer Fenn saw a man he thought had a pistol and started for him. When he got close the man started to shoot. I did not notice the man closely, but I think he is a small man and wore a black hat. I afterward saw a man looking like him running towards the International and Great Northern bridge in the direction of the Fifth Ward."

As the witness interviews progressed, police determined that the suspect possibly had an accomplice. One witness reported that after the suspect shot Officer Fenn, this accomplice was nearby and was well acquainted with the suspect. After he was taken into custody and questioned, he provided officers with the name of the suspect, Henry McGee. Thus, the accomplice, Sam Ashwood, who was a close acquaintance of the suspect, became a key eyewitness to this murder.

A description of Henry McGee was obtained and distributed as well as it could be in those days. It was learned that Henry McGee was a waiter of recent employment at both the Capitol Hotel and Grand Central Hotel in the downtown area. He was described as being a Negro male, about five feet, six inches tall, slight build, small moustache, dark complexion, lame in the left leg from rheumatism, and walks with difficulty. His clothing at the time was a small, stiff black hat, black pantaloons, dark sack coat, white shirt with a handkerchief tied around his neck. He fled with what was believed to be the murder weapon, a .44-caliber Bulldog pistol.

Henry McGee made his getaway from the scene on foot, running toward the Southern Pacific crossing, making his way eastward. It was learned that he had a brother living in Beaumont and other relatives in Louisiana. His reported sightings in other parts of Houston were checked out with negative results.

There was likely a history between Officer Fenn and Henry McGee. It will never be known, but it was thought that McGee held a grudge against Fenn regarding an arrest that took place three months prior. McGee was heard to make a threat against Fenn. As was common in those days, those threats were likely shrugged off as part of the job. In today's terms, it was "the nature of the beast."

Following the death of Officer Fenn in the doctor's office, the remains were taken to an undertaker at once. The funeral was held at 10 a.m. Monday, March 16, 1891. The Knights of Labor held charge of the ceremonies. On Sunday, funeral notices were circulated which contained the following notice:

"The officers and members of the Pioneer Assembly No. 4215, Knights of Labor, are hereby requested to meet at their hall in the Fifth ward, Monday morning at 8:30 o'clock, for the purpose of attending the funeral of our deceased brother James E. Fenn. Officers and members of sister assemblies are invited to attend."

Services would be conducted from the late officer's residence beyond the Fair grounds. Burial followed at the Washington Cemetery, then known as the German Society Cemetery. A resolution passed by the Knights of Labor was printed in the newspaper of March 22. It read:

"To the memory of our brother, James E. Fenn, deceased: Whereas, it has pleased the Almighty Master Workman of the Universe to remove from our midst our brother, James E. Fenn, and Whereas, Pioneer Assembly and the order has lost a brave, true and faithful member and his family a kind, loving and affectionate husband and father: now therefore be it Resolved, that the members of this assembly extend their heartfelt sympathy to the family of our deceased brother in this their sad bereavement, and that a copy of these resolutions be spread upon the record of this assembly and a copy be sent to the family of our deceased brother; and be it further Resolved that a copy of these resolutions be sent to the daily press for publication, and that the charter of this assembly be draped in mourning for the space of thirty days."

A newspaper account of the tragedy was headlined, THE DOGGERIES MUST GO. The story read:

"Chief Wichman has issued the edict which will drive them out of town. The wanton murder of brave Officer James E. Fenn in the Bill Davis dive (defined as 'a disreputable place for drinking and gambling') on Saturday night thoroughly aroused public sentiment against these places. Houston promises to be soon purged of them. It was the universal verdict yesterday that an efficient policeman had been slain, and that in the death of Officer Fenn, the seal of doom was stamped upon the dives of the city."

Chief Wichman, heading up the investigation, received a tip after two days and nearly two nights of diligent search for the suspect. The chief got information that the suspect was at a Negro cabin in the First ward, a block north of Koesler's store off Houston Avenue. The chief led a posse of officers in a raid of this cabin and arrested the suspect, Henry McGee. Newspaper accounts indicated that following the arrest, Chief Wichman suggested to McGee the propriety of just shooting him in the abdomen as he done Officer Fenn. McGee, of course, denied having done it that way. It is probable that in this day and time, an abdomen gunshot wound was nearly always fatal.

After the arrest, there was a good deal of talk about a mob forcing the jail and taking Henry McGee out and hanging him. The mob failed to materialize, which was fortunate since Harris County Sheriff Ellis was prepared for the worst, strongly feeling his sworn duty to protect the prisoner.

The date of the trial differs somewhat in several news publications. We can safely say that it took place during the week of April 21, 1891 in criminal court. Henry McGee's attorney moved for continuance, but Judge Cleveland overruled him. The case then went to trial. Out of a venire of sixty men, the court had obtained nine jurors by 6 p.m. and recessed until 7:30 p.m. to choose one more juror before adjourning until the next day. The case against the prisoner was considered to be very strong. What the state had to do was prove the identity of the suspect, which the officers believe they could do without a doubt.

Once chosen, the jury considered the evidence and returned a guilty verdict, assessing Henry McGee the death penalty. McGee's attorney filed an appeal and the appeals court ordered a new trial, which was set for the May 1892 term. Another jury again found McGee guilty and assessed the death penalty.

More details of both of these trials are summarized in the article which described the punishment received by Henry McGee. This lengthy newspaper article is rather graphic in the description. Here is the headline and complete story in the Galveston Daily News for Saturday, August 13,

1892:

HENRY MCGEE SUSPENDED-THE NEGRO CONVICTED OF KILLING OFFICER FENN IS DEAD

Detailed and graphic account of how the Law's decree was executed

Henry McGee, the murderer of Officer James Fenn, was hanged today in expiation of the crime and in accordance of the court. The sentence was primarily to have been executed last Friday, August 5, but by respite from the governor it was postponed to Friday, August 12, and therefore to take place today.

The newspapers this morning contained a special telegram from Governor Hogg saying he saw no reason why the sentence should not be executed and instructing the Sheriff of Harris County to carry out the law.

It set aside all doubt that might have been entertained that the execution would not take place. The result was that many Houstonians began early to prepare to witness the execution. Sheriff Ellis had given out between fifty and one hundred passes to persons to witness the hanging, in order that the law might be fully complied with in this respect.

As early as 8 o'clock, people began to gather on the street extending in front of the jail. There were only a few at this hour, but their stopping and staring up into the jail door and windows attracted others. They were men, women and children, and nearly all Negroes. Soon drays, buggies and horsemen began to stop and swell the crowd.

First they were confined to the sidewalk bordering the jail yard. Soon that was full and the outer line of the crowd extended into the street, and finally stretched across and filled the opposite sidewalk. It became a multitude of men, women and children of all ages and colors. They clustered around drays and wagons thicker than anywhere else, because there they found something upon which they could lean or rest, and perhaps from which they could get a better view, if one point had any advantage over another.

Shortly after 9 o'clock officers were placed at the front gate to admit persons who had business on the inside or whose right to admission was unquestionable. After the officers were inside one of the first to arrive was a brother of the condemned man, whose home was down about Lynchburg, near the mouth of Buffalo Bayou. He was ushered upstairs into the presence of his brother and sitting in front of the cell occupied by the condemned man, they talked of the terrible situation.

They were in the presence of others, including the death watch, and the conversation was audible to them all. Henry McGee talked cheerfully with his brother and among other things told him that Jailer Anderson would give him $3 or $4, a Bible and a Testament, they being about the only things of which he possessed. They talked mostly about the subject of religion, and Henry assured his brother of his readiness for the terrible ordeal through which he would go to meet Jesus. The situation became quite affecting before the interview ended. He told his brother to take charge of his remains and bury them.

It was considerably after 9 o'clock before the newspaper men began to arrive. It was perhaps 9:30 when the News correspondent entered. Henry was standing in his cell looking through the window over the crowd on Caroline street, but he turned, and in replying to an inquiry concerning himself he said: "I feel I can't complain, can't grumble, I feel first rate."

"Are you ready for the terrible trial?" asked the correspondent.

"Whenever God is ready to do his will I am ready."

No feature of the prisoner's face indicated terror, dread, or fear. When talking he seemed happy. It was learned that had slept well during the night, had eaten a couple of eggs and a few slices of cake for breakfast and relished them.

Jailer Anderson appeared in front of the door and the prisoner asked if he could get a razor to shave. While the jailer stepped aside to see the Sheriff the prisoner forgot it and the matter was never mentioned again.

Addressing the News correspondent, he said: "I hope everything you say about me after I am gone will be correct. I want to appear before my Maker with that report to make my showing."

Here he began in a low tone to hum a hymn, uttering at short intervals the names of God and Jesus. His voice was very weak and it was often difficult to catch his words. While humming he rolled a cigarette and asked for a match with which he lit it and began to smoke.

In answering a question he said: "I want to see my redeemer lives; I want to appear before him."

It was 9:45 when Elder Yates, one of his spiritual advisors, appeared and took his seat in front of the cell door. McGee was glad to see him and at once assured him of his readiness to go and the perfect freedom of his heart from fear. The minister repeated to him comforting passages from various parts of the Bible and impressed upon him the real importance of having truth in his heart and firm belief in God.

"Jesus said: 'Whosoever believeth in me shall not die but have everlasting life.' " At these words McGee knelt upon the floor and watched the minister eagerly. The minister then referred to the comforting words of the Savior to the thief on the cross. All must be prepared, you as well as others, to meet Jesus.

In the meantime persons to whom the sheriff had given permission to be with the prisoner during the hour of his preparation for the gallows began to arrive and at 10 o'clock, the following were in the large west corner room on the second floor, into which the prisoner was led from his cell: George Ellis, Sheriff; Deputies Pruett, Conaway, Parker, Gwynn and Sation,

Dr. Koubig, Rev. Yates, Justice Schwander, Constable W. M. Glass, Messrs. John Warren, William Schultz, Lewis Ross, A. Carmichael, Dr. H. Rutherford, and several newspaper men. At 10:01 o'clock Jailer Anderson opened the cell door and Deputy Sation escorted the prisoner into the large room.

The prisoner's face in the light showed that it had bleached a good deal. The shackles held his feet, he wore a brown shirt, striped pair of pants, socks without shoes or slippers. He was immediately taken into the bathroom, where he bathed and put on an entirely new suit of clothes. His face clearly indicated that the change pleased him and as he got into the new white shirt he smiled pleasantly. There was no attempt on his part to kill time or delay the proceedings. It was 10:20 when he began to dress and at 10:23 he stepped out of the little bathroom fully dressed. He wore a black suit, white shirt, collar, tie and gloves and gaiters, all new.

He was handed a chair and took his seat far from a window. Sheriff Ellis stepped in front of him and read the death warrant in a clear voice but not loud tone. The prisoner watched him and listened attentively to every word that was uttered. He sat with head leaning to one side.

Following these he read the governor's proclamation published in these columns this morning. At 10:40 o'clock both had been read to him.

At this juncture Rev. Watts, the leading spiritual advisor of McGee entered the room and immediately he and Rev. Yates had a whispered conversation. The three then united in singing a spiritual hymn. They stood and the prisoner showed some nervousness during the singing. He entered fully into the spirit of the lines. They sang a couple of verses and Rev. Yates prayed as follows:

"Most Holy Father, you know the cause of our meeting here today; it is to witness the execution of one man who has shed another's blood. 'Whosoever sheds the blood of man by man his blood shall be shed. So says God our Father.' In the image of our father God we thank thee, because you govern all, and we hope you will recognize our brother to the Savior. We thank thee because you have these powers in heaven and earth; you have power over all flesh and all mankind. We pray this morning that you have mercy upon Henry McGee. And, O Lord, forgive his transgressions, if it please thee, God, for Jesus' sake. Be merciful, O God, and be with us here today. Bless all the officers who are here today and may the face of Christ shine in you when you meet in another world. Amen."

During the prayer the prisoner knelt upon one knee, supporting his right elbow on the other and resting his face in his right hand. They formed an earnest group, and others in the rooms showed the same earnestness. They arose and Rev. Watts at the conclusion of the prayer approached McGee and the following conversation ensued:

Rev. Watts: How do you feel in regard to death?

McGee: I am willing and ready to die. I feel no distress and trust myself to Jesus. I know that he will forgive me for my sins.

Rev. Watts: How do you feel toward your fellow man, as the sheriff, the jury and others?

McGee: I have nothing against them. I have nothing to fear and know that I will meet my Jesus.

Rev. Watts: The hour has now come for you to go. Did you kill Officer Fenn?

McGee: I did not kill Officer Fenn. I have told you this, elder, many times when you asked me. I can not tell a lie to you. I will tell the truth, elder, and I am ready to go in his place. Thank God, he may meet me, for I go in his place.

Rev. Watts: Would you like to see your wife?

McGee: No, I do not care to see my wife. Tell my sister goodby. I will meet her in the glory land. I have no other word to send her.

Rev. Watts: Do you believe God will forgive you?

McGee: I feel that God has told me so. I feel in my heart that I am going clear to heaven. I feel that God has told me so, I know he has, I know it. I know that God loves me. I will soon have to die for another man.

Rev. Watts: You do not dread the hour of death?

McGee: Oh no, God stands to meet me in heaven. Jesus said he would be there. I know and believe the great God will be there. I do not feel scared about anything, no, I don't feel scared about anything. I want to give everybody satisfaction before I leave, but I know I can't do it. I can't satisfy all the people.

Rev. Watts: Do you feel satisfied that when you are hung on the gallows you will go to Christ?

McGee: I am depending on his word, yes sir.

Rev. Watts: Have you anything against anyone?

McGee: I have got nothing against this world.

Rev. Watts: Did you say you would like to see your sister?

Sheriff Ellis (interrupting): Your sister is in Galveston.

McGee: Oh, I am as happy as ever.

Rev. Watts: You found great virtue in prayer; you did not pray much before I visited you.

McGee: I couldn't pray downstairs, the boys bothered me. I did pray there, but was glad Sheriff Ellis put me upstairs. I had more chance. I feel like a good man, now.

Rev. Watts: You claimed to have conversion in this cell upstairs. I would like to know how you knew it and when was it?

McGee: It was between 11 and 12 o'clock one night.

Rev. Watts: How did you know you were changed?

McGee: I couldn't tell you how I felt, it was so good. I felt like I had just come out of it, thrown it off and was free.

Rev. Watts: Before conversion, how did you feel?

McGee: I couldn't eat or drink anything.

Rev. Watts: What kind of impression did it make on you?

McGee: I felt very much relieved, nothing didn't bother me and I felt good inside.

Rev. Watts: Do you feel ready to go?

McGee: Yes, I feel ready to go and good to everybody.

Rev. Watts: John the apostle says you can tell death from life and life from death when you love everybody.

McGee: Yes, Lord.

The prisoner here talked of his condition of mind and his future with cheerful enthusiasm, forcibly endeavoring to impress upon the minister the bright feeling of his heart. While talking of this condition he moved his arms and head with much animation and feeling.

Rev. Watts: Brother McGee, I am going read you "The Christian's Future Home" to encourage you on your journey.

At the conclusion of the reading of the passage it was 10:57 o'clock and Rev. Watts said, "Brother McGee, would you like to tell your friends goodby at the gallows?"

McGee: I don't know whether it would do any good. I don't feel like telling them goodby.

During the reading of the encouraging words of the "Christian's Future," the prisoner sat and watched the minister intently, looking glad as the words uttered applied to his case.

At 10:58, Dr. Red, the county physician, entered the room and everything was in readiness to go upstairs to the scaffold. Drs. Geo. McDonald and Geo. Larendon came into the room at this time. During this time Rev. Watts was talking to the prisoner, telling him that if he believed in God he would be saved and there was no power that could keep him out of heaven.

In the meantime persons who had been given passes were allowed to enter the front gate and hurry directly up to the third floor, where the hanging was to take place. There was a great jam at the gate, and several policemen were on a strain to prevent the crowd from forcing their way into the yard. The trouble was to allow those who had a right to be there to come in, and at the same time keep the others out.

They were finally upstairs, and at 11:10 o'clock Sheriff Ellis gave the signal, and the minister, with the prisoner between them, and the deputies in front and behind, started to ascend the steep steps. The way was clear and the solemn procession moved without hindrance or delay upstairs. The prisoner walked with a firm step, though he leant on the arms of the ministers for support. The party reached the floor upon which the scaffold stood and moved directly up the steps leading to the gallows. Immediately upon the landing the prisoner stepped, following the indication of the sheriff, upon the trap door, the ministers taking their places in front of him and others around. There were nineteen on the platform.

It was 11:12 o'clock when they were all arranged. The prisoner first stood with his face toward Caroline street. In a few seconds he turned, overlooking the crowd and with his back to Preston avenue. He held his hands behind him and in one grasped a handkerchief. They trembled very slightly. As all were in place the Rev. Watts started the hymn:

"Oh, thy poor soul be not afraid, If God be with us there; We will walk through the dark country and never yield to fear."

McGee joined them and sang in a firm voice. Rev. Watts then knelt down in prayer, and McGee kneeling on the trap door, the following prayer was offered by Rev. Watts:

"Ever wise and omnipotent father, we are gathered here this morning on a solemn and serious mission. We are here for the purpose of putting trust in the Lord Jesus Christ and we hope if it pleases his will that he will give him courage and assist him in this trying hour. In the name of the Lord Jesus Christ. He cometh up as a flower and is cut down in the midst of life. I am the resurrection and the life and though I may die I die not forever and my spirit lives. Though the worms may destroy our body our spirit will live and we will rise on the day of resurrection. Oh, Father, help him for God's sake. In the name of the Father, Son, and Holy Ghost I now commit Brother McGee in your hands. Save him the miseries of death, oh God. God bless the officers and those who are gathered here. In the name of the resurrection of Christ, Amen."

The silence that followed was oppressive.

Then the crowd with upturned faces and eager gaze watched everything that was done, every motion that was made by anyone. Jailer Anderson immediately began binding the prisoner's hands behind him. With this the prisoner said: God bless everybody, goodbye, God bless you Sheriff Ellis, and turning his pinioned hands to one side he sought the Sheriff's hand and shook it. He then said, God bless you Mr. Bob Sation, you have been good to me, God bless you, and you Mr. Anderson, you have been so kind to me, God bless you forever. God bless you all and with those the prisoner stepped off in his enthusiasm of the trap door, and overlooking the crowd said, God bless you all, I can't blame anybody, I got myself into it.

He was easily moved back on the trap, and at 11:17 the knot was adjusted about his neck and the black cap pulled over his head. He stood firm all the time. His knees were pinioned by Jailer Anderson and he was ready. The trap was cleared and 11:18 Sheriff Ellis pulled the lever and Henry McGee dropped into eternity. He never kicked or struggled and death must have been instantaneous. As soon as he dropped, Drs. Red and Rutherford were at his side.

At 11:21 he was declared dead, and at 11:22 the body was cut down by Jailer Anderson and carried downstairs by three colored men and the officers. His neck was examined and found by the doctors to have been broken. The body was laid in the coffin at 11:33 and turned over to his brother by being placed in charge of undertakers Ross & Wright. It was taken down to Lynchburg for burial tomorrow.

The crime which cost Henry McGee his life was committed March 14, 1891. It was the killing of Officer James Fenn. It occurred at a Negro dance house known as the old broom factory, near the International freight depot in this city. The officer had been placed there to keep order and was sitting on the end of the counter when a pistol was discharged in the room and Officer Fenn hurried to the spot and found Henry McGee with a pistol in his hand.

He extended his hand to arrest McGee when the latter shot him, the ball taking effect near the navel and passing out near the spinal column. Frank Michaels, who had gone to the aid of the officer grabbed McGee and while they were struggling McGee handed the pistol to another negro to shoot Michaels, which he did, the ball going through the shoulder and causing Michaels to release McGee, who made his escape, but was arrested Monday or Tuesday night following by Marshal Wichman in the house of Tampy Jackson in the First ward. When Fenn was shot he was brought to the house of Dr. Duffau's office on Main street and died about midnight, an hour after the shooting.

Henry McGee was twice tried for murder, found guilty of the crime both times with the death penalty assessed. The first trial was commenced on April 21, 1891, before Judge Cleveland with W. M. Baker as foreman of the jury. DA J. K. Gillespie represented the state and C. W. Bocock was appointed by the presiding judge to defend McGee. The jury returned the verdict on April 25, 1891. A motion for a new trial was made and overruled on May 2 and an appeal was taken on the grounds that the court erred in admitting the evidence of Dan Going to go to the jury because he was the father-in-law of the defendant and had been conditionally pardoned for the crime of murder of the first degree by the governor. The court of appeals sustained the objections and reversed and remanded the case for another trial in the criminal district court of Harris county.

The second trial was heard during the May term of court in 1892. J. K. P. Gillespie and James V. Lea appeared for the state and C. W. Bocock and Uvalde Burns for McGee, the defendant. G. H. Tips was foreman of the jury. The death of Judge Cleveland having occurred last fall, Judge E. C. Cavin of Galveston presided at the second trial. McGee was again found guilty of murder in the first degree, with the death penalty assessed. Judge Cavin sentenced McGee for the second time July 2, 1891, to be hanged August 5, but he was respited to August 12.

Henry McGee died on the gallows in 1892 for the murder of Houston Police Officer James Fenn.

5

Officer William A. Weiss
July 30, 1901

Officer Weiss, Father of Two, Shot to Death By a Known Drunk Having a Bad Police Day

In the summer of 1901, there resided in Houston two brothers from Powder Springs, Georgia. These two young men were cocky, confident and seemingly of means beyond appearance. They were J. T. Vaughn and his brother Newt. Their apartment/business was at 1113½ Congress Avenue between Fannin and San Jacinto. It was common knowledge in the community that they were well supplied with money since they were in the money-lending business. J. T. also was a law student at the time. It was reported that their father and a brother practiced medicine in their home state of Georgia.

Policing in the downtown area of Houston in 1901 involved the dedicated Houston officers who were charged with keeping the peace and at the same time provided some protection for one other. Their jobs didn't yet include the convenience of radios or vehicles. Any "report" came from the officers personally witnessing a crime or from citizens' word of mouth.

At 7 p.m. Monday, July 29, 1901, J. T. Vaughn, later described as having a "propensity for strong drink and drinking sprees," was arrested by Officer Herman Youngst for discharging a pistol through a window in his apartment. Officer Youngst booked him in jail but Vaughn was released about 11 p.m. that same night. Once he got this freedom J. T. Vaughn set out to find the arresting officer, claiming that his watch and $25 was missing from the effects he reclaimed upon leaving the jailhouse. He returned to the area around Yadon's Saloon at the corner of Congress and San Jacinto. Yadon's was a popular place among locals who had the means to buy themselves drinks.

J. T. found his brother Newt and told him about his missing cash and watch. At about the same time, their attorney, R. E. Kahn, with whom the two brothers had transacted considerable business, was walking toward Yadon's for a nightcap. He had just left the nearby Red Men's Hall, where he was a respected member.

The Vaughn brothers advised Kahn of the situation and he went in search of the arresting officer, Herman Youngst. While en route, they met Officer William F. Weiss, to whom Kahn explained the details of the missing money and watch. Officer Weiss, also a member of the Red Men's Lodge, was apparently a welcome ear to Kahn and J. T. Vaughn, his disgruntled client. Several citizens later identified as witnesses said it appeared to them that a conversation between Youngst, Weiss, Kahn and the Vaughn brothers went well. Officer Youngst said he had no idea what Vaughn was talking about and, further, that if J. T. Vaughn had any property missing, he needed to go back to the police station in the morning to claim it.

OFFICER WILLIAM A. WEISS

Apparently, Kahn was satisfied at this point but J. T. Vaughn was not ready to put this matter to rest for the night. Officer Bill Weiss, an acquaintance of Kahn's from the Red Men's organization, was standing nearby during the conversation involving Vaughn and Youngst. It is unknown whether J. T. Vaughn was intoxicated at this point, but it is safe to say he was definitely agitated over the matter. Information from an independent witness, Dick Miller, indicated the following chain of events leading up to the tragedy:

J. T. Vaughn pointed toward Officer Weiss and said, "Maybe he got it." Whereupon Weiss responded, "I don't know anything about it." As the officer turned to walk away, Vaughn continued with the words, "Maybe you would, too."

Weiss grew somewhat agitated. With authority, he stated to Vaughn, "Don't you accuse me of anything like that" and raised his club. Newt Vaughn stepped in between his brother and the officer, provoking Weiss to push him back.

"Don't step between us when I am talking to your brother or I will let you have it too," Weiss said. "If you are looking for trouble, I can whip you without my club."

J. T. Vaughn then reached for his hip, pulling out a pistol from his pants. He shot Weiss four times, causing the officer to fall to the street, mortally wounded.

Officers J. C. James and Henry Lee were sitting in front of the station on Caroline when they heard the shots. They ran down to the corner of San Jacinto and Congress, where they found Officer Youngst standing near the body of Officer Weiss, who was already dead at the scene. Youngst told them that "they" did it and that "they" were inside the saloon.

All three officers charged inside Yadon's, where they were told that Vaughn "did it" and that he had run out the back door. Officers Lee and James then pursued the suspect, who ran north on San Jacinto and west on Franklin before making the block by running back south on Fannin and east on Congress.

A gun battle between the two officers and Vaughn ensued around the block. Officer Rabouln and Special Officer Quinby followed, ready to help their fellow officers.

Another witness, M. A. Grant, saw the latter part of this event. Grant and his family occupied rooms upstairs in the building adjoining the Vaughn brothers' rooms. Grant was a witness to the shooting earlier in the evening that led to Officer Youngst's arrest of J. T. Vaughn. Grant heard the gunfire that killed Weiss and started downstairs to investigate when J. T. Vaughn met him on the stairway. Vaughn proceeded to push him aside, causing Grant to go back upstairs to protect his wife. Vaughn followed, running into their sitting room.

Grant had personal experience with Vaughn and was well aware of his propensity for strong drink. Thinking he was under the influence of liquor, he pushed Vaughn out into the hallway. In doing so, Vaughn was silhouetted, gun in hand. Officers Lee and James began firing at Vaughn, wounding him and causing him to stagger down the stairs. He fell down, not fifty feet from where the slain Officer Weiss lay. Newt Vaughn was allowed to go to his brother and, along with the other officers, heard his brother's last words: "I died game."

Then he breathed his last breath, leaving his .41-caliber pistol in the stairway.

After Sergeant Busey arrived, Yadon's Saloon was shut down for the night. Justice of the Peace Malsch arrived and held an inquest into the deaths of Officer Weiss and his deceased assailant, J. T. Vaughn. On orders from Justice Malsch, an autopsy was performed on the body of Weiss, who had been taken to the Westheimer undertaking establishment. There the judge continued his inquest as the autopsy was performed.

Two .41-caliber slugs were found in Officer Weiss, one that had passed through his heart and another very near it. Both were determined to be sufficient to cause his death. The judge also ruled that the wounds were inflicted from very close range – Weiss' clothing contained powder burns.

J. T. Vaughn was removed to the undertaking establishment of Ross and Wright. While no autopsy was ordered on him, Justice Malsch determined his cause of death was from one bullet wound to his abdomen. His brother Newt was taken into custody for questioning and investigators released him after concluding he had no part in the death of Officer Weiss. Newt was allowed to send messages to his brother and parents in Dallas and Powder Springs, Georgia.

William A. "Willie" Weiss was born in Houston on March 7, 1870. His parents were Mr. and Mrs. J. F. Weiss. Besides his mother and father, he left a wife and two small children. Funeral services for the beloved officer were held at his residence at 215 LaBranch at 4 p.m. Wednesday, July 31, 1901. The services were under the auspices of the Little Elk Tribe No. 94, Improved Order of the Red Men and the Maccabees, both organizations who were proud to have Willie Weiss as a member.

In addition to the members of these fraternities, the entire night police force attended as active and honorary pallbearers. The night police force met at police headquarters at 3 p.m. and marched to the residence. Active pallbearers were Deputy Chief Henry Thompson, Sergeants J. C. Busey and Charles Williford and Chief Clerk William Kessler. Serving as honorary pallbearers were Officers Lee, James, Bernner, Lahey, Gossett, Patrick, Whittington, Youngst, Newhoff, Higgins, Proctor, Howard, Charlton, Cahill, and Night Clerk Krum. Burial followed at Glenwood Cemetery on Washington Avenue.

A newspaper account about the effects Officer Weiss' death had on the community included this passage:

"Officer Weiss, very popular as an officer and as a citizen. The lawyer at the bar, the clerk behind the counter, the blacksmith as he shod a refractory colt chewing an unaccustomed bit, the street car motorman as he turned on and off the mysterious currents that propel the cars. All who knew the dead officer joined in some kind of tribute to him. At the police station the customary show of solemn bleak was made, and the crepe by the door was but the trappings and suits of woe which was felt by every member of the department with whom this reporter talked."

Officer Weiss was the fifth known HPD officer to give his life in the line of duty, the first in ten years and the first in the 20th century. What followed just four short months later continued a sad trend for the entire century. Weiss's gravesite was located at Glenwood Cemetery. From the handsome marker placed on his family plot, it appears his survivors were people of means.

His marker reads:

WILLIAM A. WEISS, MARCH 7, 1870-JULY 30, 1901.

"THERE WAS AN ANGEL CHOIR IN HEAVEN THAT WAS NOT QUITE COMPLETE,
SO GOD TOOK OUR DARLING WILLIE TO FILL THE VACANT SEAT."

With the wonderful cooperation of Mr. and Mrs. Richard Ambrus and Ms. Martha Peterson at Glenwood Cemetery, an additional marker was placed at the foot of Officer Weiss's grave in 2004. This marker is the LINE OF DUTY foot marker provided by the 100 Club of Houston and Harris County. Mr. and Mrs. Ambrus and Glenwood Cemetery donated the installation costs.

There is one other HPD Officer killed in the Line of Duty interred at Glenwood. That is Officer Rufus Daniels, one of five Houston police officers killed in 1917 during the Camp Logan riot. His gravesite has never had a marker and in 2006, his grave was marked with the 100 Club LINE OF DUTY marker, also made possible by Glenwood Cemetery management.

6 & 7

Officer Herman Youngst
Badge #7
and
Officer John C. James
December 11, 1901

Noted Gambler Got His Shotgun and Murdered Two of Houston's Finest on Tragic Day in 1901

On Wednesday, December 11, 1901, at about 4 p.m., a tragedy occurred at the intersection of Congress Avenue and San Jacinto Streets in the heart of downtown Houston. After the gunshots quieted, a large crowd shadowed the scene. There they saw two of the Houston Police Department's finest lying dead, one in the street and the other in the gutter.

They were fifty-eight-year-old Officer Herman Youngst, a twenty-eight-year veteran, and thirty-five-year-old Officer John C. James, who had been with the department going on three years. This was the same corner location where earlier in the same year – on July 30 – Officer William A Weiss was murdered. Also dead at the Youngst-James death scene was Sid Preacher, a young white man. While less than thirty years old, Preacher had lived a rather wild life and was well known to Houston police.

Two eyewitness citizens reported to the Houston Chronicle their account of the tragic event:

"We were standing in front of Yadon's saloon when our attention was attracted by Sid Preacher and another man. They were verbally abusing several HPD detectives for making it so difficult for Preacher and his cohorts, gamblers by trade, to conduct their business during the carnival season. They were 'roasting' the detectives.

"Then, Detective James came up and while I did not hear what was said, the next thing I saw was that Sid Preacher stepped up to a buggy that had just been driven up. Sid Preacher took out a double-barreled shotgun and in just an instance, the shooting began. Detective James fell."

It is unclear whether Officer Youngst was with Detective James, but he was definitely nearby when James was shot. Witnesses continued describing the scene to a reporter, who said in an article:

"They saw the uniformed Officer Youngst grappling with Sid Preacher for the shotgun. Preacher was able to grab the shotgun away from the much older Youngst. Officer Youngst, at this time, apparently felt his only safety outlet was to flee and when doing so, he was shot in the back by Sid Preacher. Preacher then ran in on top of the seriously wounded Officer Youngst and struck him three times in the head with the shotgun.

"However, Officer James, lying on the sidewalk mortally wounded, was able to raise his head less than six inches from the street and shot at Preacher three or four times with a pistol. Preacher was struck a number of times and while not totally incapacitated, he advanced on Officer James until the shotgun was taken from him by an intervening citizen."

At least six gunshots had been discharged. The result was two dead police officers and one dead gambling, cop-killing scoundrel – a terrible day at any time but this was less than two weeks before Christmas and during the festive Houston carnival season. The families of two murdered officers were left to bury their dead and mourn them during the joyous of all seasons.

While the actual eyewitness account of this tragedy was certainly no mystery, the circumstances leading up to this event were of great interest to the Police Department and the many honest citizens of early 20th century Houston.

Officer Herman Youngst was one of the best known and most respected members of the police force. Having served twenty-eight years in the department, he was the senior member of the force. He was born in Prussia in November 1845 or 1846 and had been a Confederate soldier during the Civil War, a member of Company K, 26th Texas Calvary, CSA (Confederate States of America). Private Youngst had been captured as a Union prisoner of war and following the end of hostilities he was released from Union custody in June 1865.

OFFICER HERMAN YOUNGST

Officer Youngst was not married at the time of his death. He was believed to be a widower. His only survivors were his two daughters, Mrs. J. C. Buddendorf and Mrs. S. G. Hobbs. Coincidentally, they were both at the Racket store, not fifty feet away from their father at the time of his death. Officer Youngst resided at 2218 Preston Avenue.

The bodies of both officers and their assailant were transported to the Westheimer Undertaking establishment. The doors were securely barred in order to keep back the morbid crowd which followed the death wagons from the scene to the "very portals of the house of death." Officer Youngst was found to have been shot in the back with buckshot. Several of the balls passed through his cardiac region and lodged under the skin directly above the heart. Death was instantaneous.

Funeral services for Officer Herman Youngst were held at 4 p.m. Thursday, December 12, 1901, at the residence of his daughter and son-in-law, Mr. and Mrs. S. G. Hobbs, at 1909 Congress Avenue. Burial followed at the Washington Cemetery, originally the German Society Cemetery, on Washington Avenue. When this gravesite was located in 2004, there existed a marker with the following information:

IN MEMORY OF
OUR DEAR FATHER

HERMAN YOUNGST
DIED
DEC 11, 1901
AGED
58 YEARS

Detective John C. James had been on the police force for almost three years, but prior to that he had made a good reputation as a deputy constable. Being highly esteemed by Police Chief John G. Blackburn (1898-1902), as was Officer Youngst, James had recently been selected for special detective work. James had been shot in the bowels with buckshot, which tore away a portion of the stomach walls, allowing his entrails to protrude. After being wounded, he was able to shoot and kill Sid Preacher prior to dying at the scene.

James, believed to have been born in August, 1867, was about thirty-four years old and was the head of a family. His wife, the former Miss Willie Brooks was born in Bexar County in 1874, which would have made her a widow at the young age of twenty-seven years old. They were believed to have four small children, who were among the primary mourners at the detective's funeral. This service was held at 10 a.m. Friday, December 13, 1901 at his residence at 2812 Commerce Street. Burial also took place at the Washington Cemetery.

These children were Charlie Andrew James-age eight, Leedell (Ludell)-age six, Florence B.-age four, and an infant, two months old. When this gravesite was located by way of cemetery records, it was learned that no marker had ever been placed in memory of Detective John C. James. Apparently, Mrs. James was in dire financial straits at the time, although she was able to purchase the space in 1902. Efforts are continuing to locate any distant family members in the hopes that they might approve a 100 CLUB LINE OF DUTY MARKER for Officer James.

Doctors W. R. Eckhardt and O. L. Norsworthy examined James' wounds under the supervision of Justice of the Peace W. B. Hill, who used the wound information to conduct the inquest into all three deaths.

Sid Preacher was ruled to have died from a pistol bullet which entered the left side low down and came out under the right armpit, passing entirely through the body. This wound was inflicted by Detective James while he lay in the gutter with his vitals laid bare by a charge of buckshot. C. Sidney Preacher, who lived at the southwest corner of Kentucky Avenue and Des Chaumes Street, was a native of Liberty. His remains were returned to that locale for burial. He was the son of Mrs. Ed Heard, his father having passed away six years earlier. His lived in Houston for most of his life and had spent much of this time in the local courts for the past six years. The beginning of his troubles was reported to be his stabbing of his step-father eight years earlier. He was married at the time of this offense.

Several months prior to his death, Preacher had been involved in a serious situation in Peter's Alley, a notorious locality in the Fifth Ward. Preacher and another man had shotguns (claiming to be on their way to go hunting). Preacher and his group, all white men, wound up killing three African-Americans, a woman and two men. The investigation reportedly resulted in claims of self-defense. There was no record of any charges ever having been filed in this matter.

DETECTIVE JOHN C. JAMES

The background into this tragedy gradually unfolded in the newspaper accounts in the days following the shootout. Sid Preacher, by all accounts, was a gambler by trade, having been arrested the previous day by Officer B. W. Whittington, who stated:

"I had Sid Preacher under arrest on the charge of running a gaming device in Albert Lewis' saloon. In walking him down to the station, he asked me to allow him to go upstairs to see his attorney, J. B. Brockman. I took Sid up to see Brockman. As I stepped in the door after Preacher, I heard Sid say that he had a good notion not to go anywhere (with Whittington). Brockman replied that he should go ahead this time, although they got no right to arrest you without a warrant. Then, Brockman added some words that would prove very troublesome to him and his cohorts shortly thereafter.

"Those words were in his advice to Sid Preacher – 'Don't you do it any more, if you have got to arm yourself with a six-shooter and defend yourself.' Brockman then added, 'It's getting to be a damn pretty come-off that men are getting arrested every day and thrown in jail down there without a warrant.' Brockman then went a large step further with the following words of advice to his regular client: 'You arm yourself with six-shooter and the next f---ing policeman who attempts to arrest you without a warrant for any offense, except for carrying a six-shooter, shoot his f---ing belly off.'"

When this information was learned on the same night of the deaths of these two fine officers, investigators and the district attorney turned their attention to Sid Preacher's attorney, J. B. Brockman. Deputy Police Chief Thompson requested Justice Hill, who held the inquest into the three deaths, to issue a murder warrant for Brockman. Thompson anticipated trouble and took several officers with him to make this arrest. Brockman did not resist and was taken to the police station and after paperwork was prepared, he was turned over to the sheriff. A writ of habeas corpus was filed and it was expected that a hearing would be granted shortly.

In a very strange turn of events for which newspaper accounts provide no reasoning whatsoever, J. L. Bowers, C. C. Watkins, W. C. Woodward, and Bill Brazell – all cohorts of J. B. Brockman – were all indicted for the murders of Officers Youngst and James. However, on December 23, 1901, all charges were dismissed on Brockman and his friends. While none of these men deserve mention in a story about Officers Youngst and James, it was discovered that J.B. Brockman was murdered around 1909 by a man named Henry Ransom. What goes around comes around, as the old saying goes.

When the dust settled and emotions died down, there were families of two murdered Houston police officers left to fend for themselves. Of course, one crook also was dead but it was widely considered good riddance to this individual.

Coincidentally, Officers Youngst and James also were involved with the same Yadon's Saloon at Congress and San Jacinto four short months previously in the tragic death of Officer Willie Weiss in late July 1901. That area must have been like Hill Street and Lyons Avenue of later years or similar to the 6800-7100 blocks of Harrisburg in the years 1976-1980 when three Houston officers – George Rojas, Tim Hearn and Victor Wells – were killed in separate incidents.

Records showed that Youngst was born in Prussia in November of 1845 or 1846. It is unknown when he came to the United States but it is clear that he wound up in the Army of the Confederate States during the Civil War. The Union Army took him prisoner and on the 26th day of June, 1865, documents indicate the Union released him with a Parole of Honor. In a rather interesting document, Youngst agreed to the following terms and conditions of his release:

"I will not hereafter serve in the Armies of the Confederate States, or in any military capacity whatever against the United States of America, or render aid to the enemies of the latter, until duly exchanged, or otherwise released from the obligations of this parole by the authority of the government of the United States."

He married a sixteen-year-old woman named Harriet in 1868. The couple had two daughters, Henrietta Youngst (Hobbs) and Mary Alice Youngst (Buddendorf). It is believed that Youngst's wife Harriet passed away prior to the officer's murder. So here was this individual Herman Youngst, born in mid-19th century Prussia, who immigrated to the United States in time to serve in the Confederate Army and be taken as a prisoner of war and be released, only to become a Houston police officer who died in the line of duty.

Not as much information was available about Detective James. He was about thirty-five years old and, according to newspaper accounts, was a husband and father of four young children, ages seven years old to six weeks old. He also was the main provider for his widowed sister, herself the mother of five children.

A newspaper tribute to the slain Detective James from Warrant Officer Daniel Curtin of the Galveston Police Department read as follows:

"Officer James was a fearless man. He was one of the first to reach Galveston after the storm a year ago (the great Galveston hurricane of September 1900). During the trying times immediately following the storm, he rendered valuable service here. In his death, the force at Houston loses a man of great worth. I think the whole trouble can be easily traced to the peculiar conditions that have prevailed in Houston for some time. The people of this city (Galveston) have a great deal to be thankful for that Galveston has so few undesirable characters. Only eternal vigilance on the part of the force here has kept this city free from them."

The Houston Chronicle reported in its December 14, 1901 edition that the paper had initiated a relief fund for Officer James' widow and four children, who were between the ages of seven years to six weeks. The latest tally of this relief fund was the sum of $71.50.

Other tributes to Officer James were as follows:

"All his life he worked faithfully for the support of this family, but the demands were too great to permit savings. Already his fellow officers have provided for immediate wants, but they, like he, have dear ones to remember. No one is more deserving of recognition than the family of as brave an officer as ever donned a uniform. During three years, Doc James, as he was affectionately called by his friends, proved himself to be a good officer. No man was ever braver in times of danger and no officer was ever more conscientious in obeying orders. With him to be told to do a thing was to do it. Now that he is dead, the large family that he left without means of support should be remembered. Their grief is beyond description."

8

Deputy Chief William E. Murphy
April 1, 1910

Ex-Officer Earl McFarland Kills Deputy Chief Murphy With 'Smoking Gun' but Galveston Jury Set Him Free

In April of the year 1910 Earl McFarland, a man from a prominent law enforcement and public service family in Southeast Texas, had it in for his former boss, Houston Deputy Police Chief William E. Murphy. The feeling was quite mutual. It started when it became Chief Murphy's duty to fire McFarland from his position as a patrol officer in the Houston Police Department a few months before.

Although crippled from a childhood accident, McFarland had moved around long enough on the force to develop a reputation as a hell-raising, hot-tempered maverick, a disposition that apparently did him in as an officer. Yet he held a few trump cards, including a law enforcement connection – his brother L. R. "Len" McFarland was a deputy U. S. marshal – and political tie – brother W. I. "Will" McFarland, a Richmond resident, had been the Fort Bend County tax assessor/collector. The McFarland family knew many people since it had been living in the Houston/Richmond area for more than half a century.

Earl McFarland, a man with a linebacker's build, was known to make physical threats, many with a drawn pistol, always making it clear that he wasn't the sort to back away from trouble. This attitude and the continuing conflict with Murphy, Houston's night shift chief, led to the death of Murphy, the department's highest-ranking officer killed in the line of duty.

It also set the stage for the most uniquely dramatic trial up until that point in Texas history. In many respects McFarland's trial had the same makings as the 1995 O. J. Simpson "trial of the century," complete with an all-star defense team, numerous witnesses, dramatic strategy and, yes, a surprise verdict. On a change of venue to Galveston, both sides picked the first-ever jury in Texas with as many as six African-American men.

The steps leading up to the shooting and trial unfurled in a downtown Houston where the police station was centrally located off San Jacinto and the bars, cafes, hotels, flophouses and theaters were in close proximity. Each of HPD's eight previous line-of-duty death cases involved an angry citizen, a saloon – or both – in downtown or close-by environs.

The two men had liked each other up to a point where nothing changed a person's attitude quicker than a grudge that starts building up against the man who fires him.

Murphy fired McFarland late in 1909 or early in 1910 for a variety of reasons, the primary one being a hot-tempered, almost constantly violent disposition that was unbecoming a police officer. McFarlane bore out this line of reasoning in the months leading up to the shooting in the early evening of April 1. Houston police had arrested their former colleague on different occasions for disturbing the peace, pulling his gun on an officer, fighting with the chief of detectives and literally shooting off his little finger, and – on Jan. 13, 1910 – drawing his pistol and pointing it at Murphy, prompting another officer to pull his service revolver and thwart further violence.

McFarland backed away in this latter situation, obviously outnumbered since three officers were alongside the chief, prompting him to vow angrily to Murphy, "I'll get you when you haven't got your gang." The officers filed charges against McFarland for using abusive language. But they were later dismissed. The incident was one among the many threats the two men made against each other, almost always taking turns to vow, "I'm going to kill you."

It was McFarland who followed through on his word, with smoking gun in hand on the Friday evening of April 1, 1910, as Chief Murphy finished off his evening meal and was in the process of rolling a cigarette at the Acme Restaurant at 904 Preston Avenue. Witnesses said the chief was in a good mood that night. He was known to frequent the Acme between 8 and 9:30 p.m. nightly for his "lunch hour," where patrol officers knew they could find him. McFarland also knew Murphy's habit. And sometime between 9:10 and 9:15 he arrived outside the diner with a friend, Joe Vining, to pick up some roast beef to-go.

Four witnesses in the restaurant told police investigators that McFarland entered the Acme with his gun drawn on Murphy, who was sitting on the fifth stool at the counter. McFarland pulled the trigger, his bullet causing immediate death.

One witness thought he heard Murphy say, "Oh, my God" before he expired. Martin Schleier, a waiter and night manager, said Murphy had just finished eating when McFarland came in with a pistol, fired one shot and dropped the pistol behind the counter. He said Murphy never drew his own gun. Two other diner employees agreed with Schleier's account and one customer thought he heard McFarland say, "Drop your gun" before he fired the shot. As Schleier telephoned for an ambulance, HPD night Sergeant R. L. Ward rushed in and found his night

30

chief on the floor and speechless. Ward said. "Mr. Murphy was breathing when I first got to him, but was dead within a minute or two after my arrival."

Seconds later, Dr. W. G. Priester, who had been in a nearby pharmacy, ran in to administer to Murphy. Priester was certain about two pertinent facts at the scene of the shooting – Murphy died almost instantly and had his gun still holstered. Later, the doctor and others who examined the body said the shot through Murphy's right arm rendered impossible his ability to use his right hand.

Since there was no radio or television, the quickest way to spread the news of note before the morning Post hit the streets was word of mouth. The word spread like wild fire. Other police officers from downtown beats were on the scene within minutes.

McFarland, literally holding a smoking gun containing one hot spent cartridge, didn't get far from the front entrance to the Acme. Two officers from nearby beats, H. W. Depenbrock and Thomas O'Leary, got to him first. McFarland requested to be taken to the jail and not to the police station. Officers took him to the station. O'Leary said he heard the shot from several blocks away and saw McFarland walking on Preston toward Main. "I was too quick for him," McFarland told O'Leary. "I had to defend myself." Suddenly – only minutes after the deadly shooting took place – the perpetrator laid the groundwork for his defense.

A Houston Post reporter pursued McFarland all the way to the county jail, where the suspect appeared ill at ease with beads of perspiration "upon his forehead." He allowed a few words to escape that made it into print: "I'm sorry it happened. I had to do it to defend myself."

At the Murphy residence east of downtown some fellow officers wrestled with the words they needed to break the news to Mrs. Murphy, who had been bed-ridden with illness for a number of days. They finally did so gently, yet still broke four hearts – those of the new widow, daughter Margaret Murphy and sons Willie Murphy and George Murphy.

William E. Murphy's law enforcement career began in Galveston in the late 1880s. He served there many years as a police officer and plain clothes detective. He was the first patrol wagon driver for the Galveston force, appointed to the job in 1889 on the day shift. He resigned in 1892 but returned a year later when he worked as a patrolman before returning to the job of plain-clothes detective. He joined the Houston Police Department on May 1, 1902 as a detective and served in that capacity until 1907 when he was appointed deputy chief at age forty-five. He was well-liked by the men under him, especially those serving at night.

Coincidentally, Police Chief George Ellis was out of town on a hunting trip when the shooting took place. The department had only two vehicles at this time and one was sent to fetch the chief, who was not very talkative about the tragic event other than to echo the words of Mayor H. B. Rice that Houston had lost a dedicated officer in the line of duty. Rice and Ellis vowed that the Department would conduct a full investigation in the preparation of a habeas corpus hearing and, eventually, the trial.

Funeral services were held at the Murphy residence on Sunday afternoon, April 3, 1910, with the Reverend Dyek of the German Lutheran Church officiating. Burial was in Evergreen Cemetery. The home of the deceased officer was fully decked out in floral arrangements from fellow officers and friends from all over Houston and Galveston. George Murphy, the deceased chief's brother, came up from Galveston for the service.

The active pallbearers included Galveston Police Chief W. H. Perrett, Houston Chief George Ellis and W. F. Kessler, Houston's chief of detectives. The service was under the direction of the Knights of Pythias Lodge in Houston and Settegast-Kopf Funeral Home.

After a habeas corpus hearing prosecutors took the case before a Harris County grand jury, which promptly indicted Earl McFarland for murder in the death of Chief Murphy. A judge refused bail and kept McFarland in the county jail until trial. McFarland's defense team began to take shape over the summer and fall of 1910 and succeeded in getting a change of venue to Galveston County, setting an early stage for the most celebrated case of its time. More than three hundred witnesses were subpoenaed for the February 1911 trial, most put on the train to Galveston and quartered in hotels until called to testify.

Houston's prosecution team included three or four assistant district attorneys with the DA himself, Richard G. Maury, making intermittent appearances before leading off the state's closing arguments. The trial took place almost a century ago, yet the defense team closely resembles the glamorous stalwarts of O. J. Simpson's defense team.

McFarland's group of experts included Judge John C. Williams, a former judge now on the defense side of the bar, and Henry E. Kahn, Elmo Johnson and John T. Wheeler, all of Houston; and Galveston attorney Tom C. Turnley and two of his fellow members of the Galveston bar – Lewis Fisher and the flamboyant Marsene Johnson. And Lewis Fisher also happened to be the mayor of Galveston at this time.

To say that the defense team had a decided edge with the Galveston lawyers present might be a fair assumption given what proceeded to take place at the Courthouse. They started playing their cards right during the jury selection process, a key element for the defense in every trial like this one. Obviously the local lawyers knew the jury panel far better than their opponents.

Judge C. W. Robinson called a 250-member jury panel with 161 of them making it to the building. As customary then as now, lawyers asked each prospect the same questions, taking care to learn just how much they knew from newspaper publicity and word of mouth. They challenged accordingly. Then something happened that never had before in a Texas criminal court: the first two jurors officially picked were black men! This was unheard of during this period in Texas history. Newspapers identified each man by name, occupation and address – a practice that would never pass muster in a criminal district court more than ninety years later.

The grueling process ended with the final selection of a jury consisting of six white men and six black men. Newspaper accounts quoted attorneys who were spectators in the courtroom as saying that never before in this section of the state was a jury composed of half white and "half Negroes" impaneled "to pass upon a white man's life or liberty." But both sides said publicly that they were satisfied and ready for a classic court battle.

The defense attorneys must have winked at one another, for they had plans to turn the ethnic makeup of the jury into a decided advantage before the trial was over. The stage was set and Judge Robinson told prosecutors to call their first witness in a courtroom The Houston Post described as "packed almost to the point of suffocation."

The differences in strategies were marked even from the beginning. Mrs. Murphy, still weak from her illness and unwilling to play the role of an innocent victim, avoided the courtroom. As so often happens in courtroom settings, she sat close to McFarland's family, remaining silent. It wasn't too long before she left for Houston.

Defense attorneys, on the other hand, paraded McFarland's aging, gray-haired mother and his adoring curly-haired daughter, who quickly ran to hug her daddy upon seeing him at the defense table. McFarland's sister also was present as were his brothers, Will and Len. McFarland was separated from his wife. The defendant himself was confident of acquittal. He said so to the news media, whose members noticed that McFarland's weight had dropped from 248 pounds at the time of the killing to 171 pounds as his trial began.

The state stuck to the basics, calling witnesses who recalled McFarland's almost constant thorny presence in the side of the Houston Police Department, an irritation that began as soon as Chief Murphy fired him. The police witnesses and several doctors described in their testimony how the fatal bullet from McFarland's revolver almost instantly killed Murphy. Three witnesses said the chief's gun was never in a position to be fired in self-defense. According to testimony for the prosecution, McFarland simply carried through with his vow to shoot Murphy when he didn't have his "gang" of lower-ranking officers for help. He did so in cold blood, testimony showed.

Curiously, one key state's witness, who was in the Acme Restaurant and had seen the actual shooting, was not produced in court until the defense had closed. That was not the only factor in the case that went bad for the state's team after it rested much sooner than expected.

The all-star defense team, with Marsene Johnson taking the lead, had a strategy that included what followers of today's criminal courthouse would term "the oldest trick in the book." That slick legal maneuver must have begun somewhere and it could very well have been in Galveston in 1911.

McFarland's lawyers would put Murphy on trial. The deceased deputy police chief was certainly unable to defend himself. They would call witnesses who would allude to a mysterious "Mexican woman," intimating that Murphy was engaged in an adulterous affair. The lawyers also called to the stand a Dallas woman who testified she went to see Murphy about a theft case against her nephew involving $72 the lad had taken after breaking into a Houston saloon. Mrs. John Slider also wiggled through an already-opened can of legal worms by testifying that Murphy told her in a conversation about McFarland that he intended to "fix him so that no one would trouble him again." She quoted Murphy as saying he would kill McFarland or McFarland would kill him.

Actually it was the "missing" $72 that helped the defense in its attack against the dead man. Mrs. Slider said Murphy vowed to her that if the money were repaid to the victim, no charges would be forthcoming against her nephew. All she had to do was provide it to him, Murphy, and he would turn it over to the saloon owner. The witness testified, however, that even though she provided the cash to Murphy, the saloon owner never received it and the district attorney brought charges against her nephew, who was later convicted of the theft offense.

As the defense's side of the case came to light, Mrs. Slider turned out to be one of at least nine witnesses who testified they had heard Chief Murphy make threats to take the life of Earl McFarland.

The state argued that Murphy never had a chance to protect himself in self-defense when McFarland came into the eatery with his gun drawn. Since the shooter was no longer a police officer, he was actually carrying the weapon illegally.

Harris County District Attorney Richard G. Maury took the lead for the prosecution and argued in final summation, "If he (McFarland) was afraid of Murphy and believed that he intended to take his life, would he or would any other sensible man have gone into that restaurant that night?" Maury's assistants tried to hammer home McFarland's penchant for violence and violent threats. They quoted doctors who asserted that Murphy hadn't pulled his gun before the shot was fired and that his fatal wound made it impossible to return fire. And they tried to make something of the fact that defendant McFarland never took the stand in his own defense.

The record shows that the jurors didn't buy off on the state's logic and instead went along with the defense team's charm and cleverness. The smiling Mayor Fisher spoke briefly but carefully, acknowledging defendant McFarland's devoted mother and daughter. Turning to the jurors, the mayor/defense lawyer said, "Restore to that gray-headed mother and beautiful curly-haired babe what is theirs and when you have done that you will have done your duty."

By far the most dramatic moment was saved for Marsene Johnson of Galveston – on his "home court" to argue for more than one hour. Johnson reminded those present that respect for him must be growing since reporters had begun using his full name instead of just "M. Johnson."

Johnson reminded jurors of the witnesses who quoted Murphy as saying he was going to "get that cripple," a reference to McFarland's crippling childhood accident that caused him to walk with a limp. He said, "I would not ask a one-eyed man how he lost his eye, nor would I call a colored man a Negro because he can't help it; and I would never call a Chinaman a chink nor an Italian a dago."

At last the defense team took strong advantage of its racially mixed jury with Johnson weaving in Murphy's "prejudice" against crippled men like McFarland based on his quoted comments to at least two witnesses. The defense team had captured the trial's momentum and never let up, succeeding in trying Murphy, not McFarland.

It took the jurors four hours to return a verdict of not guilty.

We have no records of what then became of Earl McFarland except that he went home with his mother and daughter a free man. It is believed that the defendant had a distinct advantage given the fact that many officers in the Houston Police Department, including Police Chief George Ellis, were friends with McFarlane's brothers.

Adding to the curiosity is the fact that Chief Ellis resigned his position shortly after the trial, never having testified or made any definitive public statement on the case. Ellis was the last police chief elected by the people. When he was in office the law was changed so that Houston's police chief became an appointed position, which it has been ever since, with each new mayor making his or her choice.

There have been some sergeants, a few detectives, fourteen solo officers, one reserve captain and many patrol officers – die in the line of duty in Houston, but no other deputy or assistant chief of police.

9

Officer John Morris Cain
August 4, 1911

Killer of Officer John M. Cain Sentenced To Die after 5-Year Homicide Investigation

On Friday morning, August 4, 1911, at approximately 3:30 a.m., Officer John Morris Cain was on patrol duty as a Houston police officer. Officer Cain's assignment, a very dangerous and lonely one, was at the North Side Railway Crossing, further described as the crossing of the International/Great Northern and the Southern Pacific Railroads intersection as it existed in 1911 in Houston. This exact location was difficult to pinpoint in 2006, but it was believed to have been in the northeast quadrant of the city near Nance Street.

OFFICER JOHN MORRIS CAIN

An investigation later determined that Officer Cain was very apprehensive about working this assignment alone. His partner of previous nights, Officer Myers, had been removed from this location to another assignment due to manpower considerations. Cain, while having been an officer for less than a year, was apparently very aware of his dangerous assignment and had requested another assignment or, in the alternative, not to work this area alone on the night shift.

Later, Officer Cain was reported to have been involved in a conversation with several citizens regarding their business at this location at this hour. These citizens, Richard Tolson and Rosa Mason, explained the nature of their business to the satisfaction of the officer. Just after this interchange, an unknown Negro male exited the rail car near Officer Cain and the two witnesses.

He was later described as a tall, brown-skinned Negro, about twenty-eight to thirty years old, wearing a dark suit of clothes, a Panama hat and being fairly well dressed. He carried two grips in his left hand, a small one and a larger one, which from appearance were tied together.

This unknown man got off a rail car and upon seeing Officer Cain, in full HPD uniform, proceeded to walk away in the opposite direction. Witnesses recall Cain, seeing this individual hurrying away, asking him, "Can't you stop when an officer is talking?" At this point, the suspect said, "Stop, hell," and whirled and fired one or two times with a pistol toward the unsuspecting Officer Cain. The suspect then fled on foot in the darkness.

One round from a .41-caliber pistol struck Officer Cain near the left nipple. This missive ranged downward, passing just along the heart and striking the backbone and the spinal cord as it made its treacherous way through his body. The above described Negro couple, standing nearby, immediately reported this shooting and remained at the scene to describe what they had observed.

Night Chief Heck, along with Detective Kessler, Chief of Police Voss, and six other officers responded immediately to the scene to begin their investigation. This was truly a whodunit.

The Houston Post of August 5, 1911 described Officer Cain's condition:

WAS CONSCIOUS TO THE LAST: "Up to the time of his death almost, Cain was conscious and conversed with his wife, other relatives and friends, realizing all of the time that he could not live. He gave an accurate description of the negro that did the shooting and told of the circumstances that preceded the infliction of the fatal wound, the story being corroborated by the negro man and woman. Chief Voss and other officers called at the infirmary all during the day and talked to the wounded man, and at once detailed extra men to search for the negro, determined that he shall be captured."

Interviews with the critically wounded Officer verified what the witnesses had told investigators. Then, at 2:30 p.m. on Friday, August 4, 1911, Officer John Morris Cain passed away. He was thirty years old.

Investigators had early on concluded that the suspect had left town. However, they were at a loss to determine which direction, as passenger trains were very popular in these days and ran day and night in and out of Houston.

The untimely death of Officer Cain cast gloom over the entire police department. During his connection with the department, he had done duty in almost every section of the city and was well liked by all who knew him. He was considered an efficient officer, fearless and always on the job, prompt and courteous in his dealings.

John M. Cain was born on March 4, 1881, in Bastrop County, near Paige, Texas. At the age of twenty, he came to Houston and engaged in the dairy business, later worked as a motorman for the Houston Electric Company, and was at one time appointed as a deputy constable under Constable Frank Smith. In September 1910, he joined the Houston Police Department.

He was survived by his wife, his mother, three brothers, and four sisters. Two of his brothers, James and Albert, lived in Houston and were motormen. The other brother lived in Austin and the four sisters lived with their mother near Paige, which is in eastern Bastrop County.

Officer Cain was a member of the Woodmen of the World, Willow Street Camp Number 64 and this organization took charge of the funeral. The service was held at 4 p.m. Sunday, August 6, 1911, from the officer's home at 1404 Cook Street. All of the officers of the Police Department attended in a body and assembled at the Police Station at 3 p.m. They were met at the home by the Woodmen Lodge members, who also attended as a body.

The funeral cortege was one of the longest in the city in many months and the floral offerings were many. The procession to the cemetery was strikingly impressive, with the mounted police officers and other members of the department being led by Chief of Police John A. "Duff" Voss and Reverend Ammons. Burial followed at Magnolia Cemetery, located at what is now West Dallas and Montrose/Studemont. Active pallbearers were Gordon Murphey, S. M. Habermacher, J. H. McNutt, C. A. Lomax, C. M. Wilson, and Duff Voss, the chief of police. Honorary pallbearers were T. R. Carr, Ed Carr, G. Wilson, Wilbur Engle, Leon George and James Ramsey.

Since the tragic death of Officer Cain and during the funeral and mourning process, the investigation into this capital murder continued. It was in the days that followed Officer Cain's funeral that the thought regarding this whodunit murder slowly sank in: Could it be actually possible that this terrible crime would never be solved? The murdered officer gave a reasonably good description but would not be available in court. The Negro couple who observed part of this crime, therefore, would become crucial witnesses if anyone could be placed before them. Even in 1911, the authorities became aware of how critical other items of physical evidence would be.

Days upon days piled up. Leads came in and were checked out with the same negative results. Frustrations mounted, but Chief Voss and the local sheriff, as well as the entire forces from both departments, were convinced that sooner or later this murderer would be captured.

In the first three weeks, there were four newspaper accounts of arrests/detainments recorded in various parts of Texas – including Conroe, Montgomery and Rogers – of suspects believed to be the killer. All were checked out thoroughly and proven to be unworthy of prosecution. In most or all of these incidents, investigators from Houston had to arrange railroad travel schedules in order to further investigate these leads.

The days, months, and even years passed. One can only imagine the thoughts that went through the mind of Chief Voss and his successor: Will the senseless murder of Officer John Morris Cain go unsolved? The year 1914 passed with the accidental shooting deaths of Houston Officer Isaac Parsons and Harris County

Deputy Arthur Taylor by two Houston officers. Morale must have reached a low point with this incident coupled with the unsolved murder of Officer Cain.

In the great State of Texas, there existed an individual by the name of Houston Sharp, a Negro male. He came from a family of four children, the father of which was a minister. His two sisters and one brother chose the upward path and became teachers and leaders. Houston, on the other hand, went another direction. He attended Prairie View Normal, but was expelled for committing campus burglaries. He definitely chose the downward path. Later, he was described in court as a professional bad man, a small chocolate colored Negro with a mustache and a look of cunning as well as a cynical smile to all who dared to look at him.

Houston Sharp's criminal record was reported as follows:

• In 1910, when Constable T.A. Haddox of Grimes County attempted to place Sharp under arrest, Sharp grabbed a rifle and drew down on the constable and disarmed him, threatening him with death if he attempted to follow him. Shortly after this incident, Grimes County Sheriff Tom Lacey and Montgomery County Sheriff Ellis attempted to arrest him from a train, but Sharp escaped in a volley of gunfire.

• Sharp was finally captured in a post office in the eastern Montgomery County town of Fostoria. Officers shot Sharp five times with a .32 pistol, once with a .45, and a citizen assisted the lawmen by shooting Sharp in the back. Somehow, this "cat with nine lives" survived. He was convicted and sent to Huntsville. However, due to his injuries, he was moved to the hospital farm and escaped five months later.

• Grimes County Sheriff Lacey attempted to arrest Sharp, but Sharp overpowered the Sheriff and took his pistol. During the fight, Sheriff Lacey nearly cut off the "pistol hand" of Sharp. Sharp, who claimed to have suffered a total of sixteen gunshot wounds during his criminal career, was found later to be missing all of his fingers on one hand from the encounter with Sheriff Lacey.

• Sharp was convicted in 1913 of eight cases of burglary, resulting in sixteen years in the penitentiary. He escaped amid a storm of bullets from the prison guards. Houston Sharp, already of much renown throughout Texas for his many acts of misdeeds, was in the Texas Prison System in Huntsville on a burglary conviction of fifty-eight years.

• It was in prison while serving this term that he told of killing a Houston police officer. He told several fellow Negro inmates from Burleson County that he had killed Officer Cain. This was reported by these inmates, even though, just as is the case today, they likely had their own well being in mind.

Throughout his career, one law officer in particular, Harris County Detective T. Binford, proved to be the nemesis of Sharp. Detective Binford, who had suspected Sharp at one point during the five years after Officer Cain's death, eventually began tracking Sharp's movements before and after the murder. He determined that there was a gap right around the week of August 3, 1911. When confronted with the suspicion of him being the murderer of Officer Cain, Sharp confessed. However, he later withdrew his confession, saying that he was threatened with a "broken neck" if he did not sign the statement. In the summer of 1916, nearly five years after the murder of Officer John M. Cain, Houston Sharp was charged with murder.

The Houston Post of September 7, 1916 said that Sharp's trial began and the confession, after a difficult fight, was introduced into evidence. During the proceeding, Houston Sharp took the stand and denied his confession, stating that it was coerced under the duress of having his neck broken. He said that he was at home for the birth of a child on the night the officer was killed. When it was proven that the birth actually occurred two weeks prior, he stated that he must have been mistaken.

In recapping this crime, his confession, which was considered by the court, he indicated that upon his being confronted by Officer Cain, he turned and fired one round from his .41-caliber pistol. He felt like he had hit the officer and fled from the scene on foot, arriving later that night at a woman's residence in the Second Ward. Police located this woman, who testified at the trial that Houston Sharp had arrived at her boardinghouse the night of the murder and had shown her a pistol. She said the barrel was hot and smelled as if it had been recently fired. She hid it for him that night, with Sharp leaving with it again the next morning.

The Post, on September 8, said that Sharp's fate was in the hands of the jury, which was locked up for the night.

One day later, the paper said that there was good news for Sharp – that he will not be required to serve the remainder of his fifty-eight-year sentence. The bad news was that he will face a death sentence for the 1911 murder of Houston Police Officer John Morris Cain. The verdict was that Houston Sharp was to be sentenced to death by hanging.

In 2004, Officer Cain's gravesite was located at Magnolia Cemetery, tastefully marked with the standard Woodmen of the World marker. This marker makes the usual note of date of birth and date of death, but nothing as to how this young thirty-year-old man died. To correct that, a 100 Club KILLED IN THE LINE OF DUTY marker has been placed there to further honor his memory.

What really happened to the infamous Houston Sharp? He was found guilty and sentenced to die at the end of a rope in Harris County. Prior to 1923, counties in the State of Texas were given the responsibility of their own executions. This changed in 1923, when the State took over this necessary duty. However, no record could be found that indicated Houston Sharp was in fact hung. It would have seemed that in 1916, with the extensive record of Houston Sharp and his proclivity to violence, that he would have been hung in a timely manner to rid society of any further actions on his part.

Convict records were thoroughly searched at

the State of Texas Library in Austin. From there, this story becomes even stranger. Records show that a 40 year old Houston Sharp, Negro Male 40, born in 1875, was convicted of Burglary, Horse Theft, and Theft over $50.00 and received in the prison system in December, 1916. He had twenty-one cases and received two years on each which sentences were to run cumulative, a total of 42 years. This was three months after he was given the death penalty for the Murder of Officer Cain. On a sentence that by TDC records was not to expire until December of 1957, Houston Sharp was pardoned in July, 1925, thirty-two years early.

While this entire scenario seems unbelievable, the following article was located in the Galveston Daily News of July 18, 1925: "Houston Sharpe, of Burleson and Grimes counties, served twelve and one-half years of a forty-two aggregate sentence on twenty-one charges of burglary and theft over $50.00, recommended by pardon board and by R.M. Wood, chairman of the committee on teachers of Sam Houston State Teachers College, Huntsville". It appears that the murder of Officer John Morris Cain fell by the wayside. One can only guess what really occurred here, knowing that his parents and siblings were notable in education circles at Prairie View A & M College. As of this writing, no information has been located regarding a date of death for Houston Sharp.

10

Officer Isaac (Ike) Parson
May 24, 1914

Tragic Case of Mistaken Identity Causes Deaths Of Special Officer Parsons and Deputy Taylor

In the afternoon hours of Saturday, May 23, 1914, there was a great deal of difficulty involving one suspect in the near Fifth Ward area. An unknown Negro male had been terrorizing the neighborhood and on several occasions, this suspect had fired shots.

Police Chief Chauffeur Granger and Police Secretary Edmund Cardona drove to this area in response to a call at one point this afternoon. A citizen pointed out the suspect, who then ran from the officers while armed with a rifle. They pursued him along some railroad tracks for some distance. They continued the pursuit as he ran through some vacant lots, taking to their feet instead of remaining on wheels. Granger emptied six rounds from his pistol, believing he had struck the suspect. However, the suspect escaped. Cardona was not armed at this point. Both men returned to headquarters.

There were two part-time Negro officers at the time, both of them very well respected throughout their department. They were HPD Special Officer Isaac Parsons, also known as "Ike" or "bunk," also a full-time barber. The other was Harris County Sheriff's Special Deputy Arthur Taylor, who had just recently been commissioned but had worked extensively with other deputies from his department prior to his commissioning.

On this night, HPD Chief Ben Davison had assigned Officer John Richardson to team up with Officer Parsons. Between 9 and 10 p.m., Officer Parsons called in to say he would not be there to meet Officer Richardson since he had gone alone into the area to work on this problem. Officer Richardson assigned Cardona to assist him.

Tragically, neither Richardson nor Cardona knew that Deputy Taylor also was in the area working on this situation. Richardson and Cardona rode the midnight Liberty Road trolley out of Houston to the intersection of Nance and Schwartz. There, they began their investigation by interviewing citizens who had knowledge of the havoc this suspect created in their neighborhood.

At about 12:35 a.m., they heard gunshots. Richardson and Cardona were aware that two other HPD Officers, Bryson and Lyons, were in the area. Fearing for their safety, they ran toward the sounds of the gunshots, which they believed to be on Barron between Cline and Meadow streets. While en route, they heard two more shots.

Unknown to all, Deputy Taylor and Officer Parsons met up in the area and were working together. They apparently also heard the gunshots and were rushing to the same area. Officer Richardson saw a Negro male running toward him in the darkness. He flashed his pocket light on this male. Without recognizing Deputy Taylor, Officer Richardson observed that this male had a pistol in his hand. Richardson ordered him to drop the pistol, but the male refused. Richardson then began shooting, striking Taylor twice, instantly killing him.

Officer Parsons then came running into the area and Richardson and Cardona saw him running

36

with a pistol in his hand. Richardson and Cardona then fired at this male, striking Parsons four times, instantly killing him. Upon closer observation of the two dead men, Richardson and Cardona recognized Parsons. They did not recognize Taylor due to his short tenure as a special deputy.

Chief Davison arrived on the scene, as did Justice of the Peace W. T. McDonald, who held an inquest. They found one of the dead men lying in a ditch. This was Officer Parsons and when ambulance attendants conducted their examination for the judge, they found his police badge in his coat, his pistol in its scabbard. He was shot twice in the side. Deputy Taylor lay dead only a few feet away, shot through the heart. Neither Parsons nor Taylor had fired their weapons.

In Taylor's clothing was found a commission appointing him a special deputy by Sheriff Hammond. The commission was dated May 23, 1914, just one day before he was shot.

Chief Davison immediately ordered a complete investigation into this tragedy. As a result of the initial investigation, there was no reason to believe that Officers Richardson and Cardona had known in the darkness that the two individuals were Officer Parsons and Deputy Taylor. However, complaints charging murder were filed against Officer John Richardson and Mr. Edmund Cardona, secretary to Police Chief Davison. The chief placed them on indefinite suspension and put them in jail. Judge McDonald set an examining trial and released each of the defendants on $250 bail.

Harris County District Attorney Clarence Kendall began a thorough investigation into the deaths of these two peace officers. He found that Deputy Taylor was killed by Officer Richardson, who said in an official statement that upon shining his light on Taylor, he did not recognize him, had never seen him before, and had not known of his commission or that he was officially on this case. He further stated that he had ordered Taylor to drop the pistol. Taylor raised the weapon and placed it on half cock. This happened in near total darkness from only a distance of six feet. Richardson fired two shots, striking and killing the deputy.

After those initial shots that took Deputy Taylor's life, Officer Parsons came running across a ditch. Not recognizing him, Richardson fired twice and Cardona four times, striking the officer four times. Again, both Richardson and Cardona stated that they had no knowledge of these officers being in the area.

On Thursday, May 28, 1914, Justice of the Peace McDonald held an examining trial which resulted in the case being bound over to a grand jury. Both Richardson and Cardona were released on bail pending their trial. DA Clarence Kendall was in charge of the prosecution and the defendants were represented by attorneys James Storey and Campbell Sewell.

Isaac Parsons was born in Houston in the Fifth Ward on September 29, 1885. Funeral services for the officer, age twenty eight, were held on Monday, May 25, 1914. Burial followed at the Evergreen Cemetery (Lockwood and Market). He was the third of his family of three brothers to die a violent death. One brother was shot to death near Sugar Land and another recently died of stab wounds. However, Special Officer Isaac Parsons, a single man, died an honorable death.

An investigation found that there were no witnesses who could in any manner implicate Officer Richardson or Mr. Cardona as having any malice toward Officer Parsons or Deputy Taylor. In other words, prosecutors couldn't prove any intent, causing the authorities to declare the deaths a tragic case of mistaken identity. It would not be the first or the last time such a tragedy happened in the history of Harris County law enforcement. In 1974, an undercover Harris County narcotics officer was tragically shot and killed by a uniformed HPD officer. A grand jury later no billed the officer.

Court documents indicated the following in January 1915:

NOLLE PROSEQUI-No Prosecution: THE STATE OF TEXAS VS. JOHN RICHARDSON AND EDMUND CARDONA. Now comes the District Attorney, and asks the Court to dismiss the above entitled and numbered criminal action, for the following reasons, to-wit: Because the evidence is insufficient to sustain a conviction. The facts viewed from defendants' standpoint as the law requires it to be viewed shows an excusable Homicide caused by mistaken identity and purpose. Signed by Criminal District Attorney John H. Crooker.

It should be noted that in 2001, retired HPD Officer Doug Hudson, who became a Harris County deputy sheriff, uncovered this tragedy while doing research into another Harris County deputy's death. His documentation of this incident led to Officer Isaac Parsons being included in the names of HPD officers who lost their lives in the LINE OF DUTY. It was further through his efforts that the names of Officer Parsons and Deputy Taylor were submitted and accepted to be included on the Police Officer Memorials in Houston, The State Memorial in Austin and the National Memorial in Washington, D.C.

Deputy Hudson's research also found that Officer Parsons was buried in the Evergreen Cemetery and that Deputy Taylor in Olivet Cemetery. Unfortunately, neither grave is marked. A retired Prairie View A&M University professor, Dr. Woody Jones, is involved in the restoration efforts at Evergreen Cemetery, which has been badly neglected through the years. This location is known to some as the Black Evergreen Cemetery, as opposed to the Evergreen Cemetery off of Harrisburg and Altic Streets. Efforts will continue in hopes of placing of a marker for both law enforcement officers if and when their actual burial sites are discovered.

11, 12, 13, 14 & 15

Officer Rufus H. Daniels,
Officer Edwin G. Meinecke,
Officer Horace Moody,
Officer Ross Patton,
and
Officer Ira D. Raney
August 23, 1917

Race-related Rumor Fueled Camp Logan Riot, Resulting in the Bloodiest Day in HPD History

In seeking locales for the training of its growing number of troops as the United States was getting into World War I, the War Department chose the Bayou City as the site for Ellington Field, south of downtown, for the training of army flyers, and Camp Logan, to the northwest and outside the city limits, for National Guard training. The latter tree-laden site eventually became Houston's renowned Memorial Park.

Houston's leaders of industry and government were taken aback when they learned that Camp Logan would house the all-black Twenty-fourth Infantry Division of the Third Battalion, whose well-disciplined minions had distinguished themselves in earlier fighting. They were treated with respect at earlier duty stations – the people of Salt Lake City even gave them a glorious send-off – and were unaccustomed to the Jim Crow laws so prevalent in the South. Seeing the bad mix of human chemistry, these leaders of the white establishment discreetly appealed to Washington, D. C., to reconsider the color of its supply of Houston soldiers. However, their effort was in vain.

The job of the Twenty-fourth was to guard and protect the construction of the "tent camp" on the 3,002 acres that would house 1,329 buildings and have a troop capacity of 44,899 men. These soldiers arrived in time for construction to begin on July 24, 1917. Segregation was so prevalent that they couldn't even room and board near their charge. They would be bivouacked away from the permanent campsite in an area actually adjoining a neighborhood located north of Washington Avenue, immediately west of the present-day Reinerman Street.

The actions taken by the army, the frustrated and angry black soldiers, the Houston Police Department and various local black and white citizens brought out the worst in racial relationships in each of the leaders involved, from the camp commander to Houston's acting mayor and a police chief who had been politically promoted from the parks department. And Houston police of this era had absolutely no training in riot control.

OFFICER RUFUS DANIELS

The genesis of the riot developed along the streetcar line on Washington Street (later Avenue), where the conductors and train operators seriously enforced laws designed to separate black passengers from their white counterparts. It didn't take the black soldiers long to resent the mean and hateful treatment they received on the streetcars, where they were routinely called "boy" and referred to using the N-word.

The cast of white characters was so unimpressive that the U. S. Army would later use such adjectives as "unfit," "incompetent" and "cowardly" to find apt descriptions. Then again, the civilians close to the mammoth investigation that was part of the largest domestic court martial in American history knew the army was describing a few of its own camp leaders with those terms.

Camp Logan was not a plumb assignment for career army officers. Although some on the all-white staff were West Point graduates, none had distinguished himself. Lieutenant Colonel William Newman, a southerner by birth, assumed command of the Third Battalion the day it left from New Mexico for the new camp in Houston. Newman paid close attention to the morale of the men and quickly instituted what he thought would be a popular order encouraging a free flow of civilian visitors from the nearby black communities known as the Fourth Ward and "the San Felipe District." He had learned lessons from racial conflict the hard way, having been the commander of a camp in Del Rio and encountering problems with local citizens when white prostitutes refused to serve the black soldiers.

Even with these precautions, which he thought would encourage high morale, Newman feared the worst from Houston's white population. He knew there could be trouble on the streetcars and in white-owned businesses downtown. He also was keenly aware of the reputation of the Houston Police Department for failing to tolerate the slightest violation of Jim Crow laws, which basically defined black people as inferior and definitely subordinate. Texas, like every other former Confederacy state, segregated streetcars, movie houses, lunch counters, schools and restrooms. If anyone thought the Lone Star State didn't believe in "proper enforcement," they weren't aware that the state was second only to Georgia in the number of lynchings in 1916. None of those left hanging were white in color.

To make matters even worse, Newman didn't have much to work with at City Hall, where the mayor/council form of government enabled the city's chief executive to appoint the chief and the rest of the police force at his will. The summer of 1917 found Houston particularly vulnerable. The incumbent mayor, Joseph Jay Pastoriza, had won a bitterly close election in February. But he died in July and Mayor Pro Tem Daniel M. Moody succeeded him while a special election was set up. (Pastoriza was born of Spanish parents and, as such, was the first Hispanic mayor of Houston.)

Like others who found themselves in this position, Moody couldn't make thoughtful decisions and was stuck with Pastoriza's police chief, a former parks director named Clarence Brock. Brock's law enforcement philosophy followed the elected mayor's vow to go easy on prostitutes – despite the ongoing citizen crusade against them – as well as gambling and the sale of alcoholic beverages. District Attorney John H. Crooker was a leader in this anti-vice crusade. Moody, the unelected, indecisive "temporary" mayor, stayed on the fence in these and any other issues that might be considered controversial. In doing so, of course, Moody supported Brock, a laughingstock among police officers, who had highly respected the previous chief, Ben Davison.

The HPD reputation of the times wreaked of racism and brutality, not unlike hundreds of police departments in America up until the Civil Rights movement made Jim Crow laws unenforceable. Since Chief Brock was ineffective at making tough decisions about delicate issues, police officers enforced the laws on their own as they saw fit, receiving their training "on the job" from their elders on the force. Houston was then a small city of 140,000 people with a black population of 30,000 (largest in the state).

The local blacks coped with discrimination by assuming what various scholars called "dissembling." Historian Ronald L. F. Davis used this term to label the "psychological ploy in which blacks assumed positions and the appearances of non-confrontation," sometimes feigning irresponsibility and accepting "a demeaning racial etiquette."

The soldiers in the Twenty-Fourth were less likely to "dissemble." Robert V. Haynes, a University of Houston history professor who earned a doctorate from Rice University, wrote a well-documented, heavily footnoted history of the riot in 1976 entitled ***A Night of Violenc***e, the Houston riot of 1917. It remains the best resource on the subject that is often used by scholars, journalists and historians. In describing the prelude to the great tragedy, Dr. Haynes wrote, "Although in retrospect there were clear signs of impending trouble, none of the authorities, civil or military had any awareness at the time that serious violence was imminent."

MEINECKE FAMILY DESCENDANTS IN 2006

Less than a month passed before circumstances would provoke a tragedy that dramatically affected racial relations in Houston and the U. S. Army. The pivotal characters in the hopeless scenario were two Houston policemen known for their callous mistreatment of black citizens and soldiers. They were Lee Sparks and his partner, Rufus Daniels, mounted patrol officers clad in the khaki uniforms that were standard issue for the times.

Sparks and Daniels were recognized as two of the "meanest" policemen on the force, according to Haynes'

39

tireless research. They regularly patrolled the all-black San Felipe District. When residents there no more than heard the hoof beats of the horses, they ducked out of the sight of Daniels, an officer so large he was called "Daniel Boone." Sparks was smaller but far more ominous, having built up a reputation as a so-called "Negro baiter" who wouldn't allow anyone of any race to run over him in the line of duty or otherwise. Sparks' background was documented with descriptions by former Chief Davison as well as Detective T. A. Binford, who would later serve as sheriff of Harris County for almost twenty years. Binford also was the only Houston officer to survive the riot after having been wounded by shots from the soldiers.

Daniels and especially Sparks were provocateurs of the Camp Logan riot. Daniels paid with his life, one of five Houston police officers to experience that sad fate, while Sparks survived and went on to preserve his reputation with one violent act after another after his HPD career. The actions of Sparks and Daniels on the morning of August 23, 1917 are well documented by HPD and the U. S. Army in the detailed investigation that followed the riot. A court of inquiry found that they had the freedom to use what Haynes described as "any tactic they desired against blacks without fear of permanent suspension from the force."

The two officers were on horseback in their routine patrol of San Felipe District when they saw two black teenagers shooting craps in an alley. As they pursued them in a vigorous trot, the chase led to the home of Mrs. Sara Travers, a scantily clad housewife and mother of five children. Sparks entered the house and got a denial when he asked Mrs. Travers if she had seen a fleeing black man. (This was not the exact term Sparks used.)

When Mrs. Travers asked a neighbor what was going on, the neighbor replied, "I don't know; I think they were shooting at crap-shooters."

Sparks' ire instantly reached a boiling point. He denied the accusation, saying, "I shot down in the ground." Witnesses said he insulted the two women and said he thought they and the black soldiers were trying to take over the town. Follow-up investigations detailed both sides of this story, which proved to be a precipitous event to the riot that would happen later in this hot, humid August day when temperatures reached 102 degrees before the rains came. It evolved into a classic "He said – she said."

She said she was wearing a scanty blouse and old dress skirt. She screamed when Sparks slapped her, attracting Daniels' attention. They both seized her by the arm and drug her from the house, discussing whether to charge her with disorderly conduct and sending her to the Pea Farm for being – in the words of one of the officers – "one of the biggety nigger women."

Mrs. Travers' side of the story was covered by the black press and is documented in a paper entitled "Voices of the Black Press: Camp Logan Mutiny and the Houston Riot of 1917," written by Amina Hassan, great-niece of one of the solders hanged for his role in the riot.

"I asked them to let me put some clothes on and Sparks says, 'No, we'll take you just as you are. If you was naked we'd take you.' Then I take the baby in my arms and asked him to let me take it. He took it out of my arms and threw it down on the sidewalk."

Sparks later said that Mrs. Travers was decently dressed aside from being barefooted, that she had used abusive language and resisted arrest. He also denied slapping her.

The two officers used a Gamewell call box at the corner of Wilson and San Felipe to call headquarters. Private Alonzo Edwards, a soldier on a twenty-four-hour pass, stood by and was offended by the treatment of Mrs. Travers. He also may have been slightly drunk. Edwards said he would pay the fine, an offer that further angered the short-tempered Sparks and provoked him to strike the soldier in the side of the head with the butt of his six-shooter "four or five times."

"I hit him until he got his heart right," Sparks later stated.

Both Mrs. Travers and Private Edwards were taken to the city jail, where the woman was released without charges later that day, while Edwards was held for two days after being charged with interfering with a lawful arrest. The word-of-mouth reports of what happened to Edwards immediately hit the streets, getting the attention of a provost marshal (military police officer), Corporal Charles W. Baltimore, who got the details of the offense from a black soldier as he stepped from a streetcar at Heiner and San Felipe.

Respectfully, Corporal Baltimore, unarmed and not on duty at the time, approached Sparks and Daniels and asked them their version of what happened. Sparks again took offense and struck Baltimore over the head with the barrel of his pistol.

The soldier quickly fled to an unoccupied house on Bailey Street, where he hid under a bed. Sparks fired three shots at the fleeing "suspect" and when he confronted him in the bedroom of this house he hit him twice over the head before the soldier could explain his conduct. Sparks and Daniels then placed Baltimore in a patrol wagon that transported him to the city jail and the same cell that held Private Edwards. Sparks later swore that Baltimore was insolent and demanding and said he only struck the provost guard because "he ran his hand into his pocket."

Haynes' documented account cited the next major event in the conflict: "Even before Baltimore was booked for misconduct at 2:40 p.m., the camp of the Twenty-fourth was alive with exaggerated and distorted stories of the incident." Word got around camp that the angry Houston police officers killed Baltimore in cold blood. The fact that it was a bald-faced untruth made no difference; the resulting wild fire spread through the bivouac quicker than the downpour of summer rain hit the ground that day all around Buffalo Bayou and the rest of Houston.

As fate would have it, Colonel Newman left on Monday, August 20, for a new assignment at Camp Dodge in Des Moines, Iowa. Newman's successor was Major Kneeland S. Snow, who only recently had been promoted to his rank. Snow quickly found Houston to be a social paradise. Snow was as far removed from a soldier's life as he could get and paid little attention to the goings-on that affected their quality of life – or lack of it.

A boiling anger dwelt underneath the smiling facade of many of the solders and the rumors of Baltimore's death stirred these feelings to a feverish level by late afternoon.

Major Snow, Mayor Moody and Chief Brock grew concerned about the growing reports of anger amongst the troops and learned of the rumor of Corporal Baltimore's death. They soon arranged for Baltimore's release before 6 p.m. and instructed him to return to camp and downplay the events of the day in a way that would calm down the men. Snow was forthright in his efforts to convince municipal authorities like District Attorney Crooker that he had things under control at the camp. The men would be confined there and disarmed. Unfortunately, he was convincing in his appeal, for his misinterpretation cost both the army and the civilian authorities important time to prepare adequately for what was to unfurl several hours later.

OFFICER HORACE MOODY

This wasn't the only unfortunate communications misstep of the day. The agreement between Brock and Snow was that the Civil Service Commission would consider punishing Officer Sparks, likely firing him, which it later did.

The camp was not the only venue for rumors and anger. Word of the Sparks/Baltimore encounter had spread all over town by the dinner hour. White citizens became fearful of an uprising by the black soldiers. There were no media to spread with accuracy and credibility the word quicker than the next day's morning newspaper. Instead, there was word of mouth, accented by fervid imaginations, stirred by fear. Major Snow – who was so "brave" that he would later need smelling salts to stay conscious – failed to see the seriousness of the situation and obviously never dreamed that the subsequent events could ever take place. He had ordered all his troops to stay at the camp that night, increased the guard and sent military police into town to patrol the black neighborhoods. Follow-up investigation showed these orders had practically no effect.

Former Chief Ben Davison, who chaired the Chamber of Commerce's training camp committee, reported to Snow that the HPD's only black detective had just told him that the black soldiers were "going to shoot up the town." Snow was reassuring that this would not happen, saying that the situation was under control. In reality, up to two hundred soldiers had either refused to give up their rifles and ammunition or had taken what they needed to be fully armed and prepared for battle. Their call to arms was enhanced by rumors that a "white mob" was headed in their direction. Actually, there was no such mob.

As the anger of several mutinous groups continued to build, one group confronted Major Snow and threatened to kill him. There was a quick debate over whether they should shoot their commanding officer and while the debate was going on Snow ran from his well armed soldiers.

Eyewitnesses later reported that while Snow fled, a huge man named Private "Big Frank" Johnson stepped to the rear of the group and yelled, "Get your guns, boys! Here comes the mob!" A shot was fired in the air and immediately the march to downtown was on, with a first sergeant and veteran soldier, Vida Henry, emerging as the leader.

The mob marched east on Center Street to Roy and turned south to cross Washington to Lillian, one block south. There the soldiers picked off two innocent white citizens who came out on their porch to find out what the noise was about. As the soldiers passed 1119 Roy, several of them saw a lone light shining in the far reaches of the single room on the second floor. They took aim at the light, shot at it and missed.

(A better aim might have had a serious effect on three people who made positive impacts on the history of the Houston Police Department. The home owner, Peter Morrison, a Southern Pacific railroad man, had carefully hidden his wife and children in the room. One of the children was in his 20s. Peter Morrison was the father of future HPD Chief L. D. Morrison Sr., whose son, L. D. Jr., would become a long-time Homicide captain. Morrison also was the great-grandfather of one-time HPD acting Police Chief John Bales, who later grew up in the same house. "Our house had bullet holes in it from the Camp Logan Riot," Bales recalled in 2004. "The house across the street also had bullet holes in the siding of it.")

Led by Sergeant Henry, the group, which numbered almost one hundred, stopped for a rest in the 1600 block of San Felipe (the present-day West Dallas). By this time word of the march had spread to downtown, where citizens began taking up arms, some by looting hardware stores. Testimony later showed most of these "looters" didn't even know how to use a firearm.

Three white soldiers and a Houston police officer, E. G. Meinecke, together informed Camp Logan Captain Joseph W. Mattes and Captain Jay A. Rossiter that Meinecke knew a short cut to the Fourth Ward where the mutineers reportedly occupied the streets. Captain Mattes accepted the offer and got into a Ford automobile, whose passengers also included the three soldiers and Officer Meinecke. Rossiter and a white soldier followed the Ford but lost it in traffic.

The vehicle carrying Mattes and his four companions hit the 1917 version of road work at the Sabine Street Bridge and took another route, crossing the bayou at Capitol Avenue and eventually reaching the San Felipe District, where they would meet Sergeant Henry and his rioting troops head-on. Henry and the men were marching easterly on San Felipe, their numbers decreasing by the minute because soldiers were coming to their senses and "deserting."

Ten minutes later the rioters reached the call box at Wilson and San Felipe where Officers Sparks and Daniels had requested help in transporting Corporal Edwards to jail earlier in the day. Two mounted police officers, Ross Patton and W. H. Long, were following orders to patrol the area "in pairs." Long was on the Gamewell telephone. Without warning, three of the rioters spotted the officers and ordered them to halt. A second or two later about a dozen soldiers opened fire, shooting Patton's horse out from under him. The two officers sought safety in a nearby house. Patton was shot once in the arm and twice in the leg, dying two weeks later.

The attention of Henry and his men was diverted from these two officers by an oncoming vehicle driven by Houston investment firm president Charles W. Hahl and containing police officers Rufus Daniels, W. C. Wilson, Horace Moody and C. E. Carter. Hahl stopped his car at a point where he and his passengers had just heard the shots being fired at Officers Patton and Long.

Sergeant Henry, an army veteran of thirteen years, signaled his men to take cover on the opposite side of the street behind tombstones in a city cemetery at that location. Daniels, literally returning to his and Sparks' earlier arrest scene, charged the entrenched soldiers armed with only his pistol. Henry and his group mowed him down with bullets, killing him instantly. Carter, Wilson and Moody retreated to a garage nearby but Moody exposed their cover when he fired two shots at the soldiers. The soldiers answered with shots of their own.

"I am shot!" Moody yelled. "My leg is shot off." Officer Carter ran to Moody's aid, applying a tourniquet to his leg while Wilson stood guard. Moody was expected to recover but died when doctors were in the process of amputating his leg. A few of the rioters approached Daniels' body and, realizing who he was, battered his face with the butts of their rifles or plunged their bayonets into his body.

The rioters weren't finished at this point. Led by Henry, they continued to march toward downtown Houston, encountering two more automobiles and causing more blood to be spilled. They spotted a seven-passenger touring car coming toward them. The driver was eighteen-year-old James E. Lyon, whose passengers were two white civilians and two Houston police officers, John E. Richardson and Ira Raney. The officers had basically hitched a ride with Lyon because they were anxious "to get into the hot of it."

Lyon drove west down San Felipe, encountering what remained of Henry's troops where Heiner Street crossed. Someone, probably Sergeant Henry, ordered them out of the car, prompting Officer Raney to say, "We are police officers." The soldiers disarmed the car's occupants, who got out of the vehicle with their hands up. Richardson accidentally let his hands down. "You don't want to throw up your hands to a colored soldier?" one of the soldiers tersely asked Richardson. Before the officer could answer, the soldier broke the butt of his rifle into two pieces on Richardson's head.

Raney and one of the civilians, Eli Smith, ran, each going in a different direction. Smith was instantly picked off and Raney was actually an easier target, having run in front of the car's headlights. He was shot and died instantly. The other civilian, Asa Bland, also an eighteen-year-old white, was knocked unconscious by one of the soldiers.

Another soldier stuck his rifle into the chest of Lyon, the driver, who jumped just as the trigger popped the bullet, which then struck him in the arm. As he fled, Lyon was shot seven more times with buckshot. Two blocks over, a police officer picked up Lyon and took him to a downtown hospital where doctors saved his life.

When Ira Raney's body was found, he had been bayoneted and beaten in the head just as Rufus Daniels had been. The scene was bloody. Bland was lying unconscious in the middle of San Felipe and Officer Richardson was nearby, pretending he was dead.

Then the Ford containing Captain Mattes, three white soldiers and Officer Meinecke had at long last found the "short cut" Meinecke promised. Not even the road work would cause enough of a delay to keep this group from its bloody fate. About forty soldiers poised with their rifles ready as the automobile approached the already deadly Heiner intersection. They opened fire at the very moment Captain Mattes chose to stand up in the open touring car. "Wait!" the captain yelled as about fifty shots blew off his head and instantly killed Officer Meinecke, seated directly in front of Mattes. The bullets also riddled one of the three white enlisted men, whose lifeless body and that of Mattes collapsed over a second white soldier in the car, thus saving his life. The driver, the third soldier present with Captain Mattes and Officer Meineke, ducked under the steering wheel, crashing the car but saving his life in the process.

At this point the soldiers' desire to kill and destroy was waning; some deserted and others wanted to go back to camp. When Henry saw all momentum was lost he called special attention to Corporal Baltimore's bruises and bandages to remind the men of how badly they had been mistreated. This emotion didn't mix well with the knowledge that the men had given no quarter to two officers who were wearing the same uniform as they wore. The location of this important conference was roughly the eastern edge of Fourth Ward near a railroad track. One group of men wanted to head back to camp, while a second group leaned toward hiding out in the nearby woods or in the homes of black friends. This fork in the road effectively ended the raid since only Henry and a few others still had the burning desire to continue.

Henry begged three or four of his close friends who had served with him for many years to shoot him so he wouldn't have to commit suicide. They refused and left Henry alone with his rifle. They bade him farewell, each shaking his hand, and one of the soldiers even asked Henry to wait some minutes before he took his own life in order to give the men time to get as far away as possible. These men later heard a single shot fired about 2:05 a.m. Friday, August 24, 1917. Some little boys playing near the railroad tracks at daybreak found Sergeant Henry's body. Most of his head was blown away after he apparently put a pistol into his mouth and pulled the trigger.

Neither civil nor military officials had enough grasp of details of the riot to assemble an effective defense. Subsequent investigations revealed somewhat of an unsung hero in the form of Brigadier General John A. Hulen, commanding officer of the Texas National Guard.

Hulen met with Chief Brock and Colonel Newman and convinced them to dispatch military patrols in the black neighborhoods, including San Felipe District. Hulen became the driving force to persuade Governor James E. Ferguson to declare a state of emergency and place Houston under martial law. The governor, battling impeachment at the time for misappropriation of public funds, placed General Hulen in charge to take whatever necessary measures to restore order. Ferguson's declaration of martial law was one of his last official acts as Texas' chief executive before he became the only governor impeached and removed from office.

The next day Hulen – from the downtown office of The Houston Post – oversaw the arrival of 350 Coast Guard troops from Galveston along with another 602 infantrymen from Fort Sam Houston in San Antonio. Hulen and other local leaders spent every waking moment convincing white citizens not to retaliate but to leave it to the Army to see that justice was done.

District Attorney John Crooker immediately opened a court of inquiry for the primary purpose of allowing citizens of Houston to vent their feelings over the violent outbreak. It soon became apparent that the Houston Police Department, led by Chief Brock, failed to respond to the riot with a coordinated plan to stop the rioters and protect civilians.

The Army pressed Southern Pacific Railroad officials into quick enough service to get all the black troops out of Houston on two trains by 9:30 a.m. Saturday, August 25. They were taken to San Antonio and New Mexico to sort out the details of the crimes, taking care to ensure that no Houstonians retaliated in any manner.

The largest domestic court martial in American history resulted in charges of mutiny, rioting and murder against one-hundred-eighteen men, one-hundred-ten of whom were ultimately found guilty of at least one charge (seven were acquitted and one was found mentally incompetent to stand trial). Haynes' research showed that eighty-two men were found guilty of all charges and twenty-nine were sentenced to be hanged at the first court martial at Fort Sam Houston in San Antonio. The evidence prevailed despite the fact that most, if not all, white witnesses could not positively identify the black soldiers at fault. Their reasoning was that all of the soldiers looked alike, a frequent excuse used by whites during this period.

Justice was swift and without appeal, at least for the soldiers convicted in the first of three courts-martial. Early in the morning of Tuesday, December 11, 1917 – not quite four months from the date of the riot – thirteen black soldiers were taken to a remote area of the Alamo City to the specially prepared gallows that were out of sight of thirteen wooden coffins sitting aside thirteen freshly dug graves. It was all over in less than one minute.

Ensuing years saw six other soldiers hanged; the rest went to prison to serve their time. Protests from black leaders, including those from the National Association for the Advancement of Colored People (NAACP) went all the way to three presidents of the United States – Woodrow Wilson, Warren G. Harding and Calvin Coolidge. The NAACP strategy and steadfastness worked in some cases and is credited with pressuring these commanders-in-chief to lessen the total number of death sentences actually carried out. Before 1930, only a few soldiers were still imprisoned and they were there because they either violated parole or had bad conduct records. The last rioter was paroled on April 5, 1938.

The findings of the various investigations of the riots and its causes and effects prominently mentioned the Houston Police Department. Mayor Pro Tem Daniel M. Moody was too insecure to take decisive action. Moody had no control over Police Chief Clarence Brock and Brock certainly had no control over the men on the force. Having come from the parks department, Brock was not familiar with policing and lacked the basic police training that usually results in earning "the respect of the men" after taking actions that spoke louder than words.

The funeral for Daniels took place on Sunday, August 26, 1917 at his home on Hussion Street, east of downtown. He is buried in Glenwood Cemetery. Daniels' pallbearers were six Houston police officers. One of them was Lee Sparks.

Sparks will go down in HPD history as the mounted patrol officer who provoked the early stages of the riot. Evidence presented at the courts-martial showed that this Fort Bend native son considered himself to be a self-appointed defender of "the southern way of life." On the very same day Sparks helped carry his partner Rufus Daniels to his final resting place he shot and killed a black Houstonian named Wallace "Snow" Williams. Two black witnesses testified against Sparks at the trial, contending that they saw it happen. Nevertheless, a jury acquitted Sparks after a one-minute deliberation on October 15, 1917.

The board of inquiry recommended the removal of Chief Brock. Yet that suggestion had no effect since incoming Mayor Joseph C. Hutcheson Jr. kept him in the job throughout his first two-year term. Sparks, on the other hand, was taken off the force. Subsequent events clearly demonstrated that this man was hard-headed and set in his ways. He definitely was not open to a change in attitude, for in early March 1918, while he served as a night watchman for the Texas Oil Company, Sparks shot at two blacks hanging out near a boxcar, severely wounding one of them. The Houston Press suggested Sparks could add yet another notch to his gun but he was unable to do so when the wounded man recovered.

Houston's police chief and some of its officers were not the only prime time players at fault. Major Kneeland S. Snow demonstrated an ability to partake of the finer establishments of the Bayou City while ignoring the problems in camp and inadequately taking precautions against the mutiny. A downtown businessman, a pharmacist, said the camp commander was so visibly shaken from the confrontation with Sergeant Henry and his mutinous group of soldiers that he almost fainted from fright and asked the pharmacist for help. Snow was recommended for court martial but the proper paperwork was never filed.

The Camp Logan Riot was by far the worst event of its kind and remains to this day a record holder of sorts; its aftermath resulted in what are still the largest mutiny and the largest domestic court martial in U. S. Army history. It remains the only race riot in which more whites perished than blacks. In all, sixteen whites were killed, including the five Houston police officers, and close to thirty others suffered violent wounds such as the loss of limbs. No black civilians were killed and only four troopers of the 24th Infantry died, including Sergeant Vida Henry, who took his own life.

Compensation for the survivors of those killed in the riots was slow to come. U. S. Representative Daniel Garrett of Houston continuously pleaded with his colleagues in Congress to help people like Mrs. Pearl Raney, widow of Officer Raney, who was left with eight children to support. Finally in February 1925, seven-plus years later, Congress awarded $46,000 to compensate the claims of twenty-one riot victims. Ultimately, Mrs. Raney received $3,500 (and a cow), while $2,500 was awarded to Mrs. D. R. Patton, Mrs. Horace Moody and Mrs. E. J. Meinecke. (Rufus Daniels had no surviving wife).

The riot set Army policy for the future: no black soldiers would be stationed in any rural part of the south. This meant that blacks in the military service were destined to train and serve in remote locations until World War II and thereafter.

After a period as a convalescent center, Camp Logan was dismantled by the end of 1918. The land was put up for sale and in July 1923 Catharine Emmott had the idea of preserving part of the camp land as a memorial to the soldiers who had died in service. Mrs. Emmott, a music teacher and widow, took her crusade to City Hall and the Chamber of Commerce. She drew the attention of developers Henry Stude and Will Hogg and Mike Hogg. By April 1924 these men bought 873 acres with a new suburb in mind. Instead, they sold the city the land at cost and convinced another developer, Reineman Land Company, to sell an adjoining 630 acres. In addition, Will Hogg gave $50,000 for improvements.

Memorial Park still has its golf course, baseball diamonds, tennis courts, picnic and polo grounds and numerous other well-shaded amenities, not the least of which is an oft-used jogging path. Only a brief notation on an obscure plaque commemorates the Camp Logan Riot and the fact that much of the premises were once used as training grounds for America's fighting forces.

OFFICER IRA D. RANEY

This concludes the history of the tragic events of the Camp Logan riot of 1917. More information about the Officers and citizens that were affected by this incident follow..

Five Houston Police Officers lost their lives IN THE LINE OF DUTY that night in August, 1917. What is known about these men, their families, and their final resting place follows:

D. ROSS PATTON:

He was born on March 21, 1888 and is buried at a small, well kept cemetery off of Oates Road in northeast Houston, the Hart-Magee-Oates-Singleton Cemetery. Established in 1868, it has been designated a State of Texas Historical Site.

Officer Patton is believed to have married into the Magee family. His gravemarker was a Woodmen of the World upright marker. Woodmen of the World was at one time a fraternal and life insurance organization similar to the Elks and Moose. His marker indicated that he died on September 8, 1917, some 16 days after the riot at the young age of 29 years. This is born out by newspaper accounts as he was the only one of the five who did not pass away that night. He reached the age of 29 years and 5 months. No record has been found as to his survivors. He had received 5-6 wounds in a hip, thigh, shoulder, and leg.

Through the cooperation of the individuals in charge of this cemetery, specifically a Darlene Hickman, a 100 Club LINE OF DUTY marker was placed by Nelson and Andy Zoch in 2005. It is interesting to note that since Officer Patton was a Mounted Officer, who owned his own horse, that the following document was part of the official City Council records on this incident:

RESOLUTION AUTHORIZING THE SALE TO D.R. PATTON OF ONE HORSE TO REPLACE THE HORSE OWNED BY HIM AND KILLED WHILE SAID PATTON WAS ON DUTY AS POLICE OFFICER OF THE CITY OF HOUSTON IN MUTINY OF COLORED SOLDIERS AUGUST 23, 1917.

Whereas, the Mayor and City Council feel that in cases such as this kind an Officer who suffers loss in the discharge of his duty should be reimbursed to the extent of his loss. In short, the City of Houston gave someone the sum of One Dollar for Officer Patton's faithful steed that was shot out from under Officer Patton.

EDWIN GUSTAV MEINECKE:

Officer Edwin Gustav Meinecke was born near Bellville, Austin County, Texas, on November 26, 1893. He died in the riot on August 23, 1917, having reached the age of 23 years and some 9 months. He was riding in the vehicle with Army Captain Mattes when they were fired upon. He was shot twice in the left leg, in the right arm and had many small wounds in his back, thought to have been from a shotgun. His bravery should be noted in that he was reported to have volunteered to show Captain Mattes a shortcut route to the scene of the worst activity that night.

After a recent television story on the Camp Logan riot, I was contacted by Jackie and Carl Schroeder of Sealy, Texas. Jackie's grandfather, Robert Meinecke, was a brother to Officer Meinecke. In February, 2006, I met these fine folks in Bellville and we traveled southbound on FM 529 from Bellville towards Houston.

Off in the countryside to the left, or north, was the Pilgrim's Rest Cemetery. Being myself of German heritage, the upkeep of this cemetery certainly made me proud to be German. A tremendous amount of pride obviously goes into the maintenance of this property. Officer Meinecke's final resting place was marked by a WOODMEN OF THE WORLD marker. His marker reads:

"THE LIGHT OF HIS YOUNG LIFE WENT DOWN AS SINKS BEHIND A HILL, THE GLORY OF A SETTING STAR SUDDENLY CALM AND STILL".

He was laid to rest next to the eventual resting place of his parents, John (1859-1947) and Dorothea (1862-1939).

From the Bellville newspaper following this death of a local young man, this article appeared: "Edward Meinecke, who was born near Kenney, Texas, and would have been 24 years old soon, was killed in Houston serving as a Houston Police Officer. He had been married to his wife, Comila, in the early part of November, 1916. His body was shipped from Houston and burial took place at Pilgrim's Rest Cemetery, where funeral services were conducted by the Reverend S.W. Stokely of the Methodist Episcopal Church. The attendance was large. He was survived by his wife Comila, his parents John Fritz and Dorothea Eber Meinecke, two brothers-Robert William Meinecke and Frederick Meinecke, and three sisters-Lydia Amsler, Alma Lehmann, and Ella Lamp".

With the cooperation of the management of the Pilgrim's Rest Cemetery and the local Knesek Funeral Home, a 100 Club LINE OF DUTY marker now commemorates forever the gravesite of Officer Edwin Gustav Meinecke and the brave and honorable manner in which he died. Knesek Funeral Home, without hesitation, volunteered to place this marker with no charge. After the marker was set, a small gathering of relatives met this writer and HPD Honor Guard Officers David Freytag and D.G. Sealy. A short dedication ceremony was held to honor Officer Meinecke's service to the City of Houston and the manner in which he was slain.

IRA D. RANEY:

Ira D. Raney was born on April 19, 1878, and died on that infamous date of August 23, 1917. It was reported that he was shot in the heart and right thigh and also bayoneted through the heart. Also, he had been shot some months previously in another incident near the same location where he was killed. He is buried at Evergreen Cemetery, a burial ground in the east end of Houston that has seen much better days in the area of maintenance. It is my understanding that this property has changed ownership on several occasions and much has been lost in the way of burial location records.

Funeral services for Officer Raney were conducted on Sunday morning, August 20, from his residence at 220 Hutcherson Street with the Reverend W.S. Lockhart officiating. Pallbearers were Peter Young, Frank Schusler, L.E. Greer, George Peyton, Arthur Gale, and J.D. Morris.

HPD Officers William Murphy (1910) and Johnnie Davidson (1921) are also believed to be interred here. However, there are no records that would indicate the existence of a marker for these two fallen heroes. Such was thought to be the case of Officer Ira Raney. However, HPD Retired Officer George (Billy) Butler recently contacted me. As it turns out, Billy's stepdad is Ira Raney III, the grandson of our slain Officer Ira Raney. Billy led me directly to the existing marker of Officer Raney. The marker reads:

I.D. RANEY, APRIL 19, 1878-AUGUST 23, 1917, "GONE, BUT NOT FORGOTTEN".

His full name is Ira Devoud Raney. A small marker with the word MOM is adjacent to this grave and this is believed to be where the widow, Mrs. Pearl Raney, is buried. Officer George (Billy) Butler passed away in November, 2006.

With the cooperation of Mr. Noe Santana, of the Santana Funeral Homes and the current operator of this cemetery, a 100 Club LINE OF DUTY marker was placed at this gravesite by Nelson and Andy Zoch.

Officer Ira Raney was only 39 years old and was reported to have left a wife, Pearl, and nine chidren. Their ages at the time of their Dad's death are unknown with the exception of Ira Jr., who was 13 and the youngest who was 10 months old and in poor health. The children were: Sons Bryan, Thomas, Quincy (Mose), Robert (Cotton), Frank, Ira, and Houston Texas Raney (Rufus), and two daughters, Susan and Vera Raney. Mrs. Raney was now a widow in her late 30's with nine children. As stated earlier, she was generously provided a cow by the City of Houston to help her support this large family.

The Raney family has extensive ties to HPD. Bryan Raney, possibly the oldest of the Ira Raney children, served over 30 years with HPD, ending his career in the Jail Division in the early 1950's. It is believed that he stepped up and assisted his Mother in raising the younger siblings. Metro Police Department Captain Mike Raney, who served a short time with HPD, is in charge of Operations at Metro. He is a grandson of Officer Ira Raney and the son of Houston Texas Raney. HPD Sergeants Michelle (Shelly) Raney Scheibe and Janice Raney Landry are both granddaughters of Officer Ira Raney's son Robert. They and their husbands are longtime HPD veterans as is their mother and stepfather, Bonnie and James Montero. Officer Ira Raney's descendants were also active in various ranks in the Houston Fire Department.

All of the Camp Logan HPD Officers exhibited bravery in their approach to the action that faced them. Newspaper accounts indicated that Officer Raney and his partner, Officer J.E. Richardson, were most anxious to get into the "hot of it and we'll get them". With young citizen James Lyon driving the Officers, they inadvertently drove right into the center of the action. The following is verbatim from newspaper accounts:

"When the troopers (rioters) surrounded the vehicle and yelled for the occupants to come out, shouting, Who are you fellows anyway?" Officer Raney replied "I am an Officer". A wild shout of derision went up from seventy-five or more throats and the unfortunate victim was pushed out in front of the car. A Negro trooper switched off the dimmer and turned on the headlights. Officer Raney bravely stood there with his hands up and shouts were directed at him. Then, the man standing next to young Lyon deliberately sent a bullet into the Officer's breast as he stood facing his captor's, bathed in the light of the car. Raney threw his hands wildly over his head and a look of agony overspread his face. Then he slowly crumpled up, fell backward, and with one compulsive heave, died". Even though mortally wounded, the body of Officer Raney was bayoneted a number of times.

HORACE CLIFTON MOODY:

Officer Horace Moody was described in newspaper accounts as an elderly married man who left a widow and married children. However, his gravemarker at Hollywood Cemetery, which is a Woodmen of the World marker, shows him to have been born on September 2, 1869, which would have made him only 48 years of age. The marker also reads FAITHFUL UNTO DEATH.

He received one wound to the left leg, which was so severe that what remained of the leg had to be amputated. He died in the Baptist Sanitarium, likely from having lost so much blood. His death certificate shows him to have been born in Clark County, Mississippi, to Martin and Cornelia Moody. Further research shows that he was the sixth of nine children in that family. It is unknown how many siblings survived him. At this time, I have been unable to determine how many children Horace and his wife Lilly had. They had been married for 18 years at the time of his death and it is possible that he or she had children from a previous marriage.

Research has produced the name of a local attorney who is a distant relative of Officer Moody. It is uncertain at this time as to whether Hollywood Cemetery will allow a LINE OF DUTY marker since the nearest survivor is so very distant.

RUFUS DANIELS:

Officer Rufus (Ruff) Daniels and his partner, Officer Lee Sparks, have been portrayed in history as the sparks that lit the fire that was this insurrection. This writer will not argue with that portrayal as he has no additional information that would prove or disprove those allegations. However, Officer Daniels will be treated with respect in this story as he certainly paid with his life and also suffered much physical abuse post mortem.

He had been shot in the left side. After the rioters identified him, he was brutally beaten and bayoneted repeatedly. The funeral for Officer Rufus Daniels was held at 2pm on Sunday, August 20, 1917, from his residence at 1818 Hussion Street, with the Reverend John Green officiating. Pallbearers were Lee Sparks, F. Dunman, Jim Fife, George Mitchell, John Spaulding, and Harry McGee. Burial followed at Glenwood Cemetery. There has never been a marker to mark his place of burial. This is likely due to his reported family situation at the time of his death-widowed and unknown how many children, if any. However, cemetery records indicate he was buried in the Flower Mound Section. A 100 Club LINE OF DUTY marker was placed in 2006 to mark his gravesite.

The death certificate indicates no date of birth but does show he was a widower and to have been 56 years old. The date of birth has been a hindrance in the ordering of the marker, but it has been completed. As usual, the 100 Club provided the marker and with the full cooperation of Mr. Richard and Mrs. Bonnie Ambrus as well as Ms. Martha Peterson of Glenwood Cemetery, this marker has been placed. Officer Willie Weiss (1901), a LINE OF DUTY death from the past, is also interred at Glenwood Cemetery.

This completes the profiles of the five Houston Police Officers who lost their lives in the Camp Logan riot. While these five men died tragically, we, as police officers, are constantly aware that we could meet a similar fate in the line of duty. In addition to the above, there were at least two HPD Officers wounded during this uprising. They were:

T.A. BINFORD: City Detective. Shot in the knee, not serious. He later became a Sheriff of Harris County and a legend in local law enforcement.

J.E. RICHARDSON: Police Officer. Shot in head with rifle by Negro soldier, but not serious. He was with Officer Raney.

The following will portray the deaths of totally innocent everyday citizens who for one reason or another found themselves caught up in this tragedy and lost their lives. This information has been derived from newspaper articles of the day and also from cemetery records. It is likely as close as possible to be a complete list of the citizen victims:

FREDERICK WINKLER: 4910 Lillian Street, shot down on the front porch of his home after turning on the porch light. Was a machinist by trade and was one week shy of being 20 years old. Buried at German Cemetery, now called the Washington Cemetery.

EARL FENDLEY: 16 years of age, 1809 Preston Avenue, believed to have been the youngest victim. He was found lying in the road near Shepherd's Dam. Had been shot through the heart and bayoneted. Last seen with a party of friends on Washington Avenue before the trouble started. Buried at Holy Cross Cemetery.

A.R. CARSTENS: Was shot down at Park and Center Streets. Survived by a widow and four children, ages 5-12. He was 48 years old and a painter by trade.

SENELTON (SENATOR) SATTON: Resided at 1218 Walker and was a barber. Was shot through both thighs. An Army shell was taken from a leg. Bayoneted through the heart and neck. Survived by a widow and a 10 month old child. Buried at Glenwood Cemetery.

E.M. JONES: He was 53 years old, was a jitney driver, residing at 1110 Cordell Street. Was found dead the next morning on a shell road near Camp Logan. Had gun shots on his body and his right arm had been neatly severed by a saber stroke. Survived by his wife, six children, and his mother. Buried near Willis, Texas.

E.A. THOMPSON: He was 34 years of age, was among the first to be hit by gunfire from the rioting soldiers. Survived by wife, parents, two brothers and two sisters. Burial was in his hometown of Hempstead, Texas.

CHARLES W. WRIGHT: Resided at 2701 Wood Street and was a barber. Shot in the abdomen after he went to investigate the commotion. Survived by his wife and a sister. Buried at Glenwood Cemetery.

MANUEL GARREDO: Resided at 4900 Washington. Shot in his body.

SMITH, ELI: Ran a shooting gallery on Congress Avenue, was bayoneted in two places-the right hip and under the left armpit, the second wound penetrating the heart. Unknown how he was involved, but he was found in a ditch at Heiner and San Felipe, near the center of the heaviest action. Buried at Glenwood Cemetery.

J.W. MATTES: Captain, Battery A, Second Illinois Field Artillery, Shot, bayoneted, skull crushed with most of head shot off of his body.

M.D. EVERTON: Soldier, Also found near Mr. Carstens. He was a member of Company H, Fifth Texas Infantry. Shot in liver and right shoulder. Abdomen mangled by bayonet thrusts. Buried at Glenwood Cemetery.

The above described nine innocent citizens, along with Captain Mattes and Soldier Everton, and the five Houston Police Officers, account for 16 lives lost. Sergeant Vida Henry and Private Bryant Watson are two rioters who were found dead after that night. As stated, the above may not be a complete list of the dead as the following were listed as wounded from the action of that night and some may have passed on a later date as Officer Patton did.

The wounded citizens were:

WILLIAM J. DRUCKS: 26 years old, of 4910 Lillian, he may have been on the porch with Frederick Winkler. He is believed to be a half-brother to Frederick Winkler. He is listed as shot in right arm, which may require amputation and as very "low" from loss of blood and surgical shock. Research shows that he recovered and lived until 1975.

W.H. BURKETT: Listed in serious condition, shot in left side and also sprinkled with shotgun pellets.

SAMMIE FOREMAN: Soldier, of Livingston, Company F, Fifth Texas Infantry, shot in the leg, not serious.

ASA BLAND: Shot over the left eye, slight graze wound.

JAMES EDWARD LYON: 4427 Walker, shot in a leg and arm.

G.W. BUTCHER: Lived in Cottage Grove, serious condition, shot in left chest and right side.

W.A. THOMPSON: Serious condition, shot through right hip.

ALMA REICHART: Resided in the Washington Avenue neighborhood, shot in the stomach, serious condition.

In conclusion to the terrible story of the Camp Logan riot of 1917, Mr. Tom Kennedy's description of this tragedy was well worded when he stated that "No one won". Unfortunately, as detailed above, many innocent people also LOST that night in August, 1917. We should not forget the five Officers nor the innocent citizens killed or wounded that night either.

16

Detective Johnnie Davidson
February 19, 1921

Detective Johnnie Davidson Shot to Death By Prowler; Partner then Kills the Shooter

On Saturday night, February 19, 1921, a cold winter night in near northeast Houston, Detectives Johnnie Davidson and Tony Margiotta left the police station to answer a call in the area of Liberty Road and Gregg Street. A citizen had called about a prowler in that vicinity at approximately 10:45 p.m. Detectives Anderson and Blalock recalled later that Davidson and Margiotta were laughing as they left, not having any idea of the danger that lay just minutes ahead.

Upon their arrival at the location, they questioned several African-American males in the area and released them after determining that they had legitimate business in the area. The officers were then approached by a citizen reportee, who directed them to a residence at 3405 Liberty Road. There, upon further investigation, they located the prowler, a forty-one-year-old black man named Joe Harris. They told Harris to come with them to the front porch of this house, where they began searching him.

They found several revolver rounds in his pocket. Margiotta was later quoted as hearing Davidson say, "Get the gun, he's got one." From this point, Harris began physically resisting the detective's efforts to arrest him. As Margiotta attempted to hold Harris on the porch, the man pushed away and began firing a revolver. The Houston Post later quoted Margiotta as saying he heard Davidson say, "Oh, shoot him, he's shot me." Margiotta saw Davidson a few feet away, blood streaming from his stomach. Margiotta pulled his weapon from underneath his heavy overcoat and return fire, striking Harris numerous times.

When the gunfire ended, Detective Davidson lay dead, having been shot twice in the abdomen. He was only one week away from his thirty-fifth birthday. Margiotta also had been grazed on the side of the head by one of Harris' bullets. Harris, who had fired five of the six bullets in his weapon, had five entry and exit wounds to his body. He also was dead at the scene.

Night Chief Dunman and Harris County Detective I. L. Nix arrived on the scene. There they found Detective Margiotta leaning up against the porch, dazed from his grazing head wound. Detective Davidson and his assailant, Joe Harris, both lay dead just several feet apart.

Detective Davidson's body was taken to the Westheimer Morgue. Within half an hour all police officers who were not on duty had arrived at the Westheimer Company to pay their respects to their slain comrade. Further investigation revealed that one of the crook's bullets had lodged in the stomach of Davidson while the other had entered his right side, exited his left shoulder and was found embedded in his detective badge, which was pinned to the left side of his coat. Both detectives and Harris were carrying 28-caliber Smith and Wesson revolvers.

DETECTIVE JOHNNIE DAVIDSON

Fellow officers described Detectives Davidson and Margiotta as inseparable partners as well as very close friends off-duty. Margiotta said, "Poor Johnny, how I tried to save him" as he gazed at no one in particular at police headquarters after being treated and released from the hospital. "He was a great pal was Johnnie. Everybody liked him. How I wished I could have saved him."

Margiotta's face was smeared with blood from a deep gash in his upper lip inflicted by a blow from Harris' gun. The hair on one side of his head was singed off by the fire from the assailant's pistol during the scuffle. He received two stitches in his lip. "I yelled for someone to call an ambulance, but it was too late. The Negro killed a good man when he killed my partner," Margiotta said as his eyes welled up with tears as he recounted the tragic story to investigators.

In an odd legal turn of events, but probably the norm for the day, Justice of the Peace Leon Lusk held an inquest at the scene. He rendered a verdict over the death of Detective Davidson as "death from gunshot wounds inflicted by Joe Harris" and a verdict over the body of Harris as "death from gunshot wounds inflicted by Tony Margiotta."

Then, strangely enough, a murder charge was filed on Detective Tony Margiotta shortly before midnight that same night. Bond was fixed at $1 and less than a minute after the bond was set, a personal bond was signed by Dr. E. T. Belheze. Detective Margiotta was released on that bond. A grand jury investigation took place and he was no-billed.

Detective Davidson was survived by his wife, who was visiting in San Antonio at the time of his death. She was immediately notified. In addition to his wife, Johnnie Davidson was survived by his parents, W. S. and Susan Stansbury Davidson. Also mourning his sudden death were four brothers, C. A., J. H., C. H. and Julius, as well as three sisters, Lois Davidson, Mrs. A. H. Hancock and Mrs. J. S. Boulle. Brothers C. A. and J. H. Davidson were Houston firefighters at the time of their brother's death.

Funeral services were held at 5 p.m. Monday, February 21, 1921, at the home of Officer Davidson's parents at 1805 Preston Avenue. Sid Westheimer Undertaking Company was in charge of arrangements. Police officers served as pallbearers and many officers formed an escort from the home to the burial at Evergreen Cemetery on Altic Street off of Harrisburg Avenue.

Efforts to locate Davidson's gravesite at Evergreen have proven to be unsuccessful. The years of inadequate care and basic total neglect of this burial ground have taken their toll. Records have been lost or destroyed through several changes of ownership of this cemetery. The grave of HPD Line of Duty Death Officer Ira Raney (1917) was recently located and marked also with a 100 Club LINE OF DUTY marker. Unfortunately, just as in Officer Davidson's case, the grave of Assistant Chief of Police William E. Murphy (1910), also interred at Evergreen, has not been located. If there had been markers, they have been destroyed by vandalism or damaged and fallen over because of neglect – a sad situation, indeed.

Johnnie Davidson was born in Louisiana and had been a police officer in Houston for a number of years. He had been on the Houston force on this tour of duty since December 4, 1918. He had seen service on the force prior to that but resigned to work as a deputy under Constable Pat O'Leary. He also had served as a deputy under Harris County Sheriff Frank Hammond.

While he had no children, he left a young wife, parents and seven siblings to mourn his death. No doubt, he also was mourned by a number of his fellow officers.

17

Officer Jeter Young
June 19, 1921

Officer Jeter Young Killed in Accident Returning from 'Short Call' Assignment

On Sunday afternoon, June 19, 1921, Officers Jeter Young and Wilbur E. Scearce were assigned to run a "short call" out on Washington Avenue. After completing this assignment, they were en route back to the main police station on Caroline with Officer Scearce driving. As their car entered the intersection of Preston and Louisiana, it collided with a large Ford truck, a delivery vehicle of the Magnolia Dairy Products Company. The collision caused the police car to roll over three times.

Officer Jeter Young received massive head injuries. A Westheimer Company Ambulance rushed him to the St. Joseph's Infirmary. He never regained consciousness and died three hours later. He was thirty-four years old.

His partner, Officer Scearce, was badly bruised and suffered a number of broken bones. The driver of the milk truck, P. J. Nicholson, received a bruised elbow and his passenger, J. C. Enright, suffered only slight injuries. Nicholson made a statement to officers in which he said he did not see the approaching police car until it was too late. Justice of the Peace J. M. Ray filed a charge of negligent homicide against him.

Officer Jeter Young was born in Grimes County, Texas, on March 14, 1887. His parents were William R. and Della Andrews Young. They were natives of Mississippi and Alabama, respectively. He was survived by his wife, Annie Lou Shaw Young, and three children, eleven-year-old daughter Inez and two sons, six-year-old Clarence Loland Young and three-year-old Cecil Young. Also mourning this tragic passing were his parents and five brothers.

Funeral services for Young were held at his residence at 509 Pinckney at 10 a.m. Tuesday, June 21, 1921. The Reverend W. A. Main officiated and burial followed at the Hollywood Cemetery on North Main Street. Serving as pallbearers were his fellow Officers, C. W. Hight, J. T. Blackshear, Jerry Wilson, R. L. Honea, D. L. Gentry and B. O. Yates.

OFFICER JETER YOUNG

Police officials were unanimous in their praise of Officer Young and many others paid tributes to his work. In all of the records at police headquarters, there was not found a scratch against Officer Jeter Young's name. He was known to the executive officers of the department as an efficient, zealous but courteous officer. Young had been a police officer previously, but had left the force briefly to work in the Southern Pacific Railway shops. Shortly after the appointment of Chief Gordon Murphy, he returned to the department and was assigned to patrol duty, being stationed at Main and Capital in downtown Houston.

He later became a "short call" officer. In this assignment, due to the shortage of automobiles and gasoline, officers like Young would remain in the police station area and venture out only when a call for their service was needed. Officers Scearce and Young were returning to their station when this tragic accident occurred.

A newspaper account reported that members of the Policeman's Burial Fund Association drew resolutions and adopted them on the death of their brother officer. The resolutions spoke of the many virtues possessed by the deceased prior to his being called by death. The year 1921 marked the inauguration of the Burial Fund Association, with Officer Young being one of five deceased members that year whose families received a death benefit. Two other line-of-duty deaths occurred that year, those involving the deaths of Officers Johnnie Davidson and David Murdock. The death benefit was less than $1,000 at the time, an amount sufficient for a burial but not helping for the future needs of Annie Young and her three children.

Police Gordon Murphy further praised Officer Young, saying, "He was one of the most reliable and good-natured officers who was often called to do short-call work. He had no difficulty with anyone." The chief went on to say, "I fully realize Ford cars used for short-call work are entirely too light and are too easily turned over. In the future, I will recommend heavier cars for this purpose."

Officer Young's gravesite was located in the Edgewood Section of Hollywood Cemetery. His grave marker reads as follows:

Jeter Young, Born March 14, 1888-Died June 19, 1921. Also-OUR DARLING ONE HATH GONE BEFORE-HUSBAND.

While his head marker indicated 1888 as the year of his birth, his death certificate indicated that he was born in 1887 and was actually thirty-four years old at the time of his death.

In 2005, through the Internet and a volunteer genealogy researcher, we were successful in locating a person believed to be the nearest living relative of Officer Young, a grandson. Clarence Loland Young Jr., sixty-three, of Moscow, Texas, goes by "C. L." and is partially disabled from an accident. He was most appreciative and very surprised to hear from anyone regarding the grandfather he never knew. With his support as well as that of the 100 Club and the HPOU, a LINE OF DUTY grave marker was placed in 2006 in Officer Jeter Young's memory at Hollywood Cemetery.

18

Officer David D. Murdock
June 27, 1921

Murdock Shot During Domestic Disturbance Call, Dies Six Days Later While on the Operating Table

David Duncan Murdock was born in Bryan, Texas on August 31, 1884. His parents were Mr. and Mrs. J. H. (Ella) Murdock. He came to the Houston Police Department on October 15, 1920, from Bryan, where he had been employed as a deputy sheriff and constable.

The best information about David Murdock's fate comes from articles from the Houston Press and the Houston Chronicle in 1921.

About 6 p.m. Tuesday, June 21, Police Officer Dave Murdock and his partner, Officer McGraw, responded to a call to 1508 George Street in Houston's Fourth Ward. The summer was hot and the sun still out. Their call for service indicated that a Negro male had shot a Negro female. The shooter was in the house at this location preparing to resist arrest.

When the officers arrived on the scene, they were met with a fusillade of shots from inside the house. One of these shots struck Officer Murdock and he fell down, struck by bullets to both the jaw and the neck. Officer McGraw then opened fire, advancing toward the house. In this brave assault aimed toward the suspect who shot his partner, Officer McGraw survived, but was injured when he slipped and fell, bursting a blood vessel. About this time, other officers who were sent to assist should trouble arise, arrived on the scene and were going to the rear of the residence when they saw someone raise a window shade. When this individual saw the police, he jerked the shade down.

With Murdock lying wounded in the front yard, the officers entered the house. Inside, they found that the suspect had crawled up into the attic. They talked him down and identified him as Will Alexander, a Negro male. Alexander surrendered and gave his two guns to the officers, who also found in the residence the body of Edna Phelps, Negro female, lying on the kitchen floor. She was shot twice at close range and was dead at the scene.

When the shooting ceased and the scene was secured, an ambulance took Officer Murdock to St. Joseph's Infirmary. The initial diagnosis was that he was not seriously wounded.

Police took Will Alexander into custody at the scene and turned him over to the protection of Harris County Sheriff T. Binford, Deputy Sheriff Rogers, and District Attorney's Investigator George Andrew. They took him to the Harris County Jail charged with the murder of Ms. Phelps and the assault to murder of Officer Murdock.

OFFICER DAVID D. MURDOCK

Additional investigation revealed that there had been an on-going domestic dispute involving Alexander and Phelps, with the police involved as recently as Monday night after some shots were fired in the George Street neighborhood.

As stated, Officer Murdock's condition was not believed to have been serious. After his transfer to the hospital for emergency medical care, upon his regaining consciousness, he was reported to have asked his fellow officers, "Boys, did you get him?"

The week wore on with the Houston Press

reporting on June 27 that the Houston City Council authorized the Mayor to have Officer Murdock, now in serious condition, transferred to the Baptist Sanitarium at the City's expense.

Medical science in 1921 was not sophisticated enough to accurately diagnose the injuries Murdock suffered. The wounds were much more serious than doctors originally thought. A bullet wound to the jaw caused a tremendous amount of pain. Doctors originally planned to place a plate into the jaw bone. A three-inch fracture had resulted in the bullet lodging in the back of Murdock's neck. Doctors went through with the procedure designed to correct the problem on June 28. An operation was planned to correct this problem. Davie Murdock died on the operating table. The cause of death was listed "From Dilation of the Heart caused by Anesthesia." He died at 11 a.m. He was thirty-six years old, married and the father of three children.

Under the headline, "Police Pay Their Last Honor to Fallen Comrade," the Wednesday, June 29 edition of the Houston Post reported the details of Murdock's funeral. The cortege formed at 918 Austin Street, the home of the officer's brother, J. H. Murdock. A cordon of mounted policemen and twenty-eight patrolmen formed as an escort of honor and moved out ahead of the hearse. Directly behind came the family in automobiles and behind them a long procession of friends.

Sergeant Claude Beverly and Patrolman Frank Gresham accompanied the body of their dead companion and his family to Rockdale. Pallbearers were George Daniel, H. H. Flannagan, P. H. Hannah, W. G. Dunham, Jake Altofer and Ed Wilsford. Burial was at the Oak Lawn Cemetery in Rockdale.

None of the city's three papers contained an obituary listing the survivors of this brave police officer. During this era, a full obituary was apparently reserved for only the wealthy citizens. Not even a slain police officer qualified for this mention.

The Rockdale Reporter, a weekly publication, reported on June 30 that the deceased officer was accompanied by relatives, friends and representatives of the Houston Police Department. A service was held that day, a Wednesday, at 4:30 p.m. from the residence of Mr. and Mrs. H. G. Ashby, parents-in-law of the slain officer. Religious services were conducted at the gravesite by the Reverend G. S. Tomlin, pastor of the Baptist Church in Rockdale.

The Reporter further reported that Dave Murdock was for years engaged in various local business enterprises and that he was one of the best known and best liked men who ever lived in Rockdale. A weathered 84-year-old grave marker stands to mark the burial site of Officer Dave Murdock. Along with the usual date of birth and death, the following is inscribed:

"GOD IN HIS WISDOM HAS RECALLED THE BOON (SIC) HIS LOVE HAD GIVEN, AND THOUGH THE BODY SLUMBERS, THE SOUL IS SAFE IN HEAVEN."

He is interred in an Ashby family plot and Helon G. Ashby (1870-1950) and Janet E. Ashby (1869-1965) are likely his in-laws previously listed as Mr. and Mrs. H. G. Ashby.

Through the excellent cooperation of Stephen Jones of the Phillips-Luckey Funeral Home and Paul Luckey of Rockdale Memorials, a special KILLED IN THE LINE OF DUTY grave marker was placed in eternal memory of this brave man interred in Oak Lawn Cemetery.

Not much was learned about Officer McGraw, not even a first name. In a side note to this tragedy, McGraw was not the regular partner of Murdock, whose regular partner, Officer W. Searce, was injured in the traffic accident several days before, a tragic event that claimed the life of Officer Jeter Young on June 19, 1921. Officer Searce obviously experienced an absolute nightmare of bad luck with his partners.

The July 1 edition of the Houston Press reported Justice of the Peace Leon Lusk denied bail for Will Alexander, the slayer of his wife and Officer Murdock. Eleven charges had piled up on Alexander, which included two murder charges, two unrelated assault to murder charges and seven forgery charges stemming from his business dealings with Fourth Ward area merchants.

The July 28 Press reported the following: "Future is dismal for Will Alexander." In September 1921, it was learned that Alexander received a sentence of ninety-nine years for the murder of Edna Phelps. That headline reported "More to come." Trial on the murder of Officer Murdock was to begin on September 6. The death penalty was a strong possibility.

The newspaper files were researched extensively, with no new information forthcoming regarding the final fate of Will Alexander. Prior to 1923, death penalties were carried out by the individual counties. However, there is nothing in death records to show that his death occurred in Harris County. Further, there is nothing in State of Texas execution records to show his death in that manner.

A thorough search of Texas Convict Records in Austin revealed that Will Alexander was sentenced to the Texas Prison System previously. In 1912, he served four years for horse theft and Burglary from Montgomery County. He was released in 1916 and less than a year later in 1917, he was returned again for horse theft and given five years to serve until a conviction expiration date of January 9, 1922. Officer Murdock and Miss Phelps were killed on June 27, 1921. Had he remained in custody for his full term, , he would not have been a free man when he killed Officer Murdock.

Genealogical research revealed that Officer Murdock's widow was left with two children, David Duncan Murdock Jr., born in 1916, and Ella Murdock, born on May 12, 1921. She was only six weeks old when her dad was killed. Mrs. Exie Ashby Murdock, the widow, apparently remarried shortly after her husband's violent death. She married a man by the name of Gray and eventually bore three children with him. Also, both David Murdock Jr. and Ella Murdock took the name of

Gray as their surname. Mrs. Exie Gray passed away in 1964.

David Jr., Ella and the three Gray children are all deceased. Contact was made with some of the Gray grandchildren, but their privacy was requested and honored.

19

Officer J. Clark Etheridge
August 23, 1924

Chasing a Speeder, Officer Clark Etheridge Struck, Killed by Hupmobile in '24 Incident

On Friday night, August 22, 1924, Motorcycle Officers J. Clark Etheridge and W. E. Sammons were on patrol on Main Street just south of downtown. Shortly after midnight, a speeding motorist traveling south on Main caught their attention. After clocking this vehicle, Officer Etheridge sped up in an effort to stop the violator, who was driving a Ford.

At the intersection of Main and McGowen, a Hupmobile traveling west on McGowen pulled out in front of Officer Etheridge, who was moving at about forty miles an hour and attempted to avoid this vehicle. In doing so, he laid his bike down and slid under the Hupmobile and out the other side.

Officer Sammons, a former ambulance driver who had been employed by the Westheimer Company, rushed into a home and called for an ambulance that he knew was nearby. Westheimer ambulance attendants found Officer Etheridge severely injured and unconscious with a gaping hole in his forehead. They rushed him to St. Joseph Infirmary. He never regained consciousness and died shortly after arrival on that Saturday morning at age twenty-six.

Newspaper accounts included quotes by Officer Sammons in further describing the tragic details of the accident. He said, "Clark was traveling about forty miles an hour and I was about a half block behind him when I saw the Hupmobile pull out from McGowen at a slow rate of speed, maybe ten-fifteen miles an hour.

"Clark evidently saw the man about the same time that the driver of the Hup saw the motorcycle. The driver stopped his car in an effort to let Clark pass in front of him and Clark whipped his machine to the left in an effort to miss the Hup. That's when Clark's machine skidded and went down."

OFFICER J. CLARK ETHERIDGE

The driver of the Hupmobile, E. K. High of 2408 Fletcher, was taken into custody by Officer Sammons and transported to Police Headquarters. A charge of assault by auto was filed against him before Justice of the Peace Overstreet and he was released on $300 bond. However, Judge Overstreet held an inquest shortly thereafter. Sammons' testimony of his eyewitness account weighed heavy on the judge's opinion on the death of Officer Etheridge. After also hearing High's account of the tragedy, Overstreet ruled the incident an accidental death.

The judge commented to the media, "As near as I can find out, it was the fault of neither party. The officer's motorcycle skidded, throwing him directly into the car." As a result of this ruling, High was cleared of any responsibility for the death of Officer Etheridge.

Officer John Clark Etheridge, who went by his middle name, was born July 12, 1898. He had been in the Houston Police Department for only two years. He was married and had no children. In addition to his young widow, left to mourn his sudden passing were his parents, Mr. and Mrs. S. H. Etheridge, and three sisters.

Funeral services were held at 4 p.m. Monday, August 25, 1924, at the home of his parents at 919 Ashland in the Houston Heights. The Reverend G. W. Thomas officiated at the service, which was under the direction of the Houston Undertaking Company. Burial followed at Forest Park Lawndale Cemetery. Pallbearers were W. E. Sammons, J. W. Polk, R. O. Martin, E. O. Fondren, J. T. McDonald and A. W. Davis. (Officer Davis was killed in the line of duty in 1928).

The young widow, who had just returned from a fortnight's trip with the officer's parents, tearfully said, "I knew it would come to this. Time and time I begged him to quit his job, but he would not. I cautioned him many times to be careful. Now's he's dead." They had been married for three years.

Officer Etheridge, who had been on the police force for only two of those three years, was assigned his first six months to a police car and joined the motorcycle squad when he and a number of other officers were afforded the opportunity. He had purchased a brand new motorcycle and had experienced several falls, the worst injury being a bruised hand.

Etheridge's father said, "Clark was daring, but careful. He was the master of a motorcycle or an automobile. He could pass through tight places at high speed where most motorists would be afraid to go in low gear. I cautioned him many times to take no chances."

Clark left school at age sixteen. He was then employed by the Houston Undertaking Company, where he frequently drove an ambulance. Later, he worked for the Sinclair Oil Company and went to Mexico with that firm. Upon returning to Houston, he worked in the local Sinclair refinery before joining the Houston Police Department.

Officer Etheridge's cemetery plot is marked with a monument to the Etheridge family name with the added inscription:

ETHERIDGE
"OUR FATHER'S WILL BE DONE."

Clark's gravesite is marked J. CLARK ETHERIDGE, BORN JULY 12, 1898. DIED AUG 23, 1924.

As an added note to this death, the speeding motorist was never pursued and went free, probably not even aware of the tragedy he inadvertently caused.

Officer Sammons continued with his HPD career and in 1940, after eighteen years as a peace officer, ran for constable of Harris County, Precinct 1. Being forced to resign from HPD to run for office, he returned to the department after his campaign was unsuccessful. He left HPD again during World War II to work in security for the nuclear energy program in Hanover, Washington. After the war he was in the process of again returning to HPD when he died suddenly in July 1945. His son, Ellis P. "Pokey" Sammons, served with HPD from 1958 until 1983, retiring as a detective in the Major Offenders Division. He had previously worked in Robbery and Internal Affairs.

20

Detective Pete Corrales
January 21, 1925

Officer Pete Corrales, Father of Seven, Killed While Investigating a Boyfriend-girlfriend Relationship Gone Bad. Both Also Died in the Shootout.

On the evening of Wednesday, January 21, 1925, the lives of three individuals came abruptly to a violent end in the 2000 block of Congress Avenue at what was then near the eastern edge of the City of Houston.

There was Houston Police Detective Pete Corrales, an officer for just four short years, having joined the force in 1921. Corrales, married and the father of seven children, was nearing the end of his tour of duty at 9 p.m. He was in the barber shop section of an establishment at 2003 Congress that served as both a barber shop and soft drink parlor.

Detective Corrales and an older gentleman, Jesus Caceras, were seated in the barber shop. Through a thin partition, they overheard a very disturbing conversation. Corrales' interest in what he heard cost him his life.

The conversation involved a twenty-five-year-old woman named Juanita Guzman, a native of Coahuila, Mexico. She had only been in the United States a short time and operated the soft drink stand at this location. She lived in the rear of 2003 Congress address. Also overheard in this conversation was Max Martinez, a Hispanic male later reported to own an interest in a restaurant on nearby Odin Avenue.

Martinez and Guzman had been dating for some time. Their relationship included numerous quarrels. Even though she had broken off the relationship, most acquaintances felt that she had remained on friendly terms with Martinez. Unfortunately, Martinez was not able to let his feelings for this young woman rest.

On this night, Juanita Guzman was seated on a chair near the end of the partition where she could keep her eye on the soft drink counter as well as listen to the barber shop conversation. Naturally, the barber, Mr. Cantu, was present.

Martinez entered the establishment and ordered a soda from Guzman. She was heard to say, "I have none." This was apparently a rebuke that Martinez was not mentally prepared to hear. The room became quiet for a few seconds. Witnesses heard muffled conversations but couldn't understand the words.

All of a sudden a shot rang out, prompting Detective Corrales to draw his pistol and run around the partition. In doing so, he confronted Martinez standing over the prostrate body of Juanita Guzman, his spurned sweetheart. The guns of both men blazed simultaneously and when the firing stopped and the smoke cleared, both Detective Corrales and his assailant Martinez were on the floor, critically wounded.

Detective Corrales managed to regain his feet and staggered to a nearby drug store where he waited for an ambulance. A Fogle-West ambulance arrived and rushed both men to St. Joseph's Infirmary. Martinez died en route and Corrales died a short time later. Neither was ever able to speak after having been shot.

Five shots were fired, in what the Houston Press reported to have been the shortest gun battle in the records of the Houston Police Department. Juanita Guzman was dead at the scene, having been shot point blank in the face. Detective Corrales was struck above the heart and seen by witnesses with blood gushing from that fatal wound. It wasn't exactly clear where Corrales' bullets hit Martinez but it was obvious that they also hit home.

While no obituary for Detective Corrales was published in the local newspapers, he left a wife and seven children. Newspaper accounts the next day reported the detective's widow as saying, "He did his duty. He died as he lived—bravely. He did as I would have had him do. He faced danger without flinching." The interview was reportedly done at their small cottage at No. 22 Chenevert as her seven children grouped around her. Some of them were too young to understand the gravity of the situation. They nodded in approval of their mother's comments.

At this point, Mrs. Corrales wasn't crying; her tears had all been shed during an seemingly endless sleepless night with her family. She also was quoted as saying, "I'll be able to take care of the children some way."

In a more detailed interview with Mr. Cacera, the following was learned:

Further investigation determined that Guzman and Martinez had been involved in a relationship for some time. Their original relationship had broken off and it was believed to be on friendly terms – except from Martinez' real point of view. He owned and operated a restaurant on nearby Odin Avenue and was still upset about the break-up. Martinez, in essence, was an early-day stalker, apparently unable to accept Guzman's refusal to continue the relationship.

DETECTIVE PETE CORRALES

Funeral services were held for Detective Corrales on Saturday, January 24, 1925, at 2:30 p.m. from the modest Corrales family home at No. 22 Chenevert. Religious services followed at 3 p.m. at the Guadalupe Church, with the Reverend Father De Anta officiating. Burial took place under the direction of the Houston Undertaking Company at the Holy Cross Cemetery on North Main. This is a Catholic Cemetery with an entrance separate from the larger Hollywood Cemetery at North Main and what is now the North Freeway.

Detective Corrales was the only Hispanic detective on the force at the time of his death. Six of his fellow officers carried him to his grave on that dark and dreary day in January. They were W. F. Blalock, W. H. Anderson, T. J. Lyons, Gus Butler, W. H. Cain and Tony Margiotta.

The Houston Post failed to carry stories about this tragic event and the Press and Chronicle provided only limited coverage. No plans were mentioned in either of the latter two publications regarding any financial assistance for Mrs. Corrales and her large family. The January 22 edition of the Chronicle ran a front-page photo of the inside of the business where the shooting happened. Featured in the photo was Mr. Caceres pointing to locations, probably in a reenactment of the crime. Also in the photo was Mrs. Eva Bacher, HPD's first-ever female officer, who was seated in the same chair where Ms. Guzman was seated. Also shown were Herman Radke and F. Berner, city detectives. Detective Berner was the grandfather of retired HPD Robbery/Homicide Detective Frederick Berner.

Retired HPD Lieutenant Eli P. Rivera had indicated to me in the past that he was in some manner related to Detective Corrales. Research through the Catholic Cemetery Association revealed an earlier date of burial than originally used in the story of Corrales' death and the above date has been proven to be correct. Rivera advised this writer of a lady who was the youngest of the seven Corrales children. She stated in a phone interview that she was three years old at the time of her father's death and originally desired to maintain her privacy. However, she was contacted in March, 2007, at which time she was eighty-five years old, and was agreeable to speak with this writer.

This daughter, Mrs. Ruby Lewis Banks, was in fact the youngest of the Corrales children. From this lady, the following was learned: Officer Pete Corrales and his wife, Mrs. Sabena Nette Corrales, were both from the area of Many, Louisiana. In 1925, this family (and their approximate ages) consisted of Pete Corrales Jr. (18-19), Mary Corrales (16), Delphine Corrales, Jesse Corrales, Thomas Corrales, Frank Corrales (5), and Ruby Corrales (3). Another son, also named Frank, was killed in a traffic accident at the age of seven. This was prior to Officer Corrales' death and another son was born and named in his memory. Son Thomas was killed in World War II on a troop carrier that was bombed. The second Frank Corrales served as a Military Policeman during WW II. The family moved from Chenevert Street on Avenue S in the east end and Mrs. Sabena Corrales worked for the National Biscuit Company. Mrs. Sabena Corrales passed away in 1970.

Prior to meeting with Mrs. Banks, I had also learned from Mark Clark, Executive Director of the HPOU, and Retired Homicide Detective J. W. Clampitte that both had been acquaintances of Pete Corrales Jr. through a fraternal organization. This information led to the discovery of an obituary from June, 1984, that indicated that Peter H. Corrales had passed away that month at the age of seventy-seven. He left a wife, three daughters, two sisters, and two brothers.

In speaking with Mrs. Banks, she fondly recalled that when her Dad would leave their house for work in the early afternoon, she would attempt to follow him. However, he would return and take her back home. Unfortunately, not much else could be recalled by this lady regarding the lives of her older siblings.

21

Officer E.C. Chavez
September 17, 1925

Detective Chavez, Corrales' Replacement, Killed In Domestic Disturbance on Houston's East Side

E. C. Chavez had been a City of Houston police detective since February 15, 1925. At that time, he replaced Detective Pete Corrales, who had recently been killed in a gun battle on Congress Avenue.

At about 2:30 a.m. Thursday, September 17, 1925, Detective Chavez went to the home of Pablino and Ysabel Ramerez at No. 13 Woods Alley in the area of what today is near Canal and Navigation. Prior to this, Chavez was socializing with Pablino Ramerez, an acquaintance, at a nearby "fiesta." Both were later reported to have been drinking heavily. Chavez left Ramerez and went to Ramerez' home. Investigators never learned the complete details of what happened next as Chavez was not able to converse before he died.

While at the Ramerez home with Ysabel Ramerez, Detective Chavez allegedly made unwanted advances. The Ramerez woman resisted those advances and, while doing so, Pablino Ramerez returned home. Pablino tapped on Detective Chavez' shoulder and said, "Hello, Mr. Chavez, I thought you were my friend as you promised to be." The two exchanged more words before Pablino Ramerez went outside toward an alley.

He returned a few minutes later with a gun.

Chavez was still there and a fight ensued over the weapon. They fought all over the house and then out into Nitz Alley, where Pablino Ramerez managed to gain control of his gun and fired into Chavez' stomach. The bullet passed through Chavez' body and he fell to the ground, mortally wounded.

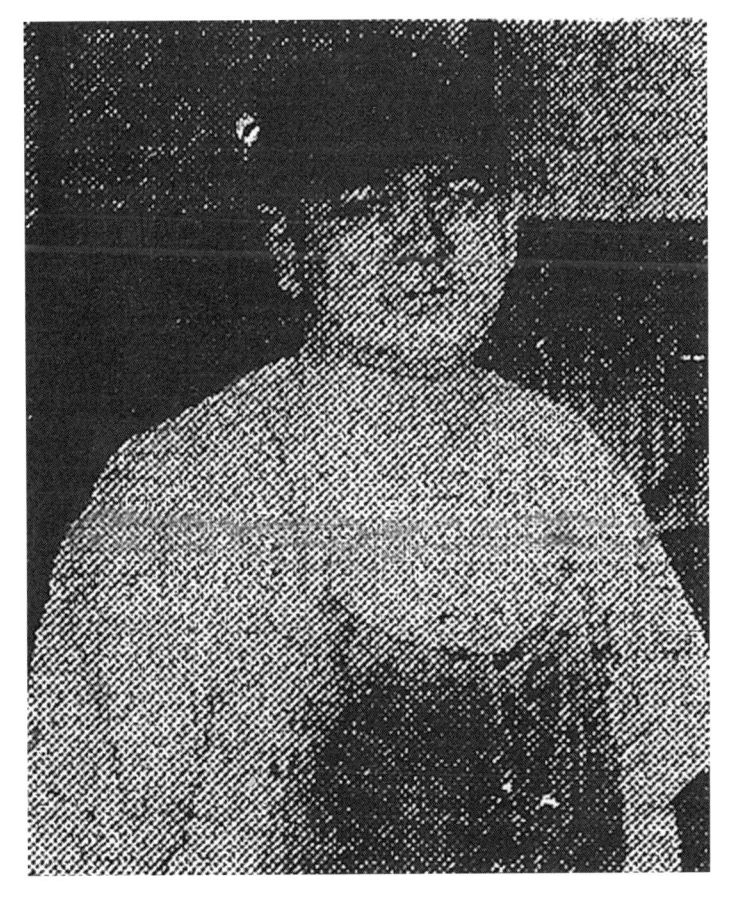

DETECTIVE E.C. CHAVEZ

Meanwhile, Ysabel Ramerez ran for help to the home of Jim Buenrosto, who lived nearby at 2203 Canal. After learning of what happened, Buenrosto ran all the way to the police station at Preston and Caroline to report what happened. Night Chief of Police R. J. Martin and short call Officers Sterling and Roberts went to the scene. There, they found Chavez lying on the ground. Ramerez had fled the scene. Also in the dirt alley lay two .45-caliber pistols on the ground next to Chavez, only one of which had been fired. Ramerez left his wife as the only witness.

An ambulance rushed Detective Chavez to Jefferson Davis Hospital, where he died at 3:37 a.m. His only words about the incident were spoken to the first officers at the scene when he stated, "a man living in that house (13 Woods Alley) shot me."

The state filed charges against Pablino Ramerez for murder in the death of Detective Chavez. At 2 p.m. Thursday, September 17, Houston Detectives William Slack and Roy Young arrested Ramerez while he was on his way to surrender at the county courthouse. The following morning, Ramerez was released from jail on a $500 bond and ordered by Justice Campbell Overstreet to return to court for an examining trial to be held on Monday, September 21 at 2 p.m.

The body of Detective Chavez was taken to Fogle-West Undertaking Company. Chavez, who lived at 907 Bagby Street, was survived by his wife, Clara, and one son, John H. Chavez. Also mourning his death were two sisters, Mrs. Josio Alvarado and Mrs. Secundina Tena, and two brothers, Steve and Golian "Will" Chavez.

Edward C. Chavez was born on October 13, 1885 and died on September 20, 1925, just short of forty years old. He was buried at the Washington Cemetery on Washington Avenue, the old German Society Cemetery. Records show Clara died in 1978 at age eighty-eight and is also buried at Washington Cemetery.

A thorough search of criminal justice records revealed no disposition of the Murder charges against Pablino Ramerez. Additionally, a search of Texas Convict records at the State of Texas library in Austin showed no record of Pablino Ramerez ever having been in the system as a convicted criminal.

In reviewing the facts and circumstances of this case with several older long-time Officers, one possible explanation is that due to the situation as described above, the charges against Pablino Remerez likely just "went away" as the best disposition for all concerned, including the Department.

22

Officer Perry Page Jones
January 30, 1927

Officer Jones' Killer Evades Death Penalty, Gets 'Sentence' Years Later by Former Special Officer

Perry Page Jones was born in Waller County, Texas, on July 3, 1893, to Mr. and Mrs. J. F. Jones. He attended Black Terrapin School and as a teenager, his family moved to both Tomball and Houston before returning to Waller County. On December 16, 1914, he married Mary Simmons and they made their home on a farm in Waller County. Their marriage was blessed with five children, Vanice Ione (Bernice) in 1915, Severn Frankline in 1917, Lyle Thurman in 1920, Howard Page in 1923, and Talmadge Ray in 1925.

Farming in Waller County and feeding a family in the 1920's was a rough life. However, it became worse when the fourth child, Howard Page Jones, passed away in 1923 from smallpox complications. Then, in August 1926, it became even tougher when Mary Jones, the wife and mother, died at age thirty-five. This left Perry Jones a widower with four children. Continuing to farm probably was not an option, with four children under age eleven. Jones left the farm and moved his motherless children to Houston, where they stayed with his parents, Mr. and Mrs. J. F. Jones, at 4202 Julian.

Jones joined the Houston Police Department on October 1, 1926 as a patrolman on the 11 p.m. – 7 a.m. shift. At approximately 3 a.m. Sunday, January 30, 1927, Officer Perry Page Jones was on foot patrol in the 400 block of Milam in downtown. He was assigned to the Milam Street beat from the City Auditorium to Commerce. As he patrolled alone, he confronted what he believed to be an intoxicated male who had just exited a bar near this location.

A city employee was in this area operating a street sweeper when he heard a gunshot. He then saw an individual, later identified as Officer Jones, sink to his knees. Just six feet away stood another person, the suspect, holding a gun in his hands. After the officer fell and lay still, the suspect pointed the gun and snapped the trigger twice at the individual with an HPD badge. Neither round fired. This witness, Ed Perry, then saw the suspect enter and quickly exit a lounge with four other people, leaving the scene in an automobile.

Police located two other witnesses later that morning. Their observations were that they saw Officer Jones struggling in an apparent attempt to arrest the individual who would shoot and kill him. They saw the suspect, a Negro male, break away from the struggle and fire a shot at the officer. They also saw the aborted shots at the fallen officer and watched the suspect enter Smith's Café at 411 Milam.

When all was said and done, Officer Perry Page Jones, thirty-three years old and a widowed father of four young children, lay dead in the street from a single gunshot wound to the head. A police career of less than four months ended and four young children were left as orphans.

The suspect at this time was unknown. Homicide detectives swung into action immediately. The suspect was seen frequently around Houston and thought by many to be from Galveston. When Homicide Detective George Peyton learned the description of the suspect, he assigned a Negro detective, Charlie Stewart, to assist him in identifying this suspect. It was determined that this black man was diminutive but violent. His name was Pete Chester. Chester had moved to Houston from Galveston, where he had an extensive criminal record. Five witnesses identified him as the man who shot Officer Jones.

Riding out San Felipe Street, Peyton spotted Chester, who was fifty-three years old. Detectives Peyton and Millsap arrested him. They searched him and found no evidence. A further search of his room revealed three cartridges which had been snapped and not exploded.

Officer Jones was survived by his children, eleven-year-old Vanice (Bernice), ten-year-old Severn, seven-year-old Lyle and two-year-old Talmadge. Other survivors were his parents, Mr. and Mrs. Frank Jones, brothers A. L. Jones and M. L. Jones; sisters, Mrs. J. M. Smith of Houston and Mrs. W. A. Scroggins of Goose Creek; an uncle J. F. Page and an aunt, Mrs. A. B. Credge. In addition to his wife, Officer Jones was preceded in death by a son, Howard, two years old, who passed away in 1923.

OFFICER PERRY PAGE JONES

Funeral services for Jones commenced when a procession of Houston officers met the hearse at the corner of Heights Boulevard and Washington Avenue at 8 a.m. Monday, January 31, 1927. This sad group of family members and police officers proceeded to Waller and from there to the New Hope Methodist Church.

Burial followed in the Fields Store Cemetery. Fogle West Funeral Home was in charge of arrangements and Christian services were conducted by the Reverends Henry Jones and John Campbell. Pallbearers were Sergeant Sid LeStrange and Officers J. H. Goodwin, T. G. Moore, J. A. Urban, A. O. Taylor and Albert Worth Davis, who later died in the line of duty in 1928.

Witnesses had identified Pete Chester as the deadly shooter in the case of Officer Jones. Chester, earlier alleged to have killed two Negroes in Galveston, pled not guilty due to self defense. In 1927, emotions ran high. While the Harris County District Attorney vowed to have a quick trial, rumors ran rampant that there would be an effort to "grab" the suspect from the Harris County jail for "some quick justice." Harris County Sheriff T. A. Binford was concerned enough that he "smuggled" Pete Chester out of his jail under the cover of darkness and took him to Huntsville, where he was placed in the protective custody of the prison system to await trial back in Houston.

(Rumors of unauthorized but quick justice came true seventeen months later when the killer of Officer Albert Worth Davis was kidnapped from Jeff Davis Hospital and lynched in far west Houston.)

District Attorney Horace Soule announced that the trial would begin on Friday, February 11, 1927. The trial was to be held in Criminal District Judge Whit Boyd's court and a venire of over two hundred men was summoned for jury duty along with fourteen witnesses. Meanwhile, Chester remained in Huntsville in protective custody. Newspaper accounts do not indicate whether Pete Chester was present at the trial.

The trial was reset to March 21. Chester's defense attorney was John M. Mathis Sr. During the trial, three snapped cartridges recovered from Chester's residence were important pieces of evidence. This matched the street sweeper's testimony that the shooter stood over the fallen Officer Jones and attempted to shoot him again.

In 1917, Pete Chester was convicted of assault to murder in Galveston. He got a five-year suspended sentence. The court dismissed another similar charge at the same time. Earlier, in 1916, Chester was found not guilty on an identical charge.

On Wednesday, March 23, 1927, the judge presented the charge to the jury. Jurors then deliberated just more than an hour before finding Chester guilty of murder in the death of Officer Jones and assessing him the death penalty. During the trial, all four of the orphaned children were in the courtroom, the youngest held in a relative's lap. The prosecution definitely exploited the children, a move that ultimately proved successful.

Research of records failed to indicate that Pete Chester was ever executed. Records did show that an appeal was upheld and granted Chester a new trial. This trial was held in Huntsville, home of Texas' Death Row, on a change of venue from Houston.

On May 11, 1928, Judge Carl Harper dropped a bombshell when he presented his charge to the jury in the second trial. Judge Harper charged the jury on manslaughter, thereby eliminating the murder verdict possibilities. Under the manslaughter statute, five years in the state pen was the maximum punishment. Needless to say, the state's attorneys, Walker County District Attorney A. T. McKinney and his assistants, were dumbfounded with this development. Was Judge Harper stating that Chester had not shot Officer Jones in malice? Had he not recalled the testimony of the street sweeper who stated that Chester had attempted to shoot the officer while he was on the ground?

Newspaper accounts of the trial shed some light (or suspicions) on this strange ruling. It seemed that Judge Harper had just recently been himself acquitted of a murder charge in Brenham, Texas. His defense was self-defense, the same as that of Pete Chester. Another even stranger twist was that Attorney Mack Gates, who assisted in Judge Harper's Brenham defense, was hired as a special prosecutor to assist District Attorney McKinney. A special fund raised by the Houston Police Department was used to retain Gates. It would take less than a suspicious mind to think that this was extremely irregular.

The jury found Pete Chester guilty of manslaughter and assessed him four years in prison. He was discharged on October 1, 1931, less than five years from the time of the murder. Chester went from Death Row to being a free man. What a bitter blow to the family of Officer Perry Page Jones. It is unknown what happened to Pete Chester after his release.

Fields Store Cemetery is off Farm Road 1488, north of the Waller/Hempstead area. In 2004 Officer Jones's grave was found to have a Woodmen of the World marker which reads:

PERRY P. JONES, 7/3/1893 – 1/30/1927

HOW DESOLATE OUR HOME BEREFT OF THEE.

Buried next to Officer Jones is the wife who passed away less than six months before, leaving him a widow with four small children. This marker reads:

MARY M. JONES, 5/3/1890 – 8/8/1926

SHE DIED AS SHE LIVED, TRUSTING IN GOD.

With the cooperation of the management of Fields Store Cemetery as well as the 100 Club and the Houston Police Officers Union, a KILLED IN THE LINE OF DUTY marker was placed in September 2004 by Nelson and Andy Zoch at Officer Perry Jones' gravesite to honor his life and tragic death.

The miracle of the Internet provided more information about the Jones children. In June 2006, a Severn Jones, who had passed away in 1998 was located on a genealogy Website. A Houston Chronicle obituary noted that there were several surviving grandchildren of Severn Jones who carried rather unusual names. These uncommon names helped tremendously in locating the grandchildren of Officer Jones.

When contact was initiated with a son of Mary Bess Jones, a daughter of Severn Jones, the young man knew immediately the story of Officer Jones due to the stories passed down to him by his mother about his great grandfather, Perry Page Jones. Mary Bess and her sister Margie and brother Larry were all apprised of the search for Jones' descendants. Later, Perry, Terry and several of the granddaughters also came forward. In July 2006, Margie and Larry and his wife Janie shared a wealth of family information for the publication of this book. Prior to this contact, even though as a family they had been at Fields Store Cemetery early in 2004, they were totally unaware of the 100 Club marker which had been placed there in memory of their grandfather, a police officer they never had the opportunity of knowing.

Vanice Ione (Bernice) attended schools in Waller County and in Houston. As a young woman, she worked for a large insurance firm in Houston. She married a man named Rufus Sawyer, whose employment took their family to a variety of locales. Eventually they settled in Houston. They had three children, Gayle, Martha and Tommy. Vanice is now deceased.

Severn Franklin "Sonny" Jones received his education in Waller County schools and Houston. He also worked for the same insurance company as his sister. He enlisted in the United States Air Corps in the early years of World War II. After training in San Antonio, he saw service in the China-Burma-India Theatre as a first sergeant in a repair squadron. After the war, he married his wife Maxine, who was from San Antonio. They lost an infant daughter while living in San Antonio and later moved to Houston, where they raised three children, Larry Severn, Marjorie and Mary Bess.

Severn Jones had a successful lengthy career in the oil transportation industry while Maxine was employed at an engineering firm. Severn Jones and his family were personal friends with HPD Honor Guard Officer David Freytag and Retired Homicide Sergeant Jim Ramsey. Severn was preceded in death by his wife. He died in 1998.

Lyle Thurman Jones received his education in Houston. Lyle suffered from eyesight problems and he was rejected for military service for World War II. However, he did serve his country by working in defense plants during the war. He was married and blessed with twin sons, Perry Page Jones and Terry Edward Jones. Lyle was involved in a variety of business interests in and around the Houston area. They included home construction, sales, real estate and used cars. He is now deceased.

Talmadge Ray Jones attended Houston schools until his induction into the United States Air Corps in 1943. He served as a gunner on a bomber and was shot down over Switzerland. Surviving this, he was reassigned to the States and contacted his family members prior to their learning of his ordeal. At one point he was listed as "Missing in Action." He worked as a carpenter and then followed his father into police work by joining the Spring Valley Police Department. He was married and was blessed with two daughters, Sharon and Neva. Talmadge passed away from a heart attack as a young man of only thirty-nine in 1964.

Had Officer Perry Page Jones not been killed by Pete Chester, he would have been the proud grandfather of ten grandchildren. His family told of a special marker that had for years adorned the officer's grave at Fields Store. The family had removed it several years ago with the thought that it might possibly be vandalized or stolen. It is of heavy brass and was severely tarnished from many years of weather. Larry has had it refurbished and it is a truly remarkable item. Who placed this marker there for Officer Jones? Basically, it consists of the wording, P. P. Jones and Honor Legion – Houston Police Department. The mystery continues.

Perry and Terry Jones, Lyle Jones' sons, believe that Pete Chester might have met his own violent and untimely death shortly after his release from prison. A Negro male had surfaced at Lyle Jones' house and told him that he was the one who killed Pete Chester. Death records show that Pete Chester did in fact die of gunshot wounds on December 22, 1933. Newspaper files indicate the following information related to Chester's death:

Charlie Stewart was the "behind the scenes" Negro investigator that assisted Homicide detectives in identifying Pete Chester. He was a special officer for about three years with HPD until April 1929. It was through him that Detectives Peyton, Millsap and the rest of the Homicide posse were able to center their investigation on Pete Chester. Officer Stewart likely operated in the later tradition of Ed Jones, Stocky Gray, Truitt Newton, Charles Banks and many other Negro officers who worked behind the scenes to assist HPD detectives in a wide variety of investigations.

In December 1933, Pete Chester learned of Charlie Stewart's employment as a cook in a café on West Dallas. Basically, Chester started coming around Stewart's job, stalking him and making it known that he was going to "take care of Stewart." Chester apparently harbored a grudge against Stewart for his part in the investigation, even though Stewart never testified against him. He merely did the leg work and obtained the name of Pete Chester based on the witness descriptions.

Charlie Stewart believed from comments Chester made to him, as well as his knowledge of Chester's behavior, that Chester was carrying a weapon when he came around his job. A week prior to Chester being killed, Chester threatened Stewart, who at the time was drinking coffee. Stewart threw hot coffee on Chester, who then retreated.

On Friday, December 22, 1933, Pete Chester approached Charlie Stewart in the 700 block of West Dallas. As they neared each other, Stewart saw Chester reach for a pistol. Feeling certain that Chester was carrying a gun, Stewart pulled his own pistol after Chester made the infamous "hip pocket move." Stewart emptied his pistol, striking Pete Chester six times in the arms and chest. Pete Chester was dead at age fifty-seven. When old Pete was loaded into the body car, a fully loaded pistol fell out of his clothes. Finally,

Officer Perry Page Jones and his family received some semblance of justice – not from the State of Texas, but from forty-six-year-old Charlie Stewart.

The same newspaper article that described the shooting indicated that Charlie Stewart was charged with murder. The disposition of that charge was unknown, but it is highly unlikely that this charge was prosecuted.

23

Officer Rodney Q. Wells
July 30, 1927

Officer R. Q. Wells, 'Running Hot,' Collides With Ice Truck, Dies from Internal Injuries

Early in the morning hours of Saturday, July 30, 1927, Short Call Officers R.Q. Wells and M. A. Gresham were summoned to a call at the home of a W. A. Stallings, who had been found dead at his home from a gunshot wound.

With Officer Wells driving, the officers approached the intersection of LaBranch and Elgin. There, they were met by an ice truck driven by R. W. Alexander of 4505 Brady. According to Gresham, Wells was running hot with red lights and siren operating. Wells tried to pass in front of the truck, but then swerved to pass behind it. The right front wheel of the police car struck the right rear wheel of the ice truck, causing the police car to overturn.

An ambulance rushed Officer Wells to Jeff Davis Hospital, where X-rays revealed broken ribs and internal injuries after he was crushed behind the steering wheel of the police car. He died in the hospital at 8:30 a.m. He was fifty years old. Justice of the Peace Campbell Overstreet ruled Wells' death due to an unavoidable accident. Officer Gresham received minor injuries and was able to remain on duty after the accident.

Officer R. Q. Wells was born in Kentucky on October 29, 1876 to John David and Emily Caroline Powell Wells. He had been a member of the Houston Police Department since May 24, 1920, having joined the department at the age of forty-three with a wife and two sons. Prior to joining the department, he was employed as a convict guard and as an electrician for a streetcar company.

One of his first assignments as an officer was to direct traffic before and after school at the McKinney Elementary School. He was well liked by the children he worked hard to protect. In the years prior to his death, Wells worked at a downtown teenager dance hall establishment. It is unknown if this was on- or off-duty. During this work a group of young boys jumped on him, forcing him to hit one of the teenagers with his pistol, causing a minor scalp wound.

Officer Wells, who lived at 1602 Crockett, was survived by his wife, Bessie Wells, and two sons, Alvin Curtis Wells and David Leroy Wells. Also mourning his death was his twin brother, John Walter Wells of Houston, and one sister, Mrs. Frank (Fannie Lee) Osburn of Huntsville.

Funeral services were held on Monday, August 1, 1927, under the direction of the Fogle West Undertaking Company. The Missouri Pacific Railroad took the body to New Waverly, where a second service was held at 1 p.m., with burial in the East Sandy Cemetery. This cemetery was located on Farm Road 1374, approximately five miles west of what is now Interstate 45 in Walker County, Texas. Officer Wells' grave marker reads:

QUINN WELLS
OCT 29, 1877
JULY 30, 1927

THOU ARE GONE,
BUT NOT FORGOTTEN.

Officer Wells' wife, Bessie Carolyn Morgan Wells, was buried next to him. She was born on November 5, 1885 and passed away on May 5, 1960. Officer Wells' parents are also interred in this cemetery. They were John D. Wells (1843-1902) and Emily C. Wells (1843-1908).

The East Sandy Cemetery Association gave approval to place a 100 Club LINE OF DUTY grave marker to honor this man. Originally, the only information available on Officer Wells was the initials R.Q. Research found him to be Rodney Quinn Wells. Information surfaced that he registered for the military draft in 1918 at the age of forty-one and was at the time employed as a ship carpenter for a Houston shipbuilding company. It is probable that industry layoffs led him to become a Houston police officer at an older age than usual.

In April 2006, the 100 Club marker was placed by Nelson and Andy Zoch at the East Sandy Cemetery gravesite of Officer Rodney Quinn Wells.

24

*Investigator Carl Greene
March 14, 1928*

Officer Greene, Assigned to Bust Bootleggers, Gets Shot to Death During Countryside Arrest

At 8:30 a.m. Wednesday, March 14, 1928, Harris County District Attorney Investigator Carl Greene and his partner, Houston Police Sergeant Claude Beverly, went to a location on East Montgomery Road, eleven miles from downtown Houston. These veteran law enforcement officers, with reputations for the relentless pursuit of bootleggers during the Prohibition era, were armed with a search warrant for the property of Sam Maglitto, an Italian farmer.

Maglitto was known to have stills operating on his rural property. He had been indicted on November 17, 1927, following a previous raid by Greene and Beverly. His case had been set for February 17, 1928, but was continued at the request of Maglitto's attorney. Meanwhile, information surfaced that Maglitto was continuing to manufacture illegal whiskey on his farm.

Upon their arrival, Greene and Beverly were met by Maglitto in the yard. He listened quietly to their reading of the search warrant and being told that he was suspected of making whiskey on the property. Maglitto denied the allegations and invited them into his house. Then Maglitto quickly headed for this abode as Greene and Beverly started toward his barn. Beverly later said that he told Greene to keep an eye on Maglitto, who Greene followed into the house.

At this point, Beverly heard Greene shout, "Don't do that! Put it up; put up the gun!"

Beverly then heard a shot from a .38, followed by a shot from Greene's larger gun. "I ran into the kitchen," Beverly said. "Maglitto was on his knees, gun in hand. Carl was staggering from the room. I fired three shots at Maglitto and he fell over dead."

Officer Beverly dragged his critically injured partner out of the house down to the road. He shouted at J. R. VanNess, who lived across the road, to call the Sheriff's Department and an ambulance. VanNess had no phone and had to drive toward town to call. Beverly flagged a passing auto and commandeered it to take his partner to Houston. They were met about halfway by a Fogle-West ambulance which carried Greene the rest of the way to the hospital.

Another Fogle-West ambulance picked up Maglitto and a Boulevard Undertaking Company ambulance picked up Bessie Maglitto, the twenty-two-year-old daughter of the dead man. She was caught in the gunfire and struck in the left leg and right arm. The ambulance took her to Methodist Hospital.

INVESTIGATOR CARL GREENE

At Baptist Hospital, Greene was found to have been shot over the heart with a .38-caliber revolver. The slug passed through both lungs and exited his back on the right side. Doctors found the missile in his shirt on the operating table. However, the officer had lost a tremendous amount of blood and died at 1:55 p.m. on this same date. He was only thirty-four years old.

As the entire Greene family anxiously waited outside the operating room, Mrs. Greene related, "I knew it had to come to this. Now I'm surprised that I can take it so bravely. For four years I have listened to that message I heard this morning. It was a little joke we had between us – my warning him to not get shot. He is so big and strong and unafraid."

Minutes later, doctors told the family that Carl Greene was dead.

Investigator Carl Greene, a native of Abbeville, Louisiana, was born on May 27, 1893. He was survived by his wife of seven years, Pearlie Walker Greene. Other survivors were his mother, Mrs. Richard Greene, two sisters, Effie Greene and Eugenia Green, and four brothers, Jules, Richard, Ellis and Robert. Another brother, Emery Greene, was killed in an auto accident just several weeks before in Beaumont.

Services for the slain Investigator were held at 3 p.m. on Friday, March 16, 1928, at the Fogle West Chapel with the Reverend T. J. Windham officiating. Burial followed at Forest Park Lawndale Cemetery. Services were also held under the auspices of the Eagles and the Woodmen of the World. Active pallbearers were Officer Claude Beverly, W. W. Way, George Andrews, Percy Heard, E. H. Tally and Jim Davlin.

Carl Greene is buried in the older section north of Lawndale. His plot is marked with a foot marker that reads:

CARL GREENE

MAY 27, 1893
MARCH 14, 1928

His widow, Pearl Walker Greene, is buried near his side. She was born on August 27, 1894 and passed away on December 31, 1940.

Shortly after the raid, neighbors reported seeing someone dragging a still away from the barn and hiding it in some brush. Sheriff T. Binford led a posse of investigators to the scene of the shooting and located a twenty-gallon still along with twenty-one gallons of whiskey in the back room of the house. Alfred Maglitto, seventeen, was charged with liquor law violations.

Justice of the Peace Campbell Overstreet held an inquest into the death of Sam Maglitto, who had been shot six times. The judge reached a verdict of death due to gunshot wounds. No charges were filed against Claude Beverly, as it was ruled he acted in self defense.

Research showed that Investigator Carl Greene was a liquor investigator for the Harris County District Attorney's Office. Yet, he was declared as KILLED IN THE LINE OF DUTY with the Houston Police Department. To date, no explanation for this has been discovered.

Further investigation shed more light on Greene. He was an ex-ironworker, ex-boxer and an ex-wrestler. He came to HPD in 1924, a man of huge physique who never used his size and strength to abuse anyone. His HPD career began on Congress Avenue and continued later on the Houston Ship Channel, where the toughest crooks in Houston hung out. He was later asked by Harris County District Attorney Horace Soule to work for him as a liquor investigator. After a short time in that assignment, he returned to work for HPD. At some point, Investigator Greene was assigned from HPD to the DA's Office in the capacity as a liquor investigator along with Officer Claude Beverly.

Sam Maglitto, who had been widowed and remarried, was survived by his second wife, Josephine and six daughters from the ages of twenty-two years to two months, Bessie, Josie, Rosie, Mary, Laura and Francie. He also had five sons from ages twenty-four to two years, Dif, Alfred, Joe, Frank and Angelo.

This was a double tragedy in the great experiment of Prohibition during the years of the Great Depression. Here were two honest and dedicated law officers attempting to enforce the laws passed by our country, along with probably an otherwise honest man who was attempting to supplement his meager farming income to feed, clothe and house his ever-growing family.

25

Officer Paul W. Whitlock
April 22, 1928

Accident on HPD Target Shooting Range Takes the Life of Officer Paul W. Whitlock

On Tuesday, April 17, 1928, a group of six uniformed Houston police officers were on the sixth floor of the Police Headquarters on Caroline Street in downtown Houston. There existed at that time a makeshift indoor pistol range and these officers, who all worked the 3-11 p.m. shift, were conducting informal pistol target practice at approximately 2:45 p.m. prior to going on their regular tours of duty.

Present were Officers Paul W. Whitlock, C. V. "Buster" Kern, H. N. Howard, G. A. Morrow, W. J. Myers and E. A. "Dutch" Boehler. All of the officers had fired several shots at targets and were preparing for the firing of additional rounds. It is unclear as to whether there was any type of organized supervision at this practice session. There probably was not.

Newspaper accounts said that Officer Whitlock was about eight feet to the side of Officer Howard and slightly in front of him. Officer Howard raised his arm to shoot his weapon and the gun went off before he could level it on the target. A .38-caliber bullet from Officer Howard's weapon struck Officer Whitlock in the right side of his abdomen.

The officers immediately carried Whitlock down the six flights of stairs, loaded him into a police vehicle and rushed him to Baptist Hospital. He was listed in critical condition from the projectile, which shattered the pelvis bone and lodged in the left hip joint. He was reported to have a "fighting chance to live." However, he passed away at 1:16 a.m. Sunday, April 22, 1928. He was twenty-seven years old.

Officer Whitlock, who had only been on the Houston Police Department since January 16, 1928, was a traffic control officer assigned to the intersection of Main and Prairie. He lived at 407 East Ninth Street.

Funeral services were held at the Fogle-West Chapel at 4 p.m. Monday, April 23, 1928. The Reverend E. P. West officiated at the service and burial followed at Forest Park Cemetery on Lawndale. Members of the Police Department served as pallbearers. Honorary pallbearers were Bill Jones, N. E. West, Earl V. Hyde, A. J. Kuenstler, T. H. Hassat, Jack Smith, Hubert Cosby, Raymond Kaufold and Joe Thornton.

In addition to his wife, Officer Whitlock was survived by his father, Arthur Whitlock of Houston, and one sister, Mrs. E. P. Goudreau, of Jennings, Louisiana.

Police Chief Tom C. Goodson immediately ordered an investigation into this tragic incident. Statements were taken from all present and were very much consistent. Officer Howard's statement indicated that as he was raising his weapon to fire, someone struck his elbow, and his weapon discharged prematurely. All officers stated that when the gun went off, Officer Whitlock doubled up and pointed to his right side, saying "right here." His only question was, "Who did it?" All of the officers who placed Officer Whitlock into Captain Tatum's car stayed at the hospital with their wounded friend until Lieutenant Meinke instructed them to return to the station and make their statements.

The investigation as well as the death certificate declared this shooting to be an accident.

For whatever reason, the death of Officer Paul Whitlock was not written up as a LINE OF DUTY death. Retired HPD Homicide Lieutenant Nelson Zoch turned up the details while researching newspaper microfilm archives for information on this HPD Line of Duty Death book. Zoch presented the research to Police Chief Harold Hurtt in 2006. In October of that year, Chief Hurtt officially approved the death of Officer Whitlock for the LINE OF DUTY status.

While the original decision could be questioned, it must be noted that early 1928 was a terrible time in the Houston Police Department, very much similar to 1982-83 when HPD lost six Officers in THE LINE OF DUTY.

Officer Carl Greene was shot and killed in March. Officer Whitlock was killed in April, followed by Officer Albert Worth Davis in June. Three more officers went down in a three-month span of 1928, and it was only June.

Officer Whitlock was born in Louisiana on January 27, 1901, to Mr. and Mrs. Arthur Whitlock. The name of Officer Whitlock's widow was never mentioned in any article, obituary or on the death certificate. While Officer Whitlock's gravesite was located in the older section of Forest Park Lawndale (north side of Lawndale), there was never a grave marker put into place. Efforts are underway to place the 100 Club/HPOU LINE OF DUTY marker for this fallen Officer.

26

Detective Albert Worth Davis
June 17, 1928

Detective Worth Davis Dies in Shootout With Fourth Ward Resident Robert Powell

On Saturday night, June 16, 1928, Detective Albert "Worth" Davis and his partner, Detective Henry Bradshaw, were working the night shift in the city's Fourth Ward. At about 2 a.m., they observed an unruly crowd gathered at the intersection of Andrews and Genessee. Sensing trouble from this gathering at this time of the morning, they sought to disperse this group. In doing so, Detective Bradshaw arrested one of the men in the group for dropping a pistol on the ground.

Another man in the crowd, later identified as Robert Powell, took to his heels and ran, with Detective Davis in hot pursuit around the corner to Robin Street. Detective Bradshaw later said, "I heard an automatic pistol shot and then two or three reports from Davis' gun. I got someone to hold my suspect and ran around the corner. I found Davis lying on the sidewalk with bullets in his head and side."

Bradshaw called Detective Sergeant Billie Cain and advised him of the shooting. An ambulance came for the wounded officer. Percy Heard, night chief of police, led a posse of fifteen men to look for the suspect. Within thirty minutes of the wounding of Detective Davis, all available officers were in the process of combing the Fourth Ward for the suspect.

DETECTIVE ALBERT WORTH DAVIS

Officers soon learned that Robert Powell was wounded in the exchange of gunfire with Davis. His brother-in-law later said that Powell ran through his house screaming that he had been shot. The posse found him at his residence at 1717 Robin, arresting him at 4:30 a.m. as he was lying in bed suffering from a gunshot wound that entered his abdomen just above the waist line and exited his back. A blood-stained blue serge suit was found near the bed, identical to the type Bradshaw saw the suspect wearing when he ran from Davis. Powell was taken immediately to Jeff Davis Hospital for treatment of his wound. Initially, two uniformed officers were assigned to guard him while the shooting investigation continued."

Unfortunately, Detective Davis' wounds were very serious. He died at 11:45 a.m. Sunday, June 17, 1928. He was thirty years old. Davis was a member of the department for six years, serving as a motorcycle officer until six months before his death, when he was promoted to the Detective department. He had earned an enviable reputation for the number of burglars and thieves he apprehended.

Detective Albert "Worth" Davis was survived by his wife Alma and two young sons, James and Felix Davis. Also surviving him were his three sisters, Marjorie Vercher, Nola Slocovich and Ruth Wiggins.

Funeral services were conducted from his home at 1238 Waverly at 5 p.m. Monday, June 18, under the direction of the Morse Undertaking Company. The Reverend J. White of the Church of Christ officiated. Pallbearers were from the Houston Police Department: R. A. Trammel, A. O. Taylor, E. H. Meinke, M. L. McGrew, J. H. Tatum and Henry Bradshaw. Burial followed at the Hollywood Cemetery.

The investigation into this tragic death continued at a rapid pace. Police took statements from a number of witnesses, all acquaintances of Powell who implicated him as the suspect who shot and killed Worth Davis. As a result, the state filed murder charges against Powell. Doctors initially felt that Powell might not survive his wounds. The day of Davis' funeral they decided that he would likely recover. At least the Houston Police Department had the culprit arrested and charged. The accounts of witnesses made the case against Powell very strong.

However, on the Monday night after the funeral, things took a definite turn for the worse. A group of unmasked white men, armed with pistols, entered the hospital and kidnapped Robert Powell. The previous report of two police guards had apparently changed, as he was under the watch of a lone hospital security guard. The kidnapping was immediately reported to the police. All available Houston officers, Harris County Sheriff T. A. Binford and his deputies, as well as investigators for District Attorney Horace Soule were assigned to search for Robert Powell and his brazen captors.

Then, at 6:15 a.m. Tuesday, Houston Detectives Ira Nix and John Gambill found Robert Powell hanging from a bridge on Post Oak Cutoff Road, eight miles west of the city. He had been lynched. This location was near what is now Interstate 10 West and Loop 610.

One can only imagine the turmoil a lynching caused in the City of Houston. City Council immediately met and committed $10,000 to the capture and conviction of the person or persons responsible. The governor of the State of Texas sent three Texas Ranger captains (one being the legendary Frank Hamer) to assist in this investigation. Local newspapers were flush with stories about the lynching. Fortunately for everyone involved, the investigation took a positive turn. By the end of the week, the state had six suspects in custody charged with murder and sought yet another who was charged but on the loose.

The following week, June 25-29, the Democratic National Convention was in Houston for their 1928 presidential nomination convention. The newspapers were relatively guarded in what was reported about the lynching during that time. The investigation continued until early July when a grand jury returned indictments for murder in the death of Robert Powell against seven suspects. Soule, the district attorney, vowed a quick trial.

In December 2006, an expert genealogy researcher helped to locate Felix Davis, the eighty-eight-year-old son of Detective Worth Davis, who lives near Humble. Felix Davis is a retired major general (two stars) of the United States Army. Detective Davis' other son, James, is deceased. Felix Davis had entered the U.S. Navy as an enlisted man in 1934 at a very young age, even attending the U. S. Navy Academy for one year. After the beginning of World War II, Felix joined the U. S. Army and served in the Pacific and Indian Ocean Theater of operations, as well as in Alaska.

He was later called for further duty during the Korean War and his total active time was fifteen years. He served in the U. S. Army Reserves. For a period of time, he was the commanding officer of the 75th Maneuver Area Command here in Houston, retiring in 1975 as a major general. In that command, he was responsible for the training of all Army reserves west of the Mississippi River. While serving in the Reserves, the general had HPD Lieutenant Jim "Pete" Gunn serving on his staff.

General Davis was certainly not without tragedy in his life. Of course, he lost his father at age ten. He married in 1938 and a son, his namesake, passed away from polio at the age of four. Shortly after his retirement in 1975, his wife of thirty-seven years died from leukemia. The general's daughter and son-in-law, Jarrie Davis McCarty and Danny McCarty, practice law in Houston. Each of the couple's three children were in the process of taking the bar exam. General Davis' other living child is Patrick, a pipeline engineer and Texas A&M graduate who was a member of the Corps of Cadets. Patrick and his wife have three children and reside in Boerne.

General Felix Davis passed away in October 2006 at the age of eighty-nine.

Much more is known about the abduction/lynching of the suspect Robert Powell and the resulting Murder charges against those suspects. However, the purpose of this story is to honor Officer Albert Worth Davis and the rest of the story will remain unwritten in this document in order to properly preserve the memory of Officer Davis.

No gravemarker could be located for Officer Davis at Hollywood Cemetery, even though the probable site was found. With cooperation of Hollywood Cemetery and family members, a 100 CLUB LINE OF DUTY marker has been placed to honor this man's life and death.

27

Officer Oscar Hope
June 22, 1929

Highly Respected Oscar Hope, Also a Rodeo Star, Shot to Death While Answering Fourth Ward Call

On Saturday night, at 8:30 p.m. one Felix Andres, a Negro male, came to Houston Police Headquarters complaining of threats on his life made by Henry Charles. Andres complained to Detective Sergeant Roy Young that Charles had come to his house at 408 Bayou, where Andres, his sister Laura Andres and a woman, Minerva Baptiste, resided along with Laura's four children.

Henry Charles had at one time lived there with Minerva, but they had separated about a month before. Charles was boisterous and brandished a .45-caliber automatic pistol, saying he was "one mean n____r and couldn't be took by any police officer." Minerva worried that Henry Charles might cause trouble, so she enlisted Felix Andres to ask the police for protection.

At just about the time this walk-in complaint arrived at the station, Officers Oscar Hope and Ira Nix came on duty. Bayou Street being in their district, they volunteered to go out on the call. The story that followed exemplified the way several law enforcement families worked together right up until the end.

Officer Oscar Hope's wife, Frankie Mae, was a supervisor at the Hadley telephone exchange who was almost through with her evening shift duties. It was normal practice for her to check in with her husband, who was just beginning his tour of duty. Upon her arrival at police headquarters, Officer Hope told his wife that she would have to wait until his call on Bayou was completed. Then he would follow her home. The officer told her that she and Edmund Nix, son of Officer Ira Nix, may as well accompany them to the call at the Bayou Street address.

While the officers and Mrs. Hope were en route to this location, Felix Andres supposedly told the officers once again the words that Henry Charles had related to them: "I'm a bad n____r, boss, and no law was going to get me."

Prior to arrival, Detective Nix told Andres to warn them before they reached the house so they could leave the car and approach Charles quietly to avoid trouble. But, as well might be expected, Andres forgot and as they rolled past the house, Officers Nix and Hope, accompanied by Felix Andres, Mrs. Hope and Edmund Nix, observed Henry Charles, Laura Andres and Minerva Baptiste all sitting on the front porch. Seeing the officers, Charles ran inside the house. The following chain of events then unfurled:

OFFICER OSCAR HOPE

Officers Hope and Nix got out of their car. Hope told Nix to go to the rear, while he, Hope, followed Charles into the house. With his gun drawn, Hope entered through the front door as Nix went around to the rear. As Nix reached the rear door, shots rang out from inside the house. Nix battered down the locked door only to see Officer Hope as he fell. He also caught a glimpse of Charles' leg as he darted into another room, where he tried to get out through another rear door.

Detective Nix then rushed outside and fired three times through the door the suspect was trying to open. The suspect went out that same door amid gunfire, which narrowly missed the detective's head as boards from the door splintered. The suspect fled in the safest direction he knew, out the front door, with Detective Nix in close pursuit.

Henry Charles fired and Nix returned fire at the fleeing suspect. Nix returned to find his son, Edmund, kneeling over the body of Detective Oscar Hope. Edmund, holding his Uncle Oscar's hand, handed Hope's gun to his dad and said, "Here is Oscar's gun, Dad. There are three shells left." Charles fled from the house and Nix fired two more shots at him as he crossed a nearby vacant lot. Nix jumped into their car and drove down to the next corner, which was Cline and Bayou. He turned down Cline in pursuit. In the 3100 block, he found Charles collapsed in the street.

Nix returned to the Bayou street house and told his son, Edmund, to stay with Officer Hope's body while he phoned to the police station. A squad of officers, headed by Senior Captain of Police Percy Heard, arrived just as the suspect, Henry Charles, died in the street.

Back at the scene, it was apparent that Officer Oscar Hope died instantly. In reconstructing the scene, officers believed that Charles had hidden behind the door connecting the front room with the kitchen and, as Officer Hope entered the kitchen, Charles opened fire. One bullet entered the rear of Hope's head. Hope's pistol was fired three times.

An inquest was held with Justice of the Peace Campbell Overstreet returning a verdict of murder in Officer Hope's death and a verdict of death by gunshot wounds in the case of Henry Charles. As a result of this inquest, no charges were filed against Detective Nix, as it was ruled that he obviously fired in the line of duty.

Detective Oscar Hope was thirty-one years old, having been born in Longview, Harrison County, on August 17, 1897. He was the second of seven children born to Robert Wert Hope and Harriet Parker Hope. He had entered the service as a mounted ward officer seven years before his death. He later served as a plain clothes man and was made head of the Vice Squad, a position he held until the new city administration came into office the previous April. He was very well respected by all officers who had served with him.

Oscar Hope was also well known as a rodeo performer, having tamed broncos, bulldogged steers and roped calves at exhibitions throughout the Southwest. In addition to performing in England, he had also seen rodeo action at the 1928 National Convention of the Shrine at Miami, Florida. He had participated in several motion pictures, including "North of 36" and "Womanhandled." In 1924, he rode before the King and Queen of England, as well as the Prince of Wales, in a traveling rodeo.

Hope, who lived at 3207 West Dallas Avenue, was survived by his wife, Frankie Mae, and his parents, Mr. and Mrs. R. W. (Harriet) Hope, Sr., two brothers, R. W. Hope Jr. (HPD officer) and Glenn Hope, and five sisters, Mrs. Norma McFarland of Longview and Mrs. Gay Osbourne of South Houston, and Mrs. Annie Mae Peterson, Mrs. Robbie Gregg and Miss Ruth Hope, all of Houston.

While the family relationship of Officers Hope and Nix has been somewhat confusing through the years, with the help of Officer Hope's nephew, HPD's own Harry Hope, and his daughter Heather, the proper information came to fore. Oscar Hope and Ira Nix were fellow officers as well as very good friends. Hope's younger brother, Ruben, later married Nix's daughter, Alma, in 1933, four years after Officer Hope's murder. Their son, Harry Hope, joined HPD as a civilian in the Identification Bureau in 1963, retiring in 2004.

Just one week prior to Officer Oscar Hope losing his life in the line of duty, Officer Ruben Hope was involved in a fatal shooting of a suspect while off-duty in near West Houston. Officer Ruben Hope, while traveling in his personal vehicle, was confronted and actually kidnapped by a crazed, drunken suspect who was fleeing on foot after killing several citizens. Officer Hope calmly accompanied the suspect. When responding HPD officers confronted this suspect, Hope took his chance with a concealed off-duty weapon and shot and killed the suspect.

One week later, his dear brother, Oscar, ten years his senior, lost his life in the line of duty. Oscar Hope is buried at Forest Park Lawndale on the north side of Lawndale. His marker reads:

OSCAR E. HOPE
1898-1929

"SWEET MEMORIES"

28

Detective Ed Jones
September 13, 1929

Well-respected Black HPD Detective Ed Jones Murdered by his Wife's Brother, Johnnie Wilson

On Friday night, September 13, 1929, veteran Houston Detective Ed Jones, a man of color, was home at his residence at 3527 McGregor Avenue. He lived there with his wife Sylvia. Sylvia's brother, Johnnie Wilson, a man later described as demented, lived there on an occasional basis. He was there this night, having been brought to this residence to stay for a few days of rest and recuperation from an illness.

Detective Jones had just gone to bed when he was awakened by a slam of the door. Upon investigation, he saw Johnnie leaving the room with his gun. He pursued Johnnie to the sidewalk, where the man, without provocation, fired a shot that struck the detective in the chest. According to Sylvia Jones and her mother, Mrs. Amanda Wilson, there had been no quarrel or dispute. Johnnie Wilson fled the scene on foot, running east and taking the .45-caliber pistol with him. Detective Jones was dead from the chest wound, while also struck in the right leg.

Almost immediately, Detectives George Peyton and Young led a posse that searched throughout the night but failed to produce the suspect. On Saturday afternoon, they located Wilson in a wooded area less than a half mile from the scene of the deadly shooting. A crowd estimated at more than five hundred people gathered nearby as the officers arrived to arrest Wilson.

Detectives Peyton, Kirk Irwin, Gambill and McGrew responded to reports that Wilson had been seen in the woods. The posse found him leaning against a tree and engaged him in a conversation while edging nearer. Wilson on several occasions caused a panic by waving the gun around in his hand. Calmly carrying on a conversation until they were at arms length, the officers reached out and grabbed the gun, with Wilson offering no resistance.

Officers took statements from Sylvia Jones and Amanda Wilson, the sister and mother of the suspect. Justice of the Peace Campbell Overstreet held an inquest, returning a verdict of death due to pistol wound from a weapon in the hands of Johnnie Wilson. After Wilson's arrest, Justice Overstreet charged the suspect with murder in Detective Jones' death.

Ed Jones was listed as being forty-five years old, although he was believed to have been born sometime in 1880 in Alabama. The supposed birth year would make him forty-nine years old at the time of his death. His death certificate showed no exact date of birth. Newspaper headlines depicted him as a veteran city detective and a Negro sleuth and further described him as "friend to the erring but a terror to the habitual law breaker." Other comments from department heads included, "He was one of our best men and I think his place will be hard to fill. In fact, I don't think it can be filled. He was fearless and always on the job." Jones had been employed as an officer with the Houston Police Department since 1924.

A verbatim story from the Houston Informer of Saturday, September 21, 1929 said:

The funeral services for Detective Jones were conducted on Tuesday, September 17, 1929, at the Saint John Baptist Church (Broadway), with Pastor N. C. Crain officiating. Several colored and white members attended the funeral in a body, with six race officers serving as pallbearers.

Sergeant of Detectives George Peyton (white)

and James (Ditty) Thompson (Negro), the latter being the deceased officer's partner, delivered brief eulogies. Peyton commended Detective Jones for his efficiency as an officer as well as his honesty and loyalty. Mr. H. P. Carter read the obituary. The services were under the direction of McCoy-Harrison Undertaking Company. The funeral cortege was escorted by a fleet of motorcycle officers. Burial followed in Olivewood Cemetery.

29

Officer C.F. (Osburn) Thomas
December 17, 1929

Officer Thomas Loved to Help Firefighters; He Died on a Motor, Run Over by a Pumper

On Monday night, December 16, 1929, Motorcycle Officer C. F. "Osburn" Thomas was on duty on his motor in the business district at approximately 7:30 p.m. when he heard the clang of a fire department apparatus rushing south on Caroline Street.

The trucks were going to a major fire reported at 1122 Capital Avenue. With his siren screaming, Thomas hurried east on Texas Avenue in an attempt to reach Caroline in advance of the fire engine. Then he would further escort the firefighters to their assigned destination.

It was his extreme devotion to his duty that caused this dedicated public servant to attempt to accomplish his self-assigned mission. However, a hose truck, two engine trucks and the fire chief's chauffeur vehicle had already gone through this intersection.

As Officer Thomas approached Texas and Caroline, another pumper truck driven by Fireman A. Giese was entering the intersection. Thomas, apparently seeing that a crash was inevitable, slammed on his brakes, causing his motorcycle to veer. Witnesses saw the motor strike the rear of the pumper and skid right under the large vehicle's wheels.

Officer Thomas sustained extensive injuries to his left chest. A Fogle-West ambulance rushed him to Baptist Hospital where he passed away from those injuries at 5:40 a.m. Tuesday, December 17, 1929. He was only twenty-three.

He was survived by his wife, Mrs. Eula Lee Thomas of 4444 Clay in Houston and his parents, Mr. and Mrs. J. A. Thomas, one sister, Mrs. Mary Edna Landrum, and three brothers, Leo Thomas of Miami, Florida, and Lynn Thomas and Fred Thomas, both of Houston.

Funeral services were held from the Westheimer Funeral Home on Thursday, December 19, 1929, with the Reverend L. H. Mathison officiating. Burial followed at the Forest Park Lawndale Cemetery, 6900 Lawndale. The escort included Houston police officers, Houston firefighters and, especially, his fellow motorcycle squad officers. Pallbearers were Emmett Bailey, R. E. Rogers, R. H. "Rimps" Sullivan (Line of Duty Death, 1935), Robert Vaughn, R. F. Johnson and W. E. "Pokey" Sammons.

Interestingly enough, of the pallbearers, Officer Sammons had been a former partner of Officer Thomas. Officer Sullivan was shot and killed in the line of duty in 1935 and is buried not far from Officer Thomas, as is Officer J. Clark Etheridge, killed in the line of duty in 1924. Officer Etheridge was riding with Officer Sammons on the night he was killed on his motorcycle just south of downtown Houston.

C. F. (initials only) Osburn Thomas was born on May 8, 1906, in Hearne, Texas. His parents were Mr. James A. Thomas (from Florida) and Mrs. Ella Osburn Thomas (from Tennessee). He had been with the Police Department since January 9, 1929 and recently been assigned to the motorcycle force. He was well known at the HFD Central Station for his willingness to assist firefighters on their way to a fire scene by preceding the fire trucks and warning motorists of their approach. It was that dedication, unfortunately, that led to his death.

The following poetic tribute was written about Officer Thomas by the Reverend F. M. Johnson, chaplain of the Houston Fire Department:

When the siren shrieked through the city's streets,
   As fireman rode a danger to meet,
   When excited crowds heard the clanging bell,
   And knew that fireman would soon face hell,
   HE CLEARED THE WAY.

His siren was heard above all the rest,
   In the line of duty he gave his best;
   When he faced danger he met the test,
   Now his duty done, he deserves his rest:
   HE CLEARED THE WAY.

No thought of self as he nightly rode,
   His duty was first he plainly showed.
   His staunch brave spirit has gone on high,
   And there for a comet in God's great sky.
   HE CLEARED THE WAY.

Such a spirit as his will ne'er grow dim,
One thinks of a cross, of the love of Him,
Who, too, saw duty, but such they slay,
For it's not easy on any day
TO CLEAR THE WAY.

Officer C. F. Thomas' gravesite was located in the old section of Forest Park on the north side of Lawndale. The marker reads:

OUR PAL
C.F. THOMAS
1906-1929
DIED IN THE LINE OF DUTY
HOUSTON MOTORCYCLE POLICE SAFETY CLUB

30 & 31

*Officer Edward Davis Fitzgerald
and
Officer William Bonner Phares
September 20, 1930*

Killer of 2 HPD Officers Gets Swift Justice: 'The Chair' 69 Days Later

In the fall of 1930 the United States of America was less than a year into the Great Depression. The economy had taken a serious blow in October 1929 and times were tough everywhere, with businesses uncertain of what the future held for their livelihood. Cash money was scarce. Most Americans had little disposable income and spent what little money they had on necessities – or were flat saving it for emergencies. Unemployment reached an all-time high.

Furniture was not considered a necessity but people were buying what pieces they absolutely needed on credit or layaway. Consequently, unlike today, furniture stores required cash for their goods.

On Saturday night, September 20, 1930, at approximately 9:45, closing time was nigh for one such establishment, the Touchy Furniture Store at 720 Milam Street. T. T. Clarke, an employee, and H. E. Hall, the credit manager, were closing up, both out on the sidewalk as they showed a customer to the door. They were in the process of lowering the awnings on the Milam Street side of the store when the armed bandits approached them and forced them back inside.

The two well-dressed young bandits were both white men about five-foot-ten and each weighing about one-hundred-thirty pounds. According to Clarke, both of the men emptied the cash registers, taking $300 in bills – which amounted to a small fortune in 1930. After taking Clarke as a hostage, they fled in a Chevrolet coupe. After-the-fact witnesses said this vehicle had been parked around the corner with the engine running. Clarke, in fear of his life, asked the bandits where they were taking him. They said they would release him down on the viaduct and admonished him not to remember the license number of their car since it was stolen anyway.

The crooks answered Clarke's plea for freedom and left him unharmed at the intersection of Bagby and Rusk. From there the armed men were seen westbound on Rusk. When Clarke got his wits about it, he was in fact able to recall the license number of the car, which was immediately flashed over police wires to all detectives and motorcycle men on duty. Upon his arrival back at the Touchy Furniture Store, Clarke and the other robbery victim provided police with as many more details as they could remember. An all-alerts bulletin was again issued for the getaway car and subsequent information was obtained from eyewitness statements.

Two officers who promptly responded were motorcycle Officers Fitzgerald and Phares. Shortly after the bulletins were issued with updated information, all hell broke loose some 25 blocks south of the furniture store. What happened there was related in the crucial statement of Officer W. B. Phares. Bleeding from the mouth and losing blood internally from a gunshot wound to the abdomen, Officer Phares told investigators:

"Fitzgerald and I reported at the police box at Dowling and Leeland. We were told to search for an automobile bearing such a license number as the occupants of the vehicle had been involved in a robbery and abduction. We were told to search for a specific automobile and were given a license number, as the occupants were reported to have been doing some hijacking. As we neared Milam and Anita, we saw an auto parked there with the license number on it. Fitzgerald was the first to alight from his cycle. I followed quickly after and parked my motorcycle. I drew my gun as a man emerged from his automobile.

"He opened fire at me and the first shot struck me, knocking me down to the pavement. I emptied my pistol at him and he slumped downward. I did not see Fitzgerald fire and I did not see whether he was shot or not. It was at this point that a man named Fred Carr came to my assistance. He placed me in a private car and this is all I remember until I reached Baptist Hospital."

Several witnesses were in the area and heard the first shots. Sewall King, operator of a filling station at Rosalie and Milam, saw most of what happened and was a key witness in the subsequent trial. He stated:

"After hearing several shots, I ran down to the corner and saw a uniformed officer standing on the northeast corner of Milam and Anita. He had been wounded already at this time. My attention was attracted to the officer because he was shouting and pointing to a Chevrolet coupe on the northwest corner of the intersection. The officer, who I later learned was Phares, was yelling, 'There he is in that coupe, the hijacker, don't let him get away.' At this time, Fitzgerald was walking up to the left side of the coupe. Just as he got opposite the door, a hand came out of the coupe window and two shots were fired. The officer never had a chance."

OFFICER EDWARD D. FITZGERALD

It was at this point that another civilian, Clark Christian, who got there with Sewall King, ran up to the wounded Officer Phares. The officer was able to hand his pistol and some more bullets to Christian, who then chased the fleeing suspect on foot south on Milam toward the Fannin School. He fired at least one shot but lost the suspect when he ran through a yard. While they were unable to assist in the identification of the gunman, these civilians agreed that there was only one shooter, a white male in his mid-thirties who fled on foot. Sadly enough, the description of the scene told the story of what happened.

Officer E. D. Fitzgerald, twenty-six, of 4714 Floyd, was dead at the scene from multiple gunshot wounds. Other later news accounts indicated he died at a hospital. Officer W. B. Phares, also twenty-six, of 1102 Bomar, was critically wounded and hurriedly removed from the scene to be treated at a hospital.

The details of the story began to fall into place after Homicide detectives interviewed these witnesses at length. These men both said that after hearing the shots they ran to find Officer Phares standing on the curb, wounded. This was when the officer shouted to them that the fleeing men were hijackers. Phares handed Christian his empty gun and fumbled with his belt, producing more rounds for a reload. At this point the gunman saw Fitzgerald come up to the rear of the vehicle and opened fire, shooting the officer numerous times.

While the witness accounts were rather confusing, physical evidence and a recreation of the scene painted an accurate picture. Officers Phares and Fitzgerald had come upon the getaway car just as the occupants were about to get into a second vehicle. Just why the suspect, later identified as J. J. Maples, remained in the wanted vehicle, is unknown to this day. It is important to remember that there were two hijackers at the furniture store and in the ensuing getaway only one was ever identified as being at the shooting scene.

Houston police strongly suspected the second hijacker went to get another vehicle. When the brave officers approached the scene, only one suspect gunned them down. It was determined that at least twenty rounds were fired. Also, in tracing the foot chase of the suspect, officers found a straw hat with a bullet hole in its crown. One of Officer Phares' rounds had nearly struck home.

Police Chief Percy Heard arrived and assigned Lieutenant George Peyton, head of the Homicide Squad, the responsibility for the investigation. Chief Heard had been appointed only a few weeks before. He praised both officers and issued the ultimate tribute to the slain Officer Fitzgerald, saying, "He died fearlessly in the line of duty."

With crime analysis being what it was in 1930, it became apparent early on in this investigation that these two hijackers had been very active in the month prior to this tragedy. In addition to detectives assigned specifically to this case, the entire day shift traffic squad remained on duty Saturday night after the shooting and acted as detectives reporting any clues they found directly to Chief Heard and Lieutenant Peyton.

At the shooting scene there remained the stolen vehicle used by the hijackers and a large amount of fired cartridges. Chief Heard and Lieutenant Peyton searched the vehicle and produced a brown leather wallet which contained a valuable clue – a card with this inscription: "J. J. Maple, painting and paperhanging, 7143 Avenue H." Elated by this find, a posse headed by Captain J. K. Irwin and Lieutenant Peyton left immediately for the location on Avenue H. Included were Lieutenant Dave Turner and Detectives Kesseler, Owens, Arnold, Jones and Jamison.

Entering this location with a pass key, they learned that J. J. Maple had recently moved his family to a housekeeping room at 2508 Fannin, which was a very short distance from the shootout scene. Finding the room unoccupied, Detectives Jones and Jamison secreted themselves inside the room to await further developments. At 8:30 a.m. Sunday, a woman later determined to be Mrs. Maple arrived alone. Officers took her to headquarters for questioning and were soon told this amazing story:

Shortly after 10:45 p.m. the previous night, Mrs. Maple said her husband came in all out of breath saying he was in a terrible jam and needed to get out of town. The pair hurriedly loaded up their small daughter and began walking out to Harrisburg Boulevard. They spent the night in a churchyard near a cemetery on Altic (probably Evergreen Cemetery) where her husband, J. J., told of shooting several men. Maple sent his wife back to their room to get more clothing while he kept the small daughter with him on the banks of Braes Bayou as people began arriving at the nearby church for Sunday morning services.

Realizing how serious the situation was, Mrs. Maple reluctantly led officers to the bayou, where Maple was arrested while holding the couple's daughter. Taken to headquarters, Maple refused to reveal the name of his partner in crime. However, Mrs. Maple had already provided the name of the man who had been with her husband on various recent drinking sprees.

She said it was unusual that both of them seemed to have money lately even though neither had found steady work. Initially, she pled ignorance to having knowledge of what her husband had been doing to support them. Later, however, she said she been present on several recent occasions when her husband and a man she knew as E. F. Grimes had come home and divied up their loot in front of her. Using this information, detectives went to an apartment at 711 Anita, also in the vicinity of the killing. They arrested Grimes there in the presence of his wife and two small children.

While Maple was initially uncooperative with Homicide investigators, he eventually confessed to the shootings and also told about numerous robberies. He steadily refused to provide the name of his partner in this crime spree. That later became unimportant since Grimes grew to be very talkative, apparently to distance himself from Maple's deadly actions. Maple seemed resigned to the fact that there was little hope for him after what he had done. He later would not help his attorneys and seemed to feel that nothing could be gained by fighting the case that was building up against him.

Grimes seemed anxious to cooperate, feeling that the more distance between him and Maple the better his chances of facing just robbery charges instead of capital murder. Officers also recovered two pistols, one hidden near the spot where Maple was arrested on the bayou. That .45-caliber gun was the weapon Maple used to commit murder in the death of Officer Fitzgerald and later Officer Phares. This means that one small clue found within several hours of the offense resulted in capital murder and attempted capital murder charges filed against J. J. Maple. Those charges were filed within two days of the tragedy and came as the result of an around-the-clock effort by many hard-charging HPD officers and supervisors.

Maple also was charged with five other robberies he and Grimes were identified as committing. Facing these same five charges, Grimes – like Maple – was held without bond. In one of the robberies, a civilian was shot but survived his wound. Newspaper accounts indicated that Grimes was the "brains" behind the robbery schemes with Maple doing "the heavy work." At one point, Grimes said, "There wasn't a damn bit of reason for him (Maple) to kill those officers like he did. He could have gotten away like I did if he hadn't been so hard and cold-blooded." Investigators felt that Grimes may have witnessed the shootings but would never admit it. Grimes wound up doing prison time for the robberies but he was not charged with murder.

HPD and a grieving family still had to bury a loved one. Officer Edward Davis Fitzgerald was born February 1, 1903. He was a Houston native who was educated in the local public schools. He entered the police service on his birthday in 1927 as a probationary patrolman. He was assigned to the downtown mounted traffic squad. His first assignment was working the intersection of Texas and Travis. Upon the dissolution of this squad, his next assignment was motorcycle duty. He also was a member of the Cavalry branch of the National Guard. One of his HPD supervisors later commented, "He came to us with training in the Texas National Guard and there apparently he had learned well the lesson of discipline. To him, an order was an order and he asked no unnecessary questions."

Officer Fitzgerald was survived by his mother, Louise Fitzgerald, and two sisters, Virginia Fitzgerald and Mrs. Lomis Eckman. Also mourning his death were his grandmother, Mrs. Edith A. Davis, and his grandfather, F. M. Fitzgerald. His father, Joseph Fitzgerald, preceded him in death in 1909 when Edward was only six years old.

On Monday afternoon, September 22, 1930, at the Morse Funeral Chapel, Houston said farewell to the gallant young officer. The Reverend E. A. Peterson, Fitzgerald's pastor, friend, and neighbor, described him as a splendid young officer. He also said, "Nations pay tributes of respect to those who lay down their lives for their country in war. Far more should we respect this man who laid down his life for us in time of peace."

The Christian burial service included several of his favorite renditions, "The Indian Love Call" and "Dancing with Tears in My Eyes." The funeral cortege headed by a squad of motorcycle officers also included the HPD band, in which Officer Fitzgerald had played the saxophone. After the service, a long procession traveled north on Caroline Street en route to a rain-soaked country cemetery at Barbers Hill, northeast of Houston, where he was laid to rest.

For nearly seventy-four years his grave has been marked with a small headstone showing only his name, date of birth and death. In July 2004, a 100 Club of Houston/HPOU-sponsored project further honored his death as being in the LINE OF DUTY as a member of the HOUSTON POLICE DEPARTMENT.

Meanwhile, the life of Officer Phares, shot many times in the melee, still lay in the balance at Baptist Hospital. His hometown newspaper, the Lufkin Daily News, provided daily updates on his condition, which amounted to an emotional rollercoaster ride for his family and many Houston friends. Initial condition reports were "favorable" while he was "putting up a fine fight with a splendid constitution" but soon degenerated to "holding his own" and, by the end of the first week, "taken turn for worse." He "showed stamina" by telling his doctors he had to survive for his wife and baby.

OFFICER EDWARD D. FITZGERALD

But on Tuesday, September 30, 1930, Officer Willie Bonner Phares succumbed to the injuries he sustained in the line of duty ten days earlier at age twenty-six.

Phares went by W. B. or Bonner, which was his mother's maiden name. He was survived by his wife, Lenore Kerr Phares, and son, William Bonner Phares. Also surviving were his parents, Johnsa and Florrie Bonner Phares and two brothers, Johnsa Jr. and Gil.

To say that justice moved swiftly in the depression era would definitely be an understatement. The lead story in one local newspaper dated Wednesday, October 1, 1930, said a court was picking a jury to try J. J. Maple for capital murder in the death of Officer Fitzgerald. That very same day many Houston officers traveled to Lufkin to bury Officer Phares. District Attorney O'Brien Stevens had played an active part in the investigation by providing legal advice to HPD as developments arose. He was the leader of the prosecution team. After a two-day selection process, twelve people were selected to serve on a jury of J. J. Maple's peers.

In Lufkin, the largest crowd in many years assembled at the Methodist Church to pay tribute to the memory of Houston Police Officer W. B. Phares. The funeral service was conducted by the Reverends C. A. Long, J. R. Nutt and J. N. Wooten in the presence of a throng gathered in respect for this young member of one of the oldest and best-known pioneer families of Angelina County. He was a descendant of the Bonner family, which had attained honor and fortune in various sections of Texas.

The funeral procession, one of the longest in the history of Lufkin, wound its way to Glendale Cemetery in the heart of this East Texas city. A squad of state highway officers led the procession, followed by Houston Police Chief Percy Heard, Senior Captain of Police J. H. Taut and City Manager George Pruter, alongside Lufkin city officials and Phares' childhood friends, who served as pallbearers.

Next in order came a car with the eight Houston officers designated as honorary pallbearers, followed by thirty Houston motorcycle officers, led by HPD Sergeant Roy Rogers. At the conclusion of the graveside service, a Houston police officer sounded Taps for a comrade who had made the supreme sacrifice while in the discharge of his sworn duty.

As early as the Monday following the shootings, criticism arose regarding the weapons used by Fitzgerald and Phares. Many veteran officers came forward to allege that police regulations restricted officers to .38-caliber pistols. Had they been allowed to use .45s the hijacker would not have escaped unscathed and the perpetrator may have been prevented from firing so many shots. Bowing to this pressure, the city business manager quickly announced that tests would be conducted to determine which weapon is best suited for officers.

It was learned during the crime scene investigation that two shots fired by the officers would have struck J. J. Maple had they contained more power. The scene revealed that one of the bullets struck the back of the coupe and could have bored into Maple's neck. Another struck the side of the coupe and – had it entered the car – would have surely struck Maple. However, both missiles merely bounced off the car, doing no harm whatsoever. Another bullet was found to have struck the rear glass, but in shattering the glass, stuck in the rear curtain after losing velocity. It was stated that the Texas Rangers were carrying .45s and possibly it was time for Houston police officers to do the same thing.

While this controversy unfurled, the trial continued. More evidence surfaced against Maple: While the two partners in crime were on their robbery spree, Grimes turned on Maple after a robbery in which a citizen was wounded. Although Maple initially refused to communicate with his attorneys, as the jury selection proceeded, he began whispering to them. A jury was selected and the state planned to seek the death penalty.

Then Maple pled guilty. In doing so, he saved the people the time, trouble and tax money needed to convict him. After a brief punishment phase of the trial, on October 4, 1930 – fourteen days after the offense – J. J. Maple, a former World War I sharpshooter, was assessed the death penalty. Then, on November 28, 1930 – sixty-nine days after the offense – the State of Texas strapped J. J. Maple in the electric chair in Huntsville and electrocuted him. This was swift justice, indeed.

Extensive research showed that common threads ran through the families of each of these two brave men. A niece and a nephew of Officer Edward Davis Fitzgerald survive to this day as well as another distant relative. Fitzgerald was born in La Porte, the son of Joseph Amos Fitzgerald and Edith Louise Davis Fitzgerald. He had two sisters, Louise Fitzgerald Eckman and Virginia Fitzgerald Lillich. A third sister died as an infant. From photos provided by Fitzgerald's niece, Mrs. Mary Eckman Pendley, a wonderful lady in her early eighties, her uncle appeared to be a handsome young man who had a love for motorcycles even before his job as a Houston police officer. A nephew said that stories about his uncle abound regarding his love for life, as well as for the young ladies. He was not married at the time of his death and left no children.

Ironically, Willie Bonner Phares and his deceased partner were both blessed with their mother's maiden name as middle names. The Bonner family was legend in the cattle business in Lufkin and Angelina County. The Fitzgerald family was tied to the oilfields in the Mont Belvieu area.

Phares apparently had an adventurous spirit. At age nineteen, as a deputy sheriff in his home county, he was the target of moon shiners' bullets. Newspaper accounts said he pursued these men and captured them. From there he ventured to the West Indies Island of Aruba in the employment of the Eagle Oil Company, attempting to tame the land and build a refinery. He survived but several of his co-workers were killed by poison arrows from the restless natives. Also, while on that job, he contracted the black water fever and narrowly survived.

In the attempt to find Phares' final resting place, several Lufkin citizens advised, "You best get some better information, as Glendale is a large cemetery and is actually not separated from two other cemeteries." It is in fact large. Entering the first gate, the investigator drove slowly through as if expecting pay dirt very quickly. Sure enough, there, while making the first circular drive, the Phares family plot was spied. It did not contain stand-up markers, either. There were flat ones that over the better part of a century had emerged upright so they could even be seen. Officer Phares is buried amongst his parents, an infant sister and his brother Johnsa.

His grave is marked thusly:

BONNER PHARES
FEBRUARY 29, 1904-SEPTEMBER 30, 1930
HIS TOILS ARE PAST, HIS WORK IS DONE,
HE FOUGHT THE FIGHT, THE VICTORY WON.

The 100 Club of Houston and HPOU LINE OF DUTY marker has been placed by Nelson and Andy Zoch to supplement the original marker.

32

Officer J.D. Landry
December 3, 1930

Motorcycle Officer Landry Collides with Car as He's Chasing a Speeder on Tuam Avenue

J. D. Landry was born in Louisiana on November 23, 1895. It is unknown how long he served as a Houston police officer.

On Tuesday, December 2, 1930, Motorcycle Officers J. D. Landry and A. O. Taylor were working traffic in the near south end of downtown. Officer Landry began chasing a speeder on Tuam Avenue near Genessee Street. While doing so, he crashed into the rear of a car driven by Fred Soland of No. 94 Fairview, who had slowed down to turn into his automobile business at that location, the Fairview Motor Company.

The impact turned Soland's car end to end. The collision threw Officer Landry to the ground and caused him literally to skid down the street. Soland rushed into his business and instructed an employee to call an ambulance. He also attempted to aid the injured officer with a towel and water. However, Officer Landry suffered severe internal injuries as well as a possible fractured skull.

A Fogle-West Company ambulance rushed him to Memorial Hospital, where he was treated but never regained consciousness. He passed away at 6 p.m. the following day, Wednesday, December 3, from the skull fracture and internal injuries. He was thirty-five years old.

Officer Landry, who lived at 7217 Avenue H, was survived by his wife, his parents, Mr. and Mrs. Adolphe Landry, three brothers, Walter, Otis and Sidney Landry, and one sister, Mrs. Edna Landry, all of Henry, Louisiana.

The investigation included an interview with both Officer Taylor and Mr. Soland. Soland stated that he was preparing to turn into his business when he was struck from the rear. He also said that he did not see the motorcycle until after the accident.

Soland was charged with assault by auto before Justice of the Peace Campbell Overstreet and released on $500 bond.

The body of Officer Landry was shipped to New Iberia, Louisiana by Fogle West Company via the Southern Pacific Railroad Line.

33

Officer Harry T. Mereness
October 16, 1933

HPD Motorcycle Officer Harry T. Mereness Struck and Killed by 16-year-old Driver

On Monday night, October 16, 1933, Houston Motorcycle Officer Harry Talcott Mereness was on duty and driving his motorcycle inbound on Old Galveston Road. He was attempting a left turn onto Broadway when his motorcycle was struck by an automobile driven by sixteen-year-old Owen Barry of La Porte. The side of young Barry's car struck the motorcycle as Barry made a turn to go into a root beer stand, throwing Officer Mereness to the pavement and causing severe injuries.

Mereness was first taken to Parkview Hospital at Harrisburg and 75th and, after the severity of his injuries was determined, he was transferred to Jeff Davis Hospital. He was treated for a fractured skull, a broken leg and numerous internal injuries. He passed away at Jeff Davis on Wednesday, October 18, 1933 at 12:15 p.m. He was thirty-nine years old.

Justice of the Peace George L. Rickey originally charged Owen Barry with assault by auto. After Officer Mereness' death, the charge was automatically changed to negligent homicide and referred to juvenile court.

Officer Harry T. Mereness was a native of Ypsalanti, Michigan, having been born there on September 15, probably in 1894. His parents were Seth and Julia Talcott Mereness. At the time of his service to HPD and his death, he resided at 8137 Joplin with his wife Gertrude Cure Mereness and sons, Lyman, ten, and Bert, five. He also was survived by his mother, Mrs. Julia Mereness and one sister, Miss Eugenia Mereness, both of Michigan. He was a member of the Eagles, the Dokes, the Odd Fellows and the Knights of Pythiae.

Funeral services were held on Thursday, October 19, 1933, at 8 p.m. at the Houston Funeral Home under the direction of the Redfield Lodge No 478 of the Knights of Pythiae. Active pallbearers were Pat Creagan, Fred Cochran, A. O. Taylor, Sam Wheatly, R. B. Hooper, and Captain R. T. Honea. Honorary pallbearers were members of the Houston Police Department motorcycle division. The body was forwarded at midnight that same night by the Houston Funeral Home to Ypsalanti, Michigan, via the Missouri Pacific Railroad Lines. Burial followed in Michigan.

OFFICER HARRY T. MERENESS

Mrs. Gertrude Mereness, faced with no pension from her husband's death and two young sons to raise in the midst of the Great Depression, obviously had few opportunities. Having a sister in the San Antonio suburb of Harlandale, she moved to that area, where she apparently did an excellent job in raising her two sons.

The oldest, Lyman, entered World War II, becoming a dive bomber pilot who flew thirty-nine missions before coming home safely. He later studied at St. Mary's University in San Antonio and, even though he had received an honorable discharge from the U. S. Navy, he chose to re-enter the service of his country. He rose to the rank of full commander in the Navy and retired at that rank after over twenty-seven years of service. He retired to the Victoria area community of Inez. He also was a gospel preacher for more than twenty years.

Lyman, who was born on June 2, 1923, died February 16, 2006, at the age of eighty-two. He was survived by his wife, Mary Lou Phillips Mereness, a daughter, Cheryl Goode, two sons, Lyman Mereness II and Ben Mereness, his brother Bert, eight grandchildren and nine great grandchildren. He was laid to rest in Victoria with full military honors.

Bert Mereness, who was born on July 16, 1928, served his country in the United States Coast Guard. He also studied at St. Mary's University, graduating with a business degree with a major in economics. In 1958, Bert made a serious career choice by joining the Federal Bureau of Investigation. He served in a number of assignments and retired as a supervisor from the Bureau in 1982 in Phoenix, Arizona. He has enjoyed a number of interesting assignments in the private sector since his retirement.

In 2006, Bert was semi-retired and living in Phoenix with his wife of many years, Kathleen. He has two daughters, Patricia and Catherine, and one grandson, Wade. A third daughter, Karen, passed away in 1995. Thanks go to retired FBI Agent Karl McLeod (ex HPD), who submitted a letter to the Houston Police Retired Officers Association advising of the passing of Lyman Mereness. He had met Bert through their years of service with the Bureau.

In an interview in April 2006, Bert Mereness said he was only five years old when his dad was killed, but recalled vividly a short motorcycle ride he took with him. He remembered the rough times his mother experienced, how she remarried a good man who treated him and Lyman very well. Unfortunately, his mom's health failed her early in life and she died in 1950. Both Lyman and Bert established themselves as responsible citizens before her death and she would have been extremely proud of how her sons served their country in the honorable manner as their father. Officer Mereness' mother and sister passed away.

As for young Owen Barry, research has found no information available to report the disposition of the charges against him. While it probably was a tragic accident, it cost the life of a fine man, an officer, husband, father, son and brother. Research did produce information about an Owen Barry that is believed to have been this young man. This man Barry, was born in 1917, which would have made him sixteen in 1933. He died in Alabama in 1954 at age thirty-seven, two years younger than Officer Mereness at the time of his death.

34

Detective Rempsey (Remps) Sullivan
March 9, 1935

'Rimps' Sullivan, Mayor Holcombe's Driver, Killed While in Plain Clothes in Dowling Street Shoe Shop

Rempsey Hayes Sullivan was born in Palestine, Texas, on July 8, 1900. His parents were Mr. and Mrs. Walter (Pearl) Sullivan.

At shortly before 6 p.m. on March 9, 1935, Detective R. H. "Rimps" Sullivan rode in a cab with a friend, Steve Conroy, to a location at 1917 Dowling Street. It was unknown what trouble Conroy had with the business at that location, but Detective Sullivan accompanied him as he sought to attend to the matter. The cab was driven by D. H. "Moon" Millican, a former ambulance driver and former deputy constable. The cabdriver later reported that they went to this location, which was a shoe repair shop. Conroy thought it was a bar where he wanted to search for a man named "Tony."

Conroy entered the business while Detective Sullivan and Millican remained in the cab. After several minutes, Sullivan and Millican heard loud voices coming from inside the shop. They then saw Conroy stumbling backwards out the front door, falling to the curb. Sullivan and Millican rushed the front door, with Sullivan reportedly shouting, "You can't do that; I'm an officer." Detective Sullivan, in plainclothes but wearing a police uniform shirt, exhibited his police badge and verbally identified himself as a police officer.

The shoe shop owner, Isaac Jones (Negro Male, 31) rushed behind the counter and grabbed a pistol, which he then used to shoot Sullivan, who fell wounded inside the shop. Conroy and Millican, both of whom were unarmed, ran out the front door and called for assistance.

A Fogle-West Company ambulance arrived

with ambulance attendants W. L. McCarley and N. A. Parsley onboard. However, Jones forced them at gunpoint to leave their cot in the shop and leave without Sullivan, shot once over the left eye. Jones vowed to shoot anyone who attempted to enter his shop.

More police were summoned and it was not until Homicide Detectives George Seber and Hugh Graham arrived that the standoff ended. Armed with their sawed-off shotguns leveled at Isaac Jones, they calmly walked in and took the man into custody.

Following the arrest of Jones, officers examined Detective Sullivan and found him to still be alive. The ambulance took him to St. Joseph's Infirmary but he was dead on arrival. He was thirty-four years old.

An investigation began immediately, supervised by Homicide Captain George Peyton. He was assisted by Detectives Seber, Graham, etc, and District Attorney Investigator E. H. Hammonds. The investigators obtained statements from Conroy and Millican, as well as a confession from Isaac Jones.

An independent witness, a young Negro male named Floyd Brown, returned to the scene after the arrest of Jones to give his version of the tragic event. He verified that Conroy, who had apparently been drinking, came in asking to see Tony. When Jones told him that Tony was not there any longer, Conroy started to leave, but stopped near the door. At that point, Jones approached Conroy, hitting him and shoving him out the front door, prompting Detective Sullivan to run in. Jones shot him.

Jones' statement to detectives somewhat verified the versions of Millican, Conroy and Brown. However, he stated that Detective Sullivan came in waving the gun. Jones shot him, claiming that he didn't know the gun-wielding man was a police officer. Of course, witnesses said that Detective Sullivan was verbally identifying himself as an officer. He was wearing civilian clothes and but displayed a uniformed police shirt. The investigation further revealed that Detective Sullivan's weapon was found underneath him and had not been fired.

Mayor Oscar Holcombe, for whom Sullivan had been acting as chauffeur for the past two years, and Public Safety Director George Woods, immediately went to Police Headquarters to monitor the investigation. Mayor Holcombe was quoted as saying, "Sullivan was a faithful and conscientious officer and I exceedingly regret his death. He was a splendid man and a fine officer."

Detective Captain George Peyton filed charges against Isaac Jones for murder in the death of Detective Sullivan in the Justice Court of Judge Tom Maes. Jones was ordered held without bail pending an examining trial.

Detective Sullivan was survived by his wife Myrtle and one son, Robert Harold Sullivan. Also mourning his death were one sister, Mrs. Hazel Benjamin, and two brothers, J. E. and Walter Sullivan, and his grandmother, Mrs. George Sullivan, all of Houston.

Funeral services were held in the chapel of the Houston Funeral Home, 1401 Crawford, at 2 p.m. Monday, March 11, 1935. The Reverends T. J. Windham and Harry G. Knowles officiated at the service. Burial followed at the Forest Park Lawndale Cemetery with the graveside services conducted under the direction of the Twentieth Century Lodge of the Oddfellows, of which Sullivan was an active member. Active pallbearers were Henry Bradshaw, Jimmy Bishop, W. E. Sammons, George Seber, A. C. Thornton and Neal Polk. Honorary pallbearers included Mayor Oscar Holcombe, Chief of Police B. W. Payne and many others notable in City of Houston businesses at the time.

DETECTIVE REMPSEY (REMPS) SULLIVAN

Detective Sullivan was Mayor Holcombe's chauffeur at the time of his death. He had served at various times as a patrolman, motorcycle officer and detective. He had left the service of the city on several occasions to work for local ambulance companies as a driver. However, his love for police work always brought him back to the department.

Officer Sullivan's gravesite was located in the northern and older section of Forest Park Lawndale. The grave marker reads:

MY BELOVED HUSBAND
R.H. (RIMPS) SULLIVAN
1900 – 1935

The judge held an examining trial at 1 p.m. Tuesday, March 12. Assistant District Attorney Tom Harris said that the judge would only allow witnesses and attorneys to attend the proceedings. Isaac Jones was indicted after this hearing and held without bond. A trial date was set for March 20 in Judge Whit Boyd's District Court.

On Monday, in the aftermath of the slaying of Detective Sullivan, City Commissioner Frank Holton announced that City Council would be asked to employ a special prosecutor to assist in the prosecution of Isaac Jones. Holton said, "I am told the Negro held off ambulance men and would not let them get to Sullivan. In view of these circumstances and others, I feel the city should employ a special prosecutor." His effort never came to fruition. More politics.

On March 20, 1935, the defense was granted a continuance until April 22. The state was represented by Assistant District Attorneys Tom Harris and Earle Adams. Isaac Jones' attorneys were John Mathis Sr. and William Glover.

The trial began as scheduled with Isaac Jones taking the stand in his own defense. His testimony was that he shot Detective Sullivan in self defense. However, his attitude likely didn't help him at all. He was described as being insolent in the way he answered questions from both sides. He also was described as swaggering in his walk to and from the witness stand.

At one point in his testimony, he was given the pistol used to kill Detective Sullivan. He then proudly showed how well he could handle the gun and described how he shot once into the floor that March day and then made the "quick shot" that struck Sullivan above his left eye. In cross examination by Harris, he was asked "Didn't you say that you would kill any white m_____ f_____ that came in your place?"

His smiling response was, "I did not."

Harris then asked Jones, "What are you grinning about? Do you think there's anything funny about killing this man?"

Jones reportedly leaned back in the witness chair and said, "I don't see any reason why I should cry about it."

Of course, Jones' attitude was not his only problem. Homicide Detectives Seber and Graham testified that when Detective Sullivan was lifted on to the stretcher after the standoff, his weapon was still in his holster.

On Thursday, April 25, after three hours of deliberation, the jury found Isaac Jones guilty of the murder of Detective Sullivan and assessed him the death penalty. His attorneys immediately announced they would ask for a new trial. When the sentence was announced, Isaac Jones showed no signs of nervousness. When asked if he had anything to say, he responded by saying, "I'm satisfied." Unfortunately, he and his attorneys were not satisfied.

They filed an appeal that resulted in the death sentence being overturned on unknown grounds. He was found guilty in a new trial but given a life sentence. Jones was paroled on July 1, 1960 and granted a full pardon by Governor John Connally on June 7, 1965. That pardon and at least one other one were granted by the governor after he was wounded on November 22, 1963 in Dallas, the day President John F. Kennedy was assassinated.

Rempsey Hayes Sullivan Jr. was raised by his grandmother after his mother remarried. For some reason, his name was changed to Robert Harold Sullivan, as he was listed in the original obituary of his father. He graduated from Jeff Davis High School in Houston and entered the service of his country in the United States Navy during World War II. He received an Honorable Discharge. After his World War II service, he took his original name back, that being that of his slain father, Rempsey Hayes Sullivan.

After many years of worldwide employment in the chemical industry, he retired from the Raytheon Corporation to the Country Place retirement community in Brazoria County along with his wife Shirley. Using searches that spotlighted the unusual first name of Rempsey, retired HPD Homicide Lieutenant Nelson Zoch tracked down Shirley Sullivan. She reported that Rempsey Sullivan Jr. passed away in December 2004 at the age of eighty-two. Mrs. Sullivan said she and her husband were married for over thirty years and how proud Rempsey was of his service to his country during the big war. Mrs. Sullivan said he initiated meetings for the other veterans at Country Place regarding veteran's benefits. He wanted all veterans to have full access to and knowledge of all benefits to which they were entitled. He continued this crusade until shortly before his death. He was also very proud of the father that he lost at such a young age, proud enough that he took his legal name back as soon as he was able to do so.

Rempsey Sullivan Jr. had one daughter, Lanelle, from a previous marriage. He also had a son who passed away at around the age of twelve from the ravages of polio. In 2006, Lanelle resided near Friendswood and had one daughter. Officer Rempsey Hayes Sullivan's mother, grandmother and brothers are also all deceased.

35

Officer James T. Gambill
December 1, 1936

Officer Gambill Dies in Violent Struggle with Giant Suspect- Suspect Shot and Killed by Partner

In 1936, with vehicles and gasoline being in short supply during the Great Depression, Houston Police Officers were on occasions referred to as Short Call Officers. This term defined them as not doing active patrol, but responding to calls for service as they were reported.

On Tuesday morning, December 1, 1936, Officer James (Jim) T. Gambill and his partner, Officer George G. Seber, left the station house on Caroline Street at 8am to answer a call from Jennie Mae Holmes, who resided at 2001 St. Charles. She had reported that her estranged husband, Martin Holmes, had come to her house at 4am and threatened her life. They had a fight, she said, and he left just before the officers arrived. She then offered to guide them to Martin's residence.

Newspaper accounts of this story were as follows:

Quoting Officer Seber, "We took the woman with us in the police car and drove to his house at 2902 Tierwester. When we got there, Holmes was standing by his truck in front of the house. As we got out of the car, Holmes reached in his truck and got a pistol. I disarmed him and put him in our car. We turned around and started to town with him. About the 2700 block of Calhoun, Holmes became unruly and tried to get out of the car. I stopped the car and both of us got out and tried to handcuff him. He was so powerful that we couldn't make it".

Officer Seber continued: "Holmes was scruffing with Jim, trying to get his gun. I got hold of Holmes and he came out of the car and grabbed me. We scuffled over the possession of my pistol until Jim got out of the car and then Holmes grabbed Jim. I then began shooting at Holmes. I shot five times while Holmes had a hold of Jim. At the fifth shot, he turned loose of Jim. During the scuffle, Jim's gun fired twice, but I don't know who fired it."

Just after the shooting, Jim fell backwards into a ditch. After the shooting, Officer Gambill and Holmes fell down together. Officer Gambill then got up, took several steps and fell again, his pistol going off once more as he fell for the final time. A civilian witness, Billie Schutte, who just happened to be driving by, saw the fierce fight in progress. His account matched that of Officer Seber. However, after the shooting, Officer Gambill lay in the ditch and died of an apparent heart attack suffered during this struggle with the suspect. He was forty-nine years old.

Martin Holmes, described as a powerful and giant man, was taken to Jeff Davis Hospital with five gunshot wounds. He expired at 4:05am the following morning, Wednesday, December 2, 1936. Once again, the old saying applied-"a shiny new silver dollar was exchanged for a rusty old penny".

OFFICER JAMES T. GAMBILL

Officer James Thomas Gambill, a member of the Houston Police Department for 14 years, was survived by his wife, Mrs. Patty Annie Gambill, and one daughter, Miss Glenna Mae Gambill. Also mourning his death were two brothers, Young

Gambill and John Gambill, and one sister, Mrs. Annie Kyle, all of Houston, as well as two aunts, Miss Mary Gambill of Rockdale and Mrs. John Gambill of Cameron. There were a number of other kinspeople of the Officer residing in Milam County.

Funeral services were held at 3:15pm on Wednesday, December 2, 1936, in the chapel of the Houston Funeral Home. Officiating at the service was Reverend D.L. Landrum of the Woodland Methodist Church. Active pallbearers were William Galbreath, Bogard Inghram, William Luce, Tim Parker, George G. Seber, and P.D. Hanna. Honorary pallbearers were all members of the Houston Police Department. Burial followed at the Resthaven Cemetery in north Harris County. Out of respect for Officer Gambill, Municipal Judge Ben Davison recessed police court for the afternoon.

This death being prior to the Medical Examiner authority over violent and/or public deaths, a Justice of the Peace was responsible for a ruling on the death. Justice Tom Maes held an inquest into the death of Officer Gambill and returned a verdict of death due to natural causes. It seemed that an important factor into this decision was that Officer Gambill had been in ill health for some time and was taking several different medications at the time of his death.

While this tragedy must have been quite a personal ordeal for Officer George G. Seber, he continued with HPD. Unfortunately, he passed away from a heart attack in 1938. However Officer Seber's son and namesake, George L. Seber, had been on the Department along with his Dad since approximately 1928.

George L. Seber was on a career path that would be distinguished beyond measure. He was one of the original Homicide investigators when the division was formed. This experience apparently served him well as in the years 1947-1953, he was the Captain in command of the Homicide Division. When I came on the department in 1968, he was second in command of the Houston Police Department. He was THE Assistant Chief of Police under then Chief Herman B. Short. With seven Inspectors (modern day Deputy Chiefs or Assistant Chiefs) on the command staff, it was widely known that he had a tremendous amount of decision making authority under Chief Short. Chief George L. Seber retired from that Assistant Chief position in 1969 and passed away in 1975. Chief Seber's only son, Marvin Seber, served on the department also for a number of years. He retired from the Auto Dealers Detail in 1988 and is now retired living near Waller, Texas.

While doing research for this story, I discovered that Officer Gambill's burial place was at Resthaven Cemetery. I was somewhat surprised that this resting place existed in 1936 as it is also the site of six other LINE OF DUTY deaths in HPD- Bobby Joe Schultea-1956, Louis Lyndon Sander-1967, Kenneth Wayne Moody-1969, Robert Wayne Lee-1971, Alberto Vasquez-2001, and Rodney Johnson-2006. With the utmost cooperation of the Earthman family, the first five of these are marked with 100 Club LINE OF DUTY markers at the sole expense and generosity of the Earthman Company. The Johnson marker will likely be placed at a later date.

With the able assistance of Mr. John B. Earthman's staff at Resthaven, I was able to locate this site. His grave is marked with a footmarker with the inscription:...................

HUSBAND, JAMES T. GAMBILL
AUGUST 27, 1887-DECEMBER 1, 1936

What was known of the family at this point is that one of his brothers, Robert Young Gambill, passed away less than two years later on 11/10/1938. Also, his only sister, Mrs. Anne Lela Kyle, passed away on 6/26/1961. Officer Gambill's widow, Mrs. Pattie Annie Gambill, born on May 1, 1892, passed away on October 22, 1978, having lived to the age of 86, nearly 42 years after her husband's untimely death. This story was originally published in the Badge and Gun with the above information. As a result of that story, a source in HPD came forward with a clue and the following was learned about Miss Glenna Gambill:

From Colonel James S. Schisser, United States Army: His Mom, Glenna Gambill Schisser, served her country as a member of the Women's Air Corp in World War II, serving in Burtonwood Hospital. She married Joseph George Schisser Sr., who had been a Japanese Prisoner of War for over three years. She was a "working Mom" to James and his brother, Joseph Schisser Jr. Back in Houston, she worked for a car dealership, the Social Security Administration, and ended up her career as the secretary to a top administrator at the Johnson Space Center. Through the years, she remained active in the American Legion and the American Ex-P.O.W.'s. Glenna was widowed in 1965 and in 2004 when I spoke to Colonel Schisser, his Mother was eighty-three years old and lived near Colonel Schisser and his family in the Washington D.C.-Virginia area.

Regarding his grandmother, Mrs. Pattie Annie Gambill, he stated that she lived out her life as a single working parent, relying solely on Social Security as she had not received anything from the Police Department as a result of her husband's death as a police officer.

Officer James Gambill's death obviously left a rather large void in the Gambill family. His death was similar in nature and cause as the death of HPD Officer Dennis Holmes in 2001. These deaths were ruled from natural causes, but it is very unlikely that either would have occurred without the involvement of the unlawful activities of others.

36

Officer Adolph P. Martial
November 8, 1937

One-time HPD Captain, A. P. Martial, Suffers Concussion and Later Dies After Complaining of a Severe Headache

On Saturday night, November 6, 1937, Officers A. P. Martial and M. R. George were on patrol in north Houston. Officer George was driving near the Travis School in Woodland Heights when he was forced to swerve the police car to avoid a collision with another machine. The police car struck the curb and Officer Martial was thrown forward, his head striking a gun rack over the windshield.

Shortly after the accident, Officer Martial complained of a headache. He took some aspirin, which did not provide him any relief. He was allowed to go home and, while his wife was preparing an ice pack for him, he lapsed into a coma. A Memorial ambulance transported him to the St. Joseph's Infirmary about 12:30 a.m. Sunday. The initial diagnosis was that he was suffering from a clot on the brain from a concussion.

However, his condition worsened throughout the day and the next night. Officer Adolph P. Martial passed away at St. Joseph's at 8:20 a.m. Monday, November 8, 1937. He was fifty-four years old.

Martial, a native Houstonian, was born on January 24, 1883. He lived at 2018 Leeland with his wife Alfreda and daughter, Dorothy Marie. He had held a variety of positions throughout his career. In 1923, he transferred from another city department to the Police Department, having been appointed by Mayor Oscar Holcombe as one of two special detectives to investigate the bootlegging industry during Prohibition. After he completed that special assignment, he remained on the force and was elevated in 1933 to the rank of lieutenant of detectives in charge of the Burglary and Theft Division. On January 2, 1936, he was promoted to the rank of captain.

However, as was the custom in this era under the political spoils system, when the newly elected Mayor Fonville took over the city in early 1937, Captain Martial, along with a number of other ranking officers, was demoted to the position of cruising patrolman. Even prior to his demotion, he was suffering some health problems and after his demotion, he took an extended leave of absence to engage in a business venture in Galveston. He had just returned to duty as a cruising patrolman in early November when the accident caused his death. This was likely a very difficult transition for Officer Martial, having been in either management or special positions throughout his working career. It is believed that he had no prior street policing experience.

OFFICER ADOLPH P. MARTIAL

Besides his wife and fifteen-year-old daughter, other survivors were his mother, Mrs. Christine Martial, and one brother, W. O. Martial, both of Houston.

Funeral services were conducted on Tuesday, November 9, 1937, at 2 p.m. at the Fogle-West Chapel with the Reverend Walker officiating. Active pallbearers were T. B. Morris, Carl Thornton, Arch Spradley, L. Z. Bryan, Gus Butler, M. M. Simpson, J. A. Stinson, and H. A. Supple, all of whom were policemen. Burial followed at the Hollywood Cemetery on North Main.

Mrs. Alfreda Martial, the widow, passed away in 1951. Miss Dorothy Martial married a man named Carlton Bry Stewart, who passed away in 1986. No obituary could be located on him, even though he died in Houston. If alive, Dorothy would be eighty-four years old in 2006. Efforts to locate her or her only child, Gregory Lee Stewart, have not been successful.

37

Officer Marion E. Palmer
March 24, 1938

Heights Boulevard Scene of Murder-Suicide That Took the Life of Officer Marion Palmer

Shortly before noon on Thursday, March 24, 1938, Houston Police Officer Marion Palmer and his cruising partner, Officer H. D. Roberts, were sent to a location at 1510 Heights Boulevard. It was reported that there was a crazed African-American male in the garage apartment behind this location, which carried the address of 1512 Heights.

Mrs. J. E. Cleveland, the resident at 1510 Heights, reported to police that her maid, Elvina Zink, and Elvina's husband, Light Zink, who lived in the servant quarters behind her residence, had recently been experiencing domestic difficulties. She called the police when Elvina came running into her house saying that her husband was crazy and had locked her out of the room. Mrs. Cleveland was aware of Light Zink being on her premises, as he had on occasion performed yard and garden duties for her.

Mrs. Cleveland was quoted in the local newspaper as saying, "I heard the officers arrive and heard them begging for Light to come out of the room. They told him that they would not hurt him, but he would not open the door. Then, one of the officers (Palmer) crawled out on a fence in the back. He must have looked in the window because I heard a shot and then the officer fell."

Mrs. Cleveland, whose sixty-five-year-old invalid mother, Mrs. M. L. Rasberry, was in her residence at the time of this tragedy, continued, "The other officer (Roberts) ran to the ledge. He had his gun out and seemed to be waiting for a chance to get a shot at Light. Just about fifteen seconds after the first shot, there was another shot. Then the officer ran up to the door of the room and broke it open. I called police headquarters again and reported that the officer had been shot."

Officer Palmer was rushed to Heights Hospital, where he died shortly after his arrival. He had been struck by shotgun pellets in the head and chest.

Officer Roberts, obviously distraught over the death of his partner, related the following account: "We were told that the Negro was in the apartment. We knocked on the door, but he refused to let us in. We stood there for awhile, knocking, then I smelled gas escaping. 'He's turned on the gas, I told my partner. You watch the back and I'll turn the gas off.' As I went to the gas meter beside the house in front of the garage apartment, my partner walked around to the back of the apartment."

OFFICER MARION E. PALMER

"A few minutes later I heard a shot and I ran to the rear of the house and found my partner lying at the foot of a ladder in a pool of blood. The Negro had shot once with a shotgun. As I was running back, I heard a second shot. I ran up the stairs to the garage apartment and burst the door open. I found the Negro lying dead, with half of his head blown away. He was clad in khaki pants and was lying against the wall of the tiny apartment. He clutched an old double-barrel shotgun. Both shells had been fired."

Roberts also stated that "the apartment was filled with gas when I broke into the door. There was a suicide note, obviously written by the Negro, lying on an open Bible on a little table by the open window out of which the Negro fired, killing my partner. The Bible was opened at the 15th chapter of Jeremiah. Verse 14 read, 'And I will make thee pass with thine enemy into a land which you knoweth not, for a fire is kindled in mine anger which shall burn you.'"

Officer Marion E. Palmer Sr. is believed to have been born in Springfield, Ohio, on March 20, possibly in 1891. He died at the age of forty-seven, had been a resident of Houston for eighteen years and was a member of the Houston Police Department since June 16, 1930. He worked out of the West End substation. He was a member of Tucker Lodge No. 297, Ancient Free and Accepted Masons.

Officer Palmer was survived by his wife Christine and two sons, Harold and Marion E. Palmer Jr., his mother, Mrs. W. D. Naus of Forest, Ohio, two sisters, Mrs. R. A. Weller of Cleveland, Ohio, and Mrs. Bernice Jones of Forest, Ohio, as well as a half-brother, R. C. Howard, of Phoenix, Arizona.

Funeral services for Officer Marion E. Palmer were held at 3:30 p.m. Saturday, March 26, 1938, at the Heights Funeral Home Chapel, just a block from the scene of his tragic death. The Reverend R. H. Tharp officiated. Burial followed at Forest Park Lawndale Cemetery.

The gravesite of Officer Palmer was located at Forest Park Lawndale. His marker reads as follows and also proudly displays the Masonic symbol:

OUR BELOVED HUSBAND AND DADDY
MARION E. PALMER SR.
1891-1938

On the same gravesite at Forest Park Lawndale, there lies a woman, Christine Connett. Mrs. Palmer apparently remarried and is interred there along with both of her husbands, Officer Palmer and Alvin Connett. Both Mr. and Mrs. Connett died in 1974, thirty-six years after this tragedy. Mrs. Connett was seventy-six years of age.

The obituary of Mrs. Christine Connett indicated that in 1974, both of her sons survived her. Harold lived in San Antonio while Marion Junior resided in Houston. Additionally, she was survived by Harold's children, grandsons David and Paul Palmer and granddaughter Patti Palmer and Marion Junior's daughter, Linda Sue Soukup, as well as one great grandson, Marion Soukup. Marion Soukup is an obvious namesake for his grandfather and great grandfather.

Linda Sue was located, but did not have much information on the remaining family except to state that both her father and her Uncle Harold were both deceased.

38

Officer George D. Edwards
Badge #259
June 30, 1939

Officer George Edwards, a Houston Favorite, Killed By an Ex-Con During a Downtown Scuffle on Franklin

George Dewey Edwards was born near the small East Texas town of Rusk on April 25, 1899. His actual home place was around the community of Sardis, where his parents and other extended families all lived and farmed. George attended school there and when World War I broke out, he served his country honorably in the United States Army. He came home safely after serving eighteen months in France. Having been raised on a farm and knowing what that tough life held for him, it didn't take long for George and his young wife Audie to decide to move to Houston where a brighter future laid ahead. At this time in 1925, he and Audie were the parents of three-year-old Kathryn and one-year-old Kenneth.

Edwards secured a job in Houston at a Ford Motor Company plant and sent for his wife and children. However, he was laid off during the depressed economic times of the mid-1920s. He regrouped by joining the Houston Police Department on June 17, 1927. He wore Badge No. 259. He became known as either "the smiling cop" or "Country Boy." Later reports indicated that he was the most liked and respected man in the department. He worked the evening shift patrolling downtown Houston throughout his twelve-year career.

On the Friday night of June 30, 1939, W. H. Everett of 1712 Elysian parked his automobile in the 300 block of Franklin. Returning to his car around 9 p.m., Everett saw someone inside attempting to start it. The would-be thief got out and walked away, and Everett followed him down Congress. At Preston and Fannin, the suspect met another man, who asked him, "What's the matter? Can't you get it started?"

The two men separated and as Everett continued

to follow the first man, he saw Officers Edwards and G. H. Harrell walking on Fannin toward Congress and pointed out the man to the officers and told them what was going on. About this time, Detectives S. T. Roe and Rufus Seay came driving by. Another squad car was there at about the same time and Officer Edwards jumped on the running board while Officer Harrell got on Roe and Seay's car.

OFFICER GEORGE D. EDWARDS

They all caught up with the suspect in the 1200 block of Franklin. Detective Roe later stated: "They were all there at the same time and we grabbed the man, who was dressed in a gaudy cowboy outfit. I slapped his pocket, felt a gun and told him to give it up."

"He wouldn't and began fighting the officers and at the same time, trying to pull the gun. Officer Edwards grabbed the man from behind and both of them bent over. Then the man got his right arm free and pulled the pistol and fired. He then fired again and I got hit in the arm. I began firing my pistol at him and Detective Seay did, as did Officer Harrell. The man fell and was trying to fire again and we took the gun away from him. It wasn't until then that we realized that Officer Edwards had been hit."

The wounded officer was rushed to St. Joseph's Infirmary in a Fogle-West ambulance, but was pronounced dead on arrival from a single gunshot wound to the head. He was forty years old.

None of the officers present could account for the man's ferocity and determination to avoid arrest. Detective Seay stated that "the man would not give up the pistol and so we started hitting him on the head with our guns. I hit him so hard I bent my gun. We kept telling him that we would have to shoot him. His comment was 'Shoot and be damned.' We had no choice but to shoot him."

Detective Roe, wounded in the line of duty for the third time in the last eighteen months, was heard to say during the struggle: "Stand back and I'll just kill him." Officer Edwards, probably still smiling, continued on with the effort to arrest the man as did the other officers.

Homicide Captain George Peyton took charge of the investigation, assisted by Detectives J. G. Irwin, Hugh Graham, J. F. Willis, Ted Walsh and George Seber. A large crowd gathered at the scene, some of whom had witnessed all or part of the tragedy. Officers took statements from numerous witnesses gathered at the scene.

KATHERINE, AUDIE, GEORGE, AND KENNETH EDWARDS

The suspect, who was dead at the scene, was identified as Carl Adams (White Male, 32), an ex-convict from El Campo. Police learned that he was sentenced in Arizona for robbery by assault and given five years in 1935; he was released in 1936. He had been arrested and released in some type of investigation in May 1939.

Officer George D. Edwards was an extremely popular member of the Houston Police Department. He was survived by his wife Audie Edwards and two children, fifteen-year-old son, Kenneth Edwards, and seventeen-year-old daughter, Mrs. Kathryn Farmer, and one grandson, Thomas Farmer, all of Houston. Also mourning his death were his parents, Mr. and Mrs. C. F. Edwards of Rusk, as well as five brothers: J. B., Robert, France, Bill and Charley, and two sisters, Mrs. Dora Berry and Mrs. Mack Dear.

Perry-Foley Funeral Home in Houston was in charge of arrangements and a funeral service was held at 4 p.m. Saturday, July 1, 1939. Police Chief L. C. Brown stated that every officer not on duty would be at the funeral. After the service in Houston, the entire motorcycle squadron escorted the body to Union Station, where the sad train journey continued to his childhood home in Cherokee County. The body went by rail to Jacksonville and another service was held at 9 a.m. Sunday, July 2, in nearby Dialville. Burial followed at the Rock Springs Cemetery in Dialville.

Audie Edwards, who by all accounts just worshipped her husband, faced tough times after his death. While Kathryn was already married and had a child, Mrs. Edwards was left to raise Kenneth as well as help Kathryn, her young husband and the couple's child. The Edwards family had resided at a small house at 2408 Princeton in the Houston Heights. It was reported that Mrs. Edwards received a total of $2,500 from the following sources: $500 from the City of Houston, $1,500 from the Police Burial Fund and $500 from a privately held insurance policy. There was no such thing as a police officer's city pension in those days or an annuity for her and the children from the 100 Club of Houston. Not only did the family lose a husband and a father, it lost a job and a paycheck.

Mrs. Edwards, determined to support her family, entered several business ventures including a restaurant, icehouse and later a night watchman service. In the early 1940s, with World War II looming on the horizon, economic times were very tough. Kenneth Edwards, due to severe financial difficulties, was forced to drop out of Reagan High School. He lived on his own in Houston for a time and later took a job in San Antonio.

Then, World War II entered the picture and Kenneth, following in the footsteps of his dad, entered the U. S. Army. He served in the India-China-Burma Theater for two years and while he saw no actual combat, this zone was known as a dangerous combat area of the war. He was awarded the Asiatic Pacific Ribbon with three Bronze Stars for his service. Fortunately, he returned safely to Houston, where he took advantage of the G. I. Bill, obtained his GED and attended the University of Houston.

It is not unusual for an officer killed in the line of duty to receive high praise from his friends and colleagues. Officer Edwards was no exception. Coincidentally, in the weeks prior to him being killed, he was chosen for what today is called a photo opportunity. One local newspaper had him pictured smiling while issuing a traffic citation to – yes – a smiling citizen. This was obviously a 1939 public relations effort on the part of the Houston Police Department to convince citizens that Officer Friendly was out there to protect their safety in the burgeoning motor vehicle traffic out there on the streets of the growing city.

To no one's surprise, the legend of George "Country Boy" Edwards extended outside of the continental United States. His son Kenneth recalled what he learned from an Army friend of his dad's:

WORLD WAR I ARMY PRIVATE GEORGE EDWARDS

"While in France during World War I and after most of the hostilities had ceased, George, the country boy, befriended a disabled French soldier whose wife had just recently given birth. Times were tough and the young mother, who had become undernourished during her pregnancy, was not able to provide an adequate amount of milk for the child. The family had a dry cow. George Edwards, the country boy from Sardis, Texas, took it upon himself to 'pull' some strings. He was able to trade the dry cow for a wet cow."

This was a happy ending to a rather strained situation. It was also indicative as to what the citizens of Houston later became accustomed to from George Edwards, a caring and compassionate Houston police officer.

Officer Edwards' parents and siblings are all deceased. After a number of phone calls to the Dialville-Rusk area of East Texas, as well as an unsuccessful search of Rock Springs Cemetery, HPD Homicide Lieutenant Nelson Zoch received a surprise call in 2005 from Kenneth Edwards, a long-time Houstonian who was eighty-one years old. Edwards was responding to Zoch's effort to locate George Edwards' gravesite. Country Boy's son shared memorabilia with Zoch and the HPD Police Museum. His sister Kathryn was eighty-three and lived with her son Thomas Farmer in Sulphur, Louisiana. Kathryn was only seventeen when her dad was killed but she was already a mother of young Thomas. She later had two daughters, Debbie and Renee. She is the grandmother of seven and is also a great-grandmother.

Kenneth Edwards worked for many years in the television industry as a transmitter engineer supervisor for KUHT-TV (Channel 8), the UH public television station. He and his wife, Leitha Joy, resided in Houston, both retired. They are the parents of a son, Bruce George (named after his grandfather) Edwards and a daughter, Nancy Joy.

Mrs. Audie Edwards, also a native of East Texas, worked hard to play the hand she was so abruptly dealt. She later remarried to Charles Wren, a man Kenneth Edwards described as very dedicated and devoted to his mother. She passed away from leukemia in 1965 in Houston. She is buried in Brenham, where her daughter Kathryn lived at the time.

There is not much remaining of the old farming and railroad community of Dialville. The Rock Springs Cemetery is next to the Rock Springs Baptist Church. It was here that the remains of Officer George Edwards were laid to rest. A World War I Veterans Administration marker designates the grave with the following wording:

GEORGE D. EDWARDS
TEXAS
PVT CO B 21 MG BN 7 DIV
WORLD WAR I
APRIL 25, 1899-JUNE 30, 1939

There was no reference to indicate how this heroic Houston police officer gave his life in the line of duty. With the permission of Kenneth Edwards, the administration of Rock Springs Cemetery has agreed that another stone, the 100 Club of Houston Line of Duty marker, can be placed at the gravesite to honor this man. The placement took place in September 2005.

39

Officer Howard B. Hammond
Badge #824
August 18, 1946

Officer Howard B. Hammond Murdered During Dowling Street Disturbance Call

Early in the morning hours of Sunday, August 18, 1946, Officers Howard B. Hammond and T. F. Hambley were on patrol in the 3700 block of Dowling. There, outside a cleaning shop, they observed a large crowd gathering around the front door as well as inside. This crowd was engaged in loud, raucous behavior while dancing and drinking alcohol after hours. This seemed rather unusual to the officers as a cleaning shop would not normally be open after midnight. The officers decided to stop and warn the owner about the illegal activity.

According to Officer Hambley, he went in the shop and walked toward the rear where he met the owner, while Officer Hammond remained on the front sidewalk near their police car and radio. Hambley found the owner of the business to be polite. He told the officer that the party would stop. Hammond came in the door to advise his partner that they needed to go answer another call.

As Hambley walked to the front, he heard some shouting outside and now rushing toward the front door, saw that an African-American man had his partner in a clinch, swaying back and forth on the sidewalk. He ran up and grabbed the suspect and when he did, someone grabbed the gun from his holster and jerked it away from him.

His flashlight was next as he was attacked by four men and a woman. As he fought for his own survival, he heard four or five shots from two different guns. Then a sudden quiet fell. Hambley had been beaten severely with his own pistol and flashlight and as he staggered to his feet, there was no one around but Officer Hammond lying on the ground with an African-American male lying across him.

Hambley called for assistance. Fifty to sixty HPD officers, deputy sheriffs, state highway patrolmen and Texas Rangers rushed to the scene. Ambulance drivers from Pat H. Foley Funeral Home picked up the wounded officer and headed toward St. Joseph's Infirmary. But he died en route. Only thirty-three years old, Officer Howard B. Hammond had been shot in the forehead and neck. The African-American male, Louis Henson, was dead at the scene, having been shot twice in the stomach and chest.

Police Chief Percy Heard, Detective Inspector C. V. "Buster" Kern and Homicide Lieutenant George Seber led the investigation into the murder of Officer Hammond and the serious mob-type assault of Officer Hambley. Nineteen suspects, all blacks, were rounded up immediately and placed in the Café Zanzibar next door at 3708 Dowling for interviews. Hambley, although badly beaten, remained at the scene to gasp his story to the investigators.

Based on the statements of witnesses at the scene, a daylight raid Sunday morning led to the arrest of Charles Jackson Jr. (African-American male, 27) of 3702 Briley. Jackson originally denied any involvement but, after questioning by Homicide detectives, as well as Chief District Attorney A. C. Winborn, led authorities to a house in the nearby 2400 block of Winbern.

OFFICER HOWARD B. HAMMOND

Investigators recovered a pistol there from underneath the house. This later proved to be Officer Hambley's pistol that was taken from him during the beating. Jackson had given this pistol to another black male after the offense to hide for him. Officer Hammond's pistol was found underneath him when he was loaded into the ambulance.

Upon piecing together the eyewitness accounts, some accurate and some not so reliable, the investigators ascertained that Louis Henson repeatedly hindered Officer Hammond's efforts to enter the front door. At one point, the two clenched in a struggle. They fell to the sidewalk, at which time Charles Jackson began shooting at the officer and Henson while they were on the ground.

Jackson shot both men while half dozen men from the crowd attacked Officer Hambley. Four witnesses supposedly provided this account of the tragedy. Charles Jackson at one point verbally admitted to investigators that he had shot the officer. However, he later denied making that admission as well as committing the offense.

Other Homicide detectives participating in the investigation were P. Y. Snow and W. C. Doss, who worked the initial scene investigation. Assisting them in sorting out the mass confusion were Detectives Hugh Graham, J. O. Graddy, W. P. Brown and L. L. Watts.

On Monday, August 19, 1946, a murder charge was filed against Charles Jackson Jr., who had later admitted the shooting. In October, a Harris County grand jury returned a murder indictment against Jackson. This jury had been convened on special call by Criminal District Judge Frank Willeford for the specific purpose of hearing this case.

Officer Howard B. Hammond, who originated from Longview in Gregg County, born on June 12, 1913, had served his country in World War II in the United States Navy in the Pacific Theater of Operations. He had been a Houston police officer for about five years. Officer Hambley was about the same age.

Funeral services were held at 9:30 a.m. Monday, August 19, 1946 at the Boulevard Funeral Home with the Reverend W. L. Faircloth officiating. On the Sunday night before, at the usual night shift roll call, fellow officers on the midnight-8 a.m. shift held a memorial service of their own in the assembly room. The deceased officer's chair was draped in black and a very impressive and touching service was held in his honor.

Officer Hammond's body was transported to Longview to the Welch Funeral Home in the Judson area on the north side of the city. Additional services were held at 10 a.m. on Tuesday, August 20 at the Judson Baptist Church with the Reverend James Morgan officiating. Burial followed at the Bussey Cemetery (now called the New Providence Cemetery) in Longview.

Officer Hammond was survived by his wife, Kathleen McAfee Hammond, and two daughters, thirteen-year-old Sara and eleven-year-old Yvonne, as well as his mother, Mrs. Alberta Hammond of Longview, brother Wilmer J. Hammond of Longview and three sisters, Mrs. I. C. Lewis (Annie Laurie) of Big Sandy, Mrs. L. P. Myers (Ruby) and Miss Mary Nell Hammond of Longview.

The Longview Daily News reported that Officer Howard Hammond was a member of a pioneer Gregg County family, having been born and reared in the

Judson community. The Kilgore Masonic Lodge also paid its respects at the funeral service. Officer Hammond's wife Kathleen was laid to rest years later in this same cemetery as most of his family.

His monument has the Masonic emblem at the top of his name and below his birth and death information, engraved in the granite marker, is a HOUSTON POLICE BADGE NO. 824. With the cooperation of the management of New Providence Cemetery, a LINE OF DUTY grave marker was ordered for this Houston police officer slain while performing his duties.

Kathleen died in 1992, forty-six years after her husband's death. She was seventy-eight, having been widowed at the age of thirty-two. Daughter Sara Hammond married and had three sons. The oldest was named Howard Hammond Fadner, a namesake of his grandfather that he never had an opportunity to know. In 2006, Howard Fadner was a Baptist minister in the Dallas area. It was the dream of Mrs. Alberta Hammond, Officer Hammond's mother, that Howard would be a minister. Sara's other two sons are Dale and Robert, both of whom were living in the Houston area. Sara was the proud grandmother of six children from her three sons. She died in 1999 and was buried near her parents and brother in Longview.

Yvonne Hammond married and was seventy years of age in 2006 and the wife of James Boyd, a retired United States Air Force veteran. They were living in San Antonio, the parents of Charlotte Boyd and James Boyd Junior as well as the grandparents of three. Officer Hammond's sister Annie Lauric is deceased. Another sister, Ruby, was ninety years old and living near Longview, as was the brother, Wilmer Joe. The youngest sister, Mary Nell, resided in the Dallas area.

A grandson of Officer Hammond's sister Annie was living in Houston. This grandson, Mark Lewis, as well as other family members, expressed great appreciation of the City of Houston in the manner in which the widow was treated. The year 1946 was prior to the police pension system and the 100 Club. Mrs. Kathleen Hammond was given a "lifetime" job with the city's' water department, very likely an important financial move for the widow and her two young daughters. Also, Mark had conducted extensive research into the death of his grandmother's brother and willingly shared the results with this writer.

On Friday, October 18, 1946, this case was brought before District Court Judge Langston King's court. A trial was held and on November 15, 1946, Charles Jackson was sentenced to life in prison. The legal process did not end with this conviction. Jackson, after serving less than eleven years of a life sentence, was paroled in April 1957 and later given a full pardon by Texas Governor John Connally in 1964. Speculation was that the governor being seriously wounded in the JFK assassination in 1963 might have played a part in this incredible leniency.

Officer Thomas Hambley had joined HPD in 1944 at the age of thirty-six. After the death of Officer Hammond and his own severe beating, he served in the Jail Division and later again in Radio Patrol. He developed health problems and took his retirement from HPD in 1970. He passed away shortly thereafter in March 1972 at the age of sixty-three.

Officer Hammond's family initially conceived the idea of a ceremony dedicating the Line of Duty Marker in Longview, which was placed in July 2006. While the HPD Honor Guard and the Longview PD Honor Guard are both willing to participating in this ceremony, it will remain on hold until the Hammond family and their health will permit.

40

Officer Smith A. (Buster) Kent, Jr.
Badge #135
Jan. 12, 1954

Officer Smith Anderson 'Buster' Kent Jr. Loses Life in 1954 Motorcycle Accident

Smith Anderson "Buster" Kent Jr. was born on March 29, 1906. A native of Louisiana, he moved to Houston in 1914. His original employment date with the Houston Police Department is uncertain, but it is known that he ranked as a special officer on December 19, 1934. He wore Badge No. 135.

On April 1, 1936, he was placed as a motorcycle officer. This was obviously well before the inception of the State Civil Service System. On August 16, 1939, he was promoted to second sergeant of police. Research into this special officer status showed that even though Officer S. A. Kent and his brother, J. E. Kent, were both hired in this capacity, their seniority did not become effective until the City of Houston Civil Service Commission formally certified them.

For whatever reason, his status as second sergeant of police did not last. History shows that promotions and demotions were very common prior to the late 1940s when HPD officers fought for and finally won a decent Civil Service job protection system, which eliminated the "spoils system" in place for many years.

On Wednesday, January 6, 1954, at approximately 9:30 a.m., Motorcycle Officers Smith A. Kent Jr. and Jack Betz were "sitting on a spot" in the 6300 block of Navigation at Greenwood when they observed a late model Chevrolet speeding at about fifty miles per hour east on Navigation. Officer Kent, who according to Officer Betz was "next up," started out in pursuit of this vehicle and, as he was doing so, a truck driven by Alfred Boulding pulled out of a private driveway in front of him. Boulding later said that he did not see the officer until the front of his truck was already out into the street.

Boulding applied his brakes and Officer Kent attempted to stop his motorcycle about eighty-four feet from the truck. However, he was not able to stop quickly enough. His motorcycle skidded in a straight line and he laid down his bike as he was attempting to stop. It is believed Officer Kent did not actually strike the truck but hit his head on the pavement as he went down.

The officer was taken to St. Joseph's Hospital in serious condition with a fractured skull, possible fractured neck and severe injuries to his right leg. Specialists were called in to assist in the emergency treatment. Officers L. W. "Lonnie" Bolton and Ernest F. McBeth investigated this accident under the direct supervision of Sergeant J. J. Easter and Lieutenant J. M. LeVrier. After the accident was reported, Motorcycle Sergeant J. E. Kent, the officer's brother, was immediately sent to St. Joseph's Hospital to be with his injured brother and his family.

While the investigation continued, the gravely injured officer did not respond to treatment. On Tuesday, January 12, 1954, at 6:35 p.m., Officer Smith Anderson Kent died from his injuries. He was forty-seven years of age and had been a Houston police officer for nineteen years, seventeen on motorcycles.

Nell Margaret Kent, his wife, and four-year-old son Smith Anderson "Butch" Kent III survived S. A. "Buster" Kent. Also mourning his death was his stepson, fifteen-year-old Bobby Ray Sublett, and his fellow officer and dear brother, Sergeant J. E. Kent. Three sisters survived him. They were Mrs. Frank Miller and Mrs. E. D. McMahon of Houston and Mrs. Palmer Hotchkiss of Pittsburgh, Pennsylvania. Another brother, H. B. Kent, also of Pittsburgh, survived him. He also left an aunt, Mrs. George Pilleran of Long Beach, California, and an uncle, W. M. Kent of Homer of Louisiana, as well as a number of nieces and nephews.

Funeral services were held at the Palms Funeral Home at 3 p.m. on Thursday, January 14, 1954. Reverend Grady Hallonquist officiated and burial followed at the Forest Park Lawndale Cemetery. Officer Kent was a member of the Fraternal Order of the Eagles.

The gravemarker for Officer Kent reads:

DADDY, MY DARLING HUSBAND
S.A. (BUSTER) KENT
MAR. 29, 1906 - JAN. 12, 1954

Officer Jack Betz continued his long career on Motorcycles and retired in 1980. He served thirty-six years in HPD from 1944 to 1980, almost thirty years of his career on motorcycles. Retired Officer Betz said Officer Kent had ridden motors for a number of years and had always ridden an Indian Brand motorcycle. He had recently begun to ride a Harley with controls significantly opposite to those of the Indian. It is unknown whether this factor contributed to the tragic accident. Officer Betz passed away in 2003 at the age of eighty-seven.

OFFICER SMITH A. (BUSTER) KENT

Officer E. F. McBeth later promoted to sergeant. He retired in 1976 and died in 1989. Officer L. W. Bolton continued his career in the Accident Division, retiring in 1988. He died in 1999. It is uncertain as to what happened to Sergeant Easter. However, Lieutenant LeVrier was later promoted to captain and was the Accident Division commander for many years before retiring in 1979. He died in 1987.

Mrs. Nell Margaret Kent died in 1985 and was laid to rest next to her husband at Forest Park. Son S. A. "Butch" Kent served his country in Vietnam. He was fifty percent disabled and in 2002 ran a vehicle storage lot on the north side. He was active in agriculture during high school in Spring Branch and had a calf sponsored by the Houston Police Officers Association (later HPOU). He enjoyed rodeoing and was injured while participating in a benefit rodeo for Officers Ben Gerhart and Bobby James, who were both killed in the line of duty on June 26, 1968.

In 2002, stepson Bobby Ray Sublett was involved in the management of a coffee service company in the downtown Houston area. All the other survivors of Officer Kent are deceased.

41

Officer Fred Maddox Jr.
Badge #1012
February 24, 1954

Drunken Hijacker Took Clear, Deadly Shot At Officer Fred Maddox in '54 Crime Spree

Fred Maddox Jr. was born on March 10, 1924 in Galatia, Illinois. At an early age, his family moved to Hot Springs, Arkansas where he attended public schools. He voluntarily went into the U. S. Army at the age of nineteen and proudly served his country during World War II, part of his service being in India. He joined the Houston Police Department on November 16, 1950, entering Police Cadet Class No. 6 and graduating on February 10, 1951.

Three years later, on Wednesday, February 24, 1954, Officer Fred Maddox was riding a north side wagon unit on the Evening Shift with his partner that day, Officer Martel Moon. Moon was a few years older than Maddox, having graduated Class No. 7. On this same evening Carrol Dayton Farrar (White Male, 34) was in the middle of a three-day drinking spree. Having committed several burglaries and armed robberies to sustain his habits, he was armed with a stolen .38-caliber super automatic pistol when he hailed a cab at Jensen and Crosstimbers.

The cab driver was told to take him to Laura Koppe and Farrar streets. However, he got out of the cab several blocks from the Gardner Liquor Store at 4819 Laura Koppe. E. W. Gardner, the owner of the liquor store, was alone when Farrar came in and hijacked him, also threatening to kill him. Farrar then fled east on Laura Koppe on foot. Officer J. E. Tucker was dispatched to the liquor store robbery. While there, the HPD Dispatcher called the liquor store with additional information. The L & J Cab Company had contacted Dispatch, advising that a suspect fitting the hijacker's description had called for a cab from George's Food Market at 5318 Laura Koppe.

This information was broadcast and Officer Tucker, riding alone, rushed to this location. As Tucker arrived, Farrar stepped out into view and fired point-blank at Tucker. Reacting, Tucker crouched behind his patrol car and returned fire. Farrar fired five more times at Tucker, peppering the patrol car, a 1953 black Ford. Farrar then fled to the rear of the store.

Officers Maddox and Moon, hearing the shots as they neared this location, pulled up in their paddy wagon on the opposite side of the store from Tucker's car. As they got out of the wagon they were unaware that they were in plain sight of the shooter, who was shielded only thirty feet away. As they rushed toward the rear of the store, Farrar jumped out in front of Moon and fired directly at him. Moon threw up his right arm in a defensive manner, likely saving his life. He was hit in the right forearm.

Farrar was then distracted by more shots from Tucker and, as this suspect fell back, he turned and saw Officer Maddox crouched near a car attempting to locate Farrar and get a shot at him. Unfortunately, Farrar saw Maddox first and fired once, striking him in the head.

During this heavy exchange of gunfire, off-duty Officer W. F. Millican, a police academy classmate of Officer Maddox, was visiting his wife's family liquor store/service station just four blocks away. Hearing the sounds of the gun battle, Millican grabbed a shotgun from the trunk of his personal car and ran toward the store. He handed the shotgun to Officer Tucker, who then sighted Farrar as he was slipping a third clip into his automatic weapon. Tucker then fired at Farrar, wounding him. Farrar fell and was rushed by Tucker, Moon and Deputy Sheriff A. J. Randio, who also had come upon the scene. Randio kicked Farrar's pistol away from him and helped take the hijacker into custody.

More than fifty shots were fired during this shootout.

Meanwhile, a large crowd had gathered around the mortally wounded Officer Maddox while awaiting arrival of an ambulance. The crowd became silent when a citizen came forward to offer a prayer. According to newspaper accounts, up to sixty people, including Night Police Chief H. "Buddy" McGill, other officers and many citizens, dropped to their knees to pray for the fallen officer. An ambulance rushed Maddox to Hermann Hospital, where he was pronounced dead at 10:47 p.m. from a gunshot wound to the head. He was two weeks away from his thirtieth birthday.

Meanwhile, at No. 60 Deboll, off the 5600 block of Airline, another part of this tragedy was unfolding. Officer Maddox's parents, Mr. and Mrs. Fred Maddox Sr., received word shortly before 9 p.m. that their son had been wounded. This was the year 1954, well before the days of the North Freeway. The father and mother hurried to Hermann Hospital by way of Airline Drive. Inbound on Airline, they went over the railroad overpass near 33rd Street.

Eleven-year-old Margie Elliot was crossing Airline Drive on foot when she was struck by the Maddox vehicle and killed instantly. The Maddox vehicle wound up in a ditch after striking a utility pole. Mrs. Maddox was knocked unconscious and both she and her husband were taken by ambulance to Hermann Hospital. Mrs. Maddox, who suffered numerous injuries, did not regain consciousness until 10 a.m. the next day. Upon being told of her son's death, she lapsed into hysteria and had to be sedated.

Officer Maddox' pregnant wife Louise and four-year-old daughter Brenda survived Officer Maddox. In addition to his parents, he left one brother, Army Corporal Billy Maddox, stationed in Korea and three sisters, Mrs. Betty Jean Lance, Mrs. Maxine Shaddo and Mrs. Charlene Brien. Other survivors were his grandmothers, Mrs. Belle Maddox and Mrs. Carroll Patterson.

His son and namesake, Fred Maddox III, was born on June 16, 1954.

Funeral services for Officer Maddox were held at 10 a.m. Monday, March 1, 1954 at Victory Baptist Church at 8100 Jensen Dr. Burial followed at Brookside Memorial Park. Officers Forrest Turbeville and Lamar Kimble were two of the HPD officers who stood as an Honor Guard for their slain friend. This is believed to be the first official HPD Honor Guard.

Marker for Officer Maddux:

FATHER-FRED MADDUX JR.
HPD BADGE #1012 AND MASONIC EMBLEM

The state filed capital murder charges against Carroll Dayton Farrar for murder in the death of Officer Maddox, as well as the attempted capital murders of Officers Moon and Tucker. Farrar was a thrice promoted and thrice demoted Army veteran of World War II. All of his problems in the service were alcohol-related. In 1948, he was convicted of criminal assault on a twelve-year-old girl. He served four years of a ten-year prison sentence, having been released in March 1952. Farrar was tried and convicted of the capital murder and was assessed the death penalty. He was properly executed January 4, 1956.

In 2001, Officer J. E. Tucker was living in the Houston County area and has been active in ranching since his retirement from HPD. He also had worked in the Jail and Narcotics divisions. Officer W. E. Millican, who very well may have saved the day with his shotgun, worked the Accident and Point Control divisions before his retirement from HPD in 1972. He was living in Cypress. The retired officer still had vivid memories of that fateful day.

Officer Moon, who was wounded in this incident, continued what would be a long career with HPD. He recovered from his gunshot wound to the arm. However, the flash from the gunshot as well as nitrate particles caused severe eyesight problems for him in his later years. He later worked the Jail and Point Control divisions, from which he retired in 1978. Officer Moon died in August 1999. His widow, Reba, was eighty-two and residing in Sargent in 2001.

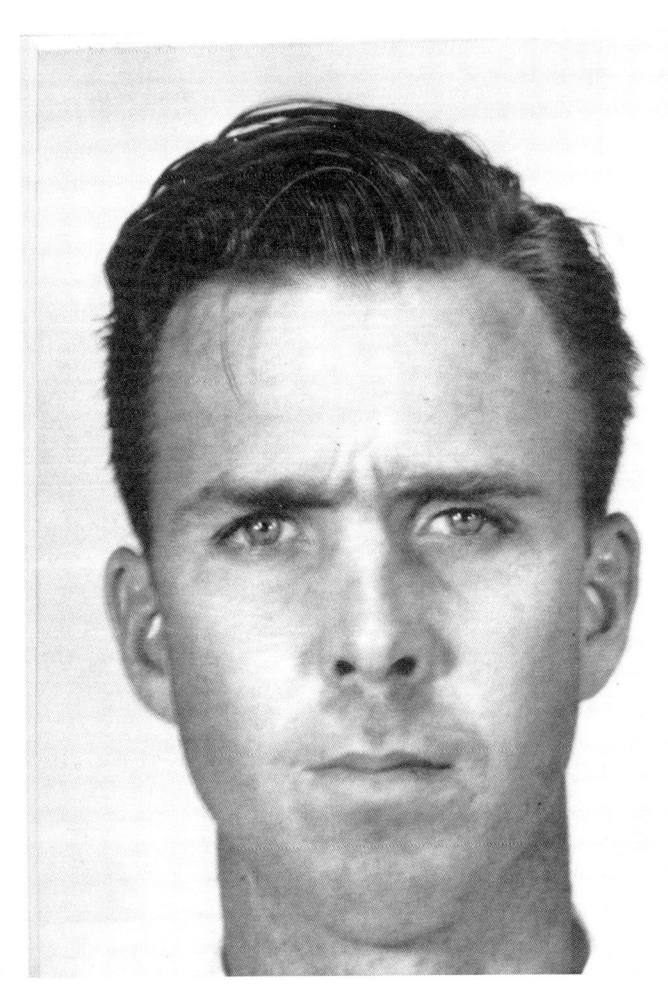

OFFICER FRED MADDUX JR.

Mrs. Moon said in an interview that year that the original information relayed to her that day in 1954 was that her husband was the officer who was shot in the head. Officer Moon's son-in-law, Accident Lieutenant Elden J. Smith, retired as a veteran of more than forty-two years of HPD service. His grandson, Central Patrol Officer Elden D. Smith, also spent more than twenty years with the department.

Gardner Liquor Store went out of business.

While it was not the scene of the shooting of Officers Maddox and Moon, the robbery of the store was the catalyst that brought about this tragedy. In this same liquor store in November 1969, Homicide Detective Jimmy L. Marquis was working an extra job for his brother-in-law, E. W. Gardner, when three armed hijackers entered the store. A shootout ensued and when the gun smoke settled, Detective Marquis was seriously wounded, one hijacker was dead and another wounded. The detective recovered from his wounds and retired in 1978. He died in 2000. One of his daughters, Sharon Garcia, became a sergeant in HPD's Burglary and Theft Division and now works Homicide Sex Crimes.

Homicide Detectives C. F. Langston, Virgil Hart, George Chapman, H. W. Rodgers, W. W. Walker, P. Y. Snow, H. E. Cole, J. E. Wilburn and C. L. Phillips investigated this offense. Supervisors were Lieutenants Breck Porter and L. L. Watts. All are deceased.

Mrs. Louise Maddox died in 1999. Officer Maddox' grandparents, father and sisters Betty Jean and Charlene are deceased. His mother, Mrs. Fred (Rissie) Maddox, passed away in 2002 at the age of ninety-seven. In 2002, Brother Bill Maddox was retired and living in the Woodlands. Fred "Trey" Maddox III was in San Antonio, the father of three sons and a daughter. Daughter Brenda was living in Santa Fe, Texas, the mother of two adult daughters and grandmother of two.

Both Trey and Brenda said the family experienced rough financial times growing up after their father's death, living off of Lyons Avenue and then in Denver Harbor. When their mother remarried, they wound up in Spring Branch, where both graduated from Spring Woods High School. Their mother had one son from a later marriage.

Bill Maddox said the Army didn't allow him to come home for his brother's funeral and that his mother attended the funeral on a stretcher. He also recalled that his father ran a service station on Baumann Road near their home and how police officers, particularly Forrest Turbeville, a close friend of Officer Fred Maddox, would drop by and visit their business.

Newspaper accounts indicated an outpouring of assistance from the Houston Police Officers Association, an automatic $200. The Fort Worth Police Officers Association made a donation. Also, Ned's Bar-B-Q on Irvington donated profits from three weekday sales. This tragedy took place just before the 100 Club was formed. Retired HPD Lieutenant Chester Massey said the tragic accident involving the Maddox family rushing to the hospital was a catalyst for changes made in the notification process. After this incident, every effort was made to make these types of notification in person. A police escort is provided when appropriate.

Also, it was suspected that Farrar was shooting at the white hat worn by police officers in those days. Class No. 11, which graduated later in 1954, was the last police academy class to be issued white hats for street duty.

42 & 43

Officer Jack Billy Beets
Badge #1214
and
Auxiliary Captain Charles Gougenheim Sr.
April 30, 1955

Drunken Substitute Bartender Guns Down Officer Beets, Auxiliary Capt. Gougenheim

Jack Billy Beets was thirty years old. He was a native of Rosser, a small town southeast of Dallas. At the age of eighteen in 1943, he joined the U. S. Navy, at the height of World War II.

Three years later, after the war ended, he left the Navy and began working as a locomotive fireman for the Southern Pacific Railroad in Houston. He had gotten married to Helen during the war and in 1947 became the proud father of a son, Billy Jack Beets.

When the railroad laid him off, Beets joined the Houston Police Department, entering Police Cadet Class No. 8 on January 7, 1952, graduating in April. After serving only a short term of his probationary period, he had an opportunity to return to work for Southern Pacific with a much better salary than what HPD was paying. So he resigned from the department in July 1952.

However, it was apparent that the Police Department and police work in general had the best of him and less than a year later, on April 1, 1953, he returned to duties as an officer.

Charles Gougenheim was fifty-three years old and a long-time employee of the Humble Refinery in Baytown. He was born in Lake Charles, Louisiana, and had been a resident of Houston since 1918. He had a wife, Evelyn, and a five-year-old son, Charles II, as well as a married daughter, Norma, and three grandchildren. His career at Humble had been successful. Too young for World War I and too old for World War II, he felt a commitment to serve his country and community in some manner. When the Houston Police Department initiated an auxiliary force near the beginning of the Second World War in 1941, Gougenheim joined immediately.

He served faithfully in this volunteer assignment and in 1947 he was wounded in the line of duty while at the Texas City explosions. He had been hit in the thigh by flying steel but recuperated and in 1954 was promoted to Captain of Company B of the Auxiliary Force. His brother Louis also had been involved with the volunteer organization and was Captain of Company A.

OFFICER JACK BILLY BEETS

On Saturday, April 30, 1955, Officer Beets was assigned to ride a one-man unit on the Evening Shift. Shortly before 6 p.m., Charles Gougenheim arrived at the Central Police Station and asked Sergeant C. R. Dietz if he could ride with Jack Beets, who was young enough to be Gougenheim's son. They had ridden together on previous occasions. The auxiliary captain enjoyed keeping company with Beets and obviously liked Officer Beets' style of police work. Dietz had Officer Beets report to the station and pick up his "partner" for the rest of the shift.

Mrs. Jessie Brown was the operator of a small tavern called Jack's Place at 3003 1/2 Nance Street in the Fifth Ward, just northeast of downtown. Earlier that day, Mrs. Brown was arrested for allowing a waitress to work at her place without a health card. She was assessed a $35 fine. In her absence, she had placed her brother, fifty-year-old Manuel Ben Smith, a cook at Rice University, to be in charge of Jack's. The more beer Smith drank that day, the more upset he became that his sister had been arrested.

With Officer Beets driving and Auxiliary Captain Gougenheim riding, the two officers were en route to their Fifth Ward beat when they observed two intoxicated males outside Jack's Place. They stopped to investigate and soon arrested the two males, placing them in back of their patrol car. Gougenheim remained outside with the suspects, while Officer Beets entered Jack's to determine if these suspects had become intoxicated on these premises. Beets was speaking to Mrs. Brown and inspecting her establishment's licenses when Manuel Ben Smith, intoxicated and enraged that the police were back, walked up behind Officer Beets.

Without warning, he shot the officer in the head.

Witnesses said Officer Beets never saw his assailant. After the first shot, he twisted around and was hit twice more – between the eyes and in the heart. The officer fell to the floor, mortally wounded.

Captain Gougenheim was standing next to the patrol car guarding the prisoners when he heard the shots. He left his prisoners and met Manuel Ben Smith just outside the front door of Jack's Place. A gun battle ensued, the cook firing the remaining three shots from his .38-caliber revolver at Gougenheim, who was firing the .45-caliber revolver he had unholstered as he rushed toward the door. Gougenheim shot five times at Smith, striking him twice in the chest. He took Smith's three rounds in the left chest, right shoulder and head.

A short two blocks away, Officers J. W. "Jean" Kindred and R. B. Brown were bogged down on a flat tire, awaiting the arrival of a tire truck. They had heard at least eleven shots and immediately ran in the direction of Jack's. What these two young officers found they would remember for the rest of their lives. Captain Gougenheim was dead alongside Smith, who was on the ground still clutching his pistol. Officer Kindred was quoted as saying, "I ran to the Negro on the sidewalk. He still had a gun in his hand and it was twitching. I stepped on his wrist, took the gun away and then I saw he was dead."

Inside they found Officer Jack Beets lying on the barroom floor, shot three times. An ambulance took him to Jefferson Davis Hospital, where he died within an hour.

The Auxiliary Force set up to supplement the HPD manpower shortage before WWII had remained a necessity due to severe budgetary restraints. Ironically, at the time of this tragic incident, Police Chief Jack Heard and several of his staff members were in Milwaukee, Wisconsin, to study its Police Department to find ways to deal with manpower problems. The facts they brought back caused a citizens' outcry after the deaths of Officer Beets and Captain Gougenheim. Milwaukee, with less than one half the square mileage of Houston, had nearly three times as many police officers. The usual political rhetoric ensued in the Bayou City and continued for several months. The end result: a lot of lip service, but nothing changed.

Officer Jack Beets died at the young age of thirty. He was survived by his wife Helen and their seven-year-old son Billy. Also surviving were his parents, Mr. and Mrs. Alvie Lee Beets Sr., of Corpus Christi, grandparents- Mr. and Mrs. G.P. Reid and Mr. John Beets, sisters-Mrs. Dorothy Garrett, Mrs. Burt Robinson, Miss Glenda Beets, Miss Kay Beets, Miss Linda Carol Beets, and Mrs. Edgar Ward, and three brothers-John Beets, Kenneth Beets, and Jerry Beets, as well as one half-brother, Alvie Lee Beets, Jr.

AUXILIARY CAPTAIN CHARLES GOUGENHEIM SR.

Funeral services were held on Tuesday, May 3, 1955, at 10am at the Bethel Baptist Church. Burial followed at the Kaufman Cemetery in Kaufman, Texas, near his hometown of Rosser. Pallbearers were Officers W.L. Kimble, E. Dominy, H.J. Timme, R.D. McClelland, K.A. McKelvey, and Sergeant J.A. Knigge. Pat H. Foley Funeral Home was in charge of arrangements. Graveside services were conducted by the Cade Rothwell Masonic Lodge, AF & AM.

The gravemarker in Kaufman for Officer Beets was located and reads as follows:

BELOVED HUSBAND & FATHER
JACK B. BEETS
FEB 14, 1925 - APRIL 30, 1955

This marker also has a Masonic emblem, Badge #1214, and a photo that has apparently withstood over 50 years without damage. A 100 Club marker has also been placed by Mary Sue and Nelson Zoch.

Auxiliary Captain Charles Gougenheim, an unpaid volunteer officer, was the first line-of-duty death for the fourteen-year-old Auxiliary Force. He was survived by his wife Evelyn, five-year-old son Charles II and married daughter Norma Haigh and her husband Donald, as well as three grandchildren-Donna Haigh, Clifford Haigh, and Earl Haigh. Other survivors were two sisters-Mrs. Adele Thompson and Mrs. Florence Rankin, and one brother, Auxiliary Captain Louis Gougenheim, whose daughter, Mary Frances Gougenheim, was a receptionist in the office of Mayor Roy Hofheinz.

Funeral services for Captain Gougenheim at 2pm on Tuesday, May 3, 1955 from the Christ Church Cathedral. Burial followed at South Park Cemetery in Pearland. Pallbearers were B.T. McKinney, J.M. Vickers, J.E. Kent, W.S. Whatley, J.O. Johnson, Bert Henry, Roy Flemming, and O.A. Carroll.

The gravemarker at South Park Cemetery reads as follows:

DADDY
CHARLES R. GOUGENHEIM
JUNE 23, 1901 - APRIL 30, 1955

Homicide Detectives Frank C. Crittenden and Chester B. Massey supervised the investigation. Detective Crittenden was later promoted to lieutenant and never left the Homicide Division, completing an illustrious career with his retirement in 1978. He died in 1992. Detective Massey also later promoted to lieutenant and served in Homicide, Robbery, Radio Patrol and the Criminal Intelligence Division. Also, for several years in the mid-1970's, he supervised a special unit of HPD named the Career Offenders Detail (COD Squad), which was a successful pilot program under a federal grant. He returned to the Homicide Division in the mid-1980's and retired from there in 1989 after having served more than thirty-nine years.

Massey said in an interview that this was without a doubt the toughest assignment of his career, seeing Captain Gougenheim dead at the scene and then Officer Beets dead at the morgue. Massey had worked with Officer Beets for a short time in the Vice Division and recalled how Captain Gougenheim still clutched in his left hand the two pocketknives he had recovered from the two "jakes" he left in the patrol car. The veteran lieutenant also recalled how the two prisoners remained in the unlocked patrol car and made no attempt to flee the scene. What was the 3000 block of Nance now sits in the middle of the East Freeway at Interstate 10 East.

R. B. Brown retired from HPD after having served

94

his entire career in Radio Patrol. He died in 1993. J. W. "Jean" Kindred promoted to detective in 1958 and was assigned to the Homicide Division. He retired in 1983 after having served twenty-five years in Homicide as a detective. He died in 1998.

Mrs. Jack (Helen) Beets died in 1995. In 1999, Jack Beets' son Bill lived in Spring Branch. He and his wife have one daughter. His mother later married another HPD officer, Marvin Seber. Bill Beets said he never had any contact with Charles Gougenheim Jr., even though this tragedy obviously had a tremendous affect on both of their lives. Beets had a scrapbook about his father, although he donated much of his memorabilia to the HPD museum. The parents, grandparents, three of Officer Beets' six sisters and three brothers died before 1999.

Mrs. Gougenheim died in 1997, having lived into her nineties. Charles Gougenheim II lived in Pearland in 1999 and also kept an extensive scrapbook about his father's death. He is a veteran of the U.S. Army, is married and the father of a daughter Jennifer, and a son, Charles III. Charles was forced to take a medical retirement but he apparently shared his father's sense of community service. He participated in the Brazoria County Sheriff's Department Citizen's Police Academy. Sister Norma Haigh had one more son, Robert, after her Dad's death. Norma lives in Katy. Her husband Donald Haigh is deceased. Captain Gougenheim's brother and sisters are also deceased.

44

Auxiliary Officer Frank Kellogg
November 30, 1955

Auxiliary Officer Frank Kellogg Dies from Wounds Suffered in Scuffle with a Drunken Wife Abuser

Auxiliary Police Officer Frank Leslie Kellogg was born in 1919 and was a native of South Haven, Michigan. By 1955 he had been a Houston resident for eighteen years and was employed by Shell Oil as a bus driver. Married with two children, he had been a City of Houston auxiliary officer for two and a half years. He lived with his family in a small home in the Pasadena area subdivision of Golden Acres. He was later described by then-Police Chief Jack Heard as "a good, dependable patrolman who knew his job."

On Friday night, October 14, 1955, Night Shift Patrol Officer J. W. "Jimmy" Vogler was assigned to East End Unit No. 172 along with Auxiliary Officer Frank L. Kellogg. Shortly after midnight, they received a call to 119 N. Bryan regarding an ex-husband breaking into his former wife's home and assaulting her. Upon arrival, Officers Vogler and Kellogg spoke to the complainant, Geraldine Taylor, and learned that the suspect, Reuben Carol Taylor, had beaten her severely and fled the scene.

Rueben Taylor administered previous beatings to Geraldine Taylor, many of them witnessed by the Taylor's three teen-aged children. The two officers searched the area. As they were driving back to the scene, one of the Taylor daughters stopped them and said that her dad had just run around the corner. The officers soon found Reuben hiding in some underbrush near Bryan and Canal. They arrested him, searched him and took him back to the scene.

When arrested, Reuben Taylor was very intoxicated and in an argumentative mood. After Geraldine Taylor and the children identified him, a verbal confrontation commenced between Officer Vogler and the suspect over the man's continuous abuse of his ex-wife. Taylor was not handcuffed. As the officers walked with him, he hit Vogler with his fist. When Officer Kellogg tried to grab Taylor, a struggle broke out. Taylor grabbed Kellogg's holster, ripped it off the Sam Browne belt and pulled the pistol out at the same time.

"Get the pistol!" Kellogg shouted at Vogler.

Vogler then heard gunfire and saw Reuben Taylor firing in the direction of the two officers. Vogler pulled his pistol and returned fire.

Vogler emptied his .45-caliber revolver, hitting Taylor numerous times, including once in the head. Taylor was dead at the scene on the day that coincidentally was his thirty-ninth birthday. The officer determined that Officer Kellogg was shot once in the chest. Liberty Ambulance was summoned to rush the wounded officer to St. Joseph's Hospital.

The morgue investigation revealed that Officer Vogler's bullets struck Reuben Taylor five times, all of which exited the suspect's body. Taylor had fired his .38 five times at Kellogg and Vogler, hitting Kellogg once in the right chest, two inches above the nipple and exiting at the top of his right shoulder. Vogler was not injured.

Once at St. Joseph, Officer Kellogg underwent immediate surgery for his chest wound and several more surgeries to correct other problems. On November 15, 1955, he was released. He was believed to be well on the road to recovery when, on November 29, he became ill at home and returned to St. Joseph's. He died on the morning of November 30, 1955, forty-six days after being wounded. He was thirty-six years old. Cause of death was ruled to be homicide due to the gunshot wound and the complications from the surgeries.

AUXILIARY OFFICER FRANK KELLOGG

Officer Kellogg was survived by his wife Mildred, seven-year-old daughter Ginger Sue and two-year-old son Robert. Also surviving him were his sister Marian Petersen and brothers Lawrence, John and Robert Kellogg.

Funeral services were arranged through the George H. Lewis and Sons Funeral Home. Kellogg was laid to rest in the Field of Honor section of Forest Park Cemetery, 6900 Lawndale. His gravesite is next to his and Mildred's first child, Sandra Lynn Kellogg. Sandra was born on August 4, 1947 and died five months later on January 6, 1948.

The officer's widow, Mildred, remarried. She died in 1998 and is buried in East Texas. In 2002, Ginger Sue and her husband of many years, James, resided in an upper Lake Livingston subdivision, Barrett's Landing. They had no children. Ginger Sue maintained her privacy over the tragic loss of her father so early in her life. Robert and his wife were living in Highlands, near Baytown, where he has been a heavy equipment operator for many years. Robert and his wife have two sons, a daughter and two grandchildren.

Only two years old at the time of his father's death, Robert remembered very little of his dad except that he loved motorcycles, owning several at the time of his death. Due to rough times financially, his mother was forced to sell the bikes. The son apparently inherited the love of motors from his father since he owned at least two of them himself.

All of Officer Frank "Buster" Kellogg's siblings – Lawrence, John, Robert, Marian and another sister, Adelaide (who was not originally listed as a survivor) – are deceased. Known to be alive in 2002 were nieces Joan Pioch, Mary Ann Petersen, Ellen Kay Van Devusse and Jo Ann Kellogg (last name unknown), as well as nephews William and Robert Kellogg.

This was a classic case of domestic violence in the mid-1950s. Reuben Taylor was apparently a heavy drinker and had been handled for molesting a minor, burglary, DWI and public drunkenness. He also had a long history of abusing his wife and children. Eventually, Mrs. Geraldine Taylor divorced him. After this divorce, he remarried for a short time and also physically abused his second wife. In addition, he kept returning to abuse Geraldine, who twice filed charges against him. Then in July 1955, she filed once again, only to have the charges dismissed for some reason on September 13. Geraldine also filed on him again three days later, but that warrant had never been served. It was outstanding at the time of this offense.

Homicide Detectives Frank Crittenden and Chester Massey investigated this case, the same team that earlier in the year had investigated the murders of Officer Jack Beets and Auxiliary Captain Charles Gougenheim. Both of these men were later promoted to Lieutenant and had lengthy successful careers with HPD. Crittenden passed away in 1992 and in 2006, Chester Massey is eighty-two years old and lives in Houston.

Patrol Supervisors at the scene were Lieutenant Otto Vahldiek and Sergeants L. P. Harrison and A. H. Moore. Vahldiek retired as an inspector and died in 1981. Harrison and Moore both retired as sergeants and are now deceased. Chief Jack Heard also made the scene. He later served with the Texas Department of Corrections as well as several terms as the sheriff of Harris County. He died in 2005. Officer Jimmy Vogler, a one-year veteran at the time of this offense, continued a long career with HPD. He retired in the early 1980s after serving most of his career in the Southwest-Beechnut Patrol Division. He died in 1985.

The Houston Police Auxiliary Force began in 1941 when the World War II military buildup left a shortage of men to keep the peace on the home front. After the loss of both Officer Frank Kellogg and Auxiliary Captain Gougenheim in 1955, the city of Houston, likely facing mounting civil liability issues, disbanded the organization in early 1956.

The grave of Auxiliary Officer Kellogg is marked

with a monument with the name KELLOGG as well as with a foot marker which reads:

FATHER
FRANK LESLIE
1919 - 1955

45

Officer Robert Joseph Schultea
Badge #1341
Aug. 24, 1956

Percy Foreman Gets Bar Maven Not Guilty Verdict in Cold-blooded Schultea Shooting

Robert Joseph Schultea was born on December 3, 1927 in McAllen in the Rio Grande Valley. His family moved to Houston in his early years and he attended Memorial Elementary, George Washington Junior High and Sam Houston High School. He served nearly two years in the United States Marine Corps. Schultea joined the Houston Police Department in April 1954, graduating from Police Cadet Class No. 11 on July 20. He was assigned to Radio Patrol and later to the Vice Division.

On Friday night, August 24, 1956, Vice Officers H. L. "Lamar" Kimble and R. J. "Bobby Joe" Schultea received a complaint from a citizen who stated that he had been ejected from Mack's Inn at 4315 Navigation on the east side. He further indicated that he had been cheated in several games of shuffleboard and after questioning the scorekeeping of the female proprietor, her husband physically ejected him.

After receiving this information, the two plainclothes officers took the citizen to Mack's Inn. The citizen pointed out to them Lillian Eggleston (White Female, 39) as the person who cheated him in the shuffleboard gambling incident. As the officers spoke to her, her intoxicated husband injected himself into the conversation. The officers identified themselves to Marvin Eggleston (White Male, 37). Marvin, described by the Houston Press as "a 6-foot-3, 240-pound brawny truck driver," was told that the place would be closed up for the night. Marvin acknowledged the officers' presence and authority by slapping the ID out of Officer Schultea's hand.

Kimble and Schultea then grabbed Marvin to arrest him for Public Intoxication and Assault. They were able to get one handcuff on this monstrous "tushhog" and, as they struggled to control Marvin, Kimble heard several gunshots and saw Schultea fall to the floor. Kimble saw Lillian behind the bar with a pistol in her hand. Lillian ducked behind the bar as he returned fire.

OFFICER ROBERT JOSEPH SCHULTEA

Kimble's pistol jammed and, after taking cover behind the jukebox to correct the problem, he emptied his pistol in Lillian's direction. He saw Schultea, mortally wounded and with pistol drawn, crawling in the direction of his assailant. Schultea, having been shot in the back, had collapsed on the barroom floor.

Kimble managed to call for help and then grabbed Schultea's weapon from the floor and confronted Lillian, hiding behind the bar, and arrested her.

An ambulance rushed Officer Schultea to Jeff Davis Hospital, but he died two hours later at the age of only twenty-eight. Lillian, described by the Houston

97

Press as a "six-foot, 200-pound barmaid" and an "auburn-tressed Amazon," was charged with Murder. Marvin was charged with drunkenness, disturbing the peace and aggravated assault on a police officer.

Officer Schultea was survived by his wife, Mrs. Jimmie Schultea, six-year-old son Patrick and his parents, Mr. and Mrs. D. D. Schultea. Also surviving were his brothers Weldon, Carl, Michael and Billy, and one sister, Marie.

Funeral services were held at 10 a.m. Monday, August 27, 1956, at the Saint Theresa Catholic Church. Burial followed at Resthaven Cemetery.

Three weeks after Officer Schultea's murder, Mrs. Jimmie Schultea and brother Weldon J. Schultea began training in Police Cadet Class No. 15. Having applied previously for this new career, both were more determined than ever to continue. They graduated and became police officers just prior to the murder trial. Patrick Schultea pinned the badge on for his mother at the swearing-in ceremony.

While the nightmare of their tragic loss was just beginning for the Schultea family and friends, a new ordeal began in the next step in the criminal justice process. Famed defense attorney Percy Foreman surfaced as Lillian Eggleston's attorney. The case was set for trial in the Criminal District Court of Judge A. C. Winborn, a former Harris County district attorney. Assistant District Attorneys Ben Woodall and Neil McKay, both of whom were experienced prosecutors who later became judges, prosecuted the case.

The trial began in February 1957, less than six months after the offense. Percy Foreman worked the courtroom magic that made him famous as one of the most successful criminal defense attorneys in Houston history. For whatever reason, much to the objections of the prosecution, Judge Winborn allowed a number of questionable defense maneuvers that harmed the prosecution.

The judge allowed a cap pistol to be fired in open court. He also permitted a plaster of Paris skull to be struck with a pistol in the presence of the jury in an attempt to demonstrate that the officers were using more force than necessary to arrest this giant of a man and to show that Lillian Eggleston had the right to use deadly force to "protect her husband."

Judge Winborn was reluctant to rule against the defense on anything. However, he did admonish Foreman for making some sarcastic remarks in front of the jury. The judge quickly instructed jurors to disregard the remarks. Foreman then mockingly said in open court, "I'll ask the jury to disregard the court's remarks." Winborn overruled Foreman even though much stronger action was warranted after openly insulting judicial authority.

Officer Schultea was the casualty of the shooting at Mack's Inn. In the courtroom, however, truth and justice became the next casualty throughout the entire trial.

How could the owners of a small Navigation Boulevard bar afford an attorney of Foreman's notoriety? Another point to ponder: How did then-Lt. Gov. Ben Ramsey come to be on the list of defense character witnesses for Mrs. Eggleston?

Judge Winborn described the charge to the jury after both sides rested their cases as the most complicated he had seen as a judge or during his four terms as district attorney. On Thursday, February 14, the twelve-man jury returned a verdict of not guilty on the woman the judge allowed Percy Foreman to refer to in open court as "the sweet little lady who runs a tea shop."

Newspaper headlines the following day declared "Eggleston Trial Acquittal Considered Legal Classic." She walked free to leave the Schultea family, Lamar Kimble and the entire Houston Police Department in a state of shock.

In the year 2000, Mrs. Schultea was remarried and lived in the Houston area. She retired from HPD in 1980 after serving most of her career in the Juvenile Division Sex Crimes Detail. Son Patrick lived in North Carolina and worked in the private sector after having retired from the United States Navy as a lieutenant commander.

Schultea's brother Weldon served most of his career in the Traffic Bureau, retired from HPD in 1982 and lived in Bryan until he passed away in 2005. Lamar Kimble made detective, worked in Burglary and Theft and retired from HPD in 1977. He later worked in the oil industry and retired in Comfort, Texas. Brother Mike was a sergeant with the Harris County Sheriff's Department. Brothers Carl and Billy, as well as sister Ruth Marie, all lived and worked in the Houston area. Mr. and Mrs. D. D. Schultea are deceased.

Although Officer Bobby Joe Schultea's promising career was cut short, the Schultea name in law enforcement lives on. Bobby Joe's cousins, brothers Vollie and Joe, joined HPD in Class Nos. 13 and 14. Joe graduated a week before Bobby Joe was murdered. Jimmie and Weldon followed in Class No. 15. Vollie retired from HPD and also retired from a second career with Harris County Constable Precinct 5. Vollie's son, Vollie Jr., also served with the constable of Precinct 5 after his HFD career. Joe left HPD early to spend a career as police chief of Hedwig Village. He came back to the department as a civilian in HPD Planning and Research. Joe's son, Joe, Jr., retired from the Harris County Sheriff's Department but went on to work there in a reserve capacity. Another of Joe's sons, James, is with HPD, assigned as a Robbery sergeant. Jim was shot and seriously wounded in the line of duty in 1986.

Homicide Detectives Frank Crittenden and Neal Todd investigated the case. Both later made lieutenant. Todd left prior to his retirement and is deceased. Crittenden retired in 1978 and died in 1992.

Whatever became of Lillian and Marvin Eggleston? As strange as the trial was, equally as strange was the fact that no record of either exists to this day. They are probably deceased, as they would both be in their early eighties after the turn of the new century. A 1964 newspaper article mentioned that the sheriff's department questioned Mrs. Eggleston regarding a barroom brawl in which she stabbed her husband. He recovered. She was last known to be leaving town for Beaumont. The northwest corner of Navigation and North Jenkins is a vacant lot.

The original marker for Officer Schultea read:

BOB SCHULTEA
DEC 3, 1928 - AUG 25, 1956

A 100 CLUB marker has also been placed to honor this fallen hero.

46

Officer Noel Ray Miller
Badge #1336
June 5, 1958

Drug Dealer in Closet with Gun Shoots, Kills Noel Ray Miller in Early War on Drugs Battle

Noel Ray Miller was born in Trenton on March 30, 1930. He attended school there, graduating from Trenton High School. He served his country in the United States Army for two years, receiving an Honorable Discharge in February 1953. After working a short time for Humble Oil, he joined the Houston Police Department through Police Cadet Class No. 11 on April 20, 1954, graduating on July 19.

On the night of Wednesday, June 4, 1958, officers in the City of West University arrested an intoxicated male who was found to be in possession of ten marijuana cigarettes. When questioned about the source of the illegal substance, the suspect implicated an individual who worked as a shoeshine man in the West U. area.

This information was turned over to Harris County Sheriff's Department Investigators L. E. Shipley and J. T. Stephenson. They joined Department of Public Safety Narcotic Agent E. J. Stutts to develop this information to the extent that on Thursday, June 5, 1958, officers had a search warrant for a house at 2813 Canfield in Houston's Third Ward. Additionally, George Moses (African American Male, 28) was identified as the suspect who was selling marijuana from the Canfield address. As this location was in the City of Houston, these investigators requested assistance from the Houston Police Department Narcotics Division in the execution of the warrant.

OFFICER NOEL RAY MILLER

Officer Noel R. Miller worked Radio Patrol until July 1955, at which time he voluntarily transferred to the Narcotics Division for a plainclothes assignment. On Thursday night, June 5, 1958, Miller and his partner, Officer A. J. Burke, were assigned to assist the county and state officers in the execution of the Canfield search warrant. It was prearranged that Agent Stutts and Officer Miller would take the front door and Officer Burke, along with Investigators Shipley and Stephenson, would cover the sides and rear of this location.

Upon arriving at 2813 Canfield on this very warm early summer evening, officers observed an individual fitting George Moses' description on the front porch. When Moses saw the officers getting out of their vehicles, he ran inside, locking the screen door. Stutts and Miller identified themselves as police officers and when they confronted the locked screen door, Officer Miller pulled it open, breaking the door latch.

Miller continued to follow Moses, who retreated into a closet where he had stashed a gun. Moses was inside the closet, armed with a .32-caliber semiautomatic pistol.

MR. AND MRS. NOEL RAY MILLER

When Officer Miller neared the partially open closet door, Moses fired twice. One shot struck the officer in his abdomen, puncturing the aorta, the large artery leading from the heart. Critically wounded, Miller returned fire, shooting once and striking the door jamb. He then fell to the floor. The other law officers arrested Moses without further incident. But the damage was done. South End Ambulance picked up Officer Miller and rushed him to Jeff Davis Hospital, arriving at 8:46 p.m.

An all-night effort then began to save the officer's life. Scores of officers from HPD and various other law enforcement agencies rushed to the hospital to offer their blood. Additionally, more than one hundred citizens from all walks of life arrived for the same purpose. Doctors administered thirty-five pints of blood by transfusion during a twelve-hour battle for his life. During the night, doctors reported that Officer Miller died four times; each time they massaged his heart back to life.

Despite the efforts of the surgeons and the all-night prayer vigil at the hospital, there was no good news. Officer Noel Ray Miller died at 8:45 a.m. Friday, June 6, 1958. He was twenty-eight years old.

He was survived by his wife, Carolyn Wondrak Miller, three-year-old daughter Janet Miller and one-year-old son Mike Miller. Also surviving were his parents, Mr. and Mrs. N. C. Miller and brothers Earl and Larry, all of Leonard, Texas. He also left behind four sisters, Tini Earwood, Joy Mammen, JoAnn Hayes and Helen Lassiter. Wife Carolyn's brother and Miller's long-time friend Houston Police Officer George P. Wondrak and his wife Rachel were also left to mourn his senseless death.

Funeral services were held at the Earthman Chapel at 2420 Fannin on Monday, June 9, 1958, at 10:30 a.m. Burial followed at the Garden of Gethsemane in Forest Park Lawndale. Pallbearers were A. J. Burke, Mike Chavez, R. D. Smith, J. D. Conley, E. J. Stutts, R. R. Boone, Buddy Hendricks and Nate Durham.

Homicide immediately began the capital murder investigation. Veteran Homicide Detectives Robert O. "Lippy" Biggs and Allen E. Rockwell were in the downtown area when the call for assistance went out on the air. Upon their arrival, the smell of gunpowder was still in the hot, musty air of this small "shotgun" house. Detective Lloyd Barrett assisted with scene photos and Criminal Investigator Gobel E. Rowell saw to the evidence collection.

The state charged George Moses, an ex-convict, with capital murder. On Friday, September 19, 1958, after a week-long trial, a jury in Judge Langston King's criminal district court brought in a guilty verdict. This jury, which according to newspaper accounts included a member of Moses' own race, assessed a sentence of death in the electric chair the next day, a mere 107 days after the offense. This sentence was properly carried out on August 12, 1960, witnessed by thirteen officers from HPD, DPS and the Harris County S.O.

Carolyn Miller remarried several years after Noel's death. She gave birth to four more children from that marriage. In 2001, she and her second husband of more than forty years lived in southeast Houston. Unfortunately, she contracted Gehrig's Disease and passed away in 2003. Daughter Janet married Wayne Bryant and they raised two children in Pearland, Shannon and Chad. Mike and his wife Missy also lived in Pearland, where they raised their two daughters, Michelle and Melissa. Shannon Bryant McCharen and her husband are the parents of Robert McCharen and Macy McCharen.

Noel's parents, his brother Larry and his sister Tini Earwood are deceased. His brother-in-law, Officer George Wondrak, also was his best friend. Noel and George attended Catholic schools together and joined the military service together prior to Noel marrying George's sister Carolyn. George, who graduated from Police Cadet Class No. 10 in early 1954, was himself involved in a shootout with an armed hijacker aboard a Rapid Transit Bus. A number of shots were fired with no injuries. George retired from HPD in 1976 after twenty-two years of service. He died in 1983. Friends in life, Noel and George are buried fifteen feet apart at Forest Park Lawndale. In 2001, George's widow Rachel resided in Shepherd, Texas.

As for the investigators, R. O. Biggs retired from HPD in 1966. He worked for a number of years with the Harris County D.A. as an investigator. He retired from there also and died in 1995. Allen Rockwell transferred from Homicide to Burglary and Theft in 1967. As a B&T Detective, he, Officer R. E. Carver and Lieutenant Leo Michna were shot in downtown Houston in 1969 in an incident with an armed shoplifter. All three recovered from their wounds. Rockwell retired from HPD and died in 1979. A. J. Burke retired from HPD in 1978 after working Solo Motorcycles for a number of years. He was active for a number of years in the Houston Police Officers Association, serving as president for a number of years. He died in 2005.

MR. AND MRS. NOEL RAY MILLER ON THEIR WEDDING DAY, AUGUST, 1954

County Officers Shipley and Stephenson are both deceased. DPS Officer Stutts resigned from the state in 1969 and later retired from the Harris County Constable Precinct 2 Office. He died in 1993. Detective Lloyd Barrett, who assisted Biggs and Rockwell in this investigation, retired from HPD and died in 1994. Officer G. E. Rowell later promoted to sergeant, lieutenant, and retired as a captain of the Traffic Division in 1983. He died in 1990.

Officer Miller was posthumously awarded the True Detective Public Service Award. The public contributed $4,000 to a trust fund for his wife and children. The war on drugs continued and even if it is ever won, it will not have been worth the loss of a man like Noel Ray Miller – a husband, father, brother, son, fellow officer.

The address of 2813 Canfield is a vacant lot, not of much less value than it was in June 1958.

Officer Miller's grave was marked as follows:
HUSBAND AND FATHER
NOEL RAY MILLER
MAR 30, 1930 - JUNE 6, 1958

A 100 Club LINE OF DUTY MARKER now marks this gravesite.

47

Officer Claude Emmett Branon

Badge #1160
March 20, 1959

Mystery Still Surrounds the Motorcycle Death of HPD Officer Claude E. Branon

Claude Emmett Branon was born in Fort Worth on November 18, 1926. He attended elementary school and junior high school in this Texas place known as "Cowtown" prior to his family's move to Houston. Once in the Bayou City, he attended Jackson Junior High School and graduated from San Jacinto High School in 1945. He proudly served his country in the United States Marine Corps for three years and nine months from February 1948 until receiving an Honorable Discharge in November 1951. A veteran of the Korean War, he was a Purple Heart recipient. He had suffered shrapnel wounds to the arms and back while in combat.

Branon joined the Houston Police Department in Police Cadet Class No. 8, which began training on January

7, 1952 and graduated on April 16. He wore Badge No. 1160. It is uncertain where his original assignment was, but it is known that he transferred to the Solo Motorcycle Detail on July 1, 1955 and was working in that capacity at the time of his injury.

OFFICER CLAUDE EMMETT BRANON

On Tuesday, January 13, 1959, at about 9 p.m., Officer Branon was working the Evening Shift in Solos along with his partner, Officer R. D. "Red" Smith. They were monitoring traffic in the 8700 block of the Gulf Freeway. As they were parked and observed feeder road traffic, Branon spotted a speeding vehicle. He took off in pursuit of this vehicle while Officer Smith remained at their original location.

What happened at this point is not exactly known and can only be speculated from the accounts of Officer Smith and the physical evidence discovered later.

When Officer Smith found Officer Branon, he was in a ditch with his wrecked motorcycle nearby. He was seriously injured and was rushed to St. Joseph's Hospital with broken ribs and possible back and head injuries, as well as some internal damage. Most importantly, he was paralyzed from the waist down and bruised throughout his body. He was not able to talk about the accident. Initial hospital diagnosis found that the paralysis was due to a crushed back and spinal cord injuries.

Patrol Officers Johnny E. Neely and Lee Wayne Redden received the call to protect the accident scene and to control traffic. The accident investigators assigned to the investigation observed what appeared to be foreign paint particles on Officer Branon's cycle and at some point following this, the Hit and Run Detail was called in to take charge of the investigation under the supervision of Sergeant Walter H. Rankin.

Officer Branon, although faced with the future of being paralyzed, improved over the next several months. Numerous Solo officers and other officers from throughout the department visited him or sat with him during his hospital confinement. Retired Lieutenant Johnny Neely recalled a conversation that happened during one of his visits with Officer Branon. While he was resigned to his probable future disability, he had a fairly good outlook on the situation and was very hopeful that he could remain an officer and possibly work in the Dispatcher's Office.

However, on Friday, March 20, 1959, at 8 a.m., sixty-six days after the accident, Officer Branon suddenly died while still in St. Joseph's Hospital. This was totally unexpected to the family, the department and the medical staff that had provided around-the-clock treatment for him. An autopsy revealed that a blood clot from an injured leg had gone directly to his heart, instantaneously causing his death. He was only thirty-two years old.

Officer Branon was survived by his wife Betty, five-year-old daughter Linda Gail and his four-year-old son Claude Emmett Branon Jr. Also mourning his death were his mother, Mrs. Leota King, and his father, Al Branon, both of Houston. One sister, Mrs. William Magee Jr. of Eagle Pass, also survived him.

Funeral services were held on Monday, March 23, 1959, at 10 a.m. at the George H. Lewis and Sons Chapel at 400 McGowen with the Reverend W. C. Webb officiating. Branon was a member of the Almeda Methodist Church as well as the Temple Lodge No. 4 of the Ancient Free and Accepted Masons (AF & AM). His fellow lodge members participated in a graveside service at Forest Park Lawndale Cemetery.

The 100 Club of Greater Houston was in the first years of practicing its honorable service to the families of officers killed in the line of duty. In addition to their contributions, Wally Gee of the Police Cafeteria at 61 Riesner and Bill Heit of Foremost Dairies jointly began a drive to assist the Branon family. At least $6,000 was collected. In 1959 dollars, this was a tremendous help.

The investigation continued and the day after the accident police located a suspect and his vehicle containing specks of white paint similar to that on a police motorcycle. However, this evidence did not work out and the suspect had an alibi for the damage as well as for the location of his vehicle at the time of the accident. This information was verified and the suspect was eliminated.

During the course of Officer Branon's hospital stay, Hit and Run Investigator Paul S. Nix, who had previously been honored in 1956 by the 100 Club for his expertise in Hit and Run, was assigned to the case. Unfortunately, this was a situation with no witness and only minute paint particles which may or may not have been a factor in the accident. A number of similar leads were investigated but no witnesses or other suspect vehicles were ever matched to the scene evidence. Nix later noted that the investigation continued well after the officer's death. The investigation never determined if this was a simple motorcycle accident or one involving another vehicle, causing Officer Branon to lose control of his motor.

Betty Branon later remarried and raised her two children as well as her new husband's two sons. Her second husband died in 1996 after having been married to Betty for thirty years. In 2002, she resided in northwest Houston. Daughter Linda Gail was a special needs schoolteacher in a suburban Houston school district. Son Claude Jr. lived in the Woodlands and had four children who never had the chance to know their grandfather.

Solo Officer T. C. "Tom" Pickens broke in Officer Branon on Motorcycles when he joined that detail in 1955. They were not only partners but also good friends. Officer Pickens left HPD in 1957 just prior to being promoted to sergeant and went to the Village Police Department, where he served as their chief of police until 1968. Following that job, he went to work for the Harris County Sheriff's Department, where he retired as a major in 1989. In 2002, he lived in Northwest Houston and remained close friends with Paul Nix.

Officer R. D. "Red" Smith left HPD at some point thereafter and his whereabouts were unknown. While this is not verified, this is believed to be the same R.D. (Red) Smith that was a close acquaintance of Officer Noel Miller, who had been killed in a Narcotics raid in 1958. The Hit and Run supervisor, Sergeant Walter H. Rankin, also left HPD to serve a number of years as the elected Harris County Constable of Precinct 1. He retired from that post in 1991 and lived in Northwest Houston.

Paul Nix promoted to detective in late 1959. After working Burglary and Theft for a short time, he found his investigative career niche in the Homicide Division. Nix was an outstanding investigator and during his career he worked on a number of high-profile homicides. Among them were the whodunit murders of Officer L. L. Sander (1967) and Officer Leon Griggs (1970). He retired from HPD in 1973 and moved to his hometown of Mineola in East Texas after doing private investigative work in Houston for several years. He died in 2006.

Of the first officers on the scene, Officer Johnny E. Neely promoted to detective and worked in the Auto Theft Division. He later made lieutenant and worked in both the Accident Division and the Radio Patrol Substation at Clear Lake. He retired in 1991 with more than thirty-seven years of service. Officer Lee Wayne Redden promoted to sergeant and was assigned to the Point Control Division for a number of years. He retired in 1982 and later died.

Officer Claude Emmett Branon served his country honorably in a time of war and survived, having suffered from wounds. He served the citizens of Houston for nearly seven years before losing his life.

The original marker at Officer Branon's grave has been replaced with the 100 Club marker. The original had the Masonic emblem and:

CLAUDE E. BRANON
NOV 18, 1926 - MAR 20, 1959

48

Officer John Wesley Suttle
Badge #1494
August 23, 1959

Drunken Freeway Driver Strikes and Kills Jack Suttle, an Officer for Just 13 Months

John Wesley Suttle was born on June 6, 1935 in Houston and grew up in his hometown, graduating from Jeff Davis High School. He went on to study at the Southwestern Bible Institute in the North Central Texas town of Waxahachie. He then served his country honorably for nearly four years in the United States Navy from February 1954 to December 1957. After the service, he was attending South Texas Junior College in Houston when he applied to become a cadet in the Houston Police Department. He entered Class No. 18 on April 28, 1958 and graduated on July 29, 1958. He wore Badge No. 1494. His first assignment was Night Shift in the Radio Patrol Bureau.

On Saturday night, August 22, 1959, Houston Police Officers John Wesley "Jack" Suttle and Kenneth G. Smelley were regular partners riding together, working the 10 p.m. to 6 a.m. shift. At approximately 1:40 a.m. on Sunday morning, August 23, they were cruising inbound in the 4800 block of the Gulf Freeway on the downside of the Lombardy overpass when they came upon an accident. A vehicle had struck the center guardrail and spun around, becoming disabled and blocking several lanes of the freeway.

Both officers got out of their vehicle and started to direct new traffic away from this hazard. They determined that one of the occupants of the disabled vehicle was injured. An ambulance was summoned. Officer Smelley went up onto the freeway to warn oncoming traffic approaching the scene from over the overpass, using his flashlight and successfully warning most of the vehicles.

Officer Suttle also was directing traffic when a vehicle came in at a high rate of speed, failing to heed officer's directions or the warning lights. This vehicle, driven by Forrest Sten Wychopin (White Male, 22) struck Officer Suttle, throwing him into the previously wrecked vehicle and onto the concrete. An ambulance rushed him to nearby St. Joseph's Hospital, where emergency room doctors amputated both of his legs in a dramatic effort to save his life. The collision also caused other massive injuries.

JOHN WESLEY SUTTLE

However, these life-saving efforts went in vain. The officer died shortly thereafter. He was only twenty-four years old.

His wife, Loy Nell Suttle, and a sixteen-month-old son, John Wesley Suttle Jr., survived the young officer. Also mourning his death were his parents, Mr. and Mrs. Oscar William Suttle, sister Mrs. Annette Anderson, and two brothers, Minor Dwayne Suttle and Carl R. "Duck" Suttle. All of these family members resided in Houston.

Funeral services were held at 10 a.m. on Tuesday, August 25, 1959, at the Pat H. Foley Funeral Home on Tidwell Road. The Reverend O. L. Davidson of the Sunnyland Assembly of God Church delivered the eulogy. Burial followed at the Brookside Cemetery at Eastex Freeway and Lauder Road.

JOHN WESLEY SUTTLE, U.S. NAVY, TAIWAN, 1956

Newspaper accounts described this tragic incident in detail in the Monday morning editions. This same article made mention of another HPD officer seriously injured later that same workday – actually on Sunday night. Motorcycle Officer J. C. Ashby was riding his motor in the 1700 block of Holcombe Boulevard when a vehicle coming out from a side street struck him.

The collision threw Officer Ashby seventeen feet off his motorcycle. Fortunately, several doctors from the nearby Veterans Administration Hospital were passing by and stopped to render emergency aid. An ambulance transported Officer Ashby to a nearby hospital where a tracheotomy was performed on him in order to keep him from choking. Fortunately, he survived his injuries.

Ashby was later instrumental with others in

forming the first HPD Dive Team. He retired in 1977 while assigned to the HPD Bomb Squad. He is an active member of the Houston Police Retired Officers Association, writing travel articles for the group's bimonthly newspaper and is also the webmaster for the HPROA website.

Forrest Sten Wychopin told investigators that he had been drinking beer in a Pasadena lounge from 9:30 p.m. Saturday night until closing time at 1 a.m. Sunday. He was charged with negligent homicide in the death of Officer Suttle. On February 4, 1960, he was convicted or pled guilty to the charge and assessed a fine of $2,000 plus court costs. This was believed to be his only brush with the law.

words, their relationship started with a shared sorrow that eventually grew into a genuine love for each other. Together, they raised John Jr. to be a good citizen and family man.

Officer Smelley was promoted to detective in 1965 and worked in both Auto Theft and Burglary and Theft. He promoted to lieutenant in 1970 and worked in Radio Patrol and the Records Division, retiring from HPD in 1979. In 2002, Loy Nell and Kenneth, known to his family and friends as "Sam," made their home near Corrigan, just north of Livingston on U. S. Highway 59 where he began a new career.

LOYNELL, WES, AND JACK SUTTLE, AUGUST, 1959

WES SUTTLE AND KENNETH PAUL SUTTLE AT THE POLICE MEMORIAL

When a tragedy of this magnitude happens, the people who believe in a Higher Power are able to draw on an inner strength that provides them the means in which to cope with their loss. In the Suttle case, this means came in different ways to different people. Loy Nell Suttle was widowed at age twenty-one, the mother of a sixteen-month-old son. Over a year after the accident that claimed the life of this officer, his widow married her husband's partner, Officer Kenneth Smelley. In their

John Jr. married and is a father to a son, Paul, and a daughter, Kathryn. Oscar Suttle died in 1963 as did Mrs. Pattie Suttle in 1998. Their son, Officer John Wesley Suttle, is buried between them at Brookside. Another tragedy struck the Suttle family when the deceased officer's brother, Carl R. "Duck" Suttle, died suddenly of a heart attack at the young age of thirty-three. The other brother, Minor D. "Dwayne" Suttle, survived him, as did the only sister, Mrs. Annette Anderson.

Marker for Officer Suttle reads:

JOHN WESLEY SUTTLE
TEXAS, U.S. NAVY, RM 3
JUNE 6, 1935-AUG 23, 1959

49

Officer Gonzalo Q. Gonzalez
Badge #1405
February 28, 1960

Officer Gonzalo Q. Gonzalez Broadsided, Killed While on Way to Burglary Call with K-9 Partner

Gonzalo Quinones Gonzalez was born in Zauzua, Nuevo Leon, Mexico, on December 23, 1931. His family moved to Houston, Texas and then to San Antonio. He attended elementary school in San Antonio and also attended Edison Junior High School and went through vocational programs in San Antonio and at Milby High School in Houston. He was granted his United States citizenship on May 19, 1952. He proudly served his country honorably in the United States Marine Corps from April 1954 to April 1956. His service included a tour of duty in Korea.

Gonzalo Q. Gonzalez joined the Houston Police Department by way of HPD Cadet Class No. 17 on September 16, 1957. Upon completing the Academy in December, 1957, he was assigned to Night Shift Radio Patrol. He wore Badge No. 1405. In his short career with HPD, he also worked the Jail Division before returning to where he began. He volunteered for duty in the newly formed Canine Detail and was accepted.

On Saturday night, February 27, 1960, Officer Gonzalez was working his shift with his partner – that night and every night – his rust-colored Doberman Pincher named Clipper. Clipper had been in Officer Gonzalez' training and custody since January 1959. While on patrol at 12:35 on Sunday morning, the officer received a call to investigate a burglary at Levitz Jewelry at 510 Main. He drove quickly and quietly without emergency equipment in order to arrive at the location without warning the possible burglars. However, while passing through the intersection of Pease and Chenevert, his patrol car was struck broadside by a vehicle driven by Victor Irvin Bryant (White Male, 52).

The impact caused Officer Gonzalez to be thrown from his patrol car. He received serious head injuries as well as a deep laceration across his abdomen. He died while being transported to Jeff Davis Hospital. He was only twenty-eight. Bryant, uninjured, was charged with murder by auto before Justice of the Peace W. C. Ragan.

Officer G. Q. Gonzalez was survived by his wife, Irene, and three small children – seven-year-old Gonzalo Gonzalez Jr., five-year-old Karen Gonzalez and two-year-old Lisa Gonzalez. Also mourning his death were his parents, Mr. and Mrs. R. C. Gonzalez of Houston, and five siblings. They were one brother, Mario Gonzalez of San Antonio, and four sisters, Mrs. Carmen Samaniego, Mrs. Delia Cruz and Mrs. Emma de la Garza of Houston and Mrs. Eva Trevino of San Antonio.

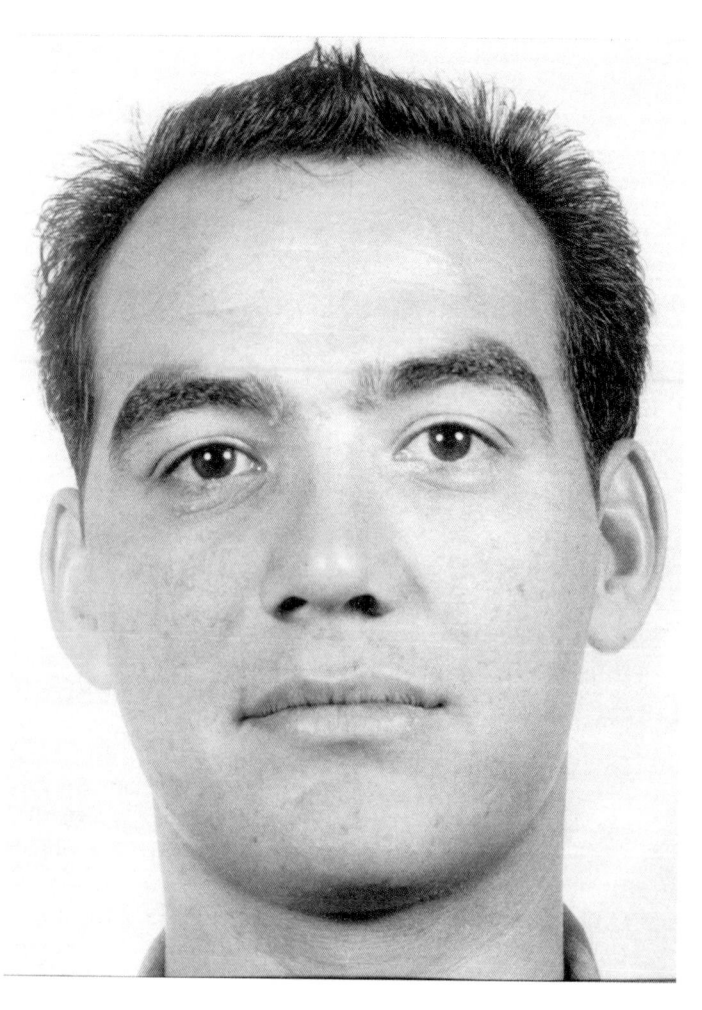

OFFICER GONZALO Q. GONZALEZ

Funeral services for Officer Gonzalez were held at the Earthman Funeral Chapel, 2420 Fannin, at 9:30 a.m. Tuesday, March 1, 1960. Burial followed in the Garden of Gethsemane Section of Forest Park Lawndale Cemetery, 6900 Lawndale.

After the accident happened and before the

arrival of other officers, Clipper, apparently scared and confused, wandered away from the accident scene. An intensive search was conducted for Clipper on Sunday but to no avail.

Newspaper accounts of the tragic accident included quotes from Harvey Richards, director of canine training for the Houston Police Department. He said it was his belief that Clipper would be docile and would not make any unprovoked attacks since he had been trained to obey his master's commands. However, he further stated that if Clipper had been injured, he might snap at anyone who attempted to touch him. Fortunately, on Tuesday morning, Clipper was found in the 600 block of Chenevert, just ten blocks north of the accident. His leash was entangled in weeds when he was spotted. He was dolefully subdued when Officer W. B. Folsam received a call from a beer distributor who spotted him while on his route.

A veterinarian summoned to examine Clipper found no injuries. Police Inspector Bill Burton said that Clipper would be boarded by the veterinarian until another officer could be selected to work with him. Further newspaper accounts brought up the question regarding K-9 officers traveling to emergency calls such as this one. K-9 cars were not equipped with sirens or emergency warning lights. Indications were that no policy change was needed but the Department's six K-9 officers were again warned to use extreme caution when answering emergency calls.

Accident Division Investigators M. J. "Joe" Chebret and H. L. Martin conducted the investigation. Bryant was apparently intoxicated since murder by auto charges were filed against him. Sergeant Chebret recalled that Bryant was a house painter and this was his ninth DWI. However, due to the lack of actual eyewitnesses to the accident, there was difficulty in placing him behind the wheel. As a result, Bryant got off very lightly, receiving a sentence of three days in jail and a $50 fine. According to Chebret, he also got credit for time served. Basically, he just "walked" after the court proceedings.

After living in California and Hawaii for a number of years, Irene and her second husband resided in Austin in 2003. Gonzalo Gonzalez Jr., known as "Gonzo," lived in Belton, the father of two sons, Kip and Carter James, and one daughter, Sarah. Gonzo is the grandfather of Kip's daughter Londyn. Karen lived in Hawaii in 2003, married with one daughter, Kaiani. Lisa lived in Austin, the mother of one daughter, Ashley.

Officer Gonzalez' father, Rodolfo Gonzalez, died in 1985. His mother, Eloisa Q. Gonzalez, died in 1989. They are interred next to their son, as is their oldest daughter, Carmen Samaniego, who died in 1998. Carmen had four children: Gilbert, Lionel (who died in 1988), Ricky and Eloisa. In 2003, Mario lived in Houston with three children, Mario, Jr., Giselle, and David. Delia lived in San Antonio, the mother of four, Tony, Tommy (deceased), Lorraine and Leticcia. The other two sisters were the twins, Emma and Eva. Emma lived in Deer Park with two children, Gail and David in 2003, while Eve was living in San Antonio, the mother of five, Gracie, Paul, Pete and twins Gerald and Geraldine.

Accident Investigator M. J. "Joe" Chebret retired as a Patrol sergeant in 1980 and lived on Lake Livingston. Officer Henry L. Martin resigned from HPD and took up a career as a gunsmith.

Retired HPD Sergeant Paul W. "Daddy Rabbit" Beeman, pictured in the 1974 HPD photo directory as one of the K-9 officers at that time of Gonzalez' death, was in Cadet Class No. 17 with Gonzalez. They both started out as K-9 Officers together. Beeman remembered him well and considered him a close, personal friend. Gonzo Jr. got to know Beeman and recalled being only six years old when he was at several K-9 training sessions with his dad. Paul retired from the Jail Division as a sergeant in 1983 and resided near Cold Spring in 2003.

Other HPD Officers who experienced this early K-9 training with Officer Gonzalez and Clipper were Paul Beeman and Satan, V. C. "Very Cautious" Holiday and Kurt, R. L. Hamilton and Shane, P. A. Leuders and Schnapps, R. D. Whitcomb and Duke and C. E. Perkins (unknown partner name).

Retired HPD Detective Doug Bostock also had fond memories of Officer Gonzalez, whom he came to know when he was a civilian clerk in the Records Division. Bostock said that he had on several occasions requested and received permission from his supervisor and Patrol supervisors to ride with Gonzales. These ride-a-long experiences aroused Bostock's interest in becoming a law enforcement officer. He worked Radio Patrol and the Jail for many years and promoted to detective, retiring from the Homicide Division. After many years with the Harris County District Attorney's Office, Doug retired and was living in Houston in 2003.

Officer Gonzalez was the third HPD officer to lose his life in a traffic accident within a year, following Claude Branon in March 1959 and John Suttle in August 1959. After Gonzalez' death, 100 Club President Leopold Meyer said Officer Gonzalez would probably be the first officer in whose name $1,000 in benefits would be paid from the newly formed club. His death also prompted the Houston Police Officer's Association (later HPOU) to form a committee to aid and console the family of an officer who loses his life in the line of duty.

When this gravesite was located, it was noticed that a very new marker had been placed recently. It read as follows:

BELOVED FATHER AND SON
GONZALO Q. BONZALEZ
DEC 23, 1931 - FEB 28, 1960
BADGE EMBLEM #1405

50

Officer James Thomas Walker
Badge #362
March 8, 1963

Solo Officer James Thomas Walker Dies Of Heart Attack in '63 Freeway Accident

James Thomas Walker was born on January 18, 1922, in Glen Flora, Wharton County, Texas. He was raised in that area, his father serving as a guard in the Texas prison system in Sugar Land. He served his country honorably in the United States Army Air Force. For a time he was a military policeman. After returning from his service during World War II he worked as a longshoreman. He began his career with the Houston Police Department on January 12, 1948, entering Police Cadet Class No. 1 and graduating on April 16, 1948. He served almost his entire career with HPD on some type of motorized vehicle, beginning on a scooter, then to three-wheelers and finally on a two-wheel solo motorcycle. He wore Badge No. 362.

On Friday morning, March 8, 1963, Officer Walker was working the 7 a.m. to 3 p.m. shift out of the Solo Motorcycle Detail. He was on the newly opened North Freeway traffic patrol assignment at approximately 8:15 a.m. and was outbound on the service road in the 6100 block. Witnesses reported that while he was driving in the left lane, he sped up and apparently observed a speeding vehicle on the freeway.

Walker accelerated in order to get on the freeway and, unfortunately, at the same time a vehicle driven by a private citizen was moving over from the right lane to the left lane, also to gain access to the freeway entry ramp.

The officer was unable to slow down and struck the rear of this vehicle. His motorcycle went down and he suffered injuries to his face and knees. The first officers on the scene later stated that he did not appear to be seriously injured. He was rushed immediately to St. Joseph's Hospital downtown for treatment. While being treated, he suddenly died at 9:15 a.m. He was forty-one years old.

It was believed at the time that he had also suffered a fractured neck. After an autopsy, A. C. Martindale, a Harris County Medical Examiner's investigator, said that the officer's injuries were superficial, such as a deep cut over the right eye and abrasions to the right side of the face and bruised ribs. The autopsy revealed that Officer Walker actually died of a coronary thrombosis – a heart attack.

OFFICER JAMES THOMAS WALKER

HPD Accident Investigator Louis M. Elliott investigated the accident. He said that the driver of the other vehicle had entered the service road from a side street and then immediately moved over into the left lane to enter the freeway. No charges were filed against the citizen.

Officer Walker was survived by his wife, Ethel Mae Walker of Houston, and five children. The four daughters were Mrs. Barbara Sullivan, Mrs. Jean Ann Montgomery, fourteen-year-old Tommye Lee Walker and twelve-year-old Jamye Lynn Walker. One son survived his father, eight-year-old James Thomas Walker Jr. Also mourning his death were four sisters, Maggie Walker of Galveston, Mrs. Irene Bradberry of Clute, and Claudia Walker and Mrs. Inez Ross, both of Houston.

Officer Walker was a member of Holy Trinity Lutheran Church and the Reagan Lodge No. 1037 of the Ancient Free and Accepted Masons, Scottish Rite Bodies, Arabia Temple Shrine. Funeral services were held on Monday, March 11, 1963, at 11:30 a.m. at the Heights Funeral Chapel on Heights Boulevard, with the Reverend Harold G. Deal officiating. Burial was at Forest Park Lawndale Cemetery with graveside services under the auspices of Reagan Lodge No. 1037 of the AF and AM.

Mrs. Ethel Walker was left with a large family to depend on her when she lost her husband so suddenly. She continued living in their home in Aldine, where the three younger children went to school. She never remarried and relocated to Florida by 2003. Barbara Sullivan, the oldest daughter, is deceased. She was the mother of one son, David, who fathered three children. In 2003, daughter Jean Ann Moreland and husband Tony lived in Houston and had three daughters. Kelly, the oldest, was born five months after Officer Walker was killed. The other two daughters were Kathy and Tiffany. The Morelands also had one son, John. Jean Ann was the grandmother of three.

In 2003, the third daughter, Tommye, who resided in Arkansas with her husband Mike, was the mother of five children. They are Tammye, Mathew (a U. S. Navy investigation team member in Iraq and also a graduate of a California Police Academy), Tracy, Michael, and Timmy. Tommye had two grandchildren. The next daughter, Jamye, lived in Conroe with her husband Rick. Jamye was a civilian employee of the Texas Department of Public Safety. She had two daughters, Lindsay and Corey.

Officer Walker's only son, James Thomas Walker, Jr., attended the University of Houston and worked in the oil industry. He and his wife Loretta lived in the Cypress area and parented three sons, James T. III, Cody and Dylan. Officer Walker and his wife had fifteen grandchildren and eight great grandchildren, none of whom he was fortunate enough to see and treasure.

Just as could happen today, it took just a split second for an accident like this one to take the life of a fine police officer and devoted family man. Even though the cause of death was not from the accident, police officers know that he very likely would not have had that heart attack had it not been for the stress incurred during the accident and the necessary medical procedures that followed.

Gravemarker for Officer Walker reads:
JAMES THOMAS WALKER
TEXAS PFC 2528 BASE UNIT AAF
WORLD WAR II
JAN 18, 1922-MARCH 8, 1963

51

Sergeant Charles R. McDaniel
August 4, 1963

Sgt. Charles R. McDaniel Killed on His Way Home After Working Overtime on an Extended Vice Investigation

Charles Raymond McDaniel was born on August 31, 1932, in Houston before the McDaniel family lived for a time in Arkansas. However, they returned to the Bayou City in the late 1940's. Charles served his country honorably in the United States Army from August 1949 through December 1952. He joined the Houston Police Department in HPD Cadet Class No. 15, which began training on October 1, 1956 and graduated on January 2, 1957. Officer McDaniel began his HPD career as an Evening Shift Patrol officer, but soon transferred to Night Shift-Radio Patrol. In 1959 the Vice Division accepted his application to become an investigator. His promotion to sergeant in August 1961 took him to the Records Division and he later transferred from Records to the Vice Division as a supervisor.

On Saturday night, August 3, 1963, Sergeant McDaniel was assigned to work the 7 p.m. until 3 a.m. shift in Vice. The Vice detail was much smaller than its modern day version and at that time Sergeant McDaniel was the Night Shift supervisor working under the command of the Vice Detail Commander, Lieutenant W. T. Higgins. Being an involved supervisor, Sergeant McDaniel was assisting Officer D. R. Perry on this night in an ongoing vice investigation, which continued past their normal tour of duty. Lieutenant Higgins provided authorization to continue the investigation, brought to a conclusion about 5 a.m. with a number of arrests.

At 5:20 a.m., Sergeant McDaniel, who lived with his family in the Cypress area, was outbound in the 14300 block of Hempstead Highway. In reviewing the accident investigation report as well as newspaper accounts of this incident, it was learned that Sergeant McDaniel veered slightly into the oncoming lane of traffic. The left front of his assigned unmarked take-home vehicle then struck the left front of a vehicle traveling inbound. This impact caused the immediate death of the sergeant and inflicted severe injuries to the two individuals in the citizen vehicle.

Charles Raymond McDaniel was dead at only thirty years of age.

SERGEANT CHARLES R. MCDANIEL

William G. Stockton drove the other vehicle in the accident. His passenger was Melvin L. Jackson. Both were postal employees on their way to work. While both were injured, they survived this tragic accident. Hempstead Highway at this time was only two lanes and was undergoing construction to widen it. A disabled boat trailer parked on the right shoulder possibly could have distracted McDaniel, causing him to veer to his left and directly into the path of the oncoming Stockton vehicle. Accident Investigators F. T. DeLoach Jr. and J. T. Leach investigated this accident. They filed no charges.

Sergeant C. R. McDaniel was survived by his wife, Jeanine, as well as two daughters, eleven-year-old Deborah Ann and nine-year-old Jacquen, and one son, six-year-old Charles Robert McDaniel. Also, he was survived by his two sisters, Mrs. A. M. Loy of Dallas and Mrs. Hazel Inman and five brothers, E. E. McDaniel of San Antonio, Ralph McGraw, Don A. McDaniel and William E. McDaniel, all of Houston, and Jerry E. McDaniel of Lubbock.

Funeral services were held at 2:30 p.m. Tuesday, August 6, 1963, at the Heights Funeral Home Chapel, with the Reverend Don Allen officiating. Burial followed at Woodlawn Garden of Memories, Old Katy Road and Antoine. Pallbearers were HPD Officers Guy McMenemy, George Brogden, J. O. "Bo" Norris, Don Perry, J. S. Oaks, and C. H. "Charlie" Culbreth.

Mrs. Jeanine McDaniel later remarried and raised her three children with her new husband. She also became the mother of four more children. In 2003, she resided near Baytown. Deborah Ann had five children, David, Lucas, Monte, Jeanine and Jennifer, as well as seven grandchildren. Jacquen was the mother of one daughter, Michele, and grandmother of two. Charles Robert McDaniel also resided in the Houston area in 2003 and had no children. Were McDaniel alive today, he and Jeanine would be the proud grandparents of six and great-grandparents of nine.

Lt. W. T. Higgins continued his long term of service, retiring as a captain in 1991. He died in 1996. Guy McMenemy retired as a sergeant in 1982 after a long period of service in both the Vice and Criminal Intelligence Divisions. "Bo" Norris also served for years in CID. He retired from Radio Patrol in 1978 and died in 1995. Don Perry, George Brogden and J. S. Oaks all resigned from the Department at various times prior to their twenty years. Investigator J. T. Leach resigned from HPD.

Charlie Culbreth became an HPD helicopter pilot and retired in 1979. He was killed that same year while piloting a chopper for the private sector. Accident Investigator Floyd T. Deloach was shot and killed in the line of duty less than two years (June 1965) after the McDaniel death.

Gravemarker for Officer McDaniel reads:

CHARLES R. MCDANIEL
TEXAS, CPL, U.S. ARMY
AUG 31, 1932-AUG 4, 1963

52

Officer James Franklin Willis
Badge #1308
July 1, 1964

Officer James F. Willis Goes After Speeder On Market, Collides with Vehicle, Perishes

Officer James Franklin Willis was born in Carthage, Texas on June 15, 1925. He attended elementary school in Galloway, Texas and graduated from Logansport High School in Louisiana in 1943. He served his country in the United States Army during World War II from February 1944 to December 1945. He joined the Houston Police Department in Cadet Class No. 15 on October 1, 1956. This class graduated on December 31, 1956, officially going to work on January 2, 1957. Willis' original assignment was to the Radio Patrol Bureau - Evening Shift. He later worked for a time in the Traffic Enforcement Division but in 1960 transferred to Radio Patrol - Night Shift.

On Monday night, June 29, 1964, Officer Willis was riding alone in Unit No. 603 in the Radio Patrol Bureau working out of the Northeast Substation. Just shortly after midnight (Tuesday morning, June 30), Officer Willis was parked on the north side of the 8800 block of Market Road. He observed traffic at this location when he pulled out onto Market Road, attempting to follow a speeding vehicle traveling east on Market. When he pulled out onto Market, the officer crossed the westbound lanes, losing control of his vehicle and slipping onto the left shoulder of the roadway and skidding sideways for more than one hundred feet on wet grass.

According to witnesses, he appeared to have regained control of his vehicle. Unfortunately, at this time a westbound 1949 Cadillac driven by Thomas Lewis Jones struck the left side of his patrol car. This tremendous collision caused the police car to break apart just behind the front seat. The rear of the vehicle – with the top still attached – came to rest 105 feet beyond the front end. Officer Willis was ejected from the car and landed in a nearby ditch. An ambulance rushed the officer to North Shore Hospital but moved him shortly thereafter to Ben Taub General Hospital with massive injuries to the head, face and chest. A doctor from North Shore Hospital rode in the ambulance with Officer Willis to the larger, better-equipped Ben Taub.

Houston Police Officer James F. Willis died from those injuries at 2:30 p.m. the following day, Wednesday, July 1, 1964. He was thirty-nine.

OFFICER JAMES FRANKLIN WILLIS

Thomas Jones was pinned inside his Cadillac. A friendly wrecker driver ripped open a door to remove him from the twisted metal. It was also too late for Jones, too. He was pronounced dead at the scene. He was forty-seven.

Fellow patrol Officers Don C. Griffin and Charles C. Dodd witnessed this tragic accident. They were traveling westbound on Market about four blocks behind Jones' Cadillac. They reported seeing an eastbound vehicle approaching them at a high rate of speed, probably the one Officer Willis was chasing. They then saw Officer Willis' headlights go over to the wrong side of the street and also saw sparks and smoke. Griffin described it as an explosion.

Accident Officers Reid A. Woodruff and Paul H. Artz conducted a thorough investigation of the two-fatality accident under the supervision of Accident

Division Captain John M. LeVrier. They determined that both vehicles were traveling in excess of fifty miles per hour at the time of impact. They never determined how or why Officer Willis lost control of his patrol car.

Officer Willis was survived by his wife, Lois, as well as two sons, seventeen-year-old Douglas Franklin Willis and ten-year-old Robert Edward Willis. Also mourning his death were his mother, Mrs. Ivous Willis of Gallaway, two sisters, Mrs. Ruby Tabor of Galloway and Mrs. Maye Peace (wife of HPD Officer James Peace) of Houston and one brother, the Reverend W. C. Willis of Houston.

Funeral services were held on Friday, July 3, 1964, at 10:30 a.m. at the Helmers Street Baptist Church, 7721 Helmers. The Reverend John Duckett officiated and the Pat H. Foley Funeral Home at 2110 Tidwell was in charge of the services. An additional service was held at 2 p.m. Saturday, July 4, at the Methodist Church in Panola County in Galloway. Burial followed at the Adams Cemetery.

Officer Willis was chairman of the Board of Deacons at the Helmers Street Baptist Church. He also was a veteran of World War II. Pallbearers were Sergeant I. H. Gaman, Officers J. T. Lum, H. M. McNutt, Curtis Simmons and Detectives George LaRue and V.O. Baker.

Lois Willis remarried and lived in Pasadena in 2003. Douglas F. Willis joined the Houston Police Department in Police Cadet Class No. 34 in 1967. He retired from HPD in 2002 after serving most of his career in the Accident Division. Robert E. Willis lived in Montana. Officer Willis' mother, Mrs. Ivous Willis, is deceased, as his sister Mrs. Ruby Tabor. Mrs. Maye Peace, who was widowed, lived in Porter. The only brother, Reverend W. C. "Jack" Willis lived in Carthage.

When Officer Doug Willis graduated from the Academy, he proudly pinned on his Dad's Badge, No. 1308.

Reid Woodruff, who investigated this terrible accident with Paul Artz, said the fact he knew Officer Willis made the accident investigation particularly difficult. Both Woodruff and Artz were later promoted to sergeant and completed long, exemplary careers with HPD. Woodruff worked Radio Patrol for many years, retiring in 1986. He lived in Magnolia. Artz worked the Accident Division and the Training Academy, retiring in 1991 to a home near Spring.

Of the witnesses, Don Griffin made detective and worked Robbery as well as Burglary and Theft before resigning from HPD. Charlie Dodd made detective and also worked in Burglary and Theft, retiring in 1989. Sergeant Gaman retired from the Police Garage in 1979. He resided in Houston. Officer J. T. Lum retired from the Police Garage in 1991 and died in 2000. Officer H. M. McNutt retired from the Academy in 1979. Officer Curtis Simmons made sergeant and retired in 1984 after a long career in HPD. He lived in Lovelady in 2003. Detective George LaRue retired from Special Thefts in 1977 and lived in Trinity until his passing in 2006. Detective V. O. Baker retired from Auto Theft in 1980 and lived in Madisonville.

Retired Assistant Chief Milton C. Simmons recalled that his father, retired Sergeant Curtis M. Simmons, was a personal friend of Officer Willis. They had been close friends since their days in Cadet Class No. 15. Chief Simmons remembered this night in particular as his family went to the hospital to be with the Willis family.

No other information was found about Thomas Lewis Jones, the other man who died in the accident.

53

Officer Herbert Planer
Badge #1377
February 18, 1965

Officer Herb Planer Shot 12 Times by Suspect Discovered Stealing Car at Apartment Complex

Officer Herbert Norman Planer was born March 3, 1932 in Irvington, New Jersey. After serving in the U. S. Navy from 1950 until 1953, he moved to Houston to live with a family he knew from New Jersey. He resumed his education, graduating from Sam Houston High School in 1954 and joined the Houston Police Department in Police Cadet Class No. 16, graduating in June 1957. After three years he resigned to do cabinet work but quickly returned six months later. During his time on HPD, he worked Night Shift Radio Patrol and Evening and Day Shift Traffic Enforcement. He wore Badge No. 1377.

At approximately 1:40 a.m. February 18, 1965, Officer Herbert Planer, a recent divorcee, returned to his apartment in the 5000 block of Navarro, near what later became known as the Galleria area. Working security at the La Fonda

West Apartments, he drove his personal 1964 Ford and was in the process of making his usual rounds when he encountered a white male in the process of stealing a 1957 Buick.

Planer was unarmed and in plain clothes. Witnesses in a nearby apartment said they heard some commotion in the parking lot and the voice of someone identifying himself as a police officer. These witnesses then looked out and saw the suspect get out of the Buick and hide behind another vehicle. When Officer Planer approached this man, he jumped out from his hiding place and opened fire.

"You've shot me enough. Please stop shooting," someone later believed to be Planer was heard to say. However, the suspect continued to shoot. Officer Planer was struck eleven times. He fell to the driveway left to die. The motor of his vehicle was still running and the suspect used it to flee the scene.

Hearing the gunfire, somebody in the complex called the police. Officer R. S. Mortenson and his rookie partner, R. M. "Speedy" Wilson, arrived and found their dead HPD comrade, whom Mortenson did not recognize. However, Officer Planer's police ID was found near his body. The officers immediately contacted the Homicide Division.

Homicide Lieutenant Frank Crittenden responded to the scene along with Detectives C. H. "Chuck" Walker and Billy Joe Rogers. Detectives B. F. "Bobby" Adams and D. A. Bolton also were assigned to the scene and later conducted the morgue investigation. While an extensive scene investigation was underway on this who dunit police officer murder, the suspect drove his victim's car to Chimney Rock and Tanglewood, where he abandoned the vehicle. He walked down Bering Street, disassembled the murder weapon as he walked and discarded it into the bushes in the 2900 block. He continued to walk to the Dobbs House Restaurant at 617 Sage Road at Richmond. Having previously worked there, he knew the night cook, whom he asked to do him a favor. Call the police, he asked.

The cook did so and district Officer D. A. "Hoot" Gibson and his rookie partner, J. D. "Jim" Tucker, responded. The suspect approached the officers and presented them with quite a surprise gift: "I shot the man up by Sage Road and I want to give myself up." This was nearly three hours after the shooting. After his arrest, he led the officers to where he had thrown the murder weapon, an inexpensive Spanish-made .22-caliber automatic, along with two clips. They found the weapon in a number of pieces.

The suspect was eighteen-year old Donald Ray Speck, who had a local record for auto theft. He gave a written confession later to Homicide Detective B. J. Rogers. He stated that he thought that the officer was a night watchman who was shining a spotlight on him. When he saw the individual had something in his hand, he shot him.

Officer Planer was holding his police identification in his hand to identify himself, but he was unarmed. Speck further stated that he was a parole violator. He said he had stolen the gun from a homosexual he had met in Oklahoma. Investigators verified the history of the pistol. They also learned that Speck was in fact a parole violator for an auto theft conviction from Coryell County, near Fort Hood. The record showed that he had received an undesirable discharge from the U. S. Army.

Houston newspapers reported Speck's comments to police: "He was spinning like a top as I shot him. Sometime I would shoot him in the front, then in the side, and sometimes in the back. He never did fall until I had shot him all twelve times. I shot him to get away."

Speck further commented: "I did wrong. I deserve to die in the electric chair."

He didn't.

OFFICER HERBERT PLANER

On March 9, 1966, Donald Ray Speck, an unemployed cook originally from Iowa, was convicted of murder in the death of Officer Herbert Planer and assessed a life sentence. The death sentence was still "constitutional" at this time and it is unknown why prosecutors did not try him for capital murder. While the officer was not in uniform, he did identify himself as police and was performing a police function at the time of his death.

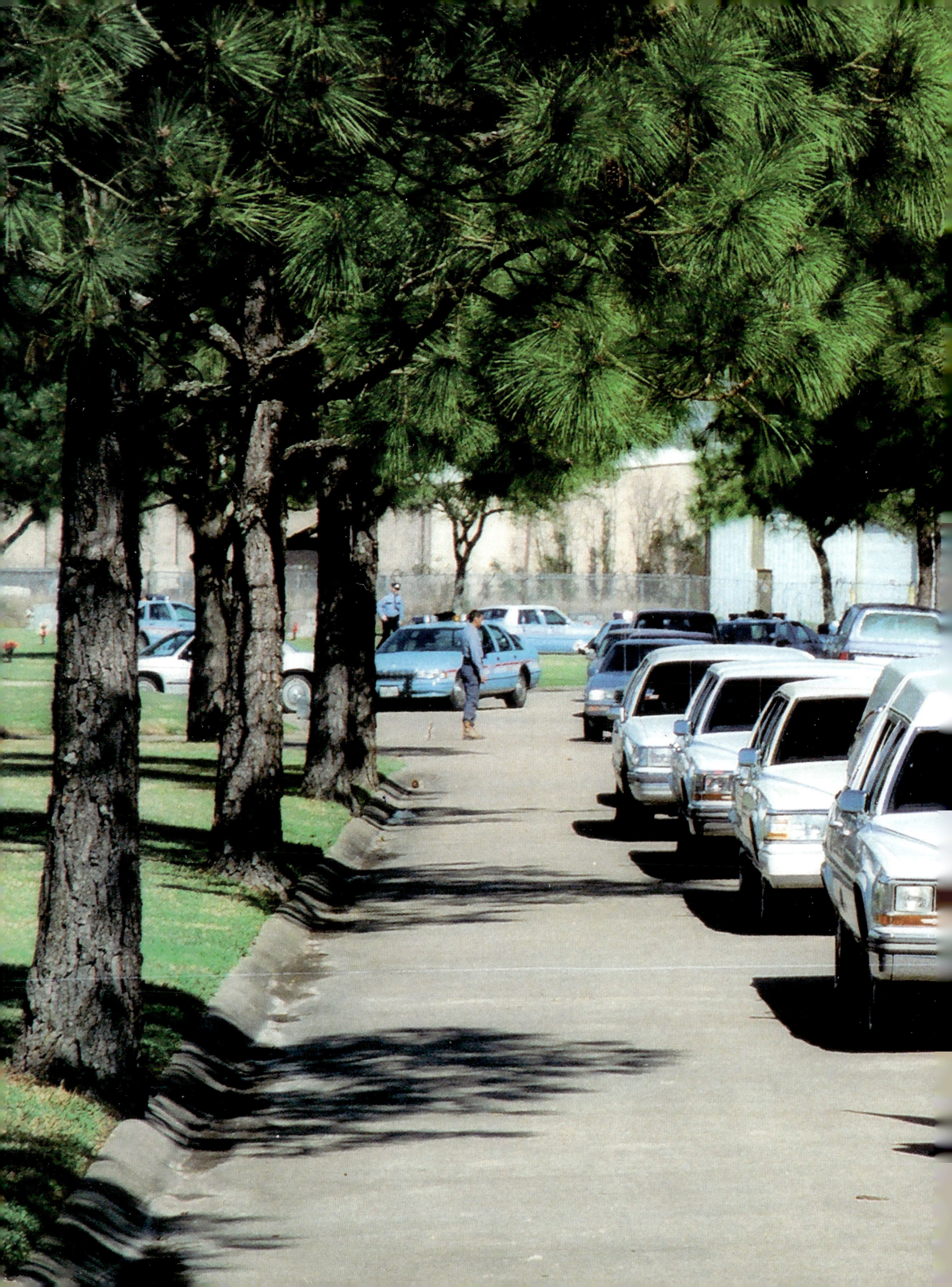

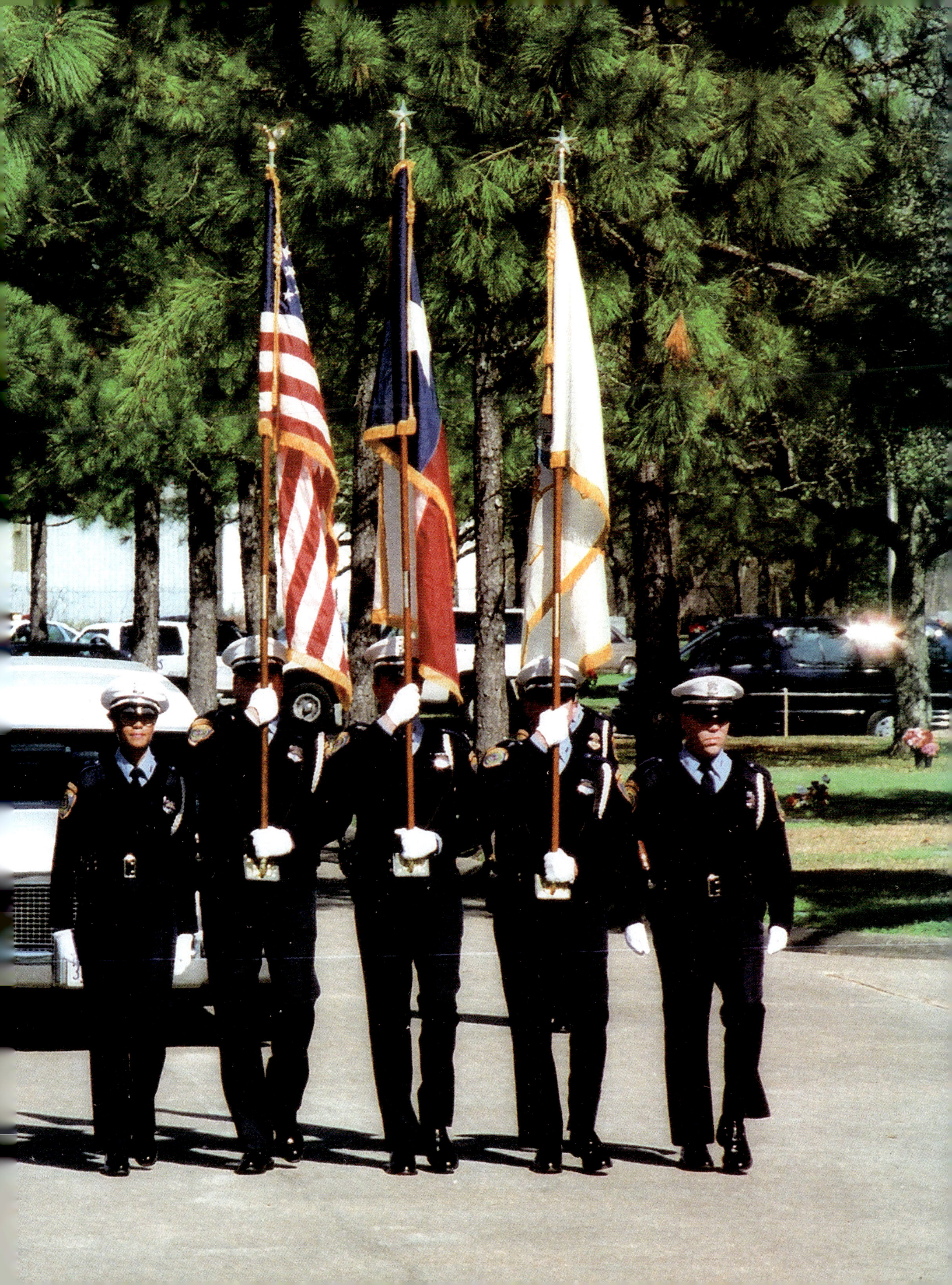

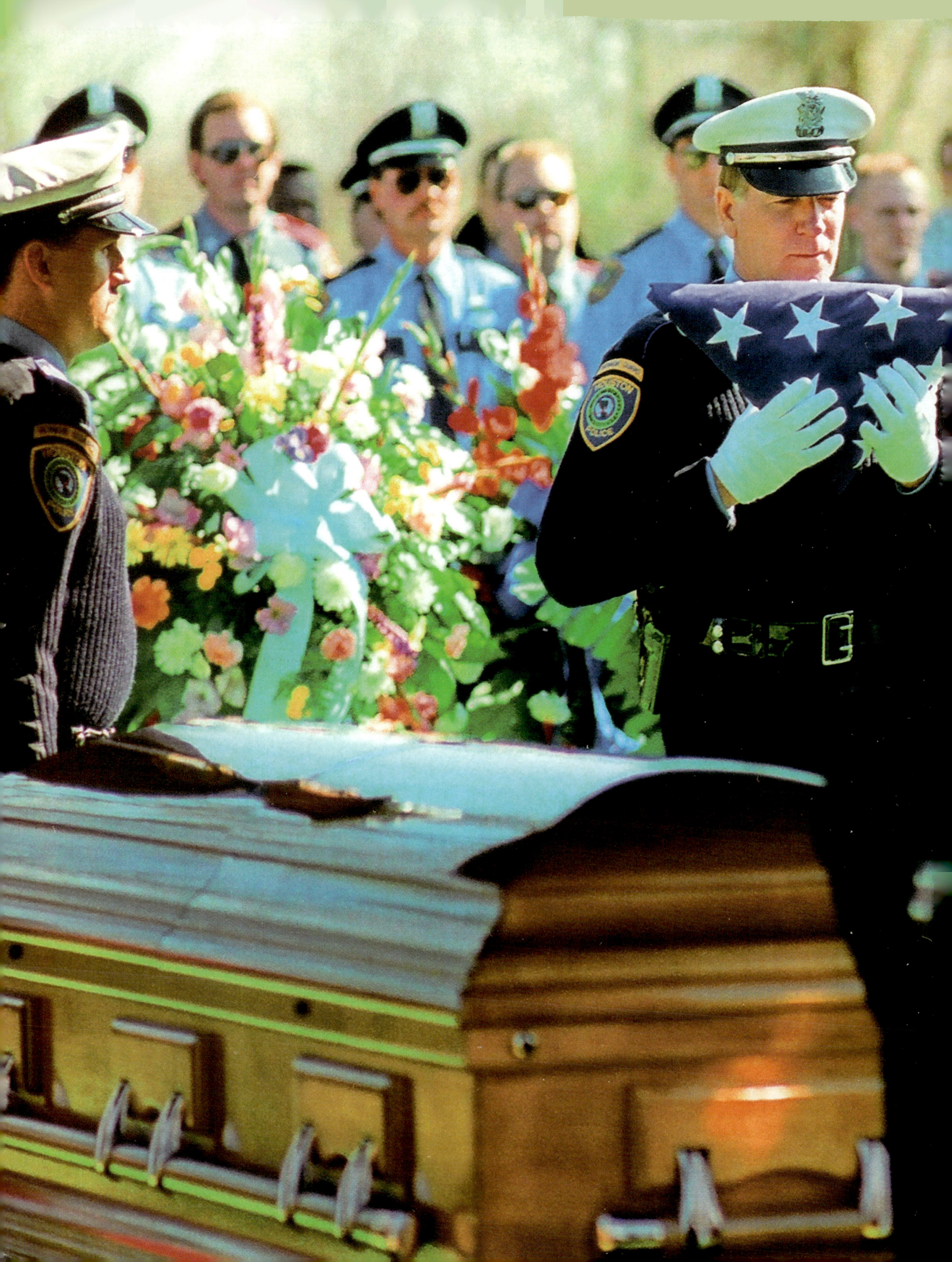

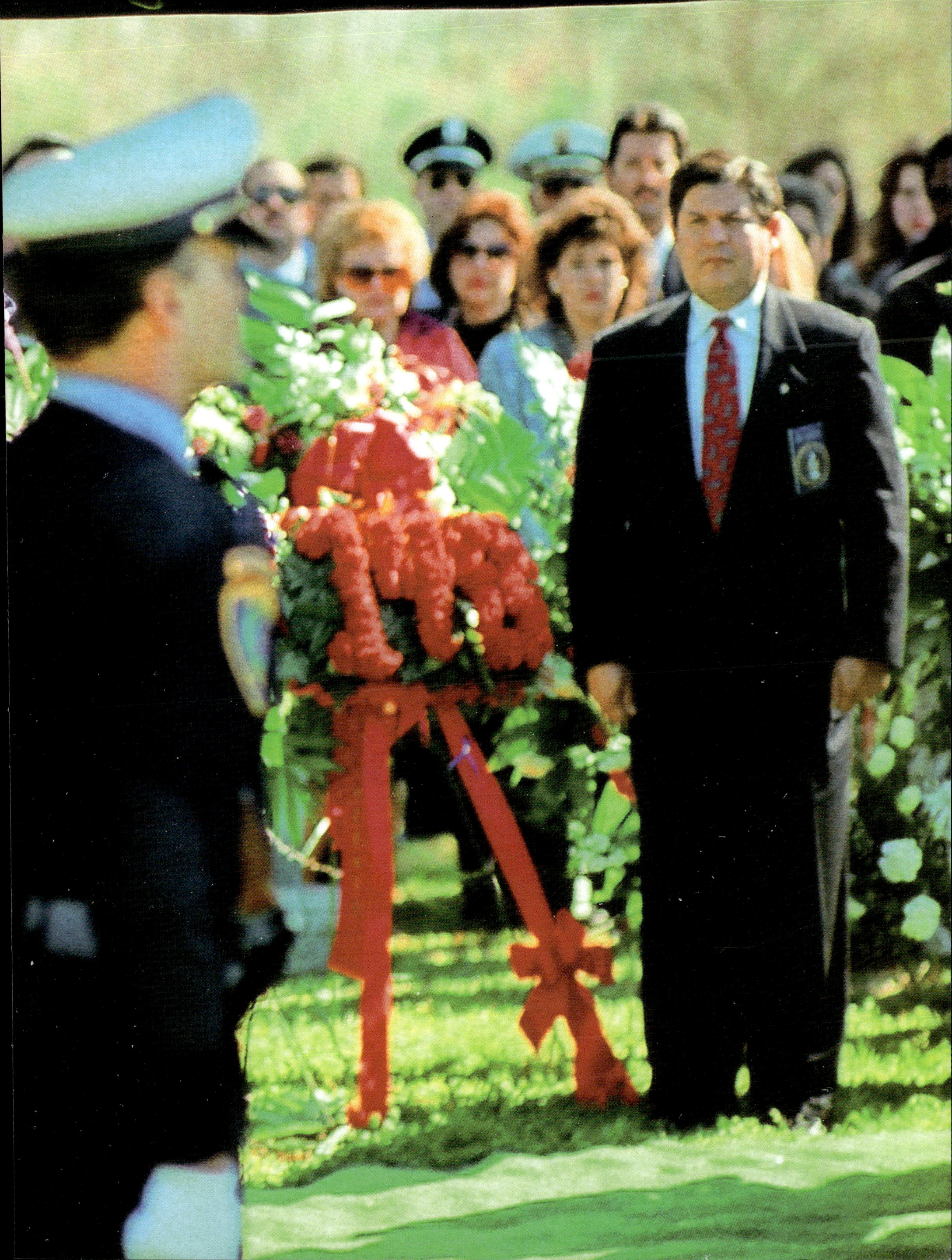

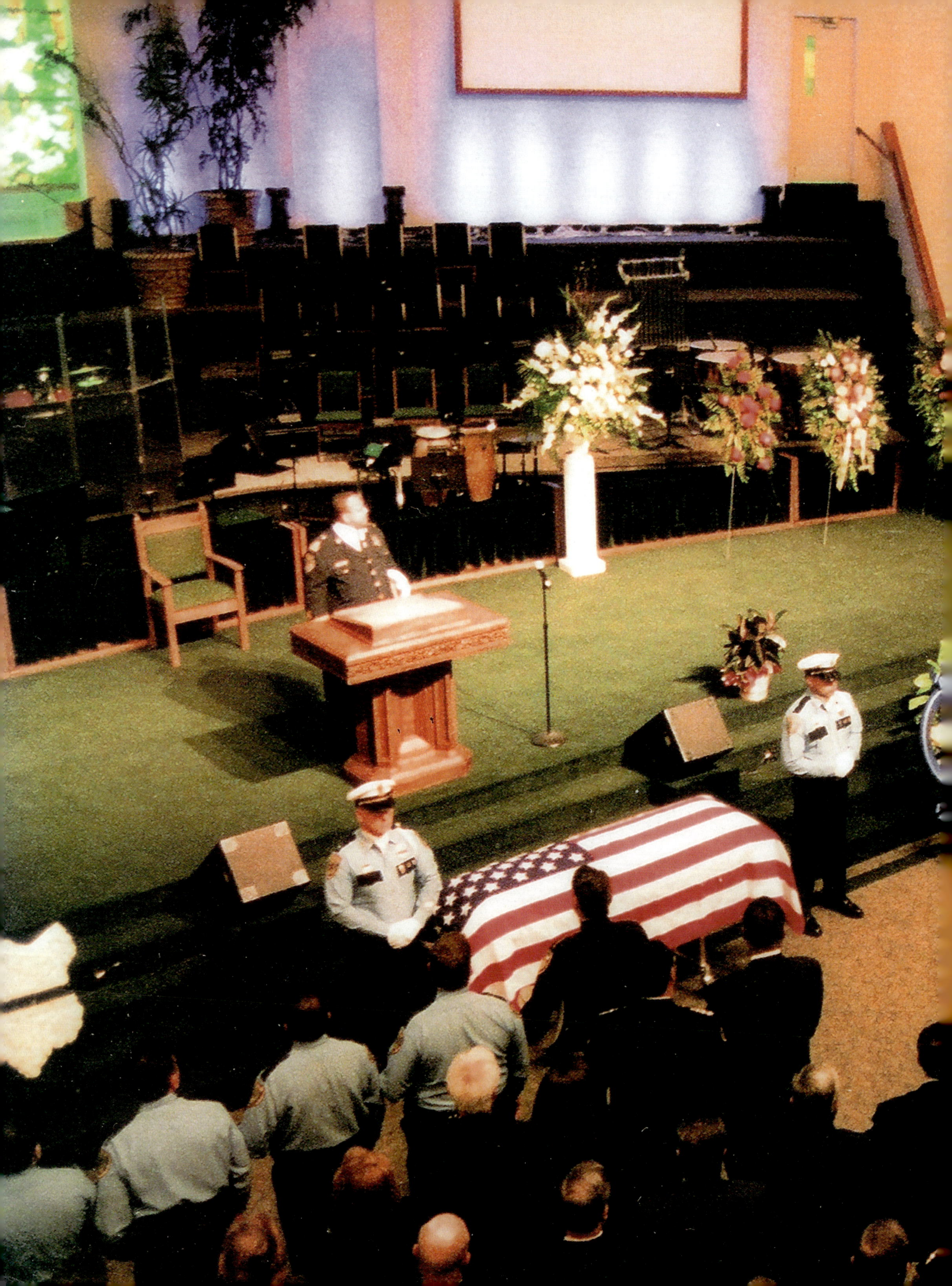

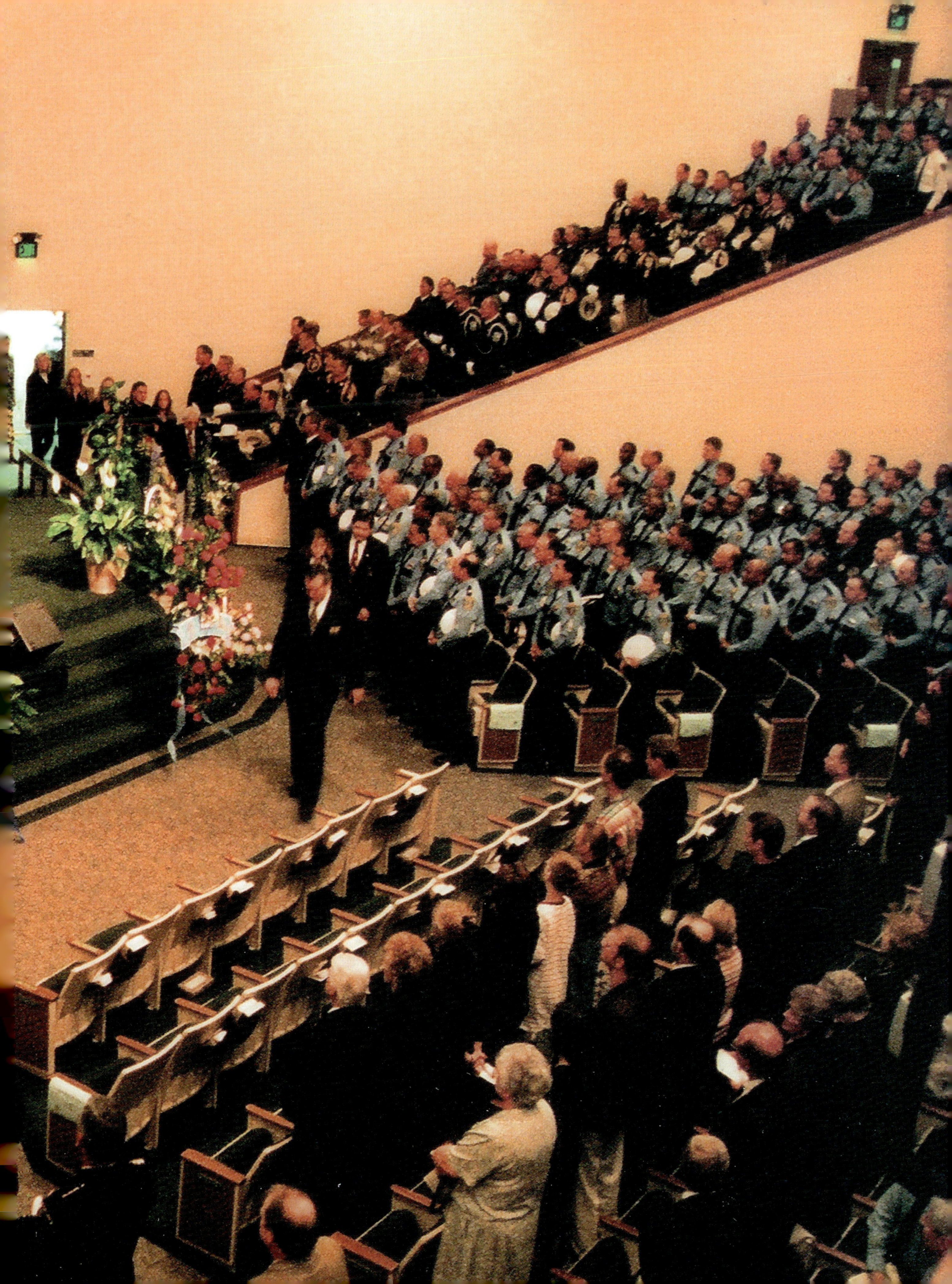

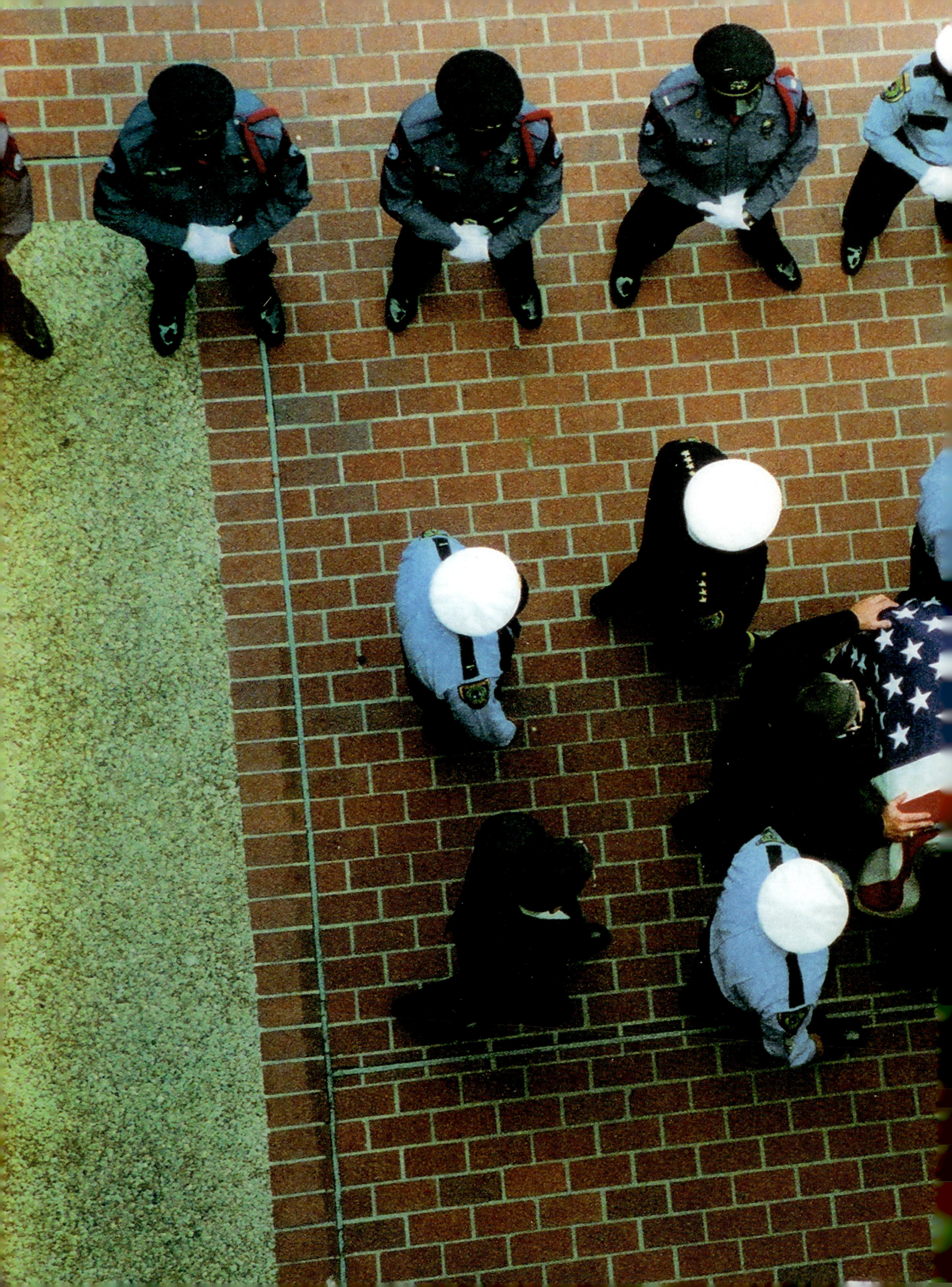

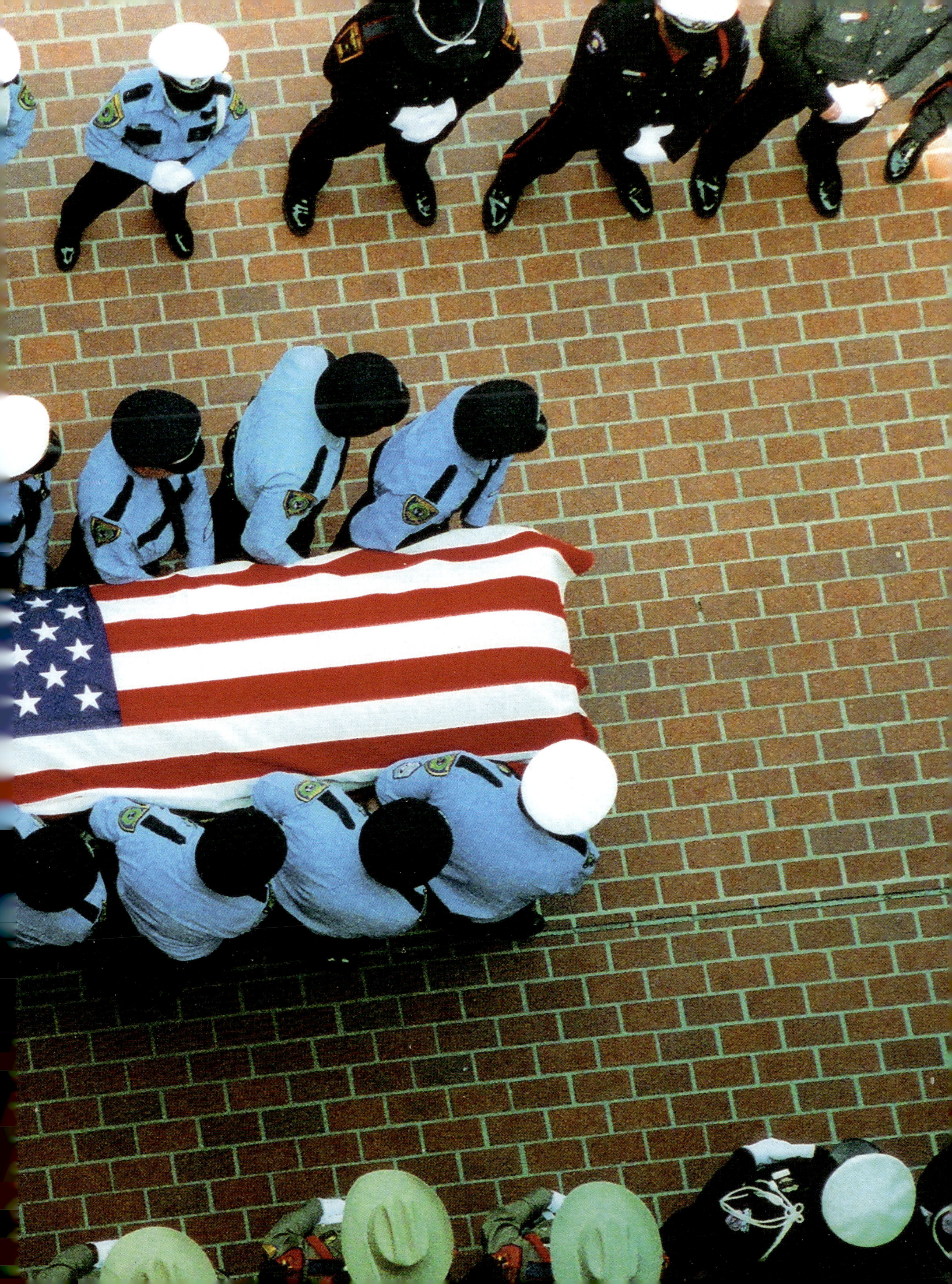

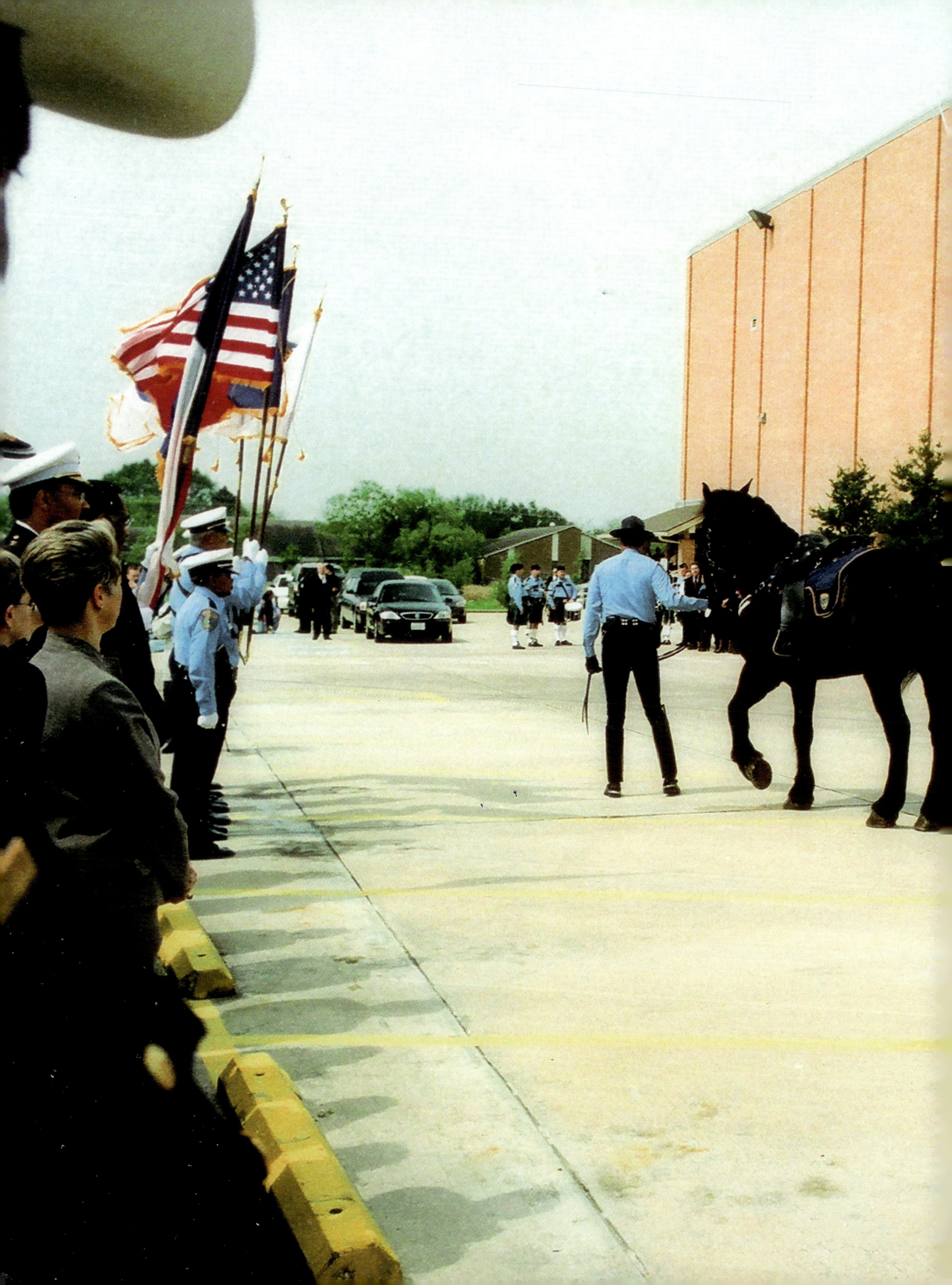

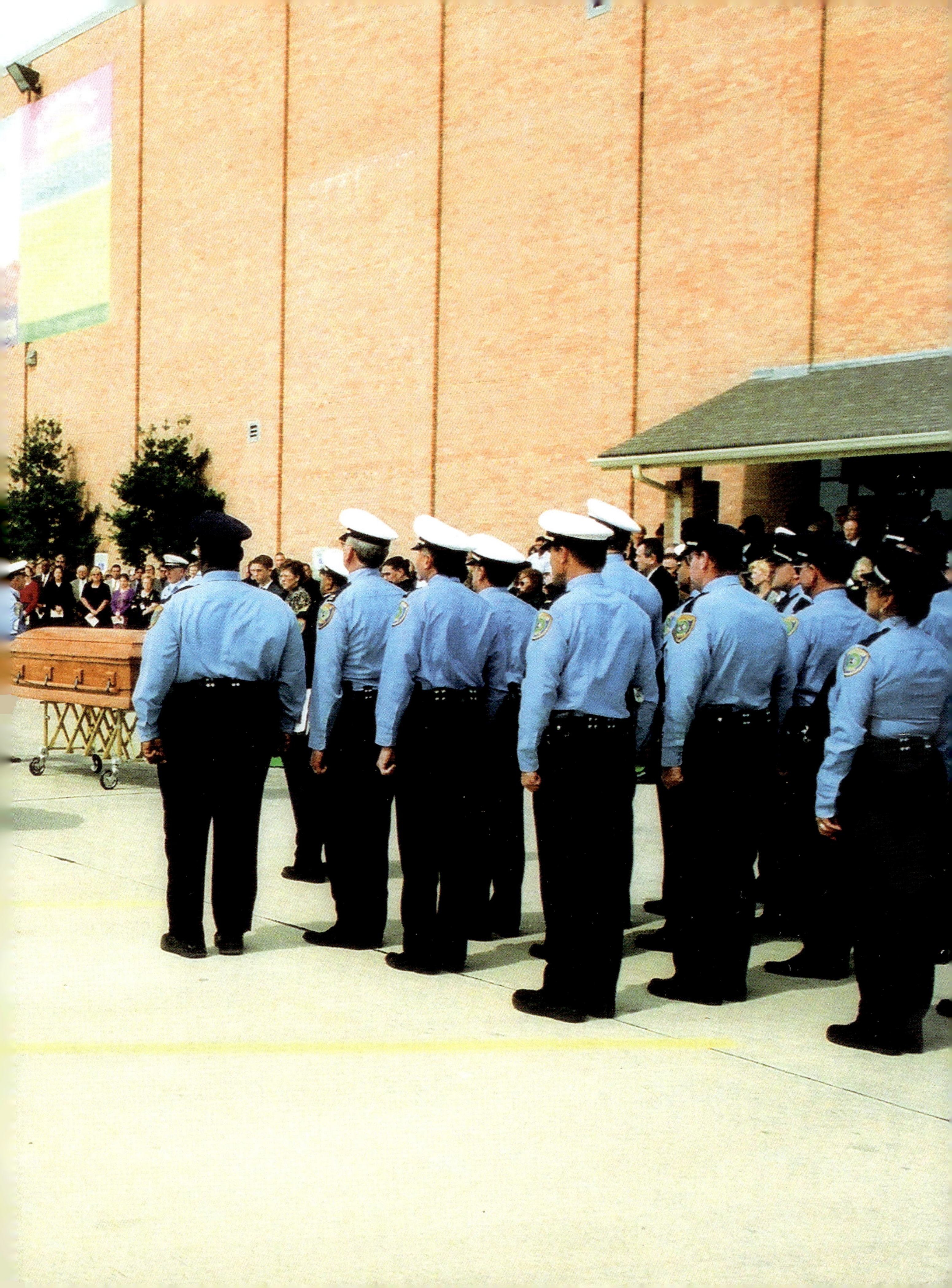

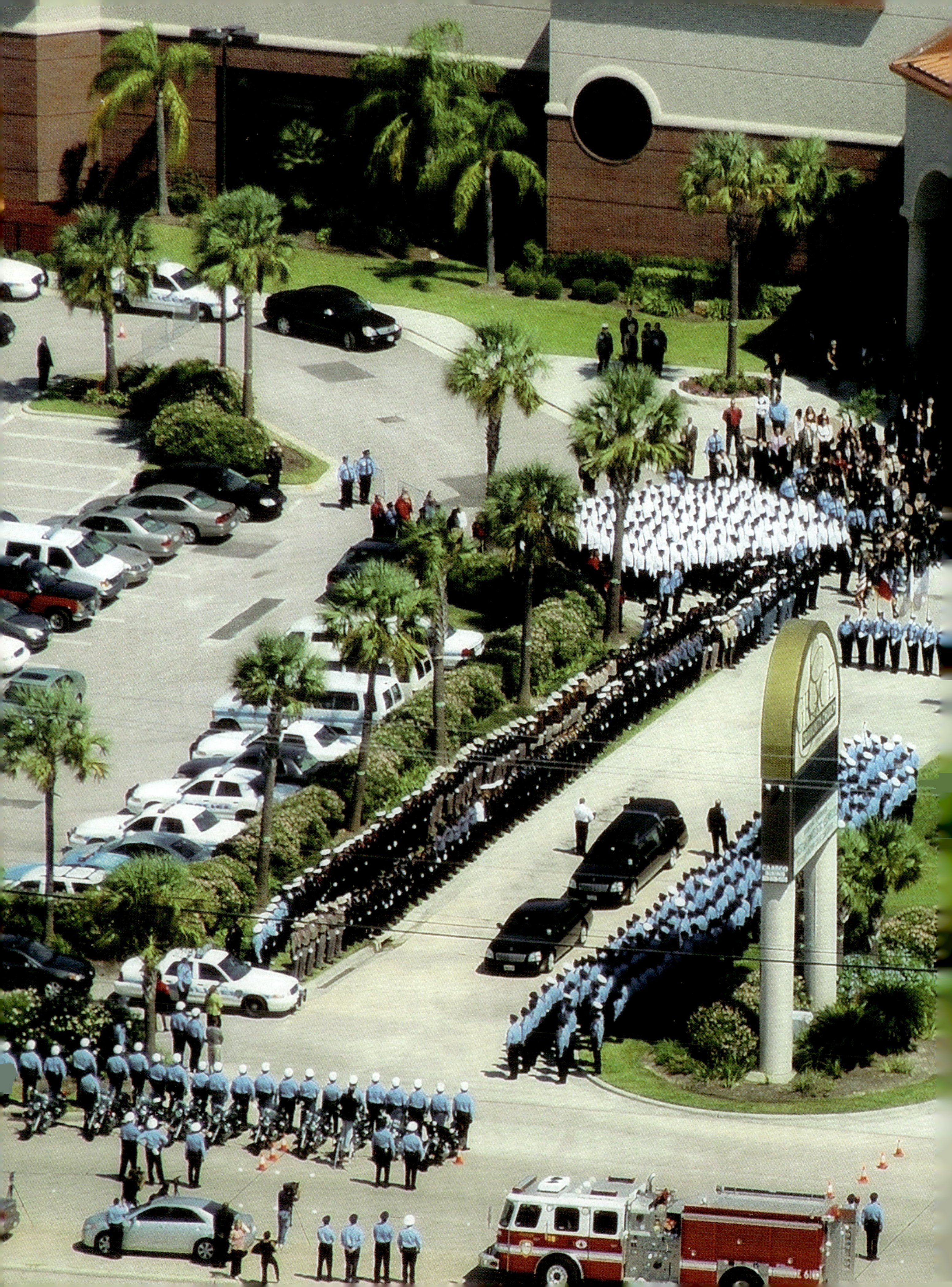
GRACE

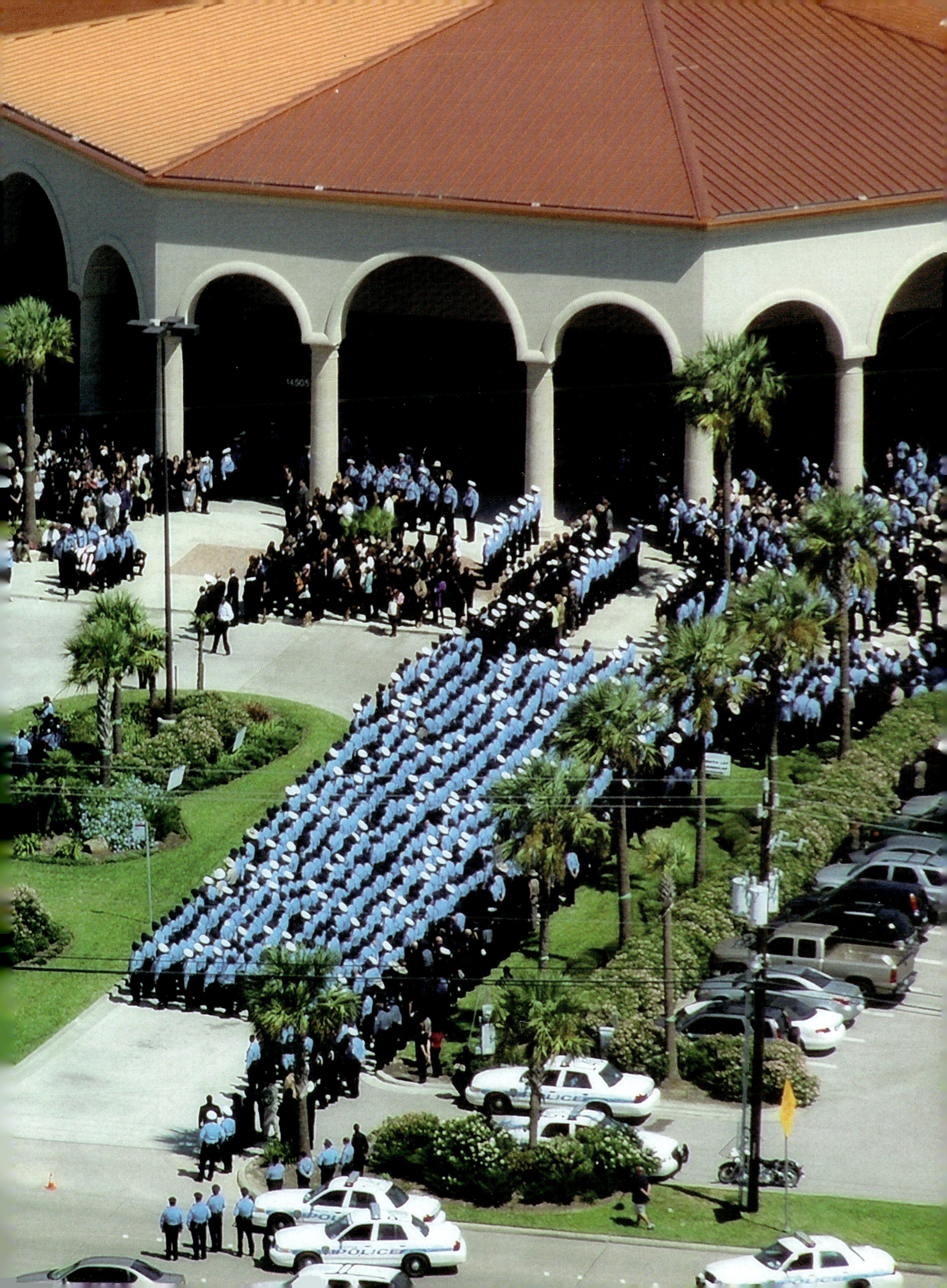
POLICE

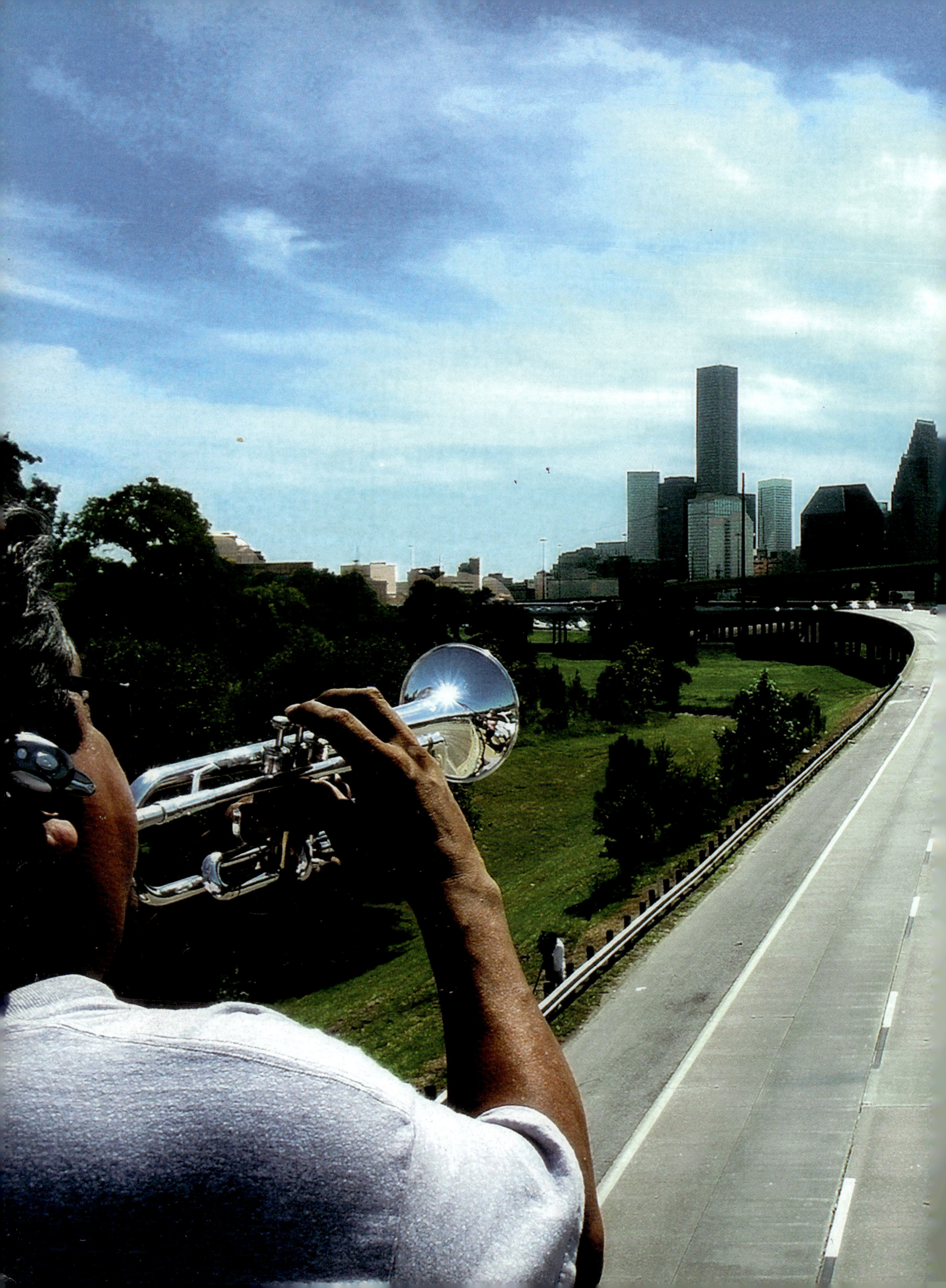

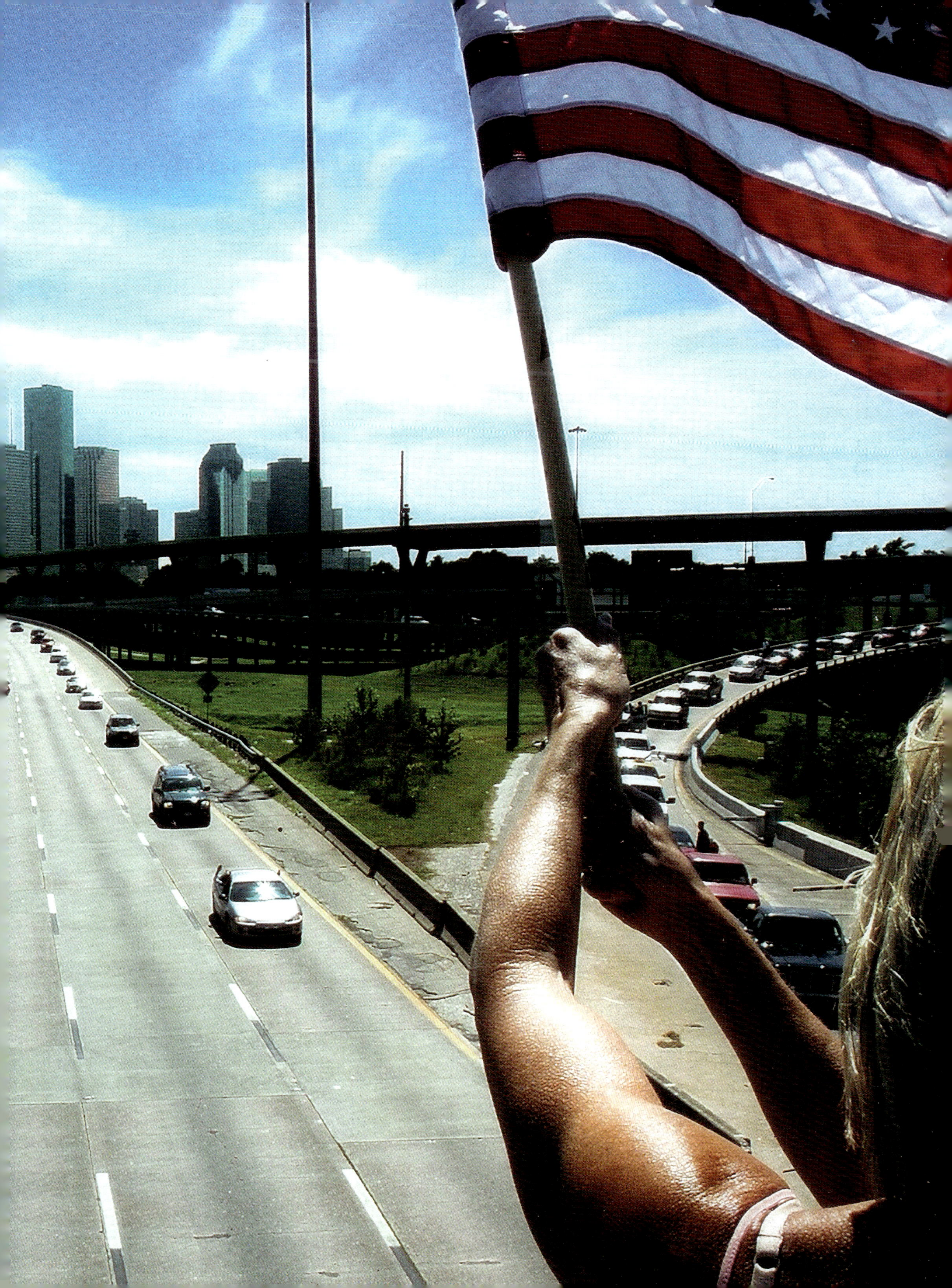

The recently divorced Planer was survived by his eight-year-old daughter, Margaret Antoinette Planer of Houston and her mother, Mrs. Betty Joan Planer. Other survivors were his father, George Planer, and three brothers, George, Eddie and Tommie, all of New Jersey.

The body of Officer Herbert Norman Planer lay in state at Forest Park Funeral Home and was then transported to Point Pleasant Beach, New Jersey. Interment was at the Beverly National Cemetery in Beverly, New Jersey.

By 1999, Lieutenant Frank Crittenden and Detective B. J. Rogers were deceased. Detective D. A. Bolton retired, as did Officer R. L. Mortenson. Detective C. H. Walker retired as a captain and Officer D. A. Gibson as a lieutenant. Then-rookie Officer J. L. Tucker was later promoted to detective and lieutenant and resigned from HPD. He died in 1998. Rookie Officer R. M. Wilson was a sergeant and helicopter pilot with HPD for a number of years. Detective Bobby Adams was promoted to lieutenant and later served as captain in several commands, including the Homicide Division. He retired after more than forty-one years of service, most of them in Homicide before serving as captain of Helicopter Division.

Donald Ray Speck adjusted to prison life very well and was called an "exemplary prisoner." He eventually earned trusty status and became a truck driver for TDC. However, on December 17, 1981, he was killed in a traffic accident in Sugar Land while driving a TDC truck.

In 2004, Eddie Planer, who was retired and lived near Edonville, Michigan, said he did not know the whereabouts of his brother's daughter. He also said that Officer Planer's father is deceased, as is his brother George. Brother Tommie lived in Florida.

In 2001, Tommie Planner (who preferred this different spelling) began his own extensive search to locate his niece. He had been contacted by this writer and this apparently aroused an old interest in finding his brother's only child. He located Margaret Shattuck in Northwest Harris County. She was married with twin seven year old sons, Nolan and Ryan, and a four-year-old son, Weston. Her mother Betty remarried and lived near Cypress in 2004. Tom Planner and his wife Sandy drove from Florida to Houston in February 2001 to meet Margaret. They chose the Houston Police Officers Memorial as their meeting place and were met at this location by this writer.

Planner said that a number of their immediate family members entered the law enforcement field. In 2004, their children, Keith and Kimberly, were both with the Florida Department of Corrections, as was Sandra's sister, Ronetta. Planner's stepson, Gary Atchison, was a deputy with Citrus County, Florida. Three of their nephews also work in law enforcement in Florida or Alabama.

54

Officer Floyd T. Deloach Jr.
Badge #1690
June 30, 1965

Lone Woman Juror Saves the Man who Killed Officer Floyd T. Deloach Jr. from Death Penalty

Floyd Taylor Deloach Jr. was born in Houston on October 20, 1936. He attended Ben Milam Elementary School, Washington Junior High and Reagan High School, graduating from Reagan in 1955. After serving his country in the United States Army for two years, he joined the Houston Police Department on September 14, 1959, graduating from Police Cadet Class No. 22 on December 16, 1959. He was elected by his classmates to be the class secretary. His first assignment was in the Accident Division.

The following chain of events was pieced together from newspaper accounts as well as with the able assistance of retired Homicide Lieutenant Chester Massey, a supervisor assigned to assist in the coordination of the Deloach investigation.

On Wednesday night, June 30, 1965, Officer Deloach reported to his extra job at the North Shepherd Bowling Lanes, 650 West Crosstimbers at North Shepherd. His hours there were from 7 p.m. until 11 p.m. His duties were to patrol the parking lot and provide security for customers' vehicles. There were no immediate eyewitnesses to what happened. About 11 p.m., a customer leaving the lanes found Officer Deloach lying on the deserted west side of the parking lot. He had been shot twice in the head, once in the abdomen and three times in his hands. An ambulance took him to Heights Hospital where he died at 11:20 p.m. He was twenty-eight.

The initial investigation determined that the officer's service revolver and personal vehicle were missing. Investigators quickly obtained registration information and by 11:45 p.m. a statewide pickup bulletin was broadcast for the officer's vehicle. Within an hour, Texas Highway Patrol put roadblocks in place on every major highway leading out of Houston.

About midnight, a hysterical woman with two

small children ran to a farmer's house on Rhodes Road near Spring Steubner Road in Northwest Harris County. The woman, Mary Davis, told the farmer that her husband had shot a policeman and had beaten her up. She further stated that her husband picked her up at the Houston Motor Inn at 5805 North Shepherd and told her that he "had to get out of here fast." Mrs. Davis' husband, Donald, in a fit of rage and covered with blood from the waist up, beat her and forced her and their children to get in a car she had never seen before. After driving aimlessly for nearly an hour, Davis got out of the car to relieve himself and when he did, Mary Davis drove off and left him. When the car quit running, she got out and ran to the farmhouse.

OFFICER FLOYD T. DELOACH JR.

Houston police initiated a massive manhunt for Donald Davis, who was on foot. By midmorning the next day, two Piper Cub airplanes, ten bloodhounds and a dozen mounted officers were searching for this killer in an area between Tomball and Spring in the Jackrabbit Road/ Spring Creek corridor. This part of Harris County was significantly different from the more thickly populated area it grew to be in the early years of the new century. In 1965, it was far away from the bright lights of even the Houston suburbs, consisting primarily of farms, oil fields and scattered farmhouses.

While the search for the killer was conducted, an investigation of the crime scene revealed that a witness had seen a red-haired man in the officer's car about 10:35 p.m. A wallet with Davis' identification was found at the scene. The description provided by this witness fit that of Donald Jay Davis (White Male, 21), who was found to be wanted on a robbery charge from Abilene. Throughout the evening and night of July 1 the search for Donald Davis intensified, but with no results. Then, on Friday, just after 7 a.m., the suspect walked into the Town and Country Beauty Salon in Huffsmith, just outside of Tomball. He asked Mrs. Berniece Jolly if he could use the phone. She recognized Davis, got scared but allowed him to call Houston.

Officer J. W. Haines in the City Jail took the call and immediately learned Davis' location. Haines motioned for someone else to call Homicide and get some units en route. He kept Davis on the line with small talk and eventually the authorities got to Huffsmith and arrested him. Davis also surrendered his gun as well as Officer Deloach's weapon.

Mrs. Jolly did her part in assisting law enforcement officers. At one point, when it seemed that Davis was getting antsy and might walk off, she offered to give him a haircut. When he accepted her offer, he calmed down. The beauty operator's move bought HPD just enough time, too.

One newspaper account of this incident was particularly enlightening. This was one year before the infamous "Miranda ruling" that would have an everlasting effect on American policing. The article began, "For the first time that veteran law officers in Harris County can remember, an arrested crime suspect was taken 'forthwith before the nearest magistrate' Friday and was provided an attorney without being questioned." It continued to say that this unprecedented procedure was carried out by the men working under Homicide Captain L. D. Morrison Jr. at the suggestion of District Attorney Frank Briscoe. Donald Davis was willing to place in writing his version of the events leading up to the death of Officer Deloach.

Captain Morrison assigned veteran Homicide Lieutenant Massey to personally interrogate the suspect. Under Massey's intense questioning, the suspect stated that he left his pregnant wife and two small children at their motel to "rob something and get some money." When Deloach halted him on the parking lot and asked him for some identification, he felt that the officer would soon find out about the Abilene robbery.

When Davis saw Deloach had a gun, he pulled out his own pistol with the intension of kidnapping the officer by taking his car and putting him in the trunk. However, Officer Deloach reacted to Davis' gun in his face by pulling his own sidearm. The two men struggled over the gun before it went off "accidentally." Davis' account did not explain the number of shots that struck and killed the officer.

Funeral services were held at 10 a.m. Saturday, July 3, 1965 at the Forest Park Funeral Home with burial following at the Forest Park Lawndale Cemetery. Officer Deloach was survived by his wife of nine years, JoAnn Deloach, and two daughters, five-year-old Terri Lynn and twenty-three-month-old Tracey Lee. Also surviving were his parents, Mr. and Mrs. Floyd Deloach, Sr., sisters Beulah Pittman, Ethel Petersen, Alta Wells and Evelyn Bearden, as well as one brother, Gilbert Nelson.

Donald Jay Davis went on trial in September 1966 for murder in the death of Officer Deloach. The state sought the death penalty. However, the jury of ten men and two women were not allowed to hear evidence in connection with the Abilene robbery. Newspaper accounts of the trial revealed that the jury was deadlocked, as there was one woman who would not vote for the death penalty under any circumstances. She felt that "Davis was a good boy who had just chanced to get into trouble." Finally, the rest of the jury gave in to her wishes and convicted Davis of murder and sentenced him to life imprisonment.

TERRY DELOACH, TRACY DELOACH JONES, AND MRS. JOANN DELOACH

Luck was on the cop killer's side. The "overcrowding" conditions during this period in Texas history along with the resulting rules inflicted upon the Texas Department of Corrections by U. S. District Judge William Wayne Justice assisted Davis in receiving an early parole. On July 26, 1983, he was paroled to Coleman County, near Abilene, having been in custody just over eighteen years. No evidence exists at this time to indicate that Davis had had further problems with the law. In this case, it was impossible to identify the primary investigators in this offense. Quite likely the entire Homicide Division participated in some aspect of the investigation and stayed on the case until it was brought together and wrapped up.

While Donald Davis was seemingly "free," Officer Floyd Deloach's family lived on with the memories of their loved one taken from them at such a young age. Jo Ann Deloach resided and worked in the Houston area in 2007 as did both daughters, Terri Lynn and Tracey Lee. Floyd's parents both died as did his sisters Beulah, Ethel and Alta and his brother, Gilbert. Sister Evelyn also resided in the Houston area.

The original marker, which has been replaced by a 100 Club marker, read as follows:

HUSBAND
FLOYD T. DELOACH JR.
OCT 20, 1936 - JUNE 30, 1965

There also exists a monument with the DELOACH family name.

55

Officer Louis Lyndon Sander
Badge #2023
January 21, 1967

Career Criminal Kenneth Hinkle Runs Stop Sign, Opens Fire and Kills HPD Officer Lyndon Sander

It was a slow Saturday night. Officers Gene E. Brown and Lyndon L. Sander were working their regular evening shift out of the Point Control Division. About 9 p.m. a thick fog settled in for the night as the two officers were stopped on the near north side of the downtown area, at the intersection of North San Jacinto and McKee. As they sat on their individual three-wheelers watching a stop sign, a railroad detective acquaintance stopped by to visit the two men. These two officers were not only partners but very close friends since their days as classmates in Police Cadet Class No. 31, from which they had graduated on January 23, 1965.

Just then a pickup truck ran the stop sign and Officer Brown followed and stopped it several blocks south on McKee. Alton Lewis, the railroad detective, stayed to talk more with Officer Sander. Sander, however, wanted to check on his partner and just as he was leaving he saw a brown Pontiac run the same stop sign. The officer dutifully pursued the Pontiac, going east on North San Jacinto (Rothwell) toward Hardy.

OFFICER LOUIS LYNDON SANDER

Just as Lewis left to check on Brown, he and the HPD officer heard five or six gunshots coming from the direction of Lyndon Sander. They both sped immediately toward the shots. When they arrived in the 900 block of Hardy, they found Officer Sander lying in the street with several Houston firefighters providing aid. The shooting happened practically in the very front of HFD Station No. 5. Officer Brown attempted to give his partner mouth-to-mouth resuscitation. An ambulance took the wounded officer to Ben Taub General Hospital. However, the man who wore Badge No. 2023 was dead on arrival from a single gunshot wound to the center of his chest.

Both Officer Brown and railroad detective Lewis saw the Pontiac leaving the general area when they went to check on Sander. Neither was able to pursue him or get close enough to get a license number. They believed that the Pontiac was involved in the murder of Officer Sander, but that was the only fact they had. A later investigation determined that Sander was likely shot shortly after he got off his three-wheeler since he had not yet retrieved his flashlight from the trunk. From Officer Sander's weapon, investigators determined that he had fired five rounds at his unknown assailant. Homicide Lieutenant C. J. "Chuck" Lofland and Detective E. D. "Sonny" Combs responded to the scene and began an extensive investigation. They were assisted by Detectives Joe Gamino and Harry Hall.

On Sunday morning, Detectives Paul Nix, Ed Horelica and Jim Pierce also were assigned to the Sander case. Lieutenant J. E. "Pete" Gunn was assigned by Homicide Captain L. D. Morrison Jr. to assist Lofland in supervising this investigation. Further assisting in the investigation were Detectives A. E. Rockwell, J. P. Paulk, C. E. Smith, I. W. Holmes and K. T. Defoor.

MR. AND MRS. LOUIS LYNDON SANDER ON THEIR WEDDING DAY

The description of the brown Pontiac was the only clue early on. HPD placed an all-points bulletin on this vehicle. The news media promptly aired this basic yet crucial information. As quickly as Sunday morning, leads began coming in and, as usual, most of them proved to be false alarms.

On Sunday afternoon, January, 22, the first big break unfurled. Point Control Officer E. M. Dobbs was on patrol and located a brown Pontiac with Arkansas license plates parked in the basement of a parking garage at 800 Franklin. It was reported stolen out of Little Rock, Arkansas on January 7. More interestingly, this vehicle had two obvious bullet creases on the upper body, from rear to front. When the license plate was broadcast on the police frequencies as well as the news media, more information began to flow.

The Galveston Police Department received a call indicating that the car was listed by a person who had registered in two Galveston motels over the past two weeks. The person driving the vehicle had registered as A. R. Johnson (White Male, mid- to late-30s). Additionally, a canvas of the area where the Pontiac was recovered turned up a parking lot attendant who said that he had parked this same vehicle on Friday, January 20, in the 100 block of Milam at Franklin. His description of the driver matched the one from Galveston.

SANDER FAMILY-MRS. SADIE, MR. WALTER, LYNDON, KENNETH, AND IN PHOTO, TAMU CADET DENNIS SANDER

Further investigation in Galveston led detectives to a bar on the Island. Investigators learned from the barmaid that she had knowledge of a Kenneth Hinkle who had been using their bar to take phone calls. An ID check revealed that one Kenneth Hinkle (White Male, 39) from West Memphis, Arkansas, fit the general description of the suspect.

The following is a summarization of a very thorough, professional investigation later presented to the Harris County District Attorney's Office:

On January 8, 1967, Kenneth Hinkle and his older brother, William, used this stolen Pontiac to commit an armed home robbery of a wealthy couple in Little Rock, Arkansas. They took jewelry, furs and a large amount of cash. A shot was fired during that robbery and the slug was later positively matched up as having been fired from the same weapon used to kill Officer Lyndon Sander. William and Kenneth Hinkle returned to Texas after the robbery to fence their stolen goods in Houston, Galveston and Beaumont. Witnesses said that after killing Officer Sander and dumping the vehicle on Franklin, Kenneth Hinkle made a long distance call to Beaumont from a bar at 800 Congress. Later, William Hinkle and his wife picked up Kenneth at a motel on Wayside. A cab had taken him there from the bar on Congress.

Based on an informant's tip, the Hinkle brothers were arrested the following week in New Orleans. Kenneth Hinkle was tried for the murder in the death of Officer Sander. On October 10, 1967, a Harris County jury convicted him and assessed him ninety-nine years and a day. William Hinkle was tried and convicted in Arkansas for his part in the robbery there.

Officer Sander was three weeks short of being twenty-five years old. He was survived by his wife Linda, who suddenly became a twenty-three-year-old widow with a three-year-old daughter, Stacie, and another child due any day. Other survivors were Lyndon's parents, Mr. and Mrs. Walter (Sadie) Sander, his brother Dennis, who was in the U. S. Army at the time, and his brother, Officer Kenneth Ray Sander, who had graduated from the same academy class with Lyndon and Officer Gene Brown. Linda Sander's due date was the day her husband and the baby's father were killed. On February 3, 1967, Kimberley Ann Sander was born, two weeks after her father died. Also mourning his death were his mother-in-law and stepfather-in-law Mr. and Mrs. Johnny Ray, stepfather-in-law John DiMacio, brother-in-law John Perry DiMacio, and sister-in-law Mrs. Karen Sander.

Funeral services were held at 2:00 p.m. on Tuesday, January 24, 1967, at the Forest Park Lawndale Funeral Chapel, with Reverend George Reck officiating. Burial followed at the Earthman Resthaven Cemetery on the North Freeway. Pallbearers were T.J. Scalise, T.L. Doty, G.E. Brown, J.A. Davis, O.H. McKissack, L.W. Redden, C.L. Simmons, and C.K. Kindall. Lyndon was a native Houstonian and a graduate of Reagan High School where he was an all-around student athlete. He also attended Blinn Junior College in Brenham, Texas.

Linda later remarried and had a son, Stephen Michael Hannah, a half-brother to Stacie and Kimberley. Linda lived in the Houston area in 2006 and unfortunately, was widowed again in 2006. Stacie Lynn Crown has two children-Lauren Elizabeth Crown, ten years old and Katherine Nicole Crown, six years old. Kimberley Anne Braswell has one son, Lyndon Tyler Braswell, ten years of age, a namesake for his grandfather that his mother never knew.

In a tragic irony, Stacie was widowed on January 21, 1987, when her husband was killed in a military aircraft accident – twenty years to the day that her father was murdered. Stacie, just like her mother, became a widow at age twenty-three. Mr. and Mrs. Sander are deceased and were laid to rest next to their son Lyndon at Resthaven. Kenneth later resigned from HPD and was employed by TCLEOSE in Austin for a number of years and now lives in Victoria. Dennis heads up his own engineering firm and lives in Houston.

LYNDON SANDER, MOST HANDSOME, REAGAN HIGH SCHOOL, 1960

When Officer Lyndon Sander stopped the brown Pontiac, two families of completely different backgrounds collided. Sander conducted a traffic stop, unknowingly stopping a career criminal, Kenneth Hinkle. The young officer very likely had no knowledge that Hinkle was wanted for the Arkansas robbery and that the driver of the vehicle possessed a prohibited weapon. He also had been proudly and openly driving a stolen vehicle for two weeks.

Lyndon and his brother Kenneth both proudly wore the uniforms of HPD. Their brother Dennis was honorably serving his country, wearing the U. S. Army uniform. All three were raised in the Houston Heights by honest, hard-working parents.

On the other end of the spectrum were the Hinkle brothers, William and Kenneth. Both were career criminals and were incarcerated for various crimes most of their adult lives. Kenneth Hinkle, after being arrested and convicted of Sander's murder, was bench warranted from Texas to Arkansas in 1984 in order to have his armed robbery case there tried while witnesses were still available. He served time in Arkansas for that crime. He died in a Tennessee Prison in 1996. It is unclear as to how he came to be in a Tennessee prison. But then, prisons were his frequent home.

As for the investigators, Captain Morrison, Lieutenants Lofland and Gunn, as well as Detectives Rockwell, Holmes, Nix, Paulk, and Combs are deceased. Detectives Horelica, Pierce, and Hall are retired. Gamino retired as a lieutenant and Smith and Defoor both retired as captains. Officer Dobbs also retired.

KIMBERLEY BRASWELL, STACIE CROWN, AND MRS. LINDA SANDER MCBRIDE

Gene Brown later promoted to sergeant and retired in 1990. Retired Officer Terry Scalisc, another close friend of Lyndon Sander who attended Reagan High School with him, said Lyndon was best man at his wedding. Brown and Scalise said they still have strong emotional feelings over the loss of their friend. They said they will never forget him and his devotion to duty.

This author has had the pleasure of meeting most of the remaining Sander family. Linda and her two daughters live with their loss in their own way each and every day. In speaking with brothers Dennis and Kenneth, it is obvious to me that the loss of their middle brother in this family, now nearly 40 years ago, is something that will never be gotten over. Mr. and Mrs. Walter Sander probably never got over the loss of that wonderful son and went to their own graves still mourning the loss of this fine young man.

The original marker for Officer Sander read as follows: A 100 Club marker has also been placed.

HUSBAND AND FATHER
LOUIS LYNDON SANDER
FEB 10, 1942 - JAN 21, 1967

56

Officer Louis Raymond Kuba
Badge #2074
May 17, 1967

Louis Kuba, a 34-Day Officer, Takes Fatal Bullet in Violent '67 TSU Campus Rioting

Louis Raymond Kuba was born on March 12, 1942 in Schwertner, Texas. His family moved to Nada, Texas. After graduating from Garwood High School in 1962, he served his country honorably for three years in the United States Army. He joined the Houston Police Department on December 27, 1966, in Police Cadet Class No. 34, graduating on April 14, 1967. His first assignment was to Radio Patrol Night Shift.

In May 1967, an atmosphere of racial unrest existed in the Houston area, particularly around the campus of the predominately African-American Texas Southern University. Demonstrations were held on May 15 and 16 at TSU, at the Holmes Road city dump (over a long promised incinerator) and at Northwood Junior High School on Homestead Road (over false rumors of an African American juvenile being shot by a white man).

On Tuesday, May 16, Criminal Intelligence Division Officers R. G. "Bobby" Blaylock and James O. "Bo" Norris were among many CID officers assigned to monitor these demonstrations. On this date, twenty-nine people were arrested for illegally demonstrating at the Holmes Road site. CID Officers A. L. Blair and C. F. Howard had received information regarding large amounts of weapons being brought onto the TSU campus. Intelligence also revealed that there were members of the Student Non-Violent Coordinating Committee (SNCC) who were agitating students on campus. Blaylock and Norris were assigned to monitor this activity on the TSU campus. There were numerous uniformed marked units in the area and CID Officers Blaylock, Norris, Blair, Howard and others were monitoring the activity.

At approximately 10:30 p.m. an individual named Charles Freeman began agitating a large crowd of students near the Student Activities Building. Then, a large watermelon was thrown onto the hood of a police car by an individual identified as Douglas Wayne Waller. At this time, Waller was arrested and found to be carrying a pistol. Leaders identified as Charles Freeman, Floyd Henry Nichols, Trazawell Franklin and John Parker continued agitating the crowd over the alleged Scenic Woods shooting. The crowd was going along with their prompting as some people threw rocks and bottles at the officers.

Unfortunately, the violence escalated. Shots were heard coming from the nearby men's dormitory. The gunfire continued and Officer Bobby Blaylock was hit in the left buttock. He was removed from the scene and taken to Ben Taub General Hospital.

OFFICER LOUIS RAYMOND KUBA

There were now several hundred Houston police officers in and around the TSU campus. Confusion and chaos reigned as shots continued from the upper floors of the dormitory in question. Police Chief Herman Short arrived to direct the police operation. Black leaders were summoned to help keep the situation from worsening. However, as they attempted to speak to the riotous crowd, they were turned back by a hail of gunfire in their direction. They were never able to negotiate.

At 2:20 a.m., a group of officers were near the northwest corner of the University Center, lined up along a wall awaiting directions from supervisors at the scene. Chief Short, like all of the other officers, took cover wherever possible. The chief directed officers to fire only when fired upon and only above the building or directly at a known source of the gunfire.

Reporters Charley Schneider of The Houston Post and Nick Gearhardt of KHOU-TV (Channel 11), were with this group of officers. Schneider said that there were two officers and a TV newsman in front of him. He said that Officer Louis Kuba was directly behind him with his hand on Schneider's shoulder. Heavy fire continued from the dorm and Schneider suddenly felt Kuba's hand become limp. Turning, he saw the officer slumping backward into Gearhardt's outstretched arms, an expressionless look on his face and blood pouring from his forehead. Schneider reported in a Post article the following day, "There was no riot at TSU. It was war."

An ambulance rushed the wounded officer to Ben Taub General Hospital. He died at 8:38 a.m. from a bullet wound above his right eye. Quiet, easy-going, even-tempered, Officer Louis Raymond Kuba, only thirty-four days out of Class No. 34, was only twenty-five.

He was survived by his wife, Patricia, who was seven months pregnant at the time. Other survivors were his parents, Mr. and Mrs. Jerry Kuba of Altair; grandparents Mr. and Mrs. Martinka of Granger; father- and mother-in-law Mr. and Mrs. James Bartlett of Houston; four sisters, Mrs. Henrietta Decker of Anto, Texas, Mrs. Mildred Squyres of Houston, Mrs. Rita Gravonic of Boling, Texas, and Miss Helen Kuba of Altair; and five brothers, Teddy Kuba of Garwood, Rudy Kuba of Beasley, Milton Kuba, a soldier in the U. S. Army, and Norbert and Andy Kuba of Altair.

A Bible Vigil service was held at 8 p.m. Thursday, May 18, at the Forest Park Lawndale Chapel. Funeral services were conducted at the St. Christopher Catholic Church at 8150 Park Place at 10 a.m. Friday, May 19. Burial followed in the Garden of Gethsemane Section of Forest Park Lawndale Cemetery.

Eventually, the shooting stopped and mass arrests were made. The record shows that 489 people were handled by local law enforcement agencies, which included not only HPD but the Harris County Sheriff's Department, District Attorney's Office and the Texas Department of Public Safety. Douglas Waller, Charles Freeman, Floyd Nichols, Trazawell Franklin and John Parker were charged with Inciting a riot and murder. There were several other casualties of the riot. Vice Officer Allen Dale Dugger received a gaping secondary bullet wound to his face, which required over three hundred stitches in three layers. One young officer went into hysteria and was treated for shock.

From a prosecutorial position, the cases were difficult. Even though it was felt that the five suspects had incited the students to riot, there was no testimony to put guns in their hands or show that they were even on campus when the fatal shot was fired. Firearms analysis of the slug indicated that it was a secondary strike, meaning that the bullet had probably ricocheted off something prior to striking Kuba. Additionally, the slug was not in very good shape for any positive matching to a particular weapon. To make matters even worse, it was not even the caliber of any of the weapons recovered at the scene.

PATRICIA AND LOUIS RAYMOND KUBA, 1965

As tough as this was to prosecute, Harris County District Attorney Carol Vance, a veteran prosecutor who had been elected to the top post in 1966, chose to take on this task. Because of extensive pre-trial publicity, a change of venue was sought and the trial was moved to Victoria, ninety miles southwest of Houston. Vance later said that he and his staff were going into uncharted waters with this prosecution. It was very difficult to prove that the inciting to riot charge led to the murder of Officer Kuba. In Victoria, District Judge Joe Kelely dealt the prosecution a heavy blow when he refused to allow the jury to consider the state's theory that Charles Freeman was guilty of the assault because he engaged in a riot.

Vance said in a newspaper article, "We were

poured out of court, so to speak in Victoria, when we could not get the riot statute to be considered as part of the evidence." The trial ended in a mistrial in October 1968. After much legal research and after all other prosecutorial avenues were studied, Vance moved to dismiss the charges against the five in November 1970. All five defendants went free.

Mrs. Patricia Kuba gave birth to a daughter, Karen Lynette, two months after her husband was killed. Patricia eventually remarried and moved on with her life, raising Karen, who now has a daughter of her own. Mr. and Mrs. Jerry Kuba lived into their nineties. In 2001, all nine of Officer Kuba's siblings were alive. Sister Mildred was the wife of retired Houston Police Officer Charles Squyres of Columbus. The other sisters and brothers lived in cities and towns all across Texas in 2001.

U.S. ARMY SPEC 4 LOUIS KUBA, 1966

Retired Officer Squyres said he remembered rushing to the hospital that night of the riot and learning with his wife and Patricia and her parents that Louis was seriously wounded. Squyres retired in 1984 from CID after twenty-five years with HPD.

Just over a year after his brother-in-law's murder, Squyres was involved in the high-speed chase after the killer of Officer Ben Gerhart, which resulted in the tragic death of Officer Bobby James. Gerhart's killer was shot and killed. Squyres not only lost his brother-in-law, but lost two close HPD friends in the Traffic Division in this violent incident thirteen months later.

The original Homicide investigation was conducted by Detectives E. D. "Sonny" Combs and I. W. "Ira" Holmes. Many others assisted in this massive investigation. Combs died in 1971 in his early forties from a Korean War POW-related condition. Holmes retired from the Forgery Division in 1987 with thirty-eight years of service and resided in Magnolia. He died in September 2001 at age seventy-six.

Officer Bobby Blaylock continued a long career of outstanding crime-fighting service in CID, retiring in 1977 after twenty years. He then worked for the Harris County District Attorney's Office for nineteen years, rising to the rank of chief investigator, retiring in 1996 and residing in Hunt, Texas. Blaylock still carried the TSU souvenir in his anatomy. Bo Norris retired from HPD in 1978 and died in 1995. A. L. Blair retired from HPD Legal Services in 1999 with forty-two years of service. C. F. Howard retired in 1984 and died in 1993. This foursome of CID officers, along with many others, played important intelligence and undercover roles, not only in the 1967 TSU riot but also again in the People's Party II incident on Dowling Street in 1970.

Officer Allen Dale Dugger retired from HPD in 1988 after thirty years and a lengthy and hardworking career in the Houston-Harris County Organized Crime Unit, doing mostly undercover work. He retired to Wimberly, Texas. Dugger said that when he was shot, he was standing next to a uniformed officer, who, coincidentally, turned out to be his brother, Joe T. Dugger. He related how as he was being led to safety with blood gushing from his face, he saw Officer Kuba lying on the ground. Kuba and Dugger had been shot at almost the same time and in close proximity to each other.

Fortunately, most police officers go through their entire career without being shot. However, in the case of Dale Dugger, he may be one of the very few HPD officer to have been shot twice in the line of duty. Dugger was shot again in a 1971 incident by Kenneth Buntion, who was then shot and killed by other officers. Kenneth Buntion was the twin brother of Carl Wayne Buntion who murdered Solo Officer Jim Irby nineteen years later, in 1990. Carl Buntion was on Death Row since March 6, 1991 in the process of exhausting his appeals.

In the Kenneth Buntion incident, Dugger, other Vice and CID Officers, as well as Pasadena officers, were attempting to arrest Buntion at 3132 Tidwell when he came out shooting. Dugger was struck in the femoral artery and would have bled to death had it not been for the medical assistance of a civilian at the scene, Norm Pullens. Pullens is the only known civilian to be recognized by the 100 Club of Greater Houston for saving an Officer's life.

Officers W. D. "Tooter" Steffenauer and Johnny R. Thornton shot and killed Kenneth Buntion. Thornton was shot in the arm and recovered from his wound. Both Steffenauer and Thornton retired from HPD.

The original marker for Officer Kuba, which has now been replaced by a 100 Club marker, read:

LOUIS RAYMOND KUBA
MAR 12, 1942 - MAY 17, 1967

57 & 58

Officers Ben Eddie Gerhart
Badge #1230
and
Bobby L. James
Badge #1142
June 26, 1968

West Loop Littering Suspect Kills Gerhart, Later Causes James' Death

Wednesday, June 26, 1968, began just like any other hot summer day in HPD's Traffic Bureau for Officer Ben Gerhart of the Traffic Enforcement Division and for Accident Investigator Bobby L. James of the Accident Division. However, before the day would be over, Houston PD would have lost two of their finest.

On this Wednesday, at approximately 11:30 a.m., Officer Gerhart, riding a one-man unit, was on patrol in the 1000 block of the West Loop North. He wore HPD Badge No. 1230. Gerhart observed glass bottles being thrown from a vehicle traveling north on the West Loop. He pulled over this vehicle and approached the driver's side. The driver was a white male driving a Buick. He had a white female by his side.

The officer obtained the driver's license from the driver and took him back to his marked blue and white traffic enforcement vehicle for a brief interview. The driver was identified as Roderick Michael Isaacks (White Male, 23). Officer Gerhart returned to the Buick to speak to the female, identified as Monica Isaacks (White Female, 19), Roderick's wife. He learned from Monica that Roderick had a gun.

Gerhart then went back and got Roderick out of the patrol car and searched him. Finding no weapon, Gerhart started toward the Buick again, apparently to search for the gun there. As he was making his approach, Roderick Isaacks ran past him, grabbed the gun from underneath the front seat and turned to face Gerhart, who had quickly pulled his revolver. Before Gerhart could defend himself, Isaacks fired one shot, hitting him in the face. The officer was not able to return fire and fell to the ground. While he lay on the ground beside the busy freeway, Isaacks picked up the police officer's weapon, ran to his car and sped away north on the West Loop. Monica was still with him.

A number of nearby witnesses observed all or part of this tragic chain of events. One of them got on the police radio and reported what happened, even providing a description of the vehicle and a license number. An ambulance was quickly dispatched to the scene, taking Officer Gerhart to Memorial Northwest Hospital, less than a mile away. However, he was dead on arrival.

OFFICER BEN EDDIE GERHART

Officers J. A. Shirley and C. F. Squyres, a two-man traffic enforcement unit, were at the Old North Loop and Jensen when they spotted the suspect vehicle. They began a hot pursuit and near the Old North Loop and Hirsch were joined by another marked unit, Accident Officer Bobby L. James, who pulled out between them and the suspect.

A high-speed chase continued east on the North Loop and then northbound on Old Beaumont Highway (U. S. 90), reaching speeds in excess of one hundred miles per hour. With James in close pursuit in his eight-cylinder vehicle, the chase continued nearly eight miles, with Isaacks firing his pistol at the

137

officer. A number of other units were behind James attempting to provide assistance. Officers Shirley and Squyres were following as close as their vehicle, a six-cylinder Plymouth, would allow. Radio Patrol Sergeant H. L. Stephens and Radio Patrol Officers J. R. Jeffcoat and J. C. Robbins, all riding one-man units, were in line behind Shirley and Squyres.

Officer James did his best to stay close to the suspect. Near U.S. 90 and Talcott, Isaack's Buick struck the rear of a Ford driven by a citizen. The collision caused both the Buick and the Ford to spin around and land crossways in the middle of the highway. It will never be known, but it is believed that Officer James was faced with a split-second decision – he had to either strike one of the two vehicles or take his chances and hit the ditch. He chose the latter, striking a three-foot-high culvert. He was killed instantly.

MRS. RUBY GERHART, DIANE GERHART, AND OFFICER BEN GERHART

Officer James A. Shirley later said it was a widely held belief among fellow officers that Officer Bobby James gave his life to avoid the possibility of hitting the civilian's Ford, which turned out to be occupied by three adults and four children. Roderick Isaacks fled on foot, still eluding officers and shooting at them. He was cornered in a small clump of woods nearby, continuing to shoot at his pursuers, who eventually included Sergeant Stephens and Officers Jeffcoat, Robbins, Shirley and Squyres. Isaacks died in the shootout of multiple gunshot wounds.

In the short span of less than half an hour, two of Houston's finest lost their lives as the result of the actions of one man. Officer Ben Gerhart was one month short of being forty-six years old. Officer Bobby James was thirty-eight.

The investigation following these two deaths revealed the following about Roderick Isaacks:

A YOUNG BEN GERHART IN HIS GENE AUTRY LOOK

Monica had left Roderick and filed for divorce due to Roderick's physical abuse. He located her and forced her to come back to live with him. When Officer Gerhart stopped their Buick, they were embroiled in a heated domestic argument. The weapon used to kill Officer Gerhart was purchased just four days before this terrible tragedy took place.

A fifteen-year veteran and graduate of Police Cadet Class No. 9, Gerhart had been a Houston policeman since May 26, 1953. He was survived by his wife Ruby, fourteen-year-old daughter Diane and his brother, HPD Officer Henry Gerhart. He was also survived by his father, John Gerhart, another brother Johnny, and sisters Mrs. Minnie Trotky, Mrs. Gladys Greer, Miss Ruth Gerhart, and Mrs. Dorothy Bell.

Funeral services for Officer Gerhart were held on Friday, June 28, 1968, from the Heights Funeral Home. Burial followed at Memorial Oaks Cemetery. Pallbearers were fellow Officers D.B. Lecour, B.K. Gordy, J.D. Evans, R. Brumley, R.B. Mize, and F.S. Brewton.

OFFICER BOBBY L. JAMES

Officer James, a sixteen-year veteran officer, graduated from Police Cadet Class No 7 on October 12, 1951. He was survived by his wife Georgia; mother and stepfather, Mary and Hubert Hayes; daughters Gayle, Cynthia and Pamela, and stepsons Don and Ronald Davenport. In March 1999, Georgia lived in Pasadena. (Georgia passed away in 2005). Officer James' mother, Mrs. Hayes, lived in Oklahoma. Stepfather Hubert Hayes is deceased, as is daughter Pamela and stepson Don. He had a number of grandchildren now, none of whom ever knew him. Note: The James family has maintained their privacy over these many years and for that reason, not much is known about the family since 1968. That privacy will continue to be respected.

Funeral services for Officer Bobby James were held at 10 a.m. on Saturday, June 29, 1968, from the North Central Baptist Church at 2100 Tidwell under the direction of Pat H. Foley Funeral Home, 2110 Tidwell. The Reverends Kenneth Trent and James Pass officiated. Pallbearers were J.E. Welch, W.K. Weiner, E.F. McBeth, J.R. Jeffcoat, G.F. Cox, and J.J. Sevcik. Burial followed at the Brookside Memorial Park, Eastex Freeway and Lauder Road.

In 2006, Mrs. Ruby Gerhart still resides in her Oak Forest home. Diane Gerhart Sullivan lives next door to her mother where she raised one son, Jonathan Sullivan, who never knew his grandfather because of what Isaacks did. Officer Henry Gerhart retired and also lives in the Oak Forest area. Officer Gerhart's father, brother John and sisters Gladys Greer and Minnie Trotky are deceased while sisters Ruth and Dorothy are still living.

Sergeant Stephens and Officers Jeffcoat, Robbins, Shirley and Squyres all retired from HPD. They lived in various parts of Texas and away from the careers that brought them very close to the same end that Officers Gerhart and James met that day in June 1968. Sergeant Stephens and Officer Jeffcoat are deceased in 2006.

A short time after this double tragedy, an article appeared in the Houston Post written by sports writer John Wilson. Mr. Wilson knew Officer Ben Gerhart from where he regularly worked Houston Astros game at Gate 2 at the Astrodome. I will include several excerpts from Mr. Wilson regarding Officer Gerhart: "Thousands knew his cheerful face and his friendly good nights. He should still be sitting there in that chair, his walkie-talkie to his ear or in his lap. Ben had already put in a full day on the force when he arrived for duty those many evenings at Gate 2. However, I never saw him in an ill-temper or heard him complain. And that is the way everyone at the Dome remembered him, a friendly, patient, human man. Every day a policeman puts on a uniform, he defends your stake in living in a civilized community. Every day Ben Gerhart put on his shield, he wore it with honor, and for the community good. And finally it cost him all. The day he had his life taken I saw tears in the eyes of honest people. There is a time for joy and a time for weeping. It is honorable for sincere men to weep when a good man dies".

Thank you, Mr. Wilson. This applies to Officer Gerhart and Officer James as well.

Marker for Officer Gerhart at Memorial Oaks:

GERHART, BEN E.
1922-1968 (HAS BADGE #1230)

Marker for Officer James at Brookside:

JAMES, BOBBY LEE
DEC 1, 1929-JUN 26, 1968

59

Officer Kenneth Wayne Moody
Badge #1850
November 26, 1969

Career Criminal Wesley Sellars Murders Officer Moody at Hamilton Junior High

Kenneth Wayne Moody was born in Center, Texas, on December 19, 1932. He spent his early school years in Center, but graduated from El Paso High School in 1951. From 1951-1955, he served in the U. S. Navy and was a Korean War veteran. On May 20, 1963, he joined HPD Police Cadet Class No. 28, graduating on September 6, 1963. His first and only assignment was to the Radio Patrol Bureau-Night Shift. He wore Badge No. 1850.

On Tuesday night, November 25, 1969, Officer Moody and his regular partner, R. R. Dietrich, were working the 11 p.m.–7 a.m. shift out of the North Shepherd Substation. Riding Unit No. 633, at 1:01 a.m. they received a silent alarm call to Hamilton Junior High School at 20th Street and Heights Boulevard. Arriving at 1:06 a.m., they parked on 22nd Street behind the school. They located a window with a broken pane of glass and carefully crawled through it.

As they walked down the darkened hallway, they came to a corner and were under a lightened EXIT sign when they were fired upon. Moody and Dietrich returned fire in the direction of their assailant, Moody twice and Dietrich four times. Dietrich then heard Moody say that he had been hit. Seeing the seriousness of the wound, Dietrich had no choice but to run to the patrol car and call for help.

This was long before the days of Handi-Talkie portable radios. After putting out the "Assist the Officer," Dietrich returned to aid his partner. The first officers to arrive were C. D. Flowers and his rookie partner, M. A. Walker. They were in front of the school when Dietrich put out the Assist. L. W. Schaeffer and J. E. Baker from the Northeast night shift and Canine Officer John Ruchti arrived shortly thereafter.

The officers searched the building. When they spotted the suspect lying in a hallway, he turned toward Officer Ruchti, who fired one shot at this suspect. The shot missed, but the officers took the already wounded suspect into custody.

Just prior to this shot being fired, rookie Officer M. A. Walker was checking the rear of the building. While doing so, he heard a metal object strike the covered walkway above him. Upon checking, he found that a .25-caliber automatic pistol had been thrown out of the fire escape near where the suspect lay just before his arrest. The suspect had apparently tried to dump his weapon as he lay wounded and heard the other officers approaching him.

Meanwhile, a private ambulance picked up Officer Moody and took him to Heights Hospital where he was pronounced DOA at 1:25 a.m. from one gunshot wound to the right chest. He was thirty-six years and eleven months old.

A private ambulance also rushed the suspect to the same hospital. He was taken into surgery in critical condition for a gunshot wound to the right chest. Investigators who later interviewed him found him to be uncooperative. He remained in the hospital until December 4, at which time he was taken to the Harris County Jail on charges of murder and assault to murder under the name of Wesley Sellars, having been identified by fingerprints. The investigation continued into this burglary and capital murder as there were a number of unanswered questions amid much speculation regarding this tragic police shooting.

Sellars (White Male, 32) was a Houston native known as the "California Kid" due to arrests in that state for burglary and robbery. He also was well known in the Houston area due to his acquittal on a robbery charge in 1965. Sellars was indicted for burglary in connection with the same incident. His trial on that charge ended in a mistrial. In a third trial, he was assessed ninety-nine years in October 1965, a conviction upheld by the Texas appeals courts in March 1966. However, a federal judge overturned that conviction, prompting Sellers' release in April 1968. In September 1969, just two months before the murder of Officer Moody, authorities arrested Sellars on auto theft and weapons charges near Nacogdoches. He was out on a $10,000 bond when he killed the officer. Sellars' brother Calvin was on Texas Death Row for his part in the 1964 Schepps family torture-robbery.

Officers immediately pondered the mystery of why a career criminal like Sellers would try to burglarize a junior high school. Also, three pry bars found at the point of entry led investigators to believe that he was not acting alone. After an extensive investigation, no other suspects were seen or could be placed at the scene. Further speculation spawned an opinion that Sellers was nothing more than a petty thief willing to burglarize any place.

Officer Kenneth Wayne Moody was survived by his wife of twelve years, Elva Joy Moody, eleven-year-old son Gregory Blake Moody and nine-year-old daughter Wendy Gayle Moody. Other survivors were his mother and stepfather, Lula and Louis Miller of Pasadena, and his father, Arvin Moody of Center, Texas. In addition to his mother-in-law and two grandparents, he also left behind one sister, Mrs. Rodney Beasley of Washington, DC.

Funeral services were held at 3 p.m. Friday, November 28, 1969 at the Church of Jesus Christ of Latter Day Saints at No. 65 Melbourne. Burial followed at the Resthaven Cemetery on Interstate 45 North.

OFFICER KENNETH WAYNE MOODY

Elva Moody remarried and lived in Thornton, Colorado in 2001 after having been widowed again after Kenneth Moody. She worked in the assisted living health care field. Son Gregory worked in Golden, Colorado, married with three children, Lucas, Meredith and Merrill. Daughter Wendy lived nearby in Arvada, also employed in the health care field. She was married with a son Brendan and a daughter Samantha. Officer Moody's mother, Mrs. Lula Miller, and his sister, Mrs. Rodney Beasley, lived in Marshall, Texas in 2001. His father, stepfather, mother-in-law, and grandparents are deceased.

The initial scene investigation was conducted by Homicide Detectives C. E. "Chuck" Smith and Max W. Lankford. Lieutenant James E. "Pete" Gunn supervised the scene and the follow-up with the assistance of E. D. "Sonny" Combs, Ken T. Defoor and Tommy E. Baker. Smith retired as a captain in 1980, having worked in Juvenile and Recruiting. He lived in the Lovelady, Texas area. Lankford worked in Homicide until the late 1970's after which time he served in Internal Affairs and Special Thefts. He retired as a detective in 1984 and served as an investigator with the Harris County District Attorney's Office, retiring from there in 2000.

Pete Gunn, after serving in Vice, SWAT and CID, retired in 1991. He died after a lengthy illness in December 2000. Sonny Combs passed away from a Korean War-related illness in 1971. Defoor retired in 1983 as a captain and Baker retired in 1985 from Homicide as a detective. J. E. Baker retired from HPD in 1990 and passed away in 2002. L. W. Schaeffer retired as a lieutenant in 1989 and died suddenly in 1990. John Ruchti retired in 1981 and resided in the Houston area. C. D. Flowers retired in 1985 from the Homicide Crime Scene Unit. M. A. Walker later worked in Robbery as a detective, in Patrol as a lieutenant and captain. He later was commander of the Tactical Operations Division (SWAT, HNT and Bomb Squad). R. R. Dietrich continued his career at North Shepherd Patrol, never forgetting that night he lost his partner and best friend. He retired in 1988, spending time at his home here in Houston as well as at his ranch near Burton, Texas.

One of K.W. Moody's best friends and pallbearers was Officer Robert E. Serres. When Officer Moody was murdered, Serres and his wife were expecting a child in February 1970. That child, a son, was named for Officer Moody. He became Houston Police Officer Kenneth Wayne Serres, an officer since 1994.

Wesley Sellars had a long criminal history and exhibited an unusual ability to beat the justice system. Harris County District Attorney Carol Vance prosecuted Sellars and sought the death penalty. A jury found him guilty. But even with his long record, he was only given a life sentence for murdering Officer Moody while in the process of committing another felony. Unfortunately, history repeated itself. The conviction was overturned on appeal. Sellars was released, pending a new trial that was never held for some unexplained reason.

He continued his life of crime and in 1984 was released on a burglary bond by State District Judge Lupe Salinas. After failing to appear in court in July 1985, his bond was forfeited and the FBI filed an unlawful flight to avoid prosecution charge against him. Assistant District Attorney Chuck Rosenthal (later the Harris County district attorney), who had argued vehemently against Sellars being released on bond, discussed the idea of Wesley Sellars surrendering with Sellars' brother Calvin. Calvin Sellars had worked himself off Death Row. Having also beaten the system, he became a paralegal. A 1986 newspaper article quoted Rosenthal as telling Calvin Sellars that someone would kill his brother Wesley if he didn't turn himself in.

On November 25, 1986, Wesley Sellars, still on the run, became involved in a one-man crime spree near Phoenix, Arizona. He was jumped in a stolen vehicle and the Scottsdale police chased him into the nearby city of Tempe. There, Sellars grabbed a six-year-old boy walking home from school. He also hijacked another vehicle at gunpoint. After having another accident, he got out of his latest vehicle with the boy as a hostage and kicked in the door of a residence, initiating a four-hour standoff.

Eventually, Sellars exposed himself for a safe shot from the local TAC Team. The house was attacked and Sergeant Ralph Tranter was shot in the eye while in the process of rescuing the little boy.

Finally, one day short of seventeen years from the day Sellars murdered HPD Officer Kenneth Wayne Moody, justice was finally served. Tempe Police Officer Les Gray felled Sellars with a single shotgun blast to the chest, leaving him dead at the scene. Sellers left Officer Gray with a graze wound and also shot and killed a police dog.

Ralph Tranter became the chief of police of the three-hundred-officer Tempe Police Department. In 2001, he said he regained some vision after several surgeries. Officer Les Gray later retired from Tempe PD and worked in law enforcement in Pine Top, Arizona. Both men still remembered the role they played in helping to end the crime-laden path of destruction caused by Wesley Sellars throughout his life.

The original marker for Officer Moody reads:

OUR DAD FOREVER
KENNETH W. MOODY, 1932-1969
BADGE #1850 AND MASONIC EMBLEM

60

Officer Leon Griggs
Badge #1018
January 31, 1970

Outstanding Detective Work Solves Case Of Officer Leon Griggs, Shot in Hijacking

On the Saturday of January 31, 1970, Officer Leon Griggs went to an approved extra job to provide for his family. He worked security at the Sacco Brothers Food Market, 2616 Blodgett, in Houston's Third Ward. Officer Griggs, who had been assigned to the Jail Division for the past ten years, was working this job on his day off and was due to be relieved at 5 p.m. that day by Officer H. L. Phillips.

At approximately 4:25 p.m., several black males approached Officer Griggs as he walked toward the front of the store. As he neared the checkout area inside the front door, the first man (later identified as Suspect No. 1) grabbed the officer's hands from the front. In the same instance, another man (Suspect No. 2) came from behind him, lifted the back of his uniform jacket and stuck a pistol in his back.

OFFICER LEON GRIGGS

As Griggs struggled with the suspect in front who was attempting to control his arms, Suspect No. 1 shot the officer from the front, causing him to fall backwards. Both suspects fired more shots and while Griggs was lying on the floor on his back, Suspect No. 1 removed the officer's service revolver from its holster. He then pulled the officer up from the floor by his tie and used the gun to fire at least three more rounds into the defenseless officer's chest. Robbery was the apparent motive for this offense, yet the suspects took no money from the store.

The two men fled the store with the store manager in hot pursuit. The manager fired once in the air in an attempt to stop the suspects. However, Suspect No. 1 then turned around and fired three shots at his pursuer, missing him all three times. After Officer Griggs was

142

shot, five other African-American males fled the store along with the two suspects. Memorial Ambulance picked up Officer Griggs and rushed him to Ben Taub General Hospital, where he was dead on arrival. He had been shot seven times.

Homicide Lieutenant J. E. "Pete" Gunn headed this investigation. P. S. "Paul" Nix and E. L. "Ed" Horelica were the primary detectives, assisted by W. J. "Bill" Wehr and Irvin E. "Mac" McComas. Witness information led to an arrest before the day was over. But the man arrested was not the right suspect. However, he remained in jail on other charges and proved to be helpful to investigators for the next several months in piecing together what happened that day at Sacco's on Blodgett Street.

Officer Griggs was a graduate of HPD Police Cadet Class No. 12 and had fourteen years and two months service at the time of his death. He was several weeks short of being forty-two years old. Funeral services were held from the Greater Zion Baptist Church, 3202 Trulley, on Wednesday, February 4, 1970. Burial followed at Cemetery Beautiful, 8205 Wheatley, in Houston.

Outstanding detective work over the next several months revealed the identities of several other subjects who were in the store at the time of the Griggs murder and fled when the shots were fired. Detectives Horelica and Nix, who both later retired from HPD, said this was a very complicated and involved case due to the fact that so many individuals fled the store after the shooting. The investigation led to the identities of three of those individuals. But the witnesses were uncertain if these particular suspects were either of the two that actually shot and killed Leon Griggs.

The first big break in the case came in late March of 1970, when the service revolver of Officer Griggs was recovered in Dallas, where police arrested three African-American male hijackers in a food store robbery. One of the arrested suspects, Elmer Porter, fit the description of the Suspect No. 1, who was behind Officer Griggs and shot him in the back. The Dallas officers recovered Griggs' pistol from Elmer Porter's car.

After Nix and Horelica went to Dallas and questioned Porter, they learned from him that it was his car that was used as the getaway vehicle in the Griggs shooting event. More importantly, Porter gave them a confession outlining his involvement as well as the name of the other shooter and the two other suspects who were part of their group. Further investigation led to murder charges against Porter and a man named Wardell Ellis. Two other suspects were present but did not shoot Officer Griggs. They were located and gave statements implicating Wardell Ellis and Elmer Porter. No charges were filed against either of these two witnesses.

Porter, who was in custody, and Ellis were charged with murder in the death of Officer Griggs. Ellis was still loose and attempts were unsuccessful in locating and arresting him. However, on February 8, 1971, more than a year after the shooting, Houston investigators received information that a robbery suspect had been involved in a shooting with police officers in Atlanta, Georgia, and that a hijacker by the name of Raymond Hunter had been killed in this shootout. Further investigation revealed the true identity of "Raymond Hunter" to be Wardell Ellis. Fingerprints taken from Hunter's body were sent to Houston and proven to be those of Wardell Ellis.

Detectives Nix and Horelica eventually reached the conclusion that Griggs' murder happened while there were two separate groups of hijackers in the Sacco Brothers Food Market. Naturally, neither knew of the other. When the Wardell Ellis-Elmer Porter team shot Officer Griggs, the other group fled the store since they also were armed and did not want to be stopped for questioning. This led to the confusion in the witnesses' accounts.

RICHARD GRIGGS, LESSIE GRIGGS, LINDA GRIGGS ROBINSON, LEON GRIGGS JR., AND LESLIE GRIGGS

The murder of a police officer going unsolved was abhorrent to all fellow police officers in the early 1970s. Fortunately, that tradition holds true right on up until today. It was also a day when the chief of police rewarded outstanding investigative work like this with a slap on the back and a Thank You. Neither the city nor the department ever officially commended Detectives Nix and Horelica for their tireless dedication to duty in this case.

Paul Nix retired in 1973 and worked a number of years as a district attorney's investigator for Wood County in the east Texas railroad town of Mineola. He completely retired in 2002 and died in 2006. He also was an accomplished western artist. Nix and Horelica had earlier been instrumental in clearing another Houston police officer whodunit, that of Officer Louis Lyndon Sander in 1967. Nix, the aspiring artist, created a cartoon strip depicting the entire Sander case investigation. He never succeeded in marketing the strip.

Detective Horelica retired in 1991 after thirty-five years with the department. After his HPD retirement, he served a number of years as security director at Baylor College of Medicine and is retired as of 2007. Lieutenant Gunn left Homicide in 1974 and continued his HPD career in the Vice amd SWAT Divisions and, for many years, in the Criminal Intelligence Division as the commander of the Houston-Harris County Organized Crime Task Force. After many years of heart problems, he died in 2000.

Bill Wehr later made lieutenant and worked for a

number of years in the Robbery Division before retiring to go into the air conditioning business. He retired from that line of work and lived in Houston to enjoy fishing around Galveston Bay. Mac McComas retired to Trinity, his wife's hometown, and continued to serve his community as municipal judge there. He died suddenly in 1996, just four months after the sudden death of his lovely wife, Jean.

Elmer Porter was tried for murder in the death of Officer Leon Griggs. A jury convicted him and gave him a life sentence. He was paroled in 1992, but this leave was revoked the following year and he was sent to the Ramsey Unit III.

Officer Griggs was survived by his wife Mrs. Iona Griggs, their son Richard Griggs, who was three and one-half years old, and by Leon's son and daughter by a previous marriage, twenty-one-year-old Leon Griggs Jr. and nineteen-year-old Linda Griggs. Also, at the time of Leon's death, Iona was pregnant with twin daughters Lessie Griggs and Leslie Griggs. In 2007, Iona resided in Houston as did Richard, Lessie and Leslie. Linda married and lived near Houston, the mother of her son Marcus, who has four daughters. Leon Jr. was the father of one daughter, Leah Griggs.

Iona Griggs raised three children without a father. Two were born after their father's death and Richard has hardly any remembrance of his father. In 2002, Lessie commented about the events her father missed out on in the summer of 1970 when she and Leslie were born on June 9, Leon Jr. was married on June 19, and Marcus was born on June 20. Additionally, two more of Officer Griggs' children grew up without their father to support and guide them.

Iona said that Leon hailed from a rural area, Cook's Point near Caldwell in Central Texas, and he loved horses. "He could ride horses," his wife said. "He tried to teach me how to ride but he was unsuccessful. I grew up in Bryan, but not on a farm or ranch."

Mrs. Iona met her future husband when he was working patrol in Third Ward with his partner, Robert Crane, who retired from HPD. Iona found Leon to be "a very quiet person who worked quite a bit. He was sociable and liked to have a little fun. He was a great teaser." Leon also was like many HPD officers – he worked extra jobs to provide a higher quality of life for his family. "He worked all these extra jobs," Iona Griggs recalled. "He worked in the jail from 5 a.m. until 2 p.m. Then he worked in some of these little clubs, like Walter's Lounge on Lockwood.

"He was always saying, 'Be careful out there in those clubs.' He also worked at a grocery store. He never knew the grocery store would be the place (that would pose the greatest danger)." When he was not working, he was deacon at Greater Zion Missionary Baptist Church. He would patrol the church parking lot on Sunday nights, accounting for the safety of people getting in and out of their cars. He also liked to travel with Iona to places in Mexico and to Louisville, Kentucky, where his sister, Ida Mae Parks, lived. Ida Mae, who was twenty years older than Leon, was like a mother to her younger brother the police officer.

On Saturdays, Leon Griggs worked an extra job at Sacco Brothers. On Saturday, January 31, 1970, he was due to get off at 5 p.m., when he would return home to Iona and Richard on the east side of Houston. Just thirty-five minutes from his normal quitting time, Leon Griggs was shot and killed by hijackers. He was the first uniformed black Houston police officer who gave his life in the line of duty.

The murder of this police officer, husband and father devastated his family. Iona was his second wife. Iona's pregnancy grew to be even more uncomfortable as she continued teaching school and caring for young Richard. "I became extremely heavy with the twins," Iona said. "There was not too much I could do. I was very uncomfortable at the time." Thankfully, she had help from Ida Mae Parks, who uprooted in Kentucky and moved to Houston to devote her life to helping Iona with Richard and the twins. She also had another plan.

"She was instrumental in raising us," Leslie Griggs, one of the twins, said. "She kept us together (with Leon Jr. and Linda), making sure we weren't raised away from each other, coming from two different marriages and everything." Iona Griggs said, "She kept them all together so they could get to know each other. They are very close now. That was a blessing. I sometimes wonder if Leon had lived if he could have pulled them together like that."

The 100 Club of Houston also pitched in to help Officer Griggs' surviving family. The Club invited Iona and Richard to the Houston Livestock Show and Rodeo in February and presented them with a $4,000 check.

"After the twins were born, I couldn't go right back to work immediately," Iona said. "I think I stayed off a year. Ida Mae moved here and helped keep the children for me when I went back to work." The twin girls, Leslie and Lessie, and Richard are all graduates of Prairie View A&M University. "My three didn't even know their father," Iona said. "Richard was three at the time and vaguely remembers a few things. Lessie and Leslie couldn't share anything. He was dead before they were born."

She raised her family as honest, church-going individuals, saying, "I thank God that they have all tried to grow up and be some kind of asset to the community instead of getting off in some kind of trouble. I'm so proud of them for that." In 2002, Leslie Griggs said she and Lessie experienced many difficult moments "not having a father, not being able to connect with whatever my other sister and brother shared. Our brother Richard was young but remembered quite a bit. We had our mother, who was great and provided what we needed. We didn't want for anything. We only have pictures of our father but not that touch or feel of knowing what that person was. It took a big adjustment. Of course, it (adjusting) is still there. A lot of our friends grew up with two parents. It was a pretty big void for both of us not having that."

Iona said, "I wanted them to be happy, peaceful and at home, and I think they were. I think the hardest time I have noticed with Leslie and Lessie were times when they were little kids and their friends would be talking about their daddies and places they went with their fathers, things they were doing. Seemed like sometimes they would kind of get emotional."

In 2002, Lessie was an accountant with a realty company, while Richard worked for a communications center. Leon Jr., a Texas Southern University graduate, was an executive for a national corporation in Rochester, N.Y., and Linda Griggs Robinson, lived in Houston and worked for the State of Texas. Linda, a University of Houston graduate, had a son, Marcus, and four granddaughters. At one time, Marcus entertained the idea of becoming a police officer, going so far as to work as a guard in the state prison system for many years. Leon's daughter, Leah, graduated from the Fordham Law School in New York.

Ida Mae Parks died in 2000 at age ninety. Iona, also a TSU graduate and a retired teacher, never really retired. She worked four days a week in Coca-Cola's "valued youth" program – which encourages high school seniors to stay in school – as a supervisor at the elementary school level.

The gravemarker for Officer Griggs at Cemetery Beautiful is a large three space monument to the GRIGGS family. In the center of the three spaces, is OFFICER LEON, 1928-1970 with his BADGE #1018 above the name. A 100 Club marker has also been placed to honor this fallen hero.

61

Officer Robert Wayne (Bob) Lee
Badge #2296
January 31, 1971

Officer Bob Lee Killed While Investigating Service Station Hi-jacking. A 25-month Career Ends in Tragedy

It began as a typical Saturday night at the 10 o'clock roll call at the Park Place substation. Officer D. W. "Wayne" Shirley was paired up on this night with Officer Robert W. "Bob" Lee on Unit 742, which normally rode far out the Gulf Freeway in the area of Almeda Mall. Lee's regular partner, Officer Mike Kardatzke, was training a rookie, J. C. Moseley, and riding Unit 712, which was an East End unit also out of Park Place.

Officers Lee and Shirley had received a call from the Pearland Police Department to pick up a juvenile prisoner and were en route to Central Station when they heard a call dispatched regarding a robbery by firearms at the Enco Station at the Gulf Freeway and Wayside. Officer Lee was driving and had just passed Wayside. He took the next exit, Telephone Road, in order to make a u-turn back to Wayside.

OFFICER ROBERT WAYNE LEE

As he did so, Officer Shirley, who was riding in the back seat (this was prior to Patrol cars having cages) with the prisoner, saw an African-American male suspect inside the Kayo Station at Telephone and the Gulf Freeway. The suspect was holding a gun to the attendant's head. Shirley made Lee aware of this. Lee immediately stopped the Patrol car and Shirley got out with his AR180 rifle. Lee continued a short distance past the station and drove into a driveway that ran behind the Kayo station. Lee reported their situation to the Police Dispatcher, got out of the car and approached the rear of the station with his weapon drawn.

Officers R. W. Carpenter and C. D. Dearing in Unit 710, having heard the radio transmissions, had arrived and parked at the intersection of

Telephone and Cumberland, a block south of the freeway. Carpenter was armed with his .357 service revolver while Dearing was carrying a .30-caliber carbine.

The suspect left the Kayo station as Officer Lee was approaching the north side of the building from the rear. As Officer Lee came forward, one shot was heard and Officers Shirley, Carpenter and Dearing saw their colleague fall to the ground. The suspect ran north toward the Gulf Freeway with the three officers shooting at him. As the suspect ran up a grassy slope toward the freeway, Officers Kardatzke and Moseley arrived. They also shot at the suspect, who fell dead at the center guardrail of the Gulf Freeway.

An ambulance quickly transported Officer Lee to Ben Taub General Hospital, where he was pronounced dead on arrival as the result of a single gunshot wound that went through the left side of his head. He was thirty-five years old.

The hijacker, twenty-four-year-old T. L. Wilson, was identified by photos as the suspect who had robbed the location of the original call at Wayside and the Gulf Freeway. Wilson had no local police record. He did have an old Texas State Prison ID number. Research into his background indicated that he was from Panola County, near Carthage, and that he had done time just prior to this incident for burglary out of Panola County. He had also been handled in that area of the state for rape and indecency with a child.

Officer Robert Wayne Lee was a native of Louisiana, having been born on December 21, 1935 and graduated from Opelousas High School in Opelousas, Louisiana in 1953. While in high school, he was involved in boxing. He was the first Opelousas area amateur boxer to enter the Lafayette District Golden Gloves boxing tournament in 1955. He fought as a welterweight at 147 pounds.

After attending college for a short time and also boxing there, he worked in the oil fields as a roughneck. In 1957, he volunteered for the service of his country and spent the next three years in the United States Marine Corps, serving overseas. After his honorable discharge, he was again employed in the oil industry for a number of years and in 1968 – at nearly thirty-three years of age – joined the Houston Police Academy. He graduated on December 14, 1968 from Class No. 39. Lee wore Badge No. 2296. He worked the night shift of Radio Patrol for the entire twenty-five months of his career.

His younger brother, Larry G. Lee, had joined him in the Houston Police Department. Larry graduated from Class No. 43 and had been a police officer less than a year when his older brother was killed in the line of duty. Larry was on patrol that night, working out of the Northwest Substation, and recently recalled the sad memory of the tragic sequence of events that followed the death of his only brother.

His wife, Betty Lee, and two stepchildren, Margaret Dierks and Jack Dierks, survived Officer Lee. Besides his brother Larry, his parents, Mr. and Mrs. Bryan Lee, grandmother, Mrs. Elma Dunn, and three sisters, Joan Kromer, Carolyn Arnold and Leticia Applegate, also survived him.

Funeral services were held at the Waltrip Funeral Home Chapel, 1415 Campbell Road, on Tuesday, February 2, 1971, at 2 p.m., with the Reverend Robert A. Dottley officiating. Graveside Masonic rites were conducted under the auspices of the Masonic Lodge. Burial took place at the Earthman Resthaven Cemetery. Pallbearers were Officers M. F. Kardatzke, D. R. Kankel, M. T. Morrison, N. E. Cox and Sergeants W. A. Perdue and M. J. Chebret.

ROBERT WAYNE LEE, USMC, 1958

Officer Larry Lee went on to serve as a police officer with the Spring Branch Independent School District after his retirement from HPD in 1990, having worked his entire career at the Northwest Patrol Division. Larry retired from that duty in 2004. Betty Lee, Mr. Bryan Lee and grandmother

Dunn are deceased. Officer Bob Lee's mother continued to reside in Spring Branch and in her later years, was cared for by Larry, who lived with her. Lee's sister Carolyn had a son, Robert Kit Arnold, who is the only Lee family grandson and is a namesake of Officer Robert W. Lee. Mrs. Lee passed away in September, 2006, at the age of 90. She was buried in Resthaven Cemetery near her husband and son. Her burial service took place on the same afternoon just prior to Officer Rodney Johnson's service at Resthaven.

Officer Daryl Wayne Shirley was later promoted to detective and on April 28, 1982. Shirley was shot and killed in the line of duty while working the Fugitive Detail in the Burglary and Theft Division. This is the only known instance where the riding partner of a murdered officer was later also killed in the line of duty.

Officer Kardatzke promoted to detective and worked for fifteen years in the Homicide Division before retiring in 1989. He worked for a short time with the District Attorney's Office and lived in the Livingston area. His rookie, J. C. Moseley, also promoted to detective and after a lengthy career in the Major Offenders Division, retired from HPD to work with the District Attorney's Office. Officer Roger Carpenter retired from the Records Division in 1991 as a lieutenant. After his retirement he went to work for the San Jacinto College Police Department in Pasadena. Officer C. D. Dearing left the department in 1975.

This offense was primarily investigated by Homicide Detectives Max Lankford and Paul Michna while the robbery phase was investigated by Robbery Detectives J.O. Parker and Weldon W. Markert. Max worked in Homicide for a number of years and after also serving in the Internal Affairs and Major Offenders divisions retired in 1984 and worked as an investigator for the D. A.'s Office. Paul Michna worked Homicide for only a short time before transferring to Auto Theft. He later promoted to lieutenant, captain and deputy chief before retiring in 1989. He served the city of Tomball as their police chief for a number of years. Parker and Markert both retired from the Robbery Division.

A 100 Club marker has been placed next to the original marker, which read as follows:

ROBERT WAYNE LEE
LOUISIANA, SGT., U.S. MARINE CORPS
DEC 21, 1935 - JAN 31, 1971

62

Officer Claude Ronnie Beck
Badge #1234
December 10, 1971

Officer Beck Dies in Routine Traffic Stop On Freeway 18 Days After He was Married

Claude Ronnie Beck was born December 29, 1947, in Warren, Arkansas. His family lived in Arizona for a few years early in his life but returned to Arkansas where Ronnie graduated from Fordyce High School in 1966. He attended Arkansas A&M College for a short time in College Heights, Arkansas. In 1967, Ronnie moved to Houston after being accepted into the Houston Police Academy.

His class, No. 35, began training on May 1, 1967, and graduated on Aug. 19, 1967. His first assignment was to Night Shift Radio Patrol. The majority of his short career was at the Park Place Substation, but several months prior to December 1971, he was assigned to the Night Shift at Central Patrol. He wore a badge with a memorable number – Badge No. 1234.

On the night of Thursday, December 9, 1971, Officer Beck and his temporary partner, S. J. Rayne, were riding the late shift out of Central Patrol. Officer Rayne was a rookie in the fifth month of his probationary period. His regularly assigned training officer had called in sick that night. Beck, who had originally been scheduled as a one-man unit, was assigned to ride with Rayne. On this night, they were assigned to the Montrose District, then known as No. 2 Police District.

At approximately 2:40 a.m., a wrecker driver friend of Officer Beck's advised him of a vehicle entering the Southwest Freeway from Smith Street that had visible evidence of a recent accident. It was Officer Beck's intention to stop this vehicle, which its driver was operating in an erratic manner. Officers Beck and Rayne suspected a possible DWI.

Officer Beck was an aggressive officer unafraid to take action in any type of situation. He was driving and successfully pulled over the driver to the right side of the freeway on the overpass above Montrose. He got out on the driver's side of his patrol car. However, as he closed his car door, the driver of a motor home veered over too far toward him and struck him as he walked forward toward the vehicle carrying the possible DWI-FSGI. He was struck and thrown fifty feet forward.

The wrecker driver friend, known to many officers as "Stuttering Danny," had followed Officers Beck and Rayne, with the obvious hope of obtaining a "prisoner's tow." When Officer Beck was struck, the driver of the motor home did not stop but continued to drive outbound (south) on the Southwest Freeway.

OFFICER CLAUDE RONNIE BECK

Danny Foster Elmore, "Stuttering Danny," immediately chased the driver of this motor home nearly 1,500 feet before the driver stopped the vehicle. Meanwhile, Officer Rayne helped his partner and called for immediate medical assistance as well as making the "assist-the-officer" call. Help arrived too late. Officer Beck was dead at the scene, just nineteen days short of his twenty-fourth birthday.

Officers arrested the driver of the motor home, Walter Meyer (White Male 47) and charged him with murder by auto.

Officer Claude Ronnie Beck was known to his friends as "Ronnie" or "Jethro," the latter name coming from his ability to consume large quantities of food. Beck was large in size and had a big heart to go with it. He also was a joy to be around. His approach to police work – while unusual at the time – was generally successful. In his own way, he was geared toward the community-oriented approach, which many police administrators have unsuccessfully attempted to imitate in later decades.

The officer was a member of the Big Brothers and attempted to help young boys who had the misfortune of not having an adult male figure in their lives. Ronnie worked a regular extra job at the Clayton Homes public housing project at 1919 Runnels. It was there that he became a legend when he befriended many youngsters of all races and genders that lived in a housing project where many young people unfortunately got off on the wrong foot. Other officers knew Ronnie regularly used money from his extra job to assist many of these young kids.

RONNIE BECK, AGE 19 YEARS

In the months just before his death, Ronnie Beck regularly attended the Faith Missionary Baptist Church, where he met a young lady by the name of Sheila. On November 23, 1971, they were married. In a matter of just eighteen days, Sheila went from a blushing bride to a grieving widow.

In addition to Sheila, his parents, Mr. and Mrs. Harold Beck of Fordyce, Arkansas, survived Officer Claude Ronnie Beck. His younger sister Lyn Bounds and her husband Rick of Bearden, Arkansas, and his grandparents, Mrs. Mary Beck of Ingalls, Arkansas and Mr. and Mrs. Claude Green of Fordyce also survive him.

RONNIE BECK AND SISTER LYNN BECK

Funeral services were held at the Forest Park Lawndale Chapel at 5 p.m. on Saturday, December 11, 1971. Following that service, Officer Beck's remains were transported overland 400 miles to Fordyce, a small town in south central Arkansas. There, on Monday, December 13, at 10 a.m., the family held additional services at the Beach Grove Baptist Church. Burial followed at the Oakland Cemetery. A native son was brought home for his final earthly resting place.

Pallbearers were Sergeant Joe Chebret and Officers Gary L. Clark, Jack Heard, R. J. "Bob" Francis, Tommy D. Crawford (another Fordyce native), Gerry L. Carter, Oscar I. Smith and Glen Thyssen. A large contingent of Houston police officers from both the Central Patrol and Park Place Substations traveled to Fordyce to pay their final respects to their fallen friend.

A jury found Walter Meyer guilty of murder by auto and assessed a very short term of probation. He was the owner of a motor home sales and service company in northwest Houston for a number of years.

Sheila Beck later joined the Houston Police Department, but resigned after only several years of service. She remarried and in 2002 resided in the Houston area. She and her husband became the parents of three daughters and the grandparents of six. Mr. and Mrs. Beck lived in Fordyce. The three grandparents who survived Ronnie died as did his brother-in-law, Rick Bounds, a heart attack victim. Ronnie Beck's sister, Lyn Bounds, was the mother of two sons, Ronald Wayne Bounds (named for his uncle) and Rodney Bounds.

It was known to some HPD officers that just before his death Ronnie Beck inquired about a job with the Arkansas State Highway Patrol. He said he wanted to be closer to home to take care of his parents. Officer Tommy Crawford, a Fordyce native who later retired from HPD and returned to his hometown, would visit the Becks in the years after their son's death. So did retired HPD Sergeant Joe Chebret.

RONNIE AND HIS PARENTS, MR. AND MRS. HAROLD BECK

Officer Ronnie Beck's rookie partner on that fateful night, S. J. Rayne, became a sergeant and served HPD for more than thirty years. Most of his career was at the Northwest Patrol Station and he retired from that assignment.

In July, 2006, this writer and his wife, Mary Sue Zoch, were traveling through Arkansas on a Sunday morning. It had for some time been an idea of mine that it would be appropriate to visit Ronnie's parents. I had spoken to them on the phone on a number of occasions, most recently when arrangements were being made to place the HPOU/100 Club LINE OF DUTY gravemarker at Ronnie's gravesite. However, I had never had the pleasure of meeting them in person.

It was about 11:30 a.m. on a Sunday morning and after taking the Fordyce exit off of a highway, I was driving rather aimlessly through Fordyce. I was not wanting to ask directions and was of the mind that someone would eventually flag me down and direct me to where I wanted to go. And, believe it or not, that happened. Prior to us arriving in Fordyce, I was reviewing my file folder on Officer Ronnie Beck and had read the name of the church his Arkansas funeral was held from, the Beach Grove Baptist Church. There, while driving down the main drag of Fordyce, Arkansas, was the Beach Grove Baptist Church. Services were just over and the parking lot was full of people.

Approaching the first person I saw, I inquired as to whether Mr. and Mrs. Harold Beck might be around. This gentleman asked me who I was and when I advised him that I was retired Houston Police Department, he asked me to standby. He hurried around the building and returned, telling me that they had already gone home, but he would be most happy to lead me to their house. This, he did.

After a very enjoyable visit with Mr. and Mrs. Beck, they led us in their vehicle to the Oakland Cemetery where their only son is buried. I cannot tell you how much this visit with this wonderful couple meant to us. While my wife and I were following them to the cemetery, I told her that this is most likely only one of many, many trips they have made to this cemetery in the last 34 plus years. In speaking to them, their faith is strong, but their memories of Claude Ronnie Beck remain forever in their hearts. May God continue to bless them as he has through these many years in the loss of their only son.

The gravemarker the Beck family placed for their son reads as follows:

BECK, CLAUDE RONNIE (Also a photo)
DEC 29, 1947-DEC 10, 1971
LET NOT YOUR HEART BE TROUBLED... I GO TO PREPARE A PLACE FOR YOU....THAT WHERE I AM, THERE YE MAY BE ALSO. JOHN 14: 1-3

Also, a footmarker with RONNIE and HPD BADGE #1234.

63

David Franklin Noel
Badge #2084
June 17, 1972

East Side Drunk Stabs and Kills David Noel Then Gets Mere 20-Year Sentence and Parole

Officer David Franklin Noel was born on September 22, 1943 in the East Texas town of Huntington, near Lufkin. After attending school there and graduating from Zavalla High School in 1962, he served his country in the United States Army for two years. David joined the Houston Police Department on December 27, 1966, graduating from the Houston Police Academy in Cadet Class No. 34 on April 14, 1967. He was initially assigned to the Evening Shift Central Patrol, later worked in the Juvenile Division for a short time but returned to the Evening Shift at Central.

On the night of Friday, June 16, 1972, Officers David Noel and J. R. "Jimmy" Davis finished their 3 p.m. – 11 p.m. tour of duty at Central and Northwest stations, respectively. Both then reported to 316 N. Nagle to work their regular departmentally approved Friday night extra job at Castillo's Lounge. An intoxicated male was bothering other patrons inside the lounge and was warned by the officers that his behavior would not be tolerated. After continuing to bother the other patrons, he was told to come outside with Officers Noel and Davis.

While they were speaking to this male, who was later identified as Paul Villalpand Deleon (Latin-American Male, 42) another intoxicated male interfered. He verbally criticized both officers, but, more importantly, he was holding an empty beer bottle in what the officers both felt was a threatening manner. He was told several times to leave, but refused to do so. At this time, Noel and Davis turned their attention to him and advised him that he was under arrest.

During this time, a small crowd gathered

and a female, Rachel Garcia (Latin-American Female, 29) verbally inserted herself into the matter. She made the comment, "If you are going to mess with that Mexican, you are going to have to mess with a bunch of us." She then said something in Spanish to Paul Deleon, which neither Officer Noel nor Davis understood. It was later learned from a witness that she was saying, "pichalo." This meant "stab him" or "stick him" in Spanish.

OFFICER DAVID FRANKLIN NOEL

While both officers were in the process of arresting the second male, Deleon pulled a knife from his waistband and struck Officer Noel once in the chest just below the left nipple. As is the case in most stabbings, only the striking motion is seen, not the weapon itself. When Officer Noel was stabbed, he slid down to the sidewalk to a sitting position. He was mortally wounded but able to tell his partner that he had been stabbed. Officer Davis took Paul Deleon into custody and summoned assistance.

Officers C. L. Landrum, P. A. Thornton, J. Deleon and J. L. Wright arrived and after they and Officer Davis realized how serious Officer Noel had been wounded, they put him in a Patrol car and rushed him to Ben Taub General Hospital. However, he was pronounced dead on arrival at 1:53 a.m. Saturday, June 17, 1972. He was only twenty-eight. Evening Shift Radio Patrol Captain L.N. Zoch and another Patrol supervisor made the emergency notification to Mrs. Noel.

Officer David Noel was survived by his wife of nearly ten years, Ina Kay Noel, and two daughters, six-year-old Sherry Diane Noel and nineteen-month-old Shannon Denise Noel. His parents, Mr. and Mrs. J. M. Noel Sr. of Huntington, as well as four older sisters-Mrs. Opal Jackson, Mrs. Bobby Ramsey, Mrs. Betty Boone, and Patsy Cosby and six older brothers-John M. Jr., James, Charles, Robert, Paul, and Ralph also survived him.

Funeral services were held at the Forest Park Lawndale Chapel at 11 a.m. Monday, June 19, with another service held later that day at 4:30 p.m. in his East Texas hometown of Zavalla. Burial followed at the Zavalla Cemetery.

DAVID, SHANNON, SHERRY, AND INA KAY NOEL, JUNE 1972

Paul Deleon and Rachel Garcia were both charged with the murder in the death of Officer Noel. Garcia was obviously charged for the encouragement and direction she provided to Paul Deleon to commit the act. They went on trial together in the 174th District Court of Judge Ed Duggan. On September 22, 1972, Rachel Garcia was found not guilty and Paul Deleon was found guilty of murder with malice aforethought and sentenced to twenty years in the Texas Department of Corrections.

Twenty years for deliberately stabbing a uniformed police officer to death was insulting to the men and women in blue and probably the vast majority of law-abiding Houstonians. To make the situation even worse, records show that Deleon apparently served less than six years of his sentence since he was arrested on a prohibited weapon (felony – licensed premises) charge in April 1978.

DAVID NOEL IN THE U.S. ARMY, AGE 18, 1962

It was believed that his parole was revoked at that time and he was returned to TDC. He became a free man, living in the Pasadena area after recently serving a two-year sentence for his fourth DWI conviction in 1997.

No follow-up was attempted on Rachel Garcia since she was not convicted.

Homicide Detectives Willie Cashmere and Earl Haring conducted this investigation. Cashmere later made lieutenant, retired in 1980 and died in 1983. Haring transferred to Auto Theft in the early 1980s and retired from HPD in 1991 to work for Harris County Constable Precinct 1. He retired from that position in May 2000.

Officer J. R. Davis continued on with his career, never forgetting the events of that tragic night in the East End when he lost a good friend. He was promoted to detective in 1976 and was assigned to the Robbery Division. Officer C. L. Landrum, one of the transporting and assisting officers, later made sergeant and was assigned to the Training Academy. P. A. Thornton resigned from HPD. Officer J. Deleon, obviously no relation to the convicted killer, retired from HPD in 1991 after a long career at Northeast Patrol. Officer J. L. Wright, a rookie at the time, left HPD after ten years. He spent the next ten years in law enforcement in Houston County, Texas, but returned to HPD in 1992 as a lateral entry officer, assigned to the Homicide Division. He retired in 2004.

In 2007, Ina Kay Noel Spurlock and husband, Retired HPD Detective Danny Spurlock, lived in Alba, Texas, near Lake Fork. Daughter Sherry Howard and her husband, Mitchell Howard, live in Tennessee and have a son, David Howard (16), a namesake for David Noel. Daughter Shannon Montes and her husband, Greg Montes, live in Lufkin and have two daughters, Hilari Montes (11) and Emily Montes (9). Kay said she and David grew up in the Huntington-Zavalla area as childhood sweethearts and that one of her brothers married David's sister Betty. Sherry and Shannon have two sisters from their Mom's second marriage- Melissa Holmes and Jamie Holmes. In a recent tragic development, Mrs. Ina Kay Noel Spurlock passed away in March, 2007, as the result of a traffic accident near Lindale, Texas. She was 62 years of age.

In 2007, both of David's parents are deceased as is David's sister, Mrs. Bobby Ramsey, and brothers James and Paul. The remainder of the Noel siblings are still living.

The original markers, which still exist next to the 100 Club marker, read as follows:

DAVID F. NOEL, HPD BADGE #2084
SEPT 22, 1943 - JUNE 17, 1972

Also, the Veterans Administration marker which indicated David Noel served in the U.S. Army in Vietnam.

Officer David Noel, a graduate of Police Cadet Class No. 34, was not the first in his class to be killed in the line of duty. Just one month after this class "hit the streets," Officer Louis R. Kuba was killed on May 17, 1967, at the Texas Southern University riot.

Unfortunately, David was not the last in that class to lose his life in the line of duty. Yet another classmate, Detective Daryl W. Shirley, was killed while attempting the arrest of a fugitive in April 1982.

64

Officer Jerry Leon Spruill
Badge #2458
October 26, 1972

Spruill Killed Outside Montrose Gay Bar as Part of Radical Group's Initiation Rite

Jerry Leon Spruill was born in Memphis, Tennessee, on March 27, 1943. In 1962, he graduated from M. B. Smiley High School in Houston and attended Alvin Junior College for a short time thereafter. He served honorably in the United States Army from 1964 until 1967. Surviving this service during the Vietnam War, he returned to the United States and on October 6, 1969, joined the Houston Police Department in Police Cadet Class No. 42. He graduated on January 24, 1970 and was assigned to the Evening Shift, Radio Patrol, North Shepherd Substation. He wore Badge No. 2458.

On the night of Thursday, October 26, 1972, Officer Jerry Spruill completed his evening shift Patrol assignment at North Shepherd. He and his regular partner, W. G. Jackson, rode the Acres Homes area and were well known to the crooks and the good guys as hard working officers. Spruill and Jackson were finishing their reports when Spruill received a phone call and as a favor for a friend, agreed to work an extra job later that night. Spruill then went to his Oak Forest home, changed clothes and went for his nightly neighborhood jog. After his jog, he showered, changed into a clean uniform and drove to the Silver Dollar Restaurant and Bar at 616 Westheimer.

At approximately 11:45 p.m., he reported to the manager that he was on duty and immediately went outside to his car, probably to obtain additional equipment. The Silver Dollar, formerly known as Art Wren's, was a well known gay establishment, right in the middle of Montrose, which had become home for the 1960s era "flower children." This also meant that the area was a haven for runaway juveniles from throughout the United States, comparable to the Haight-Asbury section of San Francisco and the Greenwich Village section of New York City.

What happened from this point may never be substantiated past educated speculation. The following facts are known:

At 11:55 p.m., while opening the driver's side door to his car, Officer Jerry Spruill was confronted by something worse than he had ever known in Vietnam or Acres Homes. Witnesses said that two gunman approached Spruill and began firing upon him. He fell mortally wounded on the parking lot just east of the restaurant.

OFFICER JERRY LEON SPRUILL

The second gunman fired several more shots into the officer as he lay dying on the parking lot next to his car. He was shot with two weapons. Spruill, an aggressive and well respected officer known as "Big Red" or "the Red Snapper" in Acres Homes, died without ever being able to draw his weapon, having been shot six times. He was dead on arrival at Ben Taub at five minutes past midnight, Friday, October 27.

Homicide Lieutenant Tim McCormick initiated an immediate response to this murder scene by assigning Detectives Pat Kainer and J. W. "John" Haines to the case with Lieutenant James E. "Pete" Gunn supervising the scene investigation. The area at this time of night was crowded with pedestrian traffic with most of the possible witnesses either homosexuals who did not wish to become involved or young juvenile runaways who certainly did not want their whereabouts made known.

However, several witnesses hung around to talk to the detectives. One in particular eventually became the star witness. Witness accounts revealed one constant

– that there were two African-American male suspects who fled south across Westheimer through a parking lot to Stanford Street. They then left in a green pickup truck with toolboxes on both sides. Witnesses further described one of the suspects in more detail as having a very noticeably protruding chin, described as being almost pointed.

JERRY SPRUILL, SMILEY HIGH SCHOOL

The two suspects apparently had been inside the Silver Dollar just prior to Officer Spruill's arrival. After the officer checked in with the manager and went outside, the two suspects went outside without touching the drinks they had ordered.

While the scene investigation was beginning, Evening Shift Patrol Captain L. N. Zoch and Sergeant Charlie Boone went to the Spruill residence with the unenviable task of notifying Mrs. Spruill. Friends as well as Officer Walter Jackson were summoned to be with the family in this difficult time.

The survivors were Spruill's wife Marcia and two sons, three-year-old Jeffery Spruill and twenty-month-old Scott Spruill. Also, there were his mother, Mrs. Mary Frances Rauscher of Mount Vernon, Arkansas, and his sisters, Mrs. Barbara Debusschere of Dearborn Heights, Michigan, and Mrs. Nancy Keathley of Mount Vernon, Arkansas, and his three brothers, Julian Spruill of the United States Air Force, Ralph Spruill of the United States Marine Corps and Bill Rauscher of Mount Vernon, Arkansas.

Funeral services were held at the Heights Funeral Home Chapel on Monday, October 30, 1972, at noon, with Police Chaplain H. L. Hannah officiating. Interment followed at the Houston Veterans Cemetery with graveside services under the auspices of VFW Post 6010. Pallbearers were W. G. Jackson, R. B. Carbo, Allen Albinus, J. H. Allen, F. W. Stewart and R. S. Davis.

This police line of duty death was a whodunit. There was no physical evidence other than the slugs later recovered from the complainant. There were a few witnesses whose credibility was an obvious concern. The autopsy showed that the slain officer had received six gunshot wounds throughout the upper torso and arms. Five slugs were recovered, four .38s and one .22. There were two shooters, two guns, no apparent motive and no leads.

In 1972, anti-Vietnam War demonstrations were taking place, the drug and free love era of the 1960's was in vogue and, more importantly, the anti-police sentiment was consuming a growing segment of society. The Black Muslims and Black Panther organizations were active throughout the country, even though their activity in Houston was perceived to be very limited. Many scenarios were pondered as the motive for this heinous offense, but there was no information forthcoming to lend credence to any possibility.

MARCIA AND U.S. ARMY PFC JERRY SPRUILL'S WEDDING, 12/18/64

Throughout the night and in the many days ahead, patrol officers stopped many green pickup trucks and checked them out. Homicide followed up every lead. The personnel involved increased. Besides E. R. "Dog" Dennis and Johnny Bonds, some of the others participating in the investigation were Max Lankford, Larry Earls, H. A. "John" Zoch, Danny Sacky, Jim Pierce, Tommy Baker and

Willie Young.

As many new murder cases flowed in and as the Spruill leads became fewer and less frequent, Homicide detectives were pulled off to work other cases. As a matter of necessity, near the end of November, only four worked it full-time. They were Kainer and his rookie detective partner-N. J. Zoch, C. J. "Chuck" Lofland, and D. A. "Hoot" Gibson. Just as important, there remained one lieutenant on the case, Peter Gunn, who was assigned to a nightshift relief lieutenant's position. Gunn was a former Homicide detective determined not to let this case die.

At some point in mid-November, the HPD Dispatcher received an anonymous call from what sounded to be an elderly African-American female. Officer Floyd Slay recorded the call. The woman was attempting to name Officer Spruill's killer and while doing her best on a bad connection to name a distant relative, she spelled out the name of one of the assailants as F-A-N-T-I-N. This name was run through the system every way possible through the pre-computer technology of 1972 with no success.

Thanksgiving, Christmas and New Year's Day passed by with nothing but an occasional lead coming forth. The detectives rechecked old clues with no positive results. One major clue was promising but after working it extensively for a period of several months, it never proved fruitful. It was dismissed. Those days in Homicide were dark. The entire HPD was faced with the possibility of an unsolved police officer murder.

The first big break in this case came in early February 1973. A neighboring law enforcement agency made an arrest. The individual involved had information on the Spruill case. Detectives Lofland and Gibson were assigned to work this information. The informant's story began back in early November 1972 when his cousin asked him to take an unknown black male to an apartment on Southmore. The informant also learned later from his cousin that this unknown male was "hot" for killing a cop.

Investigators tracked down the cousin and he reluctantly told the same story. He added several important pieces of information, however. While this unknown male stayed with him, an unknown black male and female came to pick him up. The cousin later learned that both were in the Black Panther movement. Also, the cousin stated that he had previously dated this unknown male's cousin. When this unknown male left, his host's recently purchased .45-caliber automatic pistol just magically disappeared at the same time.

Detectives Kainer and Zoch located the female cousin and interviewed her. They learned that she and other family members had suspicions about her cousin's activities. She was asked the name of her cousin and she responded, "Marvin Fentis." It was a breakthrough. The name was spelled F-E-N-T-I-S, not F-A-N-T-I-N! Words cannot describe the feeling of elation that Kainer and Zoch experienced at this point.

From this point, the investigation took a positive turn. Other police agencies provided photos of Marvin Fentis. However, of all the witnesses who saw all or part of the murder, only one gave a positive identification. This left Homicide with one eyewitness identification and not a shred of physical evidence – not much to take to Assistant District Attorney Bob Bennett, who had worked with us on various related legal questions over the past four months. However, Harris County filed murder charges against Marvin Fentis in the death of Jerry Spruill. Equally as important, the serial number was obtained on the .45 automatic believed to be in the possession of Fentis. On February 27, 1973, this serial number went into the fledgling National Crime Information Center.

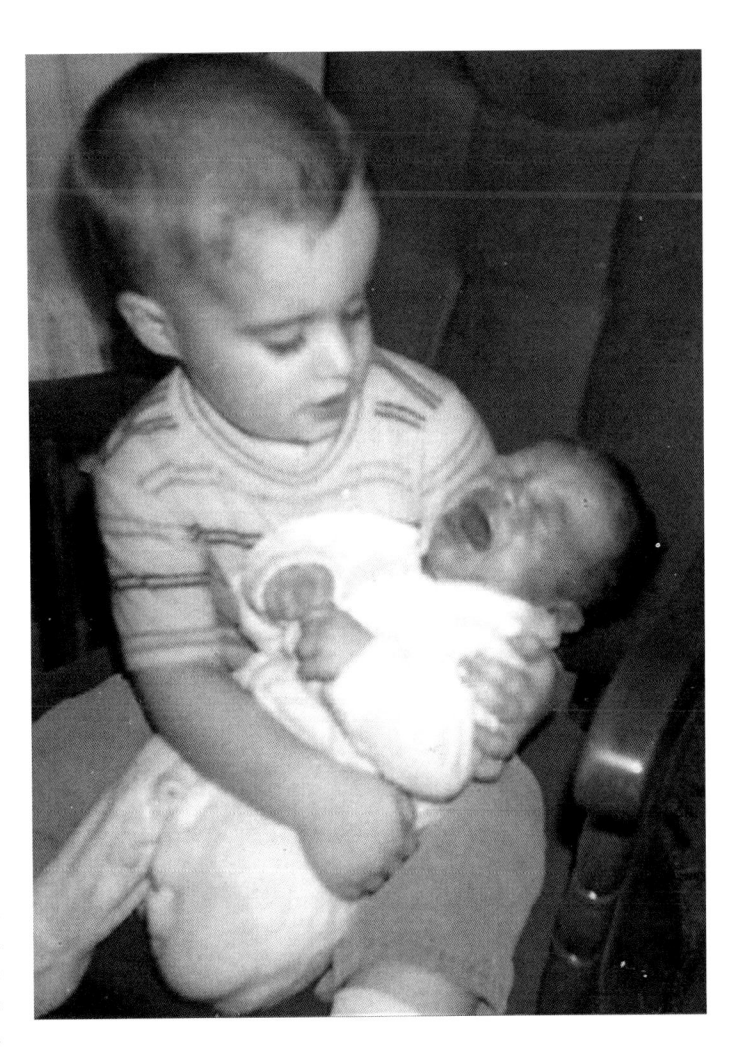

JEFFREY SPRUILL HOLDING SCOTT SPRUILL, 1971

The detectives then developed background information on Fentis. They learned that he had family in Port Arthur and Fort Smith, Arkansas. Fentis also had been arrested in Houston for disorderly conduct in Montrose along with his brother and another African-American male. Both of these individuals were checked out, but witnesses could not identify either one of them.

On Saturday night, March 3, 1973, Garland Police Officer Don Ashlock and Sergeant Bunch were on patrol in this northeast Dallas County municipality. They observed a suspicious black male walking on a street near where they had received a call. Together, they got out of their vehicles and approached this subject, prompting him to shout some profanities at them. When told to take his hands from his pockets, he did so.

However, his right hand held a .45- caliber automatic pistol and he quickly fired seven rounds in their direction, one of which ricocheted off of the pavement and struck Officer Ashlock in his foot. Both Sergeant Bunch and the wounded Officer Ashlock returned fire. The suspect fled on foot but they captured him a short distance away. Marvin Joel Fentis, aka "Sudden" (for the way he suddenly did things) and "Sharpchin" (for the shape of his chin), had been shot in – of all places – his chin. The officers recovered his pistol.

While this activity was certainly not routine for a Saturday night in this quiet suburb of Dallas, it became more unusual the next day. After checking the recovered .45 automatic in NCIC, alarms went off indicating the weapon had been stolen in Houston and was suspected to be in the possession of a suspect in the murder of a Houston police officer.

On Sunday, March 4, 1973, Garland police contacted Houston Police Burglary and Theft detectives, whose lieutenant immediately contacted Homicide Captain L. D. Morrison Jr. After learning of this break, Captain Morrison contacted lead Detective Pat Kainer and instructed Kainer and Zoch to leave immediately for Garland and Dallas, where the suspect was being treated at Parkland Memorial Hospital, the county-funded Dallas equivalent of Ben Taub. The detectives left for Dallas immediately.

After two days of intensive investigation, they returned to Houston having a feeling of relief for the first time in more than four months. Their man was in custody under two charges of assault to murder a police officer in Dallas County, then a conservative bastion of law and order.

While having Marvin Fentis in custody was a great relief, there was still the problem of the second gunman. Fentis would not give the detectives the time of day, much less talk about the Spruill murder. An eighth grade dropout, he joined the U. S. Army at age seventeen. He only served a year and was released under conditions less than honorable, having been cited several times for "lack of a positive response to authority." Fentis was diagnosed as having a passive aggressive personality, manifested by hostility and resentful of authority, impaired judgment and insight. His criminal history included arrests for burglary, auto theft, aggravated assault, and a murder that the Chicago police could not prove.

HPD detectives suspected that the murder of Officer Spruill would have been the murder of any uniformed police officer on the premises that night in October 1972. With the thought of the two possible Black Panther activists picking him up on Southmore and assisting him in leaving town, the investigation into the second gunman took Detectives Kainer and Zoch to North Texas State University in Denton. This was the base of the Black Intercommun Party. Marvin Fentis and the people he was staying with in Garland were party members. Although the detectives investigated numerous individuals, they could not charge anyone as being the second gunman.

There could have been some involvement with the Black Panthers. However, there was not any evidence to indicate the Panthers or any other radical group had ordered a "hit" on a white police officer. Information did come forth to convince the investigators that Fentis' personality was unstable enough that neither the Black Panthers nor the Black Muslims wanted anything to do with him.

Having physical custody of Marvin Joel Fentis, Dallas County quickly tried him for the attempted murders. In June 1973, a jury found Fentis guilty and assessed two life sentences. On July 24 of that year Detectives Nelson Zoch and Johnny Bonds returned Fentis to Harris County. In August 1974, Fentis went on trial for the murder of Officer Spruill. While the case was obviously weak, the one eyewitness stood tall and firm in his identification of Fentis. Two other witnesses placed Fentis inside the Silver Dollar just before the murder. Jurors found Fentis guilty and assessed him a thirty-five-year sentence in the Texas Department of Corrections.

Unfortunately, Marvin Fentis' history in our free society does not end here. In 1984, Zoch, who was now a Homicide lieutenant, and Homicide Detective Gene Yanchak visited Fentis in a TDC Unit, an encounter that failed to produce any new information. Actually, Fentis was rather hostile.

In 1985, with the assistance of Assistant District Attorney Terry Wilson, Fentis was bench-warranted back to Harris County and taken before a grand jury. He was granted full immunity for any further prosecution related to this offense. Wilson and Zoch questioned him at length. He would not provide the much-needed lead to the second gunman. Fentis, with the approval of his attorney, did participate in an interview about the murder. While it was difficult to believe his version in its entirety, new ground was broken in that he half heartedly acknowledged his presence and participation. His story included the fact that it was a rite of initiation that meant that he and the second gunman were given guns and told to go kill the uniformed officer in the parking lot of the Silver Dollar. He even went so far as to say he did not even know his gun was loaded. However, it was his duty in the initiation rite to trust the people that provided him with the weapon. Naturally, he would not provide a name since that "just would not be right."

Marvin Fentis was paroled to Harris County in 1987. He completed his parole on January 1, 1999 and moved to Fort Smith, Arkansas, where he apparently kept clean. He still does not want to talk about the second gunman. In reality, police would need a confession and some corroborating evidence to make a case on the second gunman.

In 2007, Marcia Spruill is remarried and lives in San Antonio. She was a registered nurse who sought and achieved an advanced nursing degree. Son Jeffery Spruill lived in Evanston, Wyoming and is a wire line operator with many years experience in the oil and gas exploration industry. Son Scott Spruill and his wife, Gracie Spruill, live in Corpus Christi, and are the parents of a son, Cody

Spruill.

Officer Spruill's mother, Mary Rauscher, lived in Conway, Arkansas, as does his sister, Nancy. In 2001, brother Julian resided in Lakewood, Colorado. Adopted brother Ralph was believed to be in Michigan. Brother Bill Rauscher also lived in Arkansas. Sister Barbara was in Garden City, Michigan.

As for the investigators, Lieutenant Tim McCormick was killed in a 1975 accident. Lieutenant Pete Gunn retired in 1991 and passed away in 2000. Detective Pat Kainer resigned from HPD for the second time in 1981 to go into business and lived in Katy. J. W. Haines retired in 1988 and lived near Conroe in 2007. Chuck Lofland retired as a lieutenant in 1988 and passed away in 1998. D. A. Gibson retired as a lieutenant in 1984 and after a number of years with Harris County, is retired and lives in the Houston area.

Nelson Zoch made lieutenant in 1977 and worked in that capacity in Homicide from 1980-2004, serving as the supervisor of a murder investigation squad before retiring in 2004. The prosecutor instrumental in assisting Homicide in this investigation and then later prosecuting the case, Bob Bennett, became a highly respected attorney in private practice in Houston who never lost sight of his prosecutor days. Don Ashlock, the Garland officer shot by Fentis, later resigned from that department and served four terms as an elected Dallas County constable. He then went on to become a captain in the Van Zandt County Sheriff's Department in Canton. Sergeant Bunch also resigned from Garland and lived in North Texas. Terry Wilson retired from Harris County in 1999. Officer Floyd Slay retired from HPD Crime Analysis in 2004.

In 2003, Nelson Zoch received approval from then Homicide Captain R.W. Holland to pursue this investigation. Zoch assigned Homicide Investigator Brian Harris to assist him. They traveled to Fort Smith, Arkansas, where they, along with several Fort Smith Homicide Detectives, interviewed Marvin Fentis regarding the identity of the second gunman. While Marvin refused in his usual defiant manner to identify his murder companion, he did give an interview to now Sergeant Brian Harris in which he discussed a few more details and actually admitted being there and participating in the murder of Officer Spruill. Marvin provided several pieces of information involving names of Black radicals active at the time of the murder. However, none of Marvin's information could be verified. It should be noted that when first approached in Fort Smith, Marvin's outburst included that he couldn't understand why HPD Homicide can't let this go after thirty years. Also, for him to name his partner in crime still "would just not be right". Marvin Fentis is truly a man of principle.

Marvin had, however, committed a minor parole violation while living in Fort Smith. As a result, his parole was revoked and he was returned to the Texas Department of Criminal Justice. Once again, the parole board, after several hearings, decided to again release Marvin on society after six months in custody. As far as is known, Marvin Joel Fentis is living in 2007 as a free man in Fort Smith, Arkansas.

It should be noted here that no direct evidence ever surfaced to indicate that Marvin Fentis was involved with any of the previously mentioned organizations. His mention of an initiation rite was the first verification of any connection to an organized group and with Marvin's level of credibility, not much credence could be placed in anything he stated.

It should be noted that Officer Spruill, prior to serving the citizens of the City of Houston, also served his country from 2/3/64 until 2/2/67. His final resting place of Officer Spruill at the VA Cemetery in Houston is marked as follows:

JERRY LEON SPRUILL
TENNESSEE
SP 5   US ARMY
VIETNAM
MARCH 27, 1943 - OCTOBER 26, 1972

65

Officer Antonio Guzman
Badge #1111
January 9, 1973

Drug User Shoots Officer Guzman to Death During Routine Search on Telephone Road

Antonio "Tony" Guzman Jr. was born in San Antonio on September 18, 1942. He attended Ben Milam Elementary and Brackenridge High School in San Antonio and served his country in the United States Army for seven years. Guzman joined the Houston Police Department on August 23, 1971, graduating in Police Cadet Class No. 51 on December 11, 1971. He was assigned to Patrol IV, which worked 7 p.m. until 3 a.m.

On Tuesday night, January 9, 1973, Officer Guzman and his partner, Officer Brad Mills, were assigned to Unit 4T-31 of Patrol IV, a new shift that began in August 1970. These units were assigned to supplement and overlap the existing evening and night shifts, and while they ran regular patrol calls when needed, they had the freedom to do a lot of saturation patrol duties in areas where it was deemed necessary.

On this cold night, nearly halfway through their shift, Officers Guzman and Mills were southbound on Telephone Road at 10:30 p.m. when they observed a speeding pickup truck with no taillights. Their unit, with Officer Mills driving and Officer Guzman "on the ground," stopped the pickup in the 6700 block of Telephone at Drouet. The driver, Robert Tillman Emory II (White Male, 30), got out of his vehicle, walked toward Officer Mills and offered his driver's license to the officer before even being asked for it.

OFFICER ANTONIO GUZMAN

Officer Guzman walked up to the truck and shined his flashlight inside. He then quickly returned to where Officer Mills and Emory were standing and said to Mills, "Let's search him." Emory, a railroad switchman, was wearing overalls and had his hands in the pockets. Mills told him to show his hands and repeated the order as he reached to grab Emory to begin searching him. Emory was hesitant to move his hands and Officer Guzman, who apparently had seen a box of pistol ammunition in Emory's truck, asked the man, "Where's your pistol?"

At that point, Emory pushed Officer Mills away, pulling a pistol from his overalls all in the same motion. He turned toward Guzman and pointed a small-caliber pistol at him. Without saying a word, he fired, mortally wounding the officer. Both officers pulled their weapons and began firing at Emory, who was running away. With both officers firing a total of fourteen shots at him, Emory fell in a service station driveway on the northeast corner of Telephone and Drouet. Officer Guzman also had fallen over the esplanade in the middle of the street. After Officer Mills had seen Emory fall and stay down, he turned his attention to his partner and called for assistance.

Unit 4T-33 Officers V. H. Kerchoff and R. V. Sander quickly arrived at the scene to assist. They placed Tony Guzman into their patrol car and rushed him to Ben Taub General Hospital. Doctors there pronounced him dead on arrival at 1:15 a.m., having sustained a gunshot wound to the upper left chest. He was thirty years old and had been a Houston police officer for only thirteen months.

His wife Candy and their son, eight-year old John Guzman, survived Officer Tony Guzman. Also surviving him were his parents, Mr. and Mrs. Antonio Guzman Sr., sisters Mrs. Amy Oranday and Cathy Gutierrez, and one brother, William Guzman. Funeral services were held at 9:30 a.m. Friday, January 12, at the Forest Park Lawndale Chapel with a Funeral Mass held at 10:15 a.m. at the St. Theresa Catholic Church. Military graveside services and interment took place at the Veterans Administration Cemetery in Houston.

An investigation showed that Officers Guzman and Mills had fired a total of fourteen rounds with their .45-caliber automatic pistols. The suspect Emory suffered five gunshot wounds to the top of the left shoulder and to his legs. A Houston Fire Department ambulance rushed him to Ben Taub. After surgery, he remained in the hospital, paralyzed. He was charged with murder in the death of Tony Guzman.

Emory worked in Houston for a local railroad. At the time of this shooting incident, he was on probation for five years for burglary of a boxcar and had been previously handled for several narcotics violations. He admitted to smoking marijuana and using "speed" the night he murdered Officer Guzman. In his truck, investigators found a grass pipe, a water pipe, some marijuana and a large amount of pills. However, he never went to court on his most serious charge. On April 7, 1973, he died in Ben Taub from the gunshot wounds.

In 2002, Candy Guzman had remarried and lived in the central Texas town of Belton with her husband, Ed Wade, a retired HPD officer and later a successful civilian employee in HPD's Computer Services. John Guzman, her and Tony's only son, lived nearby. Candy went to work at HPD in the Dispatcher's Office shortly after Tony's death. After several years there, she became an executive secretary in the department and retired in 1997 after having worked for several deputy and assistant chiefs. In 2002, John Guzman was a technician for a cable television firm. Officer Guzman's parents are both deceased. Both of Tony's sisters as well as his brother resided in the San Antonio area.

In an interview conducted in 2002, Candy mentioned the invaluable assistance provided to her during the rough times after her husband's murder by

A. M. "Tony" Biamonte. At the time, Tony, a Robbery detective, was the closest thing HPD had to a family assistance officer. He was on the Board of Directors of both the Houston Police Officers Association (now the Houston Police Officers Union) and the Burial Fund and provided guidance and advice to HPD family members in times of crisis. Tony retired in 1981 and died in 1996.

JOHN GUZMAN, SON OF OFFICER ANTONIO GUZMAN

Homicide Detectives C. J. "Chuck" Lofland and D. A. "Hoot" Gibson investigated this offense. Both later retired as lieutenants. Lofland died in 1998. Gibson is retired and lived in the Houston area in 2002. Brad Mills resigned from HPD in 1988 after serving seventeen years and lived in San Antonio, employed as a lieutenant with the Northside Independent School District Police Department. Of the transporting officers, V. H. "Vic" Kerckhoff worked the night shift for a number of years at the Clear Lake Patrol Division before retiring in 2004. R. V. "Richard" Sander retired as a sergeant in 1990, having worked in Narcotics, Planning and Research and Field Training during his twenty years of service. In 2007, he was the chief deputy under Harris County District Clerk Charles Bacarisse.

It is interesting to note that at some point around 2000, this writer received a phone call from a young lady who lived in Oklahoma. She was asking about this case and upon returning her call, I inquired as to why she was interested as I had not ever heard her name mentioned in the investigation nor in my inquiries while writing the original story. This young lady was very forthright in her answer. She was the daughter of Robert Emory and had heard various stories about how her Dad had died. Basically, she had been told the truth through the years and just needed to hear it from someone at HPD. She asked that I pass her condolences on to the Guzman family for what her Dad had done. To Candy and John and the rest of the Guzman family, this information is for you.

Officer Guzman, prior to losing his life in the service of the citizens of the City of Houston, spent over seven years of his life in the service of his country. His marker at the VA Cemetery in Houston reads as follows:

ANTONIO GUZMAN JR.
TEXAS
SP 5   US ARMY
VIETNAM
SEPT 18, 1942 - JAN 9, 1973

66

Officer David Huerta
Badge #2341
September 19, 1973

Officer David Huerta Senselessly Murdered In Violent Domestic Disturbance in the Heights

David Huerta was born in Houston on April 11, 1946. He was raised on the near North side of Houston and attended Looscan Elementary School. Graduating from Jeff Davis High School in 1964, he then attended South Texas Junior College in Houston for a year before his two-year service in the United States Army. After returning safely from his tour of duty in Vietnam, Huerta entered Houston Police Cadet Class No. 40 on January 13, 1969, graduating the following May 3. His initial assignment was to the Traffic Enforcement Division. In 1970, he transferred to the Narcotics Division, where he was assigned until May 1973, when he returned to Traffic Enforcement. Our story of murder begins that year.

Terry Brandt (White Female, 20) and Ronald Brandt (White Male, 21) had been married for several years. This marriage had produced a daughter who was two years old. Their relationship was stormy to say the least and had included physical violence as well as a number of separations. The situation continued to deteriorate and eventually Terry filed for a divorce and also requested a restraining order against Ronald.

On Wednesday morning, September 19, 1973, a hearing was held in a family district court (then called "domestic relations court") in Houston. The divorce would not be final for another five weeks, but the judge granted the restraining order. Terry had recently moved her and her daughter to an apartment at 918 Heights to get away from Ronald. Ronald, however, would not honor the court order and continued to bother Terry, somehow managing to move into Terry's Heights address while she was at work.

On this same Wednesday in the afternoon, Officer David Huerta was working the evening shift out of the Traffic Division. He was in the Stop-N-Go convenience store at Heights and 10th Street when Terry Brandt and several of her co-workers approached him. These friends from work said they were concerned about Terry's safety and had gone with her to see her safely to her apartment. Earlier, she had seen Ronald's car at the apartment and was afraid to go inside by herself. These same friends had recently harbored Terry from Ronald at their residence, obviously placing themselves in a precarious situation in the middle of this volatile, failing marriage of Terry and Ronald.

At the Stop-N-Go, Terry and her friends expressed their fears to Officer Huerta. Being the helpful and ready-to-serve police officer that he was, the officer agreed to go with them to the apartment in an effort to resolve the situation. Ronald met the group when they knocked on the door. Huerta explained to Ronald the seriousness of the restraining order and Ronald reluctantly agreed to move out. As he began gathering his clothes, he told Officer Huerta he would put his clothes in his car and return some of Terry's clothes he had placed there without her consent. After the clothes were returned to their proper place, Officer Huerta led Ronald, Terry and the two friends back to Terry's apartment.

Witnesses later said that Officer Huerta used the telephone to call in a report on this matter to Headquarters. (This was prior to the days of hand-held radios). While Huerta was on the phone, Ronald went into a bedroom and suddenly returned with a shotgun. Terry saw him first and screamed, but it was too late.

Officer Huerta, phone still in his hand, was struck with a shotgun blast to the head and died instantly, never having had the opportunity to draw his duty weapon. While Ronald was turning on Terry with the gun, the two witnesses fled out the door. As they ran for their lives, one of them leaping over a balcony, the two heard another shot, which apparently struck and killed Terry.

Another shot was heard and -- several minutes later – still another sounded. The fourth shot was Ronald Brandt taking his own life. Between the third and fourth shots, Ronald called Terry's father to advise him of what he had done, saying that he was about to kill himself.

OFFICER DAVID HUERTA

More police officers arrived just after these shots were heard. Inspector Wallace L. Williams, who lived just several blocks away, arrived on the scene, as did Radio Patrol Sergeants W. T. "Truitt" Bolin and Wayne Hankins. They tried unsuccessfully to communicate with Brandt – or anyone inside Apartment No. 7 – by using a bullhorn. Soon, Inspector Williams, commander of the HPD Patrol Bureau, decided to fire tear gas into the apartment. When there was still no response, Inspector Williams, Sergeants Hankins and Bolin, Officer Jerry Bench and Homicide Detective L. W. Henning entered the apartment. There they found Officer Huerta and the Brandt couple dead from shotgun wounds.

This was the tragic result of a terrible, continuing case of domestic violence. Officer Huerta was dead at the age of twenty-seven. Terry and Ronald were dead at twenty and twenty-one, respectively. One child was left without a father. Another young child was orphaned.

Officer Huerta's wife Connie, their sixteen-month-old daughter Marcie, his parents, Mr. and Mrs. Genaro Huerta, and a brother, Daniel Huerta, survived Officer David Huerta. A Rosary Service was held at the Crespo

Funeral Home, 2516 Navigation, at 8 p.m. Thursday, September 20, 1973. Religious services were held at 2 p.m. Friday, September 21, 1973, at the St. Patrick's Catholic Church. Interment followed at the Forest Park Lawndale Cemetery.

Pallbearers were Police Officers G. Gonzales, S. R. Benavides, A. A. Jasso, J. M. O'Brien, J. J. Davis, L. S. Ballesteros, and Sergeants W. S. Weaver and R. E. Hosford. The slain officer's friends – Officers H. V. Hernandez, W. T. Gower and M. Perales – performed honor guard duty.

Prior to tear-gassing the apartment, the Homicide Division was alerted to the information that there was very likely an injured police officer inside. Based on the oral statements of the two friends of Terry Brandt, Homicide Lieutenant Frank Crittenden initiated a homicide scene response by assigning Detectives L. W. "Ludwig" Henning, J. M. "John" Roescher and J. W. "John" Haines to go to the scene to begin an investigation. As a result of this tragic end, there was obviously no prosecution.

DAVID HUERTA, U.S. ARMY, VIETNAM ERA

In 2002, Officer Huerta's widow Connie had remarried and lived in Houston. Marcie Cleveland, his daughter, is married and is the mother of a son, Coby Cleveland. Mr. and Mrs. Genaro Huerta still live on the near north side where they raised their two sons. The Officer's brother, Daniel Huerta, lived in Houston in 2002 and was a police officer with the Spring Branch Independent School District. He is the father of one daughter, Nicole.

As for the officers involved in the incident on Heights Boulevard, Inspector Williams retired from HPD and died in 1991. Sergeant Hankins retired as a lieutenant in 1995 and died in 2000. Sergeant Bolin retired in 1981 and then worked a number of years as the building and maintenance director for 61 Riesner. He passed away in 2004. Officer Jerry Bench retired in 1984 and went to work in the private sector, having passed away in 2006.

Of the investigators, Detective Henning retired from Homicide in 1982 and, after working with several other law enforcement agencies, died in 1999. Detective Roescher, with forty-four years of service with HPD, died suddenly in 2000 while still assigned to the Homicide Division. Detective Haines retired in 1988 and lived near Lake Conroe in 2002. Lieutenant Crittenden retired in 1978 and died in 1992.

Slain HPD Officers David Huerta, George Rojas and Victor Ray Wells were all graduates of Jeff Davis High School in the mid 1960's. Officer Matt Perales, HPD Family Assistance Officer, grew up on the north side and went to either elementary, junior high, senior high, and/or church with these fine men, as well as a number of other HPD officers. These include retired Officer Steve Benavides, Accident Sergeant Andy Jasso, Eastside Patrol Officer Luis Ballesterors, Auto Dealer Sergeant Henry Hernandez, Homicide Sergeant Eugene Yanchak, Officer I. Iranda, and K-9 Sergeant Andy Porras.

A review of the Jeff Davis yearbook of those approximate years revealed other HPD officers such as Ray Cantwell, Richard Nieto and Robert Contreras. Another Davis student of that same era, David Clement, became a Houston police officer and died in an accidental shooting in 1971. Officer Luis Ballesteros grew up across the street from David Huerta, but later went to a different high school. Ironically, their paths crossed in Vietnam and, fortunately, both survived that war. Retired Officer Steve Benavides and Sergeant Henry Hernandez grew up in the neighborhood with David Huerta. Steve said he joined HPD after he returned from Vietnam and later encouraged David to become a Houston police officer.

Many HPD officers came out of Davis High School, which even at the time David Huerta attended there in the 1960s was in a rough neighborhood. These young men were nurtured by hard-working, law-abiding parents who raised their children to grow up obeying the law and were obviously proud that they later successfully entered law enforcement to serve and protect their fellow citizens. Officer Huerta died during his dutiful effort to protect one of those citizens.

Marker for Officer Huerta reads:

HUERTA, DAVID
APR 11, 1946-SEPT 19, 1973
SERVED IN VIETNAM 1967-1968

There is also a marker that reads:
SON-DAVID HUERTA

67

Officer Jerry Lawrence Riley
Badge #1516
June 18, 1974

Jerry L. Riley, a 4-Year Officer, Killed By 18-Wheeler on Way to Assist an Officer

Jerry Lawrence Riley was born on March 30, 1950, in the Northeast Texas town of Sulphur Springs. His family moved to Houston when Jerry was very young. He attended Hartsfield Elementary School, Hartman Junior High School and graduated from Jesse Jones High School in 1970. He joined the Houston Police Department by entering Police Cadet Class No. 45 on June 22, 1970 and graduated on October 10, 1970. His first and only assignment was to the night shift in Radio Patrol at the Park Place Police Station. He wore Badge No. 1516.

On Thursday night, June 13, 1974, Officers Jerry Riley and Ira O. Franks were assigned to Unit No. 1311. At approximately 11:27 p.m., with Officer Riley driving and Officer Franks riding, they responded to an Assist the Officer at 4401 Old Galveston Road.

They drove southbound on Old Galveston Road. As they intersected Park Terrace with red lights and siren on, they were involved in a major accident. A tractor-trailer rig had pulled out directly in their path, causing the left front and left side of the patrol car to collide with the right side of this large truck, which was westbound on Park Terrace.

Both officers sustained critical injuries. City paramedics transported Officer Riley to Ben Taub General Hospital with a depressed skull fracture. More complications set in after he underwent eight hours of surgery and another operation was required. He also had suffered rib and facial bone fractures. Fellow officers responded to the call for blood, contributing more than thirty pints in his name.

Doctors and medical personnel did all they could. Unfortunately, however, the life of Officer Jerry Lawrence Riley ended in Ben Taub on Tuesday, June 18, 1974. He was just twenty-four years old.

Officer Ira Franks was recovering from his injuries when Jerry Riley died. His injuries were diagnosed as large scalp lacerations, a concussion and cervical strain, as well as generalized abrasions. He also was initially taken to Ben Taub but was transferred to St. Joseph Hospital after being stabilized. He remained hospitalized for about six days but was released just before Officer Riley's funeral. Franks, later a Narcotics lieutenant, said that it was the only time he ever rode with Riley. He had the impression Riley considered safety first since he told Franks, an officer for less than two years, that he would "feel better" if he would buckle up his seat belt. Franks did so.

OFFICER JERRY LAWRENCE RILEY

It was well known that Officer Riley always wore his seat belt. Franks said that when the tractor-trailer rig entered Old Galveston from the left, Officer Riley veered to his right, thereby causing the brunt of the impact to his side.

Franks has always been of the opinion that had he not been wearing his seat belt he would have also died in the accident. He also said that when Riley turned to his right, he prevented more serious injuries to Franks, who considered himself very fortunate to have survived the accident.

The tractor-trailer rig was driven by Curtis Ricky Stone (White Male, 20) and was owned by the Frito Lay Company. Stone was charged with negligent collision for failing to yield right of way to an emergency vehicle. While Stone maintained that he did not hear the police siren, there were other witnesses who clearly heard it.

The accident investigation was conducted by Accident Division officers K. D. McGinn and D. W. Thompson, with Sergeant M. J. "Joe" Chebret serving as the scene supervisor.

JERRY (IN HIS ROTC UNIFORM) AND THE FUTURE SHERRY RILEY IN HIGH SCHOOL

His wife Sherry and nine-month-old daughter, Shane O'Dell Riley, survived Officer Riley. One sister, Mrs. Cathy Condon of South Houston, also survived the officer, as did his parents, Jack and Marita Riley. Jerry was predeceased by a younger brother, Teddy, who passed away at the age of eleven from a kidney disorder.

Services were held at the Forest Park Lawndale Funeral Home, 6900 Lawndale, on Friday, June 21, 1974, at 10:30 a.m. Burial followed at South Park Cemetery in Pearland. Pallbearers were Lieutenant Billy G. Ripley, Sergeants Joe Chebret and Wayne Williams and Officers C. R. "Randy" Barney, Garland Ray Estes, Roy L. Slay, Frank V. Robertson and N. W. "Wayne" Holloway.

Sherry Riley went on with her life by continuing her education in order to better provide for her young daughter. She graduated from college and in 2003 was a high school science teacher in Midland. She also remarried and had another daughter, Jill.

Shane Odell Riley graduated from Texas Tech University with a degree in fashion design. At one time, she worked in New York City for the Ralph Lauren fashion design company. While in New York, she met the man who would become her husband, Tim Heslin. After moving back to Houston, Shane Heslin became associated with Foley's and in October 2002 she and her husband became the proud parents of a daughter, Riley Blake Heslin, obviously named in memory of her father, whom she never had the opportunity to know. They are now also the proud parents of a son, Collin Heslin.

RILEY HESLIN, MRS. SHANE RILEY HESLIN, AND COLLIN HESLIN

In 2007, Mrs. Marita Riley lives in Angleton. Mr. Jack Riley passed away and is interred next to his son. Jerry's sister, Cathy Howser, lives near Fort Worth and she and her husband, Jim Howser, are the parents of four daughters-Brandy Simpson, Dena Wineinger, Dawn Howser, and Danielle Howser. Sherry lives in Midland.

Ira Franks continued his career with HPD, later working in Narcotics and the Recruiting Division. His promotion to detective took him to the Robbery Division. From that assignment, he promoted to lieutenant in 1986 and was later assigned to the Homicide Division, Internal Affairs Division and, later, returned to Homicide. Then, in 1994, he returned to Narcotics where he remained until his retirement in 2006.

The grave of Officer Riley had a very professional marker to honor this young man's life. It read:

JERRY L. RILEY
IN LOVING MEMORY OF MY HUSBAND
MAR 30, 1950 - JUNE 18, 1974

With the assistance and cooperation of South Park Cemetery, and with the support of the 100 Club and the HPOU, a LINE OF DUTY 100 Club was placed to further honor this man.

68

Officer Johnny Terrell Bamsch
Badge #1388
January 30, 1975

Robbery Suspects on Yale Murder Officer Johnny Bamsch in Cold Blood

Johnny Terrell Bamsch was born in Houston, Texas, on September 10, 1947. He attended Our Savior Lutheran School for eight years, Black Junior High and Waltrip High School, where he graduated in 1965. On December 2, 1965, Johnny joined the United States Marine Corps. This was during the massive military buildup in Vietnam and Johnny served his country proudly there for two tours of duty. He was hospitalized at one time during those tours for shell shock. He was honorably discharged on September 5, 1968, after which time he attended Sam Houston State University and graduated from there with a degree in 1973.

Johnny joined the Houston Police Department by way of Academy Class #55, which began training on June 12, 1972, and graduated on September 30, 1972.

He proudly wore Badge #1388. His wife, Cindy Bamsch, fully supported Johnny's decision to join the Houston Police Department. He spent the next two and a half years assigned to the North Shepherd Substation, night shift Radio Patrol. Policing was a job that Johnny truly loved. In a comment to his parents not long before his death, he said that he would "always be a policeman." Little did Cindy and Mr. and Mrs. Bamsch and later, Mandy, know the impact his choice to serve his city as a police officer would have on his life and theirs.

On Wednesday night, January 29, 1975, Officers Johnny Bamsch and J. D. "Pops" Ellis reported for duty as usual on the night shift at the North Shepherd Substation. Being regular partners, they were assigned to Unit No. 1161. On this particular night, Johnny was "on the ground" and Jim was driving.

OFFICER JOHNNY TERRELL BAMSCH

Just prior to 1 a.m., they were on patrol, driving south in the 4600 block of Yale. Bamsch observed some suspicious activity at the 7-Eleven Store on the northeast corner of Yale and Norview. He alerted Ellis, who made a left turn into a service station parking lot on the southeast corner of that intersection. They both observed a black male leaving the store, as well as a vehicle moving slowly west on Norview toward Yale and then turning onto Yale, going north.

At this point, Officer Bamsch got out of the patrol car and approached this man, who was apparently headed toward this suspicious vehicle. This vehicle had already left, leaving the #1 suspect behind to confront Officer Bamsch. The vehicle was going north on Yale. Ellis drove on to Yale to follow the suspect vehicle and, after traveling just half a block, heard gunshots. He immediately turned around and saw Officer Johnny Bamsch wounded and on the ground.

JOHNNY BAMSCH, U.S.M.C., 1966

Officer Ellis, seeing the suspect on the ground but holding a gun, used his shotgun, firing three shots, wounding the suspect. He put out an "Assist the Officer" on the radio and other units responded. The first officers on the scene were W.R. Elsbury and R.L. Doyle. Emergency medical personnel from the Houston Fire Department rushed Bamsch to nearby Parkway Hospital, but he was dead on arrival. He was twenty-seven years old.

Officer Johnny Terrell Bamsch was survived by his wife Cindy Bamsch and his parents, Mr. and Mrs. Roy Bamsch. Also mourning his death were his grandparents, Mrs. E.A. Bamsch of Houston, Mr. and Mrs. Jack Pigg of Lufkin and his great-grandmother, Mrs. Ida Lambert, also of Lufkin. Pat H. Foley Funeral Home, 1200 W. 34th, was in charge of arrangements. Visitation was held at that location until 1200 hours on Friday, after which time visitation was continued at Our Savior Lutheran Church, 4425 N. Shepherd, on Friday, January 31, 1975. Funeral services were held from there at 2:00pm with the Reverend John P. Schulze officiating. Burial followed at Rosewood Cemetery near Humble.

JOHNNY BAMSCH AND GRANDFATHER, MR. JACK PIGG, 1968

Pallbearers for this slain street officer were fellow Officers Jim Ellis, D.W. Thompson, Danny Wendt, Bill Elsbury, and friends Roy Horn, Bill Laurenson, J.D. Spencer, and Larry Tyree.

The Homicide Division responded in force and of course, North Shepherd Patrol units were on standby ready, willing and able to lend any assistance necessary to bring to justice the killers of their friend and fellow Officer. Homicide Lieutenant Tim McCormick made the scene and assigned Detectives Earl Haring and Tom Klawiter to the scene investigation and Detective David B. Massey to the hospital.

The investigation determined that both officers had apparently shot the wounded suspect. Richard Delain Kyles (African-American Male, 18) was taken to Ben Taub General Hospital under police guard. He survived his wounds. It was learned that the driver of the getaway car was Robert Lee Thomas (African-American Male, 30). An around the clock manhunt for Thomas began and a large of number of other Homicide and Robbery detectives were assigned to find him. Of course, patrol officers in all parts of the city, especially North Shepherd Acres Homes units were checking out leads as to Thomas' whereabouts. The stolen vehicle Thomas used to flee the scene was recovered. In the meantime, both Kyles and Thomas were charged with capital murder.

On the next day, Accident Lieutenant W.G. Eickenhorst, a former Homicide detective, located the vehicle used in this offense. Officers R.B. Carbo and C.P. Hall received information from the dispatcher regarding a vehicle believed to be occupied by Robert Lee Thomas. This vehicle was stopped and Thomas fled on foot. Officers chased and captured him and upon returning to the traffic stop location, learned that the vehicle had fled the scene with several occupants. That vehicle was located and those parties were arrested. A stolen weapon taken from a police officer in Livingston, Texas was recovered also. It was later determined that the weapon found at the scene used to shoot Officer Bamsch was purchased by Thomas earlier in the same month.

In August 1975, a jury found Robert Lee Thomas guilty of the crime and sentenced him to life imprisonment. He was paroled in 1988, but the parole was revoked in 1989. He remained confined in the Texas Department of Criminal Justice. His parole eligibility date was in November 1994. However, his parole was denied. With a projected release date classified as "undetermined," he was housed in the Ellis Unit in Huntsville.

In April 1976, a jury gave Richard Kyles, the triggerman, a life sentence. He was reviewed for parole on several occasions. Johnny's parents, Mr. and Mrs. Roy Bamsch, as well as many of Johnny's friends, were active in opposing this parole. Due greatly to their appearances before the Parole Board and through petition campaigns, this parole was not granted. Kyles was confined at the Ramsey Unit No. 1 in Rosharon. His projected release date also was classified as "undetermined."

This investigation was brought to a successful conclusion and was the result of an all-out team effort by the Homicide and Robbery Divisions. Assisting in various stages of the investigation from the Homicide Division were D.R. James, D.R. Bostock, D.R. Spurlock, P.C. Kainer, E.R. Dennis, J.M. Donovan, and N.J. Zoch. Working the robbery cases against these two hijackers were J.J. Orlando, R.J. Jeske, W.W. Markert, W.L. Burkham, J.O. Parker, and J.R. Williams.

Officer Jim "Pops" Ellis continued his HPD career. He was nearly thirty-three years old when he joined the Houston Police Department in late 1969. Being much older than most new officers, he became respectfully known to the younger officers as "Pops." Ellis was later promoted to sergeant and after working in Radio Patrol for several years, found his niche in the Narcotics Division. He had served more than twenty-eight years in HPD and was still assigned to the Narcotics Division when he died suddenly of a heart attack in April 1998. He was sixty-one years old, survived by two adult daughters.

Cindy Bamsch, the officer's wife of five and a half years, survived him. Prior to his death, Johnny and Cindy had received the good news that Cindy was possibly pregnant. Even though this had not been positively confirmed, Johnny proudly shared this with several people at North Shepherd. It was after his death that Cindy was able to confirm her pregnancy.

A daughter, Mandy, was born in August 1975, seven months after Johnny's death. Mandy Bamsch graduated from Texas A&M University in 1998 and was married in June 1999. In 2007, Mandy Derryberry and her husband Zach Derrybery are the parents of two year old Taylor Derryberry. They are also expecting another child in May, 2007. Cindy still resides in her northwest Houston home.

Cindy talked freely about being a police widow and pregnant at age twenty-five. She said she resolved to make Mandy her top priority. Knowing that she had very limited control over what happened to Johnny's killers, she placed her faith in God and the justice system. Cindy also pointed out that before Johnny's death she was not an advocate of the death penalty. Even though these killers were not given death, she grew to feel that the ultimate penalty is appropriate in certain instances.

Johnny's parents, Mr. and Mrs. Roy Bamsch, also survived Johnny. He was their only child. They continued to reside in their Oak Forest home where Johnny was raised. Since his death, his parents remained true friends of all Houston police officers, but especially to the officers at the North Shepherd Substation. For many years, prior to their failing health, they would bring doughnuts and other "goodies" to the station for the officers. Mrs. Bamsch passed away in 2001 and Mr. Bamsch followed her in 2003. Both are buried next to their only son at Rosewood Cemetery near Humble.

Many officers who were not with HPD at the time of Johnny's death knew and loved Mr. and Mrs. Bamsch, who made it a practice to attend Police Week Memorial Services. Mandy, Cindy, and former Chief of Police Harry Caldwell planted a tree in Johnny's memory at the North Shepherd Substation. Several of Johnny's police friends remained in touch with Mr. and Mrs. Bamsch. At one point, the couple gave their time to participate in an HPD training video espousing the importance and honor in volunteering to guard the Police Memorial.

More importantly, they were very active in their opposition to the parole of Richard Kyles and Robert Thomas. They actively worked toward this opposition until their health began to deteriorate.

Cindy Bamsch responded immediately to the kindness and support of the Houston Police Department by joining the 100 Club as a lifetime member and an avid supporter. She and Mandy have promoted support for slain officers through a public service television commercial. The 100 Club generously provided financial assistance for Mandy's college education.

The marker at Rosewood for Officer Bamsch consists of a foot marker which reads:
JOHN TERRELL BAMSCH
HPD BADGE #1388
CPL U.S. MARINE CORPS
SEP 10, 1947 - JAN 30, 1975

69

Officer Francis Eddie Wright
Badge #584
August 2, 1975

Freeway Driver Ignores Flashing Lights and Flares, Runs Over and Kills Officer Francis Eddie Wright

Francis Eddie Wright was born in Mansfield, Arkansas, on October 26, 1942. His parents were divorced when he was at a young age and his mother and stepfather moved to Houston, where he attended elementary and junior high school on the northeast side. He attended M. B. Smiley High School and graduated in the Class of 1961. After working in several jobs, he served his country in the United States Marine Corps in the years 1964-1967 and was a veteran of the Vietnam War.

Wright began his employment with the Houston Police Department on January 24, 1972, when he entered Police Cadet Class No. 53. He graduated and took the oath of office on May 13, 1972. He wore Badge No. 584. His initial assignment was to the Night Shift, Radio Patrol, Northeast Station, but shortly thereafter he transferred to the Evening Shift, Radio Patrol, Central Station. After a short time, he and Officer Frank B. Stachmus, an Academy classmate, teamed up and became regular partners.

On Friday night, August 1, 1975, Officers Wright and Stachmus were working the Evening Shift out of the Central Station. Riding Unit 1071, they were assigned to the near Southwest-Montrose section of the city. Just prior to 10:30 p.m., less than an hour before the end of their tour of duty, they were dispatched to the 4500 block of the Southwest Freeway (Outbound). Several auto accidents caused three disabled vehicles to block the moving lanes of traffic.

Off-duty Officer M. M. Kennedy met the two officers at the scene, having recognized the severity of the traffic problem. Kennedy wanted to assist them in any way possible. The three officers placed numerous flares in the freeway. In addition, they activated warning lights from the marked patrol unit. As they investigated the accident, carefully noting the positions of the vehicles and trying to clear the freeway by using wreckers, they directed the traffic flow away from the dangerous area.

Suddenly a vehicle arrived at a high rate of speed, apparently paying no attention to the flares and vehicle warning lights. Officer Stachmus saw this vehicle and shouted, "Look Out!"

OFFICER FRANCIS EDDIE WRIGHT

Stachmus and Kennedy reacted quickly, as did several witnesses. All of them jumped to safety. However, Officer Wright was unable to avoid this oncoming vehicle, which struck him, rolling him up onto the hood of this vehicle and knocking him off onto the pavement. The vehicle quickly fled the scene without stopping to render aid to the injured officer.

Rushing to his side, the officers present determined immediately that Wright had suffered severe injuries. They summoned a Houston Fire Department ambulance as a passing motorist, Dr. Irwin Klau, stopped to help. HFD Unit 1103 transported Officer Francis Eddie Wright to the nearest hospital, Bellaire General. Dr. Klau rode in the ambulance and, being the dedicated physician that he was, also went the extra mile, riding to Ben Taub General Hospital when the Bellaire General staff decided that the Ben Taub trauma room was the place to go to save the officer's life.

At Ben Taub doctors determined that Officer Wright had suffered massive head injuries as well as two broken legs and a broken arm. After doctors administered numerous and extensive surgeries over the next fifteen hours, they declared Officer Francis Eddie Wright dead at 2:35 p.m. on the following day, August 2, 1975.

His wife of seven years, Billie Hudson Wright, and two daughters, five-year-old Dena Ann and three-year-old Laura Nicole, survived Officer Wright. Additionally, Billie was over eight months pregnant at this time and, later the same month, gave birth to another daughter, Miranda. Wright's mother and stepfather, Mr. and Mrs. Elvin Lemley Sr. of Houston, grandmother Mrs. Mary Frances Wright of DeBarry, Florida, sisters Ann Acrey of Mt. Enterprise, Marie Davis and Leona Rucker of Houston, also survived him. Two brothers, Edwin Wright and Elvin Lemley Jr. of Houston also were left to mourn his tragic death, as were Billie's parents, Mr. and Mrs. Tom Hudson.

MRS. BILLIE WRIGHT AND DAUGHTERS DENA, MIRANDA, AND LAURA

Funeral services were held at the Hibbard Memorial Baptist Church, 8428 Green River Drive, at 10:30 a.m. on Tuesday, August 5, 1975, with the Reverend Jay B. Perkins officiating. Burial followed at Brookside Cemetery at the Eastex Freeway and Lauder Road with Pat H. Foley and Company, 2110 Tidwell Road, in charge of the arrangements.

Pallbearers were Officers Frank Stachmus, Jerry L. Wright, D. R. Sneed – all Academy classmates – along with Officers Tommy Wilcox and Jack Nelson and his longtime friends Raymond Hopkins, David Brewer and Ed Mackey.

The Accident Division assigned Accident Investigators B. D. Berryman and S. D. Nelson to begin investigating this tragic case of failure to stop and render aid, while Accident Sergeant J. C. Hartman was assigned to supervise the scene investigation. In any major accident such as this, the Hit and Run Detail was assigned the ultimate responsibility for the investigation. Then, as now, this is the Accident Division's equivalent of a who-dun-it police officer murder. More than the usual compliment of investigators was involved. Sergeant C. R. Deitz was the supervisor of this squad and assigned Officers D. G. Clifton, J. H. Parham, and E. C. Rogers to be included in the investigation of this case. Assisting them were Officers G. J. Novak and W. C. Robertson.

Fortunately, alert witnesses at the scene were able to obtain the license number of the suspect vehicle, which was driven by a young white male accompanied by a young white female. This vehicle, described as a late-model, light-colored Ford, was registered to an individual who resided in the 12600 block of Coulson, which was completely across town in the East Freeway-Federal Road area.

Radio Patrol Sergeant C. O. Warren was contacted and he and Officers F. G. Saldivar and A. R. Hughes remained in this immediate area to search for the vehicle. Shortly thereafter, this 1973 Ford was seen driving on Coulson toward the registered address. When police stopped the vehicle, they found the driver to be Mark Steven James (White Male, 20) of the Coulson address. A nineteen-year-old female accompanied him. They also found the vehicle had heavy pedestrian damage to the left front.

Officers took Mark James and his female companion into custody to the Accident Division for further questioning. The vehicle was towed to the Police Station at 61 Riesner for more detailed examination. Prior to the vehicle being towed, veteran Police Chemist Pete Christian was summoned to examine the vehicle, hoping to use the available physical evidence to place the car at the scene and identify it as the one that struck and killed Officer Wright. Officers gave the suspect his legal warnings, whereupon he waived his rights and provided a written statement to Officer W. C. Robertson. Additionally, they matched vehicle debris from the scene to the suspect's vehicle. As a result, they charged James with failure to stop and render aid. The following day, after Officer Wright died, they upgraded the charges to involuntary manslaughter.

Mrs. Billie Hudson Wright, only thirty years old, was left the task of raising three young daughters. She was a high school art teacher and, shortly after her husband's death, she purchased a home in Kingwood for the rearing of her young family. However, two years later she was diagnosed with cancer. After a three-year battle with this dreadful disease, she died on April 30, 1980. Her daughters were aged ten, eight and five. She was buried next to her husband in Brookside Cemetery.

Billie was the only child and beloved daughter of Tom and Dorothy Hudson. They were there to help her through the death of her husband, through the birth of all three of their granddaughters and through the emotional and physical suffering she experienced with her cancer treatments. When Billie died, they were there again. Mr. and Mrs. Hudson moved into Billie's Kingwood home and provided some stability in their granddaughters' lives. They lived there and raised these young women until they graduated from Kingwood High School.

In 2007, Dena Wright, thirty-seven, resides in Porter, Texas. Nicole Boufford, thirty-five, lives near Porter, is married and has three children: Mercedes Michelle Wright-eighteen, Ty Francis Bouffard-twelve (namesake of his grandfather), and Jordan Ashley Boufford-ten. Miranda Day is thirty-one, and lives near Splendora. She has three children: Devyn Renee Day-twelve, Bryce Hunter Day-thirteen, and Zane Day-seven. Miraculously, all three of Miranda's children were born on January 19th.

MIRANDA, DENA, AND LAURA WRIGHT

Also, in 2007. Mr. Tom Hudson resides in Rusk, Texas. Mrs. Dorothy Hudson passed away on Dena's 26th birthday in 1996. Officer Wright's mother, Mrs. Elvin Lemley Sr., is 80 years old and resides in Mt. Enterprise, Texas. Mr. Lemley Sr. passed away in 1996. Grandmother Wright is deceased. Brother Edwin lives in Corpus Christi. Of the three sisters, Leona lives in Crosby, Ann lives near Lake Murvaul, and Marie divides her time between Mt. Enterprise and Crosby. Elvin Jr. lives in Huffman, Texas.

Accident Sergeants Dietz and Hartman both retired, as did Officer E. C. Rogers. Dietz died in 2003 as did Rogers in 2005. Officers Berryman and Nelson both later promoted to sergeant and are both retired. Hit and Run Accident Investigators Will Robertson and Jerry Novak both made sergeant. Novak became an investigator in a Homicide Murder Squad and after a tremendous career of working Murders for twenty-four years, retired in 2004. Robertson has spent a number of years in an executive assistant chief's command office. Parham later made sergeant, but resigned, as did Officer Clifton. Chemist Pete Christian died in 1995.

Of the arresting Officers, Sergeant C. O. Warren retired from the Jail Division in 1996 and died in 2001. Officer Hughes resigned from HPD. Officer Saldivar, after serving a lengthy tour of duty in the Narcotics Division, was assigned to a Tactical Unit at Eastside Patrol in 2002. Officer M. M. Kennedy, the off-duty officer who stopped to assist, later resigned from HPD.

Officer Wright's academy classmate, close friend and partner, Officer Frank Stachmus, continued on with his police career. He worked in Narcotics for three years as well as in the Juvenile Division for a number of years. In 1993, he took his well-deserved retirement only to undertake another law enforcement career with the Tomball Police Department.

Extensive research helped to track the journey of Mark Stephen James through our often-flawed justice system. Originally charged with failure to stop and render aid, James saw the charge upgraded to involuntary manslaughter when Officer Wright died. This was his only brush with the law and this charge, for some unknown reason, was dismissed in 1978. He was charged a second time shortly thereafter and pled out for two years with the strange stipulation that the sentence could be appealed. He remained out on bond while the appeal made its way through the system. Eventually, on September 28, 1982, after all appeals were exhausted, he apparently surrendered and served all or part of his sentence. In 2002, he lived in San Antonio.

Marker for Officer Wright:

F.E. (EDDIE) WRIGHT
BELOVED HUSBAND AND FATHER

70

Officer Richard Howard Calhoun
Badge #2414
October 10, 1975

Officer Richard Calhoun Shot to Death Leading Charge toward Escaped Convicts

Richard Howard Calhoun was born on August 4, 1940 in Brooklyn, New York. His father being a career U. S. Navy man, Richard and his siblings traveled extensively in his early years. Upon graduation from Jasper High School in New Bern, North Carolina in 1959, he followed his father and older brother by enlisting in the U. S. Navy, spending the next ten years in the service of his country. His last tour of duty was as a Navy recruiter in the Houston area. He joined the Houston Police Department by way of Police Cadet Class No. 42, graduating on January 27, 1970. He wore Badge No. 2414.

After having worked the Accident Division for more than five years, he transferred to the Radio Patrol Bureau, Park Place Substation, in July 1975.

On Wednesday, October 8, 1975, three convicts escaped from the Central Unit of the Texas Department of Corrections in Sugar Land. They took a supervisor hostage and forced him to drive them to Houston. Releasing this man in southwest Houston, they took another man hostage and forced him to drive them to Dumble and Telephone in southeast Houston.

Again, they released their hostage. The three escapees were Michael Robbins (White Male, 37) and Benjamin Windberry (White Male, 29), both in for robbery, and Noel Smith (White Male, 29), doing thirty years for murder.

By the morning of Friday, October 10, Park Place Substation Lieutenant Ken DeFoor and Sergeant Fred Walschburger received a call from the Harris County Organized Crime Unit to meet them as they had information that the three escapees were in a house at 9410 Ave. J. One was reportedly dead and the other two were alive in this two-story frame house near the Houston Ship Channel. Park Place officers met Organized Crime near this location and upon discussing the information, they decided to surround this house and summon the newly formed SWAT Unit to the scene.

At 8:15 a.m., Officers Richard Calhoun and Michael J. Lyons, while securing the exterior, found a back room window unlocked and climbed in while other officers were at the front door shouting to the suspects to surrender. After making entry, Lyons opened the front door for Officers Roy Slay and Paul Thornton and County Officers Pete Cooper, Jay Evans and George Machado. Officer Calhoun took the lead and started up the stairway. He took only three steps. Suddenly an arm holding a shotgun appeared over the railing and one blast from it struck Officer Calhoun in the neck.

Officers Lyons and Thornton quickly pulled Officer Calhoun outside to shelter behind a police car, but he was already dead. Slay and the County officers returned fire up the stairway while officers outside "opened up" toward the upper floor. The Special Weapons and Tactics Team (SWAT) arrived at the scene but little gunfire came from the house after the initial barrage. SWAT began lobbing tear gas inside, which eventually burst into flames. The Houston Fire Department was called but was forced to fight the fire from several houses away due to the danger of more gunfire from the house.

OFFICER RICHARD HOWARD CALHOUN

HFD extinguished the fire at 10:47 a.m. and officers made their second entry into the gutted house. Inside they found Benjamin Windberry dead, shot and burned. An autopsy determined that he had been killed by police in the exchange of gunfire. Noel Smith was found badly burned and dead and it was later discovered that he had shot and killed himself. Michael Robbins

170

was found dead. An autopsy determined that he had died about ten hours prior to this incident, having been kicked or beaten to death by Windberry and/or Smith.

SWAT Officer P. D. Hawkins, who was on the scene of this tragic incident, was wounded when a shotgun leaning against a car accidentally fell, the shot hitting him in both legs. He later recovered from these wounds.

Officer Calhoun, thirty-five, was survived by his wife Arlene and four children: son Robert, fifteen, and three daughters Donna, fourteen, Terri, eleven, and Barbara, four. Other survivors were his parents, Mr. and Mrs. Rudolph Calhoun; a brother, Chief Robert Calhoun of the U. S. Navy; and sisters Shirley Jarvis and Donnie Wilson.

Funeral services were held at the Park Place Lutheran Church at 8130 Park Place at 10 a.m. Monday, October 13, 1975. Burial followed at Forest Park Lawndale. Pallbearers were fellow officers and friends, Captain L. D. Sherman, Sergeants W. E. Plaster, Fred Walshburger and Bobby Morgan, Detective Sam Merrill and Officers Paul Thornton, John Eaton and T. J. Buchanan.

After the dust settled, there were a number of unanswered questions as to how the three escapees came to be in an occupied residence where no one was home. The owner, a wrecker driver, was questioned about this situation. His story was that his wife was in the hospital and that he was staying in a nearby motel. An extensive investigation ensued into this individual's possible involvement with the escapees. Eventually, four other individuals with connections to the Bandidos motorcycle gang were indicted for conspiracy to commit escape. However, with the three escapees being deceased, no strong evidentiary connection could be established and the charges were dismissed.

This capital murder scene was investigated by Homicide detectives Jim Tucker and David Massey. They were assisted by J. W. "Moose" Clampitte, Jerry Carpenter and Bobby Rouse, with Carpenter and Rouse doing extensive follow-up on the escape conspiracy.

In 2007, Ken DeFoor is a retired HPD Captain, who has had a number of other interesting law enforcement positions since his 1983 retirement. Sergeant Fred Walschburger retired in 1988 from the Police Academy Pistol Range and lives in Houston. Officer Roy Slay worked in the HPD Narcotics Division for many years and retired from that division. Officer Paul Thornton, a close personal friend of Calhoun, resigned from HPD in 1979. He retired from a local chemical company and lived in Hempstead.

Mike Lyons resigned from HPD in 1981 and went to work for the Montgomery County Sheriff's Office. County Detective Pete Cooper is deceased. County Detective Jay Evans later retired from the Harris County Medical Examiner's Office and has worked as a public information officer with both HPD and HFD. George Machado's whereabouts were unknown, as his last record with TCLEOSE was 1983. P. D. Hawkins retired from HPD Westside Patrol in 1995 and went to work for the Alief School District.

Homicide Detective Jim Tucker resigned from HPD at the rank of lieutenant and died in an accident in 1998. Detective David Massey is retired as a Captain after an exemplary career with more than thirty-five years of service, having served as the Commander of the Community Services Division, the North Patrol Division, the Narcotics Division and the Police Academy. Detective Bobby Rouse lost his life in an automobile accident in 1979. Detective Jerry Carpenter retired from the Burglary and Theft Division in 1991 and resided in Baytown in 2007. Detective J.W. Clampitte retired from HPD in 1983 and was with the Harris County District Attorney's Office for a number of years and retired from that career also.

In 2001, Arlene Calhoun resided in Deer Park, as did Robert and his three children, Richard Howard Calhoun II, a namesake for Officer Calhoun, and daughters Stephanie and Christina. Donna's children are Amber and Steven. Terri has two children, Andrea and Courtney. Barbara's children are Jessica and Stephen. Arlene has been blessed with nine grandchildren, all of which were deprived the opportunity to know their paternal grandfather.

The Calhoun family has wished to retain their privacy throughout these many years since the heart and soul of their family was taken away so tragically. This writer has and always will respect that privacy. In October, 2006, however, I was contacted through the HPOU that the brother of Officer Calhoun was in Houston and was wanting to speak with someone about his brother and his brother's death.

It was my pleasure to meet with a man who has had an outstanding career with the United States Navy, Mr. Robert Calhoun, and his wife, Mary. He is now retired from the Navy and is successful in his second career. We had a pleasant breakfast together talking about his brother, whom I knew on a casual basis from both of us working night shift accident and night shift patrol both out of the Central station. It was my pleasure to provide him with contact numbers of Officers who were more closely associated with his brother that I was. More importantly, he asked me many questions about his brother's death and the procedures that were followed that tragic morning.

Officer Richard Calhoun was not the first member of Police Cadet Class No. 42 to meet a violent death in the line of duty, nor was he the last. In October 1972, Officer Jerry L. Spruill was murdered in the 600 block of Westheimer. Another class member, Officer Michael Rivers, resigned from HPD and in 1980 was shot and killed by a hijacker while on duty with the Hedwig Village Police Department.

The gravemarker for Officer Calhoun fondly refers to his departmental nickname and reads as follows:

"ROHO"
RICHARD HOWARD CALHOUN
1940 - 1975
HPD BADGE #2414

71

Officer George Garza Rojas
Badge #2199
January 28, 1976

Bonded-out Killer Cevallos Stabs Officer George G. Rojas to Death in East Side Bar

George Garza Rojas was born on February 23, 1946, in Nuevo Laredo, Mexico. When George was five years old, his parents moved to Houston and settled on the near north side. He became a naturalized citizen of the United States and attended Looscan Elementary School and Marshall Junior High before graduating from Davis High School in 1965. He was employed by the City of Houston as a lifeguard and then as an apprentice stationary engineer, working at Police Headquarters at 61 Riesner.

On January 8, 1968, a dream of George's was fulfilled when he joined the Houston Police Department in Police Cadet Class No. 37, graduating on April 26, 1968. During his seven-plus years in the department, George worked Central Patrol, Jail, Dispatcher, Narcotics and Southeast Patrol Divisions. He wore Badge No. 2199.

On the night of Tuesday, January 27, 1976, George Rojas was attending a private party at a club owned by a close personal friend. This large night club was known as the Latin World at 7035 Harrisburg. A disturbance erupted during this party over a coat which had been accidentally burnt by a cigarette. Rojas, known by many of the attendees to be a Houston police officer, stepped in to calm down the problem. After taking this action, he went about his socializing with his many friends. A perpetrator in this disturbance was a known police character, Alejandro "Alex" Cevallos (Latin American Male, 34).

At about 10:30 p.m. Officer Rojas was approached by Cevallos, who pulled a knife, prompting the officer to reach for his pistol. He identified himself to Cevallos as a police officer and told him to put the knife away and settle down. Witnesses later said Cevallos walked away saying to Rojas that he would "get him."

At about 10:55 p.m. another disturbance broke out involving the same individuals in the previous melee. As Rojas walked toward the disturbance, Cevallos walked up to Rojas and struck him in the right side of the neck. Blood began gushing from Rojas' throat. He managed to pull his off-duty revolver and start toward his assailant. However, severely weakened from the throat wound and the resulting loss of blood, Rojas dropped his pistol. Cevallos' brother picked it up and used it to keep the crowd from following him and the culprit.

The two Cevallos brothers fled the scene. Investigators later determined that Alex Cevallos, a carpet layer, had used a tool of his trade to strike Rojas in the neck, hooking and severely wounding him with the curved end of the sharpened instrument.

OFFICER GEORGE GARZA ROJAS

An ambulance crew responded and rushed Officer George Rojas to Ben Taub General Hospital. All measures were taken to save his life. However, he was pronounced dead at 3:45 a.m. Wednesday, January 28, 1976, one month short of his thirtieth birthday.

He was survived by his wife, Mary Martha Rojas, and eight-year-old daughter Sonya. Also left to mourn his death were his parents, Mr. and Mrs. Eulojio Rojas, brothers Lupe, Ernest and Edward, and one sister, Mary Ann. Religious services were held at 1 p.m. Friday, January 30, 1976, from the Crespo Funeral Home at 2516 Navigation. Burial followed at Brookside Memorial Park, Eastex Freeway and Lauder Road.

Marker for Officer Rojas:

IN LOVING MEMORY OF GEORGE G. ROJAS
(HAS AN OPEN BIBLE ON MARKER)

Upon receiving the call that an officer had been stabbed, the Homicide Division initiated an immediate scene response. This investigation was led by Homicide Lieutenant Henry Wayne Kersten, who assigned to the case veteran Homicide Detective T. E. "Tommy" Baker and his rookie partner, W. D. "David" Lott. Assisting them were Detectives E. R. "Dog" Dennis, Pat Kainer, Doug Bostock, John Donovan and Carol Stephenson.

After charges were filed on Alex Cevallos, an all-night search for him began. It was soon learned that Alex Cevallos was free on bond for a 1973 San Antonio murder and was due to be tried in March 1976 on a local murder charge.

The search continued throughout the night and a large fresh group of Homicide investigators put the "heat" on, looking for Cevallos the following morning. Those named in the offense report as searching for the crook and also doing extensive follow-up to shore up witness accounts were Homicide Detectives David Massey, Jim Tucker, Jimmy Hall, Ed Horelica, Dan McAnulty, Johnny Bonds, Nelson Zoch, Max Lankford, Larry Earls, Ray Trimble and Eli Uresti. Also, George's close friends and fellow officers from HPD's basketball team, Jim Montero and Richard Delano, joined in the search.

Famous defense attorney Percy Foreman surrendered Cevallos at 1:45 p.m. the following day on the latest murder charge, bringing Officer Rojas' pistol with him and turning it over to Homicide Lieutenant Breck Porter.

In 2001, Mrs. Mary Rojas and daughter Sonya both lived in Houston. Eulojio Rojas, George's father, passed away in January 2001. His mother resided in Houston. Sister Mary Ann and brothers Lupe, Ernest and Edward were all still alive.

Of the investigators, Detective Tommy Baker retired in 1985. David Lott, who later worked Auto Theft, Internal Affairs and B&T, retired from HPD in 1988 and went on to work with the Harris County District Attorney's Office. John Donovan died in 1991 while still on active duty. Dog Dennis died in 1989, just two years after his retirement. Pat Kainer resigned from HPD and lived in the Houston area. Doug Bostock, a former patrol partner and very close friend of Rojas, retired in 1984 and later retired a second time from the D.A.'s Office. Detective Carol Stephenson Ewton retired in 1983 and moved to the Lake Livingston-Riverside area. She died in 1999.

The criminal career of Alex Cevallos is not unlike those law enforcement authorities have seen before in cop killers. Names that come to mind are Kenneth Hinkle, who murdered Officer Lyndon Sander in 1967, Carl Buntion, who murdered Officer Jim Irby in 1990, and Wesley Sellars, who murdered Officer Kenneth Moody in 1969. In each of these instances, these individuals and their career criminal brothers seemed to always find a way to dodge or skirt the legal system through their attorneys or the fallacies of the system in general. In this case, Cevallos was out on bond on an earlier local murder charge, as well as one from San Antonio. Investigators and prosecutors were well aware that a major issue in the Rojas murder would be Cevallos' contention that he was not aware that Rojas was a police officer since he was not in uniform. This case went to trial and on July 5, 1977, the jury hung up on the question of guilt or innocence.

Another trial was held shortly thereafter and on October 10, 1977, Alex Cevallos was acquitted of the murder in the death of Officer George Rojas. He went free. If there is any consolation after such a miscarriage of justice, it is that usually individuals such as Alex Cevallos will continue to go afoul of the law and will eventually receive "some of their just due." Records indicate that in 1982, he was assessed two concurrent seven-year terms in the federal system for conspiracy to distribute cocaine. Federal time being what it is, day for day, this would have put him out of confinement in 1989. Records later reflect that in 1994 Cevallos was sentenced to eleven years and three months for money laundering in connection with conspiracy to distribute cocaine.

One of the Homicide investigators had first met George Rojas on January 8, 1968, the first day of Cadet Class No. 37. He was an extremely likeable guy who seemed to know everyone, no matter the rank and had obviously made many friends while working at Headquarters at 61 Riesner. During his academy days he was paired up by weight for a boxing match with a classmate. "As we prepared to enter the ring," Nelson Zoch recalled, "several of the instructors were laughing, as if having the time of their lives. About fifteen seconds into the match, George had taken care of me completely. I later learned that the instructors had knowledge that I was not privy to – George had been a Golden Gloves champion as a teen-ager."

Mary Rojas was a long-time employee of the City of Houston and worked in Personnel. She is now retired. Sonja worked for a major airline. Mary met George while they were in high school. She attended Milby, but liked to go the basketball games at Davis where the "good-looking guys were." George loved to play basketball and during the years he was at HPD, he played on a basketball team that would play at the various inner-city junior high schools. These games were very well attended, with all proceeds going to the school itself for athletic equipment not available from regular funding.

George had gone through elementary, junior high and high school with several other police officers, including David Huerta, who was killed in the line of duty in 1973, as well as Matt Perales, who served active and retired officers and their families in his assignment in HPD Family Assistance.

72

Officer James Frederick Kilty
Badge #1856
April 8, 1976

Popular Softball-playing Officer Jim Kilty Shot by Narc Suspect he was Investigating

James Frederick Kilty was born in Kansas City, Missouri, on November 11, 1940. He graduated from Bishop Hogan High School there in 1958 and after his graduation he served in the U. S. Coast Guard for four years. His family had moved to Houston while he was in the Coast Guard and when he moved to the Bayou City, he joined the Houston Police Department on May 20, 1963 in Police Cadet Class No. 28. He graduated on September 6, 1963 and was assigned to Radio Patrol and served there until transferring to the Narcotics Division on February 15, 1974.

Narcotics Officer Jim Kilty was conducting a self-initiated narcotics investigation, which began prior to April 7, 1976. As a result of this investigation, Kilty had learned that Willie Howard (African American, 47) was selling heroin from his home on the north side. He also learned that Howard was carrying narcotics on his person to and from his job at the Ramada Inn, 2929 Southwest Freeway, where he was employed as a cook. Further, based on his information, Officer Kilty had obtained search warrants for Willie Howard's residence and his vehicle.

In the early morning hours of Thursday, April 8, 1976, other Narcotics Division officers were assigned to assist Kilty in the planned execution of the search warrants. Officers were sent to conduct surveillance on Willie Howard's residence with instructions to contact Officer Kilty and his immediate supervisor, Narcotics Sergeant Joe Andrews, when Howard left for his job. Kilty, Andrews and Narcotics Officers M. D. Harrison and P. A. Brooks planned to be at the Ramada Inn, awaiting the suspect. Officer Kilty planned to execute the search warrant on Howard's vehicle when he arrived for work and after that execute the papers on Howard's residence.

At approximately 5 a.m., the four veteran Narcotics officers were set up at the Ramada Inn to complete this assignment. The surveillance team reported to them that Howard had left his residence. When he arrived for work, he parked at a different location than anticipated and then walked toward the front entrance rather than the kitchen door as expected. When Howard got out of his vehicle, Officer Kilty, who clearly identified himself as a police officer, confronted him. Howard pulled a small chrome revolver and shot twice at the officer.

OFFICER JAMES FREDERICK KILTY

Kilty went down and after shouting to his fellow officers that he was hit, returned fire. Officers Harrison and Brooks also returned fire, striking Howard numerous times, killing him instantly. Even though the officers summoned an ambulance, Sergeant Andrews thought Kilty's condition was quickly worsening and decided to place the wounded officer in an undercover car. With Officer Brooks driving and Sergeant Andrews in the back seat with Kilty, they sped toward Ben Taub General Hospital, where the officer was dead on arrival.

Further investigation revealed that Willie Howard possessed a small amount of heroin in the band of his wide-brimmed hat. He was an ex-convict, having served time for assault to murder and possession of heroin.

Officer Jim Kilty was thirty-five years old. He was unmarried and survived by his parents, Mr. and Mrs. William F. Kilty; three brothers, William Kilty and his wife Nancy Kilty, Tom Kilty and Mark Kilty, and one sister, Mary Anne Kilty. His grandmother, Mrs. Mary Anwander, of Kansas City, Missouri, also survived him

Funeral services were under the direction of the

Earthman Funeral Home at 6700 Ferris, in Bellaire. A Rosary service was conducted at 7pm on Friday, April 9, 1976. Funeral services were held on Saturday, April 10, 1976, at the St. Francis De Sales Catholic Church. Entombment followed at the Memorial Oaks Mausoleum. Pallbearers were Officers M.R. Woods, P.A. Brooks, M.D. Harrison, J.J. Reyes, B.J. Gallatin, Lieutenant B.G. Ripley, Sergeant Glen Cheek, and Bob Morgan.

MR. WILLIAM KILTY, JAMES KILTY, AND MRS. WILLIAM KILTY

Officer Jim Kilty was a very active patrol officer, working out of the Beechnut Substation but riding in the Montrose-Westheimer area in the late 1960's and early 1970's. The drug culture was new, but in those days it was especially strong in this area of town, which was mostly inhabited by a new group of citizens who proudly referred to themselves as "hippies."

In an interview, Jim's long-time partner, John R. Hake, recalled those days on patrol together. He mentioned the large number of arrests that the two made in this area for drug possession and the number of times they observed a number of hippies playing softball in a park. They had previously arrested many of these hippies and the group challenged them to a softball game. This game was billed as the Pigs versus the Hippies and after several cancellations was eventually held and became a national media event as the first of its kind. Whether it helped police-community relations was debatable.

As a result of Officer Kilty's initiation of many drug arrests, the 100 Club of Houston named him 1973 Officer of the Year in the Radio Patrol-Investigative Field. Also, after his death, the Houston Police Officers Association (now Houston Police Officers' Union) for a number of years conducted the Kilty Law Enforcement Softball Tournament.

Later the morning of the shooting, someone in Homicide commented, "Well, at least the crook also got killed." Another comment was made that is generally accurate when a police officer and a crook both get killed in the same incident. The comment was, "Yes, but it's like trading a shiny new gold piece for a rusty old penny."

Homicide Detectives Doug Bostock, Earl Haring, Tommy Baker and Johnny Thornton investigated this offense. By 2000, all four investigators had retired from HPD. Bostock and Thornton both went to work as investigators in the Harris County D. A.'s Office. Haring was employed by the Constable, Precinct #1. They are all completely retired in 2006. Officer John Hake retired and after several years of softball and travel was employed with the Veterans Administration Police. Another partner and close friend, J. W. Collins, served HPD as a sergeant assigned to the Bush Airport Narcotics Detail and is also retired. Sergeant Joe Andrews retired as a lieutenant and left to teach school. Officer M. D. "Mad Dog" Harrison drowned in a fishing accident in the early 1980's at Lake Conroe. Officer Phil Brooks continued with HPD and worked the Southeast Patrol Division for a number of years. He is now also retired.

JAMES KILTY ON HIS BIRTHDAY

Mrs. Kilty lives in Southwest Houston in 2007. Mr. Kilty is deceased. Kilty's brother William has three daughters-Suzanne Kilty, Meg Kilty, and Kelly Kilty. Brother Tom has a daughter, Jennifer Kilty. His only sister, Mary Ann, lives in Houston. Jim's youngest brother Mark became a Houston police officer in 1978 and worked Beechnut Patrol and Narcotics. He later became a sergeant and is currently assigned to the Vice Division. Mark's sons are James Kilty, a namesake for Officer Jim Kilty, and Justin Kilty. Most of these nieces and nephews never had an opportunity to know their Uncle Jim.

Marker for Officer Kilty on his crypt at Memorial Oaks reads:

JAMES F. KILTY
1940-1976 WITH BADGE #1856

73

Officer Timothy Lowe Hearn
Badge #1678
June 8, 1978

Lifelong Criminal Shoots to Death Popular Narc Tim Hearn, Later Gets Death Penalty

Officer Timothy Lowe Hearn was born on November 8, 1949, in Houston. After attending Oak Forest Elementary and Black Junior High, he graduated from Waltrip High School in 1968, one of a number of Waltrip graduates to become Houston police officers. He later graduated from the University of Texas in 1973 with an Accounting degree. He entered Police Cadet Class No. 67 on November 11, 1974, and was president of that class that graduated on March 6, 1975. His first assignment was to the Radio Patrol Bureau, Central Division, Evening Shift. He remained in that assignment until August 8, 1976, when he transferred to the Narcotics Division.

On Wednesday night, June 7, 1978, Officer Murray K. Jordan and his partner, Officer Tim Hearn, began their tour of duty assigned as plainclothes investigators in the Narcotics Division. Officer Jordan had developed information from a credible and reliable informant that one Rudy Ramos Esquivel was selling heroin from the Early Roberts Restaurant in the 6800 block of Harrisburg. He allegedly operated after 2 a.m. Acting on this information, Officers Jordan and Hearn set up surveillance in the parking lot of the Sears store across the street from Early Roberts.

At approximately 2:10 a.m., they observed Esquivel arriving at Early Roberts in the company of two Hispanic females. Through his previous police contacts, Jordan knew Esquivel and Esquivel knew Jordan as the arresting officer in a previous case. Shortly before 3 a.m., Esquivel and the two females left the restaurant. Jordan and Hearn met them on the sidewalk, with Jordan and Esquivel acknowledging each other. Jordan then told Rudy and the females that they needed to talk to them and asked them to come with them across the street away from the crowded sidewalk.

Officer Hearn took the purses from the two females and they all walked across the street to the patrol car. As Hearn told the two females to place their hands on the car, Jordan requested Esquivel to do the same. However, Esquivel pulled a pistol and began shooting, hitting Jordan in the left arm and back. Jordon pushed Esquivel away as attempted to pull his service pistol. More shots rang out.

OFFICER TIMOTHY LOWE HEARN

"Murray, I've been hit!" Hearn shouted.

Jordan saw Esquivel running and shot at him twice with his .357-caliber revolver before seeing him fall on the parking lot. Officer Hearn, even after having been wounded, also shot at Esquivel, firing six times with his .45-caliber automatic. Knowing Esquivel was down, Jordan called for help and turned his attention to his partner. Patrol Officers Joe Barrera and Paul Ogden, of the Park Place Substation Night Shift, were seconds away when they were dispatched to the shooting. They arrived to assist the wounded officers as well as call for Life Flight Helicopter. They also contained the two female witnesses.

LifeFlight arrived and treated both officers and took them to Hermann Hospital. Officer Jordan received two gunshot wounds to the back and one to the left forearm. Officer Hearn received one gunshot wound to the face and one to the abdomen. Hearn went into surgery but died from his wounds at 5:20 a.m. Rudy Esquivel received one gunshot wound to the back; he survived. HPD filed capital murder of a peace officer and attempted capital murder of a peace officer against him.

TIMOTHY HEARN, MOST ATTRACTIVE SENIOR, WALTRIP HIGH SCHOOL, 1968

Officer Tim Hearn was only twenty-eight years old. He was survived by his wife Jenny and two-year old son Tory. Also mourning his death were his parents, Mr. and Mrs. Robert L. Hearn, and one sister, Mrs. Sayra Hesselsweet and her husband Nick. Funeral services were held on Saturday, June 10, 1978, at the Baptist Temple at 230 West 20th. Burial followed at the Corinth Cemetery near Buckholtz, Texas.

Rudy Esquivel was first arrested and charged at the age of eighteen in 1953 for a vicious and brutal sexual assault and mutilation case that occurred in the East End of Houston, not far from where he shot Officers Hearn and Jordan. For that crime, he was assessed a ninety-nine-year sentence. He was paroled in 1964 and sent back to prison in 1969 after more trouble with the law. Paroled again, he had several other arrests for burglary and possession of controlled substances prior to 1978. At the time Esquivel shot the two officers, he was free on $20,000 bond awaiting a June 26, 1978, trial date on a charge of possession of heroin.

This plague on society, Rudy Esquivel, who should not have even been out of prison in June of 1978, was once again taken before our criminal justice system. This time, on August 18, 1978, 71 days after murdering Officer Hearn, jurors found him guilty of capital murder in the 180th Criminal District Court and assessed him the death penalty. Finally, on June 9, 1986, he was executed. Once again, and more than ever, it was "the rusty old penny for a bright shiny silver dollar or gold piece."

It is true that almost in every instance when an Officer is killed, it is discovered that this was a special person. In the case of Officer Tim Hearn, since all of his biological family has passed on, research was conducted at Waltrip High School to learn more about this young man. While I knew him personally from playing softball with him, the following was discovered about Timothy Lowe Hearn from the 1968 Waltrip yearbook: Most Attractive Senior, Senior Favorite, President of National Honor Society, President of Senior Class, member of German Club, Student Council, and American Legion Club, as well as playing on the varsity basketball team for three years. What a loss to his family, HPD, and society in general when Rudy Esquivel decided to shoot his way out of his latest problems with the law.

The area where Officer Hearn was murdered was not new to tragedy in the Houston Police Department. In January 1976, just three blocks east of the Sears Store at the Latin World Nightclub, Officer George Garza Rojas was murdered. In October 1980, across the street from Sears and almost directly in front of the Early Roberts Café, Robbery Detective Victor Ray Wells was shot and killed.

In 2006, Jenny Hearn resided in the Houston area, working in real estate. Her son Tory has completed a degree at the University of Houston. Mr. and Mrs. Hearn retired to Temple, Texas and Mr. Hearn passed away in 1998. In another family tragedy, Mr. and Mrs. Hearn's only other child, Tim's sister Sayra, passed away in the 1990s from cancer. And, in 2005, Mrs. Hearn passed away, having lived over twenty-seven years after the loss of her only son.

Officer Murray Jordan survived his wounds and continued an exemplary career with HPD, the majority of which was spent in the fight against narcotic trafficking. He retired in 1987 after twenty years on the force, returning to his Northeast Texas hometown of Gilmer. He served as chief deputy of the Upshur County Sheriff's Department with plans to retire from that job and continue his sawmill and heavy equipment businesses.

Veteran Homicide Detectives James Pierce and

Danny Spurlock investigated the murder scene. Detectives David Massey and Van Knox conducted the extensive follow-up and trial preparation. Jim Pierce retired in 1991 after nearly thirty years in the Homicide Division and moved to the Lake Sam Rayburn area. Danny Spurlock worked in Homicide for nearly eleven years, later transferring to Burglary and Theft. He retired from there in 1996 to East Texas. David Massey became a captain and retired in 2004. Van Knox later worked many years in the Auto Theft Division and retired in 2004. Officer Joe Barrera became a lieutenant and Officer Paul Ogden a sergeant. They were longtime patrol partners before their promotions and in 2006, both are assigned to the Magnolia-Eastside Division, the same area they patrolled that night when Tim Hearn's life was taken.

TIMOTHY HEARN, SENIOR CLASS FAVORITE, WALTRIP HIGH SCHOOL, 1968

Officer Hearn was an outstanding athlete and enjoyed playing softball. At the time of his death, he played with the Narcotics Division team with Murray Jordan. Cleveland Field, in the 4200 block of Scotland, was the City Park where the Houston Law Enforcement Softball League regularly played on Wednesday nights. Tim Hearn played many games on this field. On April 4, 1979, Cleveland Field was renamed Timothy Hearn Field.

Then-Mayor Jim McConn presided over a ceremony with Tim's family present. In later years, no signage indicated the name of this field. Robbery Detective Earl Musick, who later retired, was instrumental in having this field renamed for Tim Hearn. Also, just as was the case with Officer Jim Kilty, a law enforcement softball tournament was named for Tim Hearn and was held for a number of years in Houston.

The gravesite was located near Buckholtz, Texas. A monument had been placed by Tim's family to mark his final resting place, which is now near that of his beloved parents. A 100 CLUB KILLED IN THE LINE OF DUTY marker also has been placed to commemorate this fallen hero.

Few HPD softball players will ever forget the first Tim Hearn tournament, held five weeks after this tragedy. Officer Murray Jordan, who had been shot three times in June, was determined to play in these games in memory of his friend and partner. He had a "monster" tournament and was named to the All-Tournament team.

74
City Marshall Charles Henry Baker
Badge #CM122
August 16, 1979

Death Penalty Used for the Killer Of City Marshall Charles Baker

On Friday night, August 16, 1979, City Marshals Charles Baker and Ross McCammon were on the north side of Houston searching for an individual known to have traffic warrants. At about 9:30 p.m., they were en route to a location in the 1100 block of East Sunnyside where they believed this individual resided when, in the 10200 block of Silvercrest, they encountered a white male walking toward them.

Unsure of what their suspect looked like but aware that he was known to walk the streets at all hours of the night, they stopped next to him and asked him his name. Marshal Baker, who was riding, got out of their patrol car and Marshal McCammon, the driver, also got out and walked around to where Baker was already questioning this man on the side of the street. Both Marshals noticed that he was sweating profusely and appeared very nervous. In the process of beginning a search for their own protection, they found a large wad of currency and a pocketful of loose change.

They immediately suspected that he had just committed a robbery or burglary. Baker, the older of the two officers, told his rookie partner McCammon to move the car out of the street. As McCammon proceeded to do this, he heard Baker say something that provoked a scuffle with the unidentified suspect. As McCammon rushed to help his partner, he heard a shot and saw Baker fall to the ground. Then he heard another shot.

CITY MARSHALL CHARLES HENRY BAKER

McCammon then returned fire at the suspect once and was fired upon twice. As McCammon was forced to take cover behind a nearby truck, the suspect fired at him twice more, striking the truck. At this point, the suspect was running south on Silvercrest.

McCammon shot at him again and saw him fall in a ditch. After the suspect fired at him once again, McCammon started toward him, thinking that he was out of bullets. However, the suspect fired one more time and disappeared from sight. (Later, an investigation showed that McCammon fired five rounds at the suspect, who fired nine times). At this point, McCammon was able to turn his attention to his wounded partner.

It was too late. City Marshal Charles Baker was dead at the scene from gunshot wounds to the chest and groin. His service revolver was beside him on the ground. It had not been fired. Baker was fifty-one years old.

City Marshal Charles Henry Baker was born on December 27, 1927, in West Texas. Most of his childhood was spent in Houston. He served his country honorably in the United States Navy near the end of World War II. He had previously worked for the Conroe Police Department as well as the City of Houston Park Police. He had been assigned as a City Marshal since August, 1975. Just a month prior to his death, he and his wife moved into a new house near Lake Conroe, a home that he and his wife Dorothy built with their own labor.

Dorothy Baker survived him, as did a son, David Baker, and three grandchildren, all less than eight years of age, JoAnn, Renee and Paul. His parents, Mr. and Mrs. J. L. Baker of Montgomery, brother Clyde Baker of Houston and two sisters, Nelda Griggs of Conroe and Donnie Serio of Houston also mourned his death.

Funeral services for City Marshall Charles Baker were held at 10 a.m. Saturday, August 18, 1979, from the Metcalf Funeral Home Chapel of the Pines in Conroe. Burial followed at the Copeland Chapel Cemetery, which is near Lake Conroe. Pallbearers were fellow City Marshalls Ray Kimberlin, Bob Wolfe, Ross McCammon, Sherman Hicks, Lieutenant Bill Holcombe, Sergeant Bob Trojan, Richard Burge and Robert McLemore.

Evening Shift Homicide Lieutenant Guy Mason immediately assigned veteran Detective C. W. "Carl" Kent and rookie Detective P. C. "Paul" Motard to the investigation. They were assisted in their extensive scene investigation by Crime Scene Unit Officer S. P. "Speedie" Wilson.

Later that night, they learned that the north side grapevine worked well, as the individual Baker and McCammon originally sought turned himself in. He was a wanted traffic violator, but obviously wanted nothing to do with being sought in the murder of a police officer. This juvenile offender was brought in by his mother and two brothers. In interviewing the four family members, detectives ascertained the name of a suspect who was known to wear a cap similar to the one Baker and McCammon removed from the pants pocket of the shooting suspect. The physical description and cap information led detectives to seek Charles Bass (White Male, 23).

An around-the-clock investigation continued. The investigators prepared a photo spread with the latest rap sheet photo of Charles Bass. Marshal McCammon, after viewing the spread, could not make a positive identification as the photo of Charles Bass was five years old. Later that same day, a more current photo of Bass was made available to McCammon. He then made a positive identification of Charles Bass as the suspect who shot and killed his partner and shot at him numerous times.

While charges of capital murder of a police officer were being filed on Bass, Detectives Kent and Motard stepped up the investigation. They learned that Bass had been at another location in this north side neighborhood earlier in the week, shooting a pistol in a back yard of an abandoned house. They recovered slugs and hulls from this location and sent them directly to the firearms lab to be compared with firearms evidence from the Silvercrest scene as well as from Marshal Baker's body. This examination revealed a positive match. The case against Bass mounted. He could not only be placed at the scene shooting at Baker and McCammon, but could also be placed with a pistol that produced evidence matching that at the scene of the shooting.

MRS. DOROTHY AND MR. CHARLES BAKER

Working closely with Detectives Kent and Motard on this investigation were Homicide Detectives John Burmester, Mike Lewellen, Johnny Bonds and E. T. "Gene" Yanchak. Throughout the night and days following this offense, Assistant District Attorney Terry Wilson from the Harris County District Attorney's Special Crimes Division was present to assist Lieutenant Mason and lead investigator Kent with any legal decisions.

As the investigation progressed, Homicide learned that Charles Bass had a grandmother living in Covington, Kentucky. Detectives relayed this information to the proper authorities in that jurisdiction. In the early morning hours of Monday, August 20, 1979, Kentucky authorities arrested Charles Bass for capital murder in the death of Marshal Baker. He was taken to a hospital for treatment of a single gunshot wound to his left thigh. Apparently one of McCammon's shots had found its mark.

Within twenty-four hours, Detective Carl Kent flew to Cincinnati and drove to Covington. A self-serving written confession was elicited from Bass, in which he claimed to have shot Marshal Baker because he was afraid of being beaten by the two officers. He also admitted to robbing Shirlee's Lounge at 10502 Bauman Road just prior to being stopped by the two officers. Bass fought extradition but lost that battle and was returned to Texas.

Charles Bass, an unemployed sheet metal apprentice, was not a stranger to the criminal justice system. He had an extensive juvenile record which revealed he not only threatened to kill his probation officer but also stabbed his own mother. He later bitterly complained that his own mother would not visit him in jail. As an adult, he had been investigated for robbery and burglary.

His capital murder trial was held in Judge Miron Love's 178th Criminal District Court. Presenting the state's case and speaking for the deceased Police Officer were Assistant District Attorneys Bert Graham and John Holleman. Jurors convicted Bass of capital murder in July 1980 and assessed him the death penalty, which had been restored in Texas and the first death by lethal injection was administered in December 1982. Bass got his turn, too. After the usual legal maneuvering and appeals, the sentence assessed Charles William Bass was properly and justly administered on March 12, 1986.

Marshal Ross McCammon was twenty-three and had three years of law enforcement experience when this offense occurred. He stayed with the City of Houston and became a Houston police officer when the enforcement divisions of City Marshal, Park Police and Airport Police were absorbed into the HPD. He was assigned to the Special Operations Division in 2001. He retired in 2003.

Detective Carl Kent retired from HPD to become a private investigator. For a time he served as chief investigator for the Montgomery County District Attorney's Office. Mike Lewellen also retired from HPD as did Johnny Bonds, now a senior investigator with the Harris County DA's Office. Lieutenant Guy Mason continued working in Homicide for many years, supervising a Murder Squad. He, along with Gene Yanchak and John Burmester, retired in 2005. Paul Motard also continued in Homicide and is still working Murders in 2006. "Speedie" Wilson made detective and was working Homicide when he suffered a severe stroke while on duty in the mid-1980s. He retired and served as a police service officer assigned to the Homicide Print Stall. His medical problems from his stroke continued to plague him and he passed away in 2004. Terry Wilson retired after a long career working with police officers and prosecuting criminals. Bert Graham became first assistant district attorney to District Attorney Chuck Rosenthal. John Holleman was in private practice in 2001.

Dorothy remarried and lived in the Lake Conroe area in 2006. Son David was an ordained minister at the Church of Christ in Emory, Texas. David's three children are grown. Dorothy was the proud great-grandmother of Ethan, Caleb and Michael. Charles Baker's father, James L. Baker, died in 1980, while his mother Fannie lived to be ninety-two and died in 1999. Both are buried next to their oldest son Charles. Brother Clyde resided near Tomball in 2001, while Nelda Griggs resided in a nursing home and the youngest sister, Donnie Serio, lived in The Woodlands area.

CHARLES BAKER ON HIS FAVORITE HORSE

Marshall Baker's gravesite is marked with the BAKER family name and also with his and Dorothy's names and historical information. It also includes a special footstone, which consists of a five-point star representing the Houston City Marshall badge of 1979. Under this star is inscribed, "Marshal, Houston, #122." Below this is inscribed the word "Pop," a nickname given to Charles Baker by his fellow officers due to the fact he was older and was a father figure to many younger officers. A 100 Club LINE OF DUTY marker was also placed to honor the life and death of this fallen hero.

Initially, the Houston Police Officer's Memorial on Memorial Drive did not intend to include the name of a city marshall. Nevertheless, today the name of Marshall Charles Baker is now properly included with the rest of Houston's finest who gave their lives while performing their duties.

75

Detective Victor Ray Wells III
Badge #D-693
October 2, 1980

Yellow Cab Driver Opens Fire, Kills Detective Victor Wells on Harrisburg

Victor Ray Wells III was born in Houston on December 18, 1946. He attended Houston Gardens Elementary School, Marshall Junior High, and graduated from Jeff Davis Senior High School in 1964. Immediately after graduation, he enlisted in the United States Air Force and served his country for the next four years. He joined the Houston Police Department in Police Cadet Class No. 39 on August 26, 1968, graduating on December 14, 1968. He was assigned to the evening shift of Radio Patrol, Northeast Substation, and later worked the day shift at Northeast. On July 30, 1977, he was promoted to detective and assigned to the Homicide Division. On January 28, 1980, he transferred to the Robbery Division.

On Thursday night, October 2, 1980, Detective Wells was working the Evening Shift out of the Robbery Division. At 9:58 p.m., while driving west in the 6800 block of Harrisburg, Wells stopped his unmarked vehicle in front of a Yellow Cab. It is believed that there had been some erratic driving on the part of the cab driver and Wells got out of his vehicle to walk back to the cab. He was in plainclothes with his weapon in a holster and his detective badge clearly visible on his belt.

According to witnesses, the detective approached the driver's door of the cab. The nearest witnesses were a Hispanic woman and her two teenage daughters, who were sitting in their vehicle facing Harrisburg on the Sears Store parking lot. While they could not hear the conversation, they did see Wells gesturing with his hands toward the cab driver as if he were asking questions or possibly asking for an explanation. They then heard a shot and saw Wells fall to the street. As the cab hurriedly left the scene, one of the daughters was sent inside the nearby Early Roberts Café to call for assistance while the Hispanic woman and the other daughter very alertly followed the cab.

DETECTIVE VICTOR RAY WELLS III

At Wayside and the Gulf Freeway, they were finally able to obtain the license number, writing it down in the palm of the daughter's hand. Upon returning to the scene, this brave lady got on the police radio and called in an "Officer Down." First units on the scene were Park Place Patrol Officers L. N. Miller and P. D. Sybert, who were just seven blocks away. A Houston Fire Department ambulance took Detective Wells to Ben Taub Hospital. Doctors immediately cracked his chest to determine the extent of the internal injuries. They learned that he received a gunshot wound to the heart and made every effort to repair the massive damage. Unfortunately, Victor Ray Wells III, age thirty-three, died at 10:52 p.m.

Homicide Lieutenant Larry L. Earls initiated an immediate investigation involving Detective Johnny R. Thornton at the scene along with CSU Officer S. P. "Speedy" Wilson. Detectives Jim Ladd, George Dollins, Carl Kent, J. L. Waltmon, David Calhoun, Ted Thomas and Steve Arrington assisted in the initial investigation. Earls also called on Detectives Larry Webber, Vernon West and Doug Bostock from the Homicide Officer Involved Shooting Team.

Meanwhile, in the 2700 block of Main, Patrol Officers P. A. Mueller and D. R. Daniel alertly spotted the suspect vehicle. They stopped it and found Willie James Washington (African-American Male, 35) to be the driver. The officers recovered the weapon used to shoot and kill Detective Wells from the Yellow Cab. Detective Ladd obtained an oral statement from the suspect in which he indicated that this incident occurred over a traffic altercation and that he shot Detective Wells when Wells "approached him in a threatening manner." Washington said he did not know that Wells was a police officer. Washington was viewed in lineups within hours of the offense. Witnesses positively identified him. Charges of capital murder were filed on Washington in the 228th District Court.

The investigation did not end with the charges being filed. Homicide Lieutenant C. J. "Chuck" Lofland headed the Homicide Division Officer Involved Shooting Team. He, along with Homicide Captain Bobby Adams and prosecutors from the District Attorney's Office were concerned about the strength of their case in court. A likely defense would be that the defendant did not know that Detective Wells was a police officer. The defendant might contend that he felt threatened by this man in plainclothes. A scene reenactment was arranged so that a jury would be able to see how the detective was dressed, with his badge and gun clearly showing but the weapon not drawn. Homicide Detective Vernon West was assigned this responsibility.

Investigators believed that this deadly incident began when Detective Wells and his assailant were both in the same westbound lane of Harrisburg at 69th Street. Even though Willie Washington could see their light was still red, the eastbound traffic control light had changed to green and traffic was moving in that direction while the westbound light had not yet changed. Washington, with a fare to run, apparently became impatient and began honking his horn at Detective Wells, which prompted Wells to stop in front of the cab and investigate.

Wells was survived by his wife Linda Ann Wells and two children from a previous marriage, twelve-year-old Jennifer Wells and nine-year-old Kevin Wells. He also was survived by his parents, Mr. and Mrs. V. R. Wells Sr. and two brothers, William Donnie Wells and Samuel David Wells; his grandmother, Mrs. Viola Pangburn; two stepdaughters, Michelle and Christine Root, as well as the mother of Jennifer and Kevin, Susanna Wells.

Funeral Services were held at the Brookside Funeral Chapel at 3 p.m. Saturday, October 4, 1980, with burial following at the Brookside Cemetery. Police Chaplain H. L. Hannah officiated at the service. Pallbearers were Captain L. N. Zoch, Lieutenants W. J. Wehr and Roger Demny, Sergeant Freddie Black and Detectives Eugene Yanchak and Jimmy Birch.

On October 20, 1980, the case was presented to a Harris County Grand Jury, which returned an indictment for the reduced charge of voluntary manslaughter. On December 1, 1980, a trial was held and Willie Washington was found guilty of voluntary manslaughter and assessed a penalty of seven years in the Texas Department of Corrections. The conviction was overturned in 1984. Washington was out on an appeal bond most of this time. Another trial was held and on January 18, 1985, Willie Washington was acquitted and went free.

In January 2002, Linda Wells lived near Livingston. Kevin lived in Houston, the father of two daughters, Shaylen and Brittany. Jennifer resided in Livingston, the mother of four children. She had two sons, E. J. and Zachary, and two daughters, Katy and Erica. Mr. V. R. Wells Sr. passed away in 1984, as did Mrs. Wells in 1998. Grandmother Pangburn also is deceased. Brother Samuel lived near Coldspring and brother Donnie in Houston. Stepdaughters Michelle and Christine lived in Alabama and McKinney, respectively, each with two children. Kevin and Jennifer's mother Susanna lived in Galveston.

Detective Johnny R. Thornton retired from HPD to become an investigator with the Harris County DA's Office. Lieutenant Larry Earls, after a number of years in the IAD, Auto Theft and Juvenile Divisions, retired in 2004. Detectives Kent, Waltmon, Dollins, Webber, Bostock, J.W. Ladd, Thomas, Calhoun, and West all retired from Homicide. Vernon West died in 2001. Detective C. S. Arrington became a Homicide lieutenant.

D. R. Daniel was assigned to Westside Patrol in 2002. Officer P. A. Mueller resigned from the Department. The first officers on the scene, Miller and Sybert, who worked HPD Southeast Patrol and Clear Lake Patrol for many years, are also retired.

Marker for Detective Wells reads:

WELLS, VICTOR RAY III
DEC 18, 1946-OCT 2, 1980

76

Officer Jose Adolfo Zamarron Jr.
Badge #3025
April 18, 1981

Drunken Driver Strikes, Kills Officer Joe Zamarron as He Helped Investigate a Minor Accident on Market

Jose Adolfo Zamarron Jr., also known as Joseph Adolph Zamarron, was born in Houston on February 9, 1953, the son of Houston Police Officer Ignacio "Nash" Zamarron Sr. and his wife, Mrs. Guadalupe Zamarron. Jose, or "Joe," received his elementary education at the Resurrection Catholic School, attended Furr Junior High School and St. Thomas High School for a short time. He graduated from Stephen F. Austin High School in 1971 and later attended Southwest Texas State College in San Marcos.

Joe served his country in the United States Army for three years (1973-1976) during the Vietnam War. A year of that service was spent in Korea. After returning from the military, he was accepted into the Houston Police Cadet Class No. 74. Members of this class began their training on March 29, 1976 and took their oath of office on July 16, 1976. His first assignment was to the night shift of Radio Patrol, Northeast Division. He wore HPD Badge No. 3025.

While in the Police Academy, Joe, from all accounts, was a very likeable man. He met Russell Chapman, another cadet, during his training there. They became well acquainted and after graduating from Class No. 74, found themselves on the same night shift roll call in Radio Patrol at Northeast Substation. They didn't immediately become close friends, but three years later they wound up in the same patrol car together. According to Chapman, the first night they rode together, he wanted the two to become regular partners. Eventually they did.

On the Friday night of April 17, 1981, Joe and Russell were assigned to ride Unit 10C66. While on patrol they observed off-duty Officers J. M. Aldaco and

C. Roark standing outside the Illusion Club at 12774 Market, working an extra job in uniform. This was at approximately 11:35 p.m. and Joe and Russell stopped by to see if they needed any assistance on anything and especially to advise them that they were in the area. While doing so, they on-viewed an accident involving two vehicles traveling westbound on Market.

OFFICER JOSE ADOLFO ZAMARRON JR.

Officers Zamarron and Chapman immediately responded to this location to lend assistance. They were followed by Aldaco and Roark to assist in this investigation of a minor accident. Doing his duty, Officer Zamarron proceeded to the front of one of the vehicles along with both of the drivers involved in the mishap. He was standing on the dirt median in the center of the eastbound and westbound lanes of Market. Officers Chapman, Aldaco and Roark were assessing the vehicular damage when Chapman observed an eastbound vehicle traveling at a seemingly high rate of speed. Chapman shouted at his partner about the instant the speeding vehicle struck Joe Zamarron, throwing the young officer over one vehicle, onto their patrol car and into the street. Joe was rushed immediately to nearby North Shore Hospital where he was dead on arrival. Joe Zamarron died on Good Friday at age twenty-eight.

Police arrested the driver at the scene after her vehicle struck several other vehicles. She was determined to be intoxicated. Jerrie Ann Williams was charged with involuntary manslaughter after tests indicated her blood alcohol level to be .017.

Officer Zamarron was survived by his wife, Elizabeth Ann, and two sons, seven-year-old Joseph Adolph Zamarron Jr. and four-year-old Jason Anthony Zamarron. Other survivors were his parents, retired HPD Officer Ignacio "Nash" Zamarron and Mrs. Guadalupe G. Zamarron, and two sisters, Mrs. Katherine Ann Drescher and Miss Patricia Ruth Zamarron. Also mourning his death were his cousin, HPD Officer Larry Buzo (who later became a sergeant) as well as an uncle, Officer Tony Magdelano.

A Rosary was recited at 7:30 p.m. on Sunday, April 19, 1981, with a eulogy service held at 10 a.m. on Monday, April 20, 1981, at the Crespo Funeral Home, 2516 Navigation. The deceased was then taken to the Resurrection Catholic Church, 915 Zoe at Market Street, where a funeral Mass was conducted with Father Robert Carlson as celebrant. Graveside services were conducted at the Forest Park Cemetery, 6900 Lawndale, under the auspices of the Houston Police Department Military Detail.

The story of the suspect, Jerrie Ann Williams, did not end with her arrest. She also was charged with possession of a controlled substance and carrying a weapon after several guns and some pills were found in her vehicle at the time of her arrest. She was apparently able to make the appropriate bond. However, on February 23, 1982, the bond in each of the cases was forfeited when she failed to appear in court on the involuntary manslaughter charge. Williams remained a fugitive from justice until March 30, 1982, when she was apprehended hiding in a closet by HPD officers in her husband's trailer in the 200 block of Broadway. One of the arresting officers, Bobby D. Lott, had responded to a neighbor's call to an open door in this trailer. She was eventually brought to some semblance of justice in October 1982.

A jury convicted her after a trial in the manslaughter case. While she could have received ten years in prison and a $5,000 fine, Williams received a sentence of only three years in prison for striking and killing a Houston police officer while intoxicated. She was released from the Texas Department of Criminal Justice on mandatory supervision in 1985. Her whereabouts and status in 2007 are unknown. Her original driver's license number now belongs to another individual.

Officer Zamarron's father, a retired HPD officer who also had worked for the Harris County Sheriff's Department, was a close friend of retired (and now deceased) HPD Sergeant Raul Martinez, who later served as the elected constable for Precinct 6. Another retired HPD officer, Victor Trevino, succeeded Constable Martinez. A new elementary school was built in the Denver Harbor area where Officer Joe Zamarron spent his childhood. This school, located at 7211 Market, was named Raul Martinez Elementary School. In 1992, the library at this school was named after Joe Zamarron. Also, for several years, a softball tournament was held in Officer Joe Zamarron's name.

Officer Russell Chapman continued his career at Northeast after the death of his close friend and partner. The same year of this tragedy, 1981, Russell promoted from the same sergeants promotion list that contained the name of Joe Zamarron. Russell worked nights and evenings as a sergeant at Northeast until 1993, when he transferred to Mounted Patrol. Of the other two police officer witnesses, Officer Joe Aldaco was assigned to the Traffic/Accident Division and Officer Curtis Roark to the Northeast Patrol Division in 2003.

This accident was investigated by Officers Billy Chance and Mark S. Zimmerman. Chance later resigned from HPD. Officer Zimmerman was killed while en route to work one night on Memorial Drive, having been struck head-on by a DWI. Officer Bobby Lott, who was involved in the second arrest of the Zamarron case suspect, was a K-9 officer in the Narcotics Division in 2003. Another officer from this same cadet class, James Donald Harris, was shot and killed in the line of duty in 1982.

Sergeant Russell Chapman was interviewed in 2003 about the tragedy that took the life of his partner and friend. Chapman said: "Joe Zamarron and I were classmates while attending the Houston Police Academy in 1976. When we graduated, we were both assigned to the night shift at Northeast Patrol. It was only after three years in patrol that we started riding together. Joe was the best regular partner I had during the five years of working the night shift at Northeast. I knew on the first night that we rode together that I wanted him as a regular partner. We spent a lot of time together, not only at work but also in our off-duty hours. Our families became well known to each other because of our camping trips and weekend barbecues. 'Big Joe,' as he was called because of his size, was one of the most compassionate police officers that I have known in my twenty-seven-year career. He did more for unfortunate kids than anyone ever thought of during that particular time. Joe did not care what other people (police officers) thought of him for his acts of kindness as long as he thought he was doing the right thing for other human beings."

"When it came to work, we could almost read each other's minds in handling the situations that we were put in on the streets of Northeast Houston. On several occasions he would place himself in danger just to protect me and in return I always felt that protecting him was the number one priority on any workday. I wish that I could have protected him on the night he was killed. I owe my sergeant's stripes to him because he dared me to study and take the promotional exam along with him. I've tried to use him as an example for compassion as a supervisor, but I know I sometimes come up short. Police officers do not have a problem expressing themselves. It has been twenty-two years since he was killed and there is hardly a day that goes by that I am not reminded in some small way of the things that we did together as partners or as best friends. I do not have a brother, but to me he was the closest thing that I will ever have to one.

In some ways I feel that I have had an angel watching over me for the last twenty-two years." Sergeant Russell Chapman retired from HPD in 2005 after a number of years with the Mounted Patrol unit.

In 2003, Elizabeth Zamarron had remarried and lived in the Houston area. Son Joseph was an ironworker and married. Son Jason was also an ironworker and married. Elizabeth had another son by her second marriage.

Mrs. Guadalupe Zamarron, the officer's mother, died in 1983. His father, Ignacio Zamarron, died in 1988. Both are buried next to their only son at Forest Park-Lawndale. Sister Katherine was married and lived in Houston in 2003. She tragically lost one son in a motorcycle accident. Her other son, Joseph, a namesake for Joe Zamarron, was a Houston Metro officer. Sister Patricia was married and lived in Tomball with one child.

The original marker placed by the Zamarron family has been replaced by a 100 Club marker. The original marker read:

BELOVED HUSBAND & FATHER
JOSEPH ADOLPH ZAMARRON
FEB 9, 1953 - APR 18, 1981

77

Officer Winston James Rawlins
Badge #1787
March 29, 1982

Brief Career of Solo Officer Winston Rawlins Ends in Fiery Traffic Stop on South Loop 610

Winston James Rawlins was born August 1, 1958. After he attended elementary school in Shepherd, Texas, his family moved to Houston where he graduated from Saint Thomas High School in 1976. Winston attended the University of Saint Thomas for two years and followed that with one year at Sam Houston State University in Huntsville. In 1980, he joined the Houston Police Department, graduating from HPD Cadet Class No. 89. He completed his probationary period in November 1980 in Radio Patrol and went shortly thereafter to the solo motorcycle detail of the Accident Division. He wore HPD Badge No. 1787.

On Monday morning, March 29, 1982, Solo Motorcycle Officer Winston Rawlins was working the day shift on freeway patrol. At about 7:15 a.m. he stopped a Toyota vehicle for a traffic violation in the westbound 9000 block of the South Loop East. He stood beside the driver's door in the right-hand emergency lane, interviewing the driver. His motorcycle was parked in front of the alleged violator's vehicle.

There was an unusual amount of heavy morning rush-hour traffic, especially since another accident further down the freeway had caused traffic to slow to a crawl. A Kenworth gasoline transport truck slowed down as a result of this traffic buildup, stopping alongside Officer Rawlins, immediately to his left. A Mack eighteen-wheeler loaded with iron ore then struck the right rear of the gasoline truck, glancing off the Kenworth truck and striking the Toyota and Officer Rawlins, pinning him under the right front of the large truck.

Another gravel truck was able to stop behind the gasoline truck without a crash. However, the damage had been done and a number of explosions ensued. The fire destroyed all five vehicles and burned Officer Rawlins beyond recognition. Amazingly, the young officer was the only fatality. He was only twenty-three years old.

Rawlins' parents, Phillip and Edna Rawlins, survived him, as did his two brothers, Roy Julian Rawlins, and Phillip Rawlins, Jr. Also, his two young daughters, Tanuneka Allen and Nicole Allen, were left without a father. Winston James Rawlins also was a cousin of HPD Officer Lynn Williams, assigned to the Dispatcher's Division at that time, and a nephew of Harris County Sheriff's Detective T. R. Coney, who later became the U. S. Marshal in Houston.

A wake service was held for Officer Rawlins from 8 until 10 p.m. on Wednesday, March 31, at the Carl Barnes Funeral Home at 746 W. 22nd Street. Funeral services were conducted at 1 p.m. Thursday, April 1, at the Mt. Sinai Baptist Church at 902 W. 8th Street. Burial followed at the Paradise North Cemetery at 10401 W. Montgomery Road. Pallbearers were fellow Solo Officers B. E. Goodson, A. E. Coleman, J. E. Baker, J. J. Berry, T. W. Gage and R. E. Abel.

An investigation showed that the gasoline transport truck was loaded with 8,500 gallons of fuel. The heat from the blaze was so intense that the I-beams of the nearby freeway overpass melted and bent as much as six feet down. Accident investigators T. D. "Tiny" Owens, N. P. Blesener and S. E. Carr determined that it was nothing short of a miracle that no one else was seriously injured or killed.

Kenneth Wayne Morrow drove the truck that originally struck the gasoline truck, which caused Officer Rawlins to be thrown and pinned under the truck. He was charged with involuntary manslaughter and later indicted. However, the charges were dropped several years later after his company provided legal counsel. In 2002, Morrow said he is still haunted by the events of that day. At the time of this accident, he had been disabled and retired from the U. S. Military. He was living in a rural area of Central Texas.

OFFICER WINSTON JAMES RAWLINS

Officer Rawlins' parents owned and operated a service station on Interstate 10 and Waco Street, east of downtown Houston. For a number of years several solo motorcycle officers made this a regular rest stop while working morning or evening rush hour traffic assignments. Several of these officers were J. E. "Jamie" Baker and T. W. "Tommy"

Gage. Young Winston worked in the family-owned business and met these officers and many others. According to Officer Baker, Winston always wanted to know what it was like to be a policeman. These officers told him to get his education and then apply to the Houston Police Department if he still had the desire to join HPD. He was thirty hours short of a college degree when he did just that.

Police Dispatcher Lynn Williams was working one of the traffic channels the morning of this tragedy. She heard him call out on the traffic stop. Moments later, dispatchers got a call about a policeman caught in a burning accident near that same location. Williams was quoted as saying, "We knew exactly who it was," as she joined Rawlins' family in mourning this great loss. Williams, who graduated from the Police Academy shortly after her cousin, said, "Becoming a policeman was his boyhood dream. He majored in criminology."

Phillip Rawlins Sr., the officer's father, died in 1985 and was laid to rest in the family plot near his son. Edna Rawlins, his mother, retired and lived in Northwest Houston in 2002. Brother Roy Julian Rawlins lived in Houston. Brother Phillip Rawlins Jr. lived in Houston and had two sons, Phillip Riian Rawlins and Bryant Deray Rawlins. Marshal T. R. Coney died in the late 1990's. Officer Lynn Williams later resigned from HPD.

Officer Rawlins' gravesite at the Paradise North Cemetery is marked with the words "KILLED IN ACTION," a rare recognition for an initial grave marker for a Houston officer killed in the line of duty.

It read:

WINSTON J. RAWLINS
AUG 1, 1958
KILLED IN ACTION
MAR 29, 1982
BADGE EMBLEM #1787

As for investigators of this accident, Officer T. D. Owens later resigned from HPD. Officer N. P. Blesener was promoted to sergeant in 1984 and, after working Patrol at Central and South Central, was assigned to the Personnel Division in 2002. Officer S. E. Carr died suddenly of a heart attack in 1992 at the age of forty-five. All of the pallbearer friends of Officer Rawlins were retired in 2002 with the exception of J. J. Berry, still assigned as a solo unit and serving as first vice president of the Houston Police Officers Union in 2007. R.E. Abel and J.E. Baker are deceased and T.W. Gage is Sheriff of Montgomery County in Conroe.

As tragic as this day began, it would only end even worse. This same day, some thirteen hours later, at 8:30 p.m., another solo, Officer W. E. Deleon, was struck by an intoxicated driver and killed on the Southwest Freeway.

78

Officer William E. DeLeon
Badge #2280
March 29, 1982

Second HPD Solo in a Day Struck and Killed- This Time By Drunken Driver on the Southwest Freeway

William Edwin DeLeon was born on October 3, 1946 in Nacogdoches. His family moved to Houston and he attended schools in the Aldine area and graduated from Aldine High School. He then attended South Texas Junior College. He joined the Houston Police Department by entering Police Cadet Class No. 39 on August 26, 1968. This class graduated on December 14 of that year. He wore Badge No. 2280 and worked the Traffic Enforcement Division for several years before he transferred to the Solo Motorcycle Detail. Friends in HPD called him "Ponce" DeLeon after the famous explorer in history.

On the evening of Monday, March 29, 1982, the entire Houston Police Department – especially the Solo detail – was grieving over the tragic and fiery death of Solo Officer Winston J. Rawlins earlier that day. At 8:30 p.m. that same day Officer William E. "Ponce" DeLeon was working the evening shift and was set up in the emergency lane of the 1300 block of the Southwest Freeway (inbound) working radar on incoming traffic. His partner, Officer J. W. Dunbar, was inbound on the Southwest Freeway from a previous traffic stop when a blue Cadillac passed him at a high rate of speed. Dunbar clocked this vehicle at more than eighty-seven miles per hour. Dunbar then radioed ahead to DeLeon the "clock" on the Cadillac.

"I was attempting to catch up to the vehicle," Dunbar said, "but had not yet activated my emergency equipment. I observed the Cadillac drift back and forth between several lanes of traffic. Then, it passed another vehicle and drifted all the way over to the right of the freeway".

187

"There, Ponce was waiting. Like a magnet, the Cadillac headed directly toward Ponce and his motor. It looked like a bomb went off and there were motorcycle parts flying in all directions, but I did not see my partner. I saw the Cadillac was heavily damaged and at that time, I got the vehicle stopped. I immediately put out an "Assist the Officer." After I got the Cadillac driver out of his car, a patrol unit came up and took custody of him. I was then approached by a citizen who told me that there was an officer lying in the freeway."

OFFICER WILLIAM EDWIN DELEON

"We got on the radio and asked that the freeway be shut down. Myself and some other units went right back to check, going the wrong way on the freeway and found that what the citizen saw was part of the motorcycle's motor. Then I saw Ponce's weapon and helmet. We still could not find Ponce until Officer Charlie Contreras looked out over the guardrail and saw him."

Two civilian witnesses, along with Officer Dunbar, had followed this Cadillac and got it stopped three tenths of a mile from where Officer DeLeon had been struck. The driver was arrested immediately without incident. These two witnesses later stated that they saw the suspect vehicle strike Officer DeLeon and began to follow him carefully, never losing sight of him or his vehicle until Officer Dunbar took him into custody. The initial findings of the investigation revealed that Officer DeLeon had been struck and thrown 202 feet from the point of impact. The motorcycle was found 285 feet from the point of impact.

HFD ambulance personnel treated Officer DeLeon at the scene until LifeFlight Helicopter medics arrived. LifeFlight took him to Hermann Hospital, where he was pronounced dead at 9:45 p.m. He was thirty-five years old.

Officer William DeLeon was survived by his wife Patricia, his parents, Mr. and Mrs. William DeLeon Sr., eleven-year-old daughter Autumn DeLeon and eight-year-old son Michael. A sister, Kathy DeLeon, and brother, Hal Glenn DeLeon, also survived him, as did Autumn and Michael's mother, Mrs. Helen DeLeon, stepdaughter Shelley Newcomer, age fourteen, and stepson Shannon Newcomer, age ten, and brother-in-law, Houston Police Officer Manny Ortega.

Funeral services were held at 1 p.m. Friday, April 2, 1982, at the Oak Forest Baptist Church, 1700 West 43rd. Burial followed in the Field of Honor at Forest Park Lawndale Cemetery, 6900 Lawndale. Pallbearers were fellow Solo motorcycle Officers J. W. Dunbar, J. L. Woodcock, J. A. Krpec, J. M. Bell, R. M. Zumwalt and R. V. Garcia.

Officers responding to the original call of an Assist the Officer were Patrol Officers J. E. Scanlon and R. A. Dove, followed shortly thereafter by Accident Officer J. Montemayor. These initial investigators determined that this line-of-duty death should be turned over to the Hit and Run Detail of the Accident Division. Hit and Run Officers D. G. Clifton, P. Araiza, T. M. Rice and W. E. Lunsford were in the immediate response group. The investigation revealed that Officer DeLeon had received massive head, chest and abdominal injuries from being hit by the speeding Cadillac. The driver, Rogelio "Roger" Gomez Garcia (White male; 33), was arrested at the scene. He was extremely intoxicated.

Officers interviewed the husband and wife eyewitnesses, Mr. and Mrs. Edwin Lee Ubernosky, at length. They said they were driving behind the suspect and saw the Cadillac strike the officer and his motorcycle. They never lost sight of the Cadillac, followed it when it stopped and could definitely say that the arrested suspect was the driver. They were present with Officer Dunbar when he arrested the suspect. Other witnesses came forward with statements indicating that the Cadillac had passed them on the freeway at speeds estimated at one-hundred miles per hour.

The investigation continued when Sergeant C. J. Mangano and Officer A. G. Kinsel took the suspect to Central Police Station where he refused to take a breath test. He did sign a consent to search his vehicle. He said he refused the test due to his previous legal problems with DWI charges. He said that he had been drinking alcohol most of the day at the Four Palms on Telephone Road, as well as at another location in southwest Houston. The investigation determined that his head struck the inside rear view mirror and windshield of his vehicle upon impact. He was taken to Ben Taub for examination but didn't sustain any injuries.

As is the normal procedure in an investigation of an officer fatality, many officers assisted in various ways. Those who directed the investigation were Lieutenant W. G. Eickenhorst and Sergeants R. R. Schweiker and K. E. Crawford. Also assisting were Officers J. L. Scott, W. B. Johnson, C. Ramirez, P. J. Cooper, C. E. Elliott, W. G. Blair, E. C. Tyler, G. W. Anderson, S. E. Carr, J. C. Wolf, G. D. Brown, A. L. Gilbert, K. J. Howaniec, R. L. Horton, L. W. Bolton, D. L. Schultz, and F. E. Braune. HPD Support personnel instrumental in the professional examination of physical evidence were Chemist R. H. Warkentin and Latent Print Examiner Jerry Werner.

After all of the evidence was presented to the District Attorney's Office, Assistant DA Pechacek accepted charges of involuntary manslaughter and failure to stop and render aid in the 248th Criminal District Court. On October 28, 1982, a jury convicted Rogelio Garcia and sentenced him to nine years in the Texas Department of Corrections. He also was fined $5,000. Unfortunately, as seems to be the usual in these types of cases, only a short term of these nine years was actually served.

In 2003, Patricia DeLeon had remarried and lived near Lake Livingston. Daughter Autumn Marley is married and lives in the Bear Creek area. She and Jeff Marley are the parents of a son Jordan Marley and a daughter Jamie Marley. Officer DeLeon's son, Michael Edwin DeLeon, lives near Tomball. He and his wife Dianne have two daughters, Brooke Deleon and Fayth DeLeon, and one son, a namesake of his grandfather. He was named William Michael J. DeLeon. His family calls him "Will."

Autumn and Michael's mother, Helen, divorced from Officer DeLeon at the time of his death, went on with her life and raised Autumn and Michael to be productive citizens. She earned a college degree in divinity and social work. In 2003, she had become an associate minister at a Clear Lake area Presbyterian Church.

Officer DeLeon's father, retired Harris County Deputy Sheriff William Emmett DeLeon, Jr., died in June 2002. The officer's mother resided in the Houston area in 2003. Brother Hal Glenn DeLeon lived near Tomball, the father of two sons, Bobby and Matt. Sister Kathy lived with her mother. The DeLeon family also had another sibling, a sister, Janice, who died of a heart attack at age eighteen.

Helen said she and Edwin graduated from Aldine High School together but actually met at an area church they both attended. She said she supported his decision to become a police officer because he felt like that was what he was meant to be. She overcame a number of obstacles but remained close to the extended DeLeon family.

Lieutenant Eickenhorst retired in 1994 after many years as the Solo Motorcycle Detail lieutenant. He lived in Houston in 2003. Sergeants Mangano and Schweiker worked in the Accident Division that year and Sergeant Kirby Crawford died in 1983. Also in 2003, Officer Montemayor was a Hit and Run sergeant and Officer Araiza worked in the Hit and Run Unit. Officer Scanlon worked South Central Patrol. Officer Rice worked in the Inspector General's Office. Officer Dove retired in 1993 and Officers Clifton and Lunsford resigned from the Department.

As for the close friends and pallbearers of Officer DeLeon, Officer James Dunbar, a regular partner of Officer "Ponce" Deleon for five years, retired as a sergeant in 1997 and went into the private security business. Officer J. L. Woodcock worked at Westside Patrol in 2003. Officer John A. "Tony" Krpec retired in 1989. Officer J. M. Bell was no longer with HPD. Officer Randy Zumwalt was a sergeant in the Burglary and Theft Division at Westside. Officer Raymond Garcia retired in 2002.

Jim Dunbar said, "Ponce was not only my partner, but he was one of my two closest friends. He was a devoted husband and father who loved his family dearly. Before retirement, I had been a police officer for twenty-seven years and have never met anyone with more dedication and loyalty to his job than Ponce. We rode together almost five years on duty, worked most of our extra jobs together and we spent a lot of off time together with our families. Ponce was the type person that if you needed him, no matter what he was doing or where he was, he would come to help you."

"Just a few months before he was killed, my vehicle broke down on a freeway service road. I called Ponce and he immediately came to help. Before we could get my vehicle started, we were robbed at gunpoint by two males in the parking lot. Needless to say, shots were fired. One suspect was wounded and the other was DOA. As Ponce and I were en route to the Homicide Division, we spoke about how lucky we were not to have been shot. Ponce told me that if we could make it through that shooting, we could make it through anything. A few months later he was gone."

Officer DeLeon was the third member of Police Cadet Class No. 39 to meet his death in the line of duty. Officer Robert Wayne Lee was shot and killed in January 1971 as was Detective Victor Ray Wells in October 1980.

Officer DeLeon's grave was marked by the following information.

W.E. DELEON
1946 - 1982 (BADGE #2280)

This marker has been replaced with the 100 Club LINE OF DUTY marker.

79

Detective Daryl Wayne Shirley
Badge #D-638
April 28, 1982

Fugitive Shoots and Kills Detective Shirley To Avoid Arrest; Later Gets Death Penalty

Daryl Wayne Shirley was born September 1, 1947. He graduated from Sam Rayburn High School in Pasadena in 1966, and after attending San Jacinto Junior College, he joined the Houston Police Department, graduating from Police Cadet Class No. 34 in April 1967. His first assignment was to Radio Patrol – Park Place Substation, where he worked the night shift and the day shift for more than seven years until his promotion to detective in September 1974. His new assignment was in the Burglary and Theft Division, where he continued working until his tragic death.

Detective D. W. "Wayne" Shirley, a fifteen-year veteran of the Department, was assigned to the Fugitive Squad, which worked out of the Burglary and Theft Division. On Wednesday, April 28, 1982, Detective Shirley received information from the Robbery Division that Arthur Lee Williams (African-American male, age unknown) was wanted as a fugitive from the State of Minnesota. Also, that a warrant had been issued on a revocation of parole from Minnesota on a previous robbery conviction.

Shirley learned that Williams was possibly living at the Parkstone Apartments at 2801 Rolido in far west Houston. He went to the location to verify the information. According to fellow officers in the newly formed Fugitive Squad, the procedure was to verify the location of a suspect. The plan would then be for uniformed officers to attempt to make the arrest the next morning before daylight.

As the detective walked through the courtyard of the apartment project, Williams likely "made" Shirley as a police officer. Later, fellow officers who worked with him in the Fugitive Squad said they felt he would not have attempted to arrest such a fugitive by himself had he not felt he had been identified as an officer. They also felt that Shirley having been recognized and not attempting the arrest would have given the suspect an opportunity to flee. In the Fugitive Squad, officers felt that this situation would have then posed a greater hazard in the future for other officers who might attempt to apprehend the suspect.

DETECTIVE DARYL WAYNE SHIRLEY

The time was about 2:10 p.m. when Detective Shirley saw Arthur Lee Williams while walking through the apartment courtyard. The suspect's female companion at the time later told investigators that Williams whispered to her that he thought that the white male in street clothes "looked like the law." Simultaneously, Shirley stopped and said, "Williams, don't give me any trouble."

Shirley identified himself as a police officer and asked Williams for some identification, prompting him to throw some type of ID on the ground in front of him. When the detective bent over to pick it up, Williams jumped him as the female fled. Other witnesses also heard Detective Shirley identify himself as a police officer and saw the suspect on the ground with the officer on top of him. They both struggled over a metal object, which turned out to be a small two-shot derringer Williams carried.

"Call the police," Shirley shouted. "He's trying to shoot me." The struggle knocked Shirley's pistol from its holster. Probably, when the detective realized his pistol was no longer in his possession and knowing that Williams had the derringer, he attempted to bolt to safety. As he did, Williams fired both shots from the derringer, striking Wayne Shirley in the left hip and left side of his chest. The detective ran toward his police car, falling dead in the parking lot. Williams fled the scene. Detective Daryl Wayne Shirley was dead at the scene at the age of thirty-four.

Detective Shirley was the divorced father of two sons, Steven Shirley, fourteen, and Jason Shirley, ten. He was remarried at the time of his death and he and his wife Donna Shirley were the proud parents of an eleven-month-old daughter, Sara Shirley. His parents, Mr. and Mrs. Willard Shirley, and a brother, Jerry Shirley, also survived him as did Steven and Jason's mother, Margaret Shirley.

Saturday, May 1, 1982 with the Reverend John Morgan officiating. Services were handled by the Forest Park Funeral Home and burial followed at the Forest Park Cemetery, 6900 Lawndale. Pallbearers were Officers Art Petitt and Tommy Baber and John Walling, Mike Burns, Ken Bagh, and Bob Hinkson.

OFFICERS JASON SHIRLEY AND STEVE SHIRLEY

An extensive investigation was launched immediately. Homicide Captain Bobby Adams assigned Homicide Lieutenant Guy Mason to coordinate the scene investigation and Lieutenant Chuck Lofland to assist Mason from the Homicide Office by assigning additional personnel as needed. Lieutenants Wayne Kersten and Phyliss Gonzalez also remained on duty to assist as needed.

Detective J.W. Clampitte was nearby and arrived at this location to begin protecting the scene along with uniformed Officers. Officers T.D. McCabe and D.E. Rieks were the first responding Officers along with HFD paramedics. They found a dead police officer, something they likely will never forget.

Homicide shooting team members Vernon West, Bruce Frank, and Doug Bostock were assigned to make the scene. Lieutenant Mason, after arriving and assessing the situation, requested more investigators. This began a night-long investigation as Homicide Detectives P.C. Motard, W.W. Owen, L.E. Webber, L.B. Smith, T.M. Thomas, and C.S. Arrington were all assigned various segments of the investigation.

While the Fugitive Detail was aware of the subject of Detective Shirley's investigation, the folder

WAYNE SHIRLEY, SAM RAYBURN HIGH SCHOOL TRACK TEAM, 1966

He was a fifteen-year veteran of the Houston Police Department and a member of the Sagemont Baptist Church as well as of the Houston Police Officer's Association and the Houston Police Patrolman's Union.

Funeral services were held at the Sagemont Baptist Church, 11323 Hughes Road, at 10:00am on that Detective Shirley took with him that day was located in his unmarked vehicle. Information was gleaned that led investigators to an apartment in this project that Arthur Lee Williams was believed to have either relatives and/or friends. The usual professional investigation was conducted and before nightfall, it was learned that Williams had returned to an apartment in this project after the shooting. He was visibly bruised from the fierce struggle with the Detective. He had cleaned up, changed clothes, shaved his goatee, and left with the freshly loaded two-shot loaded derringer that he had used to shoot Detective Shirley.

SARA SHIRLEY

During the night before the murder of Detective Shirley, there had been two Officer involved shooting incidents in southwest Houston. In one, several suspects were killed after attempting to run down Officers with a vehicle. In another, two uniformed Officers received minor gunshot wounds in an attempt to arrest some robbery suspects. 1982 was truly a rough time in Houston, with a large number of illegal immigrants flooding into town from the south and with the economy booming, there was also a large number of citizens from the northern states arriving in Houston to obtain jobs.

With one of their own being shot down, the Burglary and Theft Division, under the command of Captain Jack Fulbright, was anxious and ready to assist in any manner deemed necessary by the Homicide Captain. The investigation continued throughout the night with an urgent need to arrest Arthur Lee Williams before he was able to harm any other officer or citizen.

Early Thursday morning, information was developed that Williams might be holed up in an apartment on Braeburn Glen. Captain Fulbright and B & T Lieutenant H.R. Trimble led a posse of investigators to this location, where surveillance was set up. This group included Detectives Steve Felchak, Wayne Jones, Charles Marcum, June Cain-Crocker, Doug Autrey, and Gerald Crutcher. Williams was arrested without incident and turned over to Homicide investigators.

Eventually, the derringer and Detective Shirley's weapon were recovered. While Williams would not provide a statement, witnesses were located that identified him as involved in the struggle with Detective Shirley. It was also learned that Williams told several witnesses that he knew Shirley was a police officer and that he had an extreme dislike for law enforcement officers.

This was a well-coordinated investigative effort by numerous supervisors and investigators from both the Homicide and Burglary and Theft Divisions.

The state tried Arthur Lee Williams for capital murder in the death of Detective Wayne Shirley. On February 28, 1983, a jury found him found guilty and assessed the death penalty in the 208th Criminal District Court. He remains on Death Row in 2007 while his appeals process takes an even slower than normal course through our system.

In 2007, Donna Harrell is remarried and resides in Lumberton, Texas, near Beaumont. Detective Shirley's two sons both entered the law enforcement field. Steven Shirley is a deputy with the Los Angeles County Sheriff's Department and has served that agency for nearly 20 years. Jason Shirley is a career police officer working in the Detective Division of the Pasadena Police Department. Daughter Sara Shirley is now working in Human Resources for industries in the Golden Triangle area. Both sons said they admired their dad and the work he did. They also said that while he had discouraged them from going into law enforcement, it must have been in their genes as both followed their Dad into law enforcement and have proven to be successful in their career choice. Detective Shirley's father served as a reserve officer with the Harris County Sheriff Department's Marine Division and Jerry Shirley is retired from the Harris County S.O. Also, Margaret, the Mother of Steven and Jason, is a longtime civilian employee of the Pasadena Police Department.

In addition, in 2007, Detective Shirley would have been the grandfather to four of his son's children. Steven and his wife, Denise Shirley, are the parents of Kannen Shirley, Kaden Shirley, and Tyler Shirley. Jason and his wife, Julie Shirley, are the parents of Natalie Shirley.

The 1982 death of Detective Shirley brought to three the number of classmates from Academy Class No. 34 who died in the line of duty. The other two were Officer Louis Raymond Kuba in 1967 and Officer David Franklin

Noel in 1972.

Originally, at Detective Shirley's gravesite, there stands a monument to the family SHIRLEY as well as a footmarker that read:

HUSBAND
D.W. SHIRLEY
SEPT. 1, 1947 -APR. 28, 1982
DETECTIVE BADGE #638

This foot marker has been replaced by the 100 Club marker.

80

Officer James Donald Harris
Badge #2973
July 13, 1982

Stalled Car Incident on Sweltering Summer Evening Proves Fatal to HPD Officer James Donald Harris

James Donald Harris was born in Syracuse, New York, on October 17, 1952. He grew up in the Syracuse-Auburn area and graduated from Auburn High School in 1971. He served his country honorably for three and a half years in the United States Air Force as a military policeman. Harris joined the Houston Police Department in Police Cadet Class No. 74 on March 29, 1976 and graduated on July 16 of that year. His first assignment was to the evening shift at the Park Place Substation. He later transferred to the K-9 Corps. He wore Badge No. 2973.

On Tuesday night, July 13, 1982, Officer Harris and his newly assigned canine partner, a German Shepherd, were working the evening shift out of Park Place. Even though nearing the end of their shift, they were still on patrol in the east end of Houston in Officer Harris' blue and white marked police unit. While in the area of Dumble and Polk, a citizen flagged down the officer to report that he had almost been run over by a recklessly driven automobile. The citizen gave Officer Harris a description of the car. Harris searched the area and found a stalled vehicle fitting this description at the intersection of Walker and Edgewood.

Harris ordered two suspects to get out of the stalled car. Both did so and came toward the officer as ordered. He placed both of the suspects up against his car in order to search them, a procedure used for his own protection. As he was searching one, the other suspect pulled a 9mm pistol and fired at the officer from close range, striking him three times in the head. These men then disarmed the fallen officer. As they were leaving on foot, a citizen, Jose Francisco Armijo (Hispanic male, 33) was driving westbound on Walker. Armijo was accompanied by his three-year-old daughter and ten-year-old son. For some unknown reason, the suspect who shot Officer Harris fired a round at Armijo's vehicle, striking Armijo in the head. His daughter received a wound from either flying glass or a bullet fragment.

OFFICER JAMES DONALD HARRIS

The suspects fled on foot north on Edgewood toward Rusk Avenue. HPD Sergeant E. Cavazos was off-duty visiting his parents in the 4900 block of Walker.

Upon hearing the shots, Cavazos retrieved his weapon and identification from his vehicle and ran west on Walker to investigate. There, he found the mortally wounded Harris and used the downed officer's handheld radio to call in an "Assist the Officer." He also reported the shooting of Armijo. His assistance was invaluable in preserving the scene from the growing crowd of neighborhood onlookers.

The Houston Fire Department ambulance paramedics assessed the officer's condition and immediately called for LifeFlight Helicopter. Another HFD paramedic team treated the wounds of Armijo as patrol units cleared a nearby baseball field for LifeFlight. When the medical helicopter landed, the doctor on board declared Officer J. D. Harris dead. He was twenty-nine years old. Armijo died from his head wound a week later on July 20, 1982.

MR. AND MRS. J.D. (PAMELA) HARRIS

Evening Shift Lieutenant R. D. Cain initiated an immediate Homicide response by assigning Detectives Richard W. Holland, Greg T. Neely, Eugene T. Yanchak and Alfred T. Hermann to the investigation. At this time, the Night Shift was coming on duty to assist. In addition, Homicide Officer Shooting Team Detectives Larry E. Webber, Vernon W. West and Douglas R. Bostock were called in for duty.

The Homicide Division Chicano Squad, under the field leadership of Detective Jim Montero, provided their usual able assistance. Assistant District Attorney Terry Wilson, then head of the DA's Civil Rights Section, also arrived on the scene. None of these investigators could ever imagine how much more involved this tragic event would become. While investigating the original scene, information surfaced that the suspects had fled to 4907 Rusk, just one block north of Walker. As a result, detectives and numerous uniformed officers surrounded this location. This clue produced no immediate results.

The search then moved next door to 4911 Rusk. While these police officials checked this house from the front, Officers L. J. "Larry" Trepagnier, Antonio Palos, Martin Rodriguez and Michael R. Edwards went around to the back. Numerous other officers also were nearby. As officers rounded the corner at the rear of the house, they were greeted by a hail of gunfire that erupted from an open garage-type building detached from the house. Trepagnier, Palos and Rodriguez returned the gunfire. Officer Edwards was unable to fire at the suspect since the other officers were in front of him, restricting his line of fire. Trepagnier was shot five times in the battle, suffering serious wounds.

After the gunfire ceased, the suspect, Roberto Carrasco Flores (Hispanic Male, 27), was dead at the scene from numerous gunshot wounds caused by Officer Rodriguez' shotgun, Officer Palos' .45-caliber automatic and Officer Trepagnier's .357 revolver. An HFD ambulance took Trepagnier, also twenty-nine years old, to a hospital. He was soon listed in critical condition. Found under Flores was a 9mm automatic later determined to be the weapon used to murder Officer Harris. Stuck in Flores' beltline was the slain officer's .357 revolver.

As other officers and Assistant DA Terry Wilson began securing yet another crime scene, Wilson observed movement from under a horse trailer in this garage. The officers then arrested Ricardo Aldape Guerra (Hispanic Male, 20). Near his hiding place was a .45-caliber automatic.

Officer J. D. Harris was survived by his wife Pamela and two daughters, four-year-old Rebecca Brooke Harris and twenty-month-old Megan Annette Harris. Other survivors were his father and stepmother, Nelson and Ruth Harris of Auburn, New York, grandparents Nelson and Gerry Harris and Robert and Carla Pierson of Syracuse, New York. There also were a sister and brother-in-law, Beverly and David Ruetsch, and nephews Jeff and Todd Ruetsch of Marcellus, New York. He was predeceased by his mother, Mrs. Beverly Jean Harris.

Funeral services were held 10:30 a.m. Friday, July 16, 1982, at the Forest Park Lawndale Chapel with the Reverends Paul Carlin and Brad Ottosen, a former police officer and friend, as well as Police Chaplin Harold Hannah, officiating. Interment was at Forest Park Lawndale Cemetery. Pallbearers were Tommy Olin and Officers Woody Phifer, Russel Hoffard, Jack Holloway, Richard Puckett, Ronnie Collingsworth and R. C. Smith.

On the extremely hot summer night of the deadly shooting, blood had been shed at four different locations, only several blocks apart. A fine young officer was dead, another seriously wounded, an innocent citizen received wounds from which he later died and an illegal Hispanic immigrant was dead as a direct result of his own actions. Officer Trepagnier received gunshot wounds that damaged his diaphragm, liver, colon and arm. In addition, he suffered the loss of a kidney. After undergoing a number of major surgeries, his survival was a miracle in itself.

While it was quite evident that the deceased suspect Flores had shot Officer Trepagnier, there was some initial concern as to whether Flores or the arrested suspect Guerra had shot Officer Harris. Diligent work by Homicide detectives produced witnesses who identified Ricardo Aldape Guerra as the suspect who shot the slain officer. The clothing description and different hair length of both suspects left no doubt in the minds of the investigators and prosecutors. The witnesses clearly described the shooter of Officer Harris as having collar-length hair and wearing a green military-type fatigue shirt. This fit Ricardo Aldape Guerra's description. The dead suspect, Flores, had shorter hair and was dressed in maroon pants and shirt and white and maroon athletic shoes.

There was an absolute clear distinction in the clothing of the two suspects. Even though Flores had the slain officer's weapon in his possession as well as the 9mm automatic that killed Officer Harris, the witnesses spoke for themselves in this part of the investigation. Ricardo Aldape Guerra was charged with capital murder in the death of Officer J. D. Harris.

Guerra was tried in the 248th Criminal District Court in Harris County for this offense and on October 14, 1982, he was found guilty and assessed the death penalty. The usual automatic appeal process began and what followed was yet another bitter pill for Houston police officers to swallow.

For whatever reason, Guerra became a cause celebre. History shows it definitely was not his lack of guilt. On May 11, 1992, his conviction was overturned. This case fell into the jurisdiction of U. S. District Judge Kenneth Hoyt in Houston. Working for Guerra throughout the appeal process were not only the Mexican state department, the Roman Catholic Church, the American Civil Liberties Union and several volunteer legal foundations well known for their "bleeding heart" attitude, but also an HPD Assistant Chief. Yes, the defense received support from one of our own, from one of the leaders of Officers Harris and Trepagnier.

Judge Hoyt severely chastised the District Attorney's Office and the Houston Police Department for their actions in the initially successful prosecution of this capital murderer. In some instances, the original prosecution witnesses, after developing their own problems in obeying the law, became uncooperative. Also, some of them were harassed by the individuals involved in the joint effort to free Guerra. Eventually, Guerra was released and returned to his native country. He was killed in an automobile accident a short time later.

There were numerous Homicide personnel involved in the massive investigation that covered four separate but related crime scenes. Other officers made important contributions but there simply were too many to mention every name herewith. Two of the primary scene detectives, Richard Holland and Greg Neely, became Homicide Captain Holland and Homicide Lieutenant Neely. Holland served as commander of the Homicide Division from 1994-2004 after serving in the Recruiting and Internal Affairs Division. In 2007, he is commander of the Criminal Intelligence Division. Neely, who later also served in Internal Affairs, retired from Homicide in 2006. Lieutenant R. D. Cain was the long-time leader of the HPD Hostage Negotiation Team and was respected throughout the country for his expertise in that area of police work. He is now assigned to the Helicoptor Division. Detective A. T. "Alfred" Hermann retired from Homicide in 2000. Detective E. T. "Gene" Yanchak retired from Homicide in 2005 after nearly thirty years of investigating murders and Officer Involved incidents. Detectives Bostock, Webber, Montero and West retired from HPD while actively working murder cases. West died in 2001.

BROOKE, MEGAN, AND PAM

Sergeant Eddie Cavazos, who worked out of North Shepherd Patrol Station at the time of this tragic event, retired in 1999 after more than twenty-eight years of service. He went to work in the private sector. In 2002, Officer Antonio Palos was assigned to the Recruiting Division after working a number of years in SWAT. Officer Martin Rodriguez made sergeant in 1982 and worked out of the Northeast Patrol Division. Officer M. R. Edwards remained an ever-present steady street officer assigned to Central Patrol and provided tremendous assistance in the 1988 Murder investigation of another HPD Officer.

While many lives were altered on this hot, sweltering July night in 1982, the life of Officer L. J. "Larry" Trepagnier was severely changed forever. After undergoing six surgeries, amazingly enough, Officer Trepagnier remained a Houston police officer. He has for a number of years been assigned to South Central Patrol. As a result of his wounds, Trepagnier suffered the loss of a kidney and eight feet of intestines. Had he not been a young, strapping, strong twenty-nine-year-old, there is no way he would have endured the aftermath of his injuries. While painful for him, he later recounted some details that were not previously known.

Trepagnier recalled lying there on the ground and after realizing how many times he was hit, thinking the logical thing: I am going to die right here. Officer Palos said he and another officer were on the scene and found Trepagnier on the ground. Both officers were fond of Vellamints. Not knowing what else to do while awaiting the arrival of HFD and LifeFlight, they used the cellophane wrappers from these candies to cover the "sucking" chest and abdomen wounds of their fellow officer and friend.

In 2002, Officer Trepagnier also shared something very likely unknown to most: As he was lying on the ground, he saw a familiar face above him – that of Sergeant Walter J. Stewart, who had been one of Larry's training officers. Walter was telling him something like, "Boy, if you are going to make it, you had better suck it up and get tough."

Stewart said he was called out on the shooting of Officer Harris as part of his training assignment as a Northeast Patrol Division Internal Affairs investigator, only to also find one of his previous rookies down and possibly out. A veteran of many Narcotics shootings in the 1970's, Stewart knew that Larry's wounds looked extremely serious. He had two gunshot wounds to the stomach and chest and one to an arm. The wounded officer remembered being given the last rites by well-meaning officer friends and hearing the HFD and LifeFlight personnel speak of his diminishing vital signs, even when he was en route to the hospital.

Pamela Harris remarried in 1990 and was a fixture at court proceedings throughout the years. In 2007, she resides in East Texas with A.C., her husband. Rebecca Brooke Harris is now Rebecca Brooke Marshall and she and her husband, Wayne Marshall, live near Waco. Megan Annette Harris is now Megan Walber and she and her husband, Shannon Walber, live near Harper, Texas. They have made Pamela Harris Rains and her husband, A.C. proud grandparents of Jace Walber, who is seven months old. Nelson Harris, J. D.'s dad, died in the 1990s. Stepmother Ruth, Grandmother Pierson, sister Beverly and nephews Jeff and Todd resided in New York State in 2002. The other three grandparents are deceased.

Pam Harris later spoke of the identity of the New York state trooper who attended J. D.'s funeral. This stiff and starched trooper in full dress wool uniform in July appeared at the funeral, his identity unknown to many HPD personnel. The officer's widow later explained that he was Jim Campbell, a childhood friend of Officer Harris who had encouraged him to enter law enforcement after his stint in the Air Force. Campbell stayed with the New York State Police and was helpful and supportive of Pam Harris and her daughters throughout the years since his friend's death.

The original gravemarker at Forest Park Lawndale read:

JAMES DONALD HARRIS
1952 - 1982
BADGE EMBLEM IN CENTER

As per Forest Park regulations, the Harris family chose to remove this marker and replace it with the 100 CLUB LINE OF DUTY marker.

81

Officer Kathleen M. Schaefer
Badge #1872
August 18, 1982

Narcotics Officer Kathy Schaefer Shot During Bust, the First Female HPD Officer to Die in Line of Duty

It was August 1982, a terrible year for the Houston Police Department. On March 29, Solo Motorcycle Officers Winston J. Rawlins and William E. DeLeon were both killed in separate freeway traffic accidents. On April 28, Burglary and Theft Fugitive Detective Daryl Wayne Shirley was shot and killed.

It got worse. On July 13, Officer J. D. Harris was shot and killed and on the same night, by the same suspects, Officer L. W. Trepegnier was shot numerous times but miraculously survived his wounds. On top of these tragedies, Officer Charlie Coates lay in a coma from injuries received after being hit by a car in May of this year of unfortunate events.

Officers were routinely asking themselves on a daily basis, "When will it end? Haven't we had enough tragedy for one year?" Could it get worse? Yes, unfortunately it could and it did.

The determinants in writing Line of Duty death stories for the Badge & Gun, the official monthly newspaper of the Houston Police Officers Union occasionally involve touchy, even embarrassing situations. The writer's intent has been to write these tragic accounts in order that HPD officers,

Houstonians and solid citizens everywhere never forget these brave sacrifices. This tragedy was unique and especially tragic for the department.

The writer long pondered whether the story should be written. He went ahead under a self-imposed stipulation. Factual information such as names of all involved as well as investigators had been routinely used in previous stories. After much soul-searching and advice from many friends and several high-ranking members of the HPD command staff, the writer persevered and decided to tell this tragic story in honor of Officer Kathy Schaefer with no intention to disparage or in any way judge the actions and intentions of any of the officers present during this tragedy. Accordingly, no name of any officer involved will be used in the Schaefer story. The focus is solely on Houston Police Officer Kathy Schaefer and is written to honor her memory with the story of her life and death. If any new planning and/or safety procedures emerge as a result of the issues described herein, then some small good will have come from this tragedy.

OFFICER KATHLEEN M. SCHAEFER

Kathleen Magdalene Cochran was born in Houston on February 24, 1948. Her parents were Houston Police Officer Harry Edward Cochran and Mrs. Theresa Cochran. Kathy attended Assumption and St. Theresa Catholic Schools as a child and then transferred to Hamilton Junior High School and Reagan Senior High School. She also studied at San Jacinto Junior College for a time.

Somewhere along this journey, she met and fell in love with Lyndon Wade Schaefer. Kathy, a daughter of a Houston police officer, married Lyndon, who had become an officer in August 1967, graduating from Police Cadet Class No. 35. They became man and wife on October 11, 1967. Two main events happened during their marriage. Lyndon Wade Schaefer Jr. was born in 1969 and Theresa Marie Schaefer was born in 1970. Lyndon Schaefer, known to many as Wade, was progressing in his career at HPD, having been promoted to sergeant in 1973 and to lieutenant in 1977. Meanwhile, Kathy was a homemaker, nurturing and raising their two children.

However, something was apparently missing in Kathy's life. After all, policing was in her blood. Having raised her children to the preteen age, she applied for employment at her husband's workplace – and her father's. It seemed that with her father and husband being police officers, she had inherited and developed a natural interest in law enforcement. This dream became reality when she was accepted into HPD Police Cadet Class No. 89. After graduating, she took her oath of office on March 21, 1980. She wore Badge No. 1872.

From all reports, Kathy Schaefer was a natural policewoman and completed her probationary period in exemplary fashion. While her original assignment was to Southwest Patrol, she was transferred as a matter of procedure to a mandatory tour of duty in the Dispatcher's Division. After that obligation she returned to Southwest Patrol. Kathy, being thirty-two, the mother of two and the wife of a career officer, was very likely deemed mature in the police service beyond her actual years of service. After a short time at Southwest, she applied for a voluntary transfer assignment to the Narcotics Division. She was accepted and began that duty on June 14, 1982.

REAGAN, STACY, LYN, LYNDON PAIGE, AND SKYLAR KATHLEEN SCHAEFER

On an extremely hot afternoon, August 18, 1982, undercover officers in Narcotics had received information regarding several individuals involved in narcotics trafficking in the Clear Lake-NASA area of the City of Houston. Following up on this information, officers made arrangements to meet with the dealers and conduct a buy-bust transaction. There were a number of plainclothes officers involved in this operation.

This transaction was set up to take place in a convenience store parking lot in the 2500 block of Bay Area Boulevard. The plan was to have an experienced male undercover officer driving an unmarked vehicle with Kathy in the front seat. When the narcotics transaction was "made," the driver was to hit his brake lights indicating to surveillance officers that the deal "had gone down." Any veteran police officer knows that these tasks are some of the most dangerous policing situations anywhere. You would have highly trained officers meeting covertly with individuals with criminal backgrounds and whom they had never met before. All precautions for officer safety are meant to be taken and there is always a plan in place to bail out if it appears to be too dangerous. Of equal importance are the arrangements made for adequate backup personnel to be available when needed.

On this day, there were two more experienced undercover narcotics officers in a Narcotics Division raid van. They were accompanied by two uniformed HPD officers, who had been approved by their supervisors to participate in the "bust" part of the operation after the "buy" had been completed. These two uniformed officers were pulled off routine patrol duty for this "special assignment." These two were in the rear of the raid van. When the brake lights were tapped, the raid van was to then move in to the location and block the suspect's vehicle from leaving. The suspects were then to be "taken down."

After the undercover vehicle was parked at the convenience store, both the male and female (Kathy) officers observed the suspect drive up and park next to them on their right. The male suspect went into the store and returned with a beer. He walked up to Kathy's side of the van, introducing himself as Bryan. Kathy opened the front passenger door, allowing Bryan to enter into the back seat area of the van. The deal went down and the undercover officer gave the brake tap signal.

The Narcotics raid van came forward, blocking the suspect's vehicle. The male officer with Kathy pulled his weapon, pointing at the suspect in the rear and at the same time identifying himself as a police officer. With the suspect directly behind her, Kathy chose to exit the front passenger door and also "drew down" on the suspect from outside the vehicle.

By now, the two undercover backups and the two uniformed backups were getting out of their raid van. However, unfortunately, there was one major detail the officers had failed to discuss when this operation was being planned – that there was a female undercover Narc involved. When the uniformed officers jumped out of the raid van, one of them saw a female in plainclothes pointing a pistol toward the inside of the van. The officer, believing that this female was pointing her pistol at the officer driving the van, was in fear that his fellow officer was in danger. He had only a split second to react. He fired his weapon one time, striking Kathy in the left side.

KEN BOUNDY, THERESA SCHAEFER BOUNDY, DAUGHTER KRISTINA, AND SON MATTHEW

The officers quickly summoned medical assistance. A female emergency medical technician stopped to assist and administered CPR to Kathy, but was unable to find a pulse. LifeFlight helicopter arrived and personnel attempted to revive Kathy, but were unsuccessful. Medical officials pronounced HPD Officer Kathy Schaefer dead at 8:14 p.m. She was the first female Houston police officer in history to die in the line of duty. She was thirty-four years old.

Kathy was survived by her husband of nearly fifteen years, HPD Lieutenant L. W. Schaefer, and a son and a daughter – thirteen-year-old Lyndon Schaefer Jr. and twelve-year-old Theresa Marie Schaefer. She also was survived by her mother, Mrs. Theresa Cochran, and three brothers, Thomas P. Cochran, Harry E.

Cochran Jr. and Daniel J. Cochran, as well as a number of aunts, uncles and cousins. Kathy's father, Harry Cochran, who retired from HPD in the early 1970's, had passed away in 1979. And, Kathy had made many, many friends from her short time with HPD.

The officer, wife and mother was a member of Holy Family Catholic Church, the Houston Police Officers Union and the Houston Police Officers Association.

A rosary and scripture service was held at the Heights Funeral Home Chapel at 7 p.m. Friday, August 20, 1982. A funeral mass was held at the Holy Family Catholic Church, 1510 5th Street, Missouri City, at 11 a.m. Saturday, August 21. Father Jay Walsh, C.S.B., officiated. Six of Kathy's best officer friends proudly served as pallbearers with all HPD officers serving as honorary pallbearers. Burial followed at Brookside Cemetery, Eastex Freeway and Lauder, next to her father.

The entire department was literally stunned from this tragedy which happened only short months after four other officers had been killed. Newspaper accounts never attempted to place blame on the young officer who was forced into that split second decision. The newspaper accounts included the following quotations:

Homicide Captain Bobby Adams: "The whole ball of wax is still under investigation, but it appears at this point to be a case of mistaken identity."

Assistant Chief of Police B. K. Johnson: "The officer's actions were within the guidelines of the police department and the rules and regulations of the State of Texas. Had Kathleen Schaefer been a crook, it would have been a clean shooting. It was a clean shooting. The unfortunate tragedy is that the victim was a police officer."

Chief Johnson went on to say, "Where we find fault at this point in time is the undercover Narcotics officers were not identified to the uniformed officers who were involved in the arrest. And, more particularly, the uniformed officers were not aware that a female officer was involved. When they got out of their van, they got out cold."

No one, not even Kathy Schaefer's children, blame the officer for what happened that hot evening in Clear Lake. Their lives have gone on. They lived not only with this tragedy, but another one some eight years later. Kathy's husband of fourteen years, Lieutenant Lyndon Schaefer, retired from HPD in January 1989. He remarried and went to work for Harris County Constable Precinct 5 and in November 1990 died from a sudden heart attack at the young age of forty-five. Lyndon Jr. and Theresa were twenty-one and twenty years old, respectively, at the time of the death of their father. Lyndon Jr. was serving his country in the United States Army at the time.

This writer has spoken to both Theresa and Lynn on the telephone. While I have not had the pleasure of meeting them, I found them to be remarkably mature about this tragedy that took their Mom from them.

They know that this was a tragic accident and hold no ill feelings toward anyone.

In 2007, Lyn Schaefer Jr. has recently opened a business in the Colorado County, Columbus, Texas area. After he served his country, be worked as a diesel mechanic. He is now in a boots, saddles, gunsmith operation. He and his wife Stacy Schaefer are the parents of three daughters-Skylar Kathleen Schaefer, age twelve, Reagan Schaefer, age nine, and Lyndy Schaefer, age five. Theresa Schaeffer Boundy and her husband Ken Boundy live in Sugarland. They are the parents of Kristina Boundy, age fourteen, and Matthew Boundy, age eleven.

Officer Kathy Schaefer's mother, Mrs. Theresa Cochran, passed away in 2005. The remainder of the Cochran family remains intact.

Marker for Officer Schaefer at Brookside Cemetery reads:

IN LOVING MEMORY
KATHLEEN C. SCHAEFER
FEB 24, 1948-AUG 18, 1982
(HAS BADGE EMBLEM #1872)

82

Officer Charles Robert Coates II
Badge #1415
February 23, 1983

Impatient Motorist Ignores Warning Lights, Strikes and Seriously Injures Officer Coates in 1982

Charles Robert Coates II was born in St. Louis, Missouri, on April 8, 1946, the first of three children of Charles R. and Jacqueline Coates. Charles attended

St. Thomas More Elementary School for six years and graduated from Normandy High School in St. Louis in 1965. From October 10, 1965 until November 15, 1967, he served his country honorably in the United States Navy.

He married Elizabeth Ann on October 8, 1966. Upon his discharge from the U.S. Navy, he returned to the St. Louis area. His public service employment began well before he came to Houston. He was employed as a firefighter with the Community Fire Department in St. Louis and later in Missouri as a patrol officer with the Frontenac Police Department and the Des Peres Police Department.

OFFICER CHARLES ROBERT COATES II

The Houston Police Department recruited nationwide in the 1970s and this fact came to the attention of Officer Coates, who came to the Bayou City on a shoestring of a budget and applied. He was accepted and began HPD Cadet Class No. 75 on September 13, 1976, graduating on January 7, 1977. His initial assignment was to the Night Shift Radio Patrol at the Beechnut Substation. He later worked Radio Patrol at Park Place Substation, Central Patrol and also completed a tour of duty in the Jail Division. His last assignment was to the Evening Shift Radio Patrol at the Northwest Substation.

On Sunday night, May 2, 1982, Officer Coates received a call shortly after 8 p.m. regarding an accident with a vehicle in a ditch in the 12600 block of Memorial Drive. Upon arrival, Coates began his investigation and selected a wrecker to assist in the removal of this vehicle. He stopped traffic from both east and westbound directions in order to clear the scene. As he was performing this duty, a vehicle with an obviously impatient driver ignored the warning lights and the officer in the street.

This vehicle, driven by a Mary Jane Eilert (White Female, 52) drove left of center and around the previously stopped traffic at a high rate of speed, striking Officer Coates and throwing him upon the hood of her vehicle, where he hit the windshield and was thrown into the air and onto the pavement. The officer was seriously injured from the impact. An ambulance rushed him to the hospital, where doctors determined that he suffered from various broken bones. However, his most severe injury was a closed head wound.

CHARLES COATES II, U.S. NAVY, AND WIFE BETTY COATES

After months of testing and attempts to assist him in rehabilitation and recovery, he remained in a comatose state and was eventually moved to a local nursing home with little or no chance of improving or ever coming home. On Wednesday, February 23, 1983, nearly ten months after the accident, Officer Charles Robert Coates II died peacefully at the Manor Care Sharpview Convalescent Home in southwest Houston. He was thirty-six years old.

His wife, Elizabeth Ann Coates, and fourteen-year-old daughter Christine survived Officer Coates. Also mourning this death were his parents, Mr. and Mrs. Charles R. Coates of St. Louis; one sister, Mrs. Carolyn Alexander; one brother, John Coates; a grandmother, Mrs. Catherine Graham; one niece and one nephew. All of the survivors resided in the St. Louis area.

Memorial services were held at 1 p.m. Friday, February 25, 1983, at the Heights Funeral Home at 1317 Heights Boulevard in Houston. Additional services were held at the Hutchens Funeral Home in Florissant, Missouri, on Saturday, February 26. Burial followed at the Florissant Cemetery. In lieu of flowers, the family respectfully requested memorial donations to the Texas Head Injury Foundation.

In a time-honored tradition, Officer Coates was not allowed to go to his final resting place alone. The HPD Honor Guard, accompanied by Northwest Patrol supervisors and close friends, Lieutenant Al Broderhausen and Sergeant W. J. "Joe" Wissel, as well as a number of other officers, traveled to Florissant with their fallen comrade, a camaraderie that warmly touched the Coates family.

The marker on Officer Coates' grave reads as follows:

CHARLES R. COATES II
APRIL 8, 1946-FEBRUARY 23, 1983

U.S. NAVY INSIGNIA

IN LOVING MEMORY
OF A FINE POLICE OFFICER
WHO LOST HIS LIFE
IN THE LINE OF DUTY

Mrs. Mary Jane Eilert was charged with aggravated assault with a motor vehicle. She eventually pled guilty in September 1982 and was assessed a sentence of ten years probation and a $1,000 fine. She lived in Southwest Houston.

Officer John L. Bertolini of the Accident Division investigated the accident. Bertolini said that after Officer Coates was struck, one of the residents of the Memorial neighborhood came out and took Ms. Eilert into their home prior to the arrival of other officers. She was hysterical and, although possibly intoxicated at the time of the incident, several hours passed before investigators were able to piece together what had actually happened and located her as the suspect.

CHRISTINE, CHARLES, MRS. JACQUELINE COATES, AND MRS. CATHERINE GRAHAM

This resulted in the problem of proving intoxication at the time of the incident as opposed to her becoming intoxicated afterwards. Most police officers would see through this defense, but yet it became a major issue.

Elizabeth Ann Coates remarried and in 2002 resided in the Hill Country. She and her husband Dan are involved in a Foster Home Placement service, which is closely involved with the State of Texas Child Protective Services in the placement of over 350 children. Daughter Christine is now Christine Sinay and was employed with this organization. Christine has a son, Jacob Sinay.

In 2002, Mr. and Mrs. Charles Coates, Sr. resided at their home in Florissant, Missouri. Their daughter Carolyn Alexander and her husband lived nearby and operated a travel agency. Their children, Officer Coates' niece and nephew, are Danielle Alexander, who lived in that same area, and Timothy Alexander, who resided in New York City. Their son John Coates lived in the St. Louis area and was the father of one son, a namesake for Officer Charles Robert Coates II. Unfortunately, Charles Robert Coates III died at age of fourteen in 1997. Grandmother, Mrs. Graham, is deceased.

Officer Bertolini continued working the Accident Division and later at the South Central and Clear Lake Patrol Divisions. He continued his career with an assignment to the Major Offenders Investigation Division and worked with the Gulf Coast Violent Offenders Task Force. Sergeant W. J. Wissel was assigned to the nightshift at the Northwest Patrol Division and retired from there in 2004. Lieutenant Al Broderhausen died in 1983.

83

Airport Police Officer William Moss
September 12, 1983

Bald Tires and Rugged, Rain-slick Streets Contribute to 1-Car Death of Officer Moss

William Moss was born in Union Point, Georgia, on August 17, 1941. He was the tenth of twelve children born to Willie and Lula Mae Moss. He graduated in 1959 from Moultrie High School in Moultrie, Georgia. From there, he moved to the New Jersey-New York City area and was employed in the engraving business with one company for more than fifteen years.

He moved to Houston in 1982 and made

application to the City of Houston Aviation Division Police Department. He successfully completed the background investigation and was sworn in as an airport police officer on September 17, 1982.

On Monday, September 12, 1983, Officer William Moss was working the evening shift at Houston Intercontinental Airport. He was in the process of responding to an accident call and driving south on JFK Boulevard on streets that were slick from a recent rain. As Officer Moss entered a curve in the boulevard, he spun out of control, striking the curb. The 1982 Ford patrol car then slid on the wet grass and into several trees, striking them with the left side. The crash pinned Officer Moss in the vehicle. After witnesses summoned assistance, responders found Officer Moss dead at the scene. He was forty-two years old.

AIRPORT POLICE OFFICER WILLIAM MOSS

Veteran Accident Investigator J. H. Lynn conducted the investigation of the scene, supervised by Accident Lieutenant E. J. Smith and Accident Sergeant Jesse Foroi. Airport Police Chief Wilfred Navarro also attended the scene of this fatality. Officer Lynn's investigation concluded that while speed and wet surfaces likely contributed to this accident, the police vehicle had a bald tire on the right rear that also was a major factor.

Lieutenant Smith and Sergeant Foroi contacted an expert from the Traffic and Transportation Department who also contributed to the investigation. They found that this roadway was worn slick from heavy use and badly in need of resurfacing. They also concluded that this type of roadway in this condition was especially dangerous when the issue of a bald tire was a factor. In summary, there were a variety of factors that contributed to the tragic death of Officer Moss.

Moss was survived by his wife Flora, a daughter, Kim Moss, age eighteen, and three sons, Barry Moss, twenty; Bryant Moss, seventeen; and Roland Moss, fourteen. He was also survived by a stepson, Michael Jones, twenty-one. He was also mourned by his parents, William and Lula Mae Moss and seven sisters, Janet Moss, Carrie Stevens, Juanita Hanks, Hattie McCullum, Mary Stallworth, Lula Carter and Sarah Richardson, as well as by two brothers, John Moss and Robert L. Moss.

Funeral Services were held at the Heights Funeral Home Chapel at 1:30 p.m. Thursday, September 15, 1983, with Police Chaplain H. L. Hannah officiating. Officer Moss' body was sent to the New York City area for burial.

84

Officer Maria Michelle Groves
Badge #4292
April 10, 1987

Officer Maria Michelle Groves, 22, Youngest Officer to Die in Line of Duty – Directing Traffic at Scene

Maria Michelle Groves was born in Fort Worth on November 13, 1964. When she was only two years old, her mother died. She and her sister Kelly, who was four years old, were raised in the loving care of their maternal grandparents in Lufkin. Maria Michelle graduated from Lufkin Hudson High School. Upon graduation, she took a few college courses while waiting to become old enough to be a Houston police officer. Known to her family and friends as Michelle, she joined HPD in Police Cadet Class No. 122. This class began their training in the new Houston Police Academy on Aldine Westfield Road on July 9, 1984, and graduated on Nov. 10, 1984.

Officer Michelle Groves' first assignment was to the Westside Patrol Division. After successfully completing her probationary term, she remained in Westside Patrol until her assignment to the Jail Division for a mandatory tour of duty. Serving that tour, she returned to Westside Patrol, Evening Shift. In March 1987, she requested and was granted a transfer to the Westside Night Shift.

On Thursday night, April 9, 1987, Officer Groves reported for duty as usual at Westside. Her assigned partner on this nightshift was Officer D. P. Jackson and they were assigned to Unit No. 20G62. At approximately 12:15 a.m., they volunteered to check on a major accident on the Katy Freeway just west of West Belt. Upon arrival, they received instructions from Sergeant W. L. Givens to begin rerouting all traffic off the freeway and onto the service road. They were on the inbound side of the 10800 block of Katy. The original call was in regards to an overturned truck/major accident near West Belt.

After arriving on the scene, Officers Groves and Jackson parked their cars across the left and center lanes and began laying out flares and rerouting traffic around the accident scene and onto the access road. Their marked vehicle's emergency lights were flashing in a further attempt to call motorists' attention to the danger that lay ahead. At this point their objective was not only to protect previously injured individuals but also prevent any additional injuries to the occupants of oncoming vehicles.

Due to the lack of vision of oncoming vehicles, this was obviously a very dangerous task. Both officers donned their HPD-approved reflective jackets. While they attempted to protect the previously involved vehicles from further damage and injury to the occupants, the officers heard a lock-up of brakes on an oncoming vehicle. This vehicle, a 1982 Chevrolet Blazer driven by Robert Andrew Richardson came upon the scene at a high rate of speed, later estimated to be more than seventy-five miles per hour. The Blazer went into a skid.

"Watch out!" Officer Jackson shouted to Michelle Groves. He quickly sought safety toward the guardrail side of the freeway.

Officer Groves, still in the process of placing warning flares, apparently saw the Chevrolet Blazer and ran toward the outside median. A later investigation showed that that she attempted to flee from the truck's path but the Blazer swerved to avoid striking the patrol car and struck the officer instead, throwing her nearly 300 feet (later accurately measured as 88 yards).

The young officer sustained a closed head injury as well as a number of other internal injuries. LifeFlight Helicopter transported her to Hermann Hospital where she was pronounced dead on arrival at 2:30 a.m. Friday, April 10, 1987. She was only twenty-two years old.

Her only sibling, a sister, Mrs. Kelley Groves O'Neal and her husband, Scott, of Fort Worth, survived Officer Maria Michelle Groves. Other survivors were her father and stepmother, Mr. and Mrs. Clyde Groves of Houston, and her maternal grandparents, Mr. and Mrs. R. S. Curtis of Lufkin.

Funeral services were held at 11 a.m. Monday, April 13, from the Second Baptist Church at 6400 Woodway with Dr. H. Edwin Young and the Reverend David Dixon officiating. A long funeral procession followed this service to Lufkin, where Officer Groves was laid to rest in the Garden of Memories on U. S. Highway 59, just south of Lufkin. Pallbearers were fellow officers.

OFFICER MARIA MICHELLE GROVES

A number of Houston police officers were present when this vehicle went out of control and struck their fellow officer. The driver, Robert Andrew Richardson (White Male, 43), was arrested immediately after this accident by Officer Groves' partner, Officer D. P. Jackson and Officer C. E. Green.

Officers Robert V. Ruiz, L. D. Ferguson and J. F. Cantu of the Accident Division investigated this case. They were assisted by a number of other Accident and Patrol officers, some of whom were Officers C. E. Green,

C. J. Grysen, S. F. Red, D. L. Wilhite, S. E. Carr, R. Ontiveros, R. D. Mosely, C. A. Webster, R. E. Tallent and J. W. Williams. Accident Sergeant J. C. Hartman was the scene supervisor.

DWI Task Force Officer C. E. Green took custody of the suspect and transported him to the Central Police Station where he was video-taped. He voluntarily submitted to an intoxilyzer exam administered by Officer A. J. Mock. This test registered at 0.18 percent, nearly twice the legal threshold for intoxication of 0.10. The suspect also consented to providing a blood specimen and was taken to the St. Joseph Hospital Emergency Room for that purpose. This later tested out to be 0.155 percent. He was charged with involuntary manslaughter in the 339th Criminal District Court and held on a $5,000 bond.

Officer Groves was the second female officer to die in the line of duty. At twenty-two, she was the youngest of the eighty-three HPD officers to have previously died in the line of duty.

Michelle was very active in her church as well as the singles group at Second Baptist. Newspaper accounts said that she while she loved her job, she had shared with friends that she would have been unable to continue doing the job without her Christian support groups. It was her feeling that dealing with the "bad sides of things" was depressing and that she needed the spiritual support she received at Second Baptist. Rather than working extra jobs, she gave of her time volunteering three days a week in the Second Baptist bookstore.

The loving maternal grandparents, Mr. and Mrs. R. S. Curtis, are now both deceased as is Michelle's father, Clyde Groves. In 2003, Mrs. Kelley O'Neal and her husband Scott resided outside of Fort Worth in Aledo. Kelley was the proud mother of Zach O'Neal and Molly Michelle O'Neal.

Officer R. V. Ruiz became a sergeant at the Eastside Patrol Tactical Unit. Officer J. F. Cantu was a sergeant in Emergency Communications in 2003, while Officers L. D. Ferguson and C. E. Green were assigned to the Accident Division. Michelle's partner on this tragic night, Officer Danny P. Jackson, later resigned from the department.

Robert Andrew Richardson, who had a previous DWI conviction in 1977, was charged with involuntary manslaughter in the death of Officer Groves. After he was convicted and sentenced to ten years in the Texas Department of Criminal Justice, he lost an appeal. He eventually served less than three years of his sentence and was released in 1991. Ironically, he relocated to a suburb of Fort Worth, the birthplace of Officer Maria Michelle Groves.

The original marker for Officer Groves read:

MARIA MICHELLE GROVES
1964 - 1987

The 100 CLUB marker has been added to this plot to honor this young fallen hero.

85

Officer Andrew Winzer
Badge #4330
February 18, 1988

Collision with Vehicle, Rusty Guardrail Causes Winzer to become the HPD's Only Drowning

Andrew Winzer was born in Newellton, Louisiana, on June 24, 1957. He attended elementary school in Newellton and Rootwood, Louisiana. His family moved to Houston and he attended and graduated from Miller Junior High School in 1972. His education continued at Jack Yates High School, where he graduated in 1976. His search for more education led him to Prairie View A&M University, where he received a degree in 1980. While at Prairie View, he was on the football and track teams. He began his career with the Houston Police Department in Police Cadet Class No. 112, graduating on September 16, 1983.

He soon resigned from the department for personal reasons but his desire to be a Houston police officer did not go away. He was reinstated on July 9, 1984 to Class No. 122. On October 15, 1984, he took the oath of office and became a Houston police officer, successfully completing his probationary period on July 9, 1985. He was assigned Badge No. 4330. His first and only assignment was the Radio Patrol Command at the North Shepherd Police Station.

On Thursday night, February 18, 1988, Officer Winzer was riding Radio Patrol Unit No. 6B42 on the evening shift at the North Shepherd Substation. As he rode a one-man unit he received a family disturbance call at 7:40 p.m. Another one-man unit, Officer W. M. Redman, was assigned to this call with Winzer. Their investigation resulted in the arrest of a female juvenile. Winzer volunteered to transport the prisoner to the Juvenile Division at 61 Riesner, as well as to complete the usual heavy paperwork.

At 9:40 p.m., Officer Winzer left the station and drove east on Franklin. He was driving through the intersection of Franklin and Louisiana when a 1975 Oldsmobile Cutlass driven by Andres Abelino Alfaro ran a red light going north on Louisiana. The front left quarter of Alfaro's vehicle collided with the right rear of Winzer's marked patrol unit. The impact caused the left rear of the suspect vehicle to spin around, sending the patrol car rolling slowly in a northeasterly direction and into a thin metal guardrail. The vehicle flipped over, crashed through a guardrail and fell forty feet down into the cold, murky waters of Buffalo Bayou.

Officer C. A. Byrd was driving a short distance behind Officer Winzer and was there when Officers T. L. Rodgers and Heidi A. Duslher also came upon the scene. Witnesses and the three officers immediately reported the accident and called for assistance. This accident happened only blocks from the Central Police Station and Houston Fire Department Headquarters. One witness reported seeing the cars collide, then sticking together by their front ends. The vehicles spun around once when the police car broke free.

OFFICER ANDREW WINZER

The witness described it as if the police vehicle was sliding on ice when it struck the railing and fell into the bayou. Both agencies responded quickly and at least three uniformed officers and two citizens jumped into the fifty-degree water in brave attempts to save Officer Winzer. Newspaper articles and interviews with those known to have been involved provide an account of the courageous efforts of everyone at the scene as well as to identify those involved.

Officers Rodgers and Duslher went to separate sides of the bayou and dove into the cold bayou after seeing bubbles from the water. So did several unidentified citizens. Officer J. P. Tyler arrived at the scene, as did Officer Mike Pappillion. Neither these two officers nor Officer Rodgers had any diving gear. Nevertheless, without regard for their own safety, they plunged into the cold water in courageous efforts to locate the vehicle.

Officer Duslher also remained in the water, acting as a safety net for those who had gone under. Officer Tyler was able to locate the vehicle and recalled how it appeared to be in a crevice at the bottom. However, without equipment to stay under for very long, they were unable to proceed any further. These brave officers stayed in the water and repeatedly attempted a rescue as their air would allow until police divers arrived.

Officer J. S. Shipley, a Dive Team member, was on duty in Radio Patrol in the Montrose area when he heard the call regarding the police car in the bayou. After collecting his gear from the Dive Team Office at 61 Riesner, he arrived on the scene at 9:59 p.m. A second dive team member, Officer S. K. Leatherman, observed the police activity as he left classes at the University of Houston-Downtown. He hurriedly made the short trip to the Dive Team Office and returned with the Dive Van and equipment, arriving at 10:10.

On his first dive, Officer Shipley, outfitted with the proper gear, located the vehicle inverted in twelve to fifteen feet of water. A short time later, Dive Team supervisor, Sergeant P. L. Blackshear arrived, as did Dive Team members M. G. Gage, D. G. Ritchey and R. J. Parker. Gage and Ritchey took over as safety officers and Parker assumed the duties as dive master.

At 10:25 p.m. Officers Shipley and Leatherman were able to dive to the vehicle together and attach two cables to the police vehicle. Their efforts to open the jammed-up doors were unsuccessful. In a last effort to remove Officer Winzer from the vehicle, both officers broke windows with their hands and finally were able to free Winzer at 10:40 p.m. They swam him to the west bank, where the Life Flight medical crew pronounced him dead at 10:55 p.m. He was thirty years old.

His wife Lavendra and eight-year old son Corey survived Officer Winzer. Also mourning his death were his parents, F. A. and Maggie Winzer, sisters Lela Jenkins, Mattie Winzer and Annie B. Williams and brothers Michael Winzer, Frank A. Winzer Jr. and Sergeant Jessie D. Winzer. Three grandparents also survived – Mavis Lewis, Nancy Sumlin and Gus Winzer. At the time of his death, Officer Andrew Winzer had custody of his fourteen-year-old brother Frank Jr.

The body of Officer Winzer lay in state on Monday, February 22, from 3 p.m. until 9 p.m. at the Carl Barnes Cathedral Chapel at 746 West 22nd Street and from 11 a.m. until 1 p.m. at the Greater Zion Baptist Church, 1620 Dolly Wright. Services were conducted from there at 1 p.m. and interment followed at the Paradise North Cemetery, 10401 West Montgomery Road.

Newspaper accounts and interviews of the officers involved in the rescue efforts quoted Officer Shipley as saying, "In any rescue, there are a lot of maybes." If the vehicle had not been so severely damaged when it hit the guard rail as well as when it struck the bottom of the bayou, there might have been a chance to get the officer out sooner. Taking only a minute to gear up, Shipley dived into the water and located the vehicle very quickly. The hope was that maybe, just maybe, the cold water slowed down the officer's body functions and gave rescuers the few extra minutes needed to revive him. Also, the officers were hopeful that maybe an air pocket had miraculously formed inside the police car.

Unfortunately, neither of these happened since the car's roof had been crushed when it landed upside down on the bayou floor. Shipley recalled that there was a lot of anger and frustration after Officer Winzer was pulled out and pronounced dead. He was quoted as saying he was angry that we couldn't get there sooner with the equipment that officers should be carrying in cars while on patrol. Officer Shipley had nothing but praise for the patrol officers who attempted a rescue dressed only in their patrol uniforms. He went on to say that he and other trained divers knew what to expect, having done it before.

However, these other officers just reacted in an effort to save a fellow officer. To this day they deserve heartfelt praise for their valiant efforts, as do both Officers Shipley and Leatherman, who sustained cuts when they broke the windows of the patrol car with their bare hands.

In 2003, Officer Redman related that he was very close friends with Officer Andrew Winzer and related the details of the original call they received that night. He also recalled that night that after it was broadcast that a police unit had gone into the bayou, North Shepherd Sergeant Frank Escobedo began a roll call via radio in an attempt to determine who was missing. When he ascertained that Officer Winzer's unit was out to Central and had already left the station, he feared that Winzer was the officer in the bayou. Those fears were confirmed a short time later.

After rescuers recovered Officer Winzer from the bayou, Sergeant Escobedo and Officer Redman were assigned the task of making the death notification to the officer's wife. His words cannot describe the emotions associated with this grim task. As with the Homicide Division when an officer is killed, the Accident Division responded in an all-out effort to conduct a thorough investigation into this tragedy, which was believed to be the first drowning death of a Houston police officer while on duty. Officers R. V. Ruiz, P. B. Nelson and S. D. Mireles conducted the original investigation. Lieutenant J. L. Davis and Sergeant B. J. Garrett supervised the overall investigation.

Officer Ruiz was assigned to be the case agent, assisted by dayshift Accident officer D. R. Boyer. Many other Accident officers assisted in various segments of the investigation. They were Officers K. E. Sampson, C. D. Deandra, J. P. Walsh, T. L. Burnett, S. Gamez, M. D. Lowder and C. B. Staggs. Homicide Division CSU Officer P. K. Breen also assisted at the scene.

The suspect, Andres Alfaro, was arrested at the scene. Breath and blood tests revealed negative alcohol in his system. Further blood tests detected no controlled substances or dangerous drugs. He was an illegal immigrant from El Salvador previously deported on July 24, 1984. He had obviously returned illegally once again and his Texas driver's license was suspended for safety responsibility issues the day before this tragedy took place.

The law was researched thoroughly by Officers Ruiz and Boyer with several assistant district attorneys. Ultimately, he was issued a citation for running a red light and charged with driving while license suspended, a misdemeanor. In August 1988, he pleaded no contest and received a three-day jail sentence and a $450 fine. He remained in the United States.

The condition of the guardrail became a major factor in this accident. The twenty-foot section was recovered from the bayou and found to be in a deplorable state of rust along with the remaining sections at the roadway. A Houston Chronicle article dated February 26, 1988 said the guardrail was thirty years old and designed to restrain pedestrians, not vehicles. The article also indicated it would not meet modern safety standards for new bridge construction. The city of Houston had no formal routine to inspect guardrails.

While this situation revealed a serious safety concern, nothing was done to begin inspecting other locations since the usual budget issues were used as an excuse. This particular guardrail was soon replaced with similar type materials. It was not until about 1995 that it was finally replaced with a heavy-duty concrete railing that hopefully would stop a vehicle going the five miles per hour, the speed that tests showed Officer Winzer's vehicle was traveling at the time of his fatal accident.

Another Chronicle article described Officer Winzer's love for kids and his use of sports as an avenue to turn kids away from the hazards of street life. He was actively involved in the Police Athletic League and used his own personal funds to take kids to Astros baseball games or to the AstroWorld amusement park.

On August 3, 1988, the Houston City Council voted to change the name of Carver Park at 7500 Carver Road to Andrew Winzer Park. Community leaders in the Acres Homes area requested the change through their council representative, then-Councilman Dale Gorczynski. All of them knew Officer Winzer personally and had deep respect for him and his influence on children.

In April 2003, Lavendra Winzer resided in Northwest Houston, as did her son Corey, who was twenty-three. F. A. Winzer and Maggie Winzer are deceased. So is Winzer's brother Jessie, who was a sergeant with the Ruston, Louisiana Police Department. Siblings Mattie, Annie and Michael all resided in Houston. Sister Lela lived in Dallas and brother Frank was in California. Grandmother Mrs. Mavis Lewis was still living but grandmother Nancy Sumlin and grandfather Gus Winzer died.

Officer Walter Redman transferred to Narcotics later the year of the accident. He resigned to join the FBI in 1995 but returned to the department shortly thereafter. He served with the U. S. State Department in Bosnia for fifteen months and returned to the Narcotics Division.

In 2003, Sergeant Frank Escobedo was still assigned to the North Division. T. L. Rodgers became a sergeant at the North Command. Heidi A. Duslher became a sergeant in the Auto Theft Division and in 2006, is retired. Officer C. A. Byrd worked in Special Operations. Officer J. P. Tyler of Special Operations, who stated he used his childhood experiences in diving in Louisiana bayous that night without any gear, was assigned to the Lake Houston Police Patrol in 2003. Officer M. L. Pappillion became a night shift jail sergeant.

Of the Dive Team members, Officer J. S. Shipley was assigned to the Vice Division in 2003. Officer D. G. Ritchey remained with the Dive Team. Officer M. G. Gage worked in Mounted Patrol. S. K. Leatherman was a sergeant in Narcotics. Officer R. J. Parker, after a lengthy term of service in SWAT, was assigned to Major Offenders. Sergeant P. L. Blackshear worked in Special Operations and retired from that assignment. As for the primary accident investigators and supervisors in 2003, Officer R. V. Ruiz was a Tactical Unit sergeant at Eastside, Officer P. B. Nelson resigned from HPD, Officer S. D. Mireles remained with the Accident Division, Lieutenant Davis was assigned to the Juvenile Division and Sergeant B. J. Garrett retired in 1994.

Marker for Officer Winzer reads as follows:

WINZER, ANDREW (ALSO HAS A PHOTO) JUNE 24, 1957-FEB 18, 1988   BADGE #4330 BELOVED, LET US LOVE ONE ANOTHER: FOR LOVE IS OF GOD: AND EVERY ONE THAT LOVETH IS BORN OF GOD, AND KNOWETH GOD. 1 JOHN 4:7

A 100 Club marker has also been placed.

86

Officer Elston Morris Howard
Badge #2818
July 19, 1988

Career Criminal Jennings Assessed Death Penalty in the Arcade Murder of Officer Elston Howard

Elston Morris Howard was born on September 18, 1963, in Houston. He attended Betsy Ross Elementary School, Burbank Junior High School and graduated from the Houston Contemporary Learning Center in 1982. He served the City of Houston as a community service officer before joining the department in HPD Cadet Class No. 111, taking the oath as a Houston police officer on June 10, 1983. After working Radio Patrol at North Shepherd and Central for two years, he transferred to the Vice Division on July 3, 1985.

On Tuesday, July 19, 1988, Officer Elston Howard and his partner, Officer Milford Sistrunk, worked the 7 p.m. to 3 a.m. shift out of the Vice Division. At about 11:15 p.m., they went to the Empire Adult Bookstore (also known as "Mr. Peepers"), located at 4330 Richmond, in the Galleria area of west Houston just inside the Loop 610. Officer Sistrunk entered the business and paid the clerk for admission to the video booths, knowing in advance that this particular establishment did not possess a current City of Houston arcade license. This location was a repeat violator of the arcade ordinance.

After Sistrunk was admitted, Howard entered the establishment and advised the clerk that he was under arrest for not having an arcade license. The clerk also was advised to call someone to take custody of the premises. Officer Howard was in plainclothes, but for the purpose of this arrest, was attired in a marked Houston Police Department raid jacket. The officer had placed his hand-held radio on the counter after calling the dispatcher for a patrol unit to make the "wagon call." He then proceeded to complete an arrest blotter while waiting for this unit.

The plan was for Officer Sistrunk, also in plainclothes, to exit the store so he would not be recognized as an officer, thereby allowing him to make future cases on the business. Sistrunk was to wait outside for Howard to complete the arrest and have the uniformed unit pick up the prisoner. While Sistrunk was outside, he had radio contact at some point with his partner, who also called the Vice Division desk officer to obtain an incident number.

Sistrunk went outside to use the pay phone and then next door to contact Howard by police radio to make sure everything was proceeding smoothly. In doing so, he heard Howard speaking by radio to Vice. He then asked him to go to Channel 8, but received no response. After Sistrunk contacted the Vice Division, he was advised that Howard had just been in touch.

OFFICER ELSTON MORRIS HOWARD

While Sistrunk waited outside, he noticed a black male leave the bookstore. Several minutes later he saw a Houston fire truck pull up in front of the building. His immediate thought: Something bad happened. He quickly entered the store and found Officer Howard lying on the floor, bleeding from the head. Houston Fire Department EMS personnel treated Officer Howard at the scene and transported him to Ben Taub General Hospital. Despite a valiant effort, Officer Elston Howard was pronounced dead at 12:35 a.m. July 20, 1988. He was only twenty-four years and ten months old.

Officer Howard was survived by his parents, Alcano and Era Mae Howard, daughter Tyesha Victoria Boudreaux Howard, and two sisters-Sheila Howard Agee and Alvonda Michelle Howard, half-brother Eugene Howard, and half-sister Virginia Howard Lane. Also, his fiance, Carolyn Ann Thompson, survived him.

Visitation for Officer Howard was held on Friday afternoon at the Lockwood Funeral Home at 9402 Lockwood from 2-5 p.m. and then from 7-9 p.m. at the Pleasant Grove Baptist Church, 2801 Conti Street at Jensen Drive. Funeral services were held at this church at 11 a.m. Saturday with the Reverends C. L. Jackson and Victor Archer, a fellow HPD officer and friend, officiating. This is a very large sanctuary but too small to accommodate the estimated crowd of 2,000, which appropriately included Mayor Kathy Whitmire and Police Chief Lee P. Brown. Burial followed at the Forest Lawn North Cemetery (now called Calvary Hill Cemetery) at 21723 Aldine Westfield Road.

Homicide Lieutenant Greg T. Neely, who supervised the scene investigation and the follow-up, directed an in-depth investigation – unquestionably an all-out effort by Homicide. Neely assigned Sergeants Ted C. Bloyd, Dennis J. Gafford and John J. Silva to begin this "who-dun-it" capital murder of a police officer investigation. Sergeant Terry M. Ross was assigned to conduct the hospital investigation.

Crime Scene Unit Officer Dec S. Wilker conducted the evidentiary segment of the scene investigation, carefully documenting all physical evidence from the store. CSU Officer Tory Tyrell assisted her. Firearms Examiner Charlie Anderson made the crime scene investigation as did Latent Fingerprint Examiner W. C. "Chuck" Sheldon. Sergeants L. B. "Boyd" Smith and John Swaim were on call on this particular night and were summoned in to begin the follow-up investigation.

Officers learned from the store clerk that while Officer Howard completed his paperwork at the counter dressed in clearly marked HPD raid attire and with a police radio on the counter, the suspect walked directly toward him and fired three shots from close range. The bullets struck him in the head and neck area. He was never able to draw his service weapon from his ankle holster to return fire. As he struggled toward the front door to get away from his assailant, he fell to the floor. The suspect then stood over the seriously wounded officer and fired once more at the officer's head.

The suspect then calmly forced the store clerk at gunpoint to empty the contents of the cash register and took the clerk's personal belongings. He then left the store.

Meanwhile, information surfaced that there had been a series of recent robberies of adult bookstores in Southwest Houston. While at the scene, Sergeant Gafford received information from Patrol Sergeant Eddie Day that a similar robbery with a suspect of the same description had happened earlier this same night at another bookstore in the area. Lieutenant Neely assigned Homicide Sergeant J. M. Castillo as well as Sergeants Smith and Swaim to begin a crime analysis on these robberies. They learned that there were in fact five other robberies with similar descriptions of an African-American suspect, as well as several in which he was accompanied by a white male.

Later the first morning after the murder, Homicide Captain Bobby Adams took command of the investigation, assigning Lieutenant G. A. Mason of a dayshift Murder Squad to coordinate this investigation with Lieutenant Neely. Also assigned to assist were Homicide Sergeants Tom Ladd, Mike Kardatzke, Jim Ladd and Eric Mehl. Working closely with Homicide were Robbery Sergeants W. H. "Bill" Lawrence and Johnny Clinton, who were investigating several of the previous robberies. Others that assisted in various segments of the investigation were Homicide Sergeants Ted Thomas, Rueben Anderson, Roy Ferguson, George Dollins, Jim Ramsey, George Alderete and Phil Trumble and Robbery Sergeant Joe Levingston, as well as a number of others who performed investigative duties as needed.

This same day, Officer M. R. Edwards of Central Patrol came forward with information regarding the robbery of an establishment known as the Kindred Spirits on Richmond Avenue. This robbery happened on July 8, 1988. Officer Edwards' information was that one of the witnesses to this robbery personally knew the black male suspect as Robert Jennings. The description of Jennings also fit that of the suspect who murdered Officer Howard. Further investigation revealed that Robert Jennings (African-American, 30) had previously been assessed a thirty-year sentence for robbery but had been paroled in May 1988.

Based on this information, investigators wanted to again interview witnesses in the July 8 robbery. They made it a top priority. Sergeants Smith, Swaim, Clinton and Lawrence began to locate these individuals. The witness who claimed to know Jennings, however, was at this time "unable" to positively identify Jennings' photo. After several other witnesses positively identified this suspect as the individual who had robbed them at gunpoint at Kindred Spirits, the original witness finally admitted that he was afraid of Jennings and was reluctant to make the identification. However, he eventually made positive ID.

Investigating officers took sworn written statements from these witnesses and obtained a probable cause warrant for the arrest of Robert Jennings on the earlier robbery. The investigation progressed in a positive direction with an all-out search for Jennings.

Later on Wednesday evening, while searching for Jennings, investigators learned from a relative of his that he had been shot in the hand and was presently in Ben Taub General Hospital being treated. Homicide Sergeants Tom Ladd, Mike Kardatzke and Eric Mehl immediately went to Ben Taub to arrest Robert Jennings on the probable cause warrant in connection with the Kindred Spirits robbery.

They found Jennings and gave him the proper legal warning. After a series of denials of any involvement in any robberies, the suspect admitted to robbing the Kindred Spirits along with a man identified as David Harvell (White Male, Age Unknown), whom Jennings said was also the one who shot him in the left hand. Investigators contacted several other robbery complainants and witnesses who picked Jennings out of photo spreads. As a result, more robbery charges were filed on him in order to keep him in custody while the capital murder investigation progressed.

On Friday, July 29, Jennings was released from Ben Taub and brought directly to 61 Riesner where a live lineup was held with the numerous witnesses from the Empire Book Store, the scene of Officer Howard's murder. After this lineup and positive identification by several witnesses, Jennings was again warned and questioned. He soon admitted to detectives that he shot a man during a robbery of the Empire Book Store. Investigators also determined from doctors at Ben Taub that the bullet in Jennings' hand could be removed. Jennings signed a consent-to-search his body for this bullet. Doctors later recovered it upon the suspect's return to the hospital.

Basically, Jennings said that his partner in crime was David Harvell, whom he had met in prison. Recently they had just by chance met up in the "Gulfton ghetto" area on the Southwest side and began hanging out, drinking, doing drugs and pulling robberies together. On the night of Officer Howard's death they were in Harvell's car. Harvell stayed outside to act as the lookout while Jennings went in to rob the place. He previously had been inside and knew the layout. After shooting the officer, he and Harvell ran back to their car and when he told Harvell that he had "screwed up really bad and shot a security guard," Harvell grew angry. He picked up Jennings' gun and shot him in the hand. Jennings jumped out the car window and fled.

Meanwhile, other detectives began the search for Harvell. His criminal record showed his mother lived in Euless in North Central Texas. It also showed that he had served time in the Texas Department of Corrections for robbery, having been paroled in February 1988 to Harris County until 1998. A probable cause warrant was issued for his arrest on the robberies. On Saturday, July 23, after Euless authorities were alerted that Harvell's mother lived there, they arrested the second suspect.

Within several hours of receiving this information, while the funeral of Officer Howard was being held, Lieutenant Neely and Sergeants Tom Ladd, Eric Mehl and Boyd Smith left for Euless, which is located between Dallas and Fort Worth.

After going over the details of the arrest with Euless police officers, Harvell was warned and questioned regarding his involvement in the robberies and the murder of Officer Elston Howard. Harvell told basically the same story as Jennings, adding that after he shot Jennings, he and his girlfriend left for San Antonio, where they spent the night. They then left west on Interstate 10, driving aimlessly to El Paso, trying to figure out how to handle his latest problem with the law. Harvell then decided that he would leave for Euless, where he could lay low at his mother's house.

Harvell said that on the way back from El Paso, he drove a short way out into the desert and buried the .38-caliber pistol used in Officer Howard's murder and the wounding of Robert Jennings. After interviewing Harvell, his girlfriend and his mother – who verified parts of his story – investigators needed to put into place the next piece of the crime's puzzle. They contacted the Texas Department of Public Safety with the gun information and DPS officials provided a Cessna airplane. While Lieutenant Neely and Sergeant Mehl drove back to Houston with stolen property recovered with Harvell's arrest in Euless, Sergeants Smith and Tom Ladd put Harvell onto the plane and flew to El Paso. There they met up with several Texas Rangers who drove them east on Interstate 10 where, miraculously, Harvell was able to show them where he buried the murder weapon. They recovered it. Harvell was returned by airplane to Houston along with the recovered pistol. Firearms Examiner Charlie Anderson matched this weapon's ballistics to the bullets recovered from Officer Howard's body and Robert Jennings' hand.

Newspaper accounts revealed that the criminal history of Robert Mitchell Jennings dated back to 1972, when at the age of fourteen he was declared a juvenile delinquent. In 1973, a court ordered him sent to a trade school in New Waverly. When his errant conduct continued there, he was sent to a Texas Youth Council Reformatory. His adult criminal record began in 1975 at age eighteen with arrests for burglary and theft and was followed by a five-year robbery conviction.

He was released early in 1978, when he promptly went on a crime spree in the South Park-Griggs area of Houston's south side. According to newspaper accounts of this spree, he committed four armed robberies and several burglaries within five days. He pled "no contest" to three of these charges and was given three thirty-year sentences, which were to run concurrently. Mysteriously, that thirty-year term became ten years and Jennings was paroled to Harris County in May 1988. His early parole led to the brutal capital murder of Officer Elston Howard.

While David Harvell did not pull the trigger of the gun that killed Officer Howard, his criminal history paralleled that of Jennings. Harvell went to the Texas Department of Corrections in 1979 and served six years of an eighteen-year sentence on robbery and theft charges. Getting out in 1985, he went back in 1986, supposedly to do five years for aggravated robbery. He did two of the five and was back out on the streets with the likes of Robert Jennings.

In July 1989, after several days of jury selection, the capital murder trial of Robert Mitchell Jennings began in state District Judge Thomas Routt's criminal court. Harris County District Attorney Johnny Holmes took personal charge of the prosecution, ably assisted by veteran Assistant DAs George Lambright and Bob Stabe. Defense attorneys Connie Williams and Grant Hardeway represented Jennings.

On July 11, 1989, a jury took just more than an hour to convict Robert Jennings of capital murder in Officer Howard's death. The trial then commenced to the punishment phase and Holmes' prosecution team paraded a number of robbery victims and witnesses before the jury to share their knowledge of Jennings' criminal escapades. On July 13, the jury came back with the verdict acknowledging that Robert Mitchell Jennings was a continuing threat to society and assessed him the death penalty.

Jennings languished on Death Row, slowly exhausting his rights to appeals. Officer Howard's dying appeals to Jennings not to shoot him anymore were not heard, but Jennings' own appeals for his life are automatically processed through the Texas criminal justice system. He is nearing eighteen years on Death Row and has lived nearly nineteen years longer than Officer Howard.

In 2002, David Lee Harvell was in the Telford Unit of the Texas Department of Criminal Justice in New Boston, having pled guilty in 1989 and receiving a fifty-five-year sentence. Even though his sentence extends to 2043, his first parole eligibility date was April 21, 2002. Houston police officers and the family of Elston Howard hope he serves his full time but aren't holding their breaths.

Long-time Homicide Captain Bobby Adams retired in March 2002 after forty-three years with HPD. Lieutenants Mason and Neely remained in Homicide, supervising murder squads. They retired in 2005 and 2006, respectively. Sergeants Gafford and Silva both made lieutenant in the early 1990s. After returning to Homicide for a short time as lieutenants, they both moved on to different assignments. In 2007, Lieutenant John Silva worked in the Criminal Intelligence Division and Lieutenant Dennis Gafford is assigned to the Narcotics Division.

In 2007, Sergeants Ted Bloyd, Tom Ladd, Jim Ladd, Jim Ramsey, Phil Trumble, Ted Thomas, George Dollins, Reuben Anderson, and John Swaim are all retired. Eric Mehl is assigned to the Homicide Division Cold Case Unit. Sergeant Mike Kardatzke retired in 1989. Robbery Sergeant Clinton retired from the Robbery Division and Robbery Sergeant W. H. Lawrence made lieutenant and headed the Forgery Detail out of Burglary and Theft from where he retired. Sergeant John Castillo left HPD. Sergeant Boyd Smith died in a shooting accident in 2003. Roy Ferguson works in the Recruiting Division and George Alderete is in an Administrative position. Joe Livingston is a Lieutenant over the Homicide Family Violence Unit.

Officer Dee Wilker retired in 1999 and Officer Tory Tyrell worked in Narcotics. Sergeant Terry Ross retired in 1993 and served as a justice of the peace in Fayette County. Firearms Examiner Charlie Anderson retired in 1998 and Fingerprint Examiner Chuck Sheldon retired in 2005. Officer M. R. Edwards stayed in Central Patrol and Sergeant Eddie Day later made lieutenant and was assigned to Burglary and Theft.

When Homicide Sergeant Ted Bloyd made the scene investigation that night at 4330 Richmond, while taking his notes he observed that Officer Elston Howard wore Badge No. 2818. It took him only an instant to realize that this was the HPD badge number assigned to him during his six years as a patrol officer from 1975 to 1981 before becoming a Homicide detective.

While this investigation progressed rapidly with some very important (and lucky) breaks along the way, an investigation of this type demanded a tremendous amount of detail in preparing a case that would withstand the rigorous defense put forth in a capital murder case. This was an outstanding piece of work, especially considering the number of Homicide and Robbery investigators involved in coordinating it and working for one common goal – identifying and convicting the persons responsible for the murder of one of their own, one of Houston's finest.

Officer Sistrunk worked Vice for several years following this offense, and in 2002, was assigned to the dayshift of the Special Operations Division.

After the death of their youngest child, Mr. and Mrs. Howard, as well as Elston's two sisters, half-brother and half-sister, nieces and nephews, aunts and uncles, had to go on with their lives. Mrs. Era Mae Howard confirmed her statement that she and her family could not have endured this tragedy without their Christian faith. While they – as do many of us – become discouraged with the slow pace of the final earthly disposition of this case in the criminal justice system, she held out the hope that justice for the tragic death of her son will ultimately prevail.

In 2007, Mr. and Mrs. Howard still resided in Houston, with Mrs. Howard no longer working outside the home but baby-sitting for three great-grandchildren. Sister Sheila Agee and her husband were the parents of Michael Jerrod Agee, twenty-nine, now a Houston Police Officer assigned to the Jail Division. Their daughter is Ashlie Renee Agee, nineteen, a graduate of SFA University. Sister Alvonda Howard resides in Austin, employed by IBM. The officer's half-brother Eugene and half-sister Virginia both resided in the Houston area.

Officer Howard's daughter, Tyesha Howard, will be graduating from SFA this year. Her mother kept her close to the Howard family through the years since Elston Howard was killed. In addition, Officer Howard had three aunts and five uncles and their families who also were survivors of this tragedy.

The original marker for Officer Howard consisted of an upright monument which read:

HOWARD, OFFICER ELSTON MORRIS
SEPT. 18, 1963 - JULY 20, 1988
AN INSPIRATION TO ALL WHO KNEW HIM
(ALSO BADGE #2818 AND A CITY OF HOUSTON LOGO)

A 100 CLUB marker has also been placed to honor his memory and the manner in which he died.

87

Officer Florentine Munoz Garcia Jr.
Badge #4412
November 10, 1989 (Veteran's Day)

Officer Garcia, Escorting Funeral Procession, Killed Instantly by Impatient Motorist

Florentino Munoz Garcia, Jr. was born January 9, 1962, in El Campo, the sixth of eight children born to his parents, Florentino R. and Mary Lou Garcia. After graduation from John H. Reagan High School in Houston, he attended Houston Community College as well as Coastal Carolina Community College. Garcia volunteered for service to his country and proudly served in the United States Marine Corps. After deciding to settle in Houston, he joined the Houston Police Department in Police Cadet Class No. 124 on October 15, 1984, graduating and taking his oath of office February 23, 1985. He wore Badge No. 4412.

His original assignment was to the Northwest Patrol Division but he soon transferred to the Accident Division. While working there, he became aware of the Solo Motorcycle Detail. Openings in Solos were rare. Yet Officer Garcia became one of a small group of individual officers who sought and received HPD's permission to work in their own divisions while working approved off-duty extra jobs. These officers, just as Solo officers, purchased their own motorcycles and had these motors appropriately marked and equipped with the necessary emergency equipment. Their goal was to provide a service to the city of Houston and at the same time supplement their income to improve the quality of life for their families.

On Friday, November 10, 1989, Officer Garcia, a divorced man with two young daughters, was officially assigned to the night shift of the Accident Division. He had received approval for an HPD extra job escorting a funeral procession in the near east end. This assignment was to escort the

211

procession from the Felix Morales Funeral Home at 2901 Canal to the gravesite. His partner, working in the same status in this assignment, was Sergeant Harry Zamora.

At 10:15 a.m. in the 3000 block of Canal, the funeral procession was eastbound, escorted by the two Houston police officers. The final destination of this procession was the Forest Lawn South Cemetery at 8701 Almeda Genoa Road. Sergeant Zamora was the lead escort in this twenty-vehicle line. His duty was to halt traffic at the major intersections on a predetermined route. Officer Garcia, after having escorted the last processional vehicle through a controlled intersection, would proceed forward as quickly as possible to relieve the sergeant.

OFFICER FLORENTINO M. GARCIA JR.

Officer Garcia had his emergency lights on and used his siren intermittently, as was his practice. He was in the right side of the roadway, heading east. He headed around the procession in order to relieve Zamora at the next controlled intersection. As he made the move, a 1978 Chevrolet Chevette, driven by Felipe Jesus Martinez Jr., was westbound on Canal. Martinez then attempted a left turn through the middle of the funeral procession.

This somewhat impatient motorist attempted to break the procession line. His goal was to get to his doctor's office by going south on North Palmer Street. In doing so, his vehicle struck Officer Garcia, toppling his motorcycle and knocking him from his machine into the rear of a parked vehicle which faced west on Canal. Even though he wore his motorcycle helmet, he received massive head injuries as well as a crushed chest and left leg.

Sergeant Zamora was just a short distance away on Canal, awaiting Officer Garcia's relief at that intersection when he observed a large gathering of citizens and vehicles around what looked like an accident scene. Zamora immediately left the procession in search of Garcia. He found a physician, Dr. Amiris Alcover, rendering medical aid to his partner. Dr. Alcover, working at a nearby medical clinic, had heard the collision and immediately came out to render emergency CPR on Officer Garcia. There was little the doctor could do. Officer Florentino Garcia, transported by a Houston Fire Department ambulance to Hermann Hospital, was pronounced dead at Hermann at 10:52 a.m. He was twenty-seven years old.

Officer Garcia was survived by his two young daughters, eight-year-old Staci Marie Garcia and six-year-old Christine Celeste Garcia, as well as his former wife, Sonya Garcia. Also mourning his untimely death were his parents, Florentino and Mary Lou Garcia Sr. of Bay City, and a large family of siblings which consisted of brothers Natividad and Raymond of Houston and five sisters, Mary Jane Montalbo and Sylvia Castaneda of Bay City, Ophelia Rodriguez of Katy, Lucy Dingas of Fort Rucker, Alabama, and Linda Gagnon of Killeen. He also left behind a grandmother, Mrs. Antonio Munoz of Bay City, and a fiancee, Wendy Ruff of Houston, as well as a growing number of nieces and nephews.

Heights Funeral Home, 1317 Heights Blvd., was in charge of funeral arrangements. Visitation was held on Sunday, November 12, 1989, from 5 p.m. until 9 p.m. A Rosary was conducted at 7:30 p.m. Monday, November 13, 1989 at the Heights Funeral Home.

Services for Officer Garcia were held at 1:30 p.m. the next day at Christ the King Catholic Church, 4400 North Main. Burial followed with full military honors at the Houston National Cemetery on Veterans Memorial Drive.

The primary accident investigators of this traffic event were Officers K. W. Sexton and D. R. Boyer. They were met at the scene by the first responding Radio Patrol officer, J. N. Landgrebe. Also at the scene was Officer D. L. Harwell, who actually transported the suspect to Ben Taub General Hospital for blood tests. Officer R. S. Cedeno questioned the suspect, Martinez, who spoke very little English. Officer R. V. Ruiz also assisted in the initial interview with the suspect, who was given an intoxilyzer examination and was determined not to have been intoxicated at the time of the deadly collision. It was learned, however, that Martinez was a consistent traffic violator, especially in the area of the State of Texas Safety Responsibility statutes.

The day of this tragedy was Veteran's Day, a city holiday. A Spanish-speaking officer was needed to perform an in-depth interview with the suspect. Homicide Division Chicano Squad Sergeant Cecil T. Mosqueda and Investigator J. L. Escalante, both veteran interviewers, were assigned to this task.

The suspect voluntarily spoke with investigators and stated that he was en route to a local clinic for treatment of an injured eye he suffered during a round of horseplay with other family members the previous night. He said that he was attempting to make a left turn and go through the funeral procession and did not see any flashing lights, nor did he hear a siren.

What role this alleged eye injury played into this tragedy remains a mystery. Newspaper accounts indicated that Martinez's right eye was swollen totally shut, deeming it highly probable that it was a significant factor. Martinez indicated that a male driver in the procession motioned for him to go ahead and make his turn. As he did so his vehicle was struck on the right side by Officer Garcia's motorcycle. Accident Division officers determined that Officer Garcia was airborne for thirty-one feet before his body struck the parked vehicle.

Officers Sexton and Boyer were assisted in this investigation by Sergeant J. Montemayor, who interviewed a passenger in the suspect's vehicle, the suspect's cousin who was an illegal immigrant from Mexico who could not speak English. This individual told basically the same story as the suspect regarding the driver motioning him through the funeral procession.

The suspect was found to be in violation for failure to yield right of way making a left turn, cutting through a funeral procession. Officers filed on him for negligent homicide in County Criminal Court at Law No. 10. Bail was set on this Class A misdemeanor at $500, considered by many officers to be light treatment for a deadly traffic violator.

In 2003, Staci was twenty-two and Christine twenty. They lived in the Katy area. Both attended college, having benefited from the 100 Club of Houston's annuity set aside for that purpose. Staci had marriage plans for the summer of 2004. An interview with the deceased officer's mother, Mrs. Mary Lou Garcia, as well as his sister Sylvia, found that they have lost contact with the two daughters.

Florentino Garcia Sr. died in 2000. In 2003, Mrs. Garcia resided in Spring Branch with her son Natividad. Sister Mary Jane died in 1999, leaving three children, Mary Lou, Theresa and Nora. Sister Sylvia lived in Bay City with seven children, Enas, Martin, Nicholas, Jessica, William and twins, Joshua and Justin.

Sister Ophelia lived in Houston and had two children, Valeria and Erica. Sister Lucy resided in Katy, the mother of Gregory, Christopher and Matthew. Brother Raymond lived in Houston, the father of Paul. Sister Linda was a Florida resident, the mother of Lindsey, Timothy and twin boys, Richard and Patrick.

Of all of the above mentioned nieces and nephews, several of them never had the opportunity to know their Uncle Florentino, the Houston police officer.

While Officer Garcia and Sergeant Zamora were off-duty as the time of the fatal incident, they were on a department-approved extra job. Additionally, City Ordinance 45-253, entitled Police Escort, mandates that "Each funeral procession shall be accompanied by a police motorcycle escort which shall be a part of the funeral procession and the police officer's motorcycle shall constitute an emergency vehicle when the siren and red lights are in operation. There shall be not less than one police motorcycle escort when the vehicles in the funeral procession, including the mortuary vehicles, do not exceed ten (10) and there shall be not less than two (2) police motorcycle escorts when such vehicles exceed ten (10)."

This line of duty death ruling was further reinforced by an opinion of the Houston city attorney. The importance of this ordinance was further indicated by the fact that after the funeral procession continued by necessity without escort, one of the vehicles was involved in a major accident with no serious injuries at the intersection of Airport and Monroe.

Sergeant Harry Zamora became a lieutenant assigned to the Northwest Patrol Division. In 2003, the primary investigators, Officers Sexton and Boyer, still worked in the Accident Division, as did Sergeant Montemayor, a Hit and Run Detail supervisor. Officer Harwell also was in the Accident Division and Officer Cedeno was assigned to Southwest Patrol. Officer Ruiz became a sergeant at the Eastside Patrol Station. The first Officer on the scene, Officer Landgrebe, retired. Sergeant Mosqueda remained a Homicide Division supervisor-investigator and Officer Escalante was assigned to the Northeast Patrol Division.

In May 1990, the suspect was sentenced by County Court-at-Law Judge Sherman Ross to nine months in jail after having been convicted on April 12 of negligent homicide. Martinez also was fined $2,000. Martinez, who was illegally in the United States at the time of this deadly accident, either returned to Mexico or kept clean since there was no further record of him.

Officer Garcia was a veteran in the service of his country also, having served nearly four full years in the United States Marine Corps. His gravemarker at the Houston VA Cemetery reads as follows:

FLORENTINO M. GARCIA JR.
CPL   US MARINE CORPS
JAN 9, 1962 - NOV 10, 1989

88

Officer James Charles Boswell
Badge #2400
December 9, 1989

DEA-Supported Drug Informant Gets Frustrated, Murders Officer Boswell

James Charles Boswell was born November 29, 1960, in Meridian, Mississippi, the oldest of four sons and one daughter born to Mr. and Mrs. Cecil (Martha) Boswell. The family moved to Texas City and James graduated from Texas City High School in 1978. After high school he attended Lamar University in Beaumont, graduating in 1982 with a Bachelor of Science degree in Physical Education. Entering the field of education, he worked for three years in the Sinton and Liberty school districts as an athletic trainer and was a member of the National Athletic Trainer's Association. He was also an active member of the Baptist Church.

However, there was apparently something missing from Jim's life: police work. He achieved his lifelong ambition to become a police officer when he entered the Houston Police Academy as a member of Police Cadet Class No. 129 on May 28, 1985, graduating on September 28, 1985. He wore Badge No. 2400. His first assignment was to the Southwest Patrol Division – Evening Shift. After several years of admirable service as a Houston police officer, however, he resigned for personal reasons on July 29, 1988.

Upon returning to the education field, J. C. Boswell realized he had experienced a potent transfusion of policing in his blood. As a result, he submitted his reapplication to the Houston Police Department on January 5, 1989, a short six months – or just one semester – after his resignation. He was immediately accepted for re-employment. His previous supervisors – a captain, lieutenant and several sergeants – thought enough of Boswell to flood the Recruiting Division with recommendations that his application be processed as quickly as possible.

After his reinstatement, he was again assigned to the Southwest Patrol Division. An energetic young officer, he was known not to be bashful or afraid to go into any policing situation. Supervisors reunited Boswell with his old partner, Officer Clay M. Gainer, this time on the Night Shift.

On an extremely cold Friday night, December 8, 1989, Officers J. C. Boswell and Clay M. Gainer were assigned to ride Unit 15E42, whose beat was the area west of the Astrodome and around the South Main string of motels. Then, as now, this area had an extremely high crime rate. It was patrolled out of the Beechnut (now Southwest) Substation.

With Gainer driving and Boswell riding shotgun, they were southbound on Main Street when they observed a red Chevrolet stopped in the left lane just south of the intersection of Main and Westridge. The time now was 1 a.m., a Saturday morning. As they approached the vehicle, the driver began moving around and continued steering the car northbound across Westridge before pulling into the parking lot of the Stop 'n' Go convenience store.

As Gainer approached the vehicle and began speaking with the driver, Boswell walked to the passenger side and began conversing with a passenger. Both officers conducted departmentally approved interrogations about the activities of both individuals. Prior to releasing the traffic violator, both officers returned to their patrol vehicle. Gainer proceeded to complete a traffic citation while Boswell began a check on the unit's MDT with information on the passengers.

At this point, a family violence situation cropped up that was in no way related to the original traffic stop on this unusually frigid night. A frustrated young female approached the patrol car on the passenger side where Boswell was seated. She had been involved in an ongoing domestic dispute and the police were called to her apartment to settle the matter. However, she feared for her safety and a friend picked her up from her nearby apartment in order to get away before the situation became violent. Boswell and Gainer had earlier received and ran this call, but cleared the scene after they learned that she had left.

The family dispute complainant had then came upon these same officers at the scene of their traffic arrest on Main Street. Boswell asked the woman to remain and told her when they were finished with the traffic violator, they would follow her back to her apartment to resolve the problem.

At this point an individual named Craig Neil Olson, aka Craig Neil Ogan, entered the scene, further complicating the job Boswell and Gainer were attending to. Craig was a rather confused individual, whose background was totally unknown to the officers. He was truly the unknown factor that Houston police officers deal with on a daily basis. With both Boswell and Gainer completing paperwork on the traffic stop and a family violence call to run, they were now confronted with Craig Ogan.

Ogan walked over to the passenger side of the patrol car and tapped on the passenger door window where Officer Boswell was seated. The officer rolled down the window and Ogan began to tell a story about a Drug Enforcement Administration agent leaving him near this location. Ogan said he had worked with the DEA and that he was freezing. Boswell told Ogan to step away from the car, at which time Ogan continued to ramble that he was an informant for the DEA and that he was cold. Boswell, feeling threatened by someone standing outside the car while he was seated, got out and stood up, telling Ogan that they needed to leave to respond to a call.

Officer Gainer overheard the conversation and saw his partner get out of the car and unholster his weapon, holding it at his side in a non-threatening manner. Gainer then observed Boswell turn as if to unlock the right rear passenger door. Then Gainer got out of the car to assist his partner. However, as he was getting out of the car, Gainer heard Ogan tell Boswell, "Fuck you, then!" Ogan fired a shot and Boswell fell to the ground. Within a split second, Ogan apparently thought he wasn't receiving the response he wanted, pulled a pistol and shot Officer Boswell one time in the head.

OFFICER JAMES CHARLES BOSWELL

The officer fell to the pavement as Ogan ran away on foot, heading south on Main across Westridge. Gainer gave chase and with the lighting from the area businesses, he could clearly see that the suspect had a pistol. Gainer fired once and his weapon jammed. Clearing it, he fired again. The suspect fell in the grassy esplanade on Main and then wisely tossed his pistol away and raised his hands. Gainer caught up to him and handcuffed him.

With the immediate threat of more danger being removed, Officer Gainer returned to his partner. The original traffic violator, who worked in an emergency room, ran up to aid the fallen officer, as did a nurse driving by after completing her shift at the nearby medical center. Emergency medical technicians from the Houston Fire Department placed Officer James Boswell into their ambulance and rushed him to Ben Taub General Hospital where he died a short time later from a close contact gunshot wound to the head. He was twenty-nine years old.

Ogan was shot in the side. He underwent surgery at Ben Taub and was listed in serious condition.

Officer James C. "Boz" Boswell was survived by his parents, Mr. Cecil and Mrs. Martha Boswell of Meridian, Mississippi. Also mourning his death were his four siblings: brothers Michael Boswell (U. S. Navy) and wife Cindy of San Diego, California; Joey Boswell and wife Julie of Texas City; and Kenneth Mark Boswell and sister Cherie and husband David Lockhart, all from Meridian. He was also survived by grandmother, Josephine Stampley Jackson, grandfather Leslie Stampley and great-grandmother Wilma H. Johnson, all of Meridian, nieces Kayli and Danielle, nephews Joey Jr. and Josh, as well as numerous aunts, uncles and cousins.

Funeral services were held under the direction of the Earthman Funeral Home, 6700 Ferris in Bellaire. The body lay in state at the Earthman chapel and visitation was held on Monday, December 11, from 8 a.m. until 9 p.m. Funeral services were held at the Second Baptist Church, 6400 Woodway at Voss Road in Houston the next day at 9 a.m., with the Reverend David Dickson officiating.

Additionally, the family held a funeral/memorial service at the James Webb Funeral Home, 2514 7th Street in Meridian at 10 a.m. Thursday, December 14, 1989. This service was conducted by the Reverend Jim Brannon of the Highland Baptist Church. Burial followed at the Memorial Park in Meridian.

Upon receiving sketchy information from the scene and through the Watch Command, Homicide Lieutenant Greg T. Neely immediately assigned Sergeants Dale A. Atchetee and Theresa M. "Terry" Ross to the scene investigation. They spoke to the first officer on the scene, I. M. Row, who said she found Officer Boswell on the ground, attended to by several citizens. She called for LifeFlight immediately after seeing Boswell's condition. Atchetee and Ross had not been aware of the severity of the officer's wounds.

As more information from the tragic scene began to filter in, Lieutenant Neely expanded the response by assigning Sergeants Ted Bloyd and Tom Murray to investigate the hospital phase of this investigation.

Neely went to the scene to coordinate the investigation. Ideally, the hospital investigator's goal would be to speak to the injured officer as soon as possible in order to ascertain his version of the event. They then learned the sad news that Officer Boswell was not expected to survive his wound despite sophisticated medical actions.

Bloyd and Murray advised Neely of the severity of Boswell's condition. Being the experienced investigators they were, they immediately turned their attention to interviewing the suspect, who was being treated in the shock room next door to where Officer Boswell lay. They spoke to Officer O. R. Warren, who had ridden in the ambulance with Ogan en route to Ben Taub. Warren advised them of several unsolicited comments Ogan had made. He told them after he advised Ogan that Boswell had been shot in the head, he responded by saying, "Damn, I'm sorry. Don't let him die. Let it be me."

Officer Warren and EMT Chris Ridge, who was also in the back of the ambulance, heard these comments and carefully made notes as to the exact wording.

The two investigators identified themselves to Ogan, who immediately blurted out, "I got nothing to hide. I f____d up." He was then given his statutory warnings. His first comment after indicating that he understood his rights was that he "would give the officers the legal right to put a bullet through my head right now."

Other than asking for his DEA control agent to be contacted, he held nothing back from Bloyd and Murray, who were electronically recording the interview. He rambled on about being a DEA informer and that he was reassigned to Houston after things became too "hot" for him in the St. Louis area. Here in Houston on that cold Friday night, he had experienced trouble in a restaurant and was having difficulties getting a motel room. Then, when he finally got a room, he was dissatisfied with the heat. Of course, his story about shooting Officer Boswell was self-serving, as he indicated that he was being threatened with going to jail. After the officer pulled his nightstick, he shot him in self-defense. The evidence at the scene indicated that Officer Boswell had not pulled his nightstick.

Homicide Sergeants William "Bill" Stephens and James L. "Jim" Ramsey were called in from home to assist in the investigation. Being assigned to a recently formed officer-involved shooting team, these two sergeants assumed ultimate responsibility for the Boswell case. Their follow-up investigation showed that the suspect had rented a room at a nearby motel and was also in possession of a vehicle. At the hospital Ogan's property consisted of more than $3,000 in cash.

Uniformed officers guarded the entrance to Ogan's motel room and his vehicle while legal authority was obtained for a complete search of both. Assisting in this investigation were Homicide Sergeants Wayne Wendel, Mike Peters, Tom Ladd and M. E. Doyle and Crime Scene Unit Officers D. S. Wilker, J. R. Davis, J. I. Kennedy and T. Q. Williams.

After Ogan signed consents for these searches, the DEA was contacted so investigating officers could learn more about Ogan's background. Those searches resulted in the recovery of a shotgun from the motel room as well as numerous phone and contact numbers from Ogan's personal property. Officers learned that Ogan was dissatisfied about the room condition as well as the heater not working properly. He had a rather "heated" argument with the motel clerk over this situation. In short, when he approached Officer Boswell, he was a very frustrated and troubled individual. He needed an outlet for his frustration and unfortunately Boswell became that outlet.

The investigation continued with the information that Sergeants Stephens and Ramsey were able to learn about the background of this suspect, later officially identified as Craig Neil Olson, also known as Gregorio Olson, Craig Neil Ogan and Gregg Olson. Whatever his name, he was in custody and on the day following this offense, he was charged with capital murder of a peace officer in the 230th Criminal District Court of Harris County. The standard no bond applied.

Officer Boswell was an outspoken individual with strong ties to the then-strong Houston Police Patrolmen's Union (HPPU). His friends knew he had very strong negative feelings toward the then-Mayor of Houston, Kathy Whitmire. A talented cartoonist, he depicted Mayor Whitmire in less than complimentary ways through his drawings in the HPOU's publication, The Sentinel. He also openly supported her challenger in the mayor's election as recently as November 1989.

Local newspapers said Officer Boswell had been of the strong opinion that Mayor Whitmire "neither respected nor supported the Houston police officers." Articles also said Boswell had made the statement to a number of fellow officers that he would not want her at his funeral should he be killed. Through negotiations with the mayor and Officer Boswell's family, she did attend his funeral without incident.

The fact that Officer James C. Boswell had been laid to rest in his native state of Mississippi and that his killer was arrested and charged did not stop the work of the Homicide Division. Investigators needed to complete a full background investigation of the killer not only to shore up the already strong case but also to rebut any ridiculous allegations that the defense might present at trial. In fact there were a number of skeletons in this man's closet that the prosecution needed to know about.

Homicide Captain Bobby Adams assigned Lieutenant Richard Holland to supervise the extensive follow-up investigation required to bring this offender to justice. Holland and Sergeants Bill Stephens and Jim Ramsey began to trace the background of the troubled suspect, at one point traveling to Missouri to thoroughly unearth the details of Ogan's background and personality.

The investigation showed that two agencies of the federal government thought enough of Ogan to continue providing him with financial assistance even though there were serious misgiving about his effectiveness and stability. Tested as a child, Ogan was found to have an IQ of 140. However, his personality made it difficult for him to get along with anyone. Possessing a fiery temper, he was discharged from the United States Navy after several disciplinary encounters. In the last one he broke a hand after striking a steel wall in anger over a supervisor's directive.

Like the 1950s television series I Led Three Lives, Craig Ogan attempted to live his fanciful lives to the fullest. His goal was to become a successful DEA informant in order to obtain a good recommendation to the CIA. To say that he resided in a dream world was no stretch of the imagination. His DEA handler described him as one who often exaggerated reality, thereby making his life as a CI more intriguing and "romantic" than it actually was. He had been a suspect in numerous situations, having become involved in traffic altercations in Missouri, caught carrying a weapon and known for continually losing his temper.

Even though DEA agents cautioned him several times to discontinue carrying a weapon, he obviously continued the practice due to his extreme paranoia. Also, he was later described as a marginally effective informant but had in his possession several thousand dollars in cash at the time of this offense. He had just received payment from both the DEA and the IRS. The DEA handler knew each of these character traits and idiosyncrasies but still advised Ogan to move to Houston to "lay low for awhile" before continuing his undercover activities.

Officer Boswell in particular and the law enforcement community in general were professionally represented at Ogan's trial by the DA's Office. Chief Prosecutor Rusty Hardin took the lead. The appointed defense attorneys were Laura Ingle and Ken McLean. They contended Boswell had gotten out of his vehicle not only with a drawn nightstick, as Ogan had stated, but also with a drawn weapon, thereby provoking the shooting.

On Wednesday, June 13, 1990, the trial began in the courtroom of Criminal District Court Joe Kegans. Testimony from the defendant as well as several DEA agents who had worked with him as an informant over a period of fifteen years showed Ogan to be an individual who had difficulties dealing with all segments of society, whether family members, authority figures or friends. He was described as a "minimally successful federal drug informant" who was jokingly referred to by his DEA handlers as "Agent 005."

Officer Clay Morgan Gainer was called to the witness stand to verify one part of Ogan's story – that Officer Boswell, who felt threatened by Ogan's irrational actions, unholstered his pistol as he exited the police vehicle, holding it at his leg. However, Officer Gainer stated unequivocally that Officer Boswell never pointed it at Ogan nor did he threaten him with it.

With no other defense, Ogan took the stand in a weak attempt to justify his actions. He testified he felt in danger of his own life and consequently was forced to shoot and kill Boswell. Of course, his own testimony was in conflict with his statements in the ambulance and later at the hospital. Hardin tore Ogan to shreds on the stand, allowing the defendant give the judge and jury a good look at what he was all about.

On Monday, June 25, 1990, a jury convicted Craig Ogan of capital murder in the death of Houston Police Officer James C. Boswell. On the following Friday, after a day and a half of deliberation, the jury sentenced Craig Neil Ogan Jr. to death by lethal injection.

Quoting from newspapers account as recently as Nov. 17, 2002, nearly thirteen years after the death of Officer Boswell, his mother Martha said:

"Jim went to Lamar University on a scholarship. He was a teacher and an athletic trainer. He was working in Liberty when he asked me what I thought about him becoming a policeman. I told him, 'Son, it's your life. You've got to do what you want.' Jim was a street cop and loved being a cop."

In May 1989, seven months prior to his death in the line of duty, Boswell was severely beaten with his nightstick during a drug bust very near the location of his eventual death scene. He was treated with a total of seventy-two stitches from wounds received in the altercation. That suspect was given eighteen years in prison and even though he has been up for parole, he likely will serve the full sentence – unusual for this day and time.

Nearly thirteen years after Officer Boswell's tragic death, justice was served on the night of Tuesday, November 19, 2002. Craig Ogan was put to death by lethal injection amid the cries of his family that he had been a victim of many different types of bad circumstances and that it was not his fault that he shot Officer Boswell in the head at point blank range.

A large contingent of the Boswell family attended the execution. While full closure for the family of Officer Boswell is likely not possible in these circumstances, it is likely that this witnessing served a purpose toward that elusive goal.

Officer Gainer continued his HPD career after that terrible night in 1989. As with all partners of slain officers, Gainer's thoughts go back to that tragedy each day, always thinking of what he could have possibly done differently. However, as is the case in almost each and every similar situation, nothing could have prevented such a person as Ogan from doing this dirty deed.

Officer Gainer's reactions were such that he was able to prevent anyone else from being injured by Ogan. In 2005, Gainer had nineteen years of excellent service with HPD. Assigned to the Bush Intercontinental Airport Detail, he had previously served stints in the Accident and Dispatcher Divisions. He appears at peace with himself that he did all he could for his partner on that fateful night.

In October 2004, Sergeant Atchetee was retired and residing near Victoria. Sergeant Terry Ross was retired, but had another career as a justice of the peace in Fayetteville (Fayette County), Texas. Sergeant Ted Bloyd was continuing his long Homicide career, working in a dayshift murder squad. He retired in 2005. Sergeant Tom Murray, after a number of years in administration, was assigned to the Bush Intercontinental Airport Detail. He has also since retired. Lieutenant Greg Neely remained in Homicide, supervising a dayshift murder squad. He retired in 2006. Captain Bobby Adams retired in 2002 with more than forty-four years of HPD service.

Lieutenant Holland, who was promoted to captain in 1991, served in the Recruiting Division and the Internal Affairs Division before becoming the commander of the Homicide Division in March 1994. During that time, his integrity and professionalism led him to a special assignment to assess and deal with problems that existed in the HPD Crime Lab. In July 2004, he was transferred to the Criminal Intelligence Division of HPD.

Sergeant Jim Ramsey returned to Homicide after tours of duty in Narcotics, SWAT and Internal Affairs. He retired in October 2004 with nearly thirty years of exemplary service. In 2005, Sergeant Bill Stephens, who also served a stint in Internal Affairs, worked in the Narcotics Division. Sergeant Tom Ladd retired in 2004. Sergeants Wendel and Doyle are both retired. Mike Peters, in 2007, is working in the Homicide Cold Case Squad.

CSU Officers Wilker and Davis are retired and are pursuing other ventures. Officer J. I. Kennedy was assigned to the Airport detail in 2005 and Officer T. Q. Williams resigned.

Mr. and Mrs. Boswell still reside in Meridian. Mrs. Boswell recently underwent knee surgery and Mr. Boswell is struggling with health problems which have him confined to a wheelchair. James was their oldest of their five children. Joey Boswell entered law enforcement after his brother's death, serving as a detective with the Meridian Police Department. He and his wife Julie are the parents of a son Joey Jr and a daughter Charly (named for her uncle James Charles). Michael Boswell was in the United States Navy in 1989 and after twenty-four years of service to his country, retired in September 2004. He now lives in Virginia Beach, Virginia, and has begun a new career. He and his wife Cindy are the parents of three sons, Josh, Zach and Adam.

Kenneth Mark Boswell and his wife Shannon reside in Clinton, Mississippi. Officer Boswell's only sister Cherie and her husband Kevin reside in Meridian. Cherie is the mother of two daughters, Kayli and Danielle. Cherie is also the stepmother of three children.

In 2004, Officer Boswell's grandmother, Mrs. Josephine Jackson, was eighty-one years old and lived in Jackson, Mississippi. His grandfather, Leslie Stampley, died in 1995. However, Boswell's great-grandmother, Mrs. Wilma Johnson, resided in Meridian at the grand old age of 102.

89

Officer James B. Irby
Badge #189
June 27, 1990

Low-life Buntion Family Produces Death In HPD Family – Officer James B. Irby

Throughout history there have been many examples of good families of people performing honest, honorable jobs not only for their loved ones but also their fellow man. Unfortunately, on the other end of the spectrum can be found the exact opposite – families with reputations for doing nothing positive; they actually spend their lives working in direct conflict with society's collective value system.

One such example in the history of the Houston Police Department came directly to light in 1967 when Officer Louis Lyndon Sander unknowingly stopped a wanted fugitive on a routine traffic violation. Sander was shot and killed by Kenneth Hinkle, who along with his older brother William, had brutally robbed and beaten a wealthy couple in Little Rock, Arkansas.

Loaded with their cache of stolen jewelry, the Hinkle brothers were in the Houston-Galveston-Beaumont triangle solely to unload their ill-gotten goods when Officer Sander stopped Kenneth Hinkle for a minor traffic violation. This was on January 21, 1967, a day when Sander died from a single bullet fired from a pistol. Both of the Hinkle brothers had been in jail most of their adult life prior to this capital murder and both later died in prison. Kenneth Hinkle, born in 1928, was a willing protégé of his older brother William. Their records practically paralleled each other and Kenneth's stretched across the South.

Kenneth Hinkle first did time in Fort Leavenworth as part of his military service in 1951. Three years later he served time in Tennessee for assault, burglary and carrying a weapon. His behavior "record" included an escape charge in Nashville. He later went to the pen in Atlanta for larceny of an auto in 1959 and basically "transferred" to an Ashville prison a year later on the same charge. By 1964 he "graduated" to federal prison for auto theft and interstate transportation of a stolen vehicle. Next it was time in the federal prison in Tallahassee,

Florida. His arrest in New Orleans in 1967 was related to Officer Sander's murder.

In comparison to the Hinkle family, Officer Sander was the middle of three sons of honest, hard-working parents. The Sanders raised their family in the shadows of Reagan High School in Houston's Heights, where they owned and operated a mom and pop grocery store and hamburger café. Other Reagan graduates of the same era share the same sentiments about the Sanders family, which showed a strong devotion to public service. The older son Dennis was serving in the United States Army when Lyndon was murdered, while the youngest son Kenneth also was serving in the Houston Police Department.

For whatever reason on this tragic night, Evil prevailed over Good for the Walter and Sadie Sander family, the citizens of Houston, HPD and the law enforcement community in general.

The dichotomy present in the Sander-Hinkle conflict also existed in the Irby-Buntion encounter about twenty-three years later. And while there is no obvious connection between the Hinkles and the Buntions – the bad guys – there are notable similarities.

The criminal antics of William and Kenneth Hinkle around the states of Arkansas and Tennessee reeked havoc for distant but promising criminal would-be playgrounds like Houston. Here were two self-proclaimed "tush-hogs" whose sole purpose in their stinking lives was to live outside of the realm of normal society. What brings brothers to this measure of success in a life of violence will remain forever a mystery to honest, decent citizens, especially those involved in day-to-day law enforcement operations.

These brothers seemed destined to be outlaws, fierce rebels against polite society. They could be compared to the Buntion family, which in this case consisted of three sons raised on Houston's Northside. All three had numerous encounters with the law in particular and any authority figure in general. Such encounters were serious and often violent.

There were the twins, Kenneth and Carl, born in 1943, and Bobby, two years their junior. Fortunately for the good of our society, law enforcement officers killed Kenneth, twenty-seven, in 1971, only after numerous skirmishes, including one in which bullets Kenneth fired wounded HPD officers on the same day.

On the other end of the spectrum there was Solo Motorcycle Officer James B. Irby, an eighteen-year HPD veteran. His honorable service had paralleled that of his grandfather, Detective V. V. Irby, an HPD retiree. Officer Irby was proud to ably wear the badge number that his grandfather wore as a patrolman. It was Badge No. 189.

James Bruce Irby was born in Houston on May 25, 1953. His got his early education at Golfcrest Elementary School, Hartman Junior High School and Jones Senior High School, from which he graduated in 1972. He joined HPD as a police trainee on November 13, 1972, entering Police Cadet Class No. 57. That class graduated on March 3, 1973, and he successfully completed his probationary period on September 15, 1973.

Officer Irby's original assignment was to the Point Control Division and from there he transferred to Radio Patrol Central in 1975. His excellent work ethic served him well when he was accepted into the prestigious Solo Motorcycle Detail in 1982.

On Wednesday afternoon, June 27, 1990, Carl Wayne Buntion (White Male, 46) had been out of prison for just a short time. On parole until 2002, Buntion was living up to his previous life style. On May 15, 1990, the Texas Department of Criminal Justice paroled Buntion for the ninth time. He was given $200 in cash and a new set of clothes and ordered to report to the Texas House on Beaumont Highway in Houston. However, consistent with his entire criminal history, Buntion chose not to conform to the freedom he had been so graciously provided. Thumbing his nose at society and its justice system, he never reported as ordered.

OFFICER JAMES B. IRBY

Six weeks later, he had no job and lived off and on with people of his own ilk on Bennington Street. He toted a pistol, as had been his lifelong habit. Technically, by not reporting to the parolee facility, he was immediately in direct violation of his parole. Additionally, he was in the constant company of another ex-con, John Earl Killingsworth (White Male, 42). Killingsworth, unlike Buntion, did have a vehicle – of questionable ownership, of course.

Finally, on June 13, 1990, his non-appearance was reported to parole officials in Huntsville and on June

28, the day after a fine HPD officer lost his life, the State of Texas issued a "blue warrant" for Buntion's arrest for the parole violation. Officers would call this the typical "day-late-dollar short" effort.

On this hot, summer afternoon, these two fine citizens, Buntion and Killingsworth, managed to scrape up enough scrap metal to cash it in for eight dollars and some change. Even though they already had run out of gas once that afternoon, they continued to drive aimlessly around the north side, drinking beer. With Killingsworth driving and Buntion toting hardware and therefore truly "riding shotgun," they cruised in search of a vulnerable robbery victim.

Officer Irby was on traffic patrol near Northline Mall about 8 p.m. when he observed an older model Pontiac driving north on Airline Drive under the North Freeway overpass. When the Pontiac left the traffic light, Officer Irby decided to stop this vehicle after it spun its tires when the light turned green.

Being summertime, it was just nearing darkness and Irby observed that the Pontiac had several other lighting violations. The traffic stop was completed when the driver of the Pontiac, Killingsworth, pulled into the parking lot of the Houston Community College's Northeast College campus near this intersection. Irby was getting off his motorcycle when the driver of the Pontiac got out, the two meeting at the left rear of the car and just in front of the parked motorcycle.

Witnesses said Officer Irby and Killingsworth were conversing in a quiet, mild manner when Irby noticed the passenger getting out of the car. Irby motioned for him to stay inside but he refused to do so. Instead, he got out, pointed a pistol at the officer and fired, striking Irby and knocking him to the ground. The shooter, later identified as parole violator Carl Wayne Buntion, then calmly walked around the Pontiac toward the fallen officer and, holding the pistol with both hands, fired at least two more times, causing Officer Irby to suffer additional gunshot wounds while lying helplessly on the pavement.

Northeast Dayshift Patrol Officer Roy E. Thompson, working an extra job at the nearby Fiesta Food Market, had two shoplifters in custody outside the store while awaiting the arrival of a patrol unit for this "wagon call." Officer Laura Smelley was dispatched to meet Thompson and passed Officer Irby while en route to the store. Slowing down, she later stated that as she looked toward Irby he acknowledged her to continue, that he needed no help with his traffic stop. Just as she entered the parking lot of the Fiesta, citizens advised her that an officer had been shot.

Hearing people shouting from the direction of the solo and fearing that the officer was involved, Smelley alertly rushed to the scene in her patrol car. Officer Thompson also heard the shots and the shouting. He immediately followed in his personal vehicle. What the two officers found was likely something that neither will ever be able to erase from their memory.

Officer Jim Irby lay mortally wounded, shot an unknown number of times. A security guard was holding a pistol – Officer Irby's – on Killingsworth. Medical assistance was summoned and while waiting their arrival, Officer Smelley attempted to perform mouth-to-mouth resuscitation on her wounded fellow officer as an "Assist the Officer" was immediately broadcast.

Unlike many shooting scenes, on this day there were a number of witnesses waiting to tell their story. In a textbook version of scene-and-witness protection, Officers Smelley and Thompson used their training by quartering these eyewitnesses inside the nearby Houston Community College building to conduct a thorough investigation. More importantly, medical aid arrived and Officer Irby was transported to Ben Taub General Hospital. However, he was pronounced dead on arrival at 8:32 p.m. as the result of four gunshot wounds, one of which was to the head from close range. Jim Irby was thirty-seven years old, a married man and the father of two young children.

Buntion fled on foot east on Lyerly Street, where he encountered two females in a vehicle. Whether he was aware of it or not, both had witnessed the shooting. He began shooting at them as the driver attempted to flee in reverse. While both escaped immediate danger, they were wounded either by bullets or glass fragments. When they successfully fled, Buntion continued his escape on foot. He ran into a delivery service business on Lyerly where he attempted to commandeer an employee's vehicle at gunpoint. In doing so, he got the vehicle started but was forced to abandon it when the engine died on him. He then ran inside the business.

His actions caused everyone inside to flee from this crazed, armed man. Officer D. G. Kalich, nearby when the "Assist the Officer" was broadcast, arrived at the shooting scene and saw other officers with Irby. He quickly noticed citizens pointing east on Lyerly and bravely drove to investigate.

A witness pointed out Buntion to Officer Kalich as he crouched behind a vehicle. At this point, Buntion decided that maybe he did not have enough ammunition or guts to shoot at an officer who might actually be in a position to shoot back. He threw his weapon out and gave up, an arrest that Officer Kalich will never forget.

Officer James B. Irby was survived by his wife Maura and two children, son Cody James Irby, just under three years old, and daughter Callie Ann Irby, who had just turned one year old.

Also mourning his death were his father, V. V. Irby Jr., and a brother, Kelly Irby, and his paternal grandmother, Mrs. Thelma Irby. There also were an uncle, Bill Folsom; a great-uncle, Bubba Irby and his wife, Madge; his father- and mother-in-law, Mr. and Mrs. Robert and Kay Mills; and Maura's two sisters, Mandie and Megan Mills. He was preceded in death by his mother, Mrs. Thelma Irby, and his grandfather, HPD Retired Detective V. V. Irby Sr.

Crespo Funeral Home at 2516 Navigation was in charge of funeral arrangements. Visitation was held beginning at 9 a.m. on Friday, June 29, 1990, with a vigil conducted at 2 p.m. that same day. Funeral services were held at the Second Baptist Church, 6400 Woodway, on Saturday, June 30, 1990, at 4 p.m. Following the church service, one of the largest funeral processions in

HPD history proceeded to the burial site at Forest Park Lawndale Cemetery, 6900 Lawndale.

Homicide Lieutenants Greg T. Neely and Bobby J. Beck were on duty when this shooting occurred. Lieutenant Neely, along with Homicide Sergeants A. J. Toepoel, John G. Burmester and Fred W. Carroll responded to the scene, which had been professionally secured by the patrol supervisors and officers. Lieutenant Beck manned the Homicide command post and assisted from that location with any additional manpower or investigation that either lieutenant deemed necessary.

At the time of the original assignments, the condition of Officer Irby was uncertain. Unfortunately, that changed for the worse. Homicide Sergeants Eric Mehl and Brad S. Rudolph were assigned to conduct the investigation at the hospitals where Officer Irby and the two wounded civilian witnesses were taken. Upon Lieutenant Neely's arrival, he was met by Assistant Chief of Police J. L. Dotson. The chief provided Neely an overall briefing on the details known at the time, as well as the fact that the suspected shooter and the driver of the vehicle were both in custody. With the principals in custody and eyewitnesses abounding, this was truly a blessing for a Homicide lieutenant's worst nightmare, a slain officer.

Yet there was a multitude of tasks to be performed and, as is the case in every homicide, these duties need to be completed in an extremely detailed manner in order to obtain evidence and eyewitness testimony. No stone would be left unturned and no item of intricate detail would be left undone.

Crime Scene Units Mary E. Lentschke, J. L. Kay and G. L. "Stoney" Burke were assigned to various segments of the scene and hospital inquiries. With a murdered officer, even with the suspects and/or witnesses available, a long night lay ahead. Additional investigators were summoned to assist. All on-duty personnel were quickly utilized and Homicide Sergeants John R. Swaim, Ken E. Vachris and Dennis J. Gafford were called in from their residences to assist. On-duty Sgt. George Alderette was assigned to conduct the crucial interview with John Lee Killingsworth, who at this time was not suspected of any criminal activity in the death of Officer Irby. While his lengthy criminal record lessened his credibility as an eyewitness, his version of the events of this tragic evening was deemed as important as if he were a choirboy.

Sergeant Dennis Gafford was assigned the task of interrogating what was believed to be the shooter, seven-time Texas ex-convict Carl Wayne Buntion. The suspect's hands had been bagged and he had refused to give officers any information at this point. CSU Officer Kay was assigned to remove the bags in order to perform the necessary tests. Buntion, however, in his usual cocky and arrogant manner toward law enforcement, did state that had he not chosen to surrender, he would still be out there "swapping lead."

After the tests were completed, Gafford provided Buntion his statutory warning. Being absolutely positive that Buntion understood his rights, Gafford proceeded in his usual professional manner in this crucial interview.

After a very short time, Buntion said, "I'm the shooter." From this point Buntion spoke freely and matter of factly about the murder. Showing no remorse whatsoever, he stated that he was in fear that Officer Irby was going to kill him and that he had decided to shoot first. Of course, this was in direct conflict with witness versions of the story. He continued to exaggerate, stating that Irby was a raging man bent on killing both him and Killingsworth for spinning his tires. As the interview continued, Sergeant Gafford condensed Buntion's oral version to writing in the form of a written confession – all done with the suspect's approval.

The investigation continued after the confession and well into the next day. Witnesses were shown a live line-up with Buntion. Their choices were unanimous: Buntion was the individual who murdered Officer Jim Irby. An autopsy was performed the following day and it determined that the officer had received a total of four entry gunshot wounds to the back, chest and head – several of which would have been fatal on their own.

Killingsworth consented to a search of his vehicle, which produced a container that held traces of heroin. Killingsworth, in addition to being a key witness in this offense, was charged with possession of a controlled substance. Much more importantly, Carl Wayne Buntion was charged with capital murder in the death of a peace officer in the 178th Criminal District Court. He was held without bond.

Finally, this predator was off the streets for good. Or, was he?

Buntion's attorneys, fully cognizant that their client faced an uphill battle in Harris County, got a change of venue in this case. The trial was moved to Fredricksburg in the heart of the Texas Hill Country. (The judicial proceedings in Fredricksburg took on a number of bizarre twists. These included the usual theatrics by the defense counsel and several strange rulings by State District Judge William Harmon, the Houston judge who also presided over the case in this country town.) After all was said and done, the optimistic view of Buntion being free no more prevailed. On January 24, 1991, a jury found him guilty of capital murder. Several days later, that same jury assessed the death penalty to career criminal Carl Wayne Buntion.

HPD investigators have long believed that Buntion's desire for revenge led him to assassinate Officer Jim Irby. The story of this possibility thickens the tragic plot.

In April 1971, Carl Wayne Buntion's twin brother Kenneth was running a forgery ring out of an apartment project near Tidwell and Jensen. Houston and Pasadena police officers conducted a three-day surveillance of these activities and eventually obtained search warrants. They had this location covered on a Saturday afternoon when they observed several of the principals, Kenneth Buntion being one of them, arrive at the project. Present along with several Pasadena officers were Vice Officer Doug "Tooter" Steffanauer and Harris County Organized Crime Task Force Officer A. D. "Dale" Dugger of HPD. From the HPD Criminal Intelligence Division there were officers Lloyd

"Sonny" Dollar, Tom Doty and Johnny Thornton.

Buntion shot Johnny Thornton through his right arm while the officers were attempting to arrest him. That same round continued and struck Dale Dugger in a main artery, very nearly causing his death. It was the second time Dugger was shot in the line of duty. Only the heroic actions of a citizen paramedic saved his life that spring day in 1971.

After shooting Dugger and Thornton, Buntion was still firing as he ran across the upstairs walkway of an apartment complex. Officer "Tooter" Steffanauer was the first to shoot Buntion, the bullet striking him in the neck. Buntion did not go down easily. Finally, the continued barrage of bullets from the guns of both Thornton and Steffanauer brought him down. As the story goes, Carl Wayne Buntion, whose sole life's ambition was to be a career criminal, took on another cause that day in 1971 – to avenge the death of his twin brother. Buntion was in the process of serving one of his many prison terms that day when his brother was killed. He and his younger brother Bobby were allowed to attend Kenneth's funeral at Bullard, Texas.

Bobby was dressed in a borrowed dark suit from his prison warden. Carl Wayne wore prison clothes. Yet their attire was identical in two respects – both wore handcuffs on their wrists and shackles on their ankles. Later, the warden of Carl's TDCJ unit called HPD officials to advise them of the threats Carl was making. Newspaper accounts said Buntion had notified the warden that he had better be locked down or he would break out of the penitentiary and come to Houston to kill Dugger and Steffanauer because they had killed his brother. He was known to voice the threat to a number of people over the next nineteen years, clearly bragging about his intentions. Dale Dugger, who spent a large portion of his HPD career working undercover in Vice and the Houston-Harris County Organized Crime Task Force, confronted Carl Buntion regarding these threats. Buntion, in his usual cowardly fashion, backed down, apologized and recanted his intentions.

Nevertheless, Carl Buntion's motives likely continued until that fateful day in 1990 when Officer Jim Irby's life was taken. A number of the officers present that day could have lost their lives in 1971 at the hands of a Buntion. Unfortunately, Officer Irby was not that lucky. One Buntion brother dead, one on Death Row, and the younger one, Bobby Joe, was in and out of jail all of this adult life.

On July 30, 1990, Officer Steffanauer was quoted in the Houston Chronicle as saying, "Instead of one rotten apple in the barrel, there's a barrel full of rotten apples."

Jim Irby is dead. However, friends and family have not forgotten this man, who volunteered many hours of his own time helping others. Just several days after his death, a local radio station held a benefit for his surviving family at the Hard Rock Café, where a large amount of money was raised. Irby had been very active with youths at the annual Houston Livestock Show and Rodeo, taking his own vacation time to work at this event. Shortly after his death, the Southeast Chapter of the Texas Peace Officer's Association held a benefit rodeo in west Houston. The proceeds of this effort established a trust fund for the Irby children.

While Buntion really deserves no more mention, it has to be noted that in 2007, while he is still on Death Row and off the streets of Houston, his conviction has been overturned partially due to "judicial misconduct". The State of Texas has the right to appeal that ruling and is doing so. In a scenario that would sicken most honest law-abiding citizens, Buntion spends his days in custody tending to his website and writing poems from his death row cell. He has become proficient in the use of the internet, a phenomenon that Officer Jim Irby had likely never dreamed of in his shortened life.

That same year, Maura Irby resided in Utah with daughter Callie, while son Cody lived near Lake Travis, just north of Austin. The slain officer's father was still alive and brother Kelly lived in Pearland and had two daughters. All of his other natural relatives died over a fourteen-year period. Mother- and father-in-law, Mr. and Mrs. Mills, resided in Austin, as did Maura's sister, Megan. Her other sister, Mandie, lived in Beaumont.

Officer Roy Thompson remained in Northeast Patrol in an undercover assignment for a number of years. He retired in April 2004 and lived in Mississippi. Officer Laura Smelley was promoted to sergeant, assigned to Northwest Patrol. Officer Kalich retired from Radio Patrol in 2005.

Of the investigators, Lieutenant Bobby Beck retired from HPD in the early 1990's. Lieutenant Greg Neely became a dayshift Homicide Murder Squad supervisor and retired in 2006. Sergeants Burmester and Carroll retired in 2003 and 2004, respectively. Sergeant John Swaim retired in 2006 as did Ken Vachris in 2007. On a sad note, Sergeant A. J. Toepoel died of a heart attack in 2000. Sergeant Eric Mehl continues to investigate Murders, at this time in the Homicide Cold Case Squad. Sergeant Brad Rudolph is now assigned to CID. Sergeant Dennis Gafford later promoted to lieutenant and after a number of years in Homicide and Internal Affairs was now assigned to the Narcotics Division.

Sergeant Alderette was assigned to an administrative position in a command office. CSU Officer Kay was still working in the Homicide Division. Officer Stoney Burke retired in 2002 and Officer Mary Lentschke was promoted to sergeant, lieutenant, and in 2007, is now the Captain over the Houston Police Training Academy.

The marker placed in memory of Officer Irby is a large monument with the Badge #189 over the name of JAMES B. IRBY with the further inscriptions of HUSBAND, FATHER, OFFICER, AND FRIEND. Also, KILLED IN THE LINE OF DUTY.

There is also a foot marker which reads: JAMES B. IRBY, MAY 25, 1953 - JUNE 27, 1990. It has the Solo Motorcycle emblem and the words: NO SOLO WILL EVER RIDE ALONE.

90

Officer John Anthony Salvaggio
Badge #2521
November 25, 1990

Katy Freeway Driver Hits, Runs, Kills Officer John Salvaggio in November 1990

John Anthony Salvaggio was born in Houston on July 23, 1951. He received his early education at Sacred Heart and Oak Forest elementary schools and later at Black Junior High School. He graduated from Waltrip Senior High School in 1969 and attended Southwest Texas State University in San Marcos for a year. Salvaggio joined the Houston Police Department by way of HPD Cadet Class No. 120. This class began its training on April 2, 1984, and upon graduation, the new officers took their oaths of office on August 4 of that year.

The new officer wore HPD Badge No. 2521. During his six and a half years on the force he worked mainly on the night shift in Radio Patrol-Northwest Station except for a short stint in the Accident Division several years before his death.

On the Saturday night of November 24, 1990, Officer John Salvaggio reported for duty on the night shift at the Northwest Substation. He went on patrol riding a one-man unit. At approximately 2am Sunday morning, using radar equipment, he stopped a motorist, Gus Mayer, for speeding in the 8500 block of the Katy Freeway. While the speeding violation had occurred in the City of Houston, by the time Officer Salvaggio had stopped the violator he was near Bingle Road, which is in the jurisdiction of the Spring Valley Police Department.

Following the proper procedures, he stopped this vehicle in the far right emergency lane. As he was trained to do, he parked to the rear and to the left of the violator's vehicle to provide a small amount of protection for him as he approached the traffic violator. Officer Salvaggio also utilized his patrol car's emergency flashing lights. As he had just approached the driver's side door, when according to Mayer, a second vehicle struck the officer and Mayer's car.

Mayer was quoted in the newspaper as saying, "I thought I was hallucinating. As soon as I felt the impact, I saw his body thrown about twenty feet in front of my car and then I tried to get a look at the car that did it. It couldn't have been more than ten seconds after he came to my car. I didn't even have time to get to my glove compartment before I was jolted by the impact." The vehicle sped off, leaving the officer lying critically injured on the side of the freeway. The impact Mayer described was his vehicle being struck on the left side by the right side of the suspect's vehicle.

OFFICER JOHN ANTHONY SALVAGGIO

A number of vehicles passed without stopping, apparently oblivious to what had happened. Shortly after the officer was struck, an off-duty HPD sergeant, Michael K. Riehl, happened along. Sergeant Riehl stated that he was en route home from an extra job. When he saw the flashing lights of the patrol car, he looked as a matter of routine to see if the officer was all right. Not seeing any officer, Riehl pulled over and backed up. It was then that he saw Officer Salvaggio on the ground. He checked the officer and then took the keys to the violator's car. He described Mayer as being totally out of it as if he were in shock. Of course, the sergeant did not exactly know at this time what had happened. He then called for assistance on Officer Salvaggio's police radio. A LifeFlight helicopter was called and Officer Salvaggio was transported to

Hermann Hospital. However, he was dead on arrival at age thirty-nine.

Officer John Anthony Salvaggio was survived by his wife, Marybess, and three children: daughters Cathy, fifteen, and Virginia, twelve, and a son, ten-month-old John Anthony Salvaggio II. Also mourning his sudden death were his parents Guy and Catherine Salvaggio, his in-laws, Mr. and Mrs. A. P. Grizaffi, and his grandmother, Mrs. Mary Salvaggio. He was also survived by his brothers Charles (wife Elizabeth) and Jack T. Salvaggio, and one sister, Tammy Martino (husband Joe).

VIRGINIA, CATHY, MARYBESS, JOHNNY, AND JOHN SALVAGGIO, FEBRUARY, 1990

Vigil for the deceased was held at 7:30 p.m. Monday, November 26, 1990, with a Rosary by the Parish, Neo-Debs, and La Amiche Club at the Earthman Hunters Creek Chapel, 8303 Katy Freeway in Houston. Funeral Mass was conducted at 10 a.m. Tuesday at the St. Michael Catholic Church at 1801 Sage Road. The Reverends Adam McClosky and Frank Fabj served as Con-Celebrants. The Rite of Committal was held at the Calvary section of Forest Park – Westheimer Cemetery.

Pallbearers were HPD Lieutenant Jerry L. Driver, Sergeant Robert Schields, fellow Officers Dan Starr and Ron Freeman, and friends and/or cousins Yance Montalbano, Johnny Whites, Michael Marino and Tony Salvaggio Jr. Honorary pallbearers were listed as all members of the Houston Police Department, his cousins, and classmates of the Waltrip High School Class of 1969.

With this offense taking place in the City of Spring Valley, their Police Department had jurisdiction in this case. However, HPD's Accident Division immediately offered the services of their experienced Hit and Run Detail, an offer Spring Valley PD graciously accepted. HPD Accident Sergeant J. E. Bickel was on the scene. This being a who-dun-it officer fatality case, a Hit and Run Detail callout was initiated. Hit and Run Sergeant J. Montemayor was summoned as well as Officers Pete Araiza and I. M. Labdi.

Spring Valley Police Lieutenant Gary Finkelman was assigned to the case from his agency. The investigation went forth as a joint effort of both departments with one goal in mind – bringing the hit-and-run driver to justice.

From the physical evidence left at the scene, investigators suspected that the wanted vehicle's right headlight and windshield were damaged. They also felt that the right side might have gray or light blue smudges from striking the Mayer vehicle. The glass of Mayer's driver's side mirror was missing and the mirror was flattened against the car. Lab examinations were already being conducted while preparations were being made for the services for Officer Salvaggio.

Accident Lieutenant E. J. Smith was HPD's lead supervisor in this investigation and was assigning additional investigators as leads surfaced. The physical evidence from the scene as well as the deceased officer's clothing was submitted to the HPD Crime Lab where Chemist Reidun Hilleman was assigned to conduct tests in this phase of the investigation.

At 4 p.m. Monday, November 26, two attorneys showed up at 61 Riesner and told authorities where to find the wanted vehicle. The attorneys did all the talking but provided little more than the vehicle's location. They did, however, identify their client as Bill Byrd. They did not explain his knowledge or involvement. Officers S. A. Galbiati and R. J. Salinas were assigned to locate and recover this vehicle.

HPD spokesman Richard Retz, himself an officer, was quoted in the Houston Chronicle as saying, "It's kind of like they said 'Here's the vehicle' and the rest is up to us. They left it up to us, and we'll do it." And, in the true fashion of HPD, whether in the Accident Division or the Homicide Division, wheels began turning and it became a high priority to determine who had "struck and killed one of our own."

Immediately after this information surfaced, investigators went to an apartment complex near Westview and Blalock, where a gold and cream colored Ford Grenada was located. As suspected by these veteran Hit and Run investigators, damage to the suspect vehicle consisted of a windshield smashed inward in a spider web of cracks, the right rear view mirror dangling over deep gashes and the right side and passenger window dotted with blood spatters. Also, the right front headlight was broken out and the right front fender was dented in nearly to the tire. Scrapes and dents along the right side were discolored by blue paint. Additionally, dark blue and light blue fabrics were discovered on the fender and windshield. The damage was consistent with what was suspected.

This was the vehicle.

Evidence was carefully recovered before the vehicle was towed under guard to the HPD Vehicle Examination Building for more extensive examinations. A computer check of the registration showed the Ford Grenada to be registered to a William Byrd. It was discovered that this suspect had been involved in a previous failure to stop and give information (FSGI) offense in 1988. However, as is the case in nearly every hit and run investigations, proving who was behind the wheel and driving the vehicle at the time of the tragedy became an extremely difficult legal issue.

Hit and Run Officer Araiza, HPD's lead investigator, and Spring Valley Lieutenant Gary Finkelman continued their investigation at the location of the vehicle's recovery. The apartment project was thoroughly canvassed for anyone who may have information about Byrd. This proved to be fruitful. One occupant had seen a man drive into the project in a damaged vehicle shortly after the accident. She said she also could testify that this driver came in alone. This after-the-fact witness later picked Byrd out of a photo array as being the man she saw drive into the project.

Investigators determined that Byrd frequently visited a female who lived in the project. Upon arriving at the complex shortly after the accident, investigators produced an individual who stated that Byrd had knocked on the door of another resident and asked for permission to park his car there, as he had been involved in an accident. The case was beginning to take shape.

The investigation continued and at 3:40 a.m. Tuesday, November 27, William E. Byrd (White Male; Age 51) was arrested on a charge of failure to stop and render assistance (FSRA) in the death of HPD Officer John Salvaggio. This arrest took place at Byrd's home in the 1200 block of Cedar Post, less than three miles from where Officer Salvaggio was killed. Under subsequent questioning, Boyd responded in the presence of his attorney, whose strategy was for Boyd to plead not guilty. Byrd did not deny driving the Grenada and only said that he knew a collision happened. He just did not know what or how it all happened. He was released on a $2,000 bond.

After the arrest, the crime lab investigation continued. After a thorough and professional examination of the evidence, Chemist Reidun M. Hilleman was able to determine that the dark and light blue cloth samples from the Grenada was consistent with the blue uniform worn by Officer Salvaggio as well as its weave pattern, fiber composition and dye components. Additionally, a large paint chip and several smaller chips recovered from the officer's uniformed pants were microscopically and chemically indistinguishable from known paint chips from the collision area of the Ford Grenada.

For a number of years John Salvaggio yearned to be a Houston police officer. The food service business was a part of his upbringing. His parents managed the restaurant portion of the Del Mar Bowling Lanes on Mangum Road. The desire to be an officer intensified during the years 1974-1977. It was during this period that John and his brother Charles managed the cafeteria in the basement of 61 Riesner. Eventually, John fulfilled his dream and became not only a police officer but also an exceptionally dedicated one.

A supervisor and friend, Lieutenant Jerry Driver, one of Salvaggio's pallbearers, described the officer as a very likeable man, the kind who would spread a little sunshine wherever he was. Driver was quoted in newspaper accounts as saying, "I had spoken to him about being safe out there, especially on the freeway. John's response was that he knew people got killed on the freeways, but that he was going to do his part in making the streets a little safer for the citizens. He was determined to do his part." The lieutenant later described Officer Salvaggio as one of those individuals who really needed no supervision. He knew what to do and was self-motivated. He just went out and did his job.

Officer Salvaggio's former partner, Officer Dan Starr, described him as a wonderful partner and friend. The two rode together for two years prior to Starr taking an assignment on a night shift fingerprint unit. He mentioned John's unique sense of humor, stating that one night prior to roll call at the station, they were looking at a physical wellness chart based on height and weight. When John located his weight on the chart, he jokingly commented that he had no idea that he was six-foot-nine.

VIRGINIA, MARYBESS, CATHY, AND JOHNNY SALVAGGIO, 2006

John also was a devoted family man, cherishing his wife, two daughters and young son, whom he had just recently videotaped taking his first steps just days before his untimely death.

In 2007, Marybess Salvaggio, a University of Houston graduate and for many years a dedicated elementary school teacher, was on temporary leave taking care of her elderly mother as well as her first grandchild, five-year-old Anthony. Daughter Cathy Birden graduated from the University of Texas in Austin and is now a fifth grade teacher. She is married to Jerry Birden. Daughter Virginia Manlove, a University of Houston graduate, is married to Jason Manlove. They are the parents of Anthony Manlove and two-year old Adrianna Manlove. Son John Anthony Salvaggio II, who was ten months old and just learning to walk when his father was taken from him, is now seventeen and an athlete in several sports at a Cypress ISD high school.

Salvaggio's parents, Mr. and Mrs. Guy Salvaggio, live in Houston. The grandmother, as well as the father of Mary Bess, Mr. Grizaffi, died in the early 1990's. Mrs. Grizaffi resides with Marybess. Sister Tammy lives in

Houston, the mother of Joseph, fourteen, and Anna, eleven, who were born after her uncle's death. Officer Salvaggio was the oldest of four children and his two brothers, who are twins, both live in the Houston area. Charles and his wife Elizabeth are the parents of Stephanie and Charlie. Jack also lives in Houston.

In January 1991, less than two months after Officer Salvaggio's death, a plea bargain agreement was near to being approved in this case. However, at the last minute, Byrd and his attorney decided that they could not agree with the summary of the incident as documented in the court charges against him. This summary said that Byrd left the scene knowing that he had struck Officer Salvaggio and knowing that the officer needed assistance. Byrd would only plea that he knew that he had hit something, but he didn't know it was a person.

Consequently, prosecutor Chuck Rosenthal, who would later become district attorney of Harris County, decided to take the case to a grand jury for indictment for failure to stop and render aid, a felony punishable up to five years in confinement. Under the tentative plea agreement, Byrd would have been sentenced by a state district judge pending an extensive background investigation. Basically, Byrd and his attorney were ready to take their chances.

In September 1991, as this case lingered on, Byrd was arrested again, this time for attempting to obtain illegal prescription drugs. He was actually charged with possession of blank prescription forms for narcotics. When he was arrested outside a West Gray pharmacy, he had the forms in his wallet. Marijuana, methadone and other unidentified pills also were recovered. He was jailed without bond.

Finally, on March 23, 1992, Byrd was sentenced to five years in prison for leaving the scene after striking Officer John Salvaggio. This was the maximum under the applicable 1990 Penal Code. Unfortunately, newspaper accounts further indicate that on or about March 23, 1994, Byrd was to be released from prison after only serving two years of his five-year sentence. He was then to be placed on ten years' probation under the supervision of a probation officer. Byrd went free, but he died on March 23, 2002, at the age of sixty-two.

Lieutenant Jerry Driver retired from the Jail Division in 2004. Sergeant Robert Schields, a good friend and high school football opponent, is retired. Officer Dan Starr still works out of the Northwest Station. Officer Ron Freeman works the Night Shift at Westside Patrol. Yance Montalbano was a nephew and close friend, Michael Marino and Anthony Salvaggio were Officer Salvaggio's cousins, and John T. Whites was a good friend.

Lieutenant E. J. Smith retired in 2002 after nearly forty-four years with HPD. Lieutenant Gary Finkelman still works with the Spring Valley PD in an investigative capacity. Accident Sergeant Bickel is now a K-9 unit supervisor for HPD. Sergeant Montemayor is assigned to the Hit and Run Detail, as is lead investigator Pete Araiza and Officers Salinas and Labdi. Officer Galbaiti is assigned to Central Patrol and Sergeant Riehl is an investigative sergeant in the Burglary and Theft Division. Chemist Reidun Hilleman continues to do her usual professional job in the Crime Lab and has been a mainstay in that division through some rough times.

The gravemarker for Officer Salvaggio reads as follows:

JOHN ANTHONY SALVAGGIO
JULY 23, 1951-NOV 25, 1990
BADGE #2521
BLESSED BE THE PEACEMAKERS FOR THEY SHALL BE CALLED THE SONS OF GOD.

91

Sergeant Bruno David Soboleski
April 12, 1991

Sgt. Bruno Soboleski Murdered in Cold Blood in the Presence of Grand Juror Ride-Along

Bruno David Soboleski was born on February 5, 1958 in Pennsylvania. He worked as an ironworker for a number of years. Layoffs occurred and he was recruited to come to Houston to join the Houston Police Department. He graduated from Houston Police Cadet Class No. 112 on August 5, 1983.

He had been a policeman for nearly eight years and a sergeant for the past two years when on Saturday night, April 6, 1991, Evening Shift Sergeant Bruno Soboleski reported for duty on his regular night off to work the Zero Tolerance Drug overtime program. Assigned to the Southeast Patrol Division, his regular assigned shift was 3-11 p.m. with Friday and Saturdays as his regular days off. On this night, Sergeant Soboleski, riding unit 91D30, was accompanied by a departmentally approved ride-along, Ms. Linda Ligon, who was currently serving on a Harris County grand jury.

While on patrol shortly before 1 a.m. Sunday, April 7, Soboleski was northbound on Calhoun from Yellowstone in the 6600 block. There he observed several males standing in the street. This being a high-crime, drug-infested area, the sergeant drove up to these individuals and inquired as to what they were doing. One of them commented that they weren't up to anything.

Soboleski got out of his vehicle and courteously told both males to place their hands on the police car so that he could conduct a pat down search for weapons. One of the men went to the front of the car and placed his hands on the hood while the other placed his hands on the left front section of the police vehicle. This placed Sergeant Soboleski between the two. Ms. Ligon remained in the car, seated in the right front seat.

The first man submitted to the search and after nothing was found, the sergeant was about to turn his attention to the second suspect when Ms. Ligon saw this man pulling a pistol from his waist. She attempted to honk the car horn and she shouted to the sergeant. However, the suspect opened fire and shot him, causing him to fall to the street after being hit at least twice. Both of these suspects then fled on foot.

Investigators later determined that there was a third man who stood and watched this happening from between several parked cars in a parking lot. When he saw his friend shoot the officer, he decided to enter the situation and fired a number of rounds at the critically wounded man in blue lying in the street. Ms. Ligon, still seated in the front, while honking the horn and screaming at the suspect in hopes of scaring him off, then frantically witnessed the suspect fire a round through the windshield at her. Fortunately, he missed. She called for assistance on the police radio.

Other police units arrived shortly as did medical help. Houston Fire Department paramedics summoned LifeFlight Helicopter for the seriously wounded Sergeant Soboleski and he was flown to Hermann Hospital in very critical condition.

On-duty Homicide Lieutenant Ken Johnson responded immediately to the scene as did his sergeants, Terry Ross and Dale Atchetee. Lieutenant Guy Mason's Day Shift murder squad was on call on this weekend. After conferring with Mason, Johnson called Mason's first two pair of investigators at home to respond to this investigation. It would be Mason squad's who would be responsible for the follow-up investigation from this night forth through prosecution.

Sergeants Ronnie Doyle and Sharon Durham were assigned to the scene investigation as the case agents who would follow through on this matter. They were assisted by Ross and Atchetee as well as Sergeants Larry Boyd Smith and Kenny Williamson, who were called in to assist in the hospital investigation and any other duties that might follow.

Early in the investigation, Ms. Linda Ligon, the grand juror, was able to provide a detailed clothing and physical description of the shooter. Additionally, there were two brothers, Johnny and Walter Green, who were working on a car nearby when the shooting happened. Both of these witnesses also were able to describe the suspects, as well as their route of travel in fleeing from the scene on foot. After all was said and done, the investigation resulted in some truly quality work not only by the Homicide investigators but also the on-duty Radio Patrol personnel.

The two mechanic brothers clearly heard the shooting and saw the suspect fleeing the scene toward them. The suspect was last seen running through a muddy field. Alert patrol officers responded and, acting on this small lead, set up a perimeter of the area north of where the suspect was last seen. Officers K. S. Fedderson and J. W. Pearson saw the suspect, who then turned south. They pursued him through some houses, losing him near England and Hull streets. At this point, they called for a K-9 Unit manned by Officer F. A. Ruffino, whose K-9 partner picked up the trail and followed it to a nearby apartment project at 4100 Hull at San Augustine. The canine lost the trail in a puddle of water but had put officers onto what later proved to be very fertile ground.

SERGEANT BRUNO DAVID SOBOLESKI

Patrol Lieutenant Gray Smith was the ranking uniformed supervisor on duty and he and a number of officers begin a full-scale canvas of the project on Hull

Street. They quickly developed information which prompted them to zero in on one particular apartment. While receiving the expected reluctant amount of cooperation, they gained permission to enter the apartment in question on a welfare check since the occupant was a teenage female caring for several small children.

This proved to be the first piece of the puzzle. Entering the unit, they located an African-American male who fit the description of the shooter. Also, they observed soiled clothing and muddy shoes, the clothing being as described by the main witness. And, of all things, a discarded 9mm pistol lay on the floor near where the suspect was found.

The officers immediately secured the location until Homicide investigators could begin the process of legal consent for a further search as well as the recovery of the evidentiary items. The investigators took this suspect, Shelton Denoria Jones, to Homicide. Sergeants Smith and Williamson, unable to interview the wounded sergeant, had returned to the Homicide office to await further instructions from Lieutenants Mason and Johnson. Mason assigned them the task of interviewing the main suspect, Shelton Jones.

Meanwhile, back at the scene, responding officers noticed a vehicle that, unlike the others around it in the parking lot, was warm to the touch of the hood. Even though it had been raining intermittently, the windows were down on the vehicle and there were items of value in plain view. Officers strongly suspected that this vehicle might be in some way involved with the suspects, all of whom fled on foot. Furthermore, they found six fired 9mm cartridges near this vehicle, the same caliber as the three found in the street where Sergeant Soboleski was shot.

The investigation was turning up clues right and left on what proved to be a hot trail. Officers checked registration on the vehicle. The finding led Lieutenant Johnson and a large posse to a nearby address on Hogue Street. From there, they learned that a man by the name of Gregory Pickrom had custody of the vehicle on this night. They also learned of a nearby location from which Pickrom had just made a rather frantic and confused phone call. Officers found Pickrom at a house on Sidney Street and he quickly upped the fact that he was there when the shooting occurred. (He was the suspect in the front of the car that Soboleski had searched and found unarmed). Pickrom became a very cooperative, concerned citizen and provided the names of Shelton Jones (arrested on Hull Street) and Chris Coleman, who was the suspect standing off in the parking lot near the vehicle when Soboleski was shot. Coleman would apparently be the one who also fired at the sergeant.

Sergeants Smith and Williamson, after conducting an at-length interview with the primary suspect, were able to obtain from Shelton Jones his admission that he had shot the sergeant. He also confirmed Gregory Pickrom's story, as well as providing not only Chris Coleman's identity, but a location in the area where he might be hiding out.

This information led Lieutenant Johnson and Sergeants Doyle and Durham and their group of very anxious patrol officers to several locations, one of which was on Maggie Street. It was there, at about daybreak, that the Johnson posse located Coleman.

As is the case of practically every incident in which a police officer is shot, a chief assistant district attorney immediately began monitoring the investigation and assisting Homicide personnel with any legal questions that might arise. ADA Keno Henderson undertook this key roll. Before the end of the day Sunday, Henderson saw to it that Shelton Denoria Jones and Christopher Dwight Coleman were charged with attempted capital murder of a peace officer. Gregory Steven Pickrom was not charged in this incident but he was jailed on outstanding forgery warrants.

Having all three suspects in custody in such a timely manner certainly uplifted every officer involved in the investigation. However, the condition of the seriously wounded Sergeant Bruno Soboleski weighed heavily on everyone's mind. Sergeants Smith and Williamson had not been able to speak with Soboleski, who received gunshot wounds in the right and left chest, left groin and right flank. Further interviews with medical personnel at Hermann Hospital revealed that the gunshots had caused a glancing blow to the heart and injuries to the lungs as well as major damage to the blood vessels leading to the lungs. A tremendous amount of internal bleeding was taking place.

In the days following, Sergeant Soboleski underwent at least four major operations in an attempt to repair the damage the 9mm missiles had done to his body. At one point, over four hundred units of blood were used as he continued to bleed internally despite all efforts to control the hemorrhaging. In a statement of support for the wounded sergeant, the Gulf Coast Regional Blood Center reported on April 11 that over 1,333 units of blood had been donated for his fight to stay alive.

Then, just shortly after midnight in the early morning hours of Friday, April 12, Sergeant Bruno David Soboleski passed away in Hermann Hospital. He was thirty-three years old.

Sergeant Soboleski was survived by his wife Sue and his daughters, Stephanie and Mallorie; his mother, Mrs. Mary Soboleski, and brothers Walter, Joseph, Frank and Leonard Soboleski; and a sister, Mary Crawley. He was preceded in death by his Father, Bruno Soboleski, and one brother, Michael Soboleski.

A vigil for the deceased was held at 7 p.m. Monday, April 15, 1991, at the Earthman Hunters Creek Chapel at 8303 Katy Freeway. Funeral services were conducted at 10 a.m. Tuesday at the Second Baptist Church, 6400 Woodway, with the Reverends David Dixon and Brad Ottosen Jr. officiating.

With burial to follow several days later at the Oak Hill Cemetery in Sandy Lake, Pennsylvania, a mock graveside service for all of his friends and fellow officers was conducted on the grassy area outside the church. The twenty-one-gun salute to Sergeant Bruno Soboleski took place, followed by a flyover of three HPD helicopters. HPD Solo motorcycle officers then escorted his remains to the airport.

The continuing investigation turned up these facts:

Shelton Jones, who was on probation for theft by receiving stolen goods, left a nearby club on Griggs with Gregory Pickrom and Christopher Coleman. Armed, their sole purpose in life that night was to find a dope dealer to rob.

Ironically, Sergeant Soboleski was working overtime on the Zero Tolerance Drug Program. Jones, in just the week prior to this offense, had purchased from a pawn shop on South Main two identical Glock 9mm automatics with successive serial numbers. Even though unemployed, he paid cash for the weapons.

When they stopped on Calhoun and Hull to do their no-good, sorry business, Coleman was in the background in the parking lot to act as the lookout. Jones admitted that when Sergeant Soboleski was successfully searching Pickrom, he decided that he "ought to be up front with the officer and show him his pistol."

Yeah, right.

In his thinking, if he just showed it to Soboleski, all would be well. Of course, when Sergeant Soboleski saw out of the corner of his eye that Jones was pulling the weapon as well as hearing his grand juror riding partner shouting, he obviously had other concerns besides being innocently shown Jones' pistol.

Then, Coleman, being the brave man his parents raised him to be, decided to join in the fun after the sergeant was shot. Investigators didn't believe that his bullets struck Sergeant Soboleski, but they later ascertained that some of the slugs from the patrol car were not from Shelton Jones' 9mm. Coleman definitely wanted to be a part of the deal, but his cowardly actions occurred only after Soboleski was down and out.

The Harris County district attorney, a county-wide elected official, is legally charged by his oath of office to enforce all laws that are broken within the confines of his jurisdiction, the most populous county in the Lone Star State. The DA is described as the chief law enforcement officer of the county. What a tremendous responsibility.

The gentlemen who have served in that awesome position for the past three decades helped Harris County earn the reputation as the Death Penalty Capital of the United States. Carol Vance firmly established the tradition. He was followed by Johnny Holmes, who held strongly to his sacred oath he gave to the citizens of Harris County. This meant that if the citizens of the great State of Texas deemed a law to be the law of the land, it should be enforced to the limit. Chuck Rosenthal, one of the most successful death penalty prosecutors in Harris County history, later succeeded Holmes.

The following sequence of events took place in this case:

October 10, 1991 – Jury selection began in Judge Woody Denson's court amid numerous objections from the defense table.

November 11 – Testimony began. DA John B. Holmes led the prosecution, ably assisted by ADAs Keno Henderson and Lyn McClellan.

Of course, the state's star witness was the grand jury member, Ms. Linda Ligon, who was riding with Sergeant Soboleski on this tragic night. Her testimony was reinforced by the taped dispatchers recordings of that night. They were, as follows:

"Help," she asked nine times. "Help, somebody help me. Help me, please, officer down." Several voices were heard on the radio asking for her location. Then: "Help me, he's dying, send an ambulance now."

Help came soon, but not soon enough.

The testimony continued, with evidence of the murder weapon being recovered from the apartment where Shelton Jones was arrested. Also, his clothing, stripped away from his sweaty body, was recovered and found to be of the exact description of the witness. Officer Gary Hicks, the first HPD officer on the scene, described the last words of Sergeant Soboleski, who expressed disbelief that this guy not only shot him, but shot him after he was on the ground. Hicks also testified to the fact that Soboleski had never been able to remove his weapon from this holster. Even though Sergeant Soboleski lived over five days after being wounded and obviously did not give up, it was mentioned by several officers that while waiting on medical assistance to arrive, the Sergeant was inquiring as to where he was. When he was told to not worry about his location, he painfully commented to the effect that he needed to "know where he was, that he wanted to know where he was going to die".

The two civilian mechanic witnesses, both men out there in the neighborhood trying to make a living and do what was right, held strong to their testimony. Johnny and Walter Green are to be commended for their forthrightness in doing their civic duty.

The court record:

November 19 – Jury finds Shelton Jones guilty of capital murder.

November 20 – Punishment phase includes testimony of a robbery victim couple who identified Jones as robbing them at gunpoint only days before murdering Soboleski.

November 21 – Jury sentences Shelton Jones to death by lethal injection. He showed no emotion just as professionals who examined him predicted he would do. He was described as a sociopath who didn't care what he did to anybody.

Jones' accomplice Chris Coleman received a twenty-year sentence for shooting at the wounded sergeant. He was eligible for parole as early as 1995. Accomplice Gregory Pickrom was not charged in this case, but had other legal issues pending against him.

In an investigation of this magnitude, it would

be impossible to mention all of the patrol officers who assisted in some manner that tragic night and the days and nights that followed. Those who should be singled out for their significant roles were the support personnel in the Crime Scene Unit and the Crime Lab. Their contributions were instrumental in this investigation. The meticulous recovery and documenting of evidence led to important identifications for prosecution purposes. CSU Officers Kevin Breen and Keith Webb conducted the scene evidentiary search, which actually comprised four locations. CSU Officers Beverly Trumble and Jim Kennedy handled the hospital and autopsy segments.

Evidence recovered by these officers enabled Firearms Examiner C. E. Anderson to positively connect evidence from Sergeant Soboleski's body and the scene to the Glock pistol recovered from the arrest location of Jones. Latent Print Examiner Peggy Frankhouser's examination of Soboleski's vehicle identified Shelton Jones' fingerprints on the fender as well as Gregory Pickrom's prints on the Glock papers recovered from the vehicle.

Members of this vast investigative team dedicated many years to HPD and the people of Houston. Lieutenant Ken Johnson retired in the 1990s to pursue another career with the U. S. State Department. Lieutenant Guy Mason retired in 2005 after twenty-seven years in the Homicide Division. Sergeants Kenny Williamson, Ronnie Doyle and Sharon Durham Evans also retired in 2005. Sergeants Dale Atchetee and Terry Ross retired in the 1990s. Sergeant L. B. Smith died in 2003 in a tragic accidental shooting.

In 2006, Mrs. Sue Soboleski resided in the Clear Lake area. Daughter Stephanie is the mother of two children, twelve-year-old Trevor and two-year-old Kaeden. Daughter Mallorie graduated from college in 2006 with a degree in Criminal Justice. The rest of the extended Soboleski remains intact.

With the assistance of Sue Soboleski, it was possible to obtain a photo of the monument that marks the gravesite of HPD Sergeant Bruno Soboleski. It reads:

SOBOLESKI

BRUNO D.
Feb. 5, 1958
Apr. 12, 1991

The reverse side of this monument reads:

SOBOLESKI

THE TIME I SPEND ALL BY MYSELF
I MOSTLY SPEND WITH YOU...

A 100 Club/HPOU LINE OF DUTY grave marker has been placed in the Oak Hill Cemetery at Sandy Lakes, Pennsylvania.

92

Officer Michael Paul Roman
Badge #5068
January 6, 1994

Motorist Strikes, Kills Officer Roman During a High Speed Chase on North Main

Michael Paul Roman was born on September 24, 1966 in Houston. He graduated from MacArthur High School and was in the United States Army Reserve for seven years, having served his country as a veteran of Desert Storm in the early 1990s. He served six months in the desert and shortly after returning home he joined the Houston Police Department in Cadet Class No. 146 on November 12, 1991. He took his oath of office as a probationary patrolman on May 6, 1992. His first assignment was to the nightshift of the Radio Patrol Division. He wore Badge No. 5068.

On Wednesday night, January 5, 1994, Officer Michael Roman was on his night off. However, with a small child and a pregnant wife, Officer Roman was working a voluntary overtime program on a 10 p.m.-1 a.m. shift. Earlier that same day, he and his wife Suelema had learned that their upcoming arrival would be a girl. Just before 11:45 p.m., Officer Roman, riding alone, heard the dispatcher put out a high-speed police pursuit situation involving Central and North Shepherd Patrol units. The latest information on the air said that the chase was approaching North Main and the 610 Loop and that officers were in pursuit of a stolen vehicle.

As any officer would do, Roman began driving in a direction that placed him in a position to assist in any manner possible. He was driving north on North Main at 28th, with both visual and audio emergency equipment engaged. However, a vehicle driven by Celia Rivas Quiroz was westbound on East 28th and failed to yield the right of way to the emergency police vehicle, going through the Stop sign controlling that intersection.

230

Ms. Quiroz entered the intersection, striking Officer Roman's vehicle. The point of impact was just to the left of the center of North Main, indicating that Officer Roman likely saw the citizen's vehicle at the last second and veered left. However, the right front of the Mitsubishi driven by Quiroz struck the right front of Officer Roman's Chevrolet Caprice. His vehicle was turned onto its left side. Taking a double blow, it slid into a utility pole on the northwest corner of North Main and 28th.

Roman was trapped inside his vehicle and, upon the Accident Investigator's arrival just moments later, Houston Fire Department paramedics were attempting to extract him from inside. The HFD personnel then rushed Roman to Ben Taub General Hospital. However, his injuries were so severe that he was declared dead at 12:45 a.m. on Thursday, January 6, 1994. He was twenty-seven years old. Other paramedics transported Celia Quiroz to Northwest Memorial Hospital with non-life-threatening injuries.

Officer Michael Paul Roman was survived by his wife Suelema and daughter Mikaela, aged two and a half. There also was the unborn daughter that was later named Marissa. Also mourning his sudden death were his parents Mr. Miguel and Mrs. Mary Roman, as well as his sister Cynthia Roman and brothers Raymond and Steven, all of Houston. Also surviving were his grandparents, Mr. and Mrs. Pablo (Ignacia) Roman of Somerville.

Brookside Funeral Home and Cemetery, 13401 Eastex Freeway at Lauder Road, was in charge of arrangements. Visitation was held at Brookside on Saturday, January 8, 1994, from 9 a.m. until 9 p.m. and continued on Sunday evening from 7 to 9 p.m. with a Rosary conducted during that time. Funeral services were held at the Second Baptist Church, 6400 Woodway, at 11 am. Monday, January 10. Burial followed at Brookside Cemetery.

Officer Roman had an extremely large extended family at HPD. They were his uncle, Public Service Officer Jose Garcia Sr.(Community Services), his cousins, Sergeants Rico Garcia, (Southwest Patrol) Andy Porras (SWAT) and J. Garcia (Eastside), and Officers D. C. Garcia (Northeast Patrol), S. M. Garcia (Central Patrol), R. Razo (Eastside Patrol), P. Razo (Southeast Patrol), Armando Ordaz (Narcotics Division), as well as Jail Attendant G. A. Garcia, PSO Supervisor C. L. Garcia (Dispatcher's Office), Civilian Clerk D. S. Gonzales (Personnel) and Administrative Aide J. Espitia (Special Operations).

The accident scene was investigated by Officers D. B. Houston and J. C. Wolfe. Their thorough investigation revealed that the suspect, whose intersection was controlled by a Stop sign, stated that she stopped and did not see or hear the emergency vehicle until she was in the intersection. She went on to say that she attempted to turn to the right to avoid the collision, but was unable to do so successfully.

A witness said that while he did not actually see the collision, he did hear Officer Roman's siren prior to the collision. Another witness arrived on the scene after the fact and stopped to inform investigators that Officer Roman had passed him with all of his emergency equipment functioning.

Accident Sergeant D. R. Hurd called in Accident Officers D. F. Willis and R. Saenz to assist in the investigation by reconstructing the accident. They reviewed photos and videotape of the scene as well as a "walk-through" that they completed. There were no skid marks from the suspect vehicle and the gouge marks in the pavement indicated that the point of impact was over into the southbound lanes, as Officer Roman had swerved in that direction in an attempt to avoid the collision.

OFFICER MICHAEL PAUL ROMAN

In summary, it was determined that the suspect failed to yield right of way leaving a Stop sign and also failed to yield right of way to an emergency vehicle. Investigators also determined that Officer Roman, while likely exceeding the speed limit, was operating within the law as he was running with full emergency equipment in order to provide backup and assistance to other officers. An assistant district attorney reviewed the investigation, resulting in charges that were only the municipal charge of failure to yield right of way (leaving a stop sign). This charge was later settled in municipal court.

In 2004, Suelema Roman, who had been married to Michael Roman nearly seven years, lived in the Spring-Klein area, where her two daughters attend Klein schools. Mikaela was thirteen years old and Marissa, born on May 4, 1994, nearly four months after her father's death, was ten. Suelema worked as a substitute teacher for several years and was now employed in the private sector.

Michael's mother died in April 1994, just three months after her son's death. His father still resides in Houston in 2004. Sister Cynthia lives in Houston and has three children, Michelle, Christina and Leo. Brother Raymond, who had a son Jess, died several years ago. Brother Steven resides in Houston. Grandmother Ignacio Roman died in 2003. Grandfather Pablo Roman is still living. As for the extended HPD family, with the exception of Uncle Jose Garcia Sr., who died in 2002, all of the cousins and surviving relatives are still with HPD in some capacity. The only other exception is Jail Attendant Gilbert Garcia, who became an officer with the HISD Police Department.

Narcotics Sergeant Rico Garcia said in an interview that he is the oldest of five brothers in law enforcement. Jose Garcia was their father. Rico also advised on the night of this tragedy he was on his way home when he heard on the police radio of this fatality. Being the kind of person he is, he said that he said a prayer for all officers as well as for his many relatives on the department. A short time later, he was advised at home that the fatality was his cousin Michael.

The stolen car involved in the deadly chase was eventually stopped near Northwest Mall. The suspect was charged with unauthorized use of a motor vehicle as well as resisting and evading arrest. Two passengers also were arrested and charged with resisting and evading while a third passenger was turned over to juvenile authorities.

Marker for Officer Roman at Brookside reads:

IN LOVING MEMORY
MICHAEL P. ROMAN
DEVOTED HUSBAND AND FATHER
(ALSO HAS BADGE #5068)

93

Officer Guy Patrick Gaddis
Badge #4539
January 31, 1994

Officer Gaddis Murdered by Lifelong Criminal Tamayo, Who Figured He Could Escape with Hands Cuffed Behind Him

Guy Patrick Gaddis was born on March 21, 1969 in Houston, Texas. He attended public schools in Pearland, graduating from Pearland High School in 1987. He served his country honorably in the United States Army and returned to the Houston area after his discharge. He joined the Houston Police Department in Police Cadet Class No. 148, which began training on April 27, 1992. His class completed training on October 15, 1992. His first assignment was to the night shift of Radio Patrol – Beechnut Substation, now called the Southwest Division. He wore Badge No. 4539.

On Sunday night, January 30, 1994, Officer Gaddis reported for duty on the night shift at the Beechnut Substation. He was assigned to ride a one-man unit, 17E23N. After running several report calls, Gaddis was flagged down in the 6700 block of Bissonnet by a citizen who reported that he had been robbed by two suspects at the Topaz Night Club. The officer reported this on-view complaint to the dispatcher and requested other units to check by with him at the Topaz, a known area trouble spot located at 6501 Chimney Rock. The reporting time was 2:21 a.m. now on the morning of Monday, January 31.

Three of Officer Gaddis' fellow units, with a total of five officers on board, immediately responded to this request. The first officer to arrive observed Officer Gaddis to have two suspects against a wall, spread-eagled and undergoing a search. This officer also observed that Gaddis had apparently completed his search of what will now be referred to as the No. 2 suspect. This first responding officer took control of this suspect and immediately handcuffed him with his hands to the rear. While doing so, this officer observed Gaddis continue his search of the No. 1 suspect. In doing so, he discovered the robbery complainant's watch. At this point, Officer Gaddis very likely ended his search of the No. 1 suspect prematurely, handcuffing him with his hands behind him.

Other officers arrived and observed the end results of the arrest. They watched as Officer Gaddis and the first arriving officer placed both suspects in the rear of Gaddis' patrol car. Suspect No. 1, later identified as Edgar Tamayo, was seated in the left rear seat while Suspect No. 2, Jesus Zarco Mendoza, was placed in the right rear seat.

OFFICER GUY PATRICK GADDIS

A very careful review of all officers present took place not only for the prosecution of the offense but also eleven years later to document the line of duty death for this publication. While no blame was assessed, important lessons were learned from the Gaddis experience.

Without a doubt, the events of this early morning will live forever in the hearts and minds of all five officers present prior to Officer Gaddis' departure with the two suspects. Their names are not used here. While they did not suffer the same consequence as Guy Gaddis, their names will not be brought forth for further questions about their actions.

These two suspects were in custody, handcuffed behind their back in the rear seat of a caged patrol car. While Gaddis transported them to the Southeast Command Station, the following is known:

Officer Gaddis drove southbound in the 8100 block of Chimney Rock. He drove through the City of Bellaire, just north of Chimney Rock and Holly. Then something went terribly awry in the back seat of the patrol car from behind the Plexiglas cage. While driving, Officer Gaddis was shot in the back of his head, causing his patrol car to veer to the left, out of control.

The unit crossed a residential yard on the northeast corner of this intersection, traveled further south across Holly and into the yard of a residence at 5229 Holly, striking the house at a high rate of speed and landing near the front door that faced north.

The crash awakened the occupants of this residence. They immediately came out the side door, only to see that a Houston police car had crashed into the front of their home. The patrol officer who had been the driver was slumped over the steering wheel. They also saw an individual in the back seat cage portion of the police vehicle bleeding from the head and apparently unconscious.

The residents immediately summoned the Bellaire police. The Bellaire dispatcher sent Officer W. T. Warner to the scene, backed up by Officer J. M. Manning. Officer Warner had been monitoring HPD's radio channel and was aware of the arrests having been made on Chimney Rock.

The Bellaire officers saw a real-life scene unlike anything they had seen in their veteran police careers: the crashed HPD patrol car and, more importantly, the condition of Officer Gaddis. They quickly called an ambulance manned by City of Bellaire paramedics Carla Breeding and Chuck Lysack. Breeding and Lysack found that the officer was not breathing and had no vital signs. They didn't give up. They made every effort possible to resuscitate Gaddis, who had three gunshot wounds to the back of his head. As they did so, the LifeFlight helicopter was in flight. Bellaire Officers Warner and Manning took control of the scene as well as the suspect Mendoza in the rear of the police car. This suspect had regained consciousness. The paramedics also examined him, finding no serious injuries.

While these activities took place, Houston police officers virtually surrounded the neighborhood.

LifeFlight rushed Officer Gaddis to Hermann Hospital, with little hope for his survival. Doctors pronounced him dead at 4:31 a.m., January 31, 1994. He was only twenty-four years old, leaving behind his pregnant wife, Mrs. Rosa Gaddis.

Besides his wife, the officer was survived his parents, Mr. And Mrs. Edwin (Gayle) Gaddis of Brookside Village; brother Glenn and his wife Angela of Houston; brother Gary and nephew Justyn Gaddis of Brookside; his aunt Patsy Reeves of Shreveport; Uncle Charles Gottlick and wife Maureen of Scotch Plains, New Jersey; aunt Bernadette Lopez and husband George and uncle Russell Gottlick and wife Joyce.

Funeral services were held at 11 a.m. Wednesday, February 2, 1994, at the Second Baptist Church in

Houston with Dr. Ed Young, Reverend David Dixon, and HPD Chaplain Ed Davis officiating. Burial followed at the South Park Cemetery in Pearland.

The on-duty Homicide supervisor, Lieutenant, C. S. "Steve" Arrington, upon learning of this tragedy, responded to the scene with several night shift on-duty investigators. He also began an immediate call to the Homicide Murder squad responsible for this particular time segment. Lieutenant Nelson Zoch was the Homicide Murder Squad lieutenant on-call at this time of the morning.

OFFICER GUY GADDIS AND HIS DAD, MR. EDWIN GADDIS, AND BROTHER GLENN GADDIS AND GARY GADDIS

"I can vividly recall arriving on the scene to find it very professionally protected not only by Lieutenant Arrington of HPD Homicide and the Beechnut Patrol officers and supervisors as well as Bellaire P.D.," Zoch said. "This offense occurred in the City of Bellaire, a municipality complete and separate from the City of Houston. As such, Bellaire had legal jurisdiction into the offenses which had occurred at that location on Chimney Rock and Holly".

"Having had previous experience with conflicting jurisdictional issues, after being assessed of the situation, Lieutenant Arrington and I approached the highest-ranking supervisor on the scene, the Bellaire chief of police. Words cannot describe the look on the chief's face when I, as a mere lieutenant of the Houston Police Department, volunteered to take complete responsibility for this investigation. That offer was graciously accepted and their full support and cooperation was pledged to provide their assistance to our department. There was never any doubt in my mind that the chief and his department could and would have conducted a professional investigation. However, as learned from previous incidents, law enforcement/justice was best served with one agency assuming total responsibility for the investigation."

Shortly after this jurisdictional matter was resolved, Criminal Investigations Assistant Chief John Gallemore and Homicide Captain W. G. "Bill" Edison arrived on the scene. Both were in complete agreement about the jurisdictional issue and assisted from that time forth in providing any additional manpower and resources necessary to pursue the goal of securing a conviction of those responsible for the capital murder of one of Houston's finest, Officer Guy Patrick Gaddis.

An important initial finding at the scene revealed that after the shooting and the crash, Edgar Tamayo had been able to kick out the window glass on the left rear door and escape on foot. HPD Officer O.R. Warren was driving southbound on Chimney Rock going toward the scene when he observed what had to have his sight of a lifetime-a suspect running with his hands cuffed behind his back. Amazingly, this was the man who had just murdered Officer Gaddis. The evidence became stronger by the minute as the handcuffs recovered from Tamayo bore Officer Guy Gaddis employee number-98834.

Lieutenant Zoch began a complete squad callout to assist the initial scene investigators, Sergeants Jerry Novak and Larry Webber, who were to be the lead investigators under the supervision of Captain Bill Edison and Lieutenant Zoch. It would be their responsibility to coordinate all investigative responsibilities through their supervisors and the Harris County District Attorney's Office.

"Lieutenant Arrington and I, while at the scene, reviewed the personnel which had been utilized to this point," Zoch recalled. As had been the practice in previous officer-involved Investigations, a Homicide investigator was assigned to be personally responsible for the care of the suspect, mainly assuring that a suspect was provided full constitutional rights under the law. In this instance, Zoch assigned Sergeant Rick Maxey the responsibility for the main suspect, Tamayo. The lieutenant gave Maxey's partner, Sergeant Stuart Hal Kennedy, the assignment to interview the second suspect, Mendoza, who at this time appeared to us not only as a robbery suspect, but as a valuable witness to a capital crime.

Sergeant Fred W. Carroll was assigned to conduct the hospital investigation while Sergeant Stuart. H. "Hal" Kennedy, who had been assigned to the suspect Mendoza, also was given the difficult task of attending the autopsy of the officer. Officer Gaddis' patrol car, heavily damaged from the impact with the house, was towed to the HPD print stall building and secured. Sergeant Eugene Yanchak was assigned to coordinate a thorough Crime Scene Unit and Lab personnel processing of this vehicle. Lieutenant Zoch assigned Sergeant David A. Ferguson as his assistant, whose job was to coordinate with the District Attorney's Office regarding any charges that would be filed in this case. Chief Prosecutor Ned Morris was present during the scene investigation, this being the norm in cases involving the death and/or serious on-duty injury of a police officer.

Further assignments were as follows: Sergeant D. D. Shirley conducted an at-length interview with the original robbery complainant. (This became more important than ever since it was this offense that eventually led to the death of Officer Gaddis); Sergeant

R. L. "Rick" Maxey began to do thorough computer background investigations into the criminal histories of both suspects, mainly Tamayo; When it became apparent that Tamayo and Mendoza's language barrier was an issue, Chicano Squad Investigators Jaime Escalante and Vincente Garcia were assigned to conduct interviews with the suspects; Veteran Detectives Maxey and Kennedy supervised these all-important proceedings while Sergeants Larry Ott and Bruce Baker assisted in the acquisition of legal consents and warrants relating to the recovery of additional evidence from both suspects. Ott and Baker also conducted extensive interviews with the home owners on Holly Street.

MRS. GAYLE GADDIS AND HER SON, OFFICER GUY GADDIS

Other observations and evidence recovered and/or noted at the scene and during the vehicle examination were that there were five bullet holes in the Plexiglas shield supposedly in place to protect the police officer. Six spent .380 hulls were recovered from the rear area of the police car as well as a Bersa .380 automatic weapon.

From the evidence recovered, as well as from a statement provided by the second robbery suspect, the following was believed to have been the chain of events leading up to this tragedy:

Somehow, during the original pat down and cursory searches conducted at the robbery scene, Edgar Tamayo had managed to secrete a semi-automatic .380 pistol on his person. After leaving the scene with both suspects, Officer Gaddis stopped to make a telephone call, believed to have been to confer with the District Attorney's Intake Office over charges he intended to file on both suspects. During this phone call while Tamayo and Mendoza were alone, but in the sight of Officer Gaddis, according to Mendoza, Tamayo spoke of shooting his way out of this situation. He was able to get the pistol in his handcuffed hands behind his back.

When Officer Gaddis drove south on Chimney Rock in the block north of Holly, Tamayo was able to turn himself around in the rear seat and place the pistol right up against the Plexiglas barrier and fire it six times.

Later, investigating officers asked themselves: Now what person in his right mind would believe he could shoot the driver of a car with your hands cuffed behind you in a locked backseat, and still be able to escape safely?

The actions of Tamayo rendered Officer Gaddis totally disabled and the police car careened out of control. It crossed a residential yard on the northeast corner of Chimney Rock and Holly, then crossed Holly, and into the yard of the Clay family home. It crashed into the front door at a high rate of speed. The impact injured both Tamayo and Mendoza, but Tamayo was able to then kick out the window glass of the left rear door and escape.

An investigation of this enormity cannot be conducted without the professional assistance of support personnel. "By this," Lieutenant Zoch said, "we are speaking not only of the Crime and Firearms Lab professionals, but also of those street 'grunts' that do much of the dirty work, the Crime Scene Units." In this investigation, CSU Officers Beverly Trumble, J. F. Goodfellow, Delinda Wilker, A. K. Williams, W. C. Cates, Ray Collins, Keith Webb, J. L. Kay, and Lorenzo Verbitskey all played important roles in the discovery and recovery of evidence. Firearms Examiner C. E. Anderson performed all of the ballistics examinations related to this offense and Latent Print Examiner Chuck Sheldon conducted the fingerprint examinations.

Edgar Tamayo, an experienced hardened criminal and also an illegal immigrant, had managed to beat the justice system of our great country by purchasing a weapon just days prior to this offense.

A violent criminal justifying his actions is truly amazing. Tamayo told Officer Escalante that it was the officer's fault for not searching him properly. He said he was searched by two different officers and went on to say that he was angry, managed to get the gun, stood up in the back of the car and shoot the officer. He had the gun on his right side when he fired the pistol. Further, he said that he had just bought the gun Wal-Mart in Dallas. Mendoza told investigators that at one point Tamayo tried to dry fire his weapon without a bullet in the chamber, but was not able to do so. Tamayo said that it was difficult to do this while handcuffed, but he did it. He seemed proud of his actions.

In October 1994, jury selection began in Judge Mike McSpadden's District Court. The lead prosecutor was District Attorney John B. Holmes, ably assisted by ADA Julian Ramirez. The Plexiglas police car cage had been removed from the car after examination. This same cage, bullet holes and all, was brought into court as further evidence of what happened that night. After the lengthy and tedious capital jury selection, testimony began. On Thursday, October 27, 1994, after a four-day trial, a jury took just thirty minutes to find Edgar Tamayo guilty of capital murder.

Next came the punishment phase of the trial. Now it would be the prosecution's objective to show that Edgar Tamayo was a continuing threat to society as proven by his violent criminal past. An illegal immigrant, he went to California and then to Texas, where he had numerous skirmishes with the law. He was found to have no regard for the laws of the country he chose to call his own. In the continuing investigation, Homicide Detective Rick Maxey and District Attorney's Investigator Johnny Bonds traveled to California, where they found that Tamayo had committed criminal acts for which he had been imprisoned. Witnesses from California as well as officers from the local area were available to testify about his unlawful demeanor. On Tuesday, November 1, 1994, after only three hours of deliberation, the jury determined that Tamayo should be sentenced to death for the murder of Officer Guy Gaddis. Twelve years later he was still on Death Row, hiding behind his appeals. Mendoza, who testified for the prosecution, received a year on the robbery charge and was released after serving his time.

In 2007, Officer Gaddis' daughter Stephanie was twelve years old and living in El Paso with her Mother, Rosa, who remarried and is the mother of two more daughters. Stephanie visits regularly in Texas with her grandparents, uncles, aunts, and cousins. Mr. and Mrs. Gaddis reside in Brookside. Mr. Gaddis is retired from the Houston Fire Department. Brother Glenn is the father of three boys-Justyn-fourteen, Taylor-nine, and Shane-seven. Brother Gary is the father of two daughters, Abigail-twelve and Mallory-nine. Glenn and Gary both reside in the Pearland area near their parents.

Sergeants Jerry Novak, Larry Webber, Fred Carroll, Larry Ott, Hal Kennedy, D. D. Shirley and Eugene Yanchak are all retired from HPD. Chief Gallemore, Captain Edison and Lieutenant Nelson Zoch also are retired. Rick Maxey is now the lieutenant over what remains of the Zoch murder squad, which still includes the resilient Sergeant David Ferguson. Lieutenant Steve Arrington supervises another day shift Murder squad. Sergeant Bruce Baker is assigned to the Homicide Six Crimes Unit. Investigator Garcia is still in the Chicano Squad and Investigator Escalante left the division. Bonds is still with the D.A.'s office and nearing retirement.

As for the CSU officers, only Verbitsky, Kay and Goodfellow are still active. Officers Wilker, Webb and Collins are retired, Cates passed away, and Trumble and Williams both left the department. As to lab personnel, Anderson and Sheldon are both retired. The officer who alertly arrested Tamayo, O. R. Warren, is still assigned to the night shift at the Southwest Station.

The Bellaire police chief retired. Officer Warner, a night shift stalwart for many years in Bellaire, retired and has since passed away. Officer Manning is still with his department. Paramedics Breeding and Lysack both left the Bellaire Fire Department.

The gravemarker at South Park Cemetery is an upright three space monument to the GADDIS family, with the name GUY PATRICK on the left, MARCH 21, 1969 - JANUARY 31, 1994.

94

Officer David Michael Healy
Badge #4642
November 12, 1994

Officer David Michael Healy, Only 26, Dies After Losing Control of Patrol Car on 288

David Michael Healy was born on July 25, 1968, in Chicago, Illinois. He was a veteran of the Persian Gulf War, having served with the United States Army 83rd Airborne Division and was discharged with the rank of sergeant. He joined the Houston Police Department by way of Police Cadet Class No. 153, which began its training on April 12, 1993. Upon completion of his academy course work, Officer Healy took his oath of office on September 30, 1993. His first and only permanent assignment in his short HPD career was to the South Central Patrol Division. He wore Badge #4642.

On Friday night, November 11, 1994, Officer David Healy was riding a one-man unit. He had completed an assignment by booking a prisoner at the Southeast Command Station at 8300 Mykawa Road and was en route back to his duty station at South Central, 2202 St. Emanuel. At approximately 2 a.m., while driving northbound on Highway 288 in the 6000 block of the freeway near North MacGregor Drive, he was in the second lane from the right.

Healy swerved to avoid slower traffic and lost control of his police vehicle, a 1993 Chevrolet Caprice. In doing so, he slid into a concrete-based lighting tower. He sustained serious injuries in the collision. A Houston Fire Department ambulance rushed him to Ben Taub General Hospital. He was pronounced dead on arrival at 2:37 a.m. Saturday, November 12, 1994. He was twenty-six years old.

Officer Healy was survived by his mother, Mrs. Judy Casey, and her husband, Gerry Casey, of Thousand Oaks, California, and his father, John B. Healy, of Chicago; his brother, John Bret Healy, and his grandmother, Mrs. Bernice Healy, both of Chicago; and numerous aunts, uncles and cousins.

Friends and fellow officers also mourned this tragic accidental death.

Visitation was held at the Earthman Hunter's Creek Chapel from 6 to 8 p.m. Monday, November 14, 1994. A funeral Mass was held at 10 a.m. the next day at the St. Michael Church, 1801 Sage Road, with the Reverend Laurence Connelly as the celebrant. The Houston Police Department Honor Guard and a United States Military Honor Guard participated at this service in honoring Officer Healy. Cremation followed.

OFFICER DAVID MICHAEL HEALY

There were several civilian eyewitnesses to this tragic accident. These witness accounts were consistent to the point that no other vehicle and/or parties were involved in any manner in the vehicular crash. A complete and thorough investigation was conducted by the Accident Division. Those participating in this review were Officers M. E. Wick, M. D. Jenkins (who actually drove upon the scene after the crash) and Hit and Run Detail Officers M.W. Potell and R. Saenz, all of whom were supervised by Accident Division Lieutenant Davis and Sergeant Hall.

Many efforts have been made to contact this officer's mother and brother; they have been unsuccessful. His father wished to keep his feelings private.

95

Officer Dawn Suzanne Erickson
Badge #5963
December 24, 1995

Young Officer Dawn Erickson Struck, Killed By Passing Motorist at Christmas Eve Service

Dawn Suzanne Erickson was born in Belleville, Illinois, on January 15, 1973. Her parents were David and Beth Erickson. She graduated from Westbury High School in southwest Houston in 1992, finishing in the top five percent of her class. Continuing her education at the Houston Community College, she earned an Associates of Arts Degree in 1993. On August 29, 1994, she joined the Houston Police Department by entering Police Cadet Class No. 160. Upon graduation on March 3, 1995, she entered her probationary training period, which she successfully completed on August 28, 1995. She wore Badge No. 5963.

Dawn's first and only assignment was to the South Central Division of Central Patrol. She had completed only four months of a promising career when on the night of December 24 – Christmas Eve 1995 – she was on a voluntary extra-job assignment of her choice at a church in southwest Houston.

At approximately 6:45 p.m. in this most joyous of seasons, Officer Erickson was directing traffic for the Christmas Eve service at the Unity Church of Christianity, 2900 Unity Drive. Erickson was wearing a reflective jacket and using an orange-tipped flashlight. At this time, a motorist was eastbound on Unity in a 1987 Honda Accord. The motorist later reported that she only saw a red light flickering in the street.

It was at this point that the passing motorist struck Officer Erickson with the left front of the vehicle. The impact caused the officer to be thrown into the vehicle's windshield and an additional twelve feet into the air and onto the pavement. Erickson suffered head and leg injuries as a result of the impact. A Houston Fire Department ambulance rushed her to Ben Taub General Hospital, where she was pronounced dead at 8:50 p.m. She was only twenty-two years old.

OFFICER DAWN SUZANNE ERICKSON

This accident was professionally investigated by the HPD Accident Division. While Officers N.E. Maurer and R. S. Cedeno were the first units on the scene, Officers J. W. Nickell and R. Hernandez were the primary investigators from the Accident Division's Hit and run Detail. Sergeant D. Hurd supervised as well as participated in the investigation. Officer R. Saenz was later assigned to assist in the investigative follow-up. Officer D. E. Henry, who was working this departmentally approved extra job with the complainant, was also on the scene to assist the responding officers.

The suspect driving the Honda Accord was quickly determined at the scene to have not had any major culpability in this offense. She was taken into custody and tested for any and all chemical substances in her body. All tests were negative.

The Accident Division conducted an extensive and thorough investigation. While investigators determined that the driver of the Honda was likely exceeding the speed limit at the time of the impact into Officer Erickson, a grand jury no billed her. Her name will not be mentioned since she was not charged with any offense.

Officer Erickson was survived by her father David Erickson of Harlingen and her mother and step-father, Beth and Scott Green of Richmond. Also, her brother Christopher Erickson as well as her sisters Deanna Nixon and husband Brent and Nicole Erickson survived her.

The Earthman Company was in charge of arrangements. Visitation was held from 8:30 a.m. until 9 p.m. at the Earthman facility at 12555 South Kirkwood on Wednesday, December 27, 1995. Funeral services were conducted at the Sugar Creek Baptist Church, 13213 Southwest Freeway, at 10 a.m. Thursday, December 28. The Reverend Gene A. Moore and Police Chaplain Edwin Davis co-officiated. Burial followed at the Forest Park-Westheimer Cemetery.

The gravemarker for Officer Erickson reads as follows:

OUR GUARDIAN ANGEL
DAWN S. ERICKSON
JAN 15, 1973 - DEC 24, 1995

It should be noted that all efforts to locate any of the Erickson family have been unsuccessful. Also, that Officer Erickson was a mere six months older than the youngest Officer killed in the line of duty, Officer Michelle Groves in 1987.

96

Officer Cuong Huy (Tony) Trinh
Badge #5891
April 6, 1997

Officer Tony Trinh, Working at Parents' Store, Shot and Killed by Man Who Steals His Jewelry

Cuong Huy Trinh was born in South Vietnam on May 18, 1971. He came to the United States along with his parents and a brother in 1983. Tony, as he was known to family, friends and fellow officers, joined the Houston Police Department by way of Police Cadet Class No. 158 on April 11, 1994. That class graduated on September 29, 1994, and Tony's first assignment was to the Westside Patrol Division. Tony completed his probation at that unit and worked there until he transferred to the Juvenile

Division in July 1996. He wore Badge No. 5891.

On Sunday morning, April 6, 1997, Officer Tony Trinh had volunteered to work at his parents' store, the Sunny's Food Store. This was a convenience store located in Southwest Houston at 2716 Westerland. Trinh opened the store at approximately 7:30 a.m. A customer arrived at 8:30 a.m. and, not seeing anyone behind the counter, began calling and searching for an employee. She then discovered Tony Trinh lying behind the counter. She called police and the Trinh was found to be dead from a single gunshot wound to the forehead. He was only twenty-four years old.

Police Officer Coung "Tony" Huy Trinh was survived by his parents, Mr. and Mrs. Nguyen Dinh Trinh, and one brother, HPD Probationary Police Officer Dat "Ricky" Huy Trinh of the Southwest Patrol Division.

Forest Park Westheimer Funeral Home, 12800 Westheimer, was in charge of arrangements. Visitation was held at that location beginning on Wednesday, April 9, 1997, from 9 a.m. until 9 p.m. Funeral services were held at the Don Coleman Community Coliseum, 1050 Dairy Ashford, at 10 a.m. Saturday, April 12. Burial followed at the Forest Park Westheimer Cemetery.

This was definitely a who-dun-it and the Homicide Division immediately sprang into action. On this weekend, the Murder Squad of Lieutenant Greg Neely was on duty. Neely had taken a vacation day and Night Shift Homicide Lieutenant Charles "Chuck" McClelland was filling in for him. Assigned to the scene investigation were Sergeant David Calhoun and Investigator Fred Hale. Lieutenant McClelland also assigned to this investigation Sergeants John Swaim and Carless Elliott, who were ably assisted by Investigators Millard "Fil" Waters and Darrell Robertson. Homicide Captain Richard Holland also made the scene with Lieutenant McClelland and they both supervised the investigation.

Crime Scene Units J. A. Ogden and J. Hammerle were summoned to record and recover any evidence the investigators deemed necessary. Firearms Examiner Mike Lyons also was called in as was Latent Print Examiner Chuck Sheldon. A chief assistant district attorney also was on hand, according to procedure in police shootings like this one. Assistant Chiefs Joe Breshears and John Gallemore also arrived to assure the Homicide supervisors of any additional resources that might be needed.

The neighborhood was canvassed and officers determined that about the time of this offense, an Asian male was seen exiting the store hurriedly and getting into the back seat of a vehicle. While this possible suspect was running, he was seen dropping an item and stopping to pick it up.

Officer Trinh was wearing several gold necklaces when he was found. He was not in uniform and his police identification was found near him in a position that probably would not have been seen.

The initial scene investigation revealed that some items of jewelry were missing from Officer Trinh, yet several were left behind. The shooter left a significant amount of cash at the store, with no signs that a ransacking or search for such had taken place. The officer's police ID remained at the scene and it was unknown whether the suspect saw the ID or the officer's weapons. The only solid physical evidence found in the initial investigation was a 9mm hull and a spent round from the scene, also possibly a 9mm slug.

The following morning, with Lieutenant Neely back on board and Captain Holland closely monitoring the investigation, Sergeant Jim Ladd and his partner, Investigator Todd Miller, were assigned to assist. Lieutenant McClelland, on the night shift, remained actively involved in the investigation. Officers ran any and all leads coming in on the night shift through him and he kept the dayshift fully informed of their activities.

OFFICER CUONG HUY TRINH

In such an involved investigation, Homicide stalwarts knew that the more experienced officers involved the better as long as the investigation and activities of all of them were closely coordinated. This again held true in this case. There have been other police officer who-dun-it investigations conducted by the Homicide Division through the years. Some of those included Officer Lyndon L. Sander (1967), Officer Leon Griggs (1970) and Officer Jerry Spruill (1972). In these instances, just as in the Trinh case, there were no immediate clues that indicated what happened or who was involved.

The major question was where to start. With

Officer Trinh being of Vietnamese background, the department's Oriental snitches were immediately pressed into service. Was this murder related to Officer Trinh's departmental assignment? Was it a botched robbery? Was there a connection with the numerous Asian gangs in the Westheimer/Alief area? Questions abounded with few answers. As the old adage goes, "Working on a mystery with no clues."

As in the cases mentioned above, months went by with officers thoroughly checking out any and all leads. Suspect after suspect were eliminated. These were very trying times for Homicide investigators and their supervisors, who are charged with the responsibility of maintaining troop morale and at the same time making sure that all leads were thoroughly checked out. Ultimately, many of them proved to be totally unrelated to the investigation. Homicide could leave no stone unturned, for this division's worst nightmare was an uncleared capital murder of an innocent citizen or, especially, the uncleared capital murder of a law enforcement officer of any jurisdiction.

Hopefully, at some point, the real story starts to unfold. Then, all of the previous work becomes well worth it. So it was on or around August 7, 1997 – four long months after this offense. Westside Asian Crimes Investigator Charlie Cash contacted Sergeant John Swaim in Homicide. Swaim was a natural leader, admired and respected by many Homicide investigators for his natural investigative instincts. Lieutenant Neely, himself an experienced investigator, recognized Swaim's abilities and readily placed him out front.

Investigator Cash' information was that a man named Chuong Tong was the person responsible for Trinh's murder. Further, Tong had been seen with Officer Trinh's missing jewelry and other individuals involved directly or indirectly were three other Asian males named Dan, Joe and yet another Joe. Also, information surfaced through Cash's informant that the murder weapon was a Glock and that Tong had been involved in a Galleria area bank robbery recently. The Glock information, as only investigators knew, was true and had been purposefully withheld for obvious reasons.

Good information is just that. However, great investigative abilities are needed to work out that information in a manner where it can be used in a criminal prosecution. Sergeant Swaim carefully had this information checked out in order to identify all of the parties mentioned. As a result of a meticulous and detailed investigation, Lieutenant Neely, Sergeant Swaim and a posse were able to obtain probable cause warrants for the parties involved to this point.

Officers made the arrests on probable cause warrants. In summary, Tong gave a statement to Investigator Fil Waters in which he implicated himself in the robbery of the Sunny's Store. He also said that he knew Officer Trinh was in fact a police officer because Trinh advised him of such and cautioned him in what he was doing. He maintained that he shot Trinh because he was intimidated by his size. (This would hardly hold any water in court due to the actual size of the slain officer).

He also later admitted to the Galleria area bank robbery and identified the other parties involved.

The two individuals who were in Dan's vehicle, the getaway car, were identified and gave statements placing themselves and Tong at the scene of the murder. Additionally, one of the witnesses who saw the suspect run across the store parking lot positively identified Tong.

The state filed capital murder charges against Cuong Tong in the death of Officer Trinh. Assistant District Attorney Julian Ramirez led the prosecution in this case. On Tuesday, March 11, 1998, the suspect pled not guilty in the 178th Criminal District Court. A jury found Tong guilty and sentenced to him to death by lethal injection. In 2007, nearly ten years after the verdict and sentence, Tong's appeal remains in the justice system.

Officer Trinh's grave is marked with a standup monument and a footmarker. Both read as follows:

TRINH, HUY CUONG (TONY)
PHAP DANK: NGUYEN GIAI
MAY 18, 1971 - APRIL 6, 1997

97

Sergeant Kent D. Kinkaid
May 23, 1998

Sgt. Kent Kinkaid Shot Suddenly After Confronting Young Men in Truck Over 'Rock' Hitting Windshield

Kent D. Kinkaid was born on August 17, 1957 in Phillipsburg, Kansas. After high school, Kent attended Fort Hays State University in Hays, Kansas. He also served on the Wichita, Kansas Police Department for four and a half years. He joined the Houston Police Department in Police Cadet Class No. 121 on May 29, 1984. He took his oath of office on September 28, 1984, proudly wearing badge No. 2251. His first assignment was to the North Shepherd Patrol Division.

After serving his mandatory tour of duty in the Jail Division, he returned to North Shepherd. In 1986, he transferred to the Special Operations Division. Upon being promoted to sergeant in 1988, his first assignment was the Dispatcher's Division. From there, he returned to Special Operations and then transferred to the night shift at Westside Patrol Command.

SERGEANT KENT D. KINKAID

On Friday night, May 22, 1998, Sergeant Kinkaid was off duty. At approximately 11 p.m. he and his wife Nancy Kincaid left their home in the Copperfield area of west Harris County. They were in their family vehicle, a Jeep Cherokee, and were en route to meet friends at a nearby restaurant. Sergeant Kinkaid was driving in his neighborhood when an unknown object struck the Jeep's front windshield. Kent and Nancy believed this unknown object had just been thrown from a pickup truck coming toward them.

Sergeant Kinkaid immediately turned around and followed this vehicle for fourteen blocks, at which time this truck turned around and headed back toward the Jeep. Kinkaid got out of his vehicle as the truck pulled up alongside him. He confronted the driver of the truck about the object that had struck his vehicle, asking the driver for identification and telling him that he was a police officer. He was reaching for his wallet to obtain his Police ID when Mrs. Kinkaid saw an arm come out of the driver's side window of the truck. She saw a flash and heard a gunshot that caused her husband to fall to the pavement as the truck fled the scene.

This offense occurred in the jurisdiction of the Harris County Sheriff's Department in the unincorporated section of the county. Quickly, the LifeFlight Helicopter transported the wounded sergeant to Hermann Hospital. He was shot once in the left eye. Given all medical attention possible, Kent Kinkaid passed away at 3:18 a.m. Saturday, May 23, 1998. He was only forty years of age.

Sergeant Kinkaid was survived by his wife Nancy Kincaid and two daughters, ten-year-old Jena Lee Kincaid and six-year-old Courtney Deanne Kincaid. Also mourning his sudden death were his mother, Mrs. Myrna Kinkaid, and one sister, Mrs. Kathy Conway, as well as numerous other relatives and friends. He was preceded in death by his father, Donald Kinkaid, in 1988.

Funeral services were under the direction of Klein Funeral Home, 16131 Champion Forest Drive in the Champions area. Visitation was held from 2 p.m. until 9 p.m. Monday, May 25. Visitation continued from 9 a.m. until 3 p.m. Tuesday, May 26 at the Bear Creek United Methodist Church. Services were held at 3 p.m. that day. Burial followed in Stockton, Kansas, on Thursday, May 28.

The Harris County Sheriff's Department had legal jurisdiction over this offense. The sheriff immediately extended professional courtesy to the Houston Police Department due to the fact that the offense involved the death of one of its own. Homicide Lieutenant Willie W. Holt and the Homicide commander, Captain Richard Holland, both made the scene of this offense. Captain Holland spoke with HCSO Homicide Captain Dick Henderson and the two agreed to a joint investigation. Since this happened on a Friday night, the weekend squad was on duty. Homicide Lieutenant Greg Neely came on duty immediately to assist HCSO Homicide investigators.

HPD Homicide Sergeants John Swaim and Carless Elliott came from home to conduct the scene investigation along with HCSO Detectives Bob Black, Roger Wedgeworth, Bill Valerio, W. A. Taber and Mark Schmidt. HCSO Crime Scene Unit Officer K. L. Culver was assisted by HPD CSU Officers C. D. Duncan and J. A. Ogden.

The physical evidence at the scene consisted of a small pool of blood and one .25 caliber hull found on the driver's side floorboard of the Kinkaid Jeep. Upon learning Mrs. Kinkaid's story, the investigators backtracked to an area fourteen blocks away where she recalled hearing the unknown object strike their vehicle. These veteran investigators examined the

Jeep's windshield more closely, causing them to believe that the object could have been an angled bullet strike. Miraculously, another .25-caliber hull was found in the street. The two were of the same brand. However, Mrs. Kinkaid could only describe the vehicle as an unknown dark-colored pickup truck with a chrome strip across the tailgate. The officers doubted that Mrs. Kinkaid could identify anyone in the truck.

HPD Sergeant C. E. Jackson lived in the area of this offense. With a teen-age stepson, he had experienced over several years a number of harassing and mischievous incidents involving his property. He learned the identity of a young man who he felt was involved in these incidents, most of which he had reported to HCSO. Just days before Kinkaid's murder, Sergeant Jackson had recovered a .25-caliber hull from the street in front of his house after the window of his vehicle had been shot out. Jackson called Homicide Sergeant Wayne Wendel, who had been called in to assist in this investigation along with his partner, Officer Fred Hale.

At the first look at this information, Sergeant Wendel probably thought it was too good to be true. Firearms Examiners Robert Baldwin and Kim Downs examined this hull with the previously recovered pair. They were a match in brand and, more importantly, all three had been fired from the same weapon.

JENA LEE, MRS. NANCY, COURTNEY, AND KENT D. KINKAID

Sergeant Jackson had named the young man he felt had been causing him these problems. Investigators further found that an attempted robbery offense had occurred in the same area the same night as Kinkaid was killed. They obtained a Texas drivers license photo on an emergency basis and used this photo in a photo spread. The robbery complainant immediately identified this suspect, Timothy Wayne "Timmy" Reese (White Male, 17). As a result of this identification, Sergeant Swaim and HCSO Detectives obtained a felony arrest warrant on the robbery case. At this point, the Homicide investigators didn't know if Reese had partners in crime.

Officers then undertook a carefully planned surveillance of Reese' residence. By late Saturday night, they had the plan in place. A vehicle drove to Reese's residence early in the hours of Sunday morning, May 24, 1998, with its occupant speaking to someone there before leaving the area. Officers stopped this vehicle on several traffic violations. Reese was in the vehicle along with a previously unknown subject, Anthony Cardell Haynes (African-American Male, 19).

The officers took Reese and Haynes to HCSO Homicide headquarters, where Sergeant Swaim began a lengthy interview with Timmy Reese, while Homicide Investigator Todd Miller questioned Haynes. Reese implicated Haynes as the shooter. He said he and a young man named Michael Tunson were just along for the ride. Haynes admitted to the shooting and before the night was over, took a joyous group of HPD and HCSO detectives on a ride which led to the weapon and the clip being recovered from two locations many miles apart.

One of the key elements to this offense was whether Haynes knew that Sergeant Kinkaid was a police officer. Early on, Mrs. Kinkaid was adamant in that she heard her husband identify himself verbally to the driver of the pickup as a police officer. As a result, capital murder charges were filed against Anthony Haynes. Timothy Wayne Reese was charged with aggravated robbery in another unrelated offense. Both of these suspects implicated a juvenile also as having been with them on this night. Officers picked him up and he admitted to being at the scene. Authorities filed on him in Juvenile Court and later certified him as a sixteen-year-old adult.

The capital murder trial was held in Judge Jim Wallace' 263rd Criminal District Court. Veteran prosecutors Mark Vinson and Don Smyth represented the State of Texas for Sergeant Kent Kinkaid. Jurors found Anthony Cardell Haynes guilty and on September 24, 1999, after three days of deliberations, sentenced him to death by lethal injection. As a matter of course, he is on death row while the appeals process winds its lengthy course. His first appeal was rejected in 2001.

Timothy Wayne Reese testified for the state in Haynes' trial and, over a period of time, was charged with an unrelated assault for which he received ninety days in jail. The juvenile certified as an adult, Michael Tunson (Turner), (White Male, 17) was given three years in TDCJ in 1999 for a robbery charge.

Life must go on for a young widow with two daughters. Mrs. Nancy Kinkaid has remained strong for her daughters and still resides in the Copperfield area.

98

Officer Troy Alan Blando
Badge #2336
May 19, 1999

Car Thief Williams Guns Down Troy Blando In Cold Blood at Southwest Freeway Motel

Troy Alan Blando was born in Bussac, France, on July 31, 1959, to Mr. and Mrs. Alvin (Della) Blando. Being the son of a career United States military man, Troy traveled extensively in his early years. He attended elementary and junior high school in San Antonio and graduated from Roosevelt High School in the Alamo City in 1977. For several years after high school, he attended Southwest Texas State University in San Marcos.

Troy came to the Houston Police Department on July 2, 1979 to enter Police Cadet Class No. 87. He took his oath of office as an HPD officer on November 3, 1979. He wore Badge No. 2336. His earliest assignment was to Central Patrol, where he served a short time before becoming a member of the Crime Scene Unit. Once the unit was transferred to be under the Homicide Division, Troy became a well known and highly respected member of the crime scene unit.

The department later assigned him to the Inspections Division, the Westside Command Center and the Chief's Administration under Police Chief Elizabeth Watson. While Troy did exceptional work in all his assignments, it seemed that he truly found his niche when in 1993, he was selected for assignment as a police officer investigator in the Auto Theft Division.

On Wednesday, May 19, 1999, Auto Theft Investigator Troy Blando was driving a city-owned unmarked vehicle, a 1995 green Jeep Cherokee. This vehicle was equipped with an MDT and he was searching the motels along the 6800 block of the Southwest Freeway for stolen vehicles. He was at the Roadrunner Motel, a location he previously had found to be ripe while searching for recoveries.

While stopped in the motel parking lot, Blando observed a new model Lexus pass by driven by an African-American male. Checking the plate, the officer learned that this vehicle had been stolen in an armed robbery several months ago. At 9:07 a.m., he reported his location to the dispatcher and stated that he had spotted an occupied stolen and wanted vehicle. Several bicycle patrol officers, L. J. Satterwhite and A. K. Hawkins, were nearby and overheard Blando's transmission and location. Riding from the 6400 block of Bellaire, they headed in Blando's direction.

OFFICER TROY ALAN BLANDO

At 9:11 a.m., they were at the Southwest Freeway at Hornwood when they heard ten to twelve gunshots coming from the direction of the Roadrunner. Just seconds later, the voice of Officer Blando came over the police radio stating that he had been shot. He also provided a description of the suspect. Within thirty seconds, Officers Hawkins and Satterwhite arrived to see Troy Blando seated in his Jeep, pointing toward the motel courtyard.

Hawkins and Satterwhite did what officers are trained to do. They split up, with Hawkins staying back to attend to Officer Blando while Satterwhite attempted to pursue the suspect, having been directed by citizens who had seen a partially handcuffed man racing away. This assistance led him to the Celebration Station amusement center at 6787 Southwest Freeway.

Other officers in patrol cars began arriving at the scene. They assisted Officer Satterwhite with the arrest of a suspect who had one handcuff on his left hand. He was also armed with the weapon used to shoot Officer Blando.

Back at the scene, Officer Hawkins had made the Assist the Officer call. Officer Blando was shot in the chest and there was a visible exit wound to his back. He had returned fire at the suspect with his .380 automatic, but had not hit him. There were numerous 9mm hulls around the scene, indicating that the suspect had fired a number of times during the shootout.

Officer Blando was bleeding internally. The delay in rushing him to a hospital became the subject of a massive investigation into the Houston Fire Department's dispatching procedures. The contention was that Blando had received injuries that could have been better treated, perhaps saving his life, had an ambulance arrived sooner. Eventually, an HFD ambulance transported him to Ben Taub General Hospital.

Homicide Captain Richard Holland assigned Lieutenant Greg Neely to lead this investigation. Lieutenant Neely assigned Sergeant Jim Ladd and his partner, Officer Todd Miller, to make the scene and be the primary investigative unit. Assigned to assist them were Sergeant John Swaim and his partner, Officer Alan Brown. Sergeant Paul Motard went to Ben Taub to interview the wounded officer. However, Motard soon learned that Officer Blando was in critical condition, undergoing surgery. The treatment was just too late. Blando had suffered a fatal loss of blood. Doctors pronounced him dead at 10:23 a.m. The veteran of almost twenty years with HPD was dead at age thirty-nine.

The motel parking lot that had been the scene of the offense was no small area to process. In addition, there was the scene of the arrest. Four Crime Scene Units responded on this weekday to assist in the most important task of Homicide investigators – to properly locate and document all items of evidence pertinent to the offense at these scenes.

Contributing in this effort were CSU Officers Larry Baimbridge, J. C. Wood, and A. G. Riddle, all of whom took part in the scene investigations. Officer D. H. Couch undertook the hospital investigation, while Officers L. Tuttle, J. A. Ogden, J. S. Hammerle, and G. H. West all participated in some manner throughout the detailed investigation.

Other than the radio transmissions from Officer Blando, investigators were left to piece together the much-needed evidence of the tragic event of this day. While there were no actual eyewitnesses, a number of people in and around the motel heard and/or saw bits and parts of the offense. The main information was the fleeing suspect's description from the scene of the shooting, which Officer Hawkins was able to obtain in more detail from Officer Blando. He in turn passed it on to the responding units.

The arrested suspect, Jeffrey Demond Williams (African-American Male, 23) ironically provided many answers to investigators' questions. Officer L. J. Satterwhite, ably assisted by Officers J. M. McPhail, J. E. Draycott, J. R. Martinez, B. J. McDonald and Sergeant G. B. Raschke, arrested Williams with not only the weapon he used to shoot Officer Blando but also with a totally indisputable piece of evidence – Officer Troy Blando's handcuffs on one of his wrists. The officers took him back to a location near the scene of the shooting, where Lieutenant Neely assigned Officer Alan Brown and Sergeant John Swaim to personally take custody of the suspect and transport him to 1200 Travis for further interviews.

OFFICER TROY ALAN BLANDO AND DANNY BLANDO

In the usual professional manner of HPD Homicide investigators, Brown and Swaim obtained utmost cooperation from the suspect. Jeffrey Williams confessed to the whole brutal ordeal, while accusing Officer Blando of disrespecting him and physically abusing him – a routine line from someone fully aware of the fact that he has just very possibly committed the final criminal act of his life. After being caught in several other falsehoods, Williams admitted to having taken the stolen Lexus two months previous in an armed robbery of a female. And, more importantly, Williams acknowledged in his confession that he knew that the plainclothes man who confronted him was a police officer.

Before the day was over, the suspect was in jail and charged with capital murder of a peace officer.

Homicide Sergeants Carless Elliott and David Calhoun were assigned the gruesome task of attending Blando's autopsy. They were accompanied by CSU Officers Leroy Tuttle and G. H. West. They needed to tie up a number of loose ends and Sergeants Ladd and Swaim and their partners, Miller and Brown, performed these duties in due time.

Officer Troy Blando was survived by his wife Judith Blando and his thirteen- year-old son, Danny Blando. Other survivors were his mother, Mrs. Della Blando; two brothers, Mike Blando and Tracy Blando; and two sisters, Vicki Sinwell and Bobi Blando; and a number of nephews.

Visitation was held at the Pat H. Foley Funeral Home at 1200 W. 34th on Saturday, May 22, 1999, from noon until 9 p.m. and then on Sunday from 9 a.m. until 9 p.m. Funeral services were held at the Second Baptist Church, 6400 Woodway, on Monday, May 24 at 10 a.m. Services were conducted by the Reverend David Dixon, Pastor Fred H. de Oliveira, Deacon F. Jay Vocelka and HPD Chaplain Edwin Davis. Interment followed at Woodlawn Garden of Memories, Antoine and Katy Freeway.

Pallbearers for Officer Troy Blando were Robert W. Irving Jr., Kenneth A Hilleman, Victor Midyett, Dennis E. Holmes, Michael D. Ingels, Collin P. Gerlich, Thomas C. Civitello and Craig L. Newman.

To police officers who attend the memorial services for fellow officers killed in the line of duty, usually some facet of the service seems to always stand out as something special to remember. Officer Troy Blando was a Boy Scout troop leader for his son Danny's troop. To witness the other adult troop leaders and Danny's fellow Scouts march out after the funeral service without troop leader Troy Blando was an unforgettable sight. What a loss, not only to HPD, but to these young men that Officer Blando served to inspire.

With the death of any police officer, Homicide investigators consider the deceased to be one of their own. In this case, most of the investigators had known Officer Troy Blando since his CSU days. Thus, this came very close to home. However, the investigation had to continue with many loose ends to wrap up tight for the prosecution.

After the initial shock of the murder and subsequent funeral, the work continued. Support personnel who assisted were Firearms Examiner Mike Lyons and Latent Print Examiner Debbie Benningfield. The weapon recovered from the suspects was positively identified as the one that fired the fatal shot. Jeffrey Williams was placed by prints in the Lexus as well as in Officer Blando's Jeep.

The capital murder trial of Jeffery Demond Williams was held in the Criminal District Court of State District Judge Carol Davies. Assistant District Attorneys Lyn McClellan and Denise Nassar were in charge of the prosecution. Williams was found guilty and on February 9, 2000, he was sentenced to die by lethal injection for the capital murder of Officer Troy Alan Blando.

Mrs. Judith Blando and son Danny moved from Houston to Meridian, Texas. Danny graduated from Meridian High School in 2004 and attended Tarleton State College for a time before deciding to enter the United States Navy. Judith, who suffers from multiple sclerosis, remained confined to a wheelchair but in good spirits. She also spends some time in her home state of Michigan.

In 2007, the extended Blando family remained intact. Mother Della lived near Fort Worth with Troy's sister, Vicki Sinwell. Vicki, as well as Bobi, Mike and Tracy all still mourn the death of brother Troy.

Officer Blando's marker at Woodlawn Cemetery reads as follows:

BLANDO, TROY A.
JULY 31, 1959 - MAY 19, 1999
(ALSO, HOUSTON POLICE BADGE #2336)

99

Officer Jerry Keith Stowe
Badge #4501
September 20, 2000

Officer Jerry Stowe Suffered Injuries in 1986; Doctors Found He Died as a Result 14 Years Later

Jerry Keith Stowe was born on February 1, 1953, in Fort Worth, Texas. His family moved to Houston and Jerry graduated from Dobie High School in Pasadena in 1971. He was a member of the Sam B. Crawford Masonic Lodge No. 1418 in New Caney and the past chairman of the East Montgomery County Fair and Rodeo. Stowe worked in the construction industry in the electrical design field for a number of years and found his calling with the Houston Police Department shortly after his twin brother, Jimmy, joined the department.

Jerry Stowe joined HPD in Police Cadet Class No. 125 on November 26, 1984, graduating on March 30, 1985. He was elected by his classmates as class president. He wore Badge No. 4501. His first assignment was to the Radio Patrol Central Division on April 1, 1985 and his probationary training was completed on December 7, 1985. He served in the Jail Division for a short time and returned to Central Patrol on July 23, 1986.

OFFICER JERRY KEITH STOWE

On the night of Tuesday, August 26, 1986, Officers T. S. Galli and J. K. Stowe were riding Unit 1A21 when they responded to a female disturbance call at 1605 Robin, just west of downtown. The call came shortly after midnight, August 27. The officers met the complainant, who advised them that she had been struck in the head by Litha Wade, also known as the "Whopper." Other units arrived and all officers went to 1506 W. Webster, where the suspect resided. Officers Galli and Stowe were accompanied to this location by Officers M. A. Calix and D. B. Casserly. They observed this address to be a typical shotgun house. There were no porch lights or working street lights in this declining ghetto area, which seemed to have immense real estate value.

The officers met a large gathering of area residents on or around the front porch. They used their flashlights and a previous description of the suspect to positively identify her. As the officers approached, they observed Litha Wade not only to be extremely intoxicated but also to be holding a beer bottle and a twelve-inch butcher knife in her hands. They talked Wade off of the porch and advised her that she was under arrest for aggravated assault. They then began to lead her to their patrol car. A mob scene erupted when she began resisting arrest.

OFFICER JERRY KEITH STOWE AND SON CODY STOWE AT ACADEMY GRADUATION

As Officers Calix and Casserly attempted to keep the crowd away from the suspect, a group of suspects, in particular Litha Wade's brother, Filo Wade, attacked them. The group also attacked Galli and Stowe while they were in the act of placing Litha Wade in their patrol car. The attackers included another Wade family member, a sister, Dolly.

After Officer Stowe and Galli had arrested Litha, violence a few feet away resulted in the stabbing of Officer Casserly. The suspect involved used a broken beer bottle. The group attacked Stowe and Galli from behind as they responded to the attack on Casserly. Someone struck Officer Stowe repeatedly from behind, using a 2X4 board and also steel reinforcement rods. During this melee, yet another sister, Jamesetta Wade, entered the fight and assaulted officers while brandishing another twelve-inch butcher knife.

An Assist the Officer call brought enough officers to the scene to get the volatile situation under control. However, the damage was already done. A number of the officers involved were injured. An ambulance took the wounded Officer Casserly to Twelve Oaks Hospital. After the assist was put out, a supervisor, Sergeant C. D. Williams, arrived, resulting in the arrest of the suspect inside a house. Officers remained in serious bodily danger for another twenty minutes while the arrest took place.

Once order was restored, the officers present determined the extent of injuries and which suspects were the actual attackers. Officer Casserly was stabbed in his left arm when he raised it in self defense after he was alerted to the fact that Dolly Wade was about to stab him from behind with a beer bottle. Casserly, who was the most seriously injured, was bleeding profusely at the scene and was later treated at Twelve Oaks. All of the officers, including Officer Stowe, complained of minor injuries but declined treatment. Fortunately, those injuries were documented in the original report.

The initial officers at the scene were the only witnesses to the attacks. They began to identify as best they could who did what. Due to the poor lighting and the swiftness of the assaults, the officers could not positively identify all of their actual attackers.

The state filed attempted capital murder of a peace officer again Jamesetta Wade and Dolly Wade. They filed the original assault charge against Litha Wade, as well as a new charge of hindering apprehension, the same charge now faced by Alma Wade, the matriarch of this model family. Filo Wade initially eluded arrest during all of the confusion but was arrested the following day on charges of assault and hindering apprehension.

After this incident, Officer Stowe stated that he had been kicked and beaten about his abdomen and the rest of his body a number of times during the melee. Being the young and strong officer that he was at only thirty-three years of age, he shrugged off the injuries as part of the job. However, as time passed, his pain intensified and became unbearable. In November 1986, he sought medical attention. Doctors determined that he had suffered a damaged spleen and removed this organ. Then medical complications multiplied as time passed, causing the development of a pulmonary embolism on a lung.

As a result of his injuries, Officer Jerry Stowe was assigned to desk duty at his home station of Central Patrol. He continued to perform those duties admirably until January 1990. His physical condition deteriorated and on January 25, 1990, the Houston Police Officers Pension System granted him a catastrophic disability pension. His health continued on a decidedly downward trend until September 20, 2000, when he succumbed to the injuries he received while on duty as a Houston police officer. He was forty-seven years old.

Officer Stowe was survived by his wife Gail and one son, Cody, his parents, Don and Geri Stowe, sisters Patti Isenberg and Vicki Stowe, and his twin brother, HPD Officer Jimmy Stowe. Also mourning his death were his daughter-in-law, Mrs. Christina Stowe, and his father and mother-in-law, C. J. and Boots Moats.

OFFICER JERRY KEITH STOWE, CODY STOWE AND GAIL STOWE AT U.S. ARMY BOOT CAMP GRADUATION

Visitation began on Sunday, September 24, 2000, at 1 p.m. at the Brookside Funeral Home, 13401 Eastex Freeway. Funeral services were held at 3 p.m. Monday, September 25 at the Brookside Chapel with Brother Richard Huth and HPD Chaplain Edwin Davis officiating. Interment and Masonic graveside services followed there at Brookside Memorial Park.

For Officer Stowe to have received the medical pension, it was necessary that a number of competent medical personnel diagnose the origin of his injuries. While this was a pending legal matter, it was never a question in the minds of his family and fellow officers. Officer Jerry Stowe died a slow and painful death. The autopsy report detailed the cause of death to be multiple organ system failure secondary to blunt force trauma. Manner of death: HOMICIDE.

A travesty of justice occurred in the system as it related to this offense. Charges were filed and the system, as it existed, prosecuted those that were known to have culpability in this offense. What was not known was the seriousness of the injuries, most specifically to Officer Stowe. Law enforcement officers do not make laws; they only enforce those that society provides for them.

Here is how the justice system treated the defendants:

- Jamesetta Wade (African-American Female, 20), charged with assault on a police officer, sentenced to ninety days in jail.
- Dolly B. Wade (African-American Female, 27), charged with attempted capital murder of a peace officer, sentenced to two years.
- Litha Wade (African-American Female, 41), the mother of the Wade family, assault charge dismissed.
- Alma Wade (African-American, 64), the mother/grandmother of this fine group of citizens, misdemeanor assault, sentenced to three days in the county jail.
- James Lester Wade (African-American, age unknown) assault charge, sentenced to four days in the county jail.

In the criminal justice system there is an animal referred to as Double Jeopardy. Basically, this means that an individual cannot be prosecuted twice for the same offense. In this case, it means that once these suspects were convicted or pled guilty to offenses related to this incident, they could not be prosecuted later for anything else relating to the original crime. This meant that these suspects could not be prosecuted for the death of Officer Stowe.

The Homicide Division of the Houston Police Department and the Harris County District Attorney's Office reviewed this offense. They carefully perused the Harris County Medical Examiner's autopsy report and determined that they could take no additional legal action against these defendants. Even though they were in fact responsible for the injuries which led to the death of Officer Stowe, they could no longer be held legally responsible.

Officer Stowe's patrol partner on that tragic night, T. S. Galli, resigned from HPD several times. On the primary backup unit were Officers Michael A. Calix and David B. Casserly. In 2006, Calix was assigned to the Inspector General's Office and Casserly worked at the Westside Patrol Division. Sergeant C. D. Williams is retired.

In 2006, Gail Stowe was remarried and lived near Lake Sam Rayburn. Son Cody, an eight-year veteran of the United States Army, is a staff sergeant with the 172nd Striker Brigade assigned in Masoul, Iraq. In May 2006, he was due to leave Iraq in two months.

In 2006, Officer Jerry Stowe's mother and two sisters were still living. His father passed away in 2005. Officer Jimmy Stowe was promoted to Sergeant and after a tour of duty at Central Patrol, was assigned to the Narcotics Division. He was widowed in 2003. Gail's father passed away in 2001 and her mother lived near Gail in East Texas in 2006.

Marker for Officer Stowe reads:

JERRY KEITH STOWE
FEB 1, 1953-SEPT 20, 2000
BLESSED ARE THE PEACEMAKERS, FOR THEY SHALL BE CALLED THE SONS OF GOD. MATTHEW 5:9.

100

Officer Dennis Edward Holmes
Badge #717
January 10, 2001

Officer Dennis Holmes Suffers Heart Attack During Arrest of Suspect on Northwest Side

Dennis Edward Holmes was born on May 1, 1955, in Washington, D.C. He grew up in Dansville, New York, graduating from high school there in 1974. He earned a Criminal Justice degree from the Community College of the Finger Lakes in Canandaigua, New York, in 1976. Holmes began his police career with the Veterans Administration Medical Center in Batavia, New York. It continued with a tour of duty with the City of Dansville, New

York. From there, he served as an officer with the State University of New York in Genesco, New York. He then worked for the U. S. government in Hot Springs, South Dakota.

Holmes joined the Houston Police Department by way of Police Cadet Class No. 101 on November 2, 1981. After taking his oath of office on March 5, 1982, he began his career with an assignment to the Northeast Patrol Division-Night Shift. He wore Badge No. 717. His career was honorable in every respect. In 1992, with the departmental wide acceptance of police officers for assignment to the investigative divisions, he was selected for assignment to the Auto Theft Division. In each of Officer Holmes' varied law enforcement assignments, he bettered himself and his family with each move and had truly found his niche with HPD and the Auto Theft Division.

All law enforcement officers go to work each day with someone expecting them to come home safely. The officers themselves, while being fully aware of what could happen during their shift, expect the same – to finish their tour of duty and return home safely. On the night of Wednesday, January 10, 2001, Officer Dennis Holmes left his family to do his tour of duty in the Auto Theft Division – just another routine night. But he never came home.

Holmes was assigned to a case outside the realm of routine auto theft assignments. An ongoing investigation was being conducted into the auto theft activities of a group of suspects strongly suspected to be involved in other organized criminal enterprises such as forgery and counterfeit currency activities. As a result, county and federal authorities were involved.

Investigations of this type involve an extensive amount of surveillance in which detailed amounts of intelligence was gathered about the principals involved. This was the case on this Wednesday night in early 2001. Surveillance of a suspect brought all investigative units involved to an area near Willowbrook Mall. While this shopping mall was in the jurisdictional area of the City of Houston, the suspects whose activities were being closely monitored were in the unincorporated areas of Harris County.

Shortly before 10:35 p.m., a suspect in this investigation made his move. The team of investigators on duty consisted of Officer Holmes and Sergeants Craig Newman and Colin Gerlich of the Auto Theft Division, all in separate vehicles. Assisting them were two Secret Service agents and a marked Harris County Sheriff's Department unit.

The county unit attempted to make the stop, but the suspect initially balked at pulling over to the curb despite the unmarked units rolling in front and to the rear of the suspect's vehicle. The marked unit used its emergency equipment to attempt to stop the suspect, who had been speeding. The suspect then attempted to pass the unmarked units in front of him. When officers finally made the stop in the 6400 block of Bourgeois Road in Harris County, Officer Holmes was still in front. Sergeants Newman and Gerlich led the other officers as they approached the suspect vehicle from the rear and side.

The officers took the suspect from the vehicle and were attempted to handcuff him when he resisted. A struggle ensued and officers finally got him on the ground and in custody. They observed Officer Holmes step forward, then backward, and then he fell to the ground. As the suspect was quickly turned over to the county officer, the Houston officers turned their attention to their fallen comrade.

OFFICER DENNIS EDWARD HOLMES

He did not appear to be breathing and the officers detected no pulse. Sergeant Gerlich began CPR while medical assistance was summoned. An ambulance arrived before LifeFlight Helicoptor was able to fly in and land. Officers deemed Holmes' condition serious enough to require the Cypress Creek Medical Service ambulance to rush the officer to Houston Northwest Medical Center. Despite all the efforts made to revive him, Officer Holmes was pronounced dead at 11:45 p.m. He was forty-five years old.

Officer Dennis Edward Holmes was survived by his wife Mrs. Kym Holmes and two daughters, fourteen-year-old Kristen Nicole Holmes and nine-year-old Ashley Ann Holmes. Also surviving him were his parents, Edward Holmes and Alta Holmes of Dansville, New York; one sister and brother-in-law, Elaine Holmes Frew and Kenneth Frew of Dansville; and two brothers and their wives, Kenneth Holmes and Linda Holmes of Hawaii and John Holmes and Theresa Holmes of Dansville; and numerous nieces, nephews and other relatives.

Kingwood Funeral Home was in charge of arrangements. Visitation began at 11 a.m. Sunday, January 14, 2001 and continued with the family present from 5 to 7 p.m., at which time a vigil was held. Funeral services were held at 10 a.m. Monday, January 15 at the St. Mary Magdalene Catholic Church, 527 South Houston Avenue in Humble, with the Monsignor Paul Procella officiating. Entombment followed at the Calvary Hill Cemetery Mausoleum, 21723 Aldine Westfield Road in north Harris County.

There were no obvious previous health conditions that might in some way explain this tragedy. An autopsy showed that Officer Holmes' sudden death was natural due to cardiomyopathy. In layman's terms, this happens when there is a tremendous amount of fibrosis or scarring on the heart muscle, which causes damage to the nerves as well as enlargement of the heart. This complicated diagnosis was well documented in correspondence to the chief of police in the investigation that resulted in Holmes' death determined to be IN THE LINE OF DUTY. This death was very similar to that of Officer James T. Gambill on December 1, 1936.

As for the suspect, the state filed no charges relating to the death of Officer Holmes against him. However, he did face counterfeiting charges.

In 2006, Mrs. Kym Holmes still resided in her home in northeast Harris County. Daughter Kristen was attending a local community college, while daughter Ashley was a local high school student. The rest of the Holmes family remained basically where they were at the time of Holmes' death. Sergeants Craig Newman and Colin Gerlich, both very close friends of Officer Dennis Holmes, were still assigned to the Auto Theft Division in 2006. The Auto Theft suffered two tremendous losses in a very short time period. First came Officer Troy Blando in May 1999 and then, less than two years later, Officer Dennis Holmes.

The crypt at Calvary Hill Mausoleum reads:

DENNIS EDWARD HOLMES
1955-2001

101

Officer Alberto Vasquez
Badge #5437
May 22, 2001

Shooting at Extra Job at Crime-infested Apartment Kills Officer Vasquez and Seriously Injures Partner

Alberto Vasquez was born on April 16, 1969 in Webb County, Texas. His parents were Mr. and Mrs. Juan (Ira Mae) Vasquez. He graduated from high school and joined the Houston Police Department in Police Cadet Class No. 155 on August 30, 1993. His class graduated on February 23, 1994 and he was assigned Badge No. 5437. His first duty was at the Westside Patrol Command Station. He later transferred to the Southwest Division of Radio Patrol, working the evening shift.

On Tuesday night, May 22, 2001, Officer Alberto Vasquez and his partner, best friend and academy classmate, Officer Enrique Duharte-Tur, had just finished their tour of duty on the Evening Shift of Radio Patrol-Southwest Division. Along with fellow Officers Major Michael Johnson and Steven O. Bryant, they traveled after 11 p.m. to an extra job at the Natchez House Apartments at 6200 Marinette in Southwest Houston.

This complex was a crime-ridden problem for the ownership, as they could not seem to avoid attracting all types of criminals who lived there and many who did not. In an effort to turn things around, they hired these HPD officers to work extra jobs by patrolling the premises and curtail the narcotics activities and prostitution believed to be taking place inside the apartments.

On this evening these officers had devised a plan of action. Upon their arrival, Officers Johnson and Bryant started on the north side of the complex in an effort to push any criminal activity to the south side where Officers Vasquez and Duharte-Tur were stationed. Shortly thereafter, Officers Johnson and

Bryant arrested a suspected drug dealer, named Reginald Bailey. They handcuffed him with his hands behind his back and began walking toward the apartment office. Meanwhile, Officers Vasquez and Duharte-Tur arrested four suspected drug dealers. They were identified as Earl Cooper, Robert Burrell, Lew Whiting and Alex Adams. Cooper and Burrell were handcuffed individually behind their backs. Adams, walking with a crutch and having a bandage on his leg, was handcuffed to Whiting. Adams' left arm was cuffed to Whiting's right arm and they were walking side by side.

OFFICER ALBERTO VASQUEZ

Near the apartment office, the four officers met where Johnson and Bryant took custody of Cooper and Burrell. Officer Vasquez was walking slowly with Adams and Whiting due to Adams' leg problem, while Officer Duharte-Tur walked just ahead of them. Then the worst thing imaginable happened. All seemed to be under control when Officer Duharte-Tur heard shots from behind him. Turning, he saw Alex Adams with a gun in his hand that he had used to shoot Officer Vasquez. Duharte-Tur then took cover and began shooting at Adams, who was by this time shooting at him also.

When the suspect fell and his weapon recovered, Officer Vasquez was found to have been shot in the back of his head. He had an exit wound in the face. He also had been shot in the left leg. Adams also had shot Officer Duharte-Tur in the chest area (exited in back) and also in a finger on his left hand. Duharte-Tur, in turn, had shot Adams once in a leg.

Houston Fire Department ambulances transported all three to Ben Taub General Hospital. Officer Alberto Vasquez, thirty-two years old, was pronounced dead on arrival at 11:22 p.m. on May 22, 2001. Officer Duharte-Tur was taken to surgery and listed in critical condition. Alex Adams was treated and kept under police guard with a non-life threatening wound.

Homicide Lieutenant Ron Walker immediately assigned Sergeant H. L. "Hub" Mayer and Investigator Brian Harris to the primary scene investigation. Sergeant Reuben Anderson and Investigators Steven Straughter and Kevin Carr were assigned to assist them in any manner deemed necessary. Lieutenant Joe Buttita, arriving for night shift duty, went to Ben Taub to monitor the wounded officer's condition. Officer Duharte-Tur provided Lieutenant Buttita with a most crucial piece of information as the hospital personnel unloaded him from the ambulance when he said, "The guy on the crutch shot us."

OFFICER ALBERTO VASQUEZ, WIFE PATTY VASQUEZ AND SONS ANDREW JOSE AND CARLOS ALBERTO

Another very vital piece of information came from Lew Whiting, who had been cuffed to Alex Adams. Whiting stated to investigators that he "felt Adams pulling on the cuffs, heard a very loud bang in his right ear and then heard several more shots." He also said he "fell to the ground and Adams fell on top of him, dropping a gun from his hand as he fell."

The investigation proceeded with the usual entourage of investigators from Internal Affairs, the District Attorney's Civil Rights Office, as well as the Crime Scene Units of the Homicide Division. District Attorney Felony Division Chief Marie Munier arrived to assist with legal advice throughout the investigation.

The atmosphere at the actual crime scene was not very pleasant. This apartment complex was not at all police-friendly and residents gathered in mob-type activity by throwing bottles, bricks and other missiles at the police officers. This activity began during the early stages when Officer Vasquez, clearly critically injured with a gunshot wound to the head, was being loaded into an HFD ambulance.

While investigators focused on Alex Adams as the shooter, they ascertained that Adams had apparently secreted a .380 automatic inside the ace bandage wrapped around his right leg. He had been searched and patted down, but this weapon inside the bandage had not been discovered. Later officers determined that Adams had fired five rounds from the hidden pistol. Officer Duharte-Tur had fired five rounds from his .45 automatic. Tests performed on Adams indicated positive firearm evidence on his right hand. His left hand, which was handcuffed to Lew Whiting, proved negative as for firearms evidence.

As the investigation progressed through the night, Lieutenants Walker and Buttita informed Homicide Division Captain Richard Holland, who also had made the scene, that more assistance was needed. As a result, Sergeants Doug Bacon and M. L. Holbrook, as well as investigators R. E. King, R. P. Martinez, Tom McCorvey, Tony Huynh, Mario Rodriguez and Danny Snow were assigned to this investigation.

The following morning Captain Holland assigned day shift Homicide Lieutenant Nelson Zoch to assist Lieutenant Ron Walker in the follow-up investigation. Lieutenant Zoch delegated the suspect portion of the investigation to Sergeants Hal Kennedy and David Ferguson. Other aspects of the case were assigned to Sergeants Jerry Novak and D. D. Shirley and their investigators, Henry Chisholm, Curtis Scales, and Breck McDaniel.

An investigation of this magnitude cannot be completed without support personnel. In this offense the expertise of Firearms Examiners Kim Downs and Robert Baldwin became invaluable in assessing the vast amount of ballistics evidence at the scene. Homicide Division Crime Scene officers, who perform a variety of duties, many not so desirable, continued their exemplary record of service. They were Officers J. S. Hammerle, E. P. Aguilera, J. S. Cruser, C. D. Duncan, D. H. Couch, D. C. Lambright and A. G. Riddle.

When all of the witness statements and evidence was reviewed, Alex Adams was charged with capital murder in the death of Officer Vasquez and attempted capital murder in the shooting of Officer Duharte-Tur.

Officer Alberto Vasquez was survived by his wife Patricia and two sons, Andrew Jose and Carlos Alberto. Also, he was survived by his father, Juan J. Vasquez; his mother, Mrs. Ira Mae Becker; his stepmother, Mrs. Ana Maria Vasquez; and his stepfather, Gerald S. Becker. Also mourning his untimely death were his sister, Valerie Lazaro and her husband, Richard, grandmothers Amelda C. Vasquez and Rose Mary Rodriguez, mother-in-law Laura Caicedo, sister-in-law Diana Caicedo, special uncle Reynaldo Sandoval, and uncle Jerry Vasquez and family. He was also mourned by a cousin, HPD Officer M. J. Ybanez.

Earthman Resthaven Funeral Home, 13102 North Freeway, was in charge of arrangements. Visitation was held on Thursday, May 24, 2001 from 5-9 p.m. and again the next day from 8 a.m. until 9 p.m. A Rosary service was conducted at 7 p.m. Friday. Funeral services were held from the St. Cyril of Alexandria Catholic Church, 10503 Westheimer, on Saturday, May 26, 2001, at 1 p.m., Father Mario Arroyo officiating. Burial followed at Earthman Resthaven Cemetery.

In October 2002, the capital murder trial began in the court of State District Judge Denise Collins. Despite testimony that Alex Adams was a violent man who had once swung an axe in anger at his own father and who also was a suspect in a Prairie View A&M University murder case, a jury deadlocked on his punishment after having previously found him guilty of capital murder. As a result of this deadlocked jury, Judge Collins was forced by law to assess him a life sentence.

In July 2003, a jury in the same court found Alex Adams guilty in the attempted capital murder of Officer Enrique Duharte-Tur. Again, the suspect was assessed a punishment of life imprisonment. This verdict and sentence assured that Adams would spend at least 70 years in custody when the cases were stacked by Judge Collins. Officer Duharte-Tur's testimony was crucial in both trials, which were prosecuted by Assistants District Attorneys Lucy Davidson and Wendy Baker.

Officer Duharte-Tur recovered from his wounds due large part to his young age and excellent physical condition. He underwent a number of medical procedures and continued his career with HPD while also working towards completing his college education. He was a strong witness against Alex Adams at both trials. Each year at the Police Week ceremony, Officer Duharte-Tur stands proudly in place of Officer Alberto Vasquez and responds when his partner's name is called.

The gravemarker for Officer Vasquez consists of a bench as well as several other markers, which read as follows:

VASQUEZ, ALBERTO
IN LOVING MEMORY, DAD AND HUSBAND
04-16-1969   05-22-2001

102

Officer Keith Alan Dees
Badge #3807
March 7, 2002

Final Patrol at End of Shift Results in Fatal Motorcycle Crash for Dees

Keith Alan Dees was born in Saudi Arabia in a United States Air Force Hospital on October 19, 1956. His parents, Mr. and Mrs. Ruby Harlon Dees, were in that country while his father was serving in the military at the time. Dee received his early education at Anderson Elementary School in Houston, Fondren and Johnston junior high schools, and graduated from Westbury High School in 1975.

Keith Dees attended the University of Houston for a time and began his employment with the City of Houston in 1978 as a fireman with the Houston Fire Department in Class 78-A. After four years of fighting fires, he applied for the Houston Police Department. He began his HPD career with Police Cadet Class No. 107 on August 9, 1982, graduating on December 10 of that year. His first assignment was to the South Radio Patrol Bureau out of the Southwest Patrol Station, night shift. He proudly wore Badge No. 3807.

Officer Dees, in the mid-1980s, began working on the Westside Traffic Enforcement Unit and in 1987 was selected to work in the Solo Motorcycle Unit of the Accident Division. He worked in that capacity until his death.

On the night of Thursday, March 7, 2002, Officer Keith Dees had nearly completed his tour of duty with the evening shift of the Solo Motorcycle Division. Just shortly before 9 p.m., he received an assignment from his supervisor, Sergeant D. J. Culak, to initiate a final inspection of his assigned freeways prior to heading home for the night.

While on his last freeway patrol of the evening, he entered the North Freeway at the Walker Street entrance. As he entered the northbound lanes, he was changing lanes to his left in an attempt to pass a slower-moving vehicle. When he did so, he was confronted with a disabled Cadillac in that lane. This automobile had lost a wheel. In an obvious attempt to avoid a collision with the disabled vehicle, Dees veered to his right and went down with the motorcycle.

The officer skidded along the freeway pavement, sustaining massive body trauma that caused a number of internal injuries. A passing motorist who was a physician stopped to render aid while an ambulance was summoned. An HFD ambulance took Dees to Memorial Hermann Hospital, where he was pronounced dead at 10:30 p.m. He was forty-five years old, a nineteen-year HPD veteran.

OFFICER KEITH ALAN DEES

Officer Keith Dees was survived by his wife Deborah Dees, his son Derek Dees, age twelve, his daughter Grace Dees, twenty-one months old, and by a stepson, Trenton, age eight. Also mourning his sudden death were his mother, Mrs. Bettye Virginia Dees, sisters Marianne Cole and Leslie Hakkola, and his brother, Kevin Dees. His siblings' spouses and their children also mourned his death, as did his inlaws, Woody Enloe and Virginia Enloe, and many aunts, uncles, cousins, nieces and nephews.

He was preceded in death by his father, Ruby Harlon Dees, as well as his grandfather,

Ruben C. Dees.

George H. Lewis and Sons, 1010 Bering Drive, was in charge of arrangements. Visitation was held from 6-8 p.m. Monday, March 11, 2002. Funeral services were held the next day at 11 a.m. at the Second Baptist Church, 6400 Woodway, with the Reverend Steve Seelig officiating. Burial followed at Forest Park Westheimer Cemetery.

Officer J. E. Tippy of the Accident Division was assigned to conduct this on-duty officer fatality investigation. Tippy, the primary investigator on the case, was supervised at the scene and in his follow-up report by Lieutenants A. F. Bukowski and S. L. Broze. He was assisted by Sergeant E. B. Robinson and Officers R. Ontiveros, R. Palomo, I. M. Labdi, R. A. Narvaez, M. W. Potell and R. Saenz. They conducted a thorough investigation and after Officer Tippy followed through and compiled all of the details, the case was presented to an Assistant District Attorney for review for possible charges. The investigation revealed no negligence or criminal intent on the part of the operator of the stalled Cadillac. After consultation with Officer Dees' family, the department decided not to pursue the matter any further.

In 2007, son Derek Dees is seventeen years old and lives in Houston with his mother, Sherri. He will graduate from high school in 2007. Grace Dees, now nearly seven years old, lives in Houston with her mother, Deborah Dees, as does Trenton. Mrs. Bettye Virginia Dees also resides in Houston; she is eighty-three. Kevin Dees lives in Houston, the father of two daughters, Karen Dees and Cynthia Dees. Sister Marianne Cole lives in Houston, the mother of Lisa and Michelle. Sister Leslie Hakkola lives in Minnesota, the mother of three daughters, Susan, Catherine and Jennifer. As a result of this tragic accident, a daughter, two sons, and seven nieces are growing up without their father or uncle.

The gravemarker in the Estate Section of Forest Park-Westheimer reads as follows:

DEES, KEITH ALAN
OCT 19, 1956 - MAR 7, 2002

103

Officer Charles R. "Charlie" Clark
Badge #4018
April 3, 2003

Clark's Gun Jams in Confrontation with Robbers, Who Kill him and Clerk at Check-Cashing Business

Charles R. "Charlie" Clark was born in Houston October 24, 1957. Raised on the southeast side in the South Park area, he attended Gregg Elementary School, Hartman Junior High and Jesse H. Jones High School. After high school, he attended San Jacinto Junior College. Clark joined the Houston Police Department in Police Cadet Class No. 112 on April 4, 1983 and graduated on August 5, 1983. Officer Charlie Clark spent his entire career at the Clear Lake and Park Place Substations and the Southeast Command Station. He was a street cop for nearly twenty years. He wore Badge No. 4018.

Mrs. Alfredia Jones was twenty-seven years old and single mother of a ten-year-old son and a three-month-old daughter. She was employed as a cashier for Ace America's Cash Express at the business' 5700 South Loop East location. On April 3, 2003, she opened the store alone. Like Officer Charlie Clark, she was "riding solo" that day.

The day began as what was expected to be a routine day in the life and career of Officer Clark and his wife, Hilde Clark, who worked for a corporation on Beltway 8 South, not far from Charlie's patrol assignment off the South Loop in the South Park area. Recently, the Clarks had planned and built their dream home in Montgomery County near Lake Conroe. Both were enduring long commutes to their jobs. Both, however, were seeing the light at the end of their commuting and job tunnel, for retirement was nearing. Life away from the daily stress of a street cop and, for Hilde, the hassle of a commute to the business world was nearing. On this day both Charlie and Hilde went to their job assignments. Nearly four hours passed in Officer Clark's tour of duty when the dispatch of one call turned their world together upside down.

Then, the world changed forever for Charlie and Hilde and the Clark family as well as for Alfredia Jones, her children and extended family.

At 9:44 a.m., HPD units were dispatched to 5700 South Loop East, Unit A, a check cashing service, regarding a robbery in progress. Officer Clark, on Unit 14D30D, was dispatched as a back-up unit. However, he was very close to this location when he was dispatched. Clark responded in the true fashion of the veteran street cop that he was, the first officer to arrive on the scene. At 9:45, he advised the dispatcher of his arrival and positioned his vehicle a short distance to the west of this strip center on the south side of the South Loop.

OFFICER CHARLES R. "CHARLIE" CLARK

Wrecker driver James Wheat, a friend of Clark's, followed the officer to the scene. Clark bravely approached the front of the Ace America Cash Express and observed three armed suspects inside, promptly advising the dispatcher and asking to speed up the other units. He then observed one of the suspects coming out of the inner office cashier's cage. Clark fired one shot at this armed suspect with his Browning 9mm automatic. That shot did not hit the suspect, but was later found to have struck the door jamb just above where he stood.

Then a cop's ultimate nightmare took place – Clark's weapon malfunctioned, leaving him defenseless against three exiting armed suspects. He moved to the right of the front door, trying to correct his weapon. The first suspect fired two shots at Officer Clark with a .380 automatic, striking him in the shoulder. As he was kneeling down and attempting to correct his weapon, he was shot in the head from close range. He fell to the sidewalk, mortally wounded.

The suspects' account, coupled with physical evidence at the scene, enabled investigators to assemble some details of the tragic chain of events. Three armed suspects, all with fear of police rushing to the scene as reinforcements, tried to take the typical actions crooks take to evade the law. When the violence was over, Officer Charlie Clark lay dead on the sidewalk. An innocent civilian employee of Ace America Cash Express, Mrs. Alfredia Jones, lay dead inside from a bullet wound to the head, having been assassinated by one of the suspects as they fled the scene, leaving Wheat the wrecker driver as the main witness.

This was one of those rare occasions when a wounded police officer is not quickly taken by LifeFlight to a hospital. A ranking Houston Fire Department official tearfully apologized later to Homicide Lieutenant Nelson Zoch at the scene for this break in tradition. He said there was nothing left for them to do; Officer Charlie Clark was dead at the scene. He was forty-five years old. Lieutenant Zoch and his squad of veteran Homicide investigators were on duty for all day shift Homicide assignments. They took the call regarding an officer and a citizen shot at 5700 South Loop East and responded to the crime scene on the South Loop East.

CHARLES AND HILDE CLARK

Homicide Captain Richard Holland immediately joined Zoch and Acting Captain Steve Jett at the scene, where they were met by Chief of Police Clarence Bradford, District Attorney Chuck Rosenthal, at least four assistant chiefs and the captain in charge of the Southeast Patrol area. Zoch assigned veteran Homicide Sergeant Ted Bloyd and his partner, Investigator Darrell Robertson, to be the lead investigators. Not knowing what to expect in the way of leads and evidence, all members of the squad – without any further communication necessary – either remained at their assigned locations or went to the scene to await further assignments.

On duty that day were Sergeants Jerry Novak, David Ferguson, and D. D. Shirley, as well as Investigators Henry Chisholm, Brian Harris, Curtis Scales and Breck McDaniel. Sergeant Hal Kennedy, who had taken off this day, was at home when a fellow investigator advised him of the situation. He reported for duty without even advising his lieutenant. Captain Holland immediately placed Lieutenants Guy Mason and Murray Smith and their squads on standby to assist Zoch's squad in this who-dun-it police officer capital murder investigation. After they completed an assessment of the known information, the Homicide crew followed up on the few scattered leads they had. Unfortunately at this point, one thing was painfully clear: there was not much to go on. They had a rather vague getaway vehicle description of a white 1993-1996 four-door Pontiac Grand Am. There also were limited descriptions of the three African-American male suspects.

Officers spent the afternoon reviewing existing information. They assiduously perused crime analyses of previous robberies of check-cashing businesses. They interviewed Wheat, the witness, without much new information surfacing.

As in any major case, when any information surfaces, officers have to take great care to investigate it, evaluate it and work through it in the manner that can later be utilized in prosecution. Later in the day, Lieutenant Zoch was advised of a call that came in to Homicide. Three females came to the Southeast Command Station to relate a chain of events that they witnessed earlier in the day. They told officers that they felt what they observed was connected to this double capital murder. Upon a phone review of this information, Lieutenant Zoch assigned Sergeants Jerry Novak, David Ferguson and Hal Kennedy to interview the three women and report back with their assessment of this information.

These veteran Homicide Detectives told Zoch that this information appeared to be very plausible but needed further verification. Basically, these witnesses – all three single mothers residing in the Villa Americanas Apartments at 5300 Selinsky, also known as the VA – were together at approximately 9 a.m. the morning of the shooting. They were at a gasoline station at the intersection of Cullen and Almeda Genoa Road, a location approximately four miles south of the scene. They observed three individuals known in some manner or the other to all three women, who said that these men acted rather suspiciously. The women saw these individuals approach a citizen they later realized was in the process of opening his own check-cashing establishment. This experience and what they later observed at the VA after the shooting caused the trio to suspect that the three men might be responsible for the murders of Officer Clark and Mrs. Jones.

The three provided sworn statements. They also identified the three individuals of interest. Additional information soon surfaced regarding a phone call one of these men made to his girlfriend just shortly after the murders. This suspect proudly alerted his female friend to watch the newscasts that morning. While he did not directly indicate his involvement, he obviously had some knowledge of the tragedy that he wanted to call to her attention.

As has been the norm for a number of years, the District Attorney, Harris County's duly elected chief law enforcement officer, attends the crime scene of an offense of this magnitude. In addition, a chief prosecutor in a felony court is immediately assigned to assist law enforcement officers from that point in the lengthy investigation that follows. This allows the prosecuting attorney to become familiar with all aspects of the investigation from the beginning right on through the prosecution of the case with the appropriate charges being filed against the suspects involved. District Attorney Chuck Rosenthal assigned veteran prosecutor Dan Rizzo to assist Captain Holland, Lieutenant Zoch and the investigators by providing legal direction throughout their investigation.

CHARLES R. "CHARLIE" CLARK ON HIS JET SKI

Based on the identifications of the three females, ADA Rizzo and Sergeant Shirley prepared probable cause arrest warrants for Dashon "Shawn" V. Glaspie, Elijah "Ghetto" Joubert and Alfred Dewayne "A. D." Brown. Even though most of the Homicide officers had worked about sixteen hours, none of them asked to be relieved, nor did they want to be. Besides assigning leads to officers as they surfaced, Lieutenants Zoch and Mason made sure that the appropriate investigative personnel remained on duty throughout the night. They also made sure that a portion of the crew left to get rest in the event that the leads began to fall together. But the captain and his lieutenants soon realized that these men could not be driven home with a horse whip. There was a police officer who-dun-it on the table that had to be taken off. Even Captain Holland, head of the Homicide Division, refused to go home, remaining a true Homicide commander in his prime.

During the night, Sergeant G. J. Novak and his partner, Investigator Henry Chisholm, had been assigned the follow-up into the activities of Dashon Glaspie. Sergeant Novak had enlisted the assistance of his son, Officer Michael Novak, and his partner, Officer R. J. Opperman. These young and energetic officers were assigned to an investigative unit out of the Westside Patrol Division and, with approval of their supervisor, Sergeant K. L. Richards, they led a posse to check motels in their patrol area. Officer Novak and this posse located a white Grand Am at a motel on the Southwest side. At 7:30 a.m., Friday morning, along with Sergeant Novak and Investigator Chisholm, they arrested Dashon Glaspie and his most recent girlfriend, a woman known as "Little Red", at this location. Recovered in this arrest was Little Red's white Pontiac Grand Am, a vehicle like the one seen leaving the scene of this crime and the one that contained three men spotted at the VA Apartments shortly after the murders.

Homicide Investigator Brian Harris interviewed Dashon Glaspie during a lengthy session and he eventually gave a statement implicating himself in the robbery. Typically, Dashon was very careful in distancing himself from the big crimes, the two murders. Dashon implicated Joubert in the slaying of Jones and Brown in the murder of Officer Clark. Sergeant Waymon Allen obtained a difficult but detailed statement from Dashon's lady friend, Little Red. At this point, investigators were reasonably satisfied with the progress of the investigation. However, they had no idea what, if anything, the other two suspects would say. If apprehended, would they both also adamantly deny being the triggermen?

In the early afternoon hours of Friday, April 4, 2006, Homicide Sergeant Doug Bacon and Investigator Tom McCorvey arrested Elijah Joubert at an apartment project near Intercontinental Airport. Bacon and McCorvey had been assigned the task of researching Joubert's background and recent haunts. After they checked a number of locations, they eventually found him near a woman friend's apartment. Homicide Detective Jim Binford interviewed Joubert, also known as "Ghetto." Joubert also confessed to his involvement in the robbery of the check-cashing business. True to form, he would not admit shooting Officer Clark or Mrs. Jones. Joubert was free on $15,000. bond on a December, 2002 felony weapon possession charge and was arrested again in March, 2003, on narcotics and evading arrest charges. Again, he was allowed to bond out so he could plan and participate in the Capital Murder of a Police Officer and an innocent gainfully employed citizen.

Having two confessions to participation in a robbery (felony) which led to the capital murders of a police officer and a civilian employee was definitely progress. However, the ultimate question hung over supervisors, investigators and Felony Chief DA Dan Rizzo: How many of these three fine citizens could be worthy of a death penalty conviction?

Rizzo and Homicide supervisors were somewhat buoyed by the existence of two confessions to participating in a robbery and capital murder. However, the remaining facts of the case would continue to haunt them for many months ahead. Those facts: Officer Clark and Mrs. Jones were murdered and obviously unavailable for testimony. And James Wheat, the wrecker driver, was unsure in his own mind which of the three suspects exited the check-cashing establishment first. The next question was what, if any, light would A. D. Brown shed on the situation? Brown was still at large.

Sergeant David Ferguson and Investigator Curtis Scales were assigned to find Brown. It didn't take long. On the evening of April 4, at approximately 7 p.m., less than thirty-four hours after the two murders, Ferguson and Scales arrested Alfred D. Brown in Southeast Houston. Veteran Detective Tom Ladd was assigned to interview Brown. He had no luck, even after a lengthy session in which a number of other detectives participated. A. D. Brown simply refused to admit any involvement in this offense. His woman friend also refused to cooperate. Many days later, when she was eventually indicted in a rare case of prosecutable perjury, she admitted that A. D. had called her at her place of employment on the day of this offense, urging her to turn on the television station that was reporting the tragedies of this terrible day.

While there is no substitute for the instincts of veteran Homicide investigators, no case could be properly investigated and documented without professional support personnel. Zoch and the investigators had to follow the proper procedures in the collection and documentation of any items that may later be introduced as evidence in court. Additionally, in a case of this magnitude, many other Homicide officers are involved in the minute aspects of the case. Those who assisted in any manner are listed herewith. The organization of this case in final report form was led by Sergeant Bloyd and Investigator Robertson through Lieutenant Zoch. Others on the team were:

- Sergeants L. B. Smith, J. L. Ramsey, Eric Mehl, Wayne Wendel, C. T. Mosqueda, Sam Kennedy and Mike Peters.
- Homicide Investigators Kevin Carr, R. E. "Bob" King, Rick Moreno, S. R. Straughter and Roy Swainson.
- Crime Scene Unit Sergeant Jesse Davila and Officers D. C. Lambright, J. C. Wood, G. H. West, J. Hammerle, J. L. Netherland, L. R. Verbitzky and F. E. Martinez.
- Latent Fingerprint Examiners Lucky Stairhime, A. Padilla and Rene Verot.
- Firearms Examiners R. D. Baldwin and Kim Downs.
- Dive Team Sergeant A. M. Oates and a large group of divers from throughout HPD.

The Homicide team conducted a very large number of unsuccessful interviews, many featuring any number of untruths, before striking a productive chord. Lieutenant Zoch found it impossible to describe the untruthfulness uncovered in many of the witness interviews. Witnesses may have held some very minute clues or bits of information in relation to the large picture. Many of them basically had nothing to hide, yet at the same time, withholding any truths that might benefit the cause was seemingly second nature to their being. Investigators exercised a tremendous amount of patience to obtain any semblance of the real truth.

The completed investigation revealed the following chain of events which occurred that morning at the Ace America location:

Mrs. Jones, according to company policy, backed up her vehicle near the front door. Feeling that she was safe, she unlocked the door, only to be rushed by the three suspects. One had remained seated in their vehicle while the other two entered the nearby furniture store to "shop" while waiting their cue. On the inside, there was an inner door to the cashier's section. An elaborate security system was in place. Mrs. Jones is believed to have told the hijackers that there was a ten-minute timed delay on the main safe and told them that she needed to call in to report that she had opened. This was an opportunity for her to report that things were bad, for she used a code to tell an Ace America employee at the other end of the line that implied a robbery was taking place.

From this point, Ace told HPD that the robbery was in progress. Soon thereafter, Officer Clark arrived. Approaching the front door and seeing armed suspects, he reported his quick assessment of the scene. He opened the front door, seeing suspect Brown. He shot at Brown, but missed. Officer Clark's weapon jammed. The hammer was in the cocked position with the slide forward. The safety was off and the clip with twelve live rounds was seated. However, a fired cartridge was still chambered, rendering it inoperable. Clark was helpless as he likely went down from a graze wound to his shoulder while he attempted to correct his weapon when Brown came out and executed him, shooting him in the forehead. At this same time, investigators believed that Joubert was leading Mrs. Jones out to the front, likely planning to use her as a hostage shield. With the officer down, she also was shot in the head.

The suspects left with nothing, leaving two innocent human beings executed in cold blood. James Wheat, the wrecker driver and friend of Officer Clark, saw the suspects leave and rushed to his friend, finding him shot in the head. Wheat then used his police radio to call for assistance. Officer Roland J. Baylous soon arrived, finding his friend dying at the scene.

Officer Clark was survived by his wife Hilde, his mother, Mrs. Ina Clark, brother Robert Clark and his wife Connie Clark, sister Marlene Keele and her husband Jimmy Keele, and sister Lora Smith. Also mourning his death were his father-in-law, Manuel E. Martinez Sr., sisters-in-law Elizabeth Richie, Monica Burns, Elfriede Whitby and husband Doug Whitby, and brothers-in-law Manuel Martinez, Henry Martinez, Frank Martinez, John Martinez and Benjamin Martinez and his wife Maria Martinez. Numerous nieces, nephews and a host of friends also survived the officer, whose father, Claude L. Clark, preceded him in death.

Visitation was held at the Forest Park Lawndale Funeral Home, 6900 Lawndale, on Sunday, April 6, 2003, from 4 to 9 p.m. and on Monday, April 7, from 8 a.m. until 9 p.m. Funeral services were conducted at the Sagemont Baptist Church, 11300 South Sam Houston Parkway East on Tuesday, April 8, 2003, at 10 a.m. Cremation followed.

With District Attorney Rosenthal making the ultimate decision, the prosecution's strategy was to offer a deal to the only non-shooter of the three suspects. He reached this decision only after many discussions with Homicide personnel and much soul-searching. Legally, Shawn Glaspie was equally as guilty of two capital murders as the two actual shooters. However, in order to prosecute anyone successfully, the prosecution was painfully aware of the fact that this deal was a necessary evil.

It was agreed with Glaspie and his attorneys that he would testify against Joubert and Brown in exchange for a plea agreement of thirty years for aggravated robbery. "I had personal knowledge of how this grated at the very core of the prosecutor's oath of office as well as their sense of right and wrong," Lieutenant Zoch remembered. "Many police officers were vocal in their opposition to this prosecutorial position. However, many of those with years of experience, as well as intricate knowledge of the evidence, knew deep down in their hearts that this had to be done."

The prosecution team, led by Dan Rizzo and Tommy LaFon, went to trial first with Elijah Joubert in October 2004. One of the first witnesses was HPD Officer Roland Baylous, a veteran of many years on the street and a friend of Officer Clark. He was the first officer to arrive after the murders, three and one-half minutes later. He tearfully testified that he had to tell his friend he was going to be all right and that help was on the way, when he knew in his heart he was lying to a dying friend. On October 11, a jury found Elijah Joubert guilty of capital murder. Ten days later, on October 21, the same jury in Judge Mark Kent Ellis' Criminal District Court sentenced him to die by lethal injection.

In October 2005, A. D. Brown went to trial in the same court. A jury found him guilty on October 18 and sentenced him one week later to die for his crime also.

As expected, a plea agreement with Dashan Vadell Glaspie allowed him to plea guilty to aggravated robbery, for which he was assessed a thirty-year sentence. The charge of capital murder against him was dismissed. While some may have felt Glaspie got off too light, the unfortunate reality was that the two death sentences would not have been possible without his testimony. Prosecutors and investigators strongly believed that Glaspie was the only one of the three suspects that day that did not fire a shot. In both trials, it was contended that Brown shot Officer Clark and Joubert shot Mrs. Jones.

Judge Ellis, upon sentencing Glaspie, told him that he even though he would be eligible for parole in fifteen years, he would always oppose his parole and would do his best that he served the full thirty years.

Certainly not to be forgotten in this terrible offense is Ms. Alfredia Jones. She was a totally innocent victim of the three hijackers that day in 2003. She was twenty-seven years of age and the single mother of a ten-year old son, Jonathan Parmer and a three-month old daughter, Brianna Butler. She had been employed with Ace for the past seven years and had just recently returned from a maternity leave. She was also survived by her parents, Mr. Tilmon Jones Sr. and Mrs. Velma Jones, and three sisters-Sandra Jackson, Kathy Haya, and Carolyn Gipson, as well as two brothers-Kenneth Jones and Tilman Jones Jr.

In speaking with Kenneth Jones in February, 2007, it was learned that Mr. and Mrs. Tilman Jones Sr. are raising Alfredia's two children with assistance from their Uncle Kenneth and the other Jones siblings. Jonathan is now fourteen and Brianna is four years old.

Mrs. Hilde Jones is now retired and resides in the Lake Conroe area home that she and Officer Charlie Clark built for their retirement years.

104

Officer Frank Manuel Cantu, Jr.
Badge #790
March 26, 2004

Drunk Driver on West Gray Strikes, Kills Dedicated HPD Veteran Frank Cantu Jr.

Frank Manuel Cantu Jr. was born on May 12, 1961 in Sacramento, California. His early years were divided between Texas and California since his parents were divorced and lived in different states. He lived with his mother in California but also spent long periods of time in and around Houston with his dad, HPD Officer Frank Cantu Sr. He attended elementary and junior high schools in California. After attending high school in Aldine and Spring, he graduated from Norte Del Rio High School in Sacramento, where he participated in football, baseball and wrestling.

Frank joined the Houston Police Department as a trainee in HPD Police Cadet Class No. 114, which began training on June 27, 1983. That class graduated on October 29 and this young man began his career as a full-fledged police officer on July 7, 1984. He wore Badge No. 790. During his career he served at the Northwest Patrol Stations and the Special Operations Division.

At approximately 2:20 a.m. Thursday, March 26, 2004, Officer F.M. Cantu, assigned to the Special Operations Division, was on patrol riding a one-man unit. While driving north on Dunlavy, he was nearly through the intersection of Dunlavy and West Gray when an eastbound Mitsubishi sports car on West Gray struck the left rear quarter of the patrol car. The impact knocked the patrol car thirty or forty feet into a flower bed.

OFFICER FRANK MANUEL CANTU, JR.

This collision caused Officer Cantu to be thrown around inside his vehicle. He suffered severe injuries and was rushed to Memorial Hermann

Hospital where he was pronounced dead at 3 a.m. Officer Cantu, a twenty-year HPD veteran, was dead at forty-two years of age.

The officer was not married. Mourning his death were his father, retired HPD Officer Frank Cantu of Mexico; his mother and stepfather, Marie and Wesley Pyevach of Canyonville, Oregon; brother, Eric Able Cantu; and two sisters, Anna Marie Ross and Deborah Ann Boyd. Also mourning his death were five nieces and nephews, ranging in age from three to nine years old.

Forest Park Westheimer Funeral Home at 12800 Westheimer was in charge of arrangements. Visitation was held on Tuesday, March 30, from 9 a.m. until 9 p.m., with a Rosary conducted at 6 p.m. Funeral Mass was held from the Saint Cyril of Alexandria Catholic Church, 10503 Westheimer, on Wednesday, March 31 at 1 p.m. Cremation followed.

Officer Rene Palomo of the Accident Division investigated this terrible tragedy. The driver of the vehicle which struck Officer Cantu was identified as Johnston Ripley Beacom IV (White Male, 29). Beacom suffered minor injuries and his passenger, Nicolas Andrew Ramirez, refused any treatment at the scene. A breath test administered at the scene showed to be more than 0.08 per cent, the legal limit to drive. As a result of that test, charges of intoxication manslaughter were filed on Beacom, a chimney sweep who resided in the 7200 block of Staffordshire.

In newspaper accounts, Officer Palomo indicated that Cantu's police vehicle apparently went airborne after being struck with such force as there were no skid marks. The police vehicle came to rest one hundred feet away from the point of impact. From Officer Cantu's injuries, it became painfully apparent that he was not using his seat belt when struck. While it could not be proven if Beacom ran a red light, it was apparent to accident investigators that he was speeding. The point of impact on the police vehicle being on the left side rear, it appeared that Officer Cantu almost made it through the intersection and probably never saw this vehicle coming toward him.

Cantu had just completed his twenty years and was planning to work another ten years, buy a boat and retire to take it easy. He was praised as a quick-witted man, easy-going and an officer who was easy to supervise. He went out and did his job with little or no direction. He was well known and very well liked at an extra job in River Oaks at the St. John's School where he directed traffic. He was known to treat the little folks as "his kids."

His mother, Mrs. Pyevach, described her son as a man who loved his job and came from a law enforcement family. In addition to his father being with HPD, his stepfather, Wesley Pyevach, served with the California Highway Patrol and the Sacramento Marshall's Office. A brother-in-law was working at the Santa Rosa, California PD and a sister with the Sacramento Sheriff's Department.

The elder Officer Cantu fondly recalled in the 1980s when he worked for HPD in the recruiting division. He particularly wanted to impress the prize recruit of his career so he personally paid for and sent a limousine to the airport to pick up his son for the next step in the application process. Mrs. Pyevach, the grieving mother, commented that her son loved being a police officer and couldn't work enough extra jobs. Officer Cantu was very close to his nieces and nephews and treated them as his own children, buying them U. S. savings bonds for birthdays and Christmas to start them on their way to saving for their college education. He was very family-oriented and loved young people, volunteering as a football coach at Davis High School.

Newspaper accounts indicated that Johnston Beacom had an extensive bad driving record. This likely contributed to his pleading guilty on the intoxication manslaughter charge and on October 28, 2004, he was sentenced to ten years in the Texas Department of Corrections.

105

Officer Rueben Becerra Deleon, Jr. Badge #6969
October, 26, 2005

Hijackers Shoot and Kill Officer Deleon In Apartment Complex on Southwest Side

Rueben Becerra Deleon Jr. was born in Houston on July 4, 1974. Rueben proudly served his country in the United States Marine Corps and continued to serve his fellow man when he joined the

Houston Police Department in Police Cadet Class No. 175 on February 22, 1999. This class graduated on July 10, 1999. The department assigned Deleon Badge No. 6969. His probationary patrolman status was completed on February 22, 2000 and his first assignment was to the Fondren Patrol Substation on the 7 p.m. to 3 a.m. shift.

On the night of Tuesday, October 25, 2005, Officer Deleon was off-duty and out with friends. Deleon and a fellow officer, Starlyn Martinez, went to the Woodscape Apartments at 9708 South Gessner to change clothes. Both officers patrolled in this area of town and, like a number of other officers, were allowed by apartment management to utilize an apartment for purposes of making reports, using the restroom and the phone during their shifts.

They arrived at the apartment at approximately 2:45 a.m. Wednesday, October 26. They entered the apartment, unaware that they were being targeted by several armed hijackers. Shortly after entering the unit and closing the door, they heard a knock on the door. Officer Martinez looked through the front door peephole and observed a young black male standing in front of the door. She advised Officer Deleon of this and then walked toward the rear of the apartment to use the restroom. Deleon went to answer the door. Officer Martinez then heard loud voices, a struggle and several gunshots. She went to retrieve a shotgun that was kept in a bedroom closet and upon returning to the front of the apartment, found Officer Deleon seriously wounded and lying on the floor. The suspects had fled.

Martinez summoned HFD paramedics, but it was too late. Officer Deleon was dead at the scene at the age of thirty-one, having been shot twice-in the left chest and the right arm.

Officer Rueben Deleon was survived by his wife, Mayra Guerrero Deleon, and three children: daughter Alejandera Deleon, age twelve, sons Rueben III, age nine, and Patrick Deleon, age four, and one stepson, John Domiguez, age eight. Also mourning his death were his mother, Mrs. Petra Saenz, his father, Rueben Deleon Sr., stepfather Guadaloupe Saenz, grandparents Frank Deleon and Juanita Deleon, sister Olga Deleon, brother Lee Deleon, stepbrother Lupe Saenz, stepsisters Martha Saenz and Dora Saenz, and father- and mother-in-law Aaron and Juana Guerra. He also was survived by a number of sisters-in-law and brothers-in-law and nieces and nephews.

Davis-Greenlawn Funeral Home in Rosenberg was in charge of arrangements. Visitation was held at their funeral home at 3900 B. F. Terry Boulevard in Rosenberg from 5 until 7 p.m. Friday, October 28, 2005. A rosary was held at 7 p.m. during this visitation. A funeral mass was conducted at 10 a.m. Saturday, October 29 from the Our Lady of Guadaloupe Catholic Church, 514 Carlisle in Rosenberg. Burial followed at the Greenlawn Memorial Park Cemetery.

The first responding police units assessed the scene and the Homicide Division immediately responded with on-duty investigators and a call-out of other personnel to assist and take charge of this investigation. The squad of Homicide Lieutenant Rick L. Maxey was called out from home and Lieutenant Maxey also responded to the scene.

Initially, there was very little useful evidence. Officer Martinez had seen a young black male through the peephole. She had been trained in observation and was able to provide a basic description of this suspect.

OFFICER RUEBEN BECERRA DELEON, JR.

This was basically another who-dun-it. Fortunately, there was an apartment resident who observed parts of the offense and was concerned as a citizen about seeing that justice prevailed. He reported to the department on Friday the 28th what he had seen on the night of this offense. He said he saw a young black male he knew as "Brandon" running from the apartment where Officer Deleon was killed. While this information was sketchy, Lieutenant Maxey and his squad made the most of it. From speaking with numerous people in the apartment complex, they determined that this Brandon was none other than Brandon Zachary, who had numerous contacts at this complex. "Brandon" was seen entering a vehicle, which was described in detail by the anonymous witness.

Information surfacing during an investigation is only "information" until experienced Homicide investigators analyze it, conduct a thorough investigation, and piece it together with other bits of intelligence. This is exactly what Lieutenant Maxey and his squad of experienced investigators proceeded to do.

Based on what they learned about Brandon Zachary, their investigation led them across the state from Beaumont to Wichita Falls. They learned of Brandon Zachary's running-mate partner-in-crime by the name of Antoine Deneil Marshall. Both Zachary and Marshall had no visible ambition in life other than to steal, rob, and more importantly, not be tied down to any gainful employment. After numerous trips to Beaumont and with the outstanding cooperation of the Beaumont Police Department, HPD investigators were able to locate Brandon Zachary. While Zachary eventually gave a statement to Homicide investigators, naturally he was naming his partner Marshall as the actual shooter. Antoine Marshall was located in Wichita Falls. He did not give a statement to HPD Homicide. After their arrests, Brandon Zachary was identified by Officer Martinez and the concerned citizen as having been at the apartment door.

During the course of this investigation, Homicide learned of one Nicholas Victoria, who had been wanted in another murder case in this same Woodscape apartment project. Victoria gave a statement to the effect that he was the driver of the getaway vehicle and had seen Zachary and Marshall running through the project toward his waiting vehicle. Naturally, Victoria would not admit knowing what they had been up to when he was asked to wait for them.

Another witness, a cellmate of Antoine Marshall, came forward to say that Marshall told him that they knew this particular apartment was used by the police and that Marshall felt he had been verbally disrespected by Officer Deleon several days previously.

When all of the pieces of this puzzle were put together, charges of capital murder were filed against Brandon Zachary, Antoine Marshall and Nicholas Victoria, who obviously would be used as a witness. The entire details of this investigation were submitted by Lieutenant Maxey through the chain of command to Police Chief Harold Hurtt, who later ruled that since the suspects knew the occupants of this particular apartment were police officers, that this death should be ruled IN THE LINE OF DUTY.

In December 2006, Antoine Marshall was tried for capital murder in the death of Officer Deleon in the Criminal District Court of Judge Don Stricklin. The lead prosecutor for the State of Texas was Assistant District Attorney Marc Brown, who did not seek the death penalty due to the unusual circumstances of the case. The jury found Antoine Marshall guilty and he was sentenced to life without parole.

In February 2007, Brandon Zachary, accused of actually shooting Officer Deleon, was placed on trial in the same court. He also was found guilty and sentenced to life in prison without parole.

106

Officer Rodney Joseph Johnson
Badge #5913
September 21, 2006

Routine Traffic Stop and Hidden Weapon Result in Officer Rodney Johnson's Death

Rodney Joseph Johnson was born October 24, 1965, in Houston. He attended school in Houston for a time, but then moved to Oakland, California, where he graduated from the Oakland Technological High School in 1984. He joined the United States Army and became a military policeman, serving honorably until 1990. After serving his country, Rodney worked for the Texas Department of Corrections as a corrections officer and was then employed as a jailer with the Houston Police Department. Rodney then joined the HPD by way of Police Cadet Class No. 159, which began training on June 20, 1994. He proudly wore HPD Badge No. 5913.

Officer Rodney Johnson was assigned to the Radio Patrol Division at the Southeast Command Station. He became a member of Southeast Gang Task Force and while a member of this unit received two Lifesaving Awards and one Medal of Valor. Following his service in this unit, he returned to the Evening Shift Radio Patrol at Southeast.

On Thursday, September 21, 2006, Officer Johnson was assigned to the Southeast Command Station on Mykawa Road, working Radio Patrol on the 3-11 p.m.

pm shift. Riding a one-man unit, 13D43, his assigned patrol area was the perimeter of Hobby Airport.

At approximately 5:20 p.m., Officer Johnson advised the Dispatcher that he had made a traffic stop on a speeding white pickup truck in the 9300 block of Randolph, southeast of the airport. He made a request to the dispatcher for a civilian wrecker to report to this location for a prisoner's tow.

Shortly thereafter, the Dispatcher was alerted that Officer Johnson's emergency signal had been activated. Repeated efforts to raise 13D43 failed and a Code 1 was initiated. Then, very likely from a citizen's call, a shooting call was reported at this location.

Wrecker driver Frank Granadas was the first to arrive at this scene. Granadas observed Officer Johnson seated in the driver's seat of the police shop, but with no visible movement. Upon closer observation, he saw Officer Johnson to be bleeding from the mouth and head. His first instinct with the driver's side door open was to lean in and grab the police radio and call for help. However, before he could do this, someone fired a shot at him from the rear seat of the vehicle. The round missed and Granadas hurriedly retreated to his wrecker and placed a call for immediate assistance.

A number of other police officers arrived, including Officers E. H. Wiggins, J. C. Pineda and H. D. Bohn. The suspect was seen holding a weapon in front of him while seated handcuffed in the rear seat. As Officers Wiggins and Pineda very carefully approached the police car from the rear, Officer Bohn used his police car as a shield as he approached from the front and side. The officers completed the arrest and the suspect was taken out of the police car without further incident.

Officer Johnson was removed from his police car and taken to Ben Taub Hospital, where he was pronounced dead at 6 p.m. He was forty years old.

The officer was survived by his wife, HPD Officer Joslyn Margaret Johnson of the Special Operations Division, and five children. They were his daughters, Jessica (nineteen), Amber (seventeen) and Astin (sixteen), and two sons, Corrigan (fourteen) and Reggie (fourteen). Also mourning his tragic sudden death were his mother, Mrs. Cynthia Johnson, and his sister Sandra.

Services were entrusted with Earthman/Southwest Funeral Home, 12555 South Kirkwood in Stafford. Visitation for family and friends was held at the Grace Community Church, 14505 Gulf Freeway, on Tuesday, September 26, 2006, from 5-9 p.m. Officer Johnson's body remained at the church overnight under constant police guard. Funeral services were conducted at the Grace Community Church at 10 a.m. Wednesday, September 27, with burial following at the Resthaven Cemetery on Interstate 45 North.

This was one of the longest funeral processions in HPD history, having originated at the Gulf Freeway and Beltway 8. It also was one of the most touching, as citizens from all walks of life lined the freeway and the overpasses to pay their respects to this fallen officer. There were numerous signs and placards throughout the thirty-mile procession. Officer Johnson was a highly respected member of the Board of Directors of the Houston Police Officers Union and was described as being 6-foot-5 and 300 pounds. However, while his physical size was intimidating, he was further referred to as "a teddy bear and a gentle giant".

Evening Shift Homicide Lieutenant Ron Walker was on duty and immediately assigned Homicide Sergeants Mark Newcomb and J. D. Padilla to the scene. Once again, the Homicide Division and its support personnel undertook an all-out investigative effort. Others assigned to the scene and to various other investigative duties were Sergeants M. K. Peters, R. Torres and Bobby Roberts, as well as Investigators Fred Mares, Kevin Carr and R. D. Young. CSU Sergeant Greg Glenn supervised the Crime Scene Unit investigation and assigned Officers C. D. Duncan, F. E. Martinez, E. P. Aguilera, L. R. Verbitzky, N. S. Kiesenwetter, D. C. Lambright, J. N. Duerer, and J. S. Cruser to various aspects of the investigation at the scene as well as the follow-ups over the next several days. Firearms Examiner Mike Lyons was called to the scene to begin his detailed examinations of the evidence.

OFFICER RODNEY JOSEPH JOHNSON

As is the norm in any type of Homicide investigation, HPD personnel handled the suspect with extreme care in order to prevent and counter any later allegations of violations of his rights. In this instance, veteran Homicide Sergeant David Ferguson was assigned the responsibility of the handling and questioning of this capital murder suspect. Assisting him were Homicide Investigators Curtis L. Scales and Roger W. Chappel. While it was rather obvious exactly what occurred at the scene, it is always helpful to obtain the "why" of the matter. This is exactly what the investigators accomplished through their lengthy interview with Juan Quintero.

After being read his legal warnings, suspect Quintero, an illegal alien who had previously been deported but returned to the United States, voluntarily spoke to investigators regarding the happenings of this afternoon. Quintero, employed by a lawn maintenance service, indicated that he, along with a co-worker, had left their normal job activities in order to retrieve his two stepdaughters from school at Sterling High School. He admitted to the speeding violation and, when stopped, he was forced to admit to Officer Johnson that he did not possess a driver's license. However, he was quick to add that he had proof of insurance. He was, after all, driving a truck owned by his employer.

In addition to his two stepdaughters, he was accompanied by a coworker. Upon being stopped for speeding, he admitted to being frustrated when Officer Johnson advised him that he was being taken into custody. Thinking that he should only receive a traffic citation for the driver's license problem, he became angry when the officer handcuffed him and proceeded to place him in the rear of the police vehicle. The two stepdaughters, who had been determined by Officer Johnson to live only several blocks away, were told by the Officer along with the coworker to leave and walk home.

It was later learned from the coworker that Quintero had consumed six or seven beers while working during the early afternoon and again while driving. He readily admitted his anger at the situation "Officer Johnson had placed him in" and after the officer sat down in the front seat of his patrol car with the center window open, he removed a 9MM automatic pistol which he had hidden on his person. He was apparently agile enough to get the cuffed hands around his legs to the front of his body. Seated on the right rear seat of the police vehicle, Quintero was able to fire a number of times at Officer Johnson through the opening in the Plexiglas screen separating the front and rear seats of the police vehicle. His bullets struck Johnson four times in the head and face. Johnson was very likely deceased when other officers were able to remove him from the vehicle.

Once again, just as in the tragic death of Officer Guy Gaddis in 1994, the mindset of the criminal is difficult for most rational people to understand. Edgar Tamayo shot and killed Officer Gaddis, while handcuffed in the backseat of a patrol car traveling at up to forty miles per hour. To summarize Quintero, it was not his fault that he shot the uniformed police officer. It was the officer who made him take the deadly action that he did. What chances of escape did Quintero possibly have in his mind, while handcuffed and locked in the back seat of a police car?

As the investigation progressed through this long, sad night, investigators learned that Quintero had been deported from the United States after being convicted of indecency with a child. The suspect was born in 1974 and, after being deported, apparently had no respect for the laws of the U. S. and just decided to return without attempting to become a legal citizen. Further, officers also learned that his wife had purchased from Carter's Country the weapon used to murder Officer Rodney Johnson.

Quintero was charged with Capital Murder of a police officer in the 248th Criminal District Court of Judge Joan Campbell.

The investigation did not end. The following morning, Homicide Lieutenant Murray J. Smith stepped up to fill in for Lieutenant Walker. He assigned Sergeant J. W. Belk and Investigators M. J. Miller and J. Sosa to continue the background investigation into the suspect and his activities. The trial date before Judge Campbell was set for May 14, 2007 with District Attorney Chuck Rosenthal expected to lead the prosecution team.

THE 100 CLUB, INC.

Prior to the 1920's and the formation of the Houston Police Officer's Burial Fund, the widow and survivors of Houston Police Officers who were Killed in the Line of Duty were usually left to fend for themselves. There were no financial benefits available for the families of the fallen heroes. There were certainly no pension benefits from the City of Houston, who for whatever reason, seemed to avoid their responsibility in these matters.

Police Officers, obviously seeing a need for assistance in these trying times, took it upon themselves to assist each other's families, whether their death was in the Line of Duty or from natural causes. Thus, the origin of the Burial Fund.

It was not until the 1950's that a group of civic leaders in the Houston business establishment saw the need for more assistance to the families of those law enforcement officers who lost their lives in the line of duty. This group stepped forward and made a difference, becoming known as the 100 Club in a concerted effort to organize 100 individuals who expressed their willingness to pay annual dues of $100.00 each.

While details of this organization's history are sketchy, the first known benefit was paid to the family of a Harris County Sheriff's Deputy in 1960. That was followed by the first benefits paid to the family of a Houston Police Officer who died in a motorcycle accident in 1963. This organization has steadily grown not only in numbers through the years, but in increased benefits to these families. From lump sums shortly after an Officer's death, while they continued to provide these funds, the 100 Club provided educational annuities for the children of these slain Officers.

Mr. Rick Hartley is the current Executive Director of the 100 Club and Mr. Clarence F. Kendall II is the current President. Past Presidents have been Mr.'s Ray Elliott, Leopold Meyer, H. Stuart Lang Jr., Leroy Gloger, Luke Johnson, Gordon Edge, R.T. "Bob" Herrin, David Morris, Charlie Worthen, Leroy Melcher, Fred Gebhardt, N.M. "Mack" Brown, Howard D. Moon, Charlie Milstead, and John R. Braniff Sr.

All of these men along with the other elected Board members of the 100 Club have worked towards continuing and improving the benefits made available to the families of slain Officers. Under Rick Hartley's leadership and that of the 100 Club's far-reaching boardroom decisions, today $10,000 is provided for emergency expenses to a family within twenty-four to forty-eight hours of a tragedy. When the time is right and the trauma has somewhat subsided, the Club compiles a unique needs assessment and proceeds accordingly. As of 2007, the average gift per family was $300,000. Overall, since 1953, the 100 Club has supplied gifts totaling over $10 million.

In addition to the above described benefits, the 100 Club has provided for area law enforcement Officers other items to save their lives-bulletproof vests, more advanced radio equipment, specialized equipment for SWAT and bomb squad teams. These benefits were later expanded to other Greater Houston law enforcement agencies and in 2001, this service was extended to the families of firefighters killed in the line of duty. The organization has provided over $10 million dollars in officer safety equipment to area law enforcement.

In 2007, the coverage for police and firefighters has been extended into over 18 area counties and just recently, the Board of Directors has voted to extend their benefits to all commissioned officers of the Texas Department of Public Safety, the Texas Rangers, Texas Parks and Wildlife, Texas Alcoholic Beverage Commission, and the Texas Department of Criminal Justice who are killed in the line of duty anywhere in the State of Texas.

When the idea of a special LINE OF DUTY GRAVEMARKER was proposed to the 100 Club of Greater Houston, the Board of Directors agreed to fund the marker portion of this project. As of 2007, this organization has funded the cost of 29 such markers. This project will continue.

From a fledgling group of civic-minded businessmen in the 1950's, this group has grown to a membership of nearly 26,000 members who pool their resources to assist the families of those public servants who gave their lives in the protection of our lives and property. Those of us in law enforcement salute this fine organization for their continued efforts to make our lives better.

Suspect Dispositions In Line Of Duty Deaths

Officer Last Name	First Name	Suspect Last Name	First Name	Disposition
Foley	C. Edward	Floeck	Michael	Unknown-Case Reset For Five Years With No Known Results.
Snow	Richard	Campbell	Henry	Death Sentence-Commuted.
Williams	Henry	Terry	Kyle	Convicted-Out On Bond, Later Was Killed In Galveston.
Fenn	James	Mcgee	Henry	Convicted-Hung In 1893
Weiss	Willie	Vaughn	J.T.	Shot Dead At Scene
Youngst	Herman	Preacher	Sid	Shot Dead At Scene
James	John C.	Preacher	Sid	Shot Dead At Scene
Murphy	William	Mcfarland	Earl	Acquitted
Cain	John	Sharp	Houston	Death Sentence-Never Executed
Parsons	Isaac	Richardson	John	Accidental-No Prosecution
		Cardona	Edmund	Accidental-No Prosecution
Daniels	Rufus	Henry	Vida	Suicide-19 More Soldiers Executed
Meinicke	Edwin	Henry	Vida	Suicide-19 More Soldiers Executed
Moody	Horace	Henry	Vida	Suicide-19 More Soldiers Executed
Patton	D. Ross	Henry	Vida	Suicide-19 More Soldiers Executed
Raney	Ira	Henry	Vida	Suicide-19 More Soldiers Executed
Davidson	Johnnie	Harris	Joe	Shot Dead At Scene
Young	Jeter	Nicholson	P.J.	Negligent Homicide-No Disposition
Murdock	David	Alexander	Will	99 Years On Other Murder Charge
Etheridge	John C.	High	E.K.	Accidental-No Prosecution
Corrales	Pete	Martinez	Max	Shot Dead At Scene
Chavez	E.	Ramerez	Pablino	Charged-No Record Of Prosecution
Jones	Perry P.	Chester	Pete	Death Penalty-Appealed, New Trial 5 Years Manslaughter, Served Time And Was Killed Harassing Witness.
Wells	Rodney Q.	Alexander	R.W.	Accidental-No Prosecution
Greene	Carl	Maglitto	Sam	Shot Dead At Scene
Whitlock	Paul W.	Howard	H.N.	Accidental-No Prosecution
Davis	Albert W.	Powell	Robert	Arrested And Charged. Kidnapped And Lynched By Mob.
Hope	Oscar	Charles	Henry	Shot Dead At Scene
Jones	Edwin	Wilson	Johnnie	Mental Case-Unknown Disposition
Thomas	C. Osburn	Giese	A.	Accidental-No Prosecution
Fitzgerald	Edward	Maple	J.J.	Executed-1930
Phares	William B.	Maple	J.J.	Executed-1930
Landry	J.	Soland	Fred	Accidental-No Prosecution
Mereness	Harry T.	Barry	Owen	Charged As Juvenile-No Disposition
Sullivan	Rempsey	Jones	Isaac	Death Penalty-Appealed, New Trial Life Sentence-Later Paroled And Fully Pardoned
Gambill	James	Holmes	Martin	Shot Dead At Scene
Martial	Adolph P.			Accidental-No Prosecution
Palmer	Marion	Zink	Light	Shot Dead At Scene
Edwards	George D.	Adams	Carl	Shot Dead At Scene
Hammond	Howard B.	Jackson	Charles	Life Sentence-Served 11 Years. Later Paroled And Fully Pardoned

Officer Last Name	First Name	Suspect Last Name	First Name	Disposition
Kent	Smith A.	Boulding	Alfred	Accidental-No Prosecution
Maddox	Fred	Farrar	Carroll D.	Executed-1956
Beets	Jack B.	Smith	Manuel B.	Shot Dead At Scene
Gougenheim	Charles	Smith	Manuel B.	Shot Dead At Scene
Kellog	Frank	Taylor	Rueben C.	Shot Dead At Scene
Schultea	Robert J.	Eggleston	Lillian	Acquitted
Miller	Noel R.	Moses	George	Executed-1960
Branon	Claude E.			Accidental
Suttle	John W.	Wychopin	Forrest S.	Negligent Homicide-Fine And Costs
Gonzalez	Gonzalo	Bryant	Victor E.	Murder By Auto-Pled To DWI, Three Days In Jail
Walker	James			Accidental-No Prosecution
McDaniel	Charles			Accidental-No Prosecution
Willis	James F.			Accidental-No Prosecution
Planer	Herbert	Speck	Donald Ray	Life Sentence-Killed In Traffic Accident In TDC In 1981
Deloach	Floyd T.	Davis	Donald Jay	Life Sentence-Paroled In 1983
Sander	Louis L.	Hinkle	Kenneth	Convicted, Bench Warranted To Arkansas For Robbery Trial, Was Convicted. Died In Tennessee Prison In 1996
Kuba	Louis R.	Waller	Douglas	Charged With Murder And Inciting A Riot. Trial Ended In A Mistrial And No Other Prosecutorial Avenues Were Available.
		Freeman	Charles	
		Nichols	Floyd	
		Franklin	Trazawell	
		Parker	John	
Gerhart	Ben E.	Isaacks	Ronald	Shot And Killed By Other Officers After Officer James Was Killed In Traffic Accident Chasing Suspect.
James	Bobby			
Moody	Kenneth W.	Sellars	Wesley	Life Sentence Was Overturned. New Trial Ordered But Never Held. Was Killed By Police In Arizona While Committing Other Felonies.
Griggs	Leon	Ellis	Wardell	Shot And Killed By Officers In Atlanta, Georgia In 1971
		Porter	Elmer	Life Sentence, Paroled, Revoked And Sent Back To TDC.
Lee	Robert W.	Wilson	T.L.	Shot Dead At Scene
Beck	Claude R.	Meyers	Walter	Murder By Auto-Found Guilty, Received A Short Probation
Noel	David F.	Deleon	Paul V.	Guilty Of Murder-20 Years, But Served Only 6 Years.
		Garcia	Rachel	Not Guilty
Spruill	Jerry L.	Fentis	Marvin	Guilty-Sentenced To 35 Years And 2 Life Sentences. Served 15 Years And Paroled.
Guzman	Antonio	Emory	Robert T.	Shot At Scene-Later Died From Wounds
Huerta	David	Brandt	Terry	Committed Suicide At Scene
Riley	Jerry L.	Stone	Curtis R.	Negligent Homicide-Unknown Disposition

Officer Last Name	First Name	Suspect Last Name	First Name	Disposition
Bamsch	Johnny T.	Kyles	Richard D.	Life Sentence-Still In TDCJ In 2007
		Thomas	Robert	Life Sentence, Paroled In 1988 But Back In TDCJ In 1989
Wright	Francis E.	James	Mark S.	Involuntary Manslaughter-Ended Up Serving About Two Years.
Calhoun	Richard H.	Robbins	Michael	Shot And Killed By Accomplices Prior To Police Involvement
		Windaberry	Benjamin	Shot Dead At Scene By Police
		Smith	Noel	Suicide At Scene
Rojas	George G.	Cevallos	Alex	Acquitted-Later Served Time In The Federal System
Kilty	James F.	Howard	Willie	Shot Dead At Scene
Hearn	Timothy L.	Esquivel	Rudy R.	Executed-1986
Baker	Charles H.	Bass	Charles W.	Executed-1986
Wells	Victor R.	Washington	Willie	Involuntary Manslaughter-Received 7 Years. Conviction Overturned, In A New Trial, Was Acquitted
Zamarron	Jose	Williams	Jerrie Ann	Involuntary Manslaughter-Received Three Years
Rawlins	Winston J.	Morrow	Kenneth W.	Involuntary Manslaughter-Charge Later Dismissed
Deleon	William E.	Garcia	Rogelio G.	Involuntary Manslaughter And FSRA-Received 9 Years And A $5,000.Fine, But Only Served Part Of Sentence
Shirley	Daryl W.	Williams	Arthur L.	Sentenced To Death But As Of 2007, Not Yet Executed
Harris	James D.	Flores	Robert C.	Shot Dead At Scene
		Guerra	Ricardo A.	Sentenced To Death. Conviction Overturned, But Was Never Retried. Killed In Mexico Auto Accident.
Schaefer	Kathleen			Accidental-No Prosecution
Coates	Charlie	Eilert	Mary Jane	Pled Guilty To Aggravated Assault With Motor Vehicle, Received 10 Years Probation And $1,000. Fine
Moss	Williams			Accident-No Prosecution
Groves	Maria M.	Richardson	Robert A.	Involuntary Manslaughter-Received 10 Years, Served 3 Years-Released
Winzer	Andrew	Alfaro	Andres	Charged With Running A Red Light & Driving While License Suspended. Three Days Jail And $450. Fine
Howard	Elston	Jennings	Robert M.	Death Penalty-Sentenced To Death But As Of 2007, Not Yet Executed.
		Harvell	David	Sentenced To 50 years For Robbery
Garcia	Florentino	Martinez	Felipe J.	Negligent Homicide, Sentenced To 9 Months In Jail And A $2,000. Fine
Boswell	James	Ogan	Craig N.	Death Penalty-Executed 2002
Irby	James	Buntion	Carl W.	Death Penalty-Overturned On Appeal. 2007-Not Yet Retried
Salvaggio	John	Byrd	William	Failure To Stop And Render Aid, Received 5 Years, Served 2 Years, Died In 2002.

Officer Last Name	First Name	Suspect Last Name	First Name	Disposition
Soboleski	Bruno D.	Jones	Shelton D.	Death Penalty-As Of 2007, Not Yet Executed
		Coleman	Chris D.	Attempted Capital Murder Of A Police Officer-Sentenced To 20 years
Roman	Michael P.	Quiroz	Celia	Failure To Yield Right Of Way At A Stop Sign-Fine Only
Gaddis	Guy P.	Tamayo	Edgar	Death Sentence-As Of 2007, Not Yet Executed
Healy	David P.			Accident-No Prosecution
Erickson	Dawn S.			Accident-No Prosecution
Thrinh	Cuong	Chuong	Tong	Sentenced To Death In 1998-As Of 2007, Not Yet Executed
Kincaid	Kent	Haynes	Anthony	Sentenced To Death In 1999-As Of 2007, Not Yet Executed
		Tunson	Michael	Three Years In TDCJ On A Robbery
		Reese	Timothy	90 Days In Jail On An Unrelated Assault
Blando	Troy	Williams	Jeffrey D.	Sentenced To Death In 2000-As Of 2007, Not Yet Executed
Stowe	Jerry	Wade		The five members of the Wade family received short jail time and little or no punishment for their actions leading to Officer Stowe's later death.
Holmes	Dennis			Heart Attach-No Prosecution
Vasquez	Alberto	Adams	Alex	Found Guilty on two charges and received Life Sentences on both convictions.
Dees	Keith			Accident-No Prosecution.
Clark	Charles	Brown	A.D.	Death Sentence-2007, not yet executed
		Joubert	Elijah	Death Sentence-2007, not yet executed
		Glaspie	Deshaun	Sentenced to 30 years in TDCJ.
Cantu	Francisco	Beacom	Johnston	Intoxicated Manslaughter, 10 years TDCJ
Deleon	Rueben	Marshall	Antoine	Convicted of Non-death Capital Murder-Sentenced to Life Without Parole
		Zachary	Brandon	Convicted of Non-death Capital Murder-Sentenced to Life Without Parole
Johnson	Rodney	Quintero	Juan	Charged with Capital Murder and as of May, 2007, not yet gone to trial

Index

Name............... Story Reference

A

Name	Ref
Abel, R.E.	77
Acrey, Ann	69
Adams, Alex	101
Adams, Bobby F.	53, 79, 81, 86, 88
Adams, Carl	38
Adams, Earl	34
Agee, Ashlie Renee	86
Agee, Michael Jerrod	86
Agee, Sheila Howard	86
Aguilera, E.P.	101, 106
Albinus, Allen	64
Alcover, Dr. Amiris	87
Aldaco, J.M.	76
Alderette, George	86, 89
Alexander, Carolyn	82
Alexander, D.B.	73
Alexander, R.W.	23
Alexander, Will	18
Alfaro, Andres Abelino	85
Allen, J.H.	64
Allen, Nicole	77
Allen, Rev. Don	51
Allen, Tanuneka	77
Allen, Waymon	103
Altofer, Jake	18
Alvarado, Josio	21
Ambrus, Bonnie	5, 11-15
Ambrus, Richard	5, 11-15
Ammons, Rev.	9
Amsler, Lydia	11-15
Anderson, Charlie E.	86, 91, 93
Anderson, G. W.	78
Anderson, Jailer	4
Anderson, Mrs. Annette	48
Anderson, Rueben	86
Anderson, W. H.	20
Andres, Felix	27
Andres, Laura	27
Andrew, George	18, 24
Andrews, Joe	72
Anwander, Mrs. Mary	72
Applegate, Leticia	61
Araiza, Pete	78, 90
Archer, Victor	86
Armijo, Jose Francisco	80
Arnold, Carolyn	61
Arnold, Detective	30/31
Arnold, Robert Kit	61
Arrington, C.S. (Steve)	75, 79, 93
Arroyo, Father Mario	101
Artz, Paul	52
Ashby, H. G.	18
Ashby, Helon G.	18
Ashby, J.C.	48
Ashby, Janet E	18
Ashby, Mrs. H. G.	18
Ashlock, Don	64
Atchetee, Dale	88, 91
Autrey, Doug	79

B

Baber, Tommy	79
Bacher, Eva	20
Bacon, Doug	101, 103
Bagh, Ken	79
Bailey, Emmett	29
Bailey, Reginald	101
Baimbridge, Larry	98
Baker, Bruce	93
BAKER, CHARLES H.	74
Baker, Clyde	74
Baker, David	74
Baker, Dorothy	74
Baker, J. E.	59, 77
Baker, JoAnn	74
Baker, Mr. J.L. Baker	74
Baker, Mrs. J.L. (Fannie)	74
Baker, Opal	74
Baker, Paul	74
Baker, Renee	74
Baker, Tommy	64, 59, 71, 72
Baker, V.O.	52
Baker, W.M.	4
Baker, Wendy	101
Baldwin, Robert D.	97, 101, 103
Bales, John	11-15
Ballesteros, L.S.	66
Baltimore, Charles W.	11-15
Bamsch, Cindy	68
BAMSCH, JOHNNY TERRELL	68
Bamsch, Mrs. E.A.	68
Bamsch, Mrs. Mickey	68
Bamsch, Roy	68
Banks, Charles	22
Banks, Ruby Lewis	20
Baptiste, Minerva	27
Barney, C.R.	67
Barrera, Joe	73
Barrett, Lloyd	46
Barry, Owen	33
Bartlett, Mr. James	56
Bartlett, Mrs. James	56
Bass, Charles William	74
Baylous, Roland J.	103
Beacom, Johnston Ripley IV	104
Bearden, Evelyn	54
Beasley, Mrs. Rodney	59
Beck, Bobby	89
BECK, CLAUDE RONNIE	62
Beck, Mr. Harold	62
Beck, Mrs. Harold	62
Beck, Mrs. Mary	62
Beck, Sheila	62
Becker, Gerald S.	101
Becker, Mrs. Ira Mae	101
Beeman, Paul W.	49
Beets, Alvie Lee Jr.	42/43
Beets, Billy Jack	42/43
Beets, Glenda	42/43
Beets, Helen	42/43
BEETS, JACK B.	42/43, 44
Beets, Jerry	42/43
Beets, Kay	42/43
Beets, Kenneth	42/43
Beets, Linda Carol	42/43
Beets, Mr. Alvie Lee Sr.	42/43
Beets, Mr. John	42/43
Beets, Mr. John (Brother)	42/43
Beets, Mrs. Alvie Lee Sr.	42/43
Belheze, Dr. E. T.	16
Belk, J.W.	106
Bell, J. M.	78
Bell, Mrs. Dorothy	57/58
Benavides, S.R.	66
Bench, Jerry	66
Benjamin, Mrs. Hazel	34
Bennett, Bob	64
Benningfield, Debbie	98
Berner, Frederick	20
Bernner, Officer	5
Berry, J. J.	77
Berry, Mrs. Dora	38
Berryman, B.D.	69
Bertolini, John L.	82
Betz, Jack	40
Beverly, Claude	18, 24
Bickel, J.E.	90
Biggs, Robert O. (Lippy)	46
Binford, T.	9, 11-15, 18, 22, 24, 26
Binford, Jim	103
Birch, Jimmy	75
Birden, Cathy	90
Birden, Jerry	90
Bishop, Jimmy	34
Black, Bob	97
Black, Freddie	75
Blackburn, Chief	6/7

Blackshear, J. T. 17
Blackshear, P.L. 85
Blair, A.L. 56
Blair, W. G. 78
Blalock, W. F. 20
Bland, Asa 11-15
Blando, Bobi 98
Blando, Danny 98
Blando, Mike 98
Blando, Mrs. Della 98
Blando, Mrs. Judith 98
Blando, Tracy 98
BLANDO, TROY ALAN 98, 100
Blaylock, R.G. (Bobby) 56
Blesener, N. P. 77
Bloyd, Ted C. 86, 88, 103
Bocock, C.W. 4
Boehler, E.A. (Dutch) 25
Bohn, H.D. 106
Bolin, W.T.(Truitt) 66
Bolton, D.A. 53
Bolton, L.W. 40, 78
Bonds, A.C. 3
Bonds, J.L. (Johnny) 64, 71, 74, 93
Boone, Betty 63
Boone, Charlie 64
Boone, R.R. 46
Bostock, Doug R. 49,68,71,72,75,79,80
Boswell, Joey Jr. 88
Boswell, Cecil 88
Boswell, Cindy 88
Boswell, Danielle 88
BOSWELL, JAMES CHARLES 88
Boswell, Joey 88
Boswell, Josh 88
Boswell, Julie 88
Boswell, Kayli 88
Boswell, Kenneth 88
Boswell, Michael 88
Boswell, Mrs. Martha 88
Boulding, Alfred 40
Boulle, J. S. 16
Bounds, Lyn 62
Bounds, Rick 62
Bounds, Rodney 62
Bounds, Ronald Wayne 62
Boundy, Ken 81
Boundy, Kristina 81
Boundy, Matthew 81
Boundy, Theresa 81
Bowers, J.L. 6/7
Boyd, Whit 34
Boyd, Charlotte 39
Boyd, Deborah Ann 104
Boyd, James 39
Boyd, James Jr. 39
Boyd, Whit 22
Boyd, Yvonne Hammond 39
Boyer, D.R. 85, 87

Boyles, Dr. T.J. 3
Bradberry, Mrs. Irene 50
Bradford, Clarence 103
Bradshaw, Henry 26, 34
Brandt, Ronald 66
Brandt, Terry 66
Brannon, Rev. Jim 88
Branon, Abigail 47
Branon, Al 47
Branon, Betty 47
BRANON, CLAUDE EMMETT ... 47, 49
Branon, Claude Emmett Jr. 47
Branon, Kiley 47
Branon, Linda Gail 47
Branon, Mindy Lee 47
Branon, Nathan 47
Braswell, Kimberley Anne 55
Braswell, Lyndon Tyler 55
Braune, F. E. 78
Brazell, Bill 6/7
Breeding, Carla 93
Breen, P.K. (Kevin) 85, 91
Breshears, Joe 96
Brewer, David 69
Brewton, F.S. 57/58
Brien, Mrs. Charlene 41
Bringhurst, Justice 2
Briscoe, Frank 54
Brock, Clarence 11-15
Brockman, J.B. 6/7
Broderhausen, Al 82
Brogden, George 51
Brooks, P.A. 72
Brooks, Willie 6/7
Brown, Alan 98
Brown, Alfred DeWayne 103
Brown, Floyd 34
Brown, G. D. 78
Brown, Gene A. 55
Brown, Jessie 42/43
Brown, L.C. 38
Brown, Lee P. 86
Brown, Marc 105
Brown, R.B. 42/43
Brown, W.P. 39
Broze, S.L. 102
Brumley, R. 57/58
Bryan, L.Z. 36
Bryant, Chad 46
Bryant, Janet 46
Bryant, Shannon 46
Bryant, Steven O. 101
Bryant, Victor Ervin 49
Bryant, Wayne 46
Bryson, Officer 10
Buchanan, T.J. 70
Buddendorf, Mary Alice 6/7
Buenrosto, Jim 21
Bukowski, A.F. 102

Bunch, Sergeant 64
Buntion, Bobby 89
Buntion, Carl Wayne 56, 71, 89
Buntion, Kenneth 56, 89
Burge, Richard 74
Burke, A.J. 46
Burke, G.L. 89
Burkett, W.H. 11-15
Burkham, W.L. 68
Burmester, John 74, 89
Burnett, T.L. 85
Burns, Mike 79
Burns, Monica 103
Burns, Uvalde 4
Burrell, Robert 101
Busey, J. C. 5
Butcher, G.W. 11-15
Butler, Brianna 103
Butler, George L. (Billy) 11-15
Butler, Gus 20, 36
Buttita, Joe 101
Buzo, Larry 76
Byrd, C.A. 85
Byrd, William (Bill)l 90

C

Caceras, Jesus 20
Cahill, Officer 5
Caicedo, Diana 101
Caicedo, Laura 101
Cain, Albert 9
Cain, Billie 26
Cain, James 9
CAIN, JOHN MORRIS 9
Cain, R. D. 80
Cain, W. H. 20
Cain-Crocker, June 79
Caldwell, Harry 68
Calhoun, Richard Howard 70
Calhoun, Barbara 70
Calhoun, David 75, 96, 98
Calhoun, Donna 70
Calhoun, Mrs. Arlene 70
Calhoun, Mrs. Rudolph 70
CALHOUN, RICHARD HOWARD 70
Calhoun, Richard Howard II 70
Calhoun, Robert (Brother) 70
Calhoun, Robert (Son) 70
Calhoun, Rudolph 70
Calhoun, Terri 70
Calix, M.A. 99
Campbell, Henry 2
Campbell, Jim 80
Campbell, Joan 106
Campbell, John 22
Cantu, Eric Able 104
CANTU, FRANCISCO JR. 104

Cantu, Frank Manuel 104	Clark, Gary 62	Corrales, Ruby 20
Cantu, Frank Manuel Jr. 104	Clark, Hilde 103	Corrales, Thomas 20
Cantu, J.F. 84	Clark, Mark 20	Cosby, Hubert 25
Cantu, Mr. 20	Clark, Mrs. Ina 103	Cosby, Patsy 63
Cantwell, Ray 66	Clark, Robert 103	Couch, D.H. 98, 101
Carbo, R.B. 64, 68	Clarke, T. T. 30/31	Cox, G.F. 57/58
Cardona, Edmund 10	Clement, David 66	Cox, Judge 3
Carlin, Paul 80	Cleveland, Grover 11-15	Cox, N.E. 61
Carlson, Father Robert 76	Cleveland, Judge 4	Crain, Pastor N.C. 28
Carmichael, A. 4	Cleveland, Mrs. J.E. 37	Crane, Robert 60
Carpenter, Jerry 70	Clifton, D.G. 69, 78	Crawford, K. E. 78
Carpenter, R.W. 61	Clinton, J.M. 86	Crawford, Tommy D. 62
Carr, Ed 9	Clipper, K-9 49	Crawley, Mary 91
Carr, Fred 30/31	Coates, Charles Robert, II 82	Creagan, Pat 33
Carr, Kevin 101, 103, 106	Coates, Charles Robert, III 82	Credge, Mrs. A. B. 22
Carr, S. E. 77, 78, 84	COATES, CHARLES ROBERT 82	Crittenden, Frank C. ....
Carr, T.R. 9	Coates, Christine 82	42/43,44,45,53,66
Carroll, A.O. 42/43	Coates, Elizabeth Ann 82	Crooker, John H. 10, 11-15
Carroll, Fred 89, 93	Coates, Jacqueline 82	Crown, Katherine Nicole 55
Carstens, A.R. 11-15	Cochran, Daniel J. 81	Crown, Lauren Elizabeth 55
Carter, C.E. 11-15	Cochran, Fred 33	Crown, Stacie Lynn 55
Carter, Gerry L. 62	Cochran, Harry E. Jr. 81	Cruser, J.S. 101, 106
Carter, H.P. 28	Cochran, Harry Edward 81	Crutcher, Jerald 79
Carter, Lula 83	Cochran, Mrs. Theresa 81	Cruz, Mrs. Delia 49
Casey, Gerry 94	Cochran, Thomas P. 81	Culak, D.J. 102
Casey, Mrs. Judy 94	Cole, H.E. 41	Culbreth, C.H. 51
Cash, Charlie 96	Cole, Marianne 102	Culver, K.L. 97
Cashmere, Willie 63	Coleman, A. E. 77	Cunningham, T.R. 73
Casserly, D.B. 99	Coleman, Christopher Dwight 91	Curtin, Officer Daniel 6/7
Castaneda, Sylvia 87	Collingsworth, Ronnie 80	Curtis, Mr. R.S. 84
Castillo, J.M. 86	Collins, J.W. 72	Curtis, Mrs. R.S. 84
Cates, W.C. 93	Collins, Judge Denise 86, 101	
Cavazos, E. 80	Collins, Ray 93	
Cavin, Judge E.C. 4	Combs, E.D. (Sonny) 55,56,59	# D
Cedeno, R.S. 87, 95	Condon, Cathy 67	
Cevallos, Alejandro (Alex) 71	Coney, T. R. 77	
Chance, Billy 76	Conley, J.D. 46	Daniel, D.R. 75
Chapman, George 41	Connally, Gov. John 39	Daniel, George 18
Chapman, Russell 76	Connally, John 34	DANIELS, RUFUS (RUFF). 5, 11-15
Chappel, Roger 106	Connelly, Rev. Laurence 94	Davenport, Don 57/58
Charles, Henry 27	Connett, Alvin 37	Davenport, Ronald 57/58
Charlton, Officer 5	Connett, Mrs. Christine 37	DAVIDSON, JOHNNIE ... 11-15, 16, 17
CHAVEZ, E.C. 6/7, 21	Conroy, Steve 34	Davidson, Susan Stansbury 16
Chavez, Clara 21	Contreras, Charlie 78	Davidson, Ben 10
Chavez, Golian (Will) 21	Contreras, Robert 66	Davidson, C. A. 16
Chavez, John H. 21	Conway, Kathy 97	Davidson, C. H. 16
Chavez, Mike 46	Conway, Deputy 4	Davidson, J. H. 16
Chavez, Steve 21	Cook, Judge Gustave 2,3	Davidson, Julius 16
Chebret, M.J. (Joe) 49, 61, 62, 67	Coolidge, Calvin 11-15	Davidson, Lois 16
Cheek, Glen 72	Cooper, Earl 101	Davidson, Lucy 101
Chester, Pete 22	Cooper, P. J. 78	Davidson, Rev. O.L. 48
Chisholm, Henry 101, 103	Cooper, Pete 70	Davidson, W. S. 16
Christian, Clark 30/31	Corrales, Ruby 20	Davies, Judge Carol 98
Christian, Pete 69	Corrales, Delphine 20	Davila, Jesse 103
Civitello, Thomas C. 98	Corrales, Frank 20	DAVIS, ALBERT WORTH 19, 22, 25
Clampitte, J. W. 20	Corrales, Jesse 20	Davis, Alma 26
Clampitte, J.W. (Moose) 20, 70, 79	Corrales, Mary 20	Davis, Bill 4
CLARK, CHARLES R. 103	Corrales, Mrs. Sabena Nette 20	Davis, Chaplain Ed 93, 95, 98, 99
Clark, Claude L. 103	CORRALES, PETE 20, 21	Davis, Donald 54
Clark, Connie 103	Corrales, Pete Jr. 20	

Davis, Edith A.	30/31	DeLeon, William E.	81	Duslher, Heidi A.	85
Davis, Felix	26	DELEON, WILLIAM E.(PONCE)	77, 78	Dyek, Rev	8
Davis, J.J.	66	DeLeon, William Emmett, Jr.	78		
Davis, J.L.	85	DeLeon, William Michael J.	78	# E
Davis, J.R.	88	DeLeon, William, Sr.	78	
Davis, J.R. (Jimmy)	63	Deloach, Floyd Sr.	54	Earls, Larry L.	64, 71, 75
Davis, James	26	DELOACH, FLOYD TAYLOR JR.	51, 54	Earthman, John B.	35
Davis, Marie	69	Deloach, Jo Ann	54	Earwood, Mrs. Tini	46
Davis, Mary	54	Deloach, Mrs. Floyd Sr.	54	Easter, J.J.	40
Davis, Patrick	26	Deloach, Terri Lynn	54	Eaton, John	70
Davis, R.S.	64	Deloach, Tracey Lee	54	Eckhardt, Dr.W.R.	6/7
Davis, Ronald L.F.	11-15	Demny, Roger	75	Eckman, Lomis	30/31
Davison, Ben	11-15, 35	Dennis, E.R.	64, 68, 71	Edison, W.G. (Bill)	93
Davlin, Jim	24	Denson, Judge Woody	91	Edwards, Alonzo	11-15
Day, Eddie	86	Depenbrock, H.W.	8	Edwards, Bill	38
de Oliveira, Rev. Fred D.	98	Derryberry, Mandy Bamsch	68	Edwards, Bruce George	38
Deal, Rev. Harold G.	50	Derryberry, Taylor Paige	68	Edwards, Charley	38
Deandra, C.D.	85	Dickson, Rev. David	88	Edwards, France	38
Dear, Mrs. Mack	38	Dierks, Jack	61	EDWARDS, GEORGE DEWEY	38
Dearing, C.D.	61	Dierks, Margaret	61	Edwards, J.B.	38
Debusschere, Barbara	64	Dietrich, R.R.	59	Edwards, Kathryn	38
Decker, Mrs. Henrietta	56	Dietz, C. R.	42/43, 69	Edwards, Kenneth	38
Dees, Cynthia	102	Dingas, Lucy	87	Edwards, Leitha Joy	38
Dees, Deborah	102	Dixon, Rev. David	84, 91, 93, 98	Edwards, Michael R.	80, 86
Dees, Derek	102	Dobbs, E.M.	55	Edwards, Mr. C.F.	38
Dees, Grace	102	Dodd, Charles C.	52	Edwards, Mrs. Audie	38
Dees, Karen	102	Dollar, Lloyd (Sonny)	89	Edwards, Mrs. C.F.	38
DEES, KEITH ALAN	102	Dollins, George	75, 86	Edwards, Nancy Joy	38
Dees, Kevin	102	Domiguez, John	105	Edwards, Robert	38
Dees, Mr. Ruby Harlon	102	Dominy, E.	42/43	Eggleston, Lillian	45
Dees, Mrs. Bettye Virginia	102	Donovan, J.M. (John)	64, 68, 71	Eggleston, Marvin	45
Dees, Mrs. Ruby Harlon	102	Doss, W.C.	39	Eickenhorst, W.G.	68, 78
Dees, Ruben C.	102	Dotson, Jimmy	89	Eilert, Mary Jane	82
DeFoor, K.T.	55, 59, 70	Dottley, Rev. Robert A.	61	Elliot, Margie	41
Dela Garza, Mrs. Emma	49	Doty, Tom	89	Elliott, C. E. (Carless)	78, 96, 97, 98
Delano, Richard	71	Dove, R. A.	78	Elliott, Louis M. Sr,	50
Deleon, Alejandera	105	Downs, Kim	97, 101, 103	Ellis, George	8
DeLeon, Autumn	78	Doyle, M.E.	88	Ellis, J.D. (Pops)	68
DeLeon, Bobby	78	Doyle, R.L.	68, 91	Ellis, Mark Kent	103
DeLeon, Brooke	78	Draycott, J.E.	98	Ellis, Sheriff George	4, 9
DeLeon, Fayth	78	Drescher, Katherine Ann	76	Ellis, Wardell	60
Deleon, Frank	105	Driver, Jerry	90	Elmore, Danny Foster	62
DcLeon, Hal Glen	78	Drucks, William J.	11-15	Elsbury, W.R. (Bill)	68
DeLeon, Helen	78	Duckett, Rev. John	52	Emmott, Catherine	11-15
Deleon, J.	63	Duerer, J.N.	106	Emory, Robert Tillman Jr.	65
DeLeon, Janice	78	Duffau, Dr.	4	Engle, Wilbur	9
Deleon, Juanita	105	Duggan, Judge Ed	63	Enloe, Virginia	102
Deleon, Kathy	78	Dugger, Allen Dale	56, 89	Enloe, Woody	102
Deleon, Lee	105	Dugger, Joe T.	56	Enright, J. C.	17
DeLeon, Matt	78	Duharte-Tur, Enrique	101	Erichson, Alex	3
DeLeon, Michael	78	Dunbar, J. W.	78	Erickson, Beth	95
Deleon, Mrs. Mayra Guerrero	105	Duncan, C.D.	97, 101, 106	Erickson, Christopher	95
DeLeon, Mrs. William, Sr	78	Dunham, W. G.	18	Erickson, David	95
Deleon, Olga	105	Dunman, F.	11-15	ERICKSON, DAWN SUZANNE	95
Deleon, Patricia	78	Dunman, Night Chief	16	Erickson, Nicole	95
Deleon, Patrick	105	Dunn, Mrs. Elma	61	Escalante, J.L. (Jaime)	87, 93
Deleon, Paul Villalpand	63	Durham, Nate	46	Escobedo, Frank	85
DELEON, REUBEN BECERRA	105	Durham, Sharon	91	Espitia, J.	92
Deleon, Reuben III	105				
Deleon, Reuben Sr.	105				

Esquivel, Rudy Ramos 73
Estes, G.R. 67
ETHERIDGE, JOHN CLARK. 19, 29
Etheridge, S. H. 19
Evans, J.D. 57/58
Evans, Jay 70
Everett, W.H. 38
Everton, M.D. 11-15
Ewton, Carol Stephenson 71

F

Fabj, Frank 90
Fadner, Dale 39
Fadner, Howard Hammond 39
Fadner, Robert 39
Faircloth, W.L. 39
Fant, Sheriff 2, 3
Fantin, Marvin 64
Farmer, Mrs. Kathryn 38
Farmer, Thomas 38
Farrar, Carrol Dayton 41
Fedderson, K.S. 91
Felchak, Steve 79
Fendley, Earl 11-15
FENN, JAMES E. 4, 6/7
Fentis, Marvin Joel 64
Ferguson, David 93, 101, 103, 106
Ferguson, James E. 11-15
Ferguson, L.D. 84
Ferguson, Roy 86
Fife, Jim 11-15
Finkelman, Gary 90
Fisher, Lewis 8
Fitzgerald, Edith Louise Davis 30/31
FITZGERALD, EDWARD DAVIS..... 30/31
Fitzgerald, F. M. 30/31
Fitzgerald, J. 3
Fitzgerald, Joseph Amos 30/31
Flannagan, H. H. 18
Flemming, Roy 42/43
Flock, Michael 1, 3
Floeck, Martin 1
Floeck, Reba 1
Flores, Roberto Carrasco 80
Flowers, C. D. 59
FOLEY, CHARLES EDWARD 1
Foley, Pat H. 39
Folsam, W.B. 49
Folsom, Bill 89
Fondren, E. O. 19
Fonville, Mayor 36
Foreman, Percy 45, 71
Foreman, Sammie 11-15
Foroi, Jesse 83
Francis, R.J. 62
Frank, Bruce 79

Frankhouser, Peggy 91
Franklin, Trazawell 56
Franks, Ira O. 67, 73
Freeman, Charles 56
Freeman, J.D. 3
Freeman, James 3
Freeman, Ron 90
Frew, Elaine Holmes 100
Frew, Kenneth 100
Freytag, David 22
Fulbright, Jack 79
Furlong, James 3

G

Gaddis, Abigail 93
Gaddis, Angela 93
Gaddis, Gary 93
Gaddis, Glenn 93
GADDIS, GUY PATRICK 93, 106
Gaddis, Justyn 93
Gaddis, Mallory 93
Gaddis, Mr. Edwin 93
Gaddis, Mrs. Gayle 93
Gaddis, Mrs. Rosa 93
Gaddis, Shane 93
Gaddis, Stephanie 93
Gaddis, Taylor 93
Gafford, Dennis 86, 89
Gage, M.G. 85
Gage, T. W. Tommy 77
Gagnon, Linda 87
Gainer, Clay M. 88
Galbiati, S.A. 90
Galbreath, William 35
Gale, Arthur 11-15
Gallatin, B.J. 72
Gallemore, John 93, 96
Galli, T.S. 99
Gaman, I.H. 52
Gambill, Detective 28
Gambill, Glenna Mae 35
GAMBILL, JAMES THOMAS 35, 100
Gambill, John 26, 35
Gambill, Mary 35
Gambill, Mrs. John 35
Gambill, Mrs. Patty Annie 35
Gambill, Young 35
Gamez, S. 85
Gamino, Joe 55
Garcia, C.L. 92
Garcia, Christine Celeste 87
Garcia, D.C. 92
GARCIA, FLORENTINO MUNOZ, JR. 87
Garcia, G.A. 92
Garcia, J. 92

Garcia, Jose Sr. 92
Garcia, Mr. Florentino R. 87
Garcia, Mrs. Mary Lou 87
Garcia, Natividad 87
Garcia, R. V. 78
Garcia, Rachel 63
Garcia, Raymond 87
Garcia, Rico 92
Garcia, S.M. 92
Garcia, Sharon 41
Garcia, Sonya 87
Garcia, Staci Marie 87
Garcia, Vincente 93
Gardner, E.W. 41
Garredo, Manuel 11-15
Garrett, B.J. 85
Garrett, Daniel 11-15
Garrett, Mrs. Dorothy 42/43
Gates, Mack 22
Gearhardt, Nick 56
Gee, Wally 47
Gentry, D. L. 17
George, Leon 9
George, M.R. 36
GERHART, BEN E. 40, 56, 57/58
Gerhart, Diane 57/58
Gerhart, Henry 57/58
Gerhart, John (Father) 57/58
Gerhart, Johnnie (Brother) 57/58
Gerhart, Mrs. Ruby 57/58
Gerhart, Ruth 57/58
Gerlich, Collin P. 98, 100
Gibson, D.A. (Hoot) 53, 64, 65
Gibson, L.E. 3
Gibson, Volney 3
Giese, A. 29
Gilbert, A. L. 78
Gillespie, J.K. 4
Gipson, Carolyn 103
Givens, W.L. 84
Glaspie, Dashon V. 103
Glass, Deputy M.W. 2, 4
Glasscock, Deputy 2
Glenn, Greg 106
Glover, William 34
Going, Dan 4
Gomez Garcia, Rogelio Roger 78
Gonzales, G. 66
Gonzalez, D.S. 92
Gonzalez, Gonzalo Jr. 49
GONZALEZ, GONZALO QUINONES 49
Gonzalez, Irene 49
Gonzalez, Karen 49
Gonzalez, Lisa 49
Gonzalez, Mario 49
Gonzalez, Mr. R.C. 49
Gonzalez, Mrs. Eloisa 49
Gonzalez, Phyliss 79
Goode, Cheryl 33

Goodfellow, J.F. ... 93
Goodson, B. E. ... 77
Goodson, Tom C. ... 25
Goodwin, J. H. ... 22
Gorczynski, Dale ... 85
Gordy, B.K. ... 57/58
Gorham, George ... 3
Gossett, Officer ... 5
Gottlick, Charles ... 93
Gottlick, Joyce ... 93
Gottlick, Maureen ... 93
Gottlick, Russell ... 93
Goudreau, Mrs. E.P. ... 25
Gougenheim, Charles II ... 42/43
Gougenheim, Charles III ... 42/43
GOUGENHEIM, CHARLES SR. ... 42/43, 44
Gougenheim, Evelyn ... 42/43
Gougenheim, Jennifer ... 42/43
Gougenheim, Louis ... 42/43
Gougenheim, Mary Frances ... 42/43
Gower, W.T. ... 66
Graddy, J.O. ... 39
Graham, Bert ... 74
Graham, Catherine ... 82
Graham, Hugh ... 34, 38, 39
Granadas, Frank ... 106
Granger, Chauffeur ... 10
Grant, M. A. ... 5
Gravonic, Mrs. Rita ... 56
Gray, Les ... 59
Gray, Stocky ... 22
Green, C.E. ... 84
Green, John ... 2
Green, Johnny ... 91
Green, Mr. Claude ... 62
Green, Mrs. Beth ... 95
Green, Mrs. Claude ... 62
Green, Rev. John ... 11-15
Green, Scott ... 95
Green, Walter ... 91
GREENE, CARL ... 24, 25
Greene, Effie ... 24
Greene, Ellis ... 24
Greene, Emery ... 24
Greene, Eugenia ... 24
Greene, Jules ... 24
Greene, Mrs. Pearlie Walker ... 24
Greene, Mrs. Richard ... 24
Greene, Richard ... 24
Greene, Robert ... 24
Greer, L.E. ... 11-15
Greer, Mrs. Gladys ... 57/58
Gregg, Robbie ... 27
Gresham, Frank ... 18
Gresham, M.A. ... 23
Griffin, Don C. ... 52
Griggs, Iona ... 60
Griggs, Leah ... 60
GRIGGS, LEON ... 47, 60, 96

Griggs, Leon Jr. ... 60
Griggs, Leslie ... 60
Griggs, Lessie ... 60
Griggs, Linda ... 60
Griggs, Mrs. Iona ... 60
Griggs, Nelda ... 74
Griggs, Richard ... 60
Grimes, E. F. ... 30/31
Grizaffi, A.P. ... 90
Grizaffi, Mrs. A.P ... 90
GROVES, MARIA MICHELLE ... 84
Groves, Mr. Clyde ... 84
Groves, Mrs. Clyde ... 84
Grysen, C.J. ... 84
Guerra, Aaron ... 105
Guerra, Juana ... 106
Guerra, Ricardo Aldape ... 80
Gunn, James E. (Pete) 26, 55, 59, 60, 64
Gutierrez, Cathy ... 65
GUZMAN, ANTONIO JR. ... 65
Guzman, Candy ... 65
Guzman, John ... 65
Guzman, Juanita ... 20
Guzman, Mr. Antonio Sr. ... 65
Guzman, Mrs. Antonio Sr. ... 65
Guzman, William ... 65
Gwynn, Deputy ... 4

H

Habermacher, S.M. ... 9
Haddox, T.A. ... 9
Hahl, Charles W. ... 11-15
Haigh, Clifford ... 42/43
Haigh, Donald ... 42/43
Haigh, Donna ... 42/43
Haigh, Earl ... 42/43
Haigh, Norma Gougenheim ... 42/43
Haigh, Robert ... 42/43
Haines, J..W. ... 54, 64, 66
Hake, John R. ... 72, 73
Hakkola, Leslie ... 102
Hale, Fred ... 96, 97
Hall, C.P. ... 68
Hall, H. E. ... 30/31
Hall, Harry ... 55
Hall, Jimmie ... 71
Hallonquist, Rev. Grady ... 40
Hambley, T.F. ... 39
Hamer, Frank ... 26
Hamilton, R.L. ... 49
Hammerle, J.S. ... 96, 98, 101, 103
Hammond, Frank ... 16
HAMMOND, HOWARD B. ... 39
Hammond, Mary Nell ... 39
Hammond, Mrs. Alberta ... 39
Hammond, Mrs. Kathleen ... 39

Hammond, Sara ... 39
Hammond, Sheriff ... 10
Hammond, Wilmer J. ... 39
Hammond, Yvonne ... 39
Hammonds, E.H. ... 34
Hancock, A. H. ... 16
Hankins, Wayne ... 66
Hanks, Juanita ... 83
Hanna, P.D. ... 35
Hannah, Chaplain Harold L. ... 64, 75, 80, 83
Hannah, P. H. ... 18
Hannah, Stephen Michael ... 55
Hardeway, Grant ... 86
Hardin, Rusty ... 88
Harding, Warren G. ... 11-15
Haring, Earl ... 63, 68, 72
Harnett, A.O. ... 3
Harper, Carl ... 22
Harrell, G.H. ... 38
Harris, Beverly Jean ... 80
Harris, Brian ... 64, 101, 103
Harris, Gerry ... 80
HARRIS, JAMES DONALD ... 76, 80
Harris, Joe ... 16
Harris, Megan Annette ... 80
Harris, Nelson (father) ... 80
Harris, Nelson (grandfather) ... 80
Harris, Pamela ... 80
Harris, Rebecca Brooke ... 80
Harris, Ruth ... 80
Harris, Tom ... 34
Harrison, L.P. ... 44
Harrison, M.D. ... 72
Hart, Virgil ... 41
Hartman, J.C. ... 69, 84
Harvell, David ... 86
Harwell, D.L. ... 87
Hassan, Amina ... 11-15
Hassat, T.H. ... 25
Hawkins, A.K. ... 98
Hawkins, P.D. ... 70
Haya, Kathy ... 103
Hayes, Hubert ... 57/58
Hayes, Mrs. JoAnn ... 46
Hayes, Mrs. Mary ... 57/58
Haynes, Anthony Cardell ... 97
Haynes, Robert V. ... 11-15
HEALY, DAVID MICHAEL ... 94
Healy, John B. (Father) ... 94
Healy, John Bret (Brother) ... 94
Healy, Mrs. Bernice ... 94
Heard, Jack ... 42/43, 44
Heard, Jack Jr. ... 62
Heard, Mrs. Ed ... 6/7
Heard, Percy ... 24, 27, 30/31, 39
Hearn, Jenny ... 73
Hearn, Mrs. Wynelle ... 73
Hearn, Robert ... 73
HEARN, TIMOTHY LOWE ... 6/7, 46,

275

73
Hearn, Tory 73
Heck, Night Chief 9
Heit, Bill 47
Henderson, Dick 97
Henderson, Keno 91
Hendricks, Buddy 46
Henning, L.W. (Lawrence) 66
Henry, Bert 42/43
Henry, D.E. 95
Henry, Jones 22
Henry, Vida 11-15
Henson, Louis 39
Hermann, Alfred T. 80
Hernandez, H.V. 66
Hernandez, R. 95
Heslin, Riley Blake 67
Hesselsweet, Sayra 73
Hickman, Darlene 11-15
Hicks, Gary 91
Hicks, Sherman 74
Higgins, Officer 5
Higgins, W.T. 51
High, E. K. 19
Hight, C. W. 17
Hill, Justice 6/7
Hill, W.B. 6/7
Hilleman, Kenneth A. 98
Hilleman, Reidun 90
Hinkle, Kenneth 55, 71, 89
Hinkle, William 55, 89
Hinkson, Bob 79
Hobbs, Henrietta 6/7
Hoffard, Russel 80
Hofheinz, Mayor Roy 42/43
Hogg, Governor 4
Hogg, Mike 11-15
Hogg, Will 11-15
Holbrook, M.L. 101
Holcombe, Bill 74
Holcombe, Oscar 34, 36
Holiday, V.C. 49
Holland, Richard W.
80,88,96,97,98,101,103
Holleman, John 74
Holloway, Jack 80
Holloway, N.W. (Wayne) 67
Holmes, Johnny 91
Holmes, Ashley Ann 100
Holmes, Dennis 35
HOLMES, DENNIS E. 98
Holmes, Dennis Edward 100
Holmes, I.W. (Ira) 55, 56
Holmes, Jamie 63
Holmes, Jennie Mae 35
Holmes, Johnny B. 86, 93, 100
Holmes, Kenneth 100
Holmes, Kristen Nicole 100
Holmes, Linda 100
Holmes, Martin 35

Holmes, Melissa 63
Holmes, Mr. Edward 100
Holmes, Mrs. Alta 100
Holmes, Mrs. Kym 100
Holmes, Theresa 100
Holt, Willie W. 97
Holton, Frank 34
Honea, R. L. 17
Honea, R. T. 33
Hooper, R. B. 33
Hope, Alma Nix 27
Hope, Frankie Mae 27
Hope, Glenn 27
Hope, Harriet Parker 27
Hope, Harry 27
Hope, Heather 27
HOPE, OSCAR 27
Hope, R.W. Jr. 27
Hope, Reuben Wert 27
Hope, Ruth 27
Hopkins, Raymond 69
Horelica, E. L. (Ed) 55, 60, 64, 71
Horn, Roy 68
Horton, R. L. 78
Hosford, R.E. 66
Hotchkiss, Mrs. Palmer 40
Houston, D.B. 92
Howaniec, K. J. 78
Howard, Alcano 86
Howard, Alvonda Michelle 86
Howard, C.F. 56
Howard, David 63
HOWARD, ELSTON MORRIS 86
Howard, Eugene 86
Howard, H.N. 25
Howard, Mitchell 63
Howard, Mrs.Era Mae 86
Howard, Officer 5
Howard, R.C. 37
Howard, Sherry 63
Howard, Tyesha Boudreaux 86
Howard, Willie 72
Howser, Cathy 67
Howser, Danielle 67
Howser, Dawn 67
Howser, Jim 67
Hoyt, Kenneth 80
Hudson, Doug M. 1, 10
Hudson, Mrs. Dorothy 69
Hudson, Tom 69
Huerta, Connie 66
Huerta, Daniel 66
HUERTA, DAVID 66, 71
Huerta, Marcie 66
Huerta, Mr. Genero 66
Huerta, Mrs. Genero 66
Hughes, A.R. 69
Hulen, John A. 11-15
Humble, William 2
Hunter, Raymond 60

Hurd, D.R. 92, 95
Hurtt, Harold 25
Hutcheson, Joseph C 11-15
Huth, Rev. Richard 99
Huynh, Tony 101
Hyde, Earl V. 25

I

Ingels, Michael D. 98
Inghram, Bogard 35
Ingle, Laura 88
Inman, Mrs. Hazel 51
Iranda, Ignacio 66
Irby, Bubba 89
Irby, Callie 89
Irby, Cody 89
IRBY, JAMES B. 56, 71, 89
Irby, Kelly 89
Irby, Madge 89
Irby, Maura 89
Irby, Mrs. Thelma 89
Irby, V.V. 89
Irby, V.V. Jr. 89
Ireland, Governor 2
Irving, Robert W. Jr. 98
Irwin, J. K. 30/31
Irwin, J.G. 38
Irwin, Kirk 28
Isaacks, Monica 57/58
Isaacks, Roderick Michael 57/58
Isenberg, Patti 99

J

Jackson, C.E. 97
Jackson, C.L. Rev. 86
Jackson, Charles Jr. 39
Jackson, D.P. 84
Jackson, Melvin L. 51
Jackson, Mrs Josephine 88
Jackson, Opal 63
Jackson, Sandra 103
Jackson, Tampy 4
Jackson, W.G. 64
JAMES, BOBBY L. 40, 56, 57/58
James, Cynthia 57/58
James, D.R. 68
James, Gayle 57/58
JAMES, JOHN C. 5, 6/7
James, Mark Steven 69
James, Mrs. Georgia 57/58
James, Officer 5
James, Pamela 57/58
Jamison, Detective 30/31
Jarvis, Shirley 70

Jasso, A.A. 66	Jones, Shelton Denoria 91	Kessler, Detective 9, 30/31
Jeffcoat, J.R. 57/58	Jones, Sylvia 28	Kessler, W.F. 8
Jenkins, Lela 85	Jones, Talmadge Ray 22	Kessler, William 5
Jenkins, M.D. 94	Jones, Terry Edward 22	Kiesenwetter, N.S. 106
Jennings, Robert Mitchell 86	Jones, Thomas Lewis 52	Killingsworth, John Earl 89
Jeske, R.J. 68	Jones, Tilmon Jr. 103	KILTY, JAMES FREDERICK 46, 72, 73
Jett, Steve 103	Jones, Vanice Ione (Bernice) 22	Kilty, Jennifer 72
Johnson, Rodney 35	Jones, Wayne 79	Kilty, Justin 72
Johnson, A.R. 55	Jones, Woody Dr. 10	Kilty, Kelly 72
Johnson, Amber 106	Jordan, Murray K. 73	Kilty, Mark 72
Johnson, Austin 2	Joubert, Elijah 103	Kilty, Mary Ann 72
Johnson, B.K. 81	Justice, William Wayne 54	Kilty, Meg 72
Johnson, Big Frank 11-15		Kilty, Mr. William F. 72
Johnson, Corrigan 106	# K	Kilty, Mrs. William F. 72
Johnson, Elmo 8		Kilty, Nancy 72
Johnson, J.O. 42/43		Kilty, Suzanne 72
Johnson, Jessica 106	Kahn, Henry 8	Kilty, Tom 72
Johnson, Ken 91	Kahn, R. E. 5	Kilty, William 72
Johnson, Major Michael 101	Kainer, P.C. (Pat) 64, 68, 71	Kimberlin, Ray 74
Johnson, Marsene 8	Kalich, D.G. 89	Kimble, Lamar 41, 42/43, 45
Johnson, Mrs. Cynthia 106	Kankel, D.R. 61	Kincaid, Courtney Deanne 97
Johnson, Mrs. Matilda 2	Kardatzke, Mike 61, 86	Kincaid, Donald 97
Johnson, Mrs. Wilma 88	Kasper, Betty Branon 47	Kincaid, Jena Lee 97
Johnson, Mrs.Joslyn Margaret 106	Kaufold, Raymond 25	KINCAID, KENT D. 97
Johnson, R.F. 29	Kay, J.L. 89, 93	Kincaid, Mrs. Myrna 97
Johnson, Rev. F.M. 29	Keathley, Nancy 64	Kincaid, Mrs. Nancy 97
JOHNSON, RODNEY JOSEPH .. 61, 106	Keegan, Deputy 2	Kindred, J.W. (Jean) 42/43
Johnson, W. B. 78	Keele, Jimmy 103	King, Langston 39, 46
Jolly, Berniece 54	Keele, Marlene 103	King, Mrs. Leota 47
Jones , Stephen 18	Kegans, Judge Joe 88	King, R.E. (Bob) 101, 103
Jones, A. L. 22	Kelely, Judge Joe 56	King, Sewall 30/31
Jones, Alfredia 103	Kellogg, Robert (Brother) 44	Kinsel, A. G. 78
Jones, Bill 25	Kellogg, Adelaide 44	Kittrell, Judge 3
Jones, Detective 30/31	KELLOGG, FRANK L. 44	Klau, Dr. Irwin 69
Jones, E.M. 11-15	Kellogg, Ginger Sue 44	Klawiter, Tom 68
JONES, ED 22, 28	Kellogg, Jo Ann 44	Knigge, J.A. 42/43
Jones, Howard Page 22	Kellogg, John 44	Knowles, Harry G. 34
Jones, Isaac 34	Kellogg, Lawrence 44	Knox, Van 73
Jones, J. F. 22	Kellogg, Mildred 44	Koubig, Dr. 4
Jones, Janie 22	Kellogg, Robert (nephew) 44	Kromer, Joan 61
Jones, Kenneth 103	Kellogg, Robert (Son) 44	Krpec, J. A. 78
Jones, Larry 22	Kellogg, Sandra Lynn 44	Krum, Night Clerk 5
Jones, Larry Severn 22	Kellogg, William 44	KUBA, LOUIS RAYMOND 79
Jones, Lyle Thurman 22	Kendall, Clarence 10	Kuba, Andy 56
Jones, M. L. 22	Kennedy, J.I. 88, 91	Kuba, Helen 56
Jones, Marjorie 22	Kennedy, M.M. 69	Kuba, Louis Raymond 56, 63
Jones, Mary Bess 22	Kennedy, Sam 103	Kuba, Milton 56
Jones, Mary Simmons 22	Kennedy, Stuart Hal 93, 101, 103	Kuba, Mr. Jerry 56
Jones, Maxine 22	Kennedy, Tom 11-15	Kuba, Mrs. Jerry 56
Jones, Michael 83	Kent, C.W. 74, 75	Kuba, Mrs. Patricia 56
Jones, Mr. Tilmon Sr. 103	Kent, H.B. 40	Kuba, Norbert 56
Jones, Mrs. Bernice 37	Kent, J.E. 40, 42/43	Kuba, Rudy 56
Jones, Mrs. J. F. 22	Kent, Nell Margaret 40	Kuba, Teddy 56
Jones, Mrs. Velma 103	KENT, SMITH A. (BUSTER) 40	Kuenstler, A.J. 25
Jones, Neva 22	Kent, Smith A. III (Butch) 40	Kyle, Mrs. Annie 35
JONES, PERRY PAGE 22	Kent, W.M. 40	Kyles, Richard Delain 68
Jones, Perry Page (Grandson) 22	Kerchkoff, V.H. 65	
Jones, Severn Frankline 22	Kern, C.V. (Buster) 25, 39	
Jones, Sharon 22	Kersten, Henry Wayne 71, 79	

L

Labdi, I.M. 90, 102
Lacey, Tom 9
Ladd, J.W. (Jim) 75, 86, 96, 98
Ladd, T.M. (Tom) 86, 88, 103
LaFon, Tommy 103
Lahey, Officer 5
Lambert, Mrs. Ida 68
Lambright, D.C. 101, 103, 106
Lambright, George 86
Lamp, Ella 11-15
Lance, Mrs. Betty Jean 41
Landgrebe, J.N. 87
Landrum, C.L. 63
Landrum, Mrs. Mary Edna 29
Landrum, Rev. D.L. 35
Landry, Edna 32
LANDRY, J.D. 32
Landry, Mr. Adolphe 32
Landry, Mrs. Adolphe 32
Landry, Mrs. J.D. 32
Landry, Otis 32
Landry, Sidney 32
Landry, Walter 32
Lane, Virginia Howard 86
Lang, John 3
Langston, C.F. 41
Lankford, Max W. 59, 61, 64, 71
Larendon, Dr. Geo. 4
Larue, George 52
Lassiter, Mrs. Helen 46
Laurenson, Bill 68
Lawrence, W.H. 86
Lazaro, Richard 101
Lazaro, Valerie 101
Lazier, A.F. 3
Lea, James V. 4
Leach, J.T. 51
Leatherman, S.K. 85
Lecour, D.B. 57/58
Lee, Betty 61
Lee, Henry 5
Lee, Larry G. 61
Lee, Mr. Bryan 61
Lee, Mrs. Bryan 61
Lee, Officer 5
LEE, ROBERT WAYNE 35, 61, 78
Lehmann, Alma 11-15
Lemley, Elvin Jr. 69
Lemley, Elvin Sr. 69
Lemley, Mrs. Elvin Sr. 69
Lentschke, Mary E. 89
LeStrange, Sid 22
Leuders, P.A. 49
Levengston, Joe 86
LeVrier, J.M. 40, 52
Lewellen, Mike 74

Lewis, Mavis 85
Lewis, Alton 55
Lewis, Mark 39
Lewis, Mrs. Annie Laurie 39
Ligon, Linda 91
Lillich, Virginia Fitzgerald 30/31
Lockhart, Cherie 88
Lockhart, David 88
Lockhart, Rev. W.S. 11-15
Lofland, C.J. (Chuck) .. 55, 64, 65, 75, 79
Lomax, C.A. 9
Long, C. A. 30/31
Long, W.H. 11-15
Lopez, Bernadette 93
Lopez, George 93
Lott, Bobbie D. 76
Lott, W.D. (David) 71
Lowder, M.D. 85
Loy, Mrs. A.M. 51
Luce, William 35
Luckey, Paul 18
Lum, J.T. 52
Lunsford, W. E. 78
Lusk, Leon 16, 18
Lynn, J. H. 83
Lyon, James Edward 11-15
Lyons, Michael J. 70
Lyons, Mike 96, 98, 106
Lyons, Officer 10
Lyons, T. J. 20
Lysack, Chuck 93

M

Machado, George 70
Mackey, Ed 69
Maddox, Billy 41
Maddox, Brenda 41
Maddox, Fred III 41
MADDOX, FRED JR. 41
Maddox, Louise 41
Maddox, Mr. Fred Sr. 41
Maddox, Mrs. Belle 41
Maddox, Mrs. Fred Sr. 41
Maes, Tom 34, 35
Magdelano, Tony 76
Magee, Mrs. William Jr. 47
Maglitto, Alfred 24
Maglitto, Angelo 24
Maglitto, Bessie 24
Maglitto, Dif 24
Maglitto, Francie 24
Maglitto, Frank 24
Maglitto, Joe, ... 24
Maglitto, Josephine 24
Maglitto, Josie 24
Maglitto, Laura 24

Maglitto, Mary 24
Maglitto, Rosie 24
Maglitto, Sam 24
Main, W. A. 17
Mammen, Mrs. Joy 46
Mangano, C. J. 78
Manlove, Adrianna 90
Manlove, Anthony 90
Manlove, Jason 90
Manlove, Virginia 90
Manning, J.M. 93
Maples, J. J. 30/31
Maples, Mrs. 30/31
Marcum, Charles 79
Mares, Fred 106
Margiotta, Tony 16, 20
Marino, Michael 90
Markert, Weldon W. 61, 68
Marquis, Jimmy 41
Marshall, Antoine Deneil 105
Marshall, Brooke 80
Marshall, Wayne 80
MARTIAL, ADOLPH P. 36
Martial, Dorothy Marie 36
Martial, Mrs. Alfreda 36
Martial, Mrs. Christine 36
Martial, W.O. 36
Martin, H.L. 49
Martin, R. O. 19
Martin, R.J. 21
Martindale, A.C. 50
Martinez, F.E. 106
Martincz, Benjamin 103
Martinez, F.E. 103
Martinez, Felipe Jesus Jr. 87
Martinez, Frank 103
Martinez, Henry 103
Martinez, J.R. 98
Martinez, John 103
Martinez, Manuel 103
Martinez, Manuel Sr. 103
Martinez, Maria 103
Martinez, Max 20
Martinez, R.P. 101
Martinez, Raul 76
Martinez, Starlyn 105
Martinka, Mr. 56
Martinka, Mrs. 56
Martino, Joe 90
Martino, Tammy 90
Mason, Guy A. 74, 79, 86, 91, 103
Mason, Rosa 9
Massey, Chester B. 41, 42/43, 44, 54
Massey, David B. 68, 70, 71, 73
Mathis, John M. 22
Mathis, John Sr. 34
Mathison, Rev. L.H. 29
Mattes, Joseph W. 11-15
Maurer, N.E. 95
Maury, Richard G. 8

Maxey, Rick L. 93, 105
Mayer, Gus 90
Mayer, H.L. (Hub) 101
McAnulty, Dan 71
McBeth, Ernest F. 40, 57/58
McCabe, T.D. 79
McCammon, Ross 74
McCarley, W.L. 34
McCarty, Danny 26
McCarty, Jarrie 26
McCharen, Macy 46
McCharen, Robert 46
McCharen, Shannon Bryant 46
McClellan, Lyn 91, 98
McClelland, Charles 96
McClelland, R.D. 42/43
McClosky, Adam 90
McComas, I.E. 60
McConn, Jim 73
McCormick, Tim 64, 68
McCorvey, Tom 101, 103
McCullum, Hattie 83
McDaniel, Breck 101, 103
MCDANIEL, CHARLES RAYMOND 51
McDaniel, Charles Robert 51
McDaniel, Deborah Ann 51
McDaniel, Don A. 51
McDaniel, E.E. 51
McDaniel, Jacquen 51
McDaniel, Jeanine 51
McDaniel, Jerry E. 51
McDaniel, William E. 51
McDonald, B.J. 98
McDonald, Dr. Geo. 4
McDonald, Judge W.T. 10, 19
McFarland, Earl 8
McFarland, L.R. 8
McFarland, Norma 27
McFarland, W.I. 8
McGee, Harry 11-15
McGee, Henry 4
McGill, H. (Buddy) 41
McGinn, K.D. 67
McGraw, Officer 18
McGraw, Ralph 51
McGrew, Detective 28
McGrew, M.L. 26
McKay, Neil 45
McKelvy, K.A. 42/43
McKinney, A. T. 22
McKinney, B.T. 42/43
McLean, Ken 88
McLemore, Robert 74
McLeod, Karl 33
McMahon, Mrs. E.D. 40
McMenemy, Guy 51
McNutt, H.M. 52
McNutt, J.H. 9
McPhail, J.M. 98
McSpadden, Judge Mike 93
Mehl, Eric S. 86, 89, 103
Meinecke, Comila 11-15
Meinecke, E.G. 11-15
MEINECKE, EDWIN GUSTAV 11-15
Meinecke, Frederick 11-15
Meinecke, John Fritz 11-15
Meinecke, Mrs. E.G. 11-15
Meinecke, Mrs.Dorothea Eber.. 11-15
Meinecke, Robert William 11-15
Meinke, E.H. 26
Meinke, Lieutenant 25
Mendoza, Jesus Zarco 93
Mereness, Ben 33
Mereness, Bert 33
Mereness, Catherine 33
Mereness, Eugenia 33
Mereness, Gertrude Cure 33
MERENESS, HARRY TALCOTT . 33
Mereness, Julia 33
Mereness, Julia Talcott 33
Mereness, Karen 33
Mereness, Kathleen 33
Mereness, Lyman 33
Mereness, Lyman II 33
Mereness, Mary Lou Phillips 33
Mereness, Patricia 33
Mereness, Seth 33
Mereness, Wade 33
Merrill, Sam 70
Meyer, Leopold 49
Meyer, Walter 62
Michaels, Frank 4
Michna, Paul 61
Midyett, Victor 98
Miller, Dick 5
Miller, Earl 46
Miller, Janet 46
Miller, L.N. 75
Miller, Larry 46
Miller, Louis 59
Miller, Lula 59
Miller, M.J. 106
Miller, Melissa 46
Miller, Michelle 46
Miller, Mike 46
Miller, Missy 46
Miller, Mr. N.C. 46
Miller, Mrs. Carolyn Wondrak 46
Miller, Mrs. Frank 40
Miller, Mrs. N.C. 46
MILLER, NOEL RAY 46
Miller, Todd 96, 97, 98
Millican, D.H. (Moon) 34
Millican, W.F. 41
Mills, Brad 65
Mills, Kay 89
Mills, Mandie 89
Mills, Megan 89
Mills, Robert 89
Millsap, Detective 22
Mireles, S.D. 85
Mistrot, Bernice 6/7
Mistrot, Gus 6/7
Mitchell, George 11-15
Mize, R.B. 57/58
Moats, Boots 99
Moats, C.J. 99
Mock, A.J. 84
Montalbano, Yance 90
Montalbo, Mary Jane 87
Montemayor, J. 78, 87, 90
Montero, Bonnie 11-15
Montero, James 11-15, 71, 80
Montes, Emily 63
Montes, Greg 63
Montes, Hilari 63
Montes, Shannon 63
Montgomery, Mrs. Jean Ann 50
Moody, Arvin 59
Moody, Cornelia 11-15
Moody, Elva Joy 59
Moody, Gregory Blake 59
MOODY, HORACE CLIFTON . 11-15
MOODY, KENNETH WAYNE 35, 59, 71
Moody, Lilly 11-15
Moody, Lucas 59
Moody, Martin 11-15
Moody, Meredith 59
Moody, Merrill 59
Moody, Mrs.Horace 11-15
Moody, Wendy Gayle 59
Moon, Martel 41
Moon, Mrs. Reba 41
Moore, A.H. 44
Moore, Rev. Gene A. 95
Moore, T. G. 22
Moreland, A.C. 3
Moreno, Rick 103
Morgan, Bob 72
Morgan, Bobby 70
Morgan, Rev. James 39
Morgan, Rev. John 79
Morris, J.D. 11-15
Morris, Ned 93
Morris, T.B. 36
Morrison, L.D. Jr. 11-15, 54, 55, 64
Morrison, L.D. Sr. 11-15
Morrison, M.T. 61
Morrison, Peter 11-15
Morrow, G.A. 25
Morrow, Kenneth Wayne 77
Mortenson, R.S. 53
Moseley, J.C. 61
Mosely, R.D. 84
Moses, George 46
Mosqueda, Cecil T. 87, 103
Moss, Barry 83

Moss, Bryant 83
Moss, Flora 83
Moss, Janet 83
Moss, John 83
Moss, Kim 83
Moss, Lula Mae 83
Moss, Robert L. 83
Moss, Roland 83
MOSS, WILLIAM 83
Moss, Willie 83
Motard, P.C. 74, 79, 98
Mueller, P.A. 75
Munier, Marie 101
Munoz, Mrs. Antonio 87
MURDOCK, DAVID DUNCAN.... 17, 18
Murdock, David Duncan Jr. 18
Murdock, Ella 18
Murdock, Ella (daughter) 18
Murdock, Exie Ashby 18
Murdock, J. H. 18
Murphey, Gordon 9
MURPHY, CHIEF WILLIAM E. 8, 11-15, 16
Murphy, George (Brother) 8
Murphy, George (Son) 8
Murphy, Gordon 17
Murphy, Margaret 8
Murray, Tom 88
Music, Bruce 73
Musick, Earl 73
Myers, Mrs. L.P. (Ruby) 39
Myers, Officer 9
Myers, W.J. 25

N

Narvaez, R.A. 102
Nassar, Denise 98
Naus, Mrs. W.D. 37
Navarro, Wilfred 83
Neely, Greg T. .. 80,86,88,89,96,97,98
Neely, Johnny E. 47
Nelson, Gilbert 54
Nelson, Jack 69
Nelson, P.B. 85
Nelson, S.D. 69
Netherland, J.L. 103
Newcomb, Mark 106
Newcomer, Shannon 78
Newcomer, Shelley 78
Newhoff, Officer 5
Newman, Craig E. 98, 100
Newman, William (Lt. Col.) 11-15
Newton, Truitt 22
Nichols, Floyd 56
Nicholson, P. J. 17
Nickell, J.W. 95

Nieto, Richard 66
Nix, Edmund 27
Nix, I.L. 16
Nix, Ira 26, 27
Nix, Paul S. 47, 55, 60, 64
Nixon, Brent 95
Nixon, Deanna 95
Noel, Charles 63
NOEL, DAVID FRANKLIN 63, 79
Noel, Ina Kay 63
Noel, James 63
Noel, John 63
Noel, John M. Sr. 63
Noel, Mrs. Flora 63
Noel, Paul 63
Noel, Ralph 63
Noel, Robert 63
Noel, Shannon Denise 63
Noel, Sherry Diane 63
Norris, James O. (Bo) 51, 56
Norsworthy, Dr. O.L. 6/7
Novak, G.J. (Jerry)... 69, 93, 101, 103
Novak, Michael 103
Nutt, J. R. 30/31

O

O'Brien, J.M. 66
O'Leary, Pat 16
O'Leary, Thomas 8
O'Neal, Molly Michelle 84
O'Neal, Mrs. Kelley Groves 84
O'Neal, Scott 84
O'Neal, Zach 84
Oaks, J.S. 51
Oates, O.A. 103
Ogan, Crain Neal 88
Ogden, J.A. 96, 97, 98
Ogden, Paul 73
Olin, Tommy 80
Olson, Craig Neal 88
Ontiveros, R. 84, 102
Opperman, R.J. 103
Oranday, Amy 65
Ordaz, Armando 92
Orlando, J.J. 68
Ortega, Manny 78
Osbourne, Gay 27
Osburn, Fannie Lee 23
Ott, Larry 93
Ottosen, Rev. Brad 80, 91
Overstreet, Judge Campbell... 23, 27, 28, 32
Owen, W.W. 79
Owens, Detective 30/31
Owens, T. D. Tiny 77

P

Padilla, A. 103
Padilla, J.D. 106
Page, J. F. 22
Palmer, David 37
Palmer, Harold 37
Palmer, Marion E. Jr. 37
PALMER, MARION E. SR. 37
Palmer, Mrs. Christine 37
Palmer, Patti 37
Palmer, Paul 37
Palomo, R. 102, 104
Palos, Antonio 80
Pangburn, Mrs. Viola 75
Pappillion, Mike 85
Parham, J.H. 69
Parker, Deputy 4
Parker, J.O. 61, 68
Parker, John 56
Parker, R.J. 85
Parker, Tim 35
Parks, Ida Mae 60
Parmer, Jonathan 103
Parsley, N.A. 34
PARSONS, ISSAC (IKE) 9, 10
Pass, Rev. James 57/58
Pastoriza, Joseph Jay 11-15
Patrick, Officer 5
Patterson, Mrs. Carroll 41
PATTON, D. ROSS 11-15
Patton, Mrs. D.R. 11-15
Paulk, J.P. 55
Payne, B.W. 34
Peace, James 52
Peace, Mrs. Mae 52
Pearson, J.W. 91
Pechacek, Asst. D.A. 78
Pendley, Mary Eckman 30/31
Perales, Matt S. 66, 71
Perdue, W.A. 61
Pereira, Theo 3
Perkins, C.E. 49
Perkins, Constable 3
Perkins, J.B. 3
Perrett, W.H. 8
Perry, D. R. 51
Perry, Ed. 22
Peters, Mike 88, 103, 106
Petersen, Ethel 54
Petersen, Marian 44
Petersen, Mary Ann 44
Peterson, Annie Mae 27
Peterson, E. A. 30/31
Peterson, Martha 5, 11
Petitt, Art 79
Peyton, George
11-15,22,28,30/31,34,38

Phares, Florrie Bonner 30/31
Phares, Gil 30/31
Phares, Johnsa 30/31
Phares, Johnsa Jr 30/31
Phares, Lenore Kerr 30/31
PHARES, WILLIAM BONNER 30/31
Phelps, Edna 18
Phifer, Woody 80
Phillips, C.L. 41
Phillips, H.L. 60
Pickens, Tom C. 47
Pickrom, Gregory Steven 91
Pierce, James A. 55, 64, 73
Pierson, Carla 80
Pierson, Robert 80
Pigg, Mr. Jack 68
Pigg, Mrs. Jack 68
Pilleran, Mrs. George 40
Pineda, J.C. 106
Pioch, JoAn 44
Pittman, Beulah 54
Planer, Eddie 53
Planer, George (Brother) 53
Planer, George (Dad) 53
PLANER, HERBERT NORMAN .. 53
Planer, Margaret Antoinette 53
Planer, Mrs. Betty Joan 53
Planner, Keith 53
Planner, Kimberly 53
Planner, Sandy 53
Planner, Tommie 53
Plaster, W.E. 70
Polk, J. W. 19
Polk, Neal 34
Porras. Andy 66, 92
Porter, Breck 41, 71
Porter, Elmer 60
Potell, M.W. 94, 102
Powell, Robert 26
Preacher, Sid 6/7
Priester, W.G. 8
Procella, Monsignor Paul 100
Proctor, Officer 5
Pruett, Deputy 4
Pruter, George 30/31
Puckett, Richard 80
Pullens, Norm 56
Pyevach, Mrs. Marie 104
Pyevach, Wesley 104

Q

Quinby, Special Officer 5
Quintero, Juan Leonardo 106
Quiroz, Celia Rivas 92

R

Rabouln, Officer 5
Radke, Herman 20
Railey, Justice J.A. 3
Raines, A.C. 80
Raines, Pamela Harris 80
Ramerez, Pablino 21
Ramerez, Ysabel 21
Ramirez, Andrew 104
Ramirez, C. 78
Ramirez, Julian 93, 96
Ramsey, James 9
Ramsey, J.L. (Jim) 22, 86, 88, 103
Ramsey, Lt. Gov. Ben 45
Ramscy, Mrs. Bobby 63
Randio, A.J. 41
Raney, Bryan 11-15
Raney, Frank 11-15
Raney, Houston Texas 11-15
RANEY, IRA DEVOUD 11-15
Raney, Ira III. 11-15
Raney, Ira Jr. 11-15
Raney, Janice 11-15
Raney, Mike 11-15
Raney, Mrs. Pearl 11-15
Raney, Quincy (Mose) 11-15
Raney, Robert (Cotton) 11-15
Raney, Susan 11-15
Raney, Thomas 11-15
Raney, Vera 11-15
Rankin, Mrs. Florencc 42/43
Rankin, W.H. 47
Rasberry, Mrs. M.L. 37
Raschke, G.B. 98
Rauscher, Bill 64
Rauscher, Mary Frances 64
Rawlins, Bryant Deray 77
Rawlins, Mrs. Edna 77
Rawlins, Phillip Riian 77
Rawlins, Phillip, Jr. 77
Rawlins, Phillip, Sr, ... 77
Rawlins, Roy Julian 77
RAWLINS, WINSTON J. 77
Ray, J. M. 17
Rayne, S.J. 62
Razo, Pete 92
Razo, R. 92
Red, Dr. 4
Red, S.F. 84
Redden, Lee Wayne 47
Redman, W.M. 85
Reese, Timothy Wayne 97
Reeves, Patsy 93
Reichart, Alma 11-15
Reid, Mr. G.P. 42/43
Reid, Mrs. G.P. 42/43
Retz, Richard 90
Reyes, J.J. 72
Rice, H.B. 8
Rice, T.M. 78
Richards, Harvey 49
Richards, K.L. 103
Richardson, John E. 10, 11-15
Richardson, Robert Andrew 84
Richardson, Sarah 83
Richie, Elizabeth 103
Rickey, George L. 33
Riddle, A.G. 98, 101
Ridge, Chris 88
Riehl, Michael K. 90
Ricks, D.E. 79
Riley, Jack 67
RILEY, JERRY LAWRENCE 67
Riley, Mrs. Marita 67
Riley, Shane Odell 67
Riley, Sherry 67
Riley, Teddy 67
Ripley, Billy G. 67, 72
Ritchey, D.G. 85
Riter, William 1
Rivera, Eli P. 20
Rivers, Michael 70
Rizzo, Dan. 103
Rizzo, J.H. 73
Roark, C. 76
Robbins, J.C. 57/58
Robbins, Michael 70
Roberts, Bobby 106
Roberts, H.D. 37
Roberts, Officer 21
Robertson, Darrell 96, 103
Robertson, F.V. 67
Robertson, W.C. 69
Robinson, C.W. 8
Robinson, E.B. 102
Robinson, Linda Griggs 60
Robinson, Mrs. Burt 42/43
Rockwell, Allen E. 46, 55
Rodgers, H.W. 41
Rodgers, T.L. 85
Rodriguez, Mario 101
Rodriguez, Martin 80
Rodriguez, Ophelia 87
Rodriguez, Rose Mary 101
Roe, S.T. 38
Roescher, John M. 66
Rogers, Billy Joe 53
Rogers, Deputy Sheriff 18
Rogers, E.C. 69
Rogers, R.E. 29
Rogers, Roy 30/31
Rojas, Edward 71
Rojas, Ernest 71
ROJAS, GEORGE GARZA 6/7, 66, 71, 73
Rojas, Lupe 71
Rojas, Mary Ann 71

Rojas, Mary Martha ... 71
Rojas, Mr. Eulojio ... 71
Rojas, Mrs. Eulojio ... 71
Rojas, Sonya ... 71
Roman, Cynthia ... 92
Roman, Ignacio ... 92
Roman, Marissa ... 92
Roman, Mary ... 92
ROMAN, MICHAEL PAUL ... 92
Roman, Miguel ... 92
Roman, Mikaela ... 92
Roman, Mrs. Suelema ... 92
Roman, Pablo ... 92
Roman, Raymond ... 92
Roman, Steven ... 92
Root, Christine ... 75
Root, Michelle ... 75
Rosenthal, Chuck ... 59, 103
Ross, Anna Marie ... 104
Ross, Henry ... 3
Ross, Judge Sherman ... 87
Ross, Lewis ... 4
Ross, Mrs. Inez ... 50
Ross, Terry M. ... 86, 88, 91
Rossiter, Jay A. ... 11-15
Rouse, Bobby ... 70
Routt, Judge Thomas ... 86
Row, I.M. ... 88
Rowell, Gobel E. ... 46
Ruchti, John ... 59
Rucker, Leona ... 69
Rudolph, Brad ... 89
Ruetsch, Beverly ... 80
Ruetsch, David ... 80
Ruetsch, Jeff ... 80
Ruetsch, Todd ... 80
Ruff, Wendy ... 87
Ruffino, F.A. ... 91
Ruiz, Robert V. ... 84, 85, 87
Rutherford, Dr. H. ... 4

S

Sacky, Danny ... 64
Saenz, R. ... 102
Saenz, Dora ... 105
Saenz, Guadaloupe ... 105
Saenz, Lupe ... 105
Saenz, Martha ... 105
Saenz, Mrs. Petra ... 105
Saenz, R. ... 92, 94, 95
Saldivar, F.G. ... 69
Salinas, Lupe ... 59
Salinas, R.J. ... 90
Salvaggio, Catherine ... 90
Salvaggio, Cathy ... 90
Salvaggio, Charles ... 90
Salvaggio, Elizabeth ... 90

Salvaggio, Guy ... 90
Salvaggio, Jack ... 90
SALVAGGIO, JOHN ANTHONY . 90
Salvaggio, John Anthony II ... 90
Salvaggio, Marybess ... 90
Salvaggio, Mrs. Mary ... 90
Salvaggio, Tony Jr. ... 90
Salvaggio, Virginia ... 90
Samaniego, Mrs. Carmen ... 49
Sammons, Ellis P. Pokey ... 19
Sammons, W.E. (Pokey) ... 19, 29, 34
Sampson, K.E. ... 85
Sander, Dennis ... 55, 89
Sander, Kenneth ... 55, 89
Sander, Kimberly Ann ... 55
Sander, Linda ... 55
SANDER, LOUIS LYNDON .. 35, 47, 55, 71, 89, 96
Sander, Mr. Walter ... 55
Sander, Mrs. Walter ... 55
Sander, Sadie ... 89
Sander, Stacie ... 55
Sander, Walter ... 89
Sanders, R.V. ... 65
Sandoval, Reynoldo ... 101
Santana, Noe ... 11-15
Sation, Deputy ... 4
Satterwhite, L.J. ... 98
Satton, Senelton ... 11-15
Sawyer, Gayle ... 22
Sawyer, Martha ... 22
Sawyer, Rufus ... 22
Sawyer, Tommy ... 22
Scales, Curtis L. ... 101, 103, 106
Scalise, Terry ... 55
Scanlan, Dan ... 3
Scanlon, J. E. ... 78
Scearce, Wilbur E. ... 17
SCHAEFER, KATHLEEN M. ... 81
Schaefer, Lyndon Wade ... 59, 81
Schaefer, Lyndon Wade Jr. ... 81
Schaefer, Lyndy ... 81
Schaefer, Reagan ... 81
Schaefer, Skylar ... 81
Schaefer, Stacy ... 81
Schaefer, Theresa Marie ... 81
Scheibe, Michelle Raney ... 11-15
Schields, Robert ... 90
Schisser, Glenna ... 35
Schisser, James S. ... 35
Schisser, Joseph George Sr. ... 35
Schisser, Joseph Jr. ... 35
Schleier, Martin ... 8
Schmidt, Mark ... 97
Schneider, Charley ... 56
Schroeder, Carl ... 11-15
Schroeder, Jackie ... 11-15
Schultea, Billy ... 45
SCHULTEA, BOBBY JOE ... 45
Schultea, Carl ... 45

Schultea, James ... 45
Schultea, Jimmie ... 45
Schultea, Joe ... 45
Schultea, Joe, Jr. ... 45
Schultea, Marie ... 45
Schultea, Michael ... 45
Schultea, Mr. D.D. ... 45
Schultea, Mrs. D.D. ... 45
Schultea, Patrick ... 45
Schultea, Robert J. ... 45
Schultea, Vollie ... 45
Schultea, Vollie, Jr. ... 45
Schultea, Weldon J. ... 45
Schultz, D. L. ... 78
Schultz, William ... 4
Schulze, Rev. John P. ... 68
Schusler, Frank ... 11-3
Schwander, Justice ... 4
Schweiker, R. R. ... 78
Scott, J. L. ... 78
Scroggins, Mrs. W. A. ... 22
Searce, W. ... 18
Seay, Rufus ... 38
Seber, George G. ... 35
Seber, George L. ... 34, 35, 38, 39
Seber, Marvin ... 35, 42/43
Seelig, Rev. Steve ... 102
Sellars, Calvin ... 59
Sellars, Wesley ... 59, 71
Serio, Donnie ... 74
Serres, Kenneth Wayne ... 59
Serres, Robert E. ... 59
Sessner, G.K. ... 3
Sevcik, J.J. ... 57/58
Sewell, Campbell ... 10
Sexton, K.W. ... 87
Shaddo, Mrs. Maxine ... 41
Sharp, Houston ... 9
Shattuck, Margaret ... 53
Shattuck, Nolan ... 53
Shattuck, Ryan ... 53
Shattuck, Weston ... 53
Sheldon, W.C. (Chuck) ... 86, 93, 96
Sherman, L.D. ... 70
Shipley, J.S. ... 85
Shipley, L.E. ... 46
Shirley, D.D. ... 93, 101, 103
SHIRLEY, DARYL WAYNE ... 61, 63, 79, 81
Shirley, Denise ... 79
Shirley, Donna ... 79
Shirley, J.A. ... 57/58
Shirley, Jason ... 79
Shirley, Jerry ... 79
Shirley, Julie ... 79
Shirley, Kaden ... 79
Shirley, Kannen ... 79
Shirley, Margaret ... 79
Shirley, Mr. Willard ... 79
Shirley, Mrs. Willard ... 79

Shirley, Natalie	79
Shirley, Sara	79
Shirley, Steven	79
Shirley, Tyler	79
Short, Herman	35, 56
Silva, John J.	86
Simmons, Curtis	52
Simmons, Milton	52
Simpson, Brandy	67
Simpson, M.M.	36
Sinwell, Vicki	98
Sistrunk, Milford	86
Slack, William	21
Slay, Floyd	64
Slay, Roy	67, 70
Slider, Mrs. John	8
Slocovich, Nola	26
Smelley, Kenneth G.	48
Smellley, Laura	89
Smith, C. E. Chuck	55, 59
Smith, Elden D.	41
Smith, Elden J.	41, 83, 90
Smith, Eli	11-15
Smith, Frank	9
Smith, Gray	91
Smith, Jack	25
Smith, L.B. (Boyd)	79, 86, 91, 103
Smith, Lora	103
Smith, Manuel Ben	42/43
Smith, Mrs. J. M.	22
Smith, Murray J.	103, 106
Smith, Noel	70
Smith, Oscar I.	62
Smith, R. C.	80
Smith, R.D. (Red)	46, 47
Smyth, Don	97
Sneed, D.R.	69
Snow, Danny	101
Snow, Kneeland S.	11-15
Snow, P.Y.	39, 41
SNOW, RICHARD	2
SOBOLESKI, BRUNO DAVID	91
Soboleski, Frank	91
Soboleski, Joseph	91
Soboleski, Leonard	91
Soboleski, Mallorie	91
Soboleski, Michael	91
Soboleski, Mr. Bruno	91
Soboleski, Mrs. Mary	91
Soboleski, Mrs. Sue	91
Soboleski, Stephanie	91
Soboleski, Walter	91
Soland, Fred	32
Sosa, J.	106
Soukup, Linda Sue	37
Soukup, Marion	37
Soule, Horace	22, 24, 26
Sparks, Lee	11-15
Spaulding, John	11-15
Speck, Donald Ray	53
Spencer, Frank	3
Spencer, J.D.	68
Spradley, Arch	36
Spruill, Cody	64
Spruill, Jeffrey	64
SPRUILL, JERRY LEON	64, 70, 96
Spruill, Julian	64
Spruill, Marcie	64
Spruill, Ralph	64
Spruill, Scott	64
Spurlock, D.R. (Danny)	63, 68, 73
Spurlock, Ina Kay Noel	63
Squyres, C. F.	56, 57/58
Squyres, Mrs. Mildred	56
Stabe, Bob	86
Stachmus, Frank B.	69
Staggs, C.B.	85
Stairhime, Lucky	103
Stallings, W.A.	23
Stallworth, Mary	83
Stampley, Lester	88
Starr, Dan	90
Steffanauer, Doug (Tooter)	89
Stephens, H.L.	57/58
Stephens, William	88
Stephenson, Carol	71
Stephenson, J.T.	46
Sterling, Officer	21
Stevens, Carrie	83
Stevens, O'Brien	30/31
Stewart, Carlton Bry	36
Stewart, Charlie	22
Stewart, F.W.	64
Stewart, Gregory Lee	36
Stewart, Walter J.	73, 80
Stinson, J.A.	36
Stockton, Wiliam G.	51
Stokely, Rev. S.W.	11-15
Stone, Curtis Ricky	67
Storey, James	10
Stowe, Christina	99
Stowe, Cody	99
Stowe, Don	99
Stowe, Gail	99
Stowe, Geri	99
STOWE, JERRY KEITH	99
Stowe, Jimmy	99
Stowe, Vicki	99
Straughter, Steven	101, 103
Stricklin, Don	105
Stude, Henry	11-15
Stutts, E.J.	46
Sublett, Bobby Ray	40
Sullivan, Diane Gerhart	57/58
Sullivan, J.E.	34
Sullivan, J.J	3
Sullivan, Jonathan	57/58
Sullivan, Lanelle	34
Sullivan, Mr. Walter	34
Sullivan, Mrs. Barbara	50
Sullivan, Mrs. George	34
Sullivan, Mrs. Myrtle	34
Sullivan, Mrs. Pearl	34
SULLIVAN, R.H. (RIMPS)	29, 34
Sullivan, Robert Harold	34
Sullivan, Shirley	34
Sullivan, Walter	34
Sumlin, Nancy	85
Supple, H.A.	36
Suttle, Carl R.	48
Suttle, John	49
SUTTLE, JOHN WESLEY (JACK)	48
Suttle, John Wesley Jr.	48
Suttle, Kenneth Paul	48
Suttle, Loy Nell	48
Suttle, Minor Dwayne	48
Suttlc, Mr. Oscar William	48
Suttle, Mrs. Oscar William	48
Suttle, Sarah Kathryn	48
Swaim, John R.	86, 89, 96, 97, 98
Swainson, Roy	103
Sybert, P.D.	75

T

Taber, W.A.	97
Tabor, Mrs. Ruby	52
Tallent, R.E.	84
Tally, E.H.	24
Tamayo, Edgar	93, 106
Tatum, Captain	25
Tatum, J.H.	26
Taut, J. H.	30/31
Taylor, A. O.	22, 26, 32, 33
Taylor, Arthur	9
Taylor, Deputy Arthur	10
Taylor, Geraldine	44
Taylor, Reuben	44
Tena, Secundina	21
Terry, A.W.	3
Terry, Frank	3
Terry, Kyle	3
Tharonat, Charlie	3
Tharp, Rev. R.H.	37
Thomas , G. W.	19
THOMAS, C.F. (OSBURN)	29
Thomas, Fred	29
Thomas, Leo	29
Thomas, Lynn	29
Thomas, Mr. J.A.	29
Thomas, Mrs. Eula Lee	29
Thomas, Mrs. J.A.	29
Thomas, Robert Lee	68
Thomas, Ted	75, 79, 86
Thompson, Carolyn Ann	86
Thompson, D.W.	67, 68
Thompson, Deputy Chief	6/7

Thompson, E.A. 11-15
Thompson, Henry 5
Thompson, James (Ditty) 28
Thompson, Mrs. Adele 42/43
Thompson, Roy E. 89
Thompson, W.A. 11-15
Thornton, A.C. 34
Thornton, Carl 36
Thornton, Joe 25
Thornton, Johnny 72, 75. 89
Thornton, P.A. (Paul) 63, 70
Thyssen, Glen 62
Timme, H.J. 42/43
Tippy, J.L. 102
Tips, G.H. 4
Todd, Neal 45
Toepoel, A.J. 89
Tolson, Richard 9
Tomlin, G. S. 18
Tong, Chuong 96
Torres, R. 106
Trammel, R.A. 26
Tranter, Ralph 59
Travers, Mrs. Sara 11-15
Trent, Rev. Kenneth 57/58
Trepagnier, L. J. Larry 80, 81
Trevino, Mrs. Eva 49
Trimble, H.R. (Ray) 71, 79
TRINH, CUONG HOY (TONY) 96
Trinh, Dat (Ricky) Huy 96
Trinh, Mr. Nguyen Dinh 96
Trinh, Mrs. Nguyen Dinh 96
Trojan, Bob 74
Trotky, Mrs. Minnie 57/58
Trumble, Beverly 91, 93
Trumble, Phil 86
Tucker, J.D. (Jim) 53, 70, 71
Tucker, J.E. 41
Tunson, Michael 97
Turbeville, Forrest 41
Turner, Dave 30/31
Turnley, Tom C. 8
Tuttle, L. 98
Tyler, E. C. 78
Tyler, J.P. 85
Tyree, Larry 68
Tyrell, Tory 86

U

Ubernosky, Edwin Lee 78
Ubernosky, Mrs. Edwin Lee 78
Urban, J. A. 22
Uresti, Eli 71

V

Vachris, Ken E. 89
Vahldiek, Otto 44
Valerio, Bill 97
Van Devusse, Ellen Kay 44
Vance, Carol 56, 59, 91
VanNess, J.R. 24
VASQUEZ, ALBERTO 35, 101
Vasquez, Amelda C. 101
Vasquez, Ana Marie 101
Vasquez, Andrew Jose 101
Vasquez, Carlos Alberto 101
Vasquez, Jerry 101
Vasquez, Mr. Juan 101
Vasquez, Mr. Juan J. 101
Vasquez, Mrs. Ira Mae 101
Vasquez, Mrs. Patricia 101
Vaughn, J. T. 5
Vaughn, Newt 5
Vaughn, Robert 29
Verbitskey, Lorenzo R. 93, 103, 106
Vercher, Marjorie 26
Verot, Rene 103
Vickers, J.M. 42/43
Victoria, Nicholas 105
Vining, Joe 8
Vinson, Mark 97
Vocelka, F. J. 98
Vogler, J.W. (Jimmie) 44
Voss, Chief John A. (Duff) 9

W

Wade, Alma 99
Wade, Dolly 99
Wade, Ed 65
Wade, Filo 99
Wade, Jamesetta 99
Wade, Litha 99
Walber, Jace 80
Walber, Megan 80
Walber, Shannon 80
Walker, C.H. 53
Walker, Claudia 50
Walker, Cody 50
Walker, Dylan 50
WALKER, JAMES THOMAS 50
Walker, James Thomas Jr. 50
Walker, Jamye Lynn 50
Walker, Joe 4
Walker, Loretta 50
Walker, M. A. 59
Walker, Maggie 50
Walker, Mrs. Ethel Mae 50
Walker, Rev. 36
Walker, Ron 101, 106
Walker, Tommye Lee 50
Walker, W.W. 41
Wallace, Judge Jim 97
Waller, Douglas 56
Walling, John 79
Walschberger, Fred 70
Walsh, Father Jay 81
Walsh, J.P. 85
Walsh, Ted 38
Waltmon, J.L. 75
Ward, Mrs. Edgar 42/43
Ward, R.L. 8
Warkentin, R. H. 78
Warner, W.T. 93
Warren O.R. 88, 93
Warren, C.O. 69
Warren, John 4
Washington, Willie James 75
Waters, Millard (Fil) 96
Watkins, C.C. 6/7
Watson, Bryant 11-3
Watson, Elizabeth 98
Watts, L.L. 39, 41
Watts, Rev. 4
Way, W.W. 24
Weaver, W.S. 66
Webb, Keith 91, 93
Webb, Rev. W.C. 47
Webber, Larry E. 75, 79, 80, 93
Webster, C.A. 84
Wedgeworth, Roger 97
Wehr, W.J. 60, 75
Weiner, W.K. 57/58
Weiss, J. F. 5
WEISS, WILLIAM A. (WILLIE) 5, 6/7, 11-15
Weiss. Mrs. J. F. 5
Welch, J.E. 57/58
Weller, Mrs. R.A. 37
Wells, Alta 54
Wells, Alvin Curtis 23
Wells, Bessie 23
Wells, Brittany 75
Wells, David Leroy 23
Wells, Emily Powell 23
Wells, Jennifer 75
Wells, John David 23
Wells, John Walter 23
Wells, Kevin 75
Wells, Linda Ann 75
Wells, Mr. V.R. Sr. 75
Wells, Mrs. V.R. Sr. 75
WELLS, RODNEY QUINN 23
Wells, Samuel David 75
Wells, Shaylen 75
Wells, Susanna 75
WELLS, VICTOR RAY 66, 73, 75, 78
Wells, William Donnie 75
Wendel, Wayne 88, 97, 103

Wendt, Danny 68
Werner, Jerry 78
West, G.H. 98, 103
West, N.E. 25
West, Rev. E.P. 25
West, Vernon W. 75, 79, 80
Whatley, W.S. 42/43
Wheat, James 103
Wheatly, Sam 33
Wheeler, John T. 8
Whitby, Doug 103
Whitby, Elfriede 103
Whitcomb, R.D. 49
White, Jack 3
White, Rev. J. 26
Whiteley, Johnny 73
Whites, Johnny 90
Whitesides, F. 3
Whiting, Lew 101
Whitlock, Arthur 25
Whitlock, Mrs. Arthur 25
Whitlock, Mrs. Paul 25
WHITLOCK, PAUL W. 25
Whitmire, Kathy 86, 88
Whittington, B.W. 6/7
Whittington, Officer 5
Wichmann, Charles 4
Wick, M.E. 94
Wiggins, E.H. 106
Wiggins, Ruth 26
Wilburn, J.E. 41
Wilcox, Tommy 69
Wilhite, D.L. 84
Wilker, Delinda S. 86, 88, 93
Willeford, Frank 39
Williams, A.K. 93
Williams, Annie B. 85
Williams, Arthur Lee 79
Williams, C.D. 99
Williams, Connie 86
WILLIAMS, HENRY 3
Williams, J.R. 68
Williams, J.W. 84
Williams, Jeffrey Demond 98
Williams, Jerrie Ann 76
Williams, John 8
Williams, Lynn 77
Williams, T.Q. 88
Williams, Wallace 66
Williams, Wayne 67
Williamson, Kenny 91
Williford, Charles 5
Willis, J.F. 38
Willis, Douglas Franklin 52, 92
WILLIS, JAMES FRANKLIN 52
Willis, Lois 52
Willis, Mrs. Ivous 52
Willis, Rev.W.C. 52
Willis, Robert Edward 52
Wilsford, Ed 18

Wilson, C.M. 9
Wilson, Donnie 70
Wilson, G. 9
Wilson, Jerry 17
Wilson, John 57/58
Wilson, Johnnie 28
Wilson, Mrs. Amanda 28
Wilson, R.M. 53
Wilson, S.P. (Speedie) 74, 75
Wilson, T.L. 61
Wilson, Terry 64, 74, 80
Wilson, W.C. 11-15
Wilson, Woodrow 11-15
Winborn, Judge A.C. 39, 45
Windberry, Benjamin 70
Windham, Rev. T.J. 24, 34
Wineinger, Dena 67
Winkler, Frederick 11-15
WINZER, ANDREW 85
Winzer, Corey 85
Winzer, Frank A. Jr. 85
Winzer, Gus 85
Winzer, Jessie 85
Winzer, Lavendra 85
Winzer, Mattie 85
Winzer, Michael 85
Winzer, Mr. F.A. 85
Winzer, Mrs. Maggie 85
Wissel, W. J. Joe 82
Wolf, J. C. 78
Wolfe, Bob 74
Wolfe, J.C. 92
Wondrak, George 46
Wondrak, Rachel 46
Wood, J.C. 98, 103
Wood, R.M. 9
Woodall, Ben 45
Woodcock, J. L. 78
Woodruff, Reid 52
Woods, George 34
Woods, M.R. 72
Woodward, W.C. 6/7
Wooten, J. N. 30/31
Wren, Charles 38
Wright, Billie Hudson 69
Wright, Charles W. 11-15
Wright, Dena Ann 69
Wright, Edwin 69
WRIGHT, FRANCIS EDDIE 69
Wright, Jerry L. 63, 69
Wright, Laura Nicole 69
Wright, Mary Frances 69
Wright, Miranda 69
Wychopin, Forrest Sten 48

Y

Yanchak, E.T. 64, 66, 74, 75, 80, 93
Yates, B. O. 17
Yates, Elder 4
Ybanez, M.J. 101
Young, Roy 21
Young, Annie Lou Shaw 17
Young, Cecil 17
Young, Clarence Loland 17
Young, Clarence Loland Jr. 17
Young, Della Andrews 17
Young, Detective 28
Young, Dr. H. Edwin 84, 93
Young, Inez 17
YOUNG, JETER 17, 18
Young, Peter 11-15
Young, R.D. 106
Young, Roy 27
Young, William R. 17
Young, Willie 64
Youngst, Harriet 6/7
YOUNGST, HERMAN 5, 6/7
Youngst, Officer 5
Yungst, H. 3

Z

Zachary, Brandon 105
Zamarron, Elizabeth Ann 76
Zamarron, Guadalupe 76
Zamarron, Ignacio 76
Zamarron, Jason Anthony 76
ZAMARRON, JOSE ADOLPHO JR.. 76
Zamarron, Joseph Adolph Jr. 76
Zamarron, Patricia Ruth 76
Zamora, Harry 87
Zimmerman, Mark 76
Zink, Elvina 37
Zink, Light 37
Zoch, Andy 11-15, 22, 23, 30/31
Zoch, H.A. (John) 64
Zoch, L.N. 63, 64, 75
Zoch, Mary Sue 42/43, 62
Zoch, Nelson J. 64, 68, 71, 79, 93, 101, 103
Zumwalt, R. M. 78

363.2092 Z84 DISCARD
Zoch, Nelson J.
Fallen heroes of the Bayou
City: Houston Police
Department:1860-2006
Central Nonfiction ADU CIRC
12/07

2/11